THE BĀBUR-NĀMA
(MEMOIRS OF BĀBUR)

The Bābur-Nāma

(Memoirs of Bābur)

Translated from the Original Turki Text of
Zahiru'd-dīn Muhammad Bābur Pādshāh Ghāzī

Volume 1

ANNETTE SUSANNAH BEVERIDGE

MANOHAR
2024

First published 1531
Reprinted 2023, 2024

ISBN 978-93-94262-56-0 (Vol. 1)
ISBN 978-93-94262-58-4 (Set)

Published by
Ajay Kumar Jain *for*
Manohar Publishers & Distributors
4753/23 Ansari Road, Daryaganj
New Delhi 110 002

Printed at
Replika Press Pvt. Ltd.

This work

is dedicate to

Bābur's

fame.

TABLE OF CONTENTS

PREFACE: Introductory.—Cap. I. Babur's exemplars in the Arts of peace, p. xxvii.—Cap. II. Problems of the mutilated Babur-nama, p. xxxi.—Cap. III. The Turki MSS. and work connecting with them, p. xxxviii. — Cap. IV. The Leyden and Erskine "Memoirs of Baber", p. lvii.— Postscript of Thanks, p. lx.

SECTION I.—FARGHĀNA

899 AH.—Oct. 12th 1493 to Oct. 2nd 1494 AD.—Bābur's age at the date of his accession—**Description of Farghāna** (pp. 1 to 12)—Death and biography of 'Umar Shaikh (13 to 19 and 24 to 28)—Biography of Yūnas *Chaghatāī* (18 to 24) — Bābur's uncles Aḥmad *Mīrān-shāhī* and Maḥmūd *Chaghatāī* (The Khān) invade Farghāna—Death and biography of Aḥmad—Misdoings of his successor, his brother Maḥmūd 1-42

900 AH.—Oct. 2nd 1494 to Sep. 21st 1495 AD.—Invasion of Farghāna continued — Bābur's adoption of orthodox observance—Death and biography of Maḥmūd *Mīrān-shāhī* —Samarkand affairs—revolt of Ibrāhīm *Sārū* defeated— Bābur visits The Khān in Tāshkīnt—tribute collected from the Jīgrak tribe—expedition into Aūrātīpā . . 43-56

901 AH.—Sep. 21st 1495 to Sep. 9th 1496 AD.—Ḥusain *Bāī-qarā's* campaign against Khusrau Shāh—Bābur receives Aūzbeg sulṭāns—Revolt of the Tarkhāns in Samarkand—. Bābur's first move for Samarkand 57-64

902 AH.—Sep. 9th 1496 to Aug. 30th 1497 AD.—Bābur's second move for Samarkand—Dissensions of Ḥusain *Bāī-qarā* and his sons—Dissensions between Khusrau Shāh and Mas'ūd *Mīrān-shāhī* 65-71

903 AH.—Aug. 30th 1497 to Aug. 19th 1498 AD.—Bābur's second attempt on Samarkand is successful—**Description of Samarkand** (pp. 74 to 86)—his action there—Mughūls demand and besiege Andijān for Bābur's half-brother Jahāngīr—his mother and friends entreat his help—he leaves Samarkand in his cousin 'Alī's hands—has a relapse of illness on the road and is believed dying—on the news Andijān is surrendered by a Mughūl to the Mughūl faction —Having lost Samarkand and Andijān, Bābur is hospitably entertained by the Khujandīs — he is forced to dismiss Khalīfa—The Khān (his uncle) moves to help him but is

persuaded to retire—many followers go to Andijān where were their families—he is left with 200–300 men—his mother and grandmother and the families of his men sent to him in Khujand—he is distressed to tears—The Khān gives help against Samarkand but his troops turn back on news of Shaibānī—Bābur returns to Khujand—speaks of his ambition to rule—goes in person to ask The Khān's help to regain Andijān—his force being insufficient, he goes back to Khujand—Affairs of Khusrau Shāh and the Tīmūrid Mīrzās—Affairs of Ḥusain *Bāī-qarā* and his sons —Khusrau Shāh blinds Bābur's cousin Mas'ūd—Bābur curses the criminal 72–96

904 AH.—Aug. 19th 1498 to Aug. 8th 1499 AD.—Bābur borrows Pashāghar for the winter and leaves Khujand—rides 70–80 miles with fever—a winter's tug-of-war with Samarkand—his force insufficient, he goes back to Khujand—unwilling to burthen it longer, goes into the summer-pastures of Aūrātīpā—invited to Marghīnān by his mother's uncle 'Alī-dost—a joyful rush over some 145 miles — near Marghīnān prudent anxieties arise and are stilled—he is admitted to Marghīnān on terms—is attacked vainly by the Mughūl faction—accretions to his force—helped by The Khān—the Mughūls defeated near Akhsī—Andijān recovered—Mughūls renew revolt—Bābur's troops beaten by Mughūls—Tambal attempts Andijān . . 97–107

905 AH.—Aug. 8th 1499 to July 28th 1500 AD.—Bābur's campaign against Aḥmad *Tambal* and the Mughūl faction—he takes Māzū—Khusrau Shāh murders Bāī-sunghar *Mīrān-shāhī*—Biography of the Mīrzā—Bābur wins his first ranged battle, from Tambal supporting Jahāngīr, at Khūbān—winter-quarters—minor successes—the winter-camp broken up by Qambar-i-'alī's taking leave — Bābur returns to Andijān—The Khān persuaded by Tambal's kinsmen in his service to support Jahāngīr—his troops retire before Bābur—Bābur and Tambal again opposed—Qambar-i-'alī again gives trouble—minor action and an accommodation made without Bābur's wish—terms of the accommodation—The self-aggrandizement of 'Alī-dost *Mughūl*—Bābur's first marriage—a personal episode—Samarkand affairs—'Alī quarrels with the Tarkhāns—The Khān sends troops against Samarkand—Mīrzā Khān invited there by a Tarkhān—'Alī defeats The Khān's Mughūls—Bābur invited to Samarkand —prepares to start and gives Jahāngīr rendezvous for the

attempt—Taṃbal's brother takes Aūsh—Bābur leaves this lesser matter aside and marches for Samarkand—Qaṃbar-i-'alī punishes himself—Shaibānī reported to be moving on Bukhārā—Samarkand begs wait on Bābur—the end of 'Alī-dost — Bābur has news of Shaibānī's approach to Samarkand and goes to Kesh — hears there that 'Alī's Aūzbeg mother had given Samarkand to Shaibānī on condition of his marriage with herself . . 108–126

906 AH.—July 28th 1500 to July 17th 1501 AD.—Shaibānī murders 'Alī — a son and two grandsons of Aḥrārī's murdered — Bābur leaves Kesh with a number of the Samarkand begs—is landless and isolated—takes a perilous mountain journey back into Aūrātīpā—comments on the stinginess shewn to himself by Khusrau Shāh and another —consultation and resolve to attempt Samarkand—Bābur's dream-vision of success—he takes the town by a surprise attack—compares this capture with Ḥusain *Bāī-qarā's* of Herī—his affairs in good position—birth of his first child—his summons for help to keep the Aūzbeg down—literary matters — his force of 240 grows to allow him to face Shaibānī at Sar-i-pul—the battle and his defeat—Mughūls help his losses—he is besieged in Samarkand—a long blockade—great privation—no help from any quarter—Futile proceedings of Taṃbal and The Khān . 127–145

907 AH.—July 17th 1501 to July 7th 1502 AD.—Bābur surrenders Samarkand—his sister Khān-zāda is married by Shaibānī—incidents of his escape to Dīzak—his 4 or 5 escapes from peril to safety and ease—goes to Dikh-kat in Aūrātīpā—incidents of his stay there—his wanderings bare-head, bare-foot—sends gifts to Jahāngīr, and to Taṃbal a sword which later wounds himself — arrival from Samarkand of the families and a few hungry followers—Shaibānī Khān raids in The Khān's country—Bābur rides after him fruitlessly—Death of Nuyān Kūkūldāsh—Bābur's grief for his friend—he retires to the Zar-afshān valley before Shaibānī—reflects on the futility of his wanderings and goes to The Khān in Tāshkīnt—Mughūl conspiracy against Taṃbal *Mughūl*—Bābur submits verses to The Khān and comments on his uncle's scant study of poetic idiom—The Khān rides out against Taṃbal—his standards acclaimed and his army numbered—of the *Chīngīz-tūrā*—quarrel of Chīrās and Begchīk chiefs for the post of danger—Ḥunting—Khujand-river reached 146–156

908 AH.—July 7th 1502 to June 26th 1503 AD.—Bābur comments on The Khān's unprofitable move—his poverty and despair in Tāshkīnt—his resolve to go to Khitāī and ruse for getting away—his thought for his mother—his plan not accepted by The Khān and Shāh Begīm—The Younger Khān (Aḥmad) arrives from Kāshghar—is met by Bābur—a half-night's family talk—gifts to Bābur—the meeting of the two Khāns—Aḥmad's characteristics and his opinion of various weapons—The Khāns march into Farghāna against Jahāngīr's supporter Tambal—they number their force—Bābur detached against Aūsh, takes it and has great accretions of following—An attempt to take Andijān frustrated by mistake in a pass-word—Author's Note on pass-words—a second attempt foiled by the over-caution of experienced begs—is surprised in his bivouac by Tambal—face to face with Tambal—his new *gosha-gīr*—his dwindling company—wounded—left alone, is struck by his gift-sword—escapes to Aūsh—The Khān moves from Kāsān against Andijān—his disposition of Bābur's lands—Qambar-i-'alī's counsel to Bābur rejected—Bābur is treated by the Younger Khān's surgeon—tales of Mughūl surgery—Qambar-i-'alī flees to Tambal in fear through his unacceptable counsel—Bābur moves for Akhsī—a lost chance—minor actions—an episode of Pāp—The Khān's do not take Andijān—Bābur invited into Akhsī—Tambal's brother Bāyazīd joins him with Nāṣir *Mīrān-shāhī*—Tambal asks help from Shaibānī—On news of Shaibānī's consent the Khāns retire from Andijān—Bābur's affairs in Akhsī—he attempts to defend it—incidents of the defence—Bābur wounded—unequal strength of the opponents—he flees with 20–30 men—incidents of the flight—Bābur left alone—is overtaken by two foes—his perilous position—a messenger arrives from Tambal's brother Bāyazīd—Bābur expecting death, quotes Niẓāmī—(the narrative breaks off in the middle of the verse) 157–182

Translator's Note.—908 to 909 AH.—1503 to 1504 AD.—Bābur will have been rescued—is with The Khāns in the battle and defeat by Shaibānī at Archīān—takes refuge in the Asfara hills—there spends a year in misery and poverty—events in Farghāna and Tāshkīnt—Shaibānī sends the Mughūl horde back to Kāshgar—his disposition of the women of The Khān's family—Bābur plans to go to Ḥusain *Bāī-qarā* in Khurāsān—changes his aim for Kābul 182–185

[End of Translator's Note.]

SECTION II.—KĀBUL

910 AH.—June 14th 1504 to June 4th 1505 AD.—Bābur halts on an alp of Ḥiṣār—enters his 22nd (lunar) year—delays his march in hope of adherents—writes a second time of the stinginess of Khusrau Shāh to himself—recalls Sherīm Ṭaghāï *Mughūl's* earlier waverings in support—is joined by Khusrau Shāh's brother Bāqī Beg—they start for Kābul—Accretions of force — their families left in Fort Ajar (Kāhmard)—Jahāngīr marries a cousin—Bāqī advises his dismissal to Khurāsān—Bābur is loyal to his half-brother—Jahāngīr is seduced, later, by disloyal Begchīk chiefs—Ḥusain *Bāī-qarā* summons help against Shaibānī—Despair in Bābur's party at Ḥusain's plan of "defence, not attack" —Qambar-i-'alī dismissed to please Bāqī—Khusrau makes abject submission to Bābur—Mīrzā Khān demands vengeance on him—Khusrau's submission having been on terms, he is let go free—Bābur resumes his march—first sees Canopus—is joined by tribesmen—Khusrau's brother Walī flees to the Aūzbegs and is executed—Risks run by the families now fetched from Kāhmard—Kābul surrendered to Bābur by Muqīm *Arghūn*—Muqīm's family protected—**Description of Kābul** (pp. 199 to 277)—Muqīm leaves for Qandahār—Allotment of fiefs—Excess levy in grain—Foray on the Sulṭān Mas'ūdī Hazāra—Bābur's first move for Hindūstān—Khaibar traversed—Bīgrām visited—Bāqī Beg prevents crossing the Sind—and persuades for Kohāt —A plan for Bangash, Bannū and thence return to Kābul—Yār-i-ḥusain *Daryā-khānī* asks for permission to raise a force for Bābur, east of the Sind—Move to Thāl, Bannū, and the Dasht—return route varied without consulting Bābur—Pīr Kānū's tomb visited—through the Pawat-pass into Dūkī—horse-food fails—baggage left behind—men of all conditions walk to Ghaznī — spectacle of the Āb-istāda—mirage and birds—Jahāngīr is Bābur's host in Ghaznī—heavy floods—Kābul reached after a disastrous expedition of four months—Nāṣir's misconduct abetted by two Begchīk chiefs—he and they flee into Badakhshān—Khusrau Shāh's schemes fail in Herāt—imbroglio between him and Nāṣir—Shaibānī attempts Ḥiṣār but abandons the siege on his brother's death—Khusrau attempts Ḥiṣār and is there killed—his followers revolt against Bābur—his death quenches the fire of sedition 188–245

911 AH.—June 4th 1505 to May 24th 1506 AD.—Death of Bābur's mother—Bābur's illness stops a move for Qandahār —an earth-quake—campaign against and capture of Qalāt-i-ghilzāī — Bāqī Beg dismissed towards Hindūstān — murdered in the Khaibar—Turkmān Hazāra raided—Nijr-aū tribute collected—Jahāngīr misbehaves and runs away—Bābur summoned by Ḥusain *Bāī-qarā* against Shaibānī—Shaibānī takes Khwārizm and Chīn Ṣūfī is killed—Death and biography of Ḥusain *Bāī-qarā* (256 to 292)—his burial and joint-successors . . . 246–293

912 AH.—May 24th 1506 to May 13th 1507 AD.—Bābur, without news of Ḥusain *Bāī-qarā's* death, obeys his summons and leaves Kābul—Jahāngīr flees from Bābur's route—Nāṣir defeats Shaibānī's men in Badakhshān—Bābur, while in Kāhmard, hears of Ḥusain's death—continues his march with anxious thought for the Tīmūrid dynasty—Jahāngīr waits on him and accompanies him to Herāt—Co-alition of Khurāsān Mīrzās against Shaibānī—their meeting with Bābur—etiquette of Bābur's reception—an entertainment to him—of the *Chīngīz-tūrā*—Bābur claims the ceremonial observance due to his military achievements—entertainments and Bābur's obedience to Muḥammadan Law against wine—his reflections on the Mīrzās—difficulties of winter-plans (300, 307)—he sees the sights of Herī—visits the Begīms—the ceremonies observed—tells of his hitherto abstention from wine and of his present inclination to drink it—Qasīm Beg's interference with those pressing Bābur to break the Law—Bābur's poor carving—engages Ma'ṣūma in marriage—leaves for Kābul—certain retainers stay behind—a perilous journey through snow to a wrong pass out of the Herīrud valley—arrival of the party in Yaka-aūlāng—joy in their safety and comfort—Shibr-tū traversed into Ghūr-bund—Turkmān Hazāra raided—News reaches Bābur of conspiracy in Kābul to put Mīrzā Khān in his place—Bābur concerts plans with the loyal Kābul garrison—moves on through snow and in terrible cold—attacks and defeats the rebels—narrowly escaped death—attributes his safety to prayer—deals mercifully, from family considerations, with the rebel chiefs—reflects on their behaviour to him who has protected them—asserts that his only aim is to write the truth — letters-of-victory sent out — Muḥ. Ḥusain *Dūghlāt* and Mīrzā Khān banished—Spring excursion to Koh-dāman—Nāṣir, driven from Badakhshān, takes refuge with Bābur 294–322

913 AH.—May 13th 1507 to May 2nd 1508 AD.—Raid on the Ghiljī Afghāns—separation of the Fifth (*Khams*)—wild-ass hunting—Shaibānī moves against Khurāsān—Irresolution of the Tīmūrid Mīrzās—Infatuation of Ẕū'n-nūn *Arghūn*—Shaibānī takes Herī—his doings there—Defeat and death of two *Bāī-qarās*—The Arghūns in Qandahār make overtures to Bābur—he starts to join them against Shaibānī—meets Ma'ṣūma in Ghaznī on her way to Kābul—spares Hindūstān traders—meets Jahāngīr's widow and infant-son coming from Herāt—The Arghūn chiefs provoke attack on Qandahār—Bābur's army—organization and terminology—wins the battle of Qandahār and enters the fort—its spoils—Nāṣir put in command—Bābur returns to Kābul rich in goods and fame—marries Ma'ṣūma—Shaibānī lays siege to Qandahār—Alarm in Kābul at his approach—Mīrzā Khān and Shāh Begīm betake themselves to Badakhshān—Bābur sets out for Hindūstān leaving 'Abdu'r-razzāq in Kābul—Afghān highwaymen—A raid for food—Māh-chuchak's marriage—Hindūstān plan abandoned—Nūr-gal and Kūnār visited—News of Shaibānī's withdrawal from Qandahār—Bābur returns to Kābul—gives Ghaznī to Nāṣir—assumes the title of Pādshāh—Birth of Humāyūn, feast and chronogram 323–344

914 AH.—May 2nd 1508 to April 21st 1509 AD.—Raid on the Mahmand Afghāns — Seditious offenders reprieved — Khusrau Shāh's former retainers march off from Kābul—'Abdu'r-razzāq comes from his district to near Kābul—not known to have joined the rebels—earlier hints to Bābur of this "incredible" rebellion—later warnings of an immediate rising 345–346

Translator's Note.—914 to 925 AH.—1508 to 1519 AD.—Date of composition of preceding narrative—Loss of matter here seems partly or wholly due to Bābur's death—Sources helping to fill the Gap—Events of the remainder of 914 AH.—The mutiny swiftly quelled—Bābur's five-fold victory over hostile champions—Sa'īd *Chaghatāī* takes refuge with him in a quiet Kābul—Shaibānī's murders of Chaghatāī and Dūghlāt chiefs 347–366

AH.—April 21st 1509 to April 11th 1510 AD.—Beginning of hostilities between Ismā'īl *Ṣafawī* and Shaibānī—Ḥaidar *Dūghlāt* takes refuge with Bābur.

AH.—April 11th 1510 to March 31st 1511 AD.—Ismā'īl defeats the Aūzbegs near Merv—Shaibānī is killed—20,000

Mughūls he had migrated to Khurāsān, return to near Qūndūz—Mīrzā Khān invites Bābur to join him against the Aūzbegs—Bābur goes to Qūndūz—The 20,000 Mughūls proffer allegiance to their hereditary Khān Sa'īd—they propose to set Bābur aside—Sa'īd's worthy rejection of the proposal—Bābur makes Sa'īd The Khān of the Mughūls and sends him and his Mughūls into Farghāna—significance of Bābur's words, "I made him Khān"—Bābur's first attempt on Ḥiṣār where were Ḥamza and Mahdī *Aūzbeg*—beginning of his disastrous intercourse with Ismā'īl *Ṣafawī*—Ismā'īl sends Khān-zāda Begīm back to him—with thanks for the courtesy, Bābur asks help against the Aūzbeg—it is promised under dangerous conditions.

917 AH.—March 31st 1511 to March 19th 1512 AD.—Bābur's second attempt on Ḥiṣār—wins the Battle of Pul-i-sangīn—puts Ḥamza and Mahdī to death—his Persian reinforcement and its perilous cost—The Aūzbegs are swept across the Zar-afshān—The Persians are dismissed from Bukhārā—Bābur occupies Samarkand after a nine-year's absence—he gives Kābul to Nāṣir—his difficult position in relation to the Shī'a Ismā'īl—Ismā'īl sends Najm Ṣānī to bring him to order.

918 AH.—March 19th 1512 to March 9th 1513 AD.—The Aūzbegs return to the attack—'Ubaid's vow—his defeat of Bābur at Kūl-i-malik—Bābur flees from Samarkand to Ḥiṣār—his pursuers retire—Najm Ṣānī from Balkh gives him rendezvous at Tīrmīẕ—the two move for Bukhārā—Najm perpetrates the massacre of Qarshī—Bābur is helpless to prevent it—Najm crosses the Zar-afshān to a disadvantageous position—is defeated and slain—Bābur, his reserve, does not fight—his abstention made a reproach at the Persian Court against his son Humāyūn (1544 AD.?)—his arrow-sped message to the Aūzbeg camp—in Ḥiṣār, he is attacked suddenly by Mughūls—he escapes to Qūndūz—the retributive misfortunes of Ḥiṣār—Ḥaidar on Mughūls—Ayūb *Begchīk's* death-bed repentance for his treachery to Bābur—Ḥaidar returns to his kinsfolk in Kāshghar.

919 AH.—March 9th 1513 to Feb. 26th 1514 AD.—Bābur may have spent the year in Khishm—Ismā'īl takes Balkh from the Aūzbegs—surmised bearing of the capture on his later action.

920 AH.—Feb. 26th 1514 to Feb. 15th 1515 AD.—Ḥaidar's account of Bābur's misery, patience and courtesy this year

in Qūndūz—Bābur returns to Kābul—his daughter Gul-rang is born in Khwāst—he is welcomed by Nāṣir who goes back to Ghaznī.

921 AH.—Feb. 15th 1515 to Feb. 5th 1516 AD.—Death of Nāṣir—Riot in Ghaznī led by Sherīm Ṭaghāī *Mughūl*—quiet restored — many rebels flee to, Kāshghar—Sherīm refused harbourage by Sa'īd Khān and seeks Bābur's protection—Ḥaidar's comment on Bābur's benevolence.

922 AH.—Feb. 5th 1516 to Jan. 24th 1517 AD.—A quiet year in Kābul apparently—Birth of 'Askarī.

923 AH.—Jan. 24th 1517 to Jan. 13th 1518 AD.—Bābur visits Balkh—Khwānd-amīr's account of the affairs of Muhammad-i-zamān Mīrza *Bāī-qarā*—Bābur pursues the Mīrzā—has him brought to Kābul—gives him his daughter Ma'ṣūma in marriage—An expedition to Qandahār returns fruitless, on account of his illness—Shāh Beg's views on Bābur's persistent attempts on Qandahār—Shāh Beg's imprisonment and release by his slave Sambal's means.

924 AH.—Jan. 13th 1518 to Jan. 3rd 1519 AD.—Shāh Beg's son Ḥasan flees to Bābur—stays two years—date of his return to his father—Bābur begins a campaign in Bajaur against Ḥaidar-i-'alī *Bajaurī*—takes two forts.

[End of Translator's Note.]

925 AH.—Jan. 3rd to Dec. 23rd 1519 AD.—Bābur takes the Fort of Bajaur—massacres its people as false to Islām—Khwāja Kalān made its Commandant — an excessive impost in grain — a raid for corn — Māhīm's adoption of Dil-dār's unborn child—Bābur marries Bībī Mubārika—Repopulation of the Fort of Bajaur—Expedition against Afghān tribesmen—Destruction of the tomb of a heretic qalandar—Bābur first crosses the Sind—his long-cherished desire for Hindūstān—the ford of the Sind—the Koh-i-jūd (Salt-range) — his regard for Bhīra, Khūsh-āb, Chīn-ab and Chīnīūt as earlier possessions of the Turk, now therefore his own—the Kalda-kahār lake and subsequent location on it of the Bāgh-i-ṣafā—Assurance of safety sent to Bhīra as a Turk possession—History of Bhīra *etc.* as Turk possessions—Author's Note on Tātār Khān *Yūsuf-khail*—envoys sent to Balūchīs in Bhīra—heavy floods in camp—Offenders against Bhīra people punished—Agreed tribute collected—Envoy sent to ask from Ibrāhīm *Lūdī* the lands once dependent on the Turk—Daulat Khān arrests and keeps

the envoy who goes back later to Bābur *re infectâ*—news of Hind-āl's birth and cause of his name—description of a drinking-party—Tātār Khān *Kakar* compels Minūchihr Khān *Turk*, going to wait on Bābur, to become his son-in-law—Account of the Kakars—excursions and drinking-parties—Bhīra appointments—action taken against Hātī Khān *Kakar*—Description and capture of Parhāla—Bābur sees the sambal plant—a tiger killed—Gūr-khattrī visited—Loss of a clever hawk—Khaibar traversed—mid-day halt in the Bāgh-i-wafā—Qarā-tū garden visited—News of Shāh Beg's capture of Kāhān—Bābur's boys carried out in haste to meet him—wine-parties—Death and biography of Dost Beg—Arrival of Sulṭānīm *Bāī-qarā* and ceremonies observed on meeting her—A long-imprisoned traitor released—Excursion to Koh-dāman—Hindū Beg abandons Bhīra—Bābur has (intermittent) fever—Visitors from Khwāst—Yūsuf-zāī chiefs wait on Bābur—Khalīfa's son sends a wedding-gift—Bābur's amusement when illness keeps him from an entertainment—treatment of his illness—A Thursday reading of theology (*see* Add. Note p. 401)—Swimming—Envoy from Mīrzā Khān—Tribesmen allowed to leave Kābul for wider grazing-grounds—Bābur sends his first *Dīwān* to Pūlād *Aūzbeg* in Samarkand—Arrivals and departures—Punitive expedition against the 'Abdu'r-rahman Afghāns—punishment threatened and inflicted (p. 405) on defaulters in help to an out-matched man—Description of the Rustam-maidān—return to Kābul—Excursion to Koh-dāman—snake incident—Tramontane begs warned for service—fish-drugging—Bābur's non-pressure to drink, on an abstainer—wine-party—misadventure on a raft—tooth-picks gathered—A new retainer—Bābur shaves his head—Hind-āl's guardian appointed—Aūzbeg raiders defeated in Badakhshān—Various arrivals—Yūsuf-zāī campaign—Bābur dislocates his wrist—*Varia*—Dilah-zāk chiefs wait on him—Plan to store corn in Hash-nagar—Incidents of the road—Khaibar traversed—Bārā urged on Bābur as a place for corn—Kābul river forded at Bārā—little corn found and the Hash-nagar plan foiled—Plan to store Pashāwar Fort—return to 'Alī-masjid—News of an invasion of Badakhshān hurries Bābur back through the Khaibar—The Khizr-khail Afghāns punished—Bābur first writes since dislocating his wrist—The beauty and fruits of the Bāgh-i-wafā—incidents of the return march to Kābul—Excursion to the Koh-dāman—beauty of its harvest crops and autumnal trees—a line offensive to Khalīfa (*see* Add. Note p. 416)—Humāyūn makes a good shot—Beauty of the harvest near Istālīf and in the Bāgh-i-pādshāhī — Return to Kābul — Bābur receives a white falcon in gift — pays a visit of consolation to an ashamed drinker—Arrivals various—he finishes copying 'Alī-sher's four *Dīwāns* — An order to exclude from future parties those who become drunk—Bābur starts for Lāmghān 367–419

926 AH.—Dec. 23rd 1519 to Dec. 12th 1520 AD.—Excursion to Koh-dāman and Kohistān—incidents of the road—Bābur shoots with an easy bow, for the first time after the dislocation of his wrist — Nijr-aū tribute fixed — Excursions in Lāmghān—Kāfir head-men bring goat-skins of wine—Halt in the Bāgh-i-wafā—its oranges, beauty and charm—Bābur records his wish and intention to return to obedience in his 40th year and his consequent excess in wine as the end approached—composes an air—visits Nūr-valley—relieves Kwāja Kalān in Bajaur—teaches a talisman to stop rain—his opinion of the ill-taste and disgusting intoxication of beer—his reason for summoning Khwāja Kalān, and trenchant words to Shāh Ḥasan relieving him — an old beggar loaded with gifts—the raft strikes a rock—Description of the Kīndīr spring—Fish taken from fish-ponds—Hunting—Accident to a tooth—Fishing with a net—A murderer made over to the avengers of blood—A Qoran chapter read and start made for Kābul—(here the diary breaks off) 420–425

Translator's Note.—926 to 932 AH.—1520 to 1525 AD.—Bābur's activities in the Gap — missing matter less interesting than that lost in the previous one—its distinctive mark is biographical — *Dramatis personæ* — Sources of information 426–444

926 AH.—Dec. 23rd 1519 to Dec. 12th 1520 AD.—Bābur's five expeditions into Hindūstān—this year's cut short by menace from Qandahār—Shāh Beg's position—particulars of his menace not ascertained—**Description of Qandahār-fort**—Bābur's various sieges—this year's raised because of pestilence within the walls—Shāh Beg pushes out into Sind.

927 AH.—Dec. 12th 1520 to Dec. 1st 1521 AD.—Two accounts of this year's siege of Qandahār—(i) that of the *Ḥabību's-siyar*—(ii) that of the *Tārīkh-i-sind*—concerning the dates involved—Mīrzā Khān's death.

928 AH.—Dec. 1st 1521 to Nov. 20th 1522 AD.—Bābur and Māhīm visit Humāyūn in Badakhshān—Expedition to Qandahār—of the duel between Bābur and Shāh Beg—the Chihil-zīna monument of victory—Death of Shāh Beg and its date—Bābur's literary work down to this year.

929 AH.—Nov. 20th 1522 to Nov. 10th 1523 AD.—Hindūstān affairs—Daulat Khān *Lūdī*, Ibrāhīm *Lūdī* and Bābur—Dilawār (son of Daulat Khān) goes to Kābul and asks help against Ibrāhīm—Bābur prays for a sign of victory—prepares for the expedition—'Ālam Khān *Lūdī* (apparently in this year) goes to Kābul and asks Bābur's help against his nephew Ibrāhīm—Birth of Gul-badan.

930 AH.—Nov. 10th 1523 to Oct. 27th 1524 AD.—Bābur's fourth expedition into Hindūstān—differs from earlier ones by its concert with malcontents in the country—Bābur defeats Bihār Khān *Lūdī* near Lāhor—Lāhor occupied—Dībalpūr stormed, plundered and its people massacred—Bābur moves onward from Sihrind but returns on news of Daulat Khān's doings—there may have been also news of Aūzbeg threat to Balkh—The Panj-āb garrison—Death of Ismā'īl *Ṣafawī* and of Shāh Beg—Bābur turns for Kābul—plants bananas in the Bāgh-i-wafā.

931 AH.—Oct. 29th 1524 to Oct. 18th 1525 AD.—Daulat Khān's large resources—he defeats 'Ālam Khān at Dībalpūr—'Ālam Khān flees to Kābul and again asks help—Bābur's conditions of reinforcement—'Ālam Khān's subsequent proceedings detailed *s.a.* 932 AH.—Bābur promises to follow him speedily—is summoned to Balkh by its Aūzbeg menace—his arrival raises the siege—he returns to Kābul in time for his start to Hindūstān in 932 426–444

[End of Translator's Note.]

SECTION III.—HINDŪSTĀN

932 AH.—Oct. 18th 1525 to Oct. 8th 1526 AD.—Bābur starts on his fifth expedition into Hindūstān—is attacked by illness at Gandamak—Humāyūn is late in coming in from Badakhshān—Verse-making on the Kābul-river—Bābur makes a satirical verse such as he had forsworn when writing the *Mubīn*—attributes a relapse of illness to his breach of vow—renews his oath—Fine spectacle of the lighted camp at Alī-masjid—Hunting near Bīgrām—Preparations for ferrying the Sind—Order to make a list of all with the army,

aside and to march to the East—Humāyūn leads out the army—Bābur makes garden, well and mosque near Āgra—Progress of Humāyūn's campaign—News of the Aūzbegs in Balkh and Khurāsān—Affairs of Gujrāt . 445–535

933 AH.—Oct. 8th 1526 to Sep. 27th 1527 AD.—Birth announced of Bābur's son Fārūq—incomplete success in casting a large mortar—*Varia*—Humāyūn summoned from the East to act against Sangā—Plundering expedition towards Bīāna—Tahangar, Gūālīār and Dūlpūr obtained—Ḥamīd Khān *Sārang-khānī* defeated—Arrival of a Persian embassy—Ibrāhīm's mother tries to poison Bābur—**Copy of Bābur's letter detailing the affair** — his dealings with the poisoner and her agents—Humāyūn's return to Āgra—Khw. Dost-i-khawānd's arrival from Kābul — Reiterated news of the approach of Rānā Sangā—Bābur sends an advance force to Bīāna—Ḥasan Khān *Miwātī*—Tramontane matters disloyal to Bābur—Trial-test of the large mortar (p. 536)—Bābur leaves Āgra to oppose Sangā—adverse encounter with Sangā by Bīāna garrison—Alarming reports of Rājpūt prowess—Spadesmen sent ahead to dig wells in Madhākūr *pargana*—Bābur halts there—arrays and moves to Sīkrī—various joinings and scoutings—discomfiture of a party reconnoitring from Sīkrī—the reinforcement also overcome—The enemy retires at sight of a larger troop from Bābur—defence of the Sīkrī camp Rūmī fashion, with ditch besides—Continued praise of Rājpūt prowess—Further defence of the camp made to hearten Bābur's men—20–25 days spent in the above preparations—arrival of 500 men from Kābul—also of Muḥ. Sharīf an astrologer who augurs ill for Bābur's success—Archers collected and Mīwāt over-run—Bābur reflects that he had always wished to cease from the sin of wine — verses about his then position — resolves to renounce wine—details of the destruction of wine and precious vessels, and of the building of a commemorative well and alms-house—his oath to remit a tax if victorious is recalled to him—he remits the *tamghā*—Shaikh Zain writes the *farmān* announcing the two acts—Copy of the *farmān* — Great fear in Bābur's army — he adjures the Ghāzī spirit in his men who vow to stand fast—his perilous position — he moves forward in considerable array—his camp is laid out and protected by ditch and carts—An omen is taken and gives hope—Khalīfa advising, the camp is moved—While tents were being set up, the

enemy appears—The battle and victory of Kānwa—described in a copy of the Letter-of-victory—Bābur inserts this because of its full particulars (pp. 559 to 574)—assumes the title of Ghāzī—Chronograms of the victory and also of that in Dībalpūr (930 AH.)—pursuit of the fugitive foe—escape of Sangā—the falsely-auguring astrologer banished with a gift —a small revolt crushed—a pillar of heads set up—Bābur visits Bīāna—Little water and much heat set aside plan to invade Sangā's territory—Bābur visits Mīwāt—give some historical account of it — Commanders rewarded — Alwār visited—Humāyūn and others allowed to leave Hindūstān —Despatch of the Letter-of-victory—Various excursions— Humāyūn bidden farewell—Chandwāṛ and Rāprī recovered —Apportionment of fiefs—Bīban flees before Bābur's men— Dispersion of troops for the Rains—Misconduct of Humāyūn and Bābur's grief—Embassy to 'Irāq—Tardī Beg *khāksār* allowed to return to the darwesh-life — Bābur's lines to departing friends — The Ramẓān-feast — Playing-cards— Bābur ill (seemingly with fever)—visits Dūlpūr and orders a house excavated—visits Bārī and sees the ebony-tree— has doubt of Bāyazīd *Farmūlī's* loyalty—his remedial and metrical exercises—his Treatise on Prosody composed— a relapse of illness—starts on an excursion to Kūl and Saṃbal 536–586

934 AH.—Sep. 27th 1527 to Sep. 15th 1528 AD.—Bābur visits Kūl and Saṃbal and returns to Āgra—has fever and ague intermittently for 20–25 days—goes out to welcome kinswomen—a large mortar bursts with fatal result—he visits Sīkrī—starts for Holy War against Chandīrī—sends troops against Bāyazīd *Farmūlī* — incidents of the march to Chandīrī—account of Kachwa—account of Chandīrī—its siege—Meantime bad news arrives from the East—Bābur keeping this quiet, accomplishes the work in hand—Chandīrī taken—change of plans enforced by defeat in the East— return northwards—Further losses in the East—Rebels take post to dispute Bābur's passage of the Ganges—he orders a pontoon-bridge—his artillery is used with effect, the bridge finished and crossed and the Afghāns worsted—Tukhta-būghā *Chaghatāī* arrives from Kāshgar — Bābur visits Lakhnau — suffers from ear-ache — reinforces Chīn-tīmūr against the rebels—Chīn-tīmūr gets the better of Bāyazīd *Farmūlī*—Bābur settles the affairs of Aūd (Oude) and plans to hunt near 587–602

Translator's Note (part of 934 AH.)—On the *cir.* half-year's missing matter—known events of the Gap:—Continued campaign against Bīban and Bāyazīd—Bābur at Jūnpūr, Chausa and Baksara—swims the Ganges—bestows Sarūn on a Farmūlī—orders a Chār-bāgh made—is ill for 40 days—is inferred to have visited Dūlpūr, recalled 'Askarī from Multān, sent Khw. Dost-i-khāwand to Kābul on family affairs which were causing him much concern—Remarks on the Gap and, incidentally, on the Rāmpūr Dīwān and verses in it suiting Bābur's illnesses of 934 AH.

[**End of Translator's Note.**]

935 AH. Sep. 15th 1528 to Sep. 5th 1529 AD.—'Askarī reaches Āgra from Multān—Khwānd-amīr and others arrive from Khurāsān—Bābur prepares to visit Gūālīār—bids farewell to kinswomen who are returning to Kābul—marches out—is given an unsavoury medicament—inspects construction-work in Dūlpūr—reaches Gūālīār—**Description of Gūālīār** (p. 607 to p. 614)—returns to Dūlpūr—suffers from ear-ache—inspects work in Sīkrī and reaches Āgra—visit and welcomes to kinswomen—sends an envoy to take charge of Rantanbhūr—makes a levy on stipendiaries—sends letters to kinsfolk in Khurāsān—News arrives of Kāmrān and Dost-i-khāwand in Kābul—of Ṭahmāsp *Ṣafawī's* defeat at Jām of 'Ubaidu'l-lāh *Aūzbeg*—of the birth of a son to Humāyūn, and of a marriage by Kāmrān—he rewards an artificer—is strongly attacked by fever—for his healing translates Aḥrārī's *Wālidiyyah-risāla*—account of the task—Troops warned for service—A long-detained messenger returns from Humāyūn—Accredited messengers-of-good-tidings bring the news of Humāyūn's son's birth—an instance of rapid travel—Further particulars of the Battle of Jām—Letters written and summarized—**Copy of one to Humāyūn inserted here**—Plans for an eastern campaign under 'Askarī—royal insignia given to him—Orders for the measurement, stations and up-keep of the Āgra-Kābul road—the *Mubīn* quoted—A feast describes—'Askarī bids his Father farewell—Bābur visits Dūlpūr and inspects his constructions—Persian account of the Battle of Jām—Bābur decides contingently to go to the East—Balūchī incursions—News reaches Dūlpūr of the loss of Bihār (town) and decides Bābur to go East—News of Humāyūn's action in Badakhshān—Bābur starts from Āgra—honoured arrivals in the assembly-camp—incidents of the march—congratula-

tions and gifts sent to Kāmrān, Humāyūn and others—also specimens of the Bāburī-script, and copies of the translation of the *Wālidiyyah-risāla* and the Hindūstān Poems—commends his building-work to his workmen—makes a new ruler for the better copying of the *Wālidiyyah-risāla* translation—letters written—**Copy of one to Khwāja Kalān inserted here**—Complaints from Kītīn-qarā *Aūzbeg* of Bābur's begs on the Balkh frontier—Bābur shaves his head—Māhīm using his style, orders her own escort from Kābul to Āgra—Bābur watches wrestling—leaves the Jumna, disembarks his guns, and goes across country to Dugdugī on the Ganges—travels by litter—'Askarī and other Commanders meet him—News of Bīban, Bāyazīd and other Afghāns—Letters despatched to meet Māhīm on her road—Bābur sends a copy of his writings to Samarkand—watches wrestling—hears news of the Afghāns—(here a surmised survival of record displaced from 934 AH.)—fall of a river-bank under his horse—swims the Ganges—crosses the Jumna at Allahābād (Piag) and re-embarks his guns—wrestling watched—the evil Tons—he is attacked by boils—a Rūmī remedy applied—a futile attempt to hunt—he sends money-drafts to the travellers from Kābul—visits places on the Ganges he had seen last year—receives various letters below Ghāzīpūr—has news that the Ladies are actually on their way from Kābul—last year's eclipse recalled—Hindu dread of the Karmā-nāśā river—wrestling watched—Rūmī remedy for boils used again with much discomfort—fall of last year's landing-steps at Baksara—wrestling—Negociations with an envoy of Naṣrat Shāh of Bengal—Examination into Muḥammad-i-zāman's objections to a Bihār appointment—despatch of troops to Bihār (town)—Muḥammad-i-zamān submits requests which are granted—a small success against Afghāns—Royal insignia given to Muhammad-i-zamān, with leave to start for Bihār—Bābur's boats—News of the Bengal army—Muḥammad-i-zāman recalled because fighting was probable—Dūdū Bībī and her son Jalāl escape from Bengal to come to Bābur—Further discussions with the Bengal envoy—Favourable news from Bihār—Bābur in Arrah—Position of the Bengal army near the confluence of Gang and Sārū (Ganges and Gogrā)—Bābur making further effort for peace, sends an envoy to Naṣrat Shāh—gives Naṣrat's envoy leave to go conveying an ultimatum—Arrival of a servant from Māhīm west of the Bāgh-i-ṣafā—Bābur visits lotus-beds near Arrah—also

Munīr and the Son—Distance measured by counting a horse's paces—care for tired horses—Bābur angered by Junaid *Barlās'* belated arrival — Consultation and plans made for the coming battle—the Ganges crossed (by the Burh-ganga channel) and move made to near the confluence — Bābur watches 'Alī-qulī's stone-discharge — his boat entered by night—Battle and victory of the Gogrā—Babur praises and thanks his Chaghatāī cousins for their great services—crosses into the Nirhun *pargana*—his favours to a Farmūlī—News of Bīban and Bāyazīd—and of the strange deaths in Saṃbal—Chīn-tīmūr sends news from the west of inconveniences caused by the Ladies' delay to leave Kābul —and of success against the Balūchī—he is ordered to Āgra—Settlement made with the Nuḥānī Afghāns—Peace made with Naṣrat Shāh—Submissions and various guerdon —Bīban and Bāyazīd pursued—Bābur's papers damaged in a storm—News of the rebel pair as taking Luknūr (?)—Disposition of Bābur's boats—move along the Sārū—(a surmised survival of the record of 934 AH.)—Account of the capture of Luknūr (?)—Dispositions against the rebel pair—fish caught by help of a lamp—incidents of the march to Adampūr on the Jumna—Bīban and Bāyazīd flee to Maḥūba—Eastern Campaign wound up—Bābur's rapid ride to Āgra (p. 686)—visits kinswomen—is pleased with Indian-grown fruits—Māhīm arrives—her gifts and Humāyūn's set before Bābur—porters sent off for Kābul to fetch fruits—Account of the deaths in Saṃbal brought in—sedition in Lāhor — wrestling watched — sedition of Raḥīm-dād in Gūālīār—Mahdī Khwāja comes to Āgra . . 605-689

936 AH.—Sep. 5th 1529 to Aug. 25th 1530 AD.—Shaikh Ghaus comes from Gūālīār to intercede for Raḥīm-dād—Gūālīār taken over 690

Translator's Note.—936 and 937 AH. — 1529 and 1530 AD.—Sources from which to fill the Gap down to Bābur's death (December 26th 1530) — Humāyūn's proceedings in Badakhshān — Ḥaidar *Dūghlāt's* narrative of them — Humāyūn deserts his post, goes to Kābul, and, arranging with Kāmrān, sends Hind-āl to Badakhshān—goes on to Āgra and there arrives unexpected by his Father—as he is unwilling to return, Sulaimān *Mīrān-shāhī* is appointed under Bābur's suzerainty—Sa'īd Khān is warned to leave Sulaimān in possession—Bābur moves westward to support him and visits Lāhor—waited on in

Sihrind by the Rāja of Kahlūr — received in Lāhor by Kāmrān and there visited from Kābul by Hind-āl — leaves Lāhor (March 4th 1530 AD.)—from Sihrind sends a punitive force against Mundāhir Rājpūts—hunts near Dihlī — appears to have started off an expedition to Kashmīr — family matters fill the rest of the year — Humāyūn falls ill in Sambal and is brought to Āgra— his disease not yielding to treatment, Bābur resolves to practise the rite of intercession and self-surrender to save his life — is urged rather to devote the great diamond (Koh-i-nūr) to pious uses—refuses the substitution of the jewel for his own life—performs the rite—Humāyūn recovers —Bābur falls ill and is bedridden till death—his faith in the rite unquestionable, belief in its efficacy general in the East—Plan to set Bābur's sons aside from the succession— The *Tabaqāt-i-akbarī* story discussed (p. 702 to 708)— suggested basis of the story (p. 705) — Bābur's death (Jūmāda I. 5th 937 AH.—Dec. 26th 1530 AD.) and burial first, near Āgra, later near Kābul—Shāh-jahān's epitaph inscribed on a tablet near the grave—Bābur's wives and children—Mr. Erskine's estimate of his character 691–716.

[**End of Translator's Note.**]

APPENDICES

A. Site and disappearance of old Akhsī.
B. The birds Qīl-qūyīrūgh and Bāghrī-qarā.
C. On the *gosha-gīr*.
D. The Rescue-passage.
E. Nagarahār and Nīng-nahār.
F. The name Dara-i-nūr.
G. On the names of two Dara-i-nūr wines.
H. On the counter-mark Bih-būd of coins.
I. The weeping-willows of f. 190*b*.
J. Bābur's excavated chamber at Qandahār.
K. An Afghan Legend.
L. Māhīm's adoption of Hind-āl.
M. On the term Bahrī-qutās.
N. Notes on a few birds.
O. Notes by Humāyūn on some Hindūstān fruits.
P. Remarks on Bābur's Revenue List.
Q. On the Rāmpūr Dīwān.
R. Plans of Chandīrī and Gūālīār.
S. The Bābur-nāma dating of 935 AH.

T. On L:knū (Lakhnau) and L:knūr (Lakhnur *i.e.* Shahābād in Rāmpūr).
U. The Inscriptions in Bābur's Mosque at Ajodhya (Oude).
V. Bābur's Gardens in and near Kābul.

Indices:—I. Personal, II. Geographical, III. General, p. 717 *et seq.*
Omissions, Corrigenda, Additional Notes.

LIST OF ILLUSTRATIONS.

Plane-tree Avenue in Babur's (later) Burial-garden[1] . . . . *facing* p. xxvii
View from above his grave and Shah-jahan's Mosque[1] . . . . *facing* p. 367
His Grave[2] . . . . *facing* p. 445
Babur in Prayer[3] . . . . *facing* p. 702
His Signature . . . . App. Q, lxi
Plans of Chandiri and Gualiar . . . . . App. R, lxvii

[1] From Atkinson's *Sketches in Afghanistan* (I.O. Lib. & B.M.).
[2] *See* p. 710 (where for "Daniels" read Atkinson).
[3] *See* Gul-badan Begim's *Humayun-nama* Index III, *in loco*.

Plane-tree Avenue in Babur's (later) Burial-garden.

to face p. xxvii]

PREFACE.

> O Spring of work! O Source of power to Be!
> Each line, each thought I dedicate to Thee;
> Each time I fail, the failure is my own,
> But each success, a jewel in Thy Throne.
>
> JESSIE E. CADELL.

INTRODUCTORY.

THIS book is a translation of Babur Padshah's Autobiography, made from the original Turki text. It was undertaken after a purely-Turki manuscript had become accessible in England, the Haidarabad Codex (1915) which, being in Babur's *ipsissima verba*, left to him the control of his translator's diction — a control that had been impracticable from the time when, under Akbar (1589), his book was translated into Persian. What has come down to us of pure text is, in its shrunken amount, what was translated in 1589. It is difficult, here and there, to interpret owing to its numerous and in some places extensive *lacunae*, and presents more problems than one the solution of which has real importance because they have favoured suggestions of malfeasance by Babur.

My translation has been produced under considerable drawback, having been issued in four *fasciculi*, at long intervals, respectively in June 1912, May 1914, October 1917, and September 1921. I have put with it of supplementary matter what may be of service to those readers whom Babur's personality attracts and to those who study Turki as a linguistic entertainment, but owing to delays in production am unable to include the *desiderata* of maps.

CHAPTER I.

BABUR'S EXEMPLARS IN THE ARTS OF PEACE.

Babur's civilian aptitudes, whether of the author and penman, the maker of gardens, the artist, craftsman or sportsman, were nourished in a fertile soil of family tradition and example. Little about his teaching and training is now with his mutilated book, little indeed of any kind about his præ-accession years, not the date of his birth even, having escaped destruction.[1] Happily Haidar Mirza (*q.v.*) possessed a more complete Codex than has come down to us through the Timurid libraries, and from it he translated many episodes of Baburiana that help to bridge gaps and are of special service here where the personalities of Bābur's early environment are being named.

Babur's home-milieu favoured excellence in the quiet Arts and set before its children high standard and example of proficiency. Moreover, by schooling him in obedience to the Law, it planted in him some of Art's essentials, self-restraint and close attention. Amongst primal influences on him, his mother Qut-luq-nigar's ranked high; she, well-born and a scholar's daughter, would certainly be educated in Turki and Persian and in the home-accomplishments her governess possessed (*ātūn* q.v.). From her and her mother Aisan-daulat, the child would learn respect for the attainments of his wise old grandfather Yunas Khan. Aisan-daulat herself brought to her grandson much that goes to the making of a man; nomad-born and sternly-bred, she was brave to obey her opinion of right, and was practically the boy's ruling counsellor through his early struggle to hold Farghana. With these two in fine influence must be counted Khan-zada, his five-years elder sister who from his birth to his death proved her devotion to him. Her life-story tempts, but is too long to tell; her girlish promise is seen fulfilled in Gul-badan's pages. 'Umar Shaikh's own mother Shah Sultan Begim brought in a type of merit widely differing from that of Aisan-daulat Begim; as a town-lady of high Tarkhan birth, used to the amenities of life in a wealthy house of Samarkand, she was, doubtless, an accomplished and cultured woman.

'Umar Shaikh's environment was dominated for many years by two great men, the scholar and lover of town-life Yunas Khan and the saintly Ahrari (*i.e.* Khwaja 'Ubaidu'l-lah) who were frequently with him in company, came at Babur's birth and assisted at his

[1] Cf. Cap. II, PROBLEMS OF THE MUTILATED BABUR-NAMA and *Tarīkh-i-rashīdi*, trs. p. 174.

naming. Ahrari died in 895–1491 when the child was about seven years old but his influence was life-long ; in 935–1529 he was invoked as a spiritual helper by the fever-stricken Babur and his mediation believed efficacious for recovery (pp. 619, 648). For the babe or boy to be where the three friends held social session in high converse, would be thought to draw blessing on him ; his hushed silence in the presence would sow the seed of reverence for wisdom and virtue, such, for example, as he felt for Jami (*q.v.*). It is worth while to tell some part at least of Yunas' attainments in the gentler Arts, because the biography from which they are quoted may well have been written on the information of his wife Aisan-daulat, and it indicates the breadth of his exemplary influence. Yunas was many things—penman, painter, singer, instrumentalist, and a past master in the crafts. He was an expert in good companionship, having even temper and perfect manners, quick perception and conversational charm. His intellectual distinction was attributed to his twelve years of wardship under the learned and highly honoured Yazdi (Sharafu'd-din 'Ali), the author of the *Zafar-nama* [Timur's Book of Victory]. That book was in hand during four years of Yunas' education ; he will thus have known it and its main basis Timur's Turki *Malfūzāt* (annals). What he learned of either book he would carry with him into 'Umar Shaikh's environment, thus magnifying the family stock of Timuriya influence. He lived to be some 74 years old, a length of days which fairly bridged the gap between Timur's death [807–1404] and Babur's birth (888–1483). It is said that no previous Khan of his (Chaghatai) line had survived his 40th year ; his exceptional age earned him great respect and would deepen his influence on his restless young son-in-law 'Umar Shaikh. It appears to have been in 'Umar's 20th year (*cir.*) that Yunas Khan began the friendly association with him that lasted till Yunas' death (892–1483), a friendship which, as disparate ages would dictate, was rather that of father and son than of equal companionship. One matter mentioned in the Khān's biography would come to Babur's remembrance in the future days when he, like Yunas, broke the Law against intoxicants and, like him, repented and returned.

That two men of the calibre and high repute of Ahrari and Yunas maintained friendly guidance so long over 'Umar cannot but be held an accreditment and give fragrance of goodness to his name. Apart from the high justice and generosity his son ascribes to him, he could set other example, for he was a reader of great books, the Qoran and the *Masnawi* being amongst his favourites. This choice, it may be, led Abu'l-fazl to say he had the darwesh-mind. Babur was old enough before 'Umar's death to profit by the sight of his father enjoying the perusal of such books. As with other parents and other children, there would follow the happy stilling to a quiet mood, the piquing of curiosity as to what was in the book, the sight of refuge taken as in a haven from self and care, and perhaps, Babur being intelligent and of inquiring mind and 'Umar a skilled reciter, the boy would marvel at the perennial miracle that a lifeless page can become eloquent—gentle hints all, pointers of the way to literary creation.

Few who are at home in Baburiana but will take Timur as Babur's great exemplar not only as a soldier but as a chronicler. Timur cannot have seemed remote from that group of people so well-informed about him and his civilian doings; his Shahrukhi grandchildren in Samarkand had carried on his author-tradition; the 74 years of Yunas Khan's life had bridged the gap between Timur's death in 807–1405 and Babur's birth in 888–1483. To Babur Timur will have been exemplary through his grandson Aulugh Beg who has two productions to his credit, the *Char-ulus* (Four Hordes) and the Kurkani Astronomical Tables. His sons, again, Babur (*qalandar*) and Ibrahim carried on the family torch of letters, the first in verse and the second by initiating and fostering Yazdi's labours on the *Zafar-nama*. Wide-radiating and potent influence for the Arts of Peace came forth from Herat during the reign of that Sultan Husain Mirza whose Court Babur describes in one of the best supplements to his autobiography. Husain was a Timurid of the elder branch of Bai-qara, an author himself but far more effective as a Macænas; one man of the shining galaxy of competence that gave him fame, set pertinent example for Babur the author, namely, the Andijani of noble Chaghatai family, 'Ali-sher *Nawa'i* who, in classic Turki verse was the master Babur was to become in its prose. That the standard of effort was high in Herat is clear from Babur's dictum (p. 233) that whatever work a man took up, he aspired to bring it to perfection. Elphinstone varies the same theme to the tune of equality of excellence apart from social status, writing to Erskine (August, 1826), that "it gives a high notion of the time to find" (in Babur's account of Husain's Court) "artists, musicians and others, described along with the learned and great of the Age".

My meagre summary of Babur's exemplars would be noticeably incomplete if it omitted mention of two of his life-long helpers in the gentler Arts, his love of Nature and his admiration for great architectural creations. The first makes joyous accompaniment throughout his book; the second is specially called forth by Timur's ennoblement of Samarkand. Timur had built magnificently and laid out stately gardens; Babur made many a fruitful pleasaunce and gladdened many an arid halting-place; he built a little, but had small chance to test his capacity for building greatly; never rich, he was poor in Kabul and several times destitute in his home-lands. But his sword won what gave wealth to his Indian Dynasty, and he passed on to it the builder's unused dower, so that Samarkand was surpassed in Hindustan and the spiritual conception Timur's creations embodied took perfect form at Sikandra where Akbar lies entombed.

CHAPTER II.

PROBLEMS OF THE MUTILATED BABUR-NAMA.

Losses from the text of Babur's book are the more disastrous because it truly embodies his career. For it has the rare distinction of being contemporary with the events it describes, is boyish in his boyhood, grows with his growth, matures as he matured. Undulled by retrospect, it is a fresh and spontaneous recital of things just seen, heard or done. It has the further rare distinction of shewing a boy who, setting a future task before him — in his case the revival of Timurid power, — began to chronicle his adventure in the book which through some 37 years was his twinned comrade, which by its special distinctions has attracted readers for nearly a half-millennium, still attracts and still is a thing apart from autobiographies which look back to recal dead years.

Much circumstance makes for the opinion that Babur left his life-record complete, perhaps repaired in places and recently supplemented, but continuous, orderly and lucid; this it is not now, nor has been since it was translated into Persian in 1589, for it is fissured by *lacunæ*, has neither Preface nor Epilogue,[1] opens in an oddly abrupt and incongruous fashion, and consists of a series of fragments so disconnected as to demand considerable preliminary explanation. Needless to say, its dwindled condition notwithstanding, it has place amongst great autobiographies, still revealing its author playing a man's part in a drama of much historic and personal interest. Its revelation is however now like a portrait out of drawing, because it has not kept the record of certain years of his manhood in which he took momentous decisions, (1) those of 1511–12 [918] in which he accepted reinforcement — at a great price — from Isma'il the Shi'a Shah of Persia, and in which, if my reading be correct, he first (1512) broke the Law against the use of wine,[2] (2) those of 1519–1525 [926–932], in which his literary occupations with orthodox Law (*see Mubin*) associated with cognate matters of 932 AH. indicate that hi return to obedience had begun, in which too was taken the decision that worked out for his fifth expedition across the Indus with its sequel of the conquest of Hind.—The loss of matter so weighty cannot but destroy the balance of his record and falsify the drawing of his portrait.

a. *Problem of Titles.*

As nothing survives to decide what was Babur's chosen title for his autobiography, a modern assignment of names to distinguish it

[1] The suggestion, implied by my use of this word, that Babur may have definitely closed his autobiography (as Timur did under other circumstances) is due to the existence of a compelling cause *viz.* that he would be expectant of death as the price of Humayun's restored life (p. 701).

[2] Cf. p. 83 and n. and Add. Note, P. 83 for further emendation of a contradiction effected by some malign influence in the note (p. 83) between parts of that note, and between it and Babur's account of his not-drinking in Herat.

from its various descendants is desirable, particularly so since the revival of interest in it towards which the Facsimile of its Haidarabad Codex has contributed.[1]

Babur-nama (History of Babur) is a well-warranted name by which to distinguish the original Turki text, because long associated with this and rarely if ever applied to its Persian translation.[2] It is not comprehensive because not covering supplementary matter of biography and description but it has use for modern readers of classing Babur's with other Timuriya and Timurid histories such as the *Zafar–Humayun–Akbar–namas.*

Waqi'āt-i-baburi (Babur's Acts), being descriptive of the book and in common use for naming both the Turki and Persian texts, might usefully be reserved as a title for the latter alone.

Amongst European versions of the book *Memoirs of Baber* is Erskine's peculium for the Leyden and Erskine Perso-English translation—*Mémoires de Baber* is Pavet de Courteille's title for his French version of the Bukhara [Persified-Turki] compilation—*Babur-nama in English* links the translation these volumes contain with its purely-Turki source.

b. *Problems of the Constituents of the Books.*

Intact or mutilated, Babur's material falls naturally into three territorial divisions, those of the lands of his successive rule, Farghana (with Samarkand), Kabul and Hindustan. With these are distinct sub-sections of description of places and of obituaries of kinsmen.

The book might be described as consisting of annals and diary, which once met within what is now the gap of 1508–19 (914–925). Round this gap, amongst others, bristle problems of which this change of literary style is one; some are small and concern the mutilation alone, others are larger, but all are too intricate for terse

[1] Teufel held its title to be *waqi'* (this I adopted in 1908), but it has no definite support and in numerous instances of its occurrence to describe the acts or doings of Babur, it could be read as a common noun.

[2] It stands on the reverse of the frontal page of the Haidarabad Codex; it is Timur-pulad's name for the Codex he purchased in Bukhara, and it is thence brought on by Kehr (with Ilminski), and Klaproth (Cap. III); it is used by Khwafi Khan (d. *cir.* 1732), *etc.*

statement and all might be resolved by the help of a second MS. *e.g.* one of the same strain as Haidar's.

Without fantasy another constituent might be counted in with the three territorial divisions, namely, the grouped *lacunæ* which by their engulfment of text are an untoward factor in an estimate either of Babur or of his book. They are actually the cardinal difficulty of the book as it now is; they foreshorten purview of his career and character and detract from its merits; they lose it perspective and distort its proportions. That this must be so is clear both from the value and the preponderating amount of the lost text. It is no exaggeration to say that while working on what survives, what is lost becomes like a haunting presence warning that it must be remembered always as an integral and the dominant part of the book.

The relative proportions of saved and lost text are highly significant:—Babur's commemorable years are about 47 and 10 months, *i.e.* from his birth on Feb. 14th 1483 to near his death on Dec. 26th 1530; but the aggregate of surviving text records some 18 years only, and this not continuously but broken through by numerous gaps. That these gaps result from loss of pages is frequently shewn by a broken sentence, an unfinished episode. The fragments—as they truly may be called—are divided by gaps sometimes seeming to remove a few pages only (cf. *s.a.* 935 AH.), sometimes losing the record of 6 and *cir.* 18 months, sometimes of 6 and 11 years; besides these actual clefts in the narrative there are losses of some 12 years from its beginning and some 16 months from its end. Briefly put we now have the record of *cir.* 18 years where that of over 47 could have been.[1]

c. *Causes of the gaps.*

Various causes have been surmised to explain the *lacunæ*; on the plea of long intimacy with Babur's and Haidar's writings, I venture to say that one and all appear to me the result of accident. This opinion rests on observed correlations between the surviving and the

[1] That Babur left a complete record much indicates beyond his own persistence and literary bias, *e.g.* cross-reference with and needed complements from what is lost; mention by other writers of Babur's information, notably by Haidar.

lost record, which demand complement—on the testimony of Haidar's extracts, and firmly on Babur's orderly and persistent bias of mind and on the prideful character of much of the lost record. Moreover occasions of risk to Babur's papers are known.

Of these occasions the first was the destruction of his camp near Hisar in 1512 (918; p. 357) but no information about his papers survives; they may not have been in his tent but in the fort. The second was a case of recorded damage to "book and sections" (p. 679) occurring in 1529 (935). From signs of work done to the Farghana section in Hindustan, the damage may be understood made good at the later date. To the third exposure to damage, namely, the attrition of hard travel and unsettled life during Humayun's 14 years of exile from rule in Hindustan (1441–1555) it is reasonable to attribute even the whole loss of text. For, assuming — as may well be done — that Babur left (1530) a complete autobiography, its volume would be safe so long as Humayun was in power but after the Timurid exodus (1441) his library would be exposed to the risks detailed in the admirable chronicles of Gul-badan, Jauhar and Bayazid (*q.v.*). He is known to have annotated his father's book in 1555 (p. 466 n. 1) just before marching from Kabul to attempt the re-conquest of Hindustan. His Codex would return to Dihli which he entered in July 1555, and there would be safe from risk of further mutilation. Its condition in 1555 is likely to have remained what it was found when 'Abdu'r-rahim translated it into Persian by Akbar's orders (1589) for Abu'l-fazl's use in the *Akbar-nama*. That Persian translation with its descendant the *Memoirs of Baber*, and the purely-Turki Haidarabad Codex with its descendant the *Babur-nama in English*, contain identical contents and, so doing, carry the date of the mutilation of Babur's Turki text back through its years of safety, 1589 to 1555, to the period of Humayun's exile and its dangers for camel-borne or deserted libraries.

d. *Two misinterpretations of lacunæ.*

Not unnaturally the frequent interruptions of narrative caused by *lacunæ* have been misinterpreted occasionally, and sometimes detractory comment has followed on Babur, ranking him below the accomplished and lettered, steadfast and honest man he was. I select two examples of this comment neither of which has a casual origin.

The first is from the *B.M. Cat. of Coins of the Shahs of Persia* p. xxiv, where after identifying a certain gold coin as shewing vassalage by Babur to Isma'il *Safawi*, the compiler of the Catalogue notes, "We can now understand the omission from Babar's 'Memoirs' of the occurrences between 914 H. and 925 H." Can these words imply other than that Babur suppressed mention of minting of the coins shewing acknowledgment of Shi'a suzerainty? Leaving aside the delicate topic of the detraction the quoted words imply, much negatives the surmise that the gap is a deliberate "omission" of text:—(1) the duration of the Shi'a alliance was 19–20 months of 917–918 AH. (p. 355), why omit the peaceful or prideful and victorious record of some 9–10 years on its either verge? (2) Babur's Transoxus campaign was an episode in the struggle between Shaibaq Khan (Shaibani) *Auzbeg* and Shah Isma'il — between Sunni and Shi'a; how could "omission" from his book, always a rare one, hide what multitudes knew already? "Omission" would have proved a fiasco in another region than Central Asia, because the Babur–Haidar story of the campaign, vassal-coinage included,[1] has been brought into English literature by the English translation of the *Tarikh-i rashidi.* Babur's frank and self-judging habit of mind would, I think, lead him to write fully of the difficulties which compelled the hated alliance and certainly he would tell of his own anger at the conduct of the campaign by Isma'il's Commanders. The alliance was a tactical mistake; it would have served Babur better to narrate its failure.

The second misinterpretation, perhaps a mere surmising gloss, is Erskine's (*Memoirs* Supp. p. 289) who, in connection with 'Alam Khan's request to Babur for reinforcement in order to oust his nephew Ibrahim, observes that "Babur probably flattered 'Alam Khan with the hope of succession to the empire of Hindustan." This idea does not fit the record of either man. Elphinstone was angered by Erskine's remark which, he wrote (Aug. 26th 1826) "had a bad

[1] App. H, xxx.

effect on the narrative by weakening the implicit confidence in Babur's candour and veracity which his frank way of writing is so well-calculated to command." Elphinstone's opinion of Babur is not that of a reader but of a student of his book; he was also one of Erskine's staunchest helpers in its production. From Erskine's surmise others have advanced on the detractor's path saying that Babur used and threw over 'Alam Khan (*q.v.*).

e. *Reconstruction.*

Amongst the problems mutilation has created an important one is that of the condition of the beginning of the book (p. 1 to p. 30) with its plunge into Babur's doings in his 12th year without previous mention of even his day and place of birth, the names and status of his parents, or any occurrences of his præ-accession years. Within those years should be entered the death of Yunas Khan (1487) with its sequent obituary notice, and the death of [Khwaja 'Ubaidu'l-lah] Ahrari (1491). Not only are these customary entries absent but the very introductions of the two great men are wanting, probably with the also missing account of their naming of the babe Babur. That these routine matters are a part of an autobiography planned as Babur's was, makes for assured opinion that the record of more than his first decade of life has been lost, perhaps by the attrition to which its position in the volume exposed it.

Useful reconstruction if merely in tabulated form, might be effected in a future edition. It would save at least two surprises for readers, one the oddly abrupt first sentence telling of Babur's age when he became ruler in Farghana (p. 1), which is a misfit in time and order, another that of the sudden interruption of 'Umar Shaikh's obituary by a fragment of Yunas Khan's (p. 19) which there hangs on a mere name-peg, whereas its place according to Babur's elsewhere unbroken practice is directly following the death. The record of the missing præ-accession years will have included at the least as follows :—Day of birth and its place—names and status of parents—naming and the ceremonial observances proper for Muhammadan children—visits to kinsfolk in Tashkint, and to Samarkand (æt. 5, p. 35) where he was betrothed—his initiation in school subjects, in sport, the use of arms—names of teachers—education in the rules of his Faith (p. 44), appointment to the Andijan Command *etc., etc.*

There is now no fit beginning to the book; the present first sentence and its pendent description of Farghana should be removed to the position Babur's practice dictates of entering the description of a territory at once on obtaining it (cf. Samarkand, Kabul, Hindustan). It might come in on p. 30 at the end of the topic (partly omitted on p. 29 where no ground is given for the manifest anxiety about Babur's safety) of the disputed succession (Haidar, trs. p. 135) Babur's partisan begs having the better of Jahangir's (*q.v.*), and having testified obeisance, he became ruler in Farghana; his statement of age (12 years), comes in naturally and the description of his newly acquired territory follows according to rule. This removal of text to a later position has the advantage of allowing the accession to follow and not precede Babur's father's death.

By the removal there is left to consider the historical matter of pp. 12–13. The first paragraph concerns matter of much earlier date than 'Umar's death in 1494 (p. 13); it may be part of an obituary notice, perhaps that of Yunas Khan. What follows of the advance of displeased kinsmen against 'Umar Shaikh would fall into place as part of Babur's record of his boyhood, and lead on to that of his father's death.

The above is a bald sketch of what might be effected in the interests of the book and to facilitate its pleasant perusal.

CHAPTER III.

THE TURKI MSS. AND WORK CONNECTING WITH THEM.

This chapter is a literary counterpart of "Babur Padshah's Stoneheap," the roadside cairn tradition says was piled by his army, each man laying his stone when passing down from Kabul for Hindustan in the year of victory 1525 (932).[1]

[1] p. 446, n. 6. Babur's order for the cairn would fit into the lost record of the first month of the year (p. 445).

For a title suiting its contents is "Babur Padshah's Book-pile," because it is fashioned of item after item of pen-work done by many men in obedience to the dictates given by his book. Unlike the cairn, however, the pile of books is not of a single occasion but of many, not of a single year but of many, irregularly spacing the 500 years through which he and his autobiography have had Earth's immortality.

Part I. The MSS. themselves.

Preliminary.—Much of the information given below was published in the Journal of the Royal Asiatic Society from 1900 onwards, as it came into my possession during a search for reliable Turki text of the *Babur-nama.* My notes were progressive; some MSS. were in distant places, some not traceable, but in the end I was able to examine in England all of whose continued existence I had become aware. It was inevitable that some of my earlier statements should be superseded later; my Notes (*see s.n.* JRAS.) need clearing of transitory matter and summarizing, in particular those on the Elphinstone Codex and Klaproth's articles. Neither they nor what is placed here makes claim to be complete. Other workers will supplement them when the World has renewed opportunity to stroll in the bye-paths of literature.

Few copies of the *Babur-nama* seem to have been made; of the few I have traced as existing, not one contains the complete autobiography, and one alone has the maximum of dwindled text shewn in the Persian translation (1589). Two books have been reputed to contain Babur's authentic text, one preserved in Hindustan by his descendants, the other issuing from Bukhara. They differ in total contents, arrangement and textual worth; moreover the Bukhara book compiles items of divers diction and origin and date, manifestly not from one pen.

The Hindustan book is a record—now mutilated—of the Acts of Babur alone; the Bukhara book as exhibited in its fullest accessible example, Kehr's Codex, is in two parts, each having its preface, the first reciting Babur's Acts, the second Humayun's.

The Bukhara book is a compilation of oddments, mostly translated from compositions written after Babur's death. Textual and circumstantial grounds warrant the opinion that it is a distinct work mistakenly believed to be Babur's own; to these grounds was added in 1903 the authoritative verdict of collation with the Haidarabad Codex, and in 1921 of the colophon of its original MS. in which its author gives his name, with the title and date of his compilation (JRAS. 1900, p. 474). What it is and what are its contents and history are told in Part III of this chapter.

Part II. Work on the Hindustan MSS.

BABUR'S ORIGINAL CODEX.

My latest definite information about Babur's autograph MS. comes from the *Padshah-nama.* (Bib. Ind. ed. ii, 4), whose author saw it in Shah-i-jahan's private library between 1628 and 1638. Inference is justified, however, that it was the archetype of the Haidarabad Codex which has been estimated from the quality of its paper as dating *cir.* 1700 (JRAS. 1906, p. 97). But two subsequent historic disasters complicate all questions of MSS. missing from Indian libraries, namely, Nadir Shah's vengeance on Dihli in 1739 and the dispersions and fires of the Mutiny. Faint hope is kept alive that the original Codex may have drifted into private hands, by what has occurred with the Rampur MS. of Babur's Hindustan verses (App. J), which also appears once to have belonged to Shah-i-jahan.

I

Amongst items of work done during Babur's life are copies of his book (or of the Hindustan section of it) he mentions sending to sons and friends.

II

The *Tabaqat-i-baburi* was written during Babur's life by his Persian secretary Shaikh Zainu'd-din of Khawaf; it paraphrases in rhetorical Persian the record of a few months of Hindustan campaigning, including the battle of Panipat.

TABLE OF THE HINDUSTAN MSS. OF THE BABUR-NAMA.[1]

Names.	Date of completion.	Folios—standard 382.[2]	Archetype.	Scribe.	Latest known location.	Remarks.
1. Babur's Codex.	1530.	Originally much over 382.	—	Babur.	Royal Library between 1628–38.	Has disappeared.
2. Khwaja Kalan *Akrari's* Codex.	1529.	Undefined 363 (?), p. 652.	No. 1.	Unknown.	Sent to Samarkand 1529.	Possibly still in Khwaja Kalan's family.
3. Humayun's Codex = (commanded and annotate?).[3]	1531 (?).	Originally = No. 1 (unmutilated).	No. 1.	'Ali'u'l-katib (?).	Royal Library between 1556–1567.	Seems the archetype of No. 5.
4. Muhammad Haidar *Dughlat's* Codex.	Between 1536 and 40 (?).	No. 1 (unmutilated).	No. 1 or No. 2.	Haidar (?)	Kashmir 1540–47.	Possibly now in Kashghar.
5. Elphinstone Codex.	Between 1556 and 1567.	In 1816 and 1907, 286 ff.	No. 3.	Unknown.	Advocates' Library (1816 to 1921).	Bought in Peshawar 1810.
6. British Museum MS.	1629.	97 (fragments).	Unknown.	'Ali'u'l-*kashmiri*.	British Museum.	—
7. Bib. Lindesiana MS. [now John Rylands]	Scribe living in 1625.	71 (an extract).	Unknown.	Nur-muhammad (nephew of 'Abu'l-fazl).	John Rylands Library.	—
8. Haidarabad Codex.	Paper indicates *cir.* 1700.	382.	(No. 1) mutilated.	No colophon.	The late Sir Salar-jang's Library.	Centupled in facsimile, 1905.

[1] Parts of the Babur-nama sent to Babur's sons are not included here.
[2] The standard of comparison is the 382 fols. of the Haidarabad Codex.
[3] This MS. is not to be confused with one Erskine misunderstood Humayun to have copied (*Memoirs*, p. 303 and JRAS. 1900, p. 443).

III

During the first decade of Humayun's reign (1530–40) at least two important codices seem to have been copied.

The earlier (*see* Table, No. 2) has varied circumstantial warrant. It meets the need of an archetype, one marginally annotated by Humayun, for the Elphinstone Codex in which a few notes are marginal and signed, others are pell-mell, interpolated in the text but attested by a scrutineer as having been marginal in its archetype and mistakenly copied into its text. This second set has been ineffectually sponged over. Thus double collation is indicated (i) with Babur's autograph MS. to clear out extra Babur matter, and (ii) with its archetype, to justify the statement that in this the interpolations were marginal.—No colophon survives with the much dwindled Elph. Codex, but one, suiting the situation, has been observed, where it is a complete misfit, appended to the Alwar Codex of the second Persian translation, (estimated as copied in 1589). Into the incongruities of that colophon it is not necessary to examine here, they are too obvious to aim at deceit; it appears fitly to be an imperfect translation from a Turki original, this especially through its odd fashion of entitling "Humayun Padshah." It can be explained as translating the colophon of the Codex (No. 2) which, as his possession, Humayun allowably annotated and which makes it known that he had ordered 'Ali'u-'l-katib to copy his father's Turki book, and that it was finished in February, 1531, some six weeks after Babur's death.[1]

The later copy made in Humayun's first decade is Haidar Mirza's (*infra*).

IV

Muhammad Haidar Mirza *Dughlat's* possession of a copy of the Autobiography is known both from his mention of it and through numerous extracts translated from it in his *Tarikh-i-rashidi*. As a good boy-penman (p. 22) he may have copied down to 1512 (918) while with Babur (p. 350), but for obtaining a transcript of it his

[1] For precise limits of the original annotation *see* p. 446 n.—For details about the E. Codex *see* JRAS. 1907, art. *The Elph. Codex*, and for the colophon AQR. 1900, July, Oct. and JRAS. 1905, pp. 752, 761.

opportunity was while with Humayun before the Timurid exodus of 1541. He died in 1551; his Codex is likely to have found its way back from Kashmir to his ancestral home in the Kashghar region and there it may still be. (*See* T.R. trs. Ney Elias' biography of him).

V

The Elphinstone Codex[1] has had an adventurous career. The enigma of its archetype is posed above; it may have been copied during Akbar's first decade (1556–67); its, perhaps first, owner was a Bai-qara rebel (d. 1567) from amongst whose possessions it passed into the Royal Library, where it was cleared of foreign matter by the expunction of Humayun's marginal notes which its scribe had interpolated into its text. At a date I do not know, it must have left the Royal Library for its fly-leaves bear entries of prices and in 1810 it was found and purchased in Peshawar by Elphinstone. It went with him to Calcutta, and there may have been seen by Leyden during the short time between its arrival and the autumn month of the same year (1810) when he sailed for Java. In 1813 Elphinstone in Poona sent it to Erskine in Bombay, saying that he had fancied it gone to Java and had been writing to 'Izzatu'l-lah to procure another MS. for Erskine in Bukhara, but that all the time it was on his own shelves. Received after Erskine had dolefully compared his finished work with Leyden's (tentative) translation, Erskine sadly recommenced the review of his own work. The Codex had suffered much defacement down to 908 (1502) at the hands of "a Persian Turk of Ganj" who had interlined it with explanations. It came to Scotland (with Erskine?) who in 1826 sent it with a covering letter (Dec. 12th, 1826), at its owner's desire, to the Advocates' Library where it now is. In 1907 it was fully described by me in the JRAS.

VI

Of two *Waqi'at-i-baburi* (Pers. trs.) made in Akbar's reign, the earlier was begun in 1583, at private instance, by two Mughuls

[1] *See* Index *s.n.* and III *ante* and JRAS. 1900-3-5-6-7.

Payanda-hasan of Ghazni and Muhammad-quli of Hisar. The Bodleian and British Museum Libraries have copies of it, very fragmentary unfortunately, for it is careful, likeable, and helpful by its small explanatory glosses. It has the great defect of not preserving autobiographic quality in its diction.

VII

The later *Waqi'at-i-baburi* translated by 'Abdu'r-rahim Mirza is one of the most important items in Baburiana, both by its special characteristics as the work of a Turkman and not of a Persian, and by the great service it has done. Its origin is well-known; it was made at Akbar's order to help Abu'l-fazl in the Akbar-nama account of Babur and also to facilitate perusal of the *Babur-nama* in Hindustan. It was presented to Akbar, by its translator who had come up from Gujrat, in the last week of November, 1589, on an occasion and at a place of admirable fitness. For Akbar had gone to Kabul to visit Babur's tomb, and was halting on his return journey at Barik-ab where Babur had halted on his march down to Hindustan in the year of victory 1525, at no great distance from "Babur Padshah's Stone-heap". Abu'l-fazl's account of the presentation will rest on 'Abdu'r-rahim's information (A.N. trs. cap. ci). The diction of this translation is noticeable; it gave much trouble to Erskine who thus writes of it (*Memoirs* Preface, lx), "Though simple and precise, a close adherence to the idioms and forms of expression of the Turki original joined to a want of distinctness in the use of the relatives, often renders the meaning extremely obscure, and makes it difficult to discover the connexion of the different members of the sentence.[1] The style is frequently not Persian. . . . Many of the Turki words are untranslated."

Difficult as these characteristics made Erskine's interpretation, it appears to me likely that they indirectly were useful to him by restraining his diction to some extent in their Turki fettering.—This Turki fettering has another aspect, apart from Erskine's difficulties,

[1] Here speaks the man reared in touch with European classics; (pure) Turki though it uses no relatives (Radloff) is lucid. Cf. Cap. IV The Memoirs of Babur.

viz. it would greatly facilitate re-translation into Turki, such as has been effected, I think, in the Farghana section of the Bukhara compilation.[1]

VIII

This item of work, a harmless attempt of Salim (*i.e.* Jahangir Padshah ; 1605–28) to provide the ancestral autobiography with certain stop-gaps, has caused much needless trouble and discussion without effecting any useful result. It is this :—In his own autobiography, the *Tuzuk-i-jahangiri s.a.* 1607, he writes of a Babur-nama Codex he examined, that it was all in Babur's "blessed handwriting" except four portions which were in his own and each of which he attested in Turki as so being. Unfortunately he did not specify his topics; unfortunately also no attestation has been found to passages reasonably enough attributable to his activities. His portions may consist of the "Rescue-passage" (App. D) and a length of translation from the *Akbarnama*, a continuous part of its Babur chapter but broken up where only I have seen it, *i.e.* the Bukhara compilation, into (1) a plain tale of Kanwa (1527), (2) episodes of Babur's latter months (1529)—both transferred to the first person—and (3) an account of Babur's death (December 26th, 1530) and Court.

Jahangir's occupation, harmless in itself, led to an imbroglio of Langlés with Erskine, for the former stating in the *Biographie Universelle* art. Babour, that Babour's Commentaries "*augmentés par Jahangir*" were translated into Persian by 'Abdu'r-rahim. Erskine made answer, "I know not on what authority the learned Langlés hazarded this assertion, which is certainly incorrect" (*Memoirs*, Preface, p. ix). Had Langlés somewhere met with Jahangir's attestations? He had authority if he had seen merely the statement of 1607, but Erskine was right also, because the Persian translation contains no more than the unaugmented Turki text. The royal stop-gaps are in Kehr's MS. and through Ilminski reached De Courteille, whence the biting and thorough analysis of the three "Fragments" by Teufel. Both episodes—the Langlés and the

[1] For analysis of a retranslated passage *see* JRAS. 1908, p. 85.

Teufel ones—are time-wasters but they are comprehensible in the circumstances that Jahangir could not foresee the consequences of his doubtless good intentions.

If the question arise of how writings that had had place in Jahangir's library reached Bukhara, their open road is through the Padshah's correspondence (App. Q and references), with a descendant of Ahrari in whose hands they were close to Bukhara.[1]

It groups scattered information to recal that Salim (Jahangir) was 'Abdu'r-rahim's ward, that then, as now, Babur's Autobiography was the best example of classic Turki, and that it would appeal on grounds of piety—as it did appeal on some sufficient ground—to have its broken story made good. Also that for three of the four "portions" Abu'l-fazl's concise matter was to hand.

IX

My information concerning Baburiana under Shah-i-jahan Padshah (1628–58) is very meagre. It consists of (1) his attestation of a signature of Babur (App. Q and photo), (2) his possession of Babur's autograph Codex (*Padshah-nama*, Bib. Ind. ed., ii, 4), and (3) his acceptance, and that by his literary entourage, of Mir Abu-talib *Husaini*'s Persian translation of Timur's Annals, the *Malfuzat* whose preparation the *Zafar-nama* describes and whose link with Babur's writings is that of the exemplar to the emulator.[2]

X

The Haidarabad Codex may have been inscribed under Aurangzib Padshah (1655–1707). So many particulars about it have been given already that little needs saying here.[3] It was the *grande trouvaille* of my search for Turki text wherewith to revive Babur's autobiography both in Turki and English. My husband in 1900 saw it in Haidarabad; through the kind offices of the late Sayyid

[1] *Tuzuk-i-jahangiri*, Rogers & Beveridge's trs. i, 110; JRAS. 1900, p. 756, for the Persian passage, 1908, p. 76 for the "Fragments", 1900, p. 476 for Ilminski's Preface (a second translation is accessible at the B.M. and I.O. Library and R.A.S.), *Memoirs* Preface, p. ix, Index *s.nn.* de Courteille, Teufel, Bukhara MSS. and Part iii *eo cap.*

[2] For Shah-i-jahan's interest in Timur *see* sign given in a copy of his note published in my translation volume of Gul-badan Begim's *Humayun-nama*, p. xiii.

[3] JRAS. 1900 p. 466, 1902 p. 655, 1905 art. *s.n.*, 1908 pp. 78, 98; Index *in loco s.n.*

Ali *Bilgrami* it was lent to me; it proved to surpass, both in volume and quality, all other Babur-nama MSS. I had traced; I made its merits known to Professor Edward Granville Browne, just when the E. J. Wilkinson Gibb Trust was in formation, with the happy and accordant result that the best prose book in classic Turki became the first item in the Memorial—*matris ad filium*—of literary work done in the name of the Turkish scholar, and Babur's very words were safeguarded in hundred-fold facsimile. An event so important for autobiography and for Turki literature may claim more than the bald mention of its occurrence, because sincere autobiography, however ancient, is human and social and undying, so that this was no mere case of multiplying copies of a book, but was one of preserving a man's life in his words. There were, therefore, joyful red-letter days in the English story of the Codex—outstanding from others being those on which its merits revealed themselves (on Surrey uplands)—the one which brought Professor Browne's acceptance of it for reproduction by the Trust—and the day of pause from work marked by the accomplished fact of the safety of the *Babur-nama.*

XI

The period from *cir.* 1700, the date of the Haidarabad Codex, and 1810, when the Elphinstone Codex was purchased by its sponsor at Peshawar, appears to have been unfruitful in work on the Hindustan MSS. Causes for this may connect with historic events, e.g. Nadir Shah's desolation of Dihli and the rise of the East India Company, and, in Baburiana, with the disappearance of Babur's autograph Codex (it was unknown to the Scots of 1800–26), and the transfer of the Elphinstone Codex from royal possession—this, possibly however, an accident of royal travel to and from Kabul at earlier dates.

The first quarter of the nineteenth century was, on the contrary, most fruitful in valuable work, useful impulse to which was given by Dr. John Leyden who in about 1805 began to look into Turki. Like his contemporary Julius Klaproth (*q.v.*), he was avid of tongues and attracted by Turki and by Babur's writings of which he had some knowledge through the 'Abdu'r-rahim (Persian) translation. His Turki text-book would be the MS. of the Asiatic Society of Bengal,[1] a part-copy of the Bukhara compilation, from which he had the India Office MS. copied. He took up Turki again in 1810, after his return from Malay and whilst awaiting orders in Calcutta for departure to Java. He sailed in the autumn of the year and died in August 1811. Much can be learned about him and his Turki occupations from letters (*infra* xiii) written to Erskine by him and by others of the Scottish band which now achieved such fine results for Babur's Autobiography.

It is necessary to say something of Leyden's part in producing the *Memoirs*, because Erskine, desiring to "lose nothing that might add to Leyden's reputation", has assigned to him an undue position of collaboration in it both by giving him premier place on its title-page and by attributing to him the beginning the translation. What one gleans of Leyden's character makes an impression of unassumption that would forbid his acceptance of the posthumous position given to him, and, as his translation shews the tyro in Turki, there can be no ground for supposing he would wish his competence in it over-estimated. He had, as dates show, nothing to do with the actual work of the *Memoirs* which was finished before Erskine had seen in 1813 what Leyden had set down before he died in 1811. As the *Memoirs* is now a rare book, I quote from it what Erskine says (Preface, p. ix) of Leyden's rough translation :—"This acquisition (*i.e.* of Leyden's trs.) reduced me to rather an awkward dilemma. The two translations (his own and Leyden's) differed in many important particulars; but as Dr. Leyden had the advantage of translating from the original, I resolved to adopt his translation as far as it went, changing only such expressions in it as seemed evidently to be inconsistent with the context, or with other parts of the *Memoirs*, or such as seemed evidently to originate in the oversights that are unavoidable in an unfinished work.[2] This labour I had completed

[1] Cf. JRAS. 1900, Nos. VI, VII, VIII.

[2] Ilminski's difficulties are foreshadowed here by the same confusion of identity between the *Babur-nama* proper and the Bukhara compilation (Preface, Part iii, p. li).

with some difficulty, when Mr. Elphinstone sent me the copy of the *Memoirs of Baber* in the original Tūrkī (*i.e.* The Elphinstone Codex) which he had procured when he went to Peshawar on his embassy to Kabul. This copy, which he had supposed to have been sent with Dr. Leyden's manuscripts from Calcutta, he was now fortunate enough to recover (in his own library at Poona). "The discovery of this valuable manuscript reduced me, though heartily sick of the task, to the necessity of commencing my work once more."

Erskine's Preface (pp. x, xi) contains various other references to Leyden's work which indicate its quality as tentative and unrevised. It is now in the British Museum Library.

XII

Little need be said here about the *Memoirs of Baber*.[1] Erskine worked on a basis of considerable earlier acquaintance with his Persian original, for, as his Preface tells, he had (after Leyden's death) begun to translate this some years before he definitely accepted the counsel of Elphinstone and Malcolm to undertake the *Memoirs*. He finished his translation in 1813, and by 1816 was able to dedicate his complete volume to Elphinstone, but publication was delayed till 1826. His was difficult pioneer-work, and carried through with the drawback of working on a secondary source. It has done yeoman service, of which the crowning merit is its introduction of Babur's autobiography to the Western world.

XIII

Amongst Erskine's literary remains are several bound volumes of letters from Elphinstone, Malcolm, Leyden, and others of that distinguished group of Scots who promoted the revival of Babur's writings. Erskine's grandson, the late Mr. Lestocq Erskine, placed these, with other papers, at our disposal, and they are now located where they have been welcomed as appropriate additions:—Elphinstone's are in the Advocates' Library, where already (1826) he, through Erskine, had deposited his own Codex — and with his

[1] Cf. Erskine's Preface *passim*, and *in loco* item XI, cap. iv. The *Memoirs of Baber*, and Index *s.n.*

letters are those of Malcolm and more occasional correspondents; Leyden's letters (and various papers) are in the Memorial Cottage maintained in his birthplace Denholm (Hawick) by the Edinburgh Border Counties Association; something fitting went to the Bombay Asiatic Society and a volume of diary to the British Muṣeum. Leyden's papers will help his fuller biography; Elphinstone's letters have special value as recording his co-operation with Erskine by much friendly criticism, remonstrance against delay, counsels and encouragement. They, moreover, shew the estimate an accomplished man of modern affairs formed of Babur Padshah's character and conduct; some have been quoted in Colebrooke's *Life of Elphinstone*, but there they suffer by detachment from the rest of his Baburiana letters; bound together as they now are, and with brief explanatory interpolations, they would make a welcome item for " Babur Padshah's Book-pile ".

XIV

In May 1921 the contents of these volumes were completed, namely, the *Babur-nama in English* and its supplements, the aims of which are to make Babur known in English diction answering to his *ipsissima verba*, and to be serviceable to readers and students of his book and of classic Turki.

XV

Of writings based upon or relating to Babur's the following have appeared :—

Denkwurdigkeiten des Zahir-uddin Muhammad Babar — A. Kaiser (Leipzig, 1828). This consists of extracts translated from the Memoirs.

An abridgement of the Memoirs — R. M. Caldecott (London, 1844).

History of India — Baber and Humayun — W. Erskine (Longmans, 1854).

Babar — Rulers of India series — Stanley Lane-Poole (Oxford, 1899)

Tuzuk-i-babari or Waqi'at-i-babari (*i.e.* the Persian trs.) — Elliot and Dowson's History of India, 1872, vol. iv.

Babur Padshah *Ghazi* — H. Beveridge (Calcutta Review, 1899).

Babur's diamond, was it the Koh-i-nur? — H. Beveridge, Asiatic Quarterly Review, April, 1899.

Was 'Abdu'r-rahim the translator of Babur's Memoirs? (*i.e.* the *Babur-nama*) — H. Beveridge, AQR., July and October, 1900.

An Empire-builder of the 16th century, Babur—Laurence F. L. Williams (Allahabad, 1918).

Notes on the MSS. of the Turki text (*Babur-nāma*) — A. S. Beveridge, JRAS. 1900, 1902, 1921, 1905, and Part II 1906, 1907, 1908, p. 52 and p. 828, 1909 p. 452 (*see* Index, *s.n.* A. S. B. for topics).

[For other articles and notes by H. B. *see* Index *s.n.*]

Part III. The "Bukhara Babur-nama".

This is a singular book and has had a career as singular as its characteristics, a very comedy of (blameless) errors and mischance. For it is a compilation of items diverse in origin, diction, and age, planned to be a record of the Acts of Babur and Humayun, dependent through its Babur portion on the 'Abdu 'r-rahim Persian translation for re-translation, or verbatim quotation, or dove-tailing effected on the tattered fragments of what had once been Kamran's Codex of the Babur-nama proper, the whole interspersed by stop-gaps attributable to Jahangir. These and other specialities notwithstanding, it ranked for nearly 200 years as a reproduction of Babur's authentic text, as such was sent abroad, as such was reconstructed and printed in Kasan (1857), translated in Paris (1871), catalogued for the Petrograd Oriental School (1894), and for the India Office (1903).

Manifest causes for the confusion of identity are, (1) lack of the guidance in Bukhara and Petrograd of collation with the true text, (2) want of information, in the Petrograd of 1700–25, about Babur's career, coupled with the difficulties of communication with Bukhara, (3) the misleading feature in the compiled book of its author's retention of the autobiographic form of his sources, without explanation as to whether he entered surviving fragments of Kamran's

[1] The last blow was given to the phantasmal reputation of the book by the authoritative Haidarabad Codex which now can be seen in facsimile in many Libraries.

Codex, patchings or extracts from 'Abdu'r-rahim's Persian translation, or quotations of Jahangir's stop-gaps. Of these three causes for error the first is dominant, entailing as it does the drawbacks besetting work on an inadequate basis.

It is necessary to enumerate the items of the Compilation here as they are arranged in Kehr's autograph Codex, because that codex (still in London) may not always be accessible,[1] and because the imprint does not obey its model, but aims at closer agreement of the Bukhara Compilation with Ilminski's gratefully acknowledged guide — *The Memoirs of Baber*. Distinction in commenting on the Bukhara and the Kasan versions is necessary; their discrepancy is a scene in the comedy of errors.

[1] But for present difficulties of intercourse with Petrograd, I would have re-examined with Kehr's the collateral Codex of 1742 (copied in 1839 and now owned by the Petrograd University). It might be useful, as Kehr's volume has lost pages and may be disarranged here and there.

The list of Kehr's items is as follows:—

1 (*not in the Imprint*). A letter from Babur to Kamran the date of which is fixed as 1527 by its committing Ibrahim *Ludi's* son to Kamran's charge (p. 544). It is heard of again in the Bukhara Compilation, is lost from Kehr's Codex, and preserved from his archetype by Klaproth who translated it. Being thus found in Bukhara in the first decade of the eighteenth century (our earliest knowledge of the Compilation is 1709), the inference is allowed that it went to Bukhara as loot from the defeated Kamran's camp and that an endorsement its companion Babur-nama (proper) bears was made by the Auzbeg of two victors over Kamran, both of 1550, both in Tramontana.[1]

2 (*not in Imp.*). Timur-pulad's memo. about the purchase of his Codex in *cir.* 1521 (*eo cap. post*).

3 (*Imp. 1*). Compiler's Preface of Praise (JRAS. 1900, p. 474).

4 (*Imp. 2*). Babur's Acts in Farghana, in diction such as to seem a re-translation of the Persian translation of 1589. How much of Kamran's MS. was serviceable is not easy to decide, because the Turki fettering of 'Abdu'r-rahim's Persian lends itself admirably to re-translation.[2]

5 (*Imp. 3*). The "Rescue-passage" (App. D) attributable to Jahangir.

6 (*Imp. 4*). Babur's Acts in Kabul, seeming (like No. 4) a re-translation or patching of tattered pages. There are also passages taken verbatim from the Persian.

7 (*Imp. omits*). A short length of Babur's Hindustan Section, carefully shewn damaged by dots and dashes.

8 (*Imp. 5*). Within 7, the spurious passage of App. L and also scattered passages about a feast, perhaps part of 7.

9 (*Imp. separates off at end of vol.*). Translated passage from the *Akbar-nama*, attributable to Jahangir, briefly telling of Kanwa (1527), Babur's latter years (both changed to first person), death and court.[3]

[1] That Babur-nama of the "Kamran-docket" is the mutilated and tattered basis, allowed by circumstance, of the compiled history of Babur, filled out and mended by the help of the Persian translation of 1589. Cf. Kehr's Latin Trs. fly-leaf entry; Klaproth *s.n.*; A.N. trs. H.B., p. 260; JRAS. 1908, 1909, on the "Kamran-docket" (where are defects needing Klaproth's second article (1824).

[2] For an analysis of an illustrative passage *see* JRAS. 1906; for facilities of re-translation *see eo cap.* p. xviii, where Erskine is quoted.

[3] *See* A.N. trans., p. 260; Prefaces of Ilminski and de Courteille; ZDMG. xxxvii, Teufel's art.; JRAS. 1906.

[Babur's history has been thus brought to an end, incomplete in the balance needed of 7. In Kehr's volume a few pages are left blank except for what shews a Russian librarian's opinion of the plan of the book, "Here end the writings of Shah Babur."]

10 (*Imp. omits*). Preface to the history of Humayun, beginning at the Creation and descending by giant strides through notices of Khans and Sultans to "Babur Mirza who was the father of Humayun Padshah". Of Babur what further is said connects with the battle of Ghaj-davan (918–1512 *q.v.*). It is ill-informed, laying blame on him as if he and not Najm Sani had commanded—speaks of his preference for the counsel of young men and of the numbers of combatants. It is noticeable for more than its inadequacy however; its selection of the Ghaj-davan episode from all others in Babur's career supports circumstantially what is dealt with later, the Ghaj-davani authorship of the Compilation.

11 (*Imp. omits*). Under a heading "Humayun Padshah" is a fragment about (his? Accession) Feast, whether broken off by loss of his pages or of those of his archetype examination of the P. Univ. Codex may show.

12 (*Imp. 6*). An excellent copy of Babur's Hindustan Section, perhaps obtained from the Ahrari house. [This Ilminski places (I think) where Kehr has No. 7.] From its position and from its bearing a scribe's date of completion (which Kehr brings over), *viz. Tamt shud 1126* (Finished 1714), the compiler may have taken it for Humayun's, perhaps for the account of his reconquest of Hind in 1555.

[The remaining entries in Kehr's volume are a quatrain which may make jesting reference to his finished task, a librarian's Russian entry of the number of pages (831), and the words *Etablissement Orientale, Fr. v. Adelung*, 1825 (the Director of the School from 1793).[1]

[1] For particulars about Kehr's Codex *see* Smirnov's Catalogue of the School Library and JRAS. 1900, 1906. Like others who have made statements resting on the mistaken identity of the Bukhara Compilation, many of mine are now given to the winds.

Outline of the History of the Compilation.

An impelling cause for the production of the Bukhara compilation is suggested by the date 1709 at which was finished the earliest example known to me. For in the first decade of the eighteenth century Peter the Great gave attention to Russian relations with foreign states of Central Asia and negociated with the Khan of Bukhara for the reception of a Russian mission.[1] Political aims would be forwarded if envoys were familiar with Turki; books in that tongue for use in the School of Oriental Languages would be desired; thus the Compilation may have been prompted and, as will be shown later, it appears to have been produced, and not merely copied, in 1709. The Mission's despatch was delayed till 1719; it arrived in Bukhara in 1721; during its stay a member of its secretariat bought a Compilation MS. noted as finished in 1714 and on a fly-leaf of it made the following note:—

[1] *See* Gregorief's "Russian policy regarding Central Asia", quoted in Schuyler's Turkistan, App. IV.

[2] The Mission was well received, started to return to Petrograd, was attacked by Turkmans, went back to Bukhara, and there stayed until it could attempt the devious route which brought it to the capital in 1725.

"I, Timur-pulad son of Mirza Rajab son of Pay-chin, bought this book Babur-nama after coming to Bukhara with [the] Russian Florio Beg Beneveni, envoy of the Padshah . . . whose army is numerous as the stars . . . May it be well received! Amen! O Lord of both Worlds!"

Timur-pulad's hope for a good reception indicates a definite recipient, perhaps a commissioned purchase. The vendor may have been asked for a history of Babur; he sold one, but "Babur-nama" is not necessarily a title, and is not suitable for the Compilation; by conversational mischance it may have seemed so to the purchaser and thus have initiated the mistake of confusing the "Bukhara Babur-nama" with the true one.

Thus endorsed, the book in 1725 reached the Foreign Office; there in 1737 it was obtained by George Jacob Kehr, a teacher of Turki, amongst other languages, in the Oriental School, who copied it with meticulous care, understanding its meaning imperfectly, in order to produce a Latin version of it. His Latin rendering was a fiasco, but his reproduction of the Arabic forms of his archetype was so obedient that on its sole basis Ilminski edited the Kasan Imprint (1857). A collateral copy of the Timur-pulad Codex was made in 1742 (as has been said).

In 1824 Klaproth (who in 1810 had made a less valuable extract perhaps from Kehr's Codex) copied from the Timur-pulad MS. its purchaser's note, the Auzbeg?(?) endorsement as to the transfer of the "Kamran-docket" and Babur's letter to Kamran (*Mémoires relatifs à l'Asie* (Paris).

In 1857 Ilminski, working in Kasan, produced his imprint, which became de Courteille's source for *Les Mémoires de Baber* in 1871. No worker in the above series shews doubt about accepting the Compilation as containing Babur's authentic text. Ilminski was in the difficult position of not having entire reliance on Kehr's transcription, a natural apprehension in face of the quality of the Latin version, his doubts sum up into his words that a reliable text could not be made from his source (Kehr's MS.), but that a Turki reading-book could — and was. As has been said, he did not obey the dual plan of the Compilation Kehr's transcript reveals, this, perhaps, because of the misnomer Babur-nama under which Timur-pulad's Codex had come to Petrograd; this, certainly, because he thought a better history of Babur could be produced by following Erskine than by obeying Kehr — a series of errors following the verbal mischance of 1725. Ilminski's transformation of the items of his source had the ill result of misleading Pavet de Courteille to over-estimate his Turki source at the expense of Erskine's Persian one which, as has been said, was Ilminski's guide — another scene in the comedy. A mischance hampering the French work was its falling to be done at a time when, in Paris 1871, there can have been no opportunity available for learning the contents of Ilminski's Russian Preface or for quiet research and the examination of collateral aids from abroad.[1]

The Author of the Compilation.

The Haidarabad Codex having destroyed acquiescence in the phantasmal view of the Bukhara book, the question may be considered, who was its author?

This question a convergence of details about the Turki MSS. reputed to contain the *Babur-nama*, now allows me to answer with some semblance of truth. Those details have thrown new light upon a colophon which I received in 1900 from Mr. C. Salemann with other particulars concerning the "*Senkovski Babur-nama*," this being an extract from the Compilation; its archetype reached Petrograd from Bukhara a century after Kehr's [*viz.* the Timur-pulad Codex]; it can be taken as a direct copy of the Mulla's original because it bears his colophon.[2] In 1900 I accepted it as merely that of a scribe who had copied Senkovski's archetype, but in 1921 reviewing the colophon for this Preface, it seems to me to be that of the original autograph MS. of the Compilation and to tell its author's name, his title for his book, and the year (1709) in which he completed it.

[1] One might say jestingly that the spirit in the book had rebelled since 1725 against enforced and changing masquerade as a phantasm of two other books!

[2] Neither Ilminski nor Smirnov mentions another "Babur-nama" Codex than Kehr's.

TABLE OF BUKHARA REPUTED-BABUR-NAMA MSS. (*Waqi'nama-i-padshahi?*).

Names.	Date of completion.	Scribe.	Last known location.	Archetype.	Remarks.
1. Waqi'nama-i-padshahi *alias* Babur-nama.	1121–1709. Date of colophon of earliest known example.	'Ābdu'l-wahhab *q.v.* Taken to be also the author.	Bukhara.	Believed to be the original compilation.	*See* Part III.
2. Nazar Bai Turkistani's MS.	Unknown.	Unknown.	In owner's charge in Petrograd, 1824.	No. 1, the colophon of which it reproduces.	Senkovski's archetype who copied its (transferred) colophon.
3. F. O. Codex (Timur-pulad's MS.).	1126–1714.	Unknown.	F.O. Petrograd, where copied in 1742.	Not stated, an indirect copy of No. 1.	Bought in Bukhara, brought to Petro. 1725.
4. Kehr's Autograph Codex.	1737.	George Jacob Kehr.	Pet. Or. School, 1894. London T.O. 1921.	No. 3.	*See* Part III.
5. Name not learned.	1155–1742.	Unknown.	Unknown.	No. 3.	Archetype of 9.
6. (Mysore) A.S.B. Codex.	Unknown. JRAS. 1900, Nos. vii and viii.	Unknown.	Asiatic Society of Bengal.	Unknown.	—
7. India Office Codex (Bib. Leydeniana).	Cir. 1810.	Unknown.	India Office, 1921.	No. 6.	Copied for Leyden.
8. "The Senkovski Babur-nama.	1824.	J. Senkovski.	Pet. Asiatic Museum, 1900.	No. 2.	Bears a copy of the colophon of No. 1.
9. Pet. University Codex.	1839?	Mulla Faizkhanov?	Pet. Univ. Library.	No. 5 (?).	—

Senkovski brought it over from his archetype; Mr. Salemann sent it to me in its original Turki form. (JRAS. 1900, p. 474). Senkovski's own colophon is as follows:—

"*J'ai achevé cette copie le 4 Mai, 1824, à St. Petersburg; elle a ète faite d'àpres un exemplaire appartenant à Nazar Bai Turkistani, négociant Boukhari, qui etait venu cette année à St. Petersburg. J. Senkovski.*"

The colophon Senkovski copied from ms archetype is to the following purport:—

"*Known and entitled Waqi'nama-i-padshahi (Record of Royal Acts), [this] autograph and composition (bayad u navisht) of Mulla 'Abdu'l-wahhab the Teacher, of Ghaj-davan in Bukhara—God pardon his mistakes and the weakness of his endeavour!—was finished on Monday, Rajab 5, 1121* (Aug. 31st, 1709).—*Thank God!*"

It will be observed that the title Waqi'nama-i-padshahi suits the plan of dual histories (of Babur and Humayun) better than does the "Babur-nama" of Timur-pulad's note, that the colophon does not claim for the Mulla to have copied the elder book (1494–1530) but to have written down and composed one under a differing title suiting its varied contents; that the Mulla's deprecation and thanks tone better with perplexing work, such as his was, than with the steadfast patience of a good scribe; and that it exonerates the Mulla from suspicion of having caused his compilation to be accepted as Babur's authentic text. Taken with its circumstanding matters, it may be the dénoument of the play.

CHAPTER IV.

THE LEYDEN AND ERSKINE MEMOIRS OF BABER.

The fame and long literary services of the *Memoirs of Baber* compel me to explain why these volumes of mine contain a verbally new English translation of the *Babur-nama* instead of a second edition of the *Memoirs*. My explanation is the simple one of textual values, of the advantage a primary source has over its derivative,

Babur's original text over its Persian translation which alone was accessible to Erskine.

If the *Babur-nama* owed its perennial interest to its valuable multifarious matter, the *Memoirs* could suffice to represent it, but this it does not; what has kept interest in it alive through some four centuries is the autobiographic presentment of an arresting personality its whole manner, style and diction produce. It is characteristic throughout, from first to last making known the personal quality of its author. Obviously that quality has the better chance of surviving a transfer of Babur's words to a foreign tongue when this can be effected by imitation of them. To effect this was impracticable to Erskine who did not see any example of the Turki text during the progress of his translation work and had little acquaintance with Turki. No blame attaches to his results; they have been the one introduction of Babur's writings to English readers for almost a century; but it would be as sensible to expect a potter to shape a vessel for a specific purpose without a model as a translator of autobiography to shape the new verbal container for Babur's quality without seeing his own. Erskine was the pioneer amongst European workers on Baburiana—Leydens's fragment of unrevised attempt to translate the Bukhara Compilation being a negligible matter, notwithstanding friendship's deference to it; he had ready to his hand no such valuable collateral help as he bequeathed to his successors in the Memoirs volume. To have been able to help in the renewal of his book by preparing a second edition of it, revised under the authority of the Haidarabad Codex, would have been to me an act of literary piety to an old book-friend; I experimented and failed in the attempt; the wording of the Memoirs would not press back into the Turki mould. Being what it is, sound in its matter and partly representative of Babur himself, the all-round safer plan, one doing it the greater honour, was to leave it unshorn of its redundance and unchanged in its wording, in the place of worth and dignity it has held so long.

Brought to this point by experiment and failure, the way lay open to make bee-line over intermediaries back to the fountain-head of re-discovered Turki text preserved in the Haidarabad Codex. Thus I have enjoyed an advantage no translator has had since 'Abdu'r-rahim in 1589.

Concerning matters of style and diction, I may mention that three distinct impressions of Babur's personality are set by his own, Erskine's and de Courteille's words and manner. These divergencies, while partly due to differing textual bases, may result mainly from the use by the two Europeans of unsifted, current English and French. Their portrayal might have been truer, there can be no doubt, if each had restricted himself to such under-lying component of his mother-tongue as approximates in linguistic stature to classic Turki. This probability Erskine could not foresee for, having no access during his work to a Turki source and no familiarity with Turki, he missed their lessoning.

Turki, as Babur writes it—terse, word-thrifty, restrained and lucid, —comes over neatly into Anglo-Saxon English, perhaps through primal affinities. Studying Babur's writings in verbal detail taught me that its structure, idiom and vocabulary dictate a certain mechanism for a translator's imitation. Such are the simple sentence, devoid of relative phrasing, copied in the form found, whether abrupt and brief or, ranging higher with the topic, gracious and dignified—the retention of Babur's use of "we" and "I" and of his frequent impersonal statement—the matching of words by their root-notion—the strict observance of Babur's limits of vocabulary, effected by allotting to one Turki word one English equivalent, thus excluding synonyms for which Turki has little use because not shrinking from the repeated word; lastly, as preserving relations of diction, the replacing of Babur's Arabic and Persian aliens by Greek and Latin ones naturalized in English. Some of these aids towards shaping a counterpart of Turki may be thought small, but they obey a model and their aggregate has power to make or mar a portrait.

(1) Of the uses of pronouns it may be said that Babur's "we" is neither regal nor self-magnifying but is co-operative, as beseems the chief whose volunteer and nomad following makes or unmakes his power, and who can lead and command only by remittent consent

accorded to him. His "I" is. individual. The *Memoirs* varies much from these uses.

(2) The value of reproducing impersonal statements is seen by the following example, one of many similar :—When Babur and a body of men, making a long saddle-journey, halted for rest and refreshment by the road-side ; "There was drinking," he writes, but Erskine, "I drank" ; what is likely being that all or all but a few shared the local *vin du pays.*

(3) The importance of observing Babur's limits of vocabulary needs no stress, since any man of few words differs from any man of many. Measured by the Babur-nama standard, the diction of the *Memoirs* is redundant throughout, and frequently over-coloured. Of this a pertinent example is provided by a statement of which a minimum of seven occurrences forms my example, namely, that such or such a man whose life Babur sketches was vicious or a vicious person (*fisq, fāsiq*). Erskine once renders the word by "vicious" but elsewhere enlarges to "debauched, excess of sensual enjoyment, lascivious, libidinous, profligate, voluptuous". The instances are scattered and certainly Erskine could not feel their collective effect, but even scattered, each does its ill-part in distorting the Memoirs portraiture of the man of the one word.[1]

Postcript of Thanks.

I take with gratitude the long-delayed opportunity of finishing my book to express the obligation I feel to the Council of the Royal Asiatic Society for allowing me to record in the Journal my Notes on the Turki Codices of the *Babur-nama* begun in 1900 and occasionally appearing till 1921. In minor convenience of work, to be able to gather those progressive notes together and review them, has been of

[1] A Correspondent combatting my objection to publishing a second edition of the *Memoirs*, backed his favouring opinion by reference to 'Umar Khayyam and Fitzgerald. Obviously no analogy exists ; Erskine's redundance is not the flower of a deft alchemy, but is the prosaic consequence of a secondary source.

value to me in noticeable matters, two of which are the finding and multiplying of the Haidarabad Codex, and the definite clearance of the confusion which had made the Bukhara (reputed) *Babur-nama* be mistaken for a reproduction of Babur's true text.

Immeasurable indeed is the obligation laid on me by the happy community of interests which brought under our roof the translation of the biographies of Babur, Humayun, and Akbar. What this has meant to my own work may be surmised by those who know my husband's wide reading in many tongues of East and West, his retentive memory and his generous communism in knowledge. One signal cause for gratitude to him from those caring for Baburiana, is that it was he made known the presence of the Haidarabad Codex in its home library (1899) and thus led to its preservation in facsimile.

It would be impracticable to enumerate all whose help I keep in grateful memory and realize as the fruit of the genial camaraderie of letters.

ANNETTE S. BEVERIDGE.

PITFOLD, SHOTTERMILL, HASLEMERE.
August, 1921.

THE MEMOIRS OF BABUR

SECTION I. FARGHĀNA.

In the name of God, the Merciful, the Compassionate.

In[1] the month of Ramẓān of the year 899 (June 1494) and in the twelfth year of my age,[2] I became ruler[3] in the country of Farghāna. Ḥaidarābād MS. fol.

(*a. Description of Farghāna.*)

Farghāna is situated in the fifth climate[4] and at the limit of settled habitation. On the east it has Kāshghar; on the west, Samarkand; on the south, the mountains of the Badakhshān border; on the north, though in former times there must have been towns such as Ālmālīgh, Ālmātū and

[1] The manuscripts relied on for revising the first section of the Memoirs, (*i.e.* 899 to 908 AH.—1494 to 1502 AD.) are the Elphinstone and the Ḥaidarābād Codices. To variants from them occurring in Dr. Kehr's own transcript no authority can be allowed because throughout this section, his text appears to be a compilation and in parts a retranslation from one or other of the two Persian translations (*Wāqi'āt-i-bāburi*) of the *Bābur-nāma*. Moreover Dr. Ilminsky's imprint of Kehr's text has the further defect in authority that it was helped out from the Memoirs, itself not a direct issue from the Turkī original.

Information about the manuscripts of the *Bābur-nāma* can be found in the JRAS for 1900, 1902, 1905, 1906, 1907 and 1908.

The foliation marked in the margin of this book is that of the Ḥaidarābād Codex and of its facsimile, published in 1905 by the Gibb Memorial Trust.

[2] Bābur, born on Friday, Feb. 14th. 1483 (Muḥarram 6, 888 AH.), succeeded his father, 'Umar Shaikh who died on June 8th. 1494 (Ramẓān 4, 899 AH.).

[3] *pād-shāh,* protecting lord, supreme. It would be an anachronism to translate *pādshāh* by King or Emperor, previous to 913 AH. (1507 AD.) because until that date it was not part of the style of any Tīmūrid, even ruling members of the house being styled Mīrzā. Up to 1507 therefore Bābur's correct style is Bābur Mīrzā. (*Cf.* f. 215 and note.)

[4] See *Āyīn-i-akbarī,* Jarrett, p. 44.

Yāngī which in books they write Tarāz,[1] at the present time all is desolate, no settled population whatever remaining because of the Mughūls and the Aūzbegs.[2]

Farghāna is a small country,[3] abounding in grain and fruits. It is girt round by mountains except on the west, *i.e.* towards Khujand and Samarkand, and in winter[4] an enemy can enter only on that side.

Fol. 2. The Saiḥūn River (*daryā*) commonly known as the Water of Khujand, comes into the country from the north-east, flows westward through it and after passing along the north of Khujand and the south of Fanākat,[5] now known as Shāhrukhiya, turns directly north and goes to Turkistān. It does not

[1] The Hai. MS. and a good many of the W.-i-B. MSS. here write Aūtrār. [Aūtrār like Tarāz was at some time of its existence known as Yāngī (New).] Tarāz seems to have stood near the modern Auliya-ātā; Ālmālīgh,—a Metropolitan see of the Nestorian Church in the 14th. century,—to have been the old capital of Kuldja, and Ālmātū (var. Ālmātī) to have been where Vernoe (Vierny) now is. Ālmālīgh and Ālmātū owed their names to the apple (*ālmā*). *Cf.* Bretschneider's Mediæval Geography p. 140 and T.R. (Elias and Ross) *s.nn.*

[2] *Mughūl u Aūzbeg jihatdīn.* I take this, the first offered opportunity of mentioning (1) that in transliterating Turkī words I follow Turkī lettering because I am not competent to choose amongst systems which *e.g.* here, reproduce Aūzbeg as Uzbeg, Özbeg and Euzbeg; and (2) that style being part of an autobiography, I am compelled, in pressing back the Memoirs on Bābur's Turkī mould, to retract from the wording of the western scholars, Erskine and de Courteille. Of this compulsion Bābur's bald phrase *Mughūl u Aūzbeg jihatdīn* provides an illustration. Each earlier translator has expressed his meaning with more finish than he himself; 'Abdu'r-raḥīm, by *az jihat 'ubūr-i (Mughūl u) Aūzbeg*, improves on Bābur, since the three towns lay in the tideway of nomad passage (*'ubūr*) east and west; Erskine writes "in consequence of the incursions" etc. and de C. "*grace aux ravages commis*" etc.

[3] Schuyler (ii, 54) gives the extreme length of the valley as about 160 miles and its width, at its widest, as 65 miles.

[4] Following a manifestly clerical error in the Second W.-i-B. the *Akbarnāma* and the Mems. are without the seasonal limitation, "in winter." Babūr here excludes from winter routes one he knew well, the Kīndīrlīk Pass; on the other hand Kostenko says that this is open all the year round. Does this contradiction indicate climatic change? (*Cf.* f. 54*b* and note; A.N. Bib. Ind. ed. i, 85 (H. Beveridge i, 221) and, for an account of the passes round Farghāna, Kostenko's *Turkistān Region*, Tables of Contents.)

[5] Var. Banākat, Banākaṣ, Fīākat, Fanākand. Of this place Dr. Rieu writes (Pers. cat. i, 79) that it was also called Shāsh and, in modern times, Tāshkīnt. Bābur does not identify Fanākat with the Tāshkīnt of his day but he identifies it with Shāhrukhiya (*cf.* Index *s.nn.*) and distinguishes between Tāshkīnt-Shāsh and Fanākat-Shāhrukhiya. It may be therefore that Dr. Rieu's Tāshkīnt-Fanākat was Old Tāshkīnt,—(Does Fanā-kint mean Old Village?) some 14 miles nearer to the Saiḥūn than the Tāshkīnt of Bābur's day or our own.

join any sea[1] but sinks into the sands, a considerable distance below [the town of] Turkistān.

Farghāna has seven separate townships,[2] five on the south and two on the north of the Saiḥūn.

Of those on the south, one is Andijān. It has a central position and is the capital of the Farghāna country. It produces much grain, fruits in abundance, excellent grapes and melons. In the melon season, it is not customary to sell them out at the beds.[3] Better than the Andijān *nāshpātī*,[4] there is none. After Samarkand and Kesh, the fort[5] of Andijān is the largest in Mawārā'u'n-nahr (Transoxiana). It has three gates. Its citadel (*ark*) is on its south side. Into it water goes by nine channels; out of it, it is strange that none comes at even a single place.[6] Round the outer edge of the ditch[7] runs a gravelled highway; the width of this highway divides the fort from the suburbs surrounding it.

Andijān has good hunting and fowling; its pheasants grow Fol. 2*b*.

[1] *hech daryā qātīlmās*. A gloss of *dīgar* (other) in the Second W.-i-B. has led Mr. Erskine to understand "meeting with no other river in its course." I understand Bābur to contrast the destination of the Saiḥūn which he [erroneously] says sinks into the sands, with the outfall of *e.g.* the Amū into the Sea of Aral.

Cf. First W.-i-B. I.O. MS. 215 f. 2; Second W.-i-B. I.O. MS. 217 f. 1*b* and Ouseley's Ibn Haukal p. 232-244; also Schuyler and Kostenko *l.c.*

[2] Bābur's geographical unit in Central Asia is the township or, with more verbal accuracy, the village *i.e.* the fortified, inhabited and cultivated oasis. Of frontiers he says nothing.

[3] *i.e.* they are given away or taken. Bābur's interest in fruits was not a matter of taste or amusement but of food. Melons, for instance, fresh or stored, form during some months the staple food of Turkistānīs. *Cf.* T.R. p. 303 and (in Kāshmīr) 425; Timkowski's *Travels of the Russian Mission* i, 419 and Th. Radloff's *Réceuils d'Itinéraires* p. 343.

N.B. At this point o folios of the Elphinstone Codex are missing.

[4] Either a kind of melon or the pear. For local abundance of pears *see* *Ayīn-i-akbarī*, Blochmann p. 6; Kostenko and Von Schwarz.

[5] *qūrghān*, *i.e.* the walled town within which was the citadel (*ark*).

[6] *Tūqūz tarnau sū kirār, bū 'ajab tūr kim bir yīrdīn ham chiqmās*. Second W.-i-B. I.O. 217 f. 2, *nuh jū'ī āb dar qila' dar mī āyid u īn 'ajab ast kah hama az yak jā ham na mī bar āyid*. (*Cf.* Mems. p. 2 and *Méms.* i, 2.) I understand Bābur to mean that all the water entering was consumed in the town. The supply of Andijān, in the present day, is taken both from the Āq Būrā (*i.e.* the Aūsh Water) and, by canal, from the Qarā Daryā.

[7] *khandaqnīng tāsh yānī*. Second W.-i-B. I.O. 217 f. 2 *dar kinār sang bast khandaq*. Here as in several other places, this Persian translation has rendered Turkī *tāsh*, outside, as if it were Turkī *tāsh*, stone. Bābur's adjective *stone* is *sangīn* (f. 45*b* l. 8). His point here is the unusual circumstance of a high-road running round the outer edge of the ditch. Moreover Andijān is built on and

so surprisnigly fat that rumour has it four people could not finish one they were eating with its stew.[1]

Andijānīs are all Turks, not a man in town or bāzār but knows Turkī. The speech of the people is correct for the pen; hence the writings of Mīr 'Alī-shīr *Nawā'ī*,[2] though he was bred and grew up in Hīrī (Harāt), are one with their dialect. Good looks are common amongst them. The famous musician, Khwāja Yūsuf, was an Andijānī.[3] The climate is malarious; in autumn people generally get fever.[4]

Again, there is Aūsh (Ūsh), to the south-east, inclining to east, of Andijān and distant from it four *yīghāch* by road.[5] It has a fine climate, an abundance of running waters[6] and a most beautiful spring season. Many traditions have their rise

---

of loess. Here, obeying his Persian source, Mr. Erskine writes "stone-faced ditch"; M. de C. obeying his Turkī one, "*bord extérieur*."

[1] *qīrghāwal āsh-kinasī bila*. *Āsh-kina*, a diminutive of *āsh*, food, is the rice and vegetables commonly served with the bird. Kostenko i, 287 gives a recipe for what seems *āsh-kina*.

[2] b. 1440; d. 1500 AD.

[3] Yūsuf was in the service of Bāī-sunghar Mīrzā *Shāhrukhī* (d. 837 AH.-1434 AD.). *Cf.* Daulat Shāh's *Memoirs of the Poets* (Browne) pp. 340 and 350-1. (H.B.)

[4] *gūzlār ail bīzkāh kūb būlūr*. Second W.-i-B. (I.O. 217 f. 2) here and on f. 4 has read Turkī *gūz*, eye, for Turkī *gūz* or *goz*, autumn. It has here a gloss not in the Ḥaidarābād or Kehr's MSS. (*Cf.* Mems. p. 4 note.) This gloss may be one of Humāyūn's numerous notes and may have been preserved in the Elphinstone Codex, but the fact cannot now be known because of the loss of the two folios already noted. (*See* Von Schwarz and Kostenko concerning the autumn fever of Transoxiana.)

[5] The Pers. trss. render *yīghāch* by *farsang*; Ujfalvy also takes the *yīghāch* and the *farsang* as having a common equivalent of about 6 *kilomètres*. Bābur's statements in *yīghāch* however, when tested by ascertained distances, do not work out into the *farsang* of four miles or the *kilomètre* of 8 *kil.* to 5 miles. The *yīghāch* appears to be a variable estimate of distance, sometimes indicating the time occupied on a given journey, at others the distance to which a man's voice will carry. (*Cf.* Ujfalvy *Expédition scientifique* ii, 179; Von Schwarz p. 124 and de C.'s Dict. *s.n. yīghāch*. In the present instance, if Bābur's 4 y. equalled 4 f. the distance from Aūsh to Andijān should be about 16 m.; but it is 33 m. 1¼ fur. *i.e.* 50 *versts*. (Kostenko ii, 33.) I find Bābur's *yīghāch* to vary from about 4 m. to nearly 8 m.

[6] *āqār sū*, the irrigation channels on which in Turkistān all cultivation depends. Major-General Gérard writes, (Report of the Pamir Boundary Commission, p. 6,) "Osh is a charming little town, resembling Islāmābād in Kāshmīr, —everywhere the same mass of running water, in small canals, bordered with willow, poplar and mulberry." He saw the Āq Būrā, the *White wolf*, mother of all these running waters, as a "bright, stony, trout-stream;" Dr. Stein saw it as a "broad, tossing river." (Buried Cities of Khotan, p. 45.) *Cf.* Réclus vi, cap. Farghāna; Kostenko i, 104; Von Schwarz *s.nn.*

in its excellencies.[1] To the south-east of the walled town (*qūrghān*) lies a symmetrical mountain, known as the Barā Koh;[2] on the top of this, Sl. Maḥmūd Khān built a retreat (*ḥajra*) and lower down, on its shoulder, I, in 902AH. (1496AD.) built another, having a porch. Though his lies the higher, mine is the better placed, the whole of the town and the suburbs being at its foot.

The Andijān torrent[3] goes to Andijān after having traversed the suburbs of Aūsh. Orchards (*bāghāt*)[4] lie along both its banks; all the Aūsh gardens (*bāghlār*) overlook it; their violets are very fine; they have running waters and in spring are most beautiful with the blossoming of many tulips and roses. Fol. 3.

On the skirt of the Barā-koh is a mosque called the Jauza

[1] *Aūshnīng faẓīlatīdā khailī aḥādīṣ wārid dūr.* Second W.-i-B. (I.O. 217 f. 2) *Faẓīlat-i-Aūsh aḥadīṣ wārid ast.* Mems. (p. 3) " The excellencies of Usb are celebrated even in the sacred traditions." *Méms.* (i, 2) " *On cite beaucoup de traditions qui célèbrent l'excellence de ce climat.*" Aūsh may be mentioned in the traditions on account of places of pilgrimage near it; Bābur's meaning may be merely that its excellencies are traditional. *Cf.* Ujfalvy ii, 172.

[2] Most travellers into Farghāna comment on Bābur's account of it. One much discussed point is the position of the Barā Koh. The personal observations of Ujfalvy and Schuyler led them to accept its identification with the rocky ridge known as the Takht-i-sulaimān. I venture to supplement this by the suggestion that Bābur, by Barā Koh, did not mean the whole of the rocky ridge, the name of which, Takht-i-sulaimān, an ancient name, must have been known to him, but one only of its four marked summits. Writing of the ridge Madame Ujfalvy says, " *Il y a quatre sommets dont le plus élevé est le troisième comptant par le nord.*" Which summit in her sketch (p. 327) is the third and highest is not certain, but one is so shewn that it may be the third, may be the highest and, as being a peak, can be described as symmetrical *i.e.* Bābur's *mauzūn*. For this peak an appropriate name would be Barā Koh.

If the name Barā Koh could be restricted to a single peak of the Takht-i-sulaimān ridge, a good deal of earlier confusion would be cleared away, concerning which have written, amongst others, Ritter (v, 432 and 732); Réclus (vi. 54); Schuyler (ii, 43) and those to whom these three refer. For an excellent account, graphic with pen and pencil, of Farghāna and of Aūsh *see* Madame Ujfalvy's *De Paris à Samarcande* cap. v.

[3] *rūd.* This is a precise word since the Āq Būrā (the White Wolf), in a relatively short distance, falls from the Kūrdūn Pass, 13,400 ft. to Aūsh, 3040 ft. and thence to Andijān, 1380 ft. *Cf.* Kostenko i, 104; Huntingdon in Pumpelly's *Explorations in Turkistān* p. 179 and the French military map of 1904.

[4] Whether Bābur's words, *bāghāt, bāghlār and bāghcha* had separate significations, such as orchard, vineyard and ordinary garden *i.e.* garden-plots of small size, I am not able to say but what appears fairly clear is that when he writes *bāghāt u bāghlār* he means *all sorts of gardens*, just as when writes *begāt u beglār*, he means *begs of all ranks*.

Masjid (Twin Mosque).[1] Between this mosque and the town, a great main canal flows from the direction of the hill. Below the outer court of the mosque lies a shady and delightful clover-meadow where every passing traveller takes a rest. It is the joke of the ragamuffins of Aūsh to let out water from the canal[2] on anyone happening to fall asleep in the meadow. A very beautiful stone, waved red and white[3] was found in the Barā Koh in 'Umar Shaikh Mīrzā's latter days; of it are made knife handles, and clasps for belts and many other things. For climate and for pleasantness, no township in all Farghāna equals Aūsh.

Again there is Marghīnān; seven *yīghāch*[4] by road to the west of Andijān,—a fine township full of good things. Its apricots (*aūrūk*) and pomegranates are most excellent. One sort of pomegranate, they call the Great Seed (*Dāna-i-kalān*); its sweetness has a little of the pleasant flavour of the small apricot (*zard-alū*) and it may be thought better than the Semnān pome-
Fol. 3*b*. granate. Another kind of apricot (*aūrūk*) they dry after stoning it and putting back the kernel;[5] they then call it *subhānī*; it is very palatable. The hunting and fowling of Marghīnān are good; *āq kīyīk*[6] are had close by. Its people are Sārts,[7] boxers,

1 Madame Ujfalvy has sketched a possible successor. Schuyler found two mosques at the foot of Takht-i-sulaiman, perhaps Bābur's Jauza Masjid.

2 *aūl shāh-jū'īdin sū qūyārlār.*

3 Ribbon Jasper, presumably.

4 Kostenko (ii, 30), 71½ versts *i.e.* 47 m. 4½ fur. by the Postal Road.

5 Instead of their own kernels the Second W.-i-B. stuffs the apricots, in a fashion well known in India by *khūbānī*, with almonds (*maghz-i badām*). The Turkī wording however allows the return to the apricots of their own kernels and Mr. Rickmers tells me that apricots so stuffed were often seen by him in the Zar-afshān Valley. My husband has shewn me that Nizāmī in his Haft Paikar appears to refer to the other fashion that of inserting almonds :—

> " I gave thee fruits from the garden of my heart,
> Plump and sweet as honey in milk ;
> Their substance gave the lusciousness of figs,
> In their hearts were the kernels of almonds."

6 What this name represents is one of a considerable number of points in the *Bābur-nāma* I am unable to decide. *Kīyīk* is a comprehensive name (*cf.* Shaw's Vocabulary); *āq kīyīk* might mean *white sheep* or *white deer*. It is rendered in the Second W.-i-B., here, by *ahū-i-wāriq* and on f. 4, by *ahū-i-safed*. Both these names Mr. Erskine has translated by "white deer," but he mentions that the first is said to mean *argālī i.e. ovis poli*, and refers to *Voyages de Pallas* iv, 325.

7 Concerning this much discussed word, Bābur's testimony is of service. It seems to me that he uses it merely of those settled in towns (villages) and

noisy and turbulent. Most of the noted bullies (*jangralār*) of Samarkand and Bukhārā are Marghīnānīs. The author of the Hidāyat[1] was from Rashdān, one of the villages of Marghīnān.

Again there is Asfara, in the hill-country and nine *yīghāch*[2] by road south-west of Marghīnān. It has running waters, beautiful little gardens (*bāghcha*) and many fruit-trees but almonds for the most part in its orchards. Its people are all Persian-speaking[3] Sārts. In the hills some two miles (*bīr shar'ī*) to the south of the town, is a piece of rock, known as the Mirror Stone.[4] It is some 10 arm-lengths (*qārī*) long, as high as a man in parts, up to his waist in others. Everything is reflected by it as by a mirror. The Asfara district (*wilāyat*) is in four sub-divisions (*balūk*) in the hill-country, one Asfara, one Warūkh, one Sūkh and one Hushyār. When Muhammad *Shaibānī* Khān defeated Sl. Maḥmūd Khān and Alacha Khān and took Tāshkīnt and Shāhrukhiya,[5] I went into the Sūkh and Hushyār hill-country and from there, after about a year spent in great misery, I set out (*'azīmat*) for Kābul.[6]

Again there is Khujand,[7] twenty-five *yīghāch* by road to the

---

without any reference to tribe or nationality. I am not sure that he uses it always as a noun; he writes of a *Sārt kishi*, a Sārt person. His Asfara Sārts may have been Turkī-speaking settled Turks and his Marghīnānī ones Persian-speaking Tājiks. *Cf.* Shaw's Vocabulary; *s.n.* Sārt; Schuyler i, 104 and note; Nalivkine's *Histoire du Khanat de Khokand* p. 45 n. Von Schwarz *s.n.*; Kostenko i, 287; Petzhold's *Turkistan* p. 32.

[1] Shaikh Burhānu'd-dīn 'Alī *Qilich*: b. *circa* 530 AH. (1135 AD.) d. 593 AH. (1197 AD.). *See* Hamilton's *Hidāyat*.

[2] The direct distance, measured on the map, appears to be about 65 m. but the road makes *détour* round mountain spurs. Mr. Erskine appended here, to the "*farsang*" of his Persian source, a note concerning the reduction of Tatar and Indian measures to English ones. It is rendered the less applicable by the variability of the *yīghāch*, the equivalent for a *farsang* presumed by the Persian translator.

[3] Ilai. MS. *Farsī-gū'ī*. The Elph. MS. and all those examined of the W.-i-B. omit the word *Farsī*; some writing *kohī* (mountaineer) for *gū'ī*. I judge that Bābur at first omitted the word *Farsī*, since it is entered in the Ilai. MS. above the word *gū'ī*. It would have been useful to Ritter (vii, 733) and to Ujfalvy (ii, 176). *Cf.* Kostenko i, 287 on the variety of languages spoken by Sārts.

[4] Of the Mirror Stone neither Fedtschenko nor Ujfalvy could get news.

[5] Bābur distinguishes here between Tāshkīnt and Shāhrukhiya. *Cf.* f. 2 and note to Fanākat.

[6] He left the hill-country above Sūkh in Muḥarram 910 AH. (mid-June 1504 AD.).

[7] For a good account of Khujand *see* Kostenko i, 346.

west of Andijān and twenty-five *yīghāch* east of Samarkand.[1] Khujand is one of the ancient towns; of it were Shaikh Maṣlaḥat and Khwāja Kamāl.[2] Fruit grows well there; its pomegranates are renowned for their excellence; people talk of a Khujand pomegranate as they do of a Samarkand apple; just now however, Marghīnān pomegranates are much met with.[3] The walled town (*qūrghān*) of Khujand stands on high ground; the Saiḥūn River flows past it on the north at the distance, may be, of an arrow's flight.[4] To the north of both the town and the river lies a mountain range called Munūghul;[5] people say there are turquoise and other mines in it and there are many snakes. The hunting and fowling-grounds of Khujand are first-rate; *āq kīyīk*,[6] *būghū-marāl*,[7] pheasant and hare are all had in great plenty. The climate is very malarious; in autumn there is much fever;[8] people rumour it about that the very sparrows get fever and say that the cause of the malaria is the mountain range on the north (*i.e.* Munūghul).

Kand-i-badām (Village of the Almond) is a dependency of Khujand; though it is not a township (*qaṣba*) it is rather a good

1 Khujand to Andijān 187 m. 2 fur. (Kostenko ii, 29-31) and, helped out by the time-table of the Transcaspian Railway, from Khujand to Samarkand appears to be some 154 m. 5½ fur.

2 Both men are still honoured in Khujand (Kostenko i, 348). For Khwāja Kamāl's Life and *Diwān*, *see* Rieu ii, 632 and Ouseley's Persian Poets p. 192. *Cf.* f. 83*b* and note.

3 *khūb artūq dūr*, perhaps brought to Hindūstān where Bābur wrote the statement.

4 Turkish arrow-flight, London, 1791, 482 yards.

5 I have found the following forms of this name,—Ḥai. MS., M:nūgh:l; Pers. trans. and Mems., Myoghil; Ilminsky, M:tugh:l; *Mēms*. Mtoughuil; Réclus, Schuyler and Kostenko, Mogul Tau; Nalivkine, "d'apres Fedtschenko," Mont Mogol; Fr. Map of 1904, M. Muzbek. It is the western end of the Kurāma Range (Kīndīr Tau), which comes out to the bed of the Sīr, is 26⅔ miles long and rises to 4000 ft. (Kostenko, i, 101). Von Schwarz describes it as being quite bare; various writers ascribe climatic evil to it.

6 Pers. trans. *ahū-i-safed*. *Cf.* f. 3*b* note.

7 These words translate into *Cervus marāl*, the Asiatic Wapiti, and to this Bābur may apply them. Dictionaries explain *marāl* as meaning *hind* or *doe* but numerous books of travel and Natural History show that it has wider application as a generic name, *i.e.* deer. The two words *būghū* and *marāl* appear to me to be used as *e.g.* drake and duck are used. *Marāl* and duck can both imply the female sex, but also both are generic, perhaps primarily so. *Cf.* for further mention of *būghū-marāl* f. 219 and f. 276. For uses of the word *marāl*, *see* the writings *e.g.* of Atkinson, Kostenko (iii, 69), Lyddeker, Littledale, Selous, Ronaldshay, Church (Chinese Turkistan), Biddulph (Forsyth's Mission).

8 *Cf.* f. 2 and note.

approach to one (*qaṣbacha*). Its almonds are excellent, hence its name; they all go to Hormuz or to Hindūstān. It is five or Fol. 4b. six *yīghāch*[1] east of Khujand.

Between Kand-i-badām and Khujand lies the waste known as Hā Darwesh. In this there is always (*hamesha*) wind; from it wind goes always (*hameshā*) to Marghīnān on its east; from it wind comes continually (*dā'im*) to Khujand on its west.[2] It has violent, whirling winds. People say that some darweshes, encountering a whirlwind in this desert,[3] lost one another and kept crying, "Hāy Darwesh! Hāy Darwesh!" till all had perished, and that the waste has been called Hā Darwesh ever since.

Of the townships on the north of the Saiḥūn River one is Akhsī. In books they write it Akhsīkīt[4] and for this reason the

[1] Schuyler (ii, 3), 18 m.

[2] Ḥai. MS. *Hamesha bū deshttā yīl bār dūr. Marghīnānghā kīm sharqī dūr, hamesha mūndīn yīl bārūr; Khujandghā kīm gharībī dūr, dā'im mūndīn yīl kīlūr.*

This is a puzzling passage. It seems to say that wind always goes east and west from the steppe as from a generating centre. E. and de C. have given it alternative directions, east or west, but there is little point in saying this of wind in a valley hemmed in on the north and the south. Bābur limits his statement to the steppe lying in the contracted mouth of the Farghāna valley (*pace* Schuyler ii, 51) where special climatic conditions exist such as (*a*) difference in temperature on the two sides of the Khujand narrows and currents resulting from this difference,—(*b*) the heating of the narrows by sun-heat reflected from the Mogol-tau,—and (*c*) the inrush of westerly wind over Mīrzā Rabāṭ. Local knowledge only can guide a translator safely but Bābur's directness of speech compels belief in the significance of his words and this particularly when what he says is unexpected. He calls the Hā Darwesh a whirling wind and this it still is. Thinkable at least it is that a strong westerly current (the prevailing wind of Farghāna) entering over Mīrzā Rabāṭ and becoming, as it does become, the whirlwind of Hā Darwesh on the hemmed-in steppe,—becoming so perhaps by conflict with the hotter indraught through the Gates of Khujand—might force that indraught back into the Khujand Narrows (in the way *e.g.* that one Nile in flood forces back the other), and at Khujand create an easterly current. All the manuscripts agree in writing to (*ghā*) Marghīnān and to (*ghā*) Khujand. It may be observed that, looking at the map, it appears somewhat strange that Bābur should take, for his wind objective, a place so distant from his (defined) Hā Darwesh and seemingly so screened by its near hills as is Marghīnān. But that westerly winds are prevalent in Marghīnān is seen *e.g.* in Middendorff's *Einblikke in den Farghāna Thal* (p. 112). *Cf.* Réclus vi, 547; Schuyler ii, 51; Cahun's *Histoire du Khanat de Khokand* p. 28 and Sven Hedin's *Durch Asien's Wüsten s.n. būrān.*

[3] *bādiya*; a word perhaps selected as punning on *bād*, wind.

[4] *i.e.* Akhsī Village. This word is sometimes spelled Akhsīkīṣ but as the old name of the place was Akhsī-kīnt, it may be conjectured at least that the *ṣā'ī maṣallaṣa* of Akhsīkīṣ represents the three points due for the *nūn* and *tā* of *kīnt*. Of those writing Akhsīkīt may be mentioned the Ḥai. and Kehr's

poet Aṣiru-d-dīn is known as *Akhsīkītī*. After Andijān no township in Farghāna is larger than Akhsī. It is nine *yīghāch*[1] by road to the west of Andijān. 'Umar Shaikh Mīrzā made it his capital.[2] The Saiḥūn River flows below its walled town (*qūrghān*). This stands above a great ravine (*buland jar*) and it has deep ravines (*'umiq jarlār*) in place of a moat. When 'Umar Shaikh Mīrzā made it his capital, he once or twice cut other ravines from the outer ones. In all Farghāna no fort is so strong as Akhsī. *Its suburbs extend some two miles further than the walled town.* People seem to have made of Akhsī the saying (*miṣal*), "Where is the village? Where are the trees?" (*Dih kujā? Dirakhtān kujā?*) Its melons are excellent; they call one kind Mīr Tīmūrī; whether in the world there is another to equal it is not known. The melons of Bukhārā are famous; when I took Samarkand, I had some brought from there and some from Akhsī; they were cut up at an entertainment and nothing from Bukhārā compared with those from Akhsī. The fowling and hunting of Akhsī are very good indeed; *āq kiyīk* abound in the waste on the Akhsī side of the Saiḥūn; in the jungle on the Andijān side *būghū-marāl*,[3] pheasant and hare are had, all in very good condition.

Again there is Kāsān, rather a small township to the north of Akhsī. From Kāsān the Akhsī water comes in the same way as the Andijān water comes from Aūsh. Kāsān has excellent air and beautiful little gardens (*bāghcha*). As these gardens all lie along the bed of the torrent (*sā'ī*) people call them the "fine front of the coat."[4] Between Kāsānīs and Aūshīs there is rivalry about the beauty and climate of their townships.

MSS. (the Elph. MS. here has a lacuna) the *Ẓafar-nāma* (Bib. Ind. i, 44) and Ibn Haukal (Ouseley p. 270); and of those writing the word with the *ṣā'ī muṣallaṣa* (*i.e.* as Akhsīkīṣ), Yāqūt's Dict. i, 162, Reinaud's Abū'l-feda I. ii, 225-6, Ilminsky (p. 5) departing from his source, and I.O. Cat. (Ethé) No. 1029. It may be observed that Ibn Haukal (Ouseley p. 280) writes Banākaṣ for Banākat. For Aṣiru'd-dīn *Akhsīkītī*, see Rieu ii, 563; Daulat Shāh (Browne) p. 121 and Ethé I.O. Cat. No. 1029.

[1] Measured on the French military map of 1904, this may be 80 kil. *i.e.* 50 miles.
[2] Concerning several difficult passages in the rest of Bābur's account of Akhsī, see Appendix A.
[3] The W.-i-B. here translates *būghū-marāl* by *gazawn* and the same word is entered, under-line, in the Ḥai. MS. *Cf.* f. 3b and note and f. 4 and note.
[4] *postīn pesh b:r:h.* This obscure Persian phrase has been taken in the following ways:—

In the mountains round Farghāna are excellent summer-pastures (*yīlāq*). There, and nowhere else, the *tabalghū*[1] grows, a tree (*yīghāch*) with red bark; they make staves of it; they make bird-cages of it; they scrape it into arrows;[2] it is an excellent wood (*yīghāch*) and is carried as a rarity[3] to distant places. Some books write that the mandrake[4] is found in these mountains but for this long time past nothing has been heard of it. A plant called *Āyīq aūtī*[5] and having the qualities of the mandrake (*mihr-giyāh*), is heard of in Yītī-kīnt;[6] it seems to be Fol. 5b.

(*a*) W.-i-B. I.O. 215 and 217 (*i.e.* both versions) reproduce the phrase.
(*b*) W.-i-B. MS., quoted by Erskine, p. 6 note, *postīn-i mīsh burra.*
(*c*) Leyden's MS. Trs., a sheepskin mantle of five lambskins.
(*d*) Mems., Erskine, p. 6, a mantle of five lambskins.
(*e*) The Persian annotator of the Elph. MS., underlining *pesh*, writes, *panj*, five.
(*f*) Klaproth (Archives, p. 109), *pustini pisch breh, d.h. gieb den vorderen Pelz.*
(*g*) Kehr, p. 12 (Ilminsky p. 6) *postīn bīsh b:r:h.*
(*h*) De. C., i, 9, *fourrure d'agneau de la première qualité.*

The "lambskins" of L. and E. carry on a notion of comfort started by their having read *sayāh*, shelter, for Turkī *sā'ī*, torrent-bed; de C. also lays stress on fur and warmth, but would not the flowery border of a mountain stream prompt rather a phrase bespeaking ornament and beauty than one expressing warmth and textile softness? If the phrase might be read as *postīn pesh perā*, what adorns the front of a coat, or as *postīn pesh bar rah*, the fine front of the coat, the phrase would recall the gay embroidered front of some leathern postīns.

[1] Var. *tabarkhūn*. The explanation best suiting its uses, enumerated here, is Redhouse's second, the Red Willow. My husband thinks it may be the Hyrcanian Willow.

[2] Steingass describes this as "an arrow without wing or point" (barb?) and tapering at both ends; it may be the practising arrow, *t'alīm aūqī*, often headless.

[3] *tabarraklūq*. Cf. f. 48*b* foot, for the same use of the word.

[4] *yabrūju'ṣ-ṣannam*. The books referred to by Bābur may well be the *Rauzatu'ṣ-ṣafā* and the *Habību's-siyār*, as both mention the plant.

[5] The Turkī word *āyīq* is explained by Redhouse as *awake* and *alert*; and by Meninski and de Meynard as *sobered* and as *a return to right senses*. It may be used here as a equivalent of *mihr* in *mihr-giyāh*, the plant of love.

[6] Mr. Ney Elias has discussed the position of this group of seven villages. (*Cf.* T. R. p. 180 n.) Arrowsmith's map places it (as Iti-kint) approximately where Mr. Th. Radloff describes seeing it *i.e.* on the Farghāna slope of the Kurāma range. (*Cf. Réceuil d'Itinéraires* p. 188.) Mr. Th. Radloff came into Yītī-kīnt after crossing the Kīndīrlik Pass from Tāshkīnt and he enumerates the seven villages as traversed by him before reaching the Sīr. It is hardly necessary to say that the actual villages he names may not be those of Bābur's Yītī-kīnt. Wherever the word is used in the *Bābur-nāma* and the *Tārīkh-i-rashidī*, it appears from the context allowable to accept Mr. Radloff's location but it should be borne in mind that the name Yītī-kīnt (Seven

the mandrake (*mihr-giyāh*) the people there call by this name (*i.e. āyīq aūtī*). There are turquoise and iron mines in these mountains.

If people do justly, three or four thousand men[1] may be maintained by the revenues of Farghāna.

(*b. Historical narrative resumed.*)[2]

As 'Umar Shaikh Mīrzā was a ruler of high ambition and great pretension, he was always bent on conquest. On several occasions he led an army against Samarkand; sometimes he was beaten, sometimes retired against his will.[3] More than once he asked his father-in-law into the country, that is to say, my grandfather, Yūnas Khān, the then Khān of the Mughūls in the camping ground (*yūrt*) of his ancestor, Chaghatāī Khān, the second son of Chīngīz Khān. Each time the Mīrzā brought The Khān into the Farghāna country he gave him lands, but, partly owing to his misconduct, partly to the thwarting of the Fol. 6. Mughūls,[4] things did not go as he wished and Yūnas Khān, not being able to remain, went out again into Mughūlistān. When the Mīrzā last brought The Khān in, he was in possession of

villages or towns) might be found as an occasional name of Altī-shahr (Six towns). *See* T.R. *s.n.* Altī-shahr.

[1] *kishī*, person, here manifestly fighting men.

[2] Elph. MS. f. 2*b*; First W.-i-B. I.O. 215 f. 4*b*; Second W.-i-B. I.O. 217 f. 4; Mems. p. 6; Ilminsky p. 7; *Mém's*. i. 10.

The rulers whose affairs are chronicled at length in the Farghāna Section of the B.N. are, (I) of Tīmūrid Turks, (always styled Mīrzā), (*a*) the three Mīrān-shāhī brothers, Aḥmad, Maḥmūd and 'Umar Shaikh with their successors, Bāī-sunghar, 'Alī and Bābur; (*b*) the Bāī-qarā, Ḥusain of Harāt: (II) of Chīngīz Khānīds, (always styled Khān,) (*a*) the two Chaghatāī Mughūl brothers, Maḥmūd and Aḥmad; (*b*) the Shaibānid Aūzbeg, Muḥammad *Shaibānī* (Shāh-i-bakht or Shaibāq or Shāhī Beg).

In electing to use the name *Shaibānī*, I follow not only the Ḥai. Codex but also Shaibānī's Boswell, Muḥammad Ṣāliḥ Mīrzā. The Elph. MS. frequently uses *Shaibāq* but its authority down to f. 198 (Ḥai. MS. f. 243*b*) is not so great as it is after that folio, because not till f. 198 is it a direct copy of Bābur's own. It may be more correct to write "the Shaibānī Khān" and perhaps even "the Shaibānī."

[3] *bī murād*, so translated because retirement was caused once by the over-ruling of Khwāja 'Ubaidu'l-lāh *Aḥrārī*. (T.R. p. 113.)

[4] Once the Mīrzā did not wish Yūnas to winter in Akhsī; once did not expect him to yield to the demand of his Mughūls to be led out of the cultivated country (*wilāyat*). His own misconduct included his attack in Yūnas on account of Akhsī and much falling-out with kinsmen. (T.R. *s.nn.*)

Tāshkīnt, which in books they write Shash, and sometimes Chāch, whence the term, a Chāchī, bow.[1] He gave it to The Khān, and from that date (890AH.-1485AD.) down to 908AH. (1503AD.) it and the Shāhrukhiya country were held by the Chaghatāī Khāns.

At this date (*i.e.*, 899AH.-1494AD.) the Mughūl Khānship was in Sl. Maḥmūd Khān, Yūnas Khān's younger son and a half-brother of my mother. As he and 'Umar Shaikh Mīrzā's elder brother, the then ruler of Samarkand, Sl. Aḥmad Mīrzā were offended by the Mīrzā's behaviour, they came to an agreement together; Sl. Aḥmad Mīrzā had already given a daughter to Sl. Maḥmūd Khān;[2] both now led their armies against 'Umar Shaikh Mīrzā, the first advancing along the south of the Khujand Water, the second along its north.

Meantime a strange event occurred. It has been mentioned that the fort of Akhsī is situated above a deep ravine;[3] along this ravine stand the palace buildings, and from it, on Monday, Ramẓān 4, (June 8th.) 'Umar Shaikh Mīrzā flew, with his pigeons and their house, and became a falcon.[4] Fol. 6*b*.

He was 39 (lunar) years old, having been born in Samarkand, in 860AH. (1456AD.) He was Sl. Abū-sa'īd Mīrzā's fourth son,[5] being younger than Sl. Aḥmad M. and Sl. Muḥammad

[1] *i.e.* one made of non-warping wood (Steingass), perhaps that of the White Poplar. The *Shāh-nāma* (Turner, Maçon ed. i, 71) writes of a Chāchī bow and arrows of *khadang*, *i.e.* white poplar. (H.B.)

[2] *i.e.* Rābi'a-sulṭān, married *circa* 893 AH.-1488 AD. For particulars about her and all women mentioned in the B.N. and the T.R. see Gulbadan Begīm's *Humāyūn-nāma*, Or. Trs. Series.

[3] *jar*, either that of the Kāsān Water or of a deeply-excavated canal. The palace buildings are mentioned again on f. 110*b*. *Cf.* Appendix A.

[4] *i.e.* soared from earth, died. For some details of the accident *see* A.N. (H. Beveridge, i, 220.)

[5] H.S. ii, 192, Firishta, lith. ed. p. 191 and D'Herbélot, sixth.

It would have accorded with Bābur's custom if here he had mentioned the parentage of his father's mother. Three times (fs. 17*b*, 70*b*, 96*b*) he writes of "Shāh Sulṭān Begīm" in a way allowing her to be taken as 'Umar Shaikh's own mother. Nowhere, however, does he mention her parentage. One even cognate statement only have we discovered, *viz.* Khwānd-amīr's (H.S. ii, 192) that 'Umar Shaikh was the own younger brother (*barādar khurdtar khūd*) of Aḥmad and Maḥmūd. If his words mean that the three were full-brothers, 'Umar Shaikh's own mother was Ābū-sa'īd's Tarkhān wife. Bābur's omission (f. 21*b*) to mention his father with A. and M. as a nephew of Darwesh Muḥ. Tarkhān would be negative testimony against taking Khwānd-amīr's statement to mean "full-brother," if clerical slips were not easy and if Khwānd-amīr's

M. and Sl. Maḥmūd Mīrzā. His father, Sl. Abū-sa'īd Mīrzā, was the son of Sl. Muḥammad Mīrzā, son of Tīmūr Beg's third son, Mīrān-shāh M. and was younger than 'Umar Shaikh Mīrzā, (the elder) and Jahāngīr M. but older than Shāhrukh Mīrzā.

c. 'Umar Shaikh Mīrzā's country.

His father first gave him Kābul and, with Bābā-i-Kābulī[1] for his guardian, had allowed him to set out, but recalled him from the Tamarisk Valley[2] to Samarkand, on account of the Mīrzās' Circumcision Feast. When the Feast was over, he gave him Andijān with the appropriateness that Tīmūr Beg had given Farghāna (Andijān) to his son, the elder 'Umar Shaikh Mīrzā. This done, he sent him off with Khudāī-bīrdī *Tūghchī Tīmūr-tāsh*[3] for his guardian.

d. His appearance and characteristics.

He was a short and stout, round-bearded and fleshy-faced Fol. 7. person.[4] He used to wear his tunic so very tight that to fasten the strings he had to draw his belly in and, if he let himself out after tying them, they often tore away. He was not choice in dress or food. He wound his turban in a fold (*dastar-pech*); all turbans were in four folds (*chār-pech*) in those days; people

---

means of information were less good. He however both was the son of Maḥmūd's wāzir (Ḥ.S. ii, 194) and supplemented his book in Bābur's presence.

To a statement made by the writer of the biographies included in Kehr's B.N. volume, that 'U.S.'s family (*aūmāgh*) is not known, no weight can be attached, spite of the co-incidence that the Mongol form of *aūmāgh, i.e. aūmāk* means *Mutter-leib*. The biographies contain too many known mistakes for their compiler to outweigh Khwānd-amīr in authority.

1 *Cf. Rauzatu'ṣ-ṣafā* vi, 266. (H.B.)

2 Dara-i-gaz, south of Balkh. This historic feast took place at Merv in 870 AH. (1465 AD.). As 'Umar Shaikh was then under ten, he may have been one of the Mīrzās concerned.

3 Khudāī-bīrdī is a Pers.-Turkī hybrid equivalent of Theodore; *tūghchī* implies the right to use or (as hereditary standard-bearer,) to guard the *tūgh*; Tīmūr-tāsh may mean *i.a.* Friend of Tīmūr (a title not excluded here as borne by inheritance. *Cf.* f. 12*b* and note), Sword-friend (*i.e.* Companion-in-arms), and Iron-friend (*i.e.* stanch). *Cf.* Dict. *s.n.* Tīmūr-bāsh, a sobriquet of Charles XII.

4 Elph. and Ḥai. MSS. *qūbā yūzlūq*; this is under-lined in the Elph. MS. by *ya'nī pur ghosht*. *Cf.* f. 68*b* for the same phrase. The four earlier trss. *viz.* the two W.-i-B., the English and the French, have variants in this passage.

wore them without twisting and let the ends hang down.[1] In the heats and except in his Court, he generally wore the Mughūl cap.

e. His qualities and habits.

He was a true believer (*Ḥanafī maẕhablīk*) and pure in the Faith, not neglecting the Five Prayers and, his life through, making up his Omissions.[2] He read the Qur'ān very frequently and was a disciple of his Highness Khwāja 'Ubaidu'l-lāh (*Aḥrārī*) who honoured him by visits and even called him son. His current readings[3] were the two Quintets and the *Masnawī*;[4] of histories he read chiefly the *Shāh-nāma*. He had a poetic nature, but no taste for composing verses. He was so just that when he heard of a caravan returning from Khitāī as overwhelmed by snow in the mountains of Eastern Andijān,[5] and that of its thousand heads of houses (*awīlūq*) two only had escaped, he sent his overseers to take charge of all goods and, though no heirs were near and though he was in want himself, summoned the heirs from Khurāsān and Samarkand, and in the course of a year or two had made over to them all their property safe and sound. Fol. 7*b*.

He was very generous; in truth, his character rose altogether to the height of generosity. He was affable, eloquent and sweet-spoken, daring and bold. Twice out-distancing all his

1 The apposition may be between placing the turban-sash round the turban-cap in a single flat fold and winding it four times round after twisting it on itself. *Cf.* f. 18 and Hughes *Dict. of Islām s.n.* turban.

2 *qaẓālār*, the prayers and fasts omitted when due, through war, travel sickness, etc.

3 *rawān sawādī bār īdī;* perhaps, wrote a running hand. De C. i, 13, *ses lectures courantes étaient . . .*

4 The dates of 'Umar Shaikh's limits of perusal allow the Quintets (*Khamsatīn*) here referred to to be those of Niẓāmī and Amīr Khusrau of Dihlī. The *Masnawī* must be that of Jalālu'd-dīn *Rūmī*. (H.B.)

5 Probably below the Tīrāk (Poplar) Pass, the caravan route much exposed to avalanches.

Mr. Erskine notes that this anecdote is erroneously told as of Bābur by Firishta and others. Perhaps it has been confused with the episode on f. 207*b*. Firishta makes another mistaken attribution to Bābur, that of Ḥasan of Yaq'ūb's couplet. (H.B.) *Cf.* f. 13*b* and Dow's *Hindustan* ii, 218.

braves,[1] he got to work with his own sword, once at the Gate of Akhsī, once at the Gate of Shāhrukhiya. A middling archer, he was strong in the fist,—not a man but fell to his blow. Through his ambition, peace was exchanged often for war, friendliness for hostility.

In his early days he was a great drinker, later on used to have a party once or twice a week. He was good company, on occasions reciting verses admirably. Towards the last he rather preferred intoxicating confects[2] and, under their sway, used to lose his head. His disposition[3] was amorous, and he bore many a lover's mark.[4] He played draughts a good deal, sometimes even threw the dice.

f. His battles and encounters.

He fought three ranged battles, the first with Yūnas Khān,
Fol. 8. on the Saiḥūn, north of Andijān, at the Goat-leap,[5] a village so-called because near it the foot-hills so narrow the flow of the water that people say goats leap across.[6] There he was beaten and made prisoner. Yūnas Khān for his part did well by him and gave him leave to go to his own district (Andijān). This fight having been at that place, the Battle of the Goat-leap became a date in those parts.

His second battle was fought on the Urūs,[7] in Turkistān, with Aūzbegs returning from a raid near Samarkand. He crossed the river on the ice, gave them a good beating, separated off all their prisoners and booty and, without coveting a single thing for himself, gave everything back to its owners.

1 *yīgītlār*, young men, the modern *jighit*. Bābur uses the word for men on the effective fighting strength. It answers to the "brave" of North American Indian story; here de C. translates it by *braves*.

2 *ma'jūn*. *Cf.* Von Schwarz p. 286 for a recipe.

3 *mutaiyam*. This word, not clearly written in all MSS., has been mistaken for *yitim*. *Cf.* JRAS 1910 p. 882 for a note upon it by my husband to whom I owe the emendation.

4 *na'l u dāghī bisyār īdī*, that is, he had inflicted on himself many of the brands made by lovers and enthusiasts. *Cf.* Chardin's *Voyages* ii, 253 and Lady M. Montague's *Letters* p. 200.

5 *tīka sikritkū*, lit. likely to make goats leap, from *sikrīmāk* to jump close-footed (Shaw).

6 *sīkrīkān dūr*. Both *sīkrītkū* and *sikrīkān dūr*, appear to dictate translation in general terms and not by reference to a single traditional leap by one goat.

7 *i.e.* Russian; it is the Arys tributary of the Sīr.

His third battle he fought with (his brother) Sl. Aḥmad Mīrzā at a place between Shāhrukhiya and Aūrā-tīpā, named Khwāṣ.[1] Here he was beaten.

g. His country.

The Farghāna country his father had given him; Tāshkīnt and Sairām, his elder brother, Sl. Aḥmad Mīrzā gave, and they were in his possession for a time; Shāhrukhiya he took by a ruse and held awhile. Later on, Tāshkīnt and Shāhrukhiya passed out of his hands; there then remained the Farghāna country and Khujand,—some do not include Khujand in Farghāna,—and Aūrā-tīpā, of which the original name was Aūrūshnā and which some call Aūrūsh. In Aūrā-tīpā, at the time Sl. Aḥmad Mīrzā went to Tāshkīnt against the Mughūls, and was beaten on the Chīr[2] (893AH.-1488AD.) was Ḥafiẓ Beg *Dūldāī*; he made it over to 'Umar Shaikh M. and the Mīrzā held it from that time forth. Fol. 8*b*.

h. His children.

Three of his sons and five of his daughters grew up. I, Ẓahīru'd-dīn Muḥammad Bābur,[3] was his eldest son; my mother was Qūtlūq-nigār Khānīm. Jahāngīr Mīrzā was his second son, two years younger than I; his mother, Fāṭima-sulṭān by name, was of the Mughūl *tūmān*-begs.[4] Nāṣir Mīrzā was his third son; his mother was an Andijānī, a mistress,[5] named Umīd. He was four years younger than I.

'Umar Shaikh Mīrzā's eldest daughter was Khān-zāda Begīm,[6] my full sister, five years older than I. The second

[1] The Fr. map of 1904 shows Kas, in the elbow of the Sīr, which seems to represent Khwāṣ.

[2] *i.e.* the Chīr-chīk tributary of the Sīr.

[3] Concerning his name, *see* T.R. p. 173.

[4] *i.e.* he was a head-man of a horde sub-division, nominally numbering 10,000, and paying their dues direct to the supreme Khān. (T.R. p. 301.)

[5] *ghūnchachī* *i.e.* one ranking next to the four legal wives, in Turkī *aūdālīq*, whence odalisque. Bābur and Gul-badan mention the promotion of several to Begīm's rank by virtue of their motherhood.

[6] One of Bābur's quatrains, quoted in the *Abūshqā*, is almost certainly addressed to Khān-zāda. *Cf.* A.Q. Review, Jan. 1911, p. 4; H. Beveridge's *Some verses of Bābur*. For an account of her marriage *see Shaibānī-nāma* (Vambéry) cap. xxxix.

time I took Samarkand (905AH.-1500AD.), spite of defeat at Sar-i-pul,[1] I went back and held it through a five months' siege, but as no sort of help or reinforcement came from any beg or ruler thereabouts, I left it in despair and got away; in that throneless time (*fatrat*) Khān-zāda Begīm fell[2] to Muḥammad *Shaibānī* Khān. She had one child by him, a pleasant boy,[3]
Fol. 9. named Khurram Shāh. The Balkh country was given to him; he went to God's mercy a few years after the death of his father (916AH.-1510AD.). Khān-zāda Begīm was in Merv when Shāh Ismā'īl (*Ṣafawī*) defeated the Aūzbegs near that town (916AH.-1510AD.); for my sake he treated her well, giving her a sufficient escort to Qūndūz where she rejoined me. We had been apart for some ten years; when Muḥammadī *kūkūldāsh* and I went to see her, neither she nor those about her knew us, although I spoke. They recognized us after a time.

Mihr-bānū Begīm was another daughter, Nāṣir Mīrzā's full-sister, two years younger than I. Shahr-bānū Begīm was another, also Nāṣir Mīrzā's full-sister, eight years younger than I. Yādgār-sulṭān Begīm was another, her mother was a mistress, called Āghā-sulṭān. Ruqaiya-sulṭān Begīm was another; her mother, Makhdūm-sulṭān Begīm, people used to call the Dark-eyed Begīm. The last-named two were born after the Mīrzā's death. Yādgār-sulṭān Begīm was brought up by my grandmother, Aīsān-daulat Begīm; she fell to 'Abdu'l-laṭīf Sl., a son of Ḥamza Sl. when Shaibānī Khān took Andijān and Akhsī (908AH.-1503AD.). She rejoined me when (917AH.-1511AD.) in Khutlān I defeated Ḥamza Sl. and other sulṭāns and took Ḥiṣār. Ruqaiya-sulṭān Begīm fell in that
Fol. 9b. same throneless time (*fatrat*) to Jānī Beg Sl. (*Aūzbeg*). By him she had one or two children who did not live. In these days

[1] Kehr's MS. has a passage here not found elsewhere and seeming to be an adaptation of what is at the top of Ilai. MS. f. 88. (Ilminsky, p. 10, *ba wujūd* ... *tāpīb*.)

[2] *tūshti*, which here seems to mean that she fell to his share on division of captives. Muḥ. Ṣāliḥ makes it a love-match and places the marriage before Bābur's departure. *Cf.* f. 95 and notes.

[3] *aūghlān*. Khurram would be about five when given Balkh in *circa* 911 AH. (1505 AD.). He died when about 12. *Cf.* H.S. ii, 364.

of our leisure (*furṣatlār*)[1] has come news that she has gone to God's mercy.

i. His ladies and mistresses.

Qūtlūq-nigār Khānīm was the second daughter of Yūnas Khān and the eldest (half-) sister of Sl. Maḥmūd Khān and Sl. Aḥmad Khān.

(*j. Interpolated account of Bābur's mother's family.*)

Yūnas Khān descended from Chaghatāī Khān, the second son of Chīngīz Khān (as follows,) Yūnas Khān, son of Wais Khān, son of Sher-'alī *Aūghlān*, son of Muḥammad Khān, son of Khiẓr Khwāja Khān, son of Tūghlūq-tīmūr Khān, son of Aīsān-būghā Khān, son of Dāwā Khān, son of Barāq Khān, son of Yīsūntawā Khān, son of Mūātūkān, son of Chaghatāī Khān, son of Chīngīz Khān.

Since such a chance has come, set thou down[2] now a summary of the history of the Khāns.

Yūnas Khān (d. 892 AH.-1487 AD.) and Aīsān-būghā Khān (d. 866 AH.-1462 AD.) were sons of Wais Khān (d. 832 AH.-1428 AD.).[3] Yūnas Khān's mother was either a daughter or a grand-daughter of Shaikh Nūru'd-dīn Beg, a Turkistānī Qīpchāq favoured by Tīmūr Beg. When Wais Khān died, the Mughūl horde split in two, one portion being for Yūnas Khān, the greater for Aīsān-būghā Khān. For help in getting the upper hand in the horde, Aīrzīn (var. Aīrāzān) one of the Bārīn *tūmān*-begs and Beg Mīrik *Turkmān*, one of the Chīrās *tūmān*-begs, took Yūnas Khān (aet. 13) and with him three or four thousand Mughūl heads of houses (*awīlūq*), to Aūlūgh Beg Mīrzā (*Shāhrukhī*) with the fittingness that Aūlūgh Beg M. had taken Yūnas Khān's elder sister for his son, 'Abdu'l- Fol. 10.

[1] This *fatrat* (interregnum) was between Bābur's loss of Farghāna and his gain of Kābul; the *furṣatlār* were his days of ease following success in Hindūstān and allowing his book to be written.

[2] *qīlālīng*, lit. do thou be (setting down), a verbal form recurring on f. 227*b* l. 2. With the same form (*aīt*)*ālīng*, lit. do thou be saying, the compiler of the *Abūshqā* introduces his quotations. Shaw's paradigm, *qīlīng* only. *Cf.* A.Q.R. Jan. 1911, p. 2.

[3] Kehr's MS. (Hminsky p. 12) and its derivatives here interpolate the erroneous statement that the sons of Yūnas were Afāq and Bābā Khāns.

'azīz Mīrzā. Aūlūgh Beg Mīrzā did not do well by them: some he imprisoned, some scattered over the country[1] one by one. The Dispersion of Aīrzīn became a date in the Mughūl horde.

Yūnas Khān himself was made to go towards 'Irāq; one year he spent in Tabrīz where Jahān Shāh *Barānī* of the Black Sheep Turkmāns was ruling. From Tabrīz he went to Shīrāz where was Shāhrukh Mīrzā's second son, Ibrāhīm Sulṭān Mīrzā.[2] He having died five or six months later (Shawwal 4, 838 AH.-May 3rd, 1435 AD.), his son, 'Abdu'l-lāh Mīrzā sat in his place. Of this 'Abdu'l-lāh Mīrzā Yūnas Khān became a retainer and to him used to pay his respects. The Khān was in those parts for 17 or 18 years.

In the disturbances between Aūlūgh Beg Mīrzā and his sons, Aīsān-būghā Khān found a chance to invade Farghāna; he plundered as far as Kand-i-badām, came on and, having plundered Andijān, led all its people into captivity.[3] Sl. Abū-sa'īd Mīrzā, after seizing the throne of Samarkand, led an army out to beyond Yāngī (Tarāz) to Aspara in Mughūlistān,
Fol. 10*b*. there gave Aīsān-būghā a good beating and then, to spare himself further trouble from him and with the fittingness that he had just taken to wife[4] Yūnas Khān's elder sister, the former wife of 'Abdu'l-'azīz Mīrzā (*Shāhrukhī*), he invited Yūnas Khān from Khurāsān and 'Irāq, made a feast, became friends and proclaimed him Khān of the Mughūls. Just when he was speeding him forth, the Sāghārīchī *tūmān*-begs had all come into Mughūlistān, in anger with Aīsān-būghā Khān.[5] Yūnas Khān went amongst them and took to wife Aīsān-daulat Begīm, the daughter of their chief, 'Alī-shīr

[1] *i.e.* broke up the horde. *Cf.* T.R. p. 74.

[2] *See* f. 50*b* for his descent.

[3] Descendants of these captives were in Kāshghar when Ḥaidar was writing the T.R. It was completed in 953 AH. (1547 AD.). *Cf.* T.R. pp. 81 and 149.

[4] An omission from his Persian source misled Mr. Erskine here into making Abū-sa'īd celebrate the Khānīm's marriage, not with himself but with his defeated foe, 'Abdu'l-'azīz who had married her 28 years earlier.

[5] Aīsān-būghā was at Āq Sū in Eastern Turkistān; Yūnas Khān's head-quarters were in Yitī-kīnt. The Sāghārīchī *tūmān* was a subdivision of the Kūnchī Mughūls.

Beg. They then seated him and her on one and the same white felt and raised him to the Khānship.[1]

By this Aīsān-daulat Begīm, Yūnas Khān had three daughters. Mihr-nigār Khānīm was the eldest; Sl. Abū-sa'īd Mīrzā set her aside[2] for his eldest son, Sl. Aḥmad Mīrzā; she had no child. In a throneless time (905 AH.) she fell to Shaibānī Khān; she left Samarkand[3] with Shāh Begīm for Khurāsān (907 AH.) and both came on to me in Kābul (911 AH.). At the time Shaibānī Khān was besieging Nāṣir Mīrzā in Qandahār and I set out for Lamghān[4] (913 AH.) they went to Badakhshān with Khān Mīrzā (Wais).[5] When Mubārak Shāh invited Khān Mīrzā into Fort Victory,[6] they were Fol. 11 captured, together with the wives and families of all their people, by marauders of Ābā-bikr *Kāshgharī* and, as captives to that ill-doing miscreant, bade farewell to this transitory world (*circa* 913 AH.-1507 AD.).

Qūtlūq-nigār Khānīm, my mother, was Yūnas Khān's second daughter. She was with me in most of my guerilla expeditions and throneless times. She went to God's mercy in Muḥarram 911 AH. (June 1505 AD.) five or six months after the capture of Kābul.

Khūb-nigār Khānīm was his third daughter. Her they gave to Muḥammad Ḥusain *Kūrkān Dūghlāt* (899 AH.). She had one son and one daughter by him. 'Ubaid Khān (*Aūzbeg*) took the daughter (Ḥabība).[7] When I captured Samarkand and

1 *Khān kūtārdīlār.* The primitive custom was to lift the Khān-designate off the ground; the phrase became metaphorical and would seem to be so here, since there were two upon the felt. *Cf.*, however, Th. Radloff's *Réceuil d'Itinéraires* p. 326.

2 *qūyūb īdī*, probably in childhood.

3 She was divorced by Shaibānī Khān in 907 AH. in order to allow him to make lawful marriage with her niece, Khān-zāda.

4 This was a prudential retreat before Shaibānī Khān. *Cf.* f. 213.

5 The "Khān" of his title bespeaks his Chaghatāī-Mughūl descent through his mother, the "Mīrzā," his Tīmūrid-Turkī, through his father. The capture of the women was facilitated by the weakening of their travelling escort through his departure. *Cf.* T.R. p. 203.

6 Qila'-i-ẓafar. Its ruins are still to be seen on the left bank of the Kukcha. *Cf.* T.R. p. 220 and Kostenko i, 140. For Mubārak Shāh *Muẓaffarī* *see* f. 213 and T.R. *s.n.*

7 Ḥabība, a child when captured, was reared by Shaibānī and by him given in marriage to his nephew. *Cf.* T.R. p. 207 for an account of this marriage as saving Ḥaidar's life.

Bukhārā (917 AH.-1511 AD.), she stayed behind,[1] and when her paternal uncle, Sayyid Muḥammad *Dūghlāt* came as Sl. Sa'īd Khān's envoy to me in Samarkand, she joined him and with him went to Kāshghar where (her-cousin), Sl. Sa'īd Khān took her. Khūb-nigār's son was Ḥaidar Mīrzā.[2] He was in my service for three or four years after the Aūzbegs slew his father, then (918 AH.-1512 AD.) asked leave to go to Kāshghar to the presence of Sl. Sa'īd Khān.

> " Everything goes back to its source,
> Pure gold, or silver or tin." [3]

People say he now lives lawfully (*tā'ib*) and has found the right way (*ṭarīqā*).[4] He has a hand deft in every thing, penmanship and painting, and in making arrows and arrow, barbs and string-grips; moreover he is a born poet and in a petition written to me, even his style is not bad.[5]

Fol. 11*b*.

Shāh Begīm was another of Yūnas Khān's ladies. Though he had more, she and Aīsān-daulat Begīm were the mothers of his children. She was one of the (six) daughters of Shāh Sulṭān Muḥammad, Shāh of Badakhshān.[6] His line, they say, runs back to Iskandar Fīlkūs.[7] Sl. Abū-sa'īd Mīrzā took another daughter and by her had Ābā-bikr Mīrzā.[8] By this

[1] *i.e.* she did not take to flight with her husband's defeated force, but, relying on the victor, her cousin Bābur, remained in the town. *Cf.* T.R. p. 268. Her case receives light from Shahr-bānū's (f. 169).

[2] Muḥammad Ḥaidar Mīrzā *Kūrkān Dūghlāt Chaghatāī Mūghūl*, the author of the *Tārīkh-i-rashidī*; b. 905 AH. d. 958 AH. (b. 1499 d. 1551 AD.). Of his clan, the " Oghlāt " (Dūghlāt) Muḥ. Ṣāliḥ says that it was called " Oghlāt " by Mughūls but Qūngūr-āt (Brown Horse) by Aūzbegs.

[3] *Baz garadad ba aṣl-i-khūd hama chīz,*
Zar-i-ṣāfī u naqra u airzīn.

These lines are in Arabic in the introduction to the *Anwar-i-suhaili*. (H.B.) The first is quoted by Ḥaidar (T.R. p. 354) and in Field's *Dict. of Oriental Quotations* (p. 160). I understand them to refer here to Ḥaidar's return to his ancestral home and nearest kin as being a natural act.

[4] *tā'ib* and *ṭarīqa* suggest that Ḥaidar had become an orthodox Musalmān in or about 933 AH. (1527 AD.).

[5] Abū'l-faẓl adds music to Ḥaidar's accomplishments and Ḥaidar's own Prologue mentions yet others.

[6] *Cf.* T.R. *s.n.* and Gul-badan's H.N. *s.n.* Ḥaram Begīm.

[7] *i.e.* Alexander of Macedon. For modern mention of Central Asian claims to Greek descent *see i.a.* Kostenko, Von Schwarz, Holdich and A. Durand. *Cf.* Burnes *Kābul* p. 203 for an illustration of a silver *patera* (now in the V. and A. Museum), once owned by ancestors of this Shāh Sulṭān Muḥammad.

[8] *Cf.* f. 6*b* note

Shāh Begīm Yūnas Khān had two sons and two daughters. Her first-born but younger than all Aīsān-daulat Begīm's daughters, was Sl. Maḥmūd Khān, called Khānika Khān[1] by many in and about Samarkand. Next younger than he was Sl. Aḥmad Khān, known as Alacha Khān. People say he was called this because he killed many Qālmāqs on the several occasions he beat them. In the Mughūl and Qālmāq tongues, one who will kill (*aūltūrgūchī*) is called *ālāchī*; Alāchī they called him therefore and this by repetition, became Alacha.[2] As occasion arises, the acts and circumstances of these two Khāns will find mention in this history (*tārīkh*).

Sulṭān-nigār Khānīm was the youngest but one of Yūnas Khān's children. Her they made go forth (*chīqārīb īdīlār*) Fol. 12. to Sl. Maḥmūd Mīrzā; by him she had one child, Sl. Wais (Khān Mīrzā), mention of whom will come into this history. When Sl. Maḥmūd Mīrzā died (900 AH.-1495 AD.), she took her son off to her brothers in Tāshkīnt without a word to any single person. They, a few years later, gave her to Adik (Aūng) Sulṭan,[3] a Qāzāq sulṭān of the line of Jūjī Khān, Chīngīz Khān's eldest son. When Shaibānī Khān defeated the Khāns (her brothers), and took Tāshkīnt and Shāhrukhiya (908 AH.), she got away with 10 or 12 of her Mughūl servants, to (her husband), Adik Sulṭān. She had two daughters by Adik Sulṭān; one she gave to a Shaibān sulṭān, the other to Rashīd Sulṭān, the son of (her cousin) Sl. Sa'īd Khān. After Adik Sulṭān's death, (his brother), Qāsim Khān, Khān of the Qāzāq horde, took her.[4] Of all the Qāzaq khāns and sulṭāns, no one, they say, ever kept the horde in such good order as he;

[1] *i.e.* Khān's child.

[2] The careful pointing of the Ḥai. MS. clears up earlier confusion by showing the narrowing of the vowels from *ālāchī* to *alacha*.

[3] The Elph. MS. (f. 7) writes *Aūng*, Khān's son, Prester John's title, where other MSS. have Adik. Bābur's brevity has confused his account of Sulṭān-nigār. Widowed of Maḥmūd in 900 AH. she married Adik; Adik, later, joined Shaibānī Khān but left him in 908 AH. perhaps secretly, to join his own Qāzāq horde. He was followed by his wife, apparently also making a private departure. As Adik died shortly after 908 AH. his daughters were born before that date and not after it as has been understood. *Cf.* T.R. and G.B.'s H.N. *s.nn.*; also Mems. p. 14 and *Méms.* i, 24.

[4] Presumably by tribal custom, *yīnkālīk*, marriage with a brother's widow. Such marriages seem to have been made frequently for the protection of women left defenceless.

his army was reckoned at 300,000 men. On his death the Khānīm went to Sl. Sa'īd Khān's presence in Kāshghar. Daulat-sulṯān Khānīm was Yūnas Khān's youngest child. Fol. 12b. In the Tāshkīnt disaster (908 AH.) she fell to Tīmūr Sulṯān, the son of Shaibānī Khān. By him she had one daughter; they got out of Samarkand with me (918 AH.-1512 AD.), spent three or four years in the Badakhshān country, then went (923 AH.-1420 AD.) to Sl. Sa'īd Khān's presence in Kāshghar.[1]

(k. Account resumed of Bābur's father's family.)

In 'Umar Shaikh Mīrzā's *ḥaram* was also Aūlūs Āghā, a daughter of Khwāja Ḥusain Beg; her one daughter died in infancy and they sent her out of the *ḥaram* a year or eighteen months later. Fāṯima-sulṯān Āghā was another; she was of the Mughūl *tūmān*-begs and the first taken of his wives. Qarā-gūz (Makhdūm sulṯān) Begīm was another; the Mīrzā took her towards the end of his life; she was much beloved, so to please him, they made her out descended from (his uncle) Minūchihr Mīrzā, the elder brother of Sl. Abū-sa'īd Mīrzā. He had many mistresses and concubines; one, Umīd Āghāchā died before him. Latterly there were also Tūn-sulṯān (var. Yun) of the Mughūls and Āghā Sulṯān.

l. 'Umar Shaikh Mīrzā's Amīrs.

There was Khudāī-bīrdī *Tūghchī Tīmūr-tāsh*, a descendant of the brother of Āq-būghā Beg, the Governor of Hīrī (Herāt, for Tīmūr Beg.) When Sl. Abū-sa'īd Mīrzā, after besieging Jūkī Mīrzā (*Shāhrukhī*) in Shāhrukhiya (868AH.-1464AD.) gave the Farghāna country to 'Umar Shaikh Mīrzā, he put this Khudāī-
Fol. 13. bīrdī Beg at the head of the Mīrzā's Gate.[2] Khudāī-bīrdī was

1 Sa'īd's power to protect made him the refuge of several kinswomen mentioned in the B.N. and the T.R. This mother and child reached Kāshghar in 932 AH. (1526 AD.).

Here Bābur ends his [interpolated] account of his mother's family and resumes that of his father's.

2 Bābur uses a variety of phrases to express Lordship in the Gate. Here he writes *aīshikni bāshlātib*; elsewhere, *aīshik ikhtiyāri qilmāq* and *mining aīshikimdā ṣāḥib ikhtiyāri qilmāq*. Von Schwarz (p. 159) throws light on the duties of the Lord of the Gate (*Aīshik Āghāsī*). "Das Thür . . . führt in eine

then 25 but youth notwithstanding, his rules and management were very good indeed. A few years later when Ibrāhīm *Begchīk* was plundering near Aūsh, he followed him up, fought him, was beaten and became a martyr. At the time, Sl. Aḥmad Mīrzā was in the summer pastures of Āq Qāchghāī, in Aūrā-tīpā, 18 *yīghāch* east of Samarkand, and Sl. Abū-sa'īd Mīrzā was at Bābā Khākī, 12 *yīghāch* east of Hirī. People sent the news post-haste to the Mīrzā(s),[1] having humbly represented it through 'Abdu'l-wahhāb *Shaghāwal*. In four days it was carried those 120 *yīghāch* of road.[2]

Ḥāfiẓ Muḥammad Beg *Dūldāī* was another, Sl. Malik *Kāshgharī's* son and a younger brother of Aḥmad Ḥājī Beg. After the death of Khudāī-bīrdī Beg, they sent him to control 'Umar Shaikh Mīrzā's Gate, but he did not get on well with the Andijān begs and therefore, when Sl. Abū-sa'īd Mīrza died, went to Samarkand and took service with Sl. Aḥmad Mīrzā. At the time of the disaster on the Chīr, he was in Aūrā-tīpā and made it over to 'Umar Shaikh Mīrzā when the Mīrzā passed through on his way to Samarkand, himself taking service with him. The Mīrzā, for his part, gave him the Andijān Command. Later on he went to Sl. Maḥmūd Khān Fol. 13*b*.

---

grosse, vier-eckige, höhe Halle, deren Boden etwa 2 m. über den Weg erhoben ist. In dieser Halle, welche alle passiren muss, der durch das Thor eingeht, reitet oder fahrt, ist die Thorwache placiert. Tagsüber sind die Thore beständig öffen, nach Eintritt der Dunkelheit aber werden dieselben geschlossen und die Schlüssel dem zuständigen Polizeichef abgeliefert. . . . In den erwähnten Thorhallen nehmen in den hoch unabhängigen Gebieten an Bazartagen haufig die Richter Platz, um jedem der irgend ein Anliegen hat, so fort Recht zu sprechen. Die zudiktierten Strafen werden auch gleich in diesem selben locale vollzogen und eventuell die zum Hangen verurteilten Verbrecher an den Deckbalken aufgehängt, so dass die Besucher des Bazars unter den gehenkten durchpassieren müssen."

[1] *bu khabarnī 'Abdu'l-wahhāb shaghāwaldīn 'arẓa-dāsht qīlīb Mīrzāghā chāptūrdīlār.* This passage has been taken to mean that the *shaghāwal, i.e.* chief scribe, was the courier, but I think Bābur's words shew that the *shaghāwal's* act preceded the despatch of the news. Moreover the only accusative of the participle and of the verb is *khabarnī.* 'Abdu'l-wahhāb had been 'Umar Shaikh's and was now Aḥmad's officer in Khujand, on the main road for Aūrā-tīpā whence the courier started on the rapid ride. The news may have gone verbally to 'Abdu'l-wahhāb and he have written it on to Aḥmad and Abū-sa'īd.

[2] Measured from point to point even, the distance appears to be over 500 miles. Concerning Bābā Khākī *see* H.S. ii. 224; for rapid riding *i.a.* Kostenko iii, cap. Studs.

in Tāshkīnt and was there entrusted with the guardianship of Khān Mīrzā (Wais) and given Dīzak. He had started for Makka by way of Hind before I took Kābul (910AH. Oct. 1504AD.), but he went to God's mercy on the road. He was a simple person, of few words and not clever.

Khwāja Ḥusain Beg was another, a good-natured and simple person. It is said that, after the fashion of those days, he used to improvise very well at drinking parties.[1]

Shaikh Mazīd Beg was another, my first guardian, excellent in rule and method. He must have served (*khidmat qīlghān dūr*) under Bābur Mīrzā (*Shāhrukhī*). There was no greater beg in 'Umar Shaikh Mīrzā's presence. He was a vicious person and kept catamites.

'Alī-mazīd *Qūchīn* was another;[2] he rebelled twice, once at Akhsī, once at Tāshkīnt. He was disloyal, untrue to his salt, vicious and good-for-nothing.

Ḥasan (son of) Yaq'ūb was another, a small-minded, good-tempered, smart and active man. This verse is his:—

> "Return, O Huma, for without the parrot-down of thy lip,
> The crow will assuredly soon carry off my bones."[3]

Fol. 14. He was brave, a good archer, played polo (*chaughān*) well and leapt well at leap-frog.[4] He had the control of my Gate after 'Umar Shaikh Mīrzā's accident. He had not much sense, was narrow-minded and somewhat of a strife-stirrer.

Qāsim Beg *Qūchīn*, of the ancient army-begs of Andijān, was another. He had the control of my Gate after Ḥasan Yaq'ūb Beg. His life through, his authority and consequence waxed without decline. He was a brave man; once he gave some Aūzbegs a good beating when he overtook them raiding near Kāsān; his sword hewed away in 'Umar Shaikh Mīrzā's

[1] *qūshūqlārnī yakhshī aītūrā īkān dūr.* Elph. MS. for *qūshūq, tūyūk. Qūshūq* is allowed, both by its root and by usage, to describe improvisations of combined dance and song. I understand from Bābur's tense, that his information was hearsay only.

[2] *i.e.* of the military class. *Cf.* Vullers *s.n.* and T.R. p. 301.

[3] The Hūma is a fabulous bird, overshadowing by whose wings brings good-fortune. The couplet appears to be addressed to some man, under the name Hūma, from whom Ḥasan of Yaq'ūb hoped for benefit.

[4] *khāk-bīla*; the *Sanglākh*, (quoting this passage) gives *khāk-p:l:k* as the correct form of the word.

presence; and in the fight at the Broad Ford (Yāsī-kījīt *circa* 904AH.-July, 1499AD.) he hewed away with the rest. In the guerilla days he went to Khusrau Shāh (907AH.) at the time I was planning to go from the Macha hill-country[1] to Sl. Maḥmūd Khān, but he came back to me in 910AH. (1504AD.) and I shewed him all my old favour and affection. When I attacked the Turkmān Hazāra raiders in Dara-i-khwush (911AH.) he made better advance, spite of his age, than the younger men; I gave him Bangash as a reward and later on, after returning to Kābul, made him Humāyūn's guardian. He went to God's mercy Fol. 14*b*. about the time Zamīn-dāwar was taken (*circa* 928AH.-1522AD.). He was a pious, God-fearing Musalmān, an abstainer from doubtful aliments; excellent in judgment and counsel, very facetious and, though he could neither read nor write (*ummiy*), used to make entertaining jokes.

Bābā Beg's Bābā Qulī ('Alī) was another, a descendant of Shaikh 'Alī *Bahādur*.[2] They made him my guardian when Shaikh Mazīd Beg died. He went over to Sl. Aḥmad Mīrzā when the Mīrzā led his army against Andijān (899AH.), and gave him Aūrā-tīpā. After Sl. Maḥmūd Mīrzā's death, he left Samarkand and was on his way to join me (900AH.) when Sl. 'Alī Mīrzā, issuing out of Aūrā-tīpā, fought, defeated and slew him. His management and equipment were excellent and he took good care of his men. He prayed not; he kept no fasts; he was like a heathen and he was a tyrant.

'Alī-dost Ṭaghāī[3] was another, one of the Sāghārīchī *tumān*-begs and a relation of my mother's mother, Aīsān-daulat Begīm. I favoured him more than he had been favoured in 'Umar Shaikh Mīrzā's time. People said, "Work will come from his hand." But in the many years he was in my presence, no work to speak of[4] came to sight. He must have served Sl. Fol. 15. Abū-sa'īd Mīrzā. He claimed to have power to bring on rain with the jade-stone. He was the Falconer (*qūshchī*), worthless

[1] *Cf.* f. 99*b*.
[2] One of Tīmūr's begs.
[3] *i.e.* uncle on the mother's side, of any degree, here a grandmother's brother. The title appears to have been given for life to men related to the ruling House. Parallel with it are Madame Mère, Royal Uncle, Sultān Wālida.
[4] *kīm dīsā būlghāī*, perhaps meaning, "Nothing of service to me."

by nature and habit, a stingy, severe, strife-stirring person, false, self-pleasing, rough of tongue and cold-of-face.

Wais *Lāgharī*,[1] one of the Samarkand *Tūghchī* people, was another. Latterly he was much in 'Umar Shaikh Mīrzā's confidence; in the guerilla times he was with me. Though somewhat factious, he was a man of good judgment and counsel.

Mīr Ghiyāṣ Ṭaghāi was another, a younger brother of 'Alī-dost Ṭaghāī. No man amongst the leaders in Sl. Abū-sa'īd Mīrzā's Gate was more to the front than he; he had charge of the Mīrzā's square seal[2] and was much in his confidence latterly. He was a friend of Wais *Lāgharī*. When Kāsān had been given to Sl. Maḥmūd Khān (899AH.-1494AD.), he was continuously in The Khān's service and was in high favour. He was a laugher, a joker and fearless in vice.

'Ali-darwesh *Khurāsānī* was another. He had served in the Khurāsān Cadet Corps, one of two special corps of serviceable young men formed by Sl. Abū-sa'īd Mīrzā when he first began Fol. 15*b*. to arrange the government of Khurāsān and Samarkand, and, presumably, called by him the Khurāsān Corps and the Samarkand Corps. 'Alī-darwesh was a brave man; he did well in my presence at the Gate of Bīshkārān.[3] He wrote the *naskh ta'līq* hand clearly.[4] His was the flatterer's tongue and in his character avarice was supreme.

Qambar-'alī *Mughūl* of the Equerries (*akhtachī*) was another. People called him The Skinner because his father, on first coming into the (Farghāna) country, worked as a skinner. Qambar-'alī had been Yūnas Khān's water-bottle bearer,[5] later on he became a beg. Till he was a made man, his conduct was excellent; once arrived, he was slack. He was full of talk and of foolish talk,—a great talker is sure to be a foolish one,—his capacity was limited and his brain muddy.

[1] Wais the Thin.

[2] *Cf.* Chardin ed. Langlès v, 461 and ed. 1723 AD. v, 183.

[3] n.e. of Kāsān. *Cf.* f. 74. Hai MS., erroneously, Samarkand.

[4] An occasional doubt arises as to whether a *ṭaurī* of the text is Arabic and dispraises or Turkī and laudatory. *Cf.* Mems. p. 17 and *Mém*s. i, 3.

[5] Elph. and Ḥai. MSS. *aftābachī*, water-bottle bearer on journeys; Kehr (p. 82) *aftābchī*, ewer-bearer; Ilminsky (p. 19) *akhtachi*, squire or groom. Circumstances support *aftābachī*. Yūnas was town-bred, his ewer-bearer would hardly be the rough Mughūl, Qambar-'alī, useful as an *aftābachī*.

(l. Historical narrative.)

At the time of 'Umar Shaikh Mīrzā's accident, I was in the Four Gardens (*Chār-bāgh*) of Andijān.[1] The news reached Andijān on Tuesday, Ramẓan 5 (June 9th); I mounted at once, with my followers and retainers, intending to go into the fort but, on our getting near the Mīrzā's Gate, Shīrīm Ṭaghāī[2] took hold of my bridle and moved off towards the Praying Place.[3] It had crossed his mind that if a great ruler like Sl. Aḥmad Mīrzā came in force, the Andijān begs would make over to him me and the country,[4] but that if he took me to Aūzkīnt and the foothills thereabouts, I, at any rate, should not be made over and could go to one of my mother's (half-) brothers, Sl. Maḥmūd Khān or Sl. Aḥmad Khān.[5] When Khwāja Maulānā-i-qāẓī[6] Fol. 16.

(*Author's note on Khwāja Maulānā-i-qāẓī.*) He was the son of Sl. Aḥmad Qāẓī, of the line of Burhānu'd-dīn 'Alī *Qīlīch*[7] and through his mother, traced back to Sl. Aīlīk *Māẓī*.[8] By hereditary right

---

[1] Bābur was Governor of Andijān and the month being June, would be living out-of-doors. *Cf.* H.S. ii, 272 and Schuyler ii, 37.

[2] To the word Sherīm applies Abū'l-ghāzī's explanation of Nūrūm and Ḥājīm, namely, that they are abbreviations of Nūr and Ḥājī Muḥammad. It explains Sulṭānīm also when used (f. 72) of Sl. Muḥammad Khānika but of Sulṭānīm as the name is common with Bābur, Ḥaidar and Gul-badan, *i.e.* as a woman's, Busbecq's explanation is the better, namely, that it means My Sulṭān and is applied to a person of rank and means. This explains other women's titles *e.g.* Khānīm, my Khān and Ākām (Ākīm), My Lady. A third group of names formed like the last by enclitic *'m* (my), may be called names of affection, *e.g.* Māhīm, My Moon, Jānīm, My Life. (*Cf.* Persian equivalents.) *Cf.* Abū'l-ghāzī's *Shajarat-i-Turkī* (Désmaisons p. 272); and Ogier Ghiselin de Busbecq's *Life and Letters* (Forster and Daniel i, 38.)

[3] *Namāz-gāh*; generally an open terrace, with a wall towards the Qibla and outside the town, whither on festival days the people go out in crowds to pray. (Erskine.)

[4] *Bēglār (nīng) mīnī u wilāyatnī tāpshūrghūlārī dūr*; a noticeably idiomatic sentence. *Cf.* f. 16*b* l. 6 and l. 7 for a repetition.

[5] Maḥmūd was in Tāshkīnt, Aḥmad in Kāshghār or on the Āq-sū.

[6] The B.N. contains a considerable number of what are virtually foot-notes. They are sometimes, as here, entered in the middle of a sentence and confuse the narrative; they are introduced by *kīm*, a mere sign of parenthetical matter to follow, and some certainly, known not to be Bābur's own, must have stood first on the margin of his text. It seems best to enter them as Author's notes.

[7] *i.e.* the author of the Hidāyat. *Cf.* f. 3*b* and note; Blochmann *Āyīn-i-akbarī s.n. qulij* and note; Bellew's *Afghan Tribes* p. 100, *Khilich*.

[8] Ar. dead, gone. The precision of Bābur's words *khānwādalār* and *yūsūnlūq* is illustrated by the existence in the days of Tīmūr, in Marghīnān, (Burhānu'd-dīn's township) of a ruler named Aīlīk Khān, apparently a

(*yūsūnlūq*) his high family (*khānwādalār*) must have come to be the Refuge (*marji'*) and Pontiffs (*Shaikhu'l-islām*) of the (Farghāna) country.

and the begs in the fort heard of (the intended departure), they sent after us Khwāja Muḥammad, the tailor,[1] an old servant (*bāyrī*) of my father and the foster-father of one of his daughters. He dispelled our fears and, turning back from near the Praying
Fol. 16*b*. Place, took me with him into the citadel (*ark*) where I dismounted. Khwāja Maulānā-i-qāẓī and the begs came to my presence there and after bringing their counsels to a head,[2] busied themselves in making good the towers and ramparts of the fort.[3] A few days later, Ḥasan, son of Yaq'ūb, and Qāsim *Qūchīn*, arrived, together with other begs who had been sent to reconnoitre in Marghīnān and those parts.[4] They also, after waiting on me, set themselves with one heart and mind and with zeal and energy, to hold the fort.

Meantime Sl. Aḥmad Mīrzā took Aūrā-tīpā, Khujand and Marghīnān, came on to Qabā,[5] 4 *yīghāch* from Andijān and there made halt. At this crisis, Darwesh Gau, one of the Andijān notables, was put to death on account of his improper proposals; his punishment crushed the rest.

Khwāja Qāẓī and Aūzūn (Long) Ḥasan,[6] (brother) of Khwāja Ḥusain, were then sent to Sl. Aḥmad Mīrzā to say in effect that, as he himself would place one of his servants in the country and as I was myself both a servant and (as) a son, he would attain his end most readily and easily if he entrusted the service to me. He was a mild, weak man, of few words who, without his begs, decided no opinion or compact (*aun*), action

---

descendant of Sātūq-būghrā Khān (b. 384 AH.-994 AD.) so that in Khwāja Qāẓī were united two dynasties, (*khānwādalār*), one priestly, perhaps also regal, the other of bye-gone ruling Khāns. *Cf.* D'Herbélot p. 433; *Yarkand Mission*, Bellew p. 121; *Tazkirat-i Sulṭān Sātūq-būghrā Khān Ghāzī Pādshāh* and *Tārīkh-i-nāṣirī* (Raverty *s.n.*)

1 *darzī*; H.S. *khaiyāṭ*.

2 *bīr yīrgā* (*qūyūb*), lit. to one place.

3 *i.e.* reconstructed the earthern defences. *Cf.* Von Schwarz *s.n.* loess.

4 They had been sent, presumably, before 'Umar Shaikh's death, to observe Sl. Ahmad M.'s advance. *Cf.* f. 6.

5 The time-table of the Andijān Railway has a station, Kouwa (Qabā).

6 Bābur, always I think, calls this man Long Ḥasan; Khwānd-amīr styles him Khwāja Ḥasan; he seems to be the brother of one of 'Umar Shaikh's fathers-in-law, Khwāja Ḥusain.

or move; they paid attention to our proposal, gave it a harsh answer and moved forward.

But the Almighty God, who, of His perfect power and without mortal aid, has ever brought my affairs to their right issue, made such things happen here that they became disgusted at having advanced (*i.e.* from Qabā), repented indeed that they had ever set out on this expedition and turned back with nothing done.

One of those things was this: Qabā has a stagnant, morass-like Water,[1] passable only by the bridge. As they were many, there was crowding on the bridge and numbers of horses and Fol. 17. camels were pushed off to perish in the water. This disaster recalling the one they had had three or four years earlier when they were badly beaten at the passage of the Chīr, they gave way to fear. Another thing was that such a murrain broke out amongst their horses that, massed together, they began to die off in bands.[2] Another was that they found in our soldiers and peasants a resolution and single-mindedness such as would not let them flinch from making offering of their lives[3] so long as there was breath and power in their bodies. Need being therefore, when one *yīghāch* from Andijān, they sent Darwesh Muḥammad Tarkhān[4] to us; Ḥasan of Yaq'ūb went out from those in the fort; the two had an interview near the Praying Place and a sort of peace was made. This done, Sl. Aḥmad Mīrzā's force retired.

Meantime Sl. Maḥmūd Khān had come along the north of the Khujand Water and laid siege to Akhsī.[5] In Akhsī was

[1] *bātqāq*. This word is underlined in the Elph. MS. by *dil-dil* and in the Hai. MS. by *jam-jama*. It is translated in the W.-i-B. by *āb pur hīla*, water full of deceit; it is our Slough of Despond. It may be remarked that neither Zenker nor Steingass gives to *dil-dil* or *jam-jama* the meaning of morass; the *Akbar-nāma* does so. (H.B. ii, 112.)

[2] *ṭawīla ṭawīla ūllār yīghīlīb aūlā kīrīshtī*. I understand the word *yīghilib* to convey that the massing led to the spread of the murrian.

[3] *jān tārātmāqlār i.e.* as a gift to their over-lord.

[4] Perhaps, Bābur's maternal great-uncle. It would suit the privileges bestowed on Tarkhāns if their title meant *Khān of the Gifts* (Turkī *tar*, gift). In the *Bāburnāma*, it excludes all others. Most of Aḥmad's begs were Tarkhāns, Arghūns and Chīngīz Khānids, some of them ancestors of later rulers in Tatta and Sind. Concerning the Tarkhāns *see* T.R. p. 55 and note; A.N. (H.B. *s.n.*) Elliot and Dowson's *History of India* , 498.

[5] *Cf.* f. 6.

Jahāngīr Mīrzā (aet. 9) and of begs, 'Alī-darwesh Beg, Mīrzā Qulī *Kūkūldāsh*, Muḥ. Bāqir Beg and Shaikh 'Abdu'l-lāh, Lord of the Gate. Wais *Lāgharī* and Mīr Ghiyāṣ Ṭaghāī had been there too, but being afraid of the (Akhsī) begs had gone off to Kāsān, Wais *Lāgharī's* district, where, he being Nāṣir Mīrzā's guardian, the Mīrzā was.[1] They went over to Sl. Maḥmūd Fol. 17*b*. Khān when he got near Akhsī; Mīr Ghiyāṣ entered his service; Wais *Lāgharī* took Nāṣir Mīrzā to Sl. Aḥmad Mīrzā, who entrusted him to Muh. Mazīd Tarkhān's charge. The Khān, though he fought several times near Akhsī, could not effect anything because the Akhsī begs and braves made such splendid offering of their lives. Falling sick, being tired of fighting too, he returned to his own country (*i.e.* Tāshkīnt).

For some years, Ābā-bikr *Kāshgharī Dūghlāt*,[2] bowing the head to none, had been supreme in Kāshgar and Khutan. He now, moved like the rest by desire for my country, came to the neighbourhood of Aūzkīnt, built a fort and began to lay the land waste. Khwāja Qāzī and several begs were appointed to drive him out. When they came near, he saw himself no match for such a force, made the Khwāja his mediator and, by a hundred wiles and tricks, got himself safely free.

Throughout these great events, 'Umar Shaikh Mīrzā's former begs and braves had held resolutely together and made daring offer of their lives. The Mīrzā's mother, Shāh Sulṭān Begīm,[3] and Jahāngīr Mīrzā and the *ḥaram* household and the begs came from Akhsī to Andijān; the customary mourning was fulfilled and food and victuals spread for the poor and destitute.[4]

Fol. 18. In the leisure from these important matters, attention was given to the administration of the country and the ordering of the army. The Andijān Government and control of my Gate were settled (*mukarrar*) for Ḥasan (son) of Yaq'ūb; Aūsh was decided on (*qarār*) for Qāsim *Qūchīn;* Akhsī and Marghīnān assigned (*ta'īn*) to Aūzun Ḥasan and 'Alī-dost Ṭaghāī. For the rest of 'Umar Shaikh Mīrzā's begs and braves, to each accord-

[1] *beg ātākā*, lit. beg for father.
[2] T.R. *s.n.* Ābā-bikr.
[3] *Cf.* f. 6*b* and note.
[4] *faqra u masākin*, *i.e.* those who have food for one day and those who have none in hand. (Steingass.)

ing to his circumstances, were settled and assigned district (*wilāyat*) or land (*yīr*) or office (*mauja*) or charge (*jīrga*) or stipend (*wajh*).

When Sl. Aḥmad Mīrzā had gone two or three stages on his return-march, his health changed for the worse and high fever appeared. On his reaching the Āq Sū near Aūrā-tīpā, he bade farewell to this transitory world, in the middle of Shawwāl of the date 899 (mid July 1494 AD.) being then 44 (lunar) years old.

m. Sl. Aḥmad Mīrzā's birth and descent.

He was born in 855 AH. (1451 AD.) the year in which his father took the throne (*i.e.* Samarkand). He was Sl. Abū-sa'īd Mīrzā's eldest son; his mother was a daughter of Aūrdū-būghā Tarkhān (*Arghūn*), the elder sister of Darwesh Muḥammad Tarkhān, and the most honoured of the Mīrzā's wives.

n. His appearance and habits.

He was a tall, stout, brown-bearded and red-faced man. He had beard on his chin but none on his cheeks. He had very Fol. 18*b*. pleasing manners. As was the fashion in those days, he wound his turban in four folds and brought the end forward over his brows.

o. His characteristics and manners.

He was a True Believer, pure in the Faith; five times daily, without fail, he recited the Prayers, not omitting them even on drinking-days. He was a disciple of his Highness Khwāja 'Ubaidu'l-lāh (*Aḥrārī*), his instructor in religion and the strengthener of his Faith. He was very ceremonious, particularly when sitting with the Khwāja. People say he never drew one knee over the other[1] at any entertainment of the Khwāja. On one occasion contrary to his custom, he sat with his feet together. When he had risen, the Khwāja ordered the place he had sat in to be searched; there they found, it may have been, a bone.[2] He had read nothing whatever and was ignorant

[1] For fashions of sitting, *see Tawārīkh-i-guzīda Naṣrat-nāma* B.M. Or. 3222. Aḥmad would appear to have maintained the deferential attitude by kneeling and sitting back upon his heels.

[2] *bīr sūnkāk bār īkān dūr.* I understand that something defiling must have been there, perhaps a bone.

(*'amī*), and though town-bred, unmannered and homely. Of genius he had no share. He was just and as his Highness the Khwāja was there, accompanying him step by step,[1] most of his affairs found lawful settlement. He was true and faithful to his vow and word; nothing was ever seen to the contrary. He had courage, and though he never happened to get in his own hand to work, gave sign of it, they say, in some of his en-
Fol. 19. counters. He drew a good bow, generally hitting the duck[2] both with his arrows (*aūq*) and his forked-arrows (*tīr-giz*), and, as a rule, hit the gourd[3] in riding across the lists (*maidān*). Latterly, when he had grown stout, he used to take quail and pheasant with the goshawks,[4] rarely failing. A sportsman he was, hawking mostly and hawking well; since Aūlūgh Beg Mīrzā, such a sporting *pādshāh* had not been seen. He was extremely decorous; people say he used to hide his feet even in the privacy of his family and amongst his intimates. Once settled down to drink, he would drink for 20 or 30 days at a stretch; once risen, would not drink again for another 20 or 30 days. He was a good drinker;[5] on non-drinking days he ate without conviviality (*basīṭ*). Avarice was dominant in his character. He was kindly, a man of few words whose will was in the hands of his begs.

p. His battles.

He fought four battles. The first was with Ni'mat *Arghūn*, Shaikh Jamāl *Arghūn's* younger brother, at Āqār-tūzī, near Zamīn. This he won. The second was with 'Umar Shaikh Mīrzā at Khwaṣ; this also he won. The third affair was when he encountered Sl. Maḥmūd Khān on the Chīr, near Tāshkīnt
Fol. 19b. (895 AH.-1469 AD.). There was no real fighting, but some Mughūl plunderers coming up, by ones and twos, in his rear and laying hands on his baggage, his great army, spite of its numbers,

[1] *Khwājaning ham āyāghlārī ūrādā īdī.*

[2] *īlbāsūn*, a kind of mallard (*Abūshqā*), here perhaps a popinjay. *Cf.* H.S. ii, 193 for Aḥmad's skill as an archer, and Payne-Gallwey's *Cross-bow* p. 225.

[3] *qabāq*, an archer's mark. Abū'l-ghāzī (Kāsān ed. p. 18 l. 5) mentions a hen (*tūqūq*) as a mark. *Cf.* Payne-Gallwey *l.c.* p. 231.

[4] *qīrghīcha, astar palumbarius.* (Shaw's Voc. Scully.)

[5] Perhaps, not quarrelsome.

broke up without a blow struck, without an effort made, without a coming face to face, and its main body was drowned in the Chīr.[1] His fourth affair was with Ḥaidar *Kūkūldāsh* (*Mughūl*), near Yār-yīlāq; here he won.

q. His country.

Samarkand and Bukhārā his father gave him; Tāshkīnt and Sairām he took and held for a time but gave them to his younger brother, 'Umar Shaikh Mīrzā, after 'Abdu'l-qadūs (*Dūghlāt*) slew Shaikh Jamāl (*Arghūn*); Khujand and Aūrā-tīpā were also for a time in his possession.

r. His children.

His two sons did not live beyond infancy. He had five daughters, four by Qātāq Begīm.[2]

Rābi'a-sulṭān Begīm, known as the Dark-eyed Begīm, was his eldest. The Mīrzā himself made her go forth to Sl. Maḥmūd Khān;[3] she had one child, a nice little boy, called Bābā Khān. The Aūzbegs killed him and several others of age as unripe as his when they martyred (his father) The Khān, in Khujand, (914 AH.-1508 AD.). At that time she fell to Jānī Beg Sulṭān (*Aūzbeg*). Fol. 20.

Ṣāliha-sulṭān (Ṣalīqa) Begīm was his second daughter; people called her the Fair Begīm. Sl. Maḥmūd Mīrzā, after her father's death, took her for his eldest son, Sl. Mas'ūd Mīrzā and made the wedding feast (900 AH.). Later on she fell to the Kāshgharī with Shāh Begīm and Mihr-nigār Khānim.

'Āyisha-sulṭān Begīm was the third. When I was five and went to Samarkand, they set her aside for me; in the guerilla times[4] she came to Khujand and I took her (905 AH.); her one little daughter, born after the second taking of Samarkand,

[1] The T.R. (p. 116) attributes the rout to Shaibānī's defection. The H.S. (ii, 192) has a varied and confused account. An error in the T.R. trs. making Shaibānī plunder the Mughūls, is manifestly clerical.

[2] *i.e.* condiment, *ce qu'on ajoute au pain.*

[3] *Cf.* f. 6.

[4] *qāzāqlār*; here, if Bābur's, meaning his conflicts with Tambal, but as the Begīm may have been some time in Khujand, the *qāzāqlār* may be of Samarkand.

went in a few days to God's mercy and she herself left me at the instigation of an older sister.

Sulṭānīm Begīm was the fourth daughter; Sl. 'Alī Mīrzā took her; then Tīmūr Sulṭān (*Aūzbeg*) took her and after him, Mahdī Sulṭān (*Aūzbeg*).

Ma'sūma-sulṭān Begīm was the youngest of Sl. Aḥmad Mīrzā's daughters. Her mother, Ḥabība-sulṭān Begīm, was of the Arghūns, a daughter of Sl. Ḥusain *Arghūn's* brother. I saw her when I went to Khurāsān (912 AH.-1506 AD.), liked her, asked for her, had her brought to Kābul and took her (913 AH.-1507 AD.). She had one daughter and there and then, went to God's mercy, through the pains of the birth. Her name was at once given to her child.

s. *His ladies and mistresses.*

Mihr-nigār Khānīm was his first wife, set aside for him by his father, Sl. Abū-sa'īd Mīrzā. She was Yūnas Khān's eldest
Fol. 20b. daughter and my mother's full-sister.

Tarkhān Begīm of the Tarkhāns was another of his wives.

Qātāq Begīm was another, the foster-sister of the Tarkhān Begīm just mentioned. Sl. Aḥmad Mīrzā took her *par amours* (*'āshiqlār bīlā*) : she was loved with passion and was very dominant. She drank wine. During the days of her ascendancy (*tīrīklīk*), he went to no other of his *ḥaram;* at last he took up a proper position (*aūlnūrdī*) and freed himself from his reproach.[1]

[1] All the (Turkī) Bābur-nāma MSS. and those examined of the W.-i-B. by writing *aūltūrdī* (killed) where I suggest to read *aūlnūrdī* (*devenir comme il faut*) state that Aḥmad killed Qātāq. I hesitate to accept this (1) because the only evidence of the murder is one diacritical point, the removal of which lifts Aḥmad's reproach from him by his return to the accepted rules of a polygamous household; (2) because no murder of Qātāq is chronicled by Khwāndamīr or other writers; and (3) because it is incredible that a mild, weak man living in a family atmosphere such as Bābur, Ḥaidar and Gul-badan reproduce for us, should, while possessing facility for divorce, kill the mother of four out of his five children.

Reprieve must wait however until the word *tīrīklīk* is considered. This Erskine and de C. have read, with consistency, to mean *life-time*, but if *aūlnūrdī* be read in place of *aūltūrdī* (killed), *tīrīklīk* may be read, especially in conjunction with Bābur's *'āshīqlīklār*, as meaning *living power* or *ascendancy*. Again, if read as from *tīrik*, a small arrow and a consuming pain, *tīrīklīk* may represent Cupid's darts and wounds. Again it might be taken as from *tīrāmāk*, to hinder, or forbid.

Under these considerations, it is legitimate to reserve judgment on Aḥmad.

Khān-zāda Begīm, of the Tīrmīẕ Khāns, was another. He had just taken her when I went, at five years old, to Samarkand; her face was still veiled and, as is the Turkī custom, they told me to uncover it.[1]

Laṯīf Begīm was another, a daughter's child of Aḥmad Ḥājī Beg *Dūldāī* (*Barlās*). After the Mīrzā's death, Ḥamza Sl. took her and she had three sons by him. They with other sulṯāns' children, fell into my hands when I took Ḥiṣār (916 AH.-1510 AD.) after defeating Ḥamza Sulṯān and Tīmūr Sulṯān. I set all free.

Ḥabība-sulṯān Begīm was another, a daughter of the brother of Sl. Ḥusain *Arghūn*.

t. His amīrs.

Jānī Beg *Dūldāī* (*Barlās*) was a younger brother of Sl. Malik *Kāshgharī*. Sl. Abū-sa'īd Mīrzā gave him the Government of Samarkand and Sl. Aḥmad Mīrzā gave him the control of his own Gate.[2] He must have had singular habits and manners;[3] many strange stories are told about him. One is this:—While he was Governor in Samarkand, an envoy came to him from the Aūzbegs renowned, as it would seem, for his strength. An Aūzbeg, is said to call a strong man a bull (*būkuh*). "Are you a *būkuh?*" said Jānī Beg to the envoy, "If you are, come, let's have a friendly wrestle together (*kūrāshālīng*)." Whatever objections the envoy raised, he refused to accept. They wrestled and Jānī Beg gave the fall. He was a brave man. Fol. 21.

Aḥmad Ḥājī (*Dūldāī Barlās*) was another, a son of Sl. Malik *Kāshgharī*. Sl. Abū-sa'īd Mīrzā gave him the Government of Hīrī (Harāt) for a time but sent him when his uncle, Jānī Beg

[1] It is customary amongst Turks for a bride, even amongst her own family, to remain veiled for some time after marriage; a child is then told to pluck off the veil and run away, this tending, it is fancied, to the child's own success in marriage. (Erskine.)

[2] Bābur's anecdote about Jānī Beg well illustrates his caution as a narrator. He appears to tell it as one who knowing the point of a story, leads up to it. He does not affirm that Jānī Beg's habits were strange or that the envoy was an athlete but that both things must have been (*ikān dūr*) from what he had heard or to suit the point of the anecdote. Nor does he affirm as of his own knowledge that Aūzbegs calls a strong man (his *zor kīshī*) a *būkuh* (bull) but says it is so understood (*dīr imīsh*).

[3] *Cf.* f. 170.

died, to Samarkand with his uncle's appointments. He was pleasant-natured and brave. Wafā'ī was his pen-name and he put together a dīwān in verse not bad. This couplet is his:—

> "I am drunk, Inspector, to-day keep your hand off me,
> "Inspect me on the day you catch me sober."

Mīr 'Alī-sher Nawā'ī when he went from Hīrī to Samarkand, was with Aḥmad Ḥājī Beg but he went back to Hīrī when Sl. Ḥusain Mīrzā (Bāī-qarā) became supreme (873 AH.-1460 AD.) and he there received exceeding favour.

Fol. 21b. Aḥmad Ḥājī Beg kept and rode excellent *tīpūchāqs*,[1] mostly of his own breeding. Brave he was but his power to command did not match his courage; he was careless and what was necessary in his affairs, his retainers and followers put through. He fell into Sl. 'Alī Mīrzā's hands when the Mīrzā defeated Bāī-sunghar Mīrzā in Bukhārā (901 AH.), and was then put to a dishonourable death on the charge of the blood of Darwesh Muḥammad Tarkhān.[2]

Darwesh Muḥammad Tarkhān (*Arghūn*) was another, the son of Aūrdū-būghā Tarkhān and full-brother of the mother of Sl. Aḥmad Mīrzā and Sl. Maḥmūd Mīrzā.[3] Of all begs in Sl. Aḥmad Mīrzā's presence, he was the greatest and most honoured. He was an orthodox Believer, kindly and darwesh-like, and was a constant transcriber of the Qu'rān.[4] He played chess often and well, thoroughly understood the science of fowling and flew his birds admirably. He died in the height of his greatness, with a bad name, during the troubles between Sl. 'Alī Mīrzā and Bāī-sunghar Mīrzā.[5]

'Abdu'l-'alī Tarkhān was another, a near relation of Darwesh Muḥammad Tarkhān, possessor also of his younger sister,[6] that is to say, Bāqī Tarkhān's mother. Though both by the Mughūl rule (*tūrā*) and by his rank, Darwesh Muḥammad

---

[1] The points of a *tīpūchāq* are variously stated. If the root notion of the name be movement (*tīp*), Erskine's observation, that these horses are taught special paces, is to the point. To the verb *tīprāmāq* dictionaries assign the meaning of *movement with agitation of mind*, an explanation fully illustrated in the B.N. The verb describes fittingly the dainty, nervous action of some trained horses. Other meanings assigned to *tūpūchāq* are roadster, round-bodied and swift.

[2] *Cf.* f. 37b.   [3] *Cf.* f. 6b and note.   [4] *mashaf kitābat qīlūr īdī*.
[5] *Cf.* f. 36 and H.S. ii. 271.   [6] *sinkīlīsī ham mūndā īdī*.

Tarkhān was the superior of 'Abdu'l-'alī Tarkhān, this Pharoah regarded him not at all. For some years he had the Government of Bukhārā. His retainers were reckoned at Fol. 22. 3,000 and he kept them well and handsomely. His gifts (*bakhshīsh*), his visits of enquiry (*purshīsh*), his public audience (*dīwān*), his work-shops (*dast-gāh*), his open-table (*shīlān*) and his assemblies (*majlis*) were all like a king's. He was a strict disciplinarian, a tyrannical, vicious, self-infatuated person. Shaibānī Khān, though not his retainer, was with him for a time; most of the lesser (Shaibān) sulṭāns did themselves take service with him. This same 'Abdu'l-'alī Tarkhān was the cause of Shaibānī Khān's rise to such a height and of the downfall of such ancient dynasties.[1]

Sayyid Yūsuf, the Grey Wolfer[2] was another; his grandfather will have come from the Mughūl horde; his father was favoured by Aūlūgh Beg Mīrzā (*Shāhrukhī*). His judgment and counsel were excellent; he had courage too. He played well on the guitar (*qūbuz*). He was with me when I first went to Kābul; I shewed him great favour and in truth he was worthy of favour. I left him in Kābul the first year the army rode out for Hindūstān; at that time he went to God's mercy.[3]

Darwesh Beg was another; he was of the line of Aīku-tīmūr Beg,[4] a favourite of Tīmūr Beg. He was a disciple of his Highness Khwāja 'Ubaidu'l-lāh (*Aḥrārī*), had knowledge of the science of music, played several instruments and was naturally Fol. 22b. disposed to poetry. He was drowned in the Chīr at the time of Sl. Aḥmad Mīrzā's discomfiture.

Muḥammad Mazīd Tarkhān was another, a younger full-brother of Darwesh Muḥ. Tarkhān. He was Governor in Turkistān for some years till Shaibānī Khān took it from him. His judgment and counsel were excellent; he was an unscrupulous and vicious person. The second and third times

[1] *khāna-wādalār*, *viz.* the Chaghatāī, the Tīmūrid in two Mīrān-shāhī branches, 'Alī's and Bābur's and the Bāī-qarā in Harāt.

[2] *aūghlāqchī i.e.* player at *kūk-būrā*. Concerning the game, *see* Shaw's Vocabulary; Schuyler i, 268; Kostenko iii, 82; Von Schwarz *s.n. baiga*.

[3] Ẕū'l-ḥijja 910 AH.-May 1505 AD. *Cf.* f. 154. This statement helps to define what Bābur reckoned his expeditions into Hindūstān.

[4] Aīkū (Ayāgū)-tīmūr *Tarkhān Arghūn* d. *circa* 793 AH.-1391 AD. He was a friend of Tīmūr. *See* Ẕ.N. i, 525 etc.

I took Samarkand, he came to my presence and each time I shewed him very great favour. He died in the fight at Kūl-i-malik (918 AH.-1512 AD.).

Bāqī Tarkhān was another, the son of 'Abdu'l-'alī Tarkhān and Sl. Aḥmad Mīrzā's aunt. When his father died, they gave him Bukhārā. He grew in greatness under Sl. 'Alī Mīrzā, his retainers numbering 5 or 6,000. He was neither obedient nor very submissive to Sl. 'Alī Mīrzā. He fought Shaibānī Khān at Dabūsī (905AH.) and was crushed; by the help of this defeat, Shaibānī Khān went and took Bukhārā. He was very fond of hawking; they say he kept 700 birds. His manners and habits were not such as may be told;[1] he grew up with a Mīrzā's state and splendour. Because his father had shewn favour to Shaibānī Khān, he went to the Khān's presence, but that inhuman ingrate made him no sort of return in favour and kind-
Fol. 23. ness. He left the world at Akhsī, in misery and wretchedness.

Sl. Ḥusain *Arghūn* was another. He was known as Qarā-kūlī because he had held the Qarā-kūl government for a time. His judgment and counsel were excellent; he was long in my presence also.

Qulī Muḥammad *Būghdā*[2] was another, a *qūchīn*; he must have been a brave man.

'Abdu'l-karīm *Ishrit*[3] was another; he was an Aūīghūr, Sl. Aḥmad Mīrzā's Lord of the Gate, a brave and generous man.

(*u. Historical narrative resumed.*)

After Sl. Aḥmad Mīrzā's death, his begs in agreement, sent a courier by the mountain-road to invite Sl. Maḥmūd Mīrzā.[4]

Malik-i-Muḥammad Mīrzā, the son of Minūchihr Mīrzā, Sl.

[1] *āndāq ikhlāq u aṭawārī yūq idī kīm dīsā būlghāī.* The *Shāh-nāma* cap. xviii, describes him as a spoiled child and man of pleasure, caring only for eating, drinking and hunting. The *Shaibānī-nāma* narrates his various affairs.

[2] *i.e., cutlass*, a parallel sobriquet to *qīlīch*, sword. If it be correct to translate by "cutlass," the nickname may have prompted Bābur's brief following comment, *mardāna īkān dūr, i.e.* Qulī Muḥ. must have been brave because known as the Cutlass. A common variant in MSS. from *Būghdā* is Bāghdād; Bāghdād was first written in the Ḥai. MS. but is corrected by the scribe to *būghdā*.

[3] So pointed in the Ḥai. MS. I surmise it a clan-name.

[4] *i.e.* to offer him the succession. The mountain road taken from Aūrā-tīpā would be by Āb-burdan, Sara-tāq and the Kām Rūd defile.

Abū-sa'īd Mīrzā's eldest brother, aspired for his own part to rule. Having drawn a few adventurers and desperadoes to himself, they dribbled away[1] from (Sl. Aḥmad Mīrzā's) camp and went to Samarkand. He was not able to effect anything, but he brought about his own death and that of several innocent persons of the ruling House.

At once on hearing of his brother's death, Sl. Maḥmūd Mīrzā went off to Samarkand and there seated himself on the throne, without difficulty. Some of his doings soon disgusted and alienated high and low, soldier and peasant. The first of these was that he sent the above-named Malik-i-Muḥammad to the Kūk-sarāī,[2] although he was his father's brother's son and his own son-in-law.[3] With him he sent others, four Mīrzās in all. Two of these he set aside; Malik-i-Muḥammad and one other he martyred. Some of the four were not even of ruling rank and had not the smallest aspiration to rule; though Malik-i-Muḥammad Mīrzā was a little in fault, in the rest there was no blame whatever. A second thing was that though his methods and regulations were excellent, and though he was expert in revenue matters and in the art of administration, his nature inclined to tyranny and vice. Directly he reached Samarkand, he began to make new regulations and arrangements and to rate and tax on a new basis. Moreover the dependants of his (late) Highness Khwāja 'Ubaid'l-lāh, under whose protection formerly many poor and destitute persons had lived free from the burden of dues and imposts, were now themselves treated with harshness and oppression. On what ground should hardship have touched them? Nevertheless oppressive exactions were made from them, indeed from the Khwāja's very children. Yet another thing was that just as he was vicious and tyrannical, so were his begs, small and great, and his retainers and followers. The Ḥiṣārīs and in particular the followers of Khusrau Shāh

Fol. 23*b*.

[1] *īrildī*. The departure can hardly have been open because Aḥmad's begs favoured Maḥmūd; Malik-i-Muḥammad's party would be likely to slip away in small companies.

[2] This well-known Green, Grey or Blue palace or halting-place was within the citadel of Samarkand. *Cf.* f. 37. It served as a prison from which return was not expected.

[3] *Cf.* f. 27. He married a full-sister of Bāī-sunghar.

engaged themselves unceasingly with wine and fornication. Once one of them enticed and took away a certain man's wife. Fol. 24. When her husband went to Khusrau Shāh and asked for justice, he received for answer: "She has been with you for several years; let her be a few days with him." Another thing was that the young sons of the townsmen and shopkeepers, nay! even of Turks and soldiers could not go out from their houses from fear of being taken for catamites. The Samarakandīs, having passed 20 or 25 years under Sl. Aḥmad Mīrzā in ease and tranquillity, most matters carried through lawfully and with justice by his Highness the Khwāja, were wounded and troubled in heart and soul, by this oppression and this vice. Low and high, the poor, the destitute, all opened the mouth to curse, all lifted the hand for redress.

> "Beware the steaming up of inward wounds,
> For an inward wound at the last makes head;
> Avoid while thou canst, distress to one heart,
> For a single sigh will convulse a world."[1]

By reason of his infamous violence and vice Sl. Maḥmud Mīrzā did not rule in Samarkand more than five or six months.

[1] *Gulistān* Part I. Story 27. For "steaming up," *see* Tennyson's Lotus-eaters Choric song, canto 8 (H.B.).

900 AH.—OCT. 2ND. 1494 TO SEP. 21ST. 1495 AD.[1]

THIS year Sl. Maḥmūd Mīrzā sent an envoy, named 'Abdu'l-qadūs Beg,[2] to bring me a gift from the wedding he had made with splendid festivity for his eldest son, Mas'ūd Mīrzā with (Ṣāliḥa-sulṭān), the Fair Begīm, the second daughter of his elder brother, Sl. Aḥmad Mīrzā. They had sent gold and silver almonds and pistachios.

There must have been relationship between this envoy and Ḥasan-i-yaq'ūb, and on its account he will have been the man sent to make Ḥasan-i-yaq'ūb, by fair promises, look towards Sl. Maḥmūd Mīrzā. Ḥasan-i-yaq'ūb returned him a smooth answer, made indeed as though won over to his side, and gave him leave to go. Five or six months later, his manners changed entirely; he began to behave ill to those about me and to others, and he carried matters so far that he would have dismissed me in order to put Jahāngīr Mīrzā in my place. Moreover his conversation with the whole body of begs and soldiers was not what should be; every-one came to know what was in his mind. Khwāja-i-Qāzī and (Sayyid) Qāsim *Qūchīn* and 'Alī-dost Ṭaghāī met other well-wishers of mine in the presence of my grandmother, Āīsān-daulat Begīm and decided to give quietus to Ḥasan-i-yaq'ūb's disloyalty by his deposition.

Few amongst women will have been my grandmother's equals for judgment and counsel; she was very wise and far-sighted and most affairs of mine were carried through under her advice. She and my mother were (living) in the Gate-house of the outer fort;[3] Ḥasan-i-yaq'ūb was in the citadel.

[1] Elph. MS. f. 16*b*; First W.-i-B. I.O. 215 f. 19; Second W.-i-B. I.O. 217 f. 15*b*; Memoirs p. 27.

[2] He was a *Dūghlāt*, uncle by marriage of Ḥaidar Mīrzā and now holding Khost for Maḥmūd. *See* T.R. s.n. for his claim on Āīsān-daulat's gratitude.

[3] *tāsh qūrghān dā chiqār dā*. Here (as *e.g.* f. 110*b* l. 9) the Second W.-i-B. translates *tāsh* as though it meant *stone* instead of outer. *Cf.* f. 47 for an

When I went to the citadel, in pursuance of our decision, he had ridden out, presumably for hawking, and as soon as he had
Fol. 25. our news, went off from where he was towards Samarkand. The begs and others in sympathy with him,[1] were arrested; one was Muḥammad Bāqir Beg; Sl. Maḥmud *Dūldāī*, Sl. Muḥammad *Dūldāī's* father, was another; there were several more; to some leave was given to go for Samarkand. The Andijān Government and control of my Gate were settled on (Sayyid) Qāsim *Qūchīn*.

A few days after Ḥasan-i-yaq'ūb reached Kand-i-badām on the Samarkand road, he went to near the Khūqān sub-division (*aūrchīn*) with ill-intent on Akhsī. Hearing of it, we sent several begs and braves to oppose him; they, as they went, detached a scouting party ahead; he, hearing this, moved against the detachment, surrounded it in its night-quarters[2] and poured flights of arrows (*shība*) in on it. In the darkness of the night an arrow (*aūq*), shot by one of his own men, hit him just (*aūq*) in the vent (*qāchār*) and before he could take vent (*qāchār*),[3] he became the captive of his own act.

> "If you have done ill, keep not an easy mind,
> For retribution is Nature's law."[4]

This year I began to abstain from all doubtful food, my obedience extended even to the knife, the spoon and the table-cloth;[5] also the after-midnight Prayer (*taḥajjud*) was
Fol. 25b. less neglected.

---

adjectival use of *tāsh*, stone, with the preposition (*tāsh*) *din*. The places contrasted here are the citadel (*ark*) and the walled-town (*qūrghān*). The *chīqār* (exit) is the fortified Gate-house of the mud circumvallation. *Cf.* f. 46 for another example of *chīqār*.

[1] Elph. Ḥai. Kehr's MSS., *āning bila bār kishi bār beglārnī tūtūrūldī*. This idiom recurs on f. *76b* l. 8. A palimpsest entry in the Elph. MS. produces the statement that when Ḥasan fled, his begs returned to Andijān.

[2] Ḥai. MS. *awī mūnkūzī*, underlined by *sāgh-i-gāū*, cows' thatched house. [*T. mūnkūz*, lit. horn, means also cattle.] Elph. MS., *awī mūnkūsh*, underlined by *dar jā'ī khwāb alfakhta*, sleeping place. [T. *mūnkūṣh*, retired.]

[3] The first *qāchār* of this pun has been explained as *gurez-gāh, sharm-gāh*, hinder parts, *fuite* and *vertèbre inférieur*. The Ḥ.S. (ii, 273 l. 3 fr. ft.) says the wound was in a vital (*maqattal*) part.

[4] From Niẓāmī's *Khusrau u Shirīn*, Lahore lith. ed. p. 137 l. 8. It is quoted also in the A.N. Bib. Ind. ed. ii, 207 (H.B., ii, 321). (H.B.).

[5] *See* Hughes *Dictionary of Islām s.nn.* Eating and Food.

(*a. Death of Sl. Maḥmūd Mīrzā.*)

In the month of the latter Rabī' (January 1495 AD.), Sl. Maḥmūd Mīrzā was confronted by violent illness and in six days, passed from the world. He was 43 (lunar) years old.

b. His birth and lineage.

He was born in 857 AH. (1453 AD.), was Sl. Abū-sa'īd Mīrzā's third son and the full-brother of Sl. Aḥmad Mīrzā.[1]

c. His appearance and characteristics.

He was a short, stout, sparse-bearded and somewhat ill-shaped person. His manners and his qualities were good, his rules and methods of business excellent; he was well-versed in accounts, not a *dinār* or a *dirhām*[2] of revenue was spent without his knowledge. The pay of his servants was never disallowed. His assemblies, his gifts, his open table, were all good. Everything of his was orderly and well-arranged;[3] no soldier or peasant could deviate in the slightest from any plan of his. Formerly he must have been hard set (*qātīrār*) on hawking but latterly he very frequently hunted driven game.[4] He carried violence and vice to frantic excess, was a constant wine-bibber and kept many catamites. If anywhere in his territory, there was a handsome boy, he used, by whatever means, to have him brought for a catamite; of his begs' sons and of his sons' begs' sons he made catamites; and laid command for this service on Fol. 26.
his very foster brothers and on their own brothers. So common in his day was that vile practice, that no person was without his catamite; to keep one was thought a merit, not to keep one, a defect. Through his infamous violence and vice, his sons died in the day of their strength (*tamām juwān*).

1 *Cf.* f. 6*b* and note. If 'Umar Shaikh were Maḥmūd's full-brother, his name might well appear here.

2 *i.e.* "Not a farthing, not a half-penny."

3 Here the Mems. enters a statement, not found in the Turkī text, that Maḥmūd's dress was elegant and fashionable.

4 *n:h:l:m.* My husband has cleared up a mistake (Mems. p. 28 and *Méms.* i, 54) of supposing this to be the name of an animal. It is explained in the A.N. (i, 255. H.B. i, 496) as a Badakhshī equivalent of *tasqāwal; tasqāwal* var. *tāshqāwal*, is explained by the *Farhang-i-azfarī*, a Turkī-Persian Dict. seen in the Mullā Fīroz Library of Bombay, to mean *rāh band kunanda*, the stopping of the road. *Cf.* J.R.A.S. 1900 p. 137.

He had a taste for poetry and put a *dīwān*[1] together but his verse is flat and insipid,—not to compose is better than to compose verse such as his. He was not firm in the Faith and held his Highness Khwāja 'Ubaidu'l-lāh (*Aḥrārī*) in slight esteem. He had no heart (*yūruk*) and was somewhat scant in modesty,—several of his impudent buffoons used to do their filthy and abominable acts in his full Court, in all men's sight. He spoke badly, there was no understanding him at first.

d. His battles.

He fought two battles, both with Sl. Ḥusain Mīrzā (*Bāī-qarā*). The first was in Astarābād; here he was defeated. The second was at Chīkman (Sarāī),[2] near Andikhūd; here also he was defeated. He went twice to Kāfiristān, on the
Fol. 26b. south of Badakhshān, and made Holy War; for this reason they wrote him Sl. Maḥmūd *Ghāzī* in the headings of his public papers.

e. His countries.

Sl. Abū-sa'īd Mīrzā gave him Astarābād.[3] After the 'Irāq disaster (*i.e.*, his father's death,) he went into Khurāsān. At that time, Qaṃbar-'alī Beg, the governor of Ḥiṣār, by Sl. Abū-sa'īd Mīrzā's orders, had mobilized the Hindūstān[4] army and was following him into 'Irāq; he joined Sl. Maḥmūd Mīrzā in Khurāsān but the Khurāsānīs, hearing of Sl. Ḥusain Mīrzā's approach, rose suddenly and drove them out of the country. On this Sl. Maḥmūd Mīrzā went to his elder brother, Sl. Aḥmad Mīrzā in Samarkand. A few months later Sayyid Badr and Khusrau Shāh and some braves under Aḥmad

1 *i.e.* "a collection of poems in the alphabetical order of the various end rhymes." (Steingass.)

2 At this battle Daulat-shāh was present. *Cf.* Browne's D.S. for Astarābād p. 523 and for Andikhūd p. 532. For this and all other references to D.S. and H.S. I am indebted to my husband.

3 The following dates will help out Bābur's brief narrative. Maḥmūd *æt.* 7, was given Astarābād in 864 AH. (1459-60 AD.); it was lost to Ḥusain at Jauz-wilāyat and Maḥmūd went into Khurāsān in 865 AH.; he was restored by his father in 866 AH.; on his father's death (873 AH.-1469 AD.) he fled to Harāt, thence to Samarkand and from there was taken to Ḥiṣār *æt.* 16. *Cf.* D'Herbélot *s.n.* Abū-sa'ad; H.S. i, 209; Browne's D.S. p. 522.

4 Presumably the "Hindūstān the Less" of Clavijo (Markham p. 3 and p. 113), approx. Qaṃbar—'alī's districts. Clavijo includes Tīrmīẓ under the name.

Mushtāq[1] took him and fled to Qambar-'alī in Ḥiṣār. From that time forth, Sl. Maḥmūd Mīrzā possessed the countries lying south of Quhqa (Quhlugha) and the Kohtin Range as far as the Hindū-kush Mountains, such as Tīrmīẕ, Chaghānīān, Ḥiṣār, Khutlān, Qūndūz and Badakhshān. He also held Sl. Aḥmad Mīrzā's lands, after his brother's death.

f. His children.

He had five sons and eleven daughters.

Sl. Mas'ūd Mīrzā was his eldest son; his mother was Khān-zāda Begīm, a daughter of the Great Mīr of Tīrmīẕ. Bāī-sunghar Mīrzā was another; his mother was Pasha (or Pāshā) Begīm. Sl. 'Alī Mīrzā was another; his mother was an Aūzbeg, a concubine called Zuhra Begī Āghā. Sl. Ḥusain Mīrzā was another; his mother was Khān-zāda Begīm, a grand-daughter of the Great Mīr of Tīrmīẕ; he went to God's mercy in his father's life-time, at the age of 13. Sl. Wais Mīrzā (Mīrzā Khān) was another; his mother, Sulṭān-nigār Khānīm was a daughter of Yūnas Khān and was a younger (half-) sister of my mother. The affairs of these four Mīrzās will be written of in this history under the years of their occurrence. Fol. 27.

Of Sl. Maḥmūd Mīrzā's daughters, three were by the same mother as Bāī-sunghar Mīrzā. One of these, Bāī-sunghar Mīrzā's senior, Sl. Maḥmūd Mīrzā made to go out to Malik-i-muḥammad Mīrzā, the son of his paternal uncle, Minūchihr Mīrzā.[2]

* * * * * *

Five other daughters were by Khān-zāda Begīm, the grand-daughter of the Great Mīr of Tīrmīẕ. The oldest of these,

[1] Perhaps a Ṣufī term,—longing for the absent friend. For particulars about this man *see* Ḥ.S. ii, 235 and Browne's D.S. p. 533.

[2] Here in the Ḥai. MS. is one of several blank spaces, waiting for information presumably not known to Bābur when writing. The space will have been in the archetype of the Ḥai. MS. and it makes for the opinion that the Ḥai. MS. is a direct copy of Bābur's own. This space is not left in the Elph. MS. but that MS. is known from its scribe's note (f. 198) down to f. 198 (Ḥai. MS. f. 243*b*) to have been copied from "other writings" and only subsequent to its f. 198 from Bābur's own. *Cf.* JRAS 1906 p. 88 and 1907 p. 143.

(Khān-zāda Begīm)[1] was given, after her father's death, to Abā-
Fol. 27*b*. bikr (*Dūghlāt*) *Kāshgharī*. The second was Bega Begīm. When Sl. Ḥusain Mīrzā besieged Ḥiṣār (901 AH.), he took her for Ḥaidar Mīrzā, his son by Pāyanda Begīm, Sl. Abū-sa'īd Mīrzā's daughter, and having done so, rose from before the place.[2] The third daughter was Āq (Fair) Begīm; the fourth[3]—,was betrothed to Jahāngīr Mīrzā (*aet.* 5, *circa* 895 AH.) at the time his father, 'Umar Shaikh Mīrzā sent him to help Sl. Maḥmūd Mīrzā with the Andijān army, against Sl. Ḥusain Mīrzā, then attacking Qūndūz.[4] In 910 AH. (1504 AD.) when Bāqī *Chaghān-īānī*[5] waited on me on the bank of the Amū (Oxus), these (last-named two) Begīms were with their mothers in Tīrmīẕ and joined me then with Bāqī's family. When we reached Kahmard, Jahāngīr Mīrzā took ——— Begīm; one little daughter was born; she now[6] is in the Badakhshān country with her grandmother. The fifth daughter was Zainab-sulṭān Begīm; under my mother's insistance, I took her at the time of the capture of Kābul (910 AH.–Oct. 1504 AD.). She did not become very congenial; two or three years later, she left the world, through small-pox. Another daughter was Makhdūm-sulṭān Begīm, Sl. 'Alī Mīrzā's full-sister; she is now in the Badakhshān country. Two others of his daughters, Rajab-sulṭān and Muḥibb-sulṭān, were by mistresses (*ghūnchachī*).

g. His ladies (*khwātīnlār*) *and concubines* (*sarārī*).

His chief wife, Khān-zāda Begīm, was a daughter of the
Fol. 28. Great Mīr of Tīrmīẕ; he had great affection for her and must have mourned her bitterly; she was the mother of Sl. Mas'ūd Mīrzā. Later on, he took her brother's daughter, also called Khān-zāda Begīm, a grand-daughter of the Great Mīr of Tīrmīẕ.

[1] The T.R. (p. 330) supplies this name.

[2] *Cf.* f. 35*b*. This was a betrothal only, the marriage being made in 903 AH. *Cf.* H.S. ii, 260 and Gul-badan's H.N. f. 24*b*.

[3] Kehr's MS. supplies Aī (Moon) as her name but it has no authority. The Elph. MS. has what may be *lā nām*, no name, on its margin and over *tūrūtūnchī* (4th.) its usual sign of what is problematical.

[4] *See* H.S. ii, 250. Here Pīr-i-Muḥammad *Aīlchī-būghā* was drowned. *Cf.* f. 29.

[5] Chaghānīān is marked in Erskine's (Mems.) map as somewhere about the head of (Fr. map 1904) the Ilyak Water, a tributary of the Kāfir-nighān.

[6] *i.e.* when Bābur was writing in Hindūstān.

She became the mother of five of his daughters and one of his sons. Pasha (or Pāshā) Begīm was another wife, a daughter of 'Alī-shukr Beg, a Turkmān Beg of the Black Sheep Bahārlū Aīmāq.[1] She had been the wife of Jahān-shāh (*Barānī*) of the Black Sheep Turkmāns. After Aūzūn (Long) Ḥasan Beg of the White Sheep had taken Āẕar-bāījān and 'Irāq from the sons of this Jahān-shāh Mīrzā (872 AH.-1467 AD.), 'Alī-shukr Beg's sons went with four or five thousand heads-of-houses of the Black Sheep Turkmāns to serve Sl. Abū-sa'īd Mīrzā and after the Mīrzā's defeat (873 AH. by Aūzūn Ḥasan), came down to these countries and took service with Sl. Maḥmūd Mīrzā. This happened after Sl. Maḥmūd Mīrzā came to Ḥiṣār from Samarkand, and then it was he took Pasha Begīm. She became the mother of one of his sons and three of his daughters. Sulṭān-nigār Khānīm was another of his ladies; her descent has been mentioned already in the account of the (Chaghatāī) Khāns. Fol. 28*b*.

He had many concubines and mistresses. His most honoured concubine (*mu'atabar ghūma*) was Zuhra Begī Āghā; she was taken in his father's life-time and became the mother of one son and one daughter. He had many mistresses and, as has been said, two of his daughters were by two of them.

h. His amirs.

Khusrau Shāh was of the Turkistānī Qīpchāqs. He had been in the intimate service of the Tarkhān begs, indeed had been a catamite. Later on he became a retainer of Mazīd Beg (Tarkhān) *Arghūn* who favoured him in all things. He was favoured by Sl. Maḥmūd Mīrzā on account of services done by him when, after the 'Irāq disaster, he joined the Mīrzā on his way to Khurāsān. He waxed very great in his latter days; his retainers, under Sl. Maḥmūd Mīrzā, were a clear five or six thousand. Not only Badakhshān but the whole country from the Amū to the Hindū-kush Mountains depended on him and he devoured its whole revenue (*darobast yīr īdī*). His open table was good, so too his open hand; though he was a rough getter,[2]

[1] For his family *see* f. 55*b* note to Yār-'alī *Balāl*.
[2] *bā wujūd turklūk muhkam paidā kunanda īdī.*

what he got, he spent liberally. He waxed exceeding great after Sl. Maḥmūd Mīrzā's death, in whose sons' time his retainers approached 20,000. Although he prayed and abstained from forbidden aliments, yet was he black-souled and vicious, dunder-headed and senseless, disloyal and a traitor to his salt. For the sake of this fleeting, five-days world,[1] he blinded one of his benefactor's sons and murdered another. A sinner before God, reprobate to His creatures, he has earned curse and execration till the very verge of Resurrection. For this world's sake he did his evil deeds and yet, with lands so broad and with such hosts of armed retainers, he had not pluck to stand up to a hen. An account of him will come into this history.

Pīr-i-muḥammad *Aīlchī-būghā*[2] *Qūchīn* was another. In Hazārāspī's fight[3] he got in on challenge with his fists in Sl. Abū-saʿīd Mīrzā's presence at the Gate of Balkh. He was a brave man, continuously serving the Mīrzā (Maḥmūd) and guiding him by his counsel. Out of rivalry to Khusrau Shāh, he made a night-attack when the Mīrzā was besieging Qūndūz, on Sl. Ḥusain Mīrzā, with few men, without arming[4] and without plan; he could do nothing; what was there he could do against such and so large a force? He was pursued, threw himself into the river and was drowned.

Ayūb (*Begchīk Mughūl*)[5] was another. He had served in Sl. Abū-saʿīd Mīrzā's Khurāsān Cadet Corps, a brave man, Bāi-sunghar Mīrzā's guardian. He was choice in dress and food;

---

[1] Roebuck's *Oriental Proverbs* (p. 232) explains the *five* of this phrase where *seven* might be expected, by saying that of this Seven days' world (qy. days of Creation) one is for birth, another for death, and that thus five only are left for man's brief life.

[2] The cognomen *Aīlchī-būghā*, taken with the bearer's recorded strength of fist, may mean Strong man of Aīlchī (the capital of Khutan). One of Tīmūr's commanders bore the name. *Cf.* f. 21*b* for *būghū* as *athlete*.

[3] Hazārāspī seems to be Mīr Pīr Darwesh Hazārāspī. With his brother, Mīr ʿAlī, he had charge of Balkh. See *Rauzatu'ṣ-ṣafā* B.M. Add. 23506, f. 242*b*; Browne's D.S. p. 432. It may be right to understand a hand-to-hand fight between Hazārāspī and Aīlchī-būghā. The affair was in 857 AH. (1453 AD.).

[4] *yārāq siz*, perhaps trusting to fisticuffs, perhaps without mail. Bābur's summary has confused the facts. Muḥ. Aīlchī-būghā was sent by Sl. Maḥmūd Mīrzā from Ḥiṣār with 1,000 men and did not issue out of Qūndūz. (H.S. ii, 251.) His death occurred not before 895 AH.

[5] See T.R. *s.nn.* Mīr Ayūb and Ayūb.

a jester and talkative, nicknamed Impudence, perhaps because the Mīrzā called him so. Fol. 29b.

Walī was another, the younger, full-brother of Khusrau Shāh. He kept his retainers well. He it was brought about the blinding of Sl. Mas'ūd Mīrzā and the murder of Bāī-sunghar Mīrzā. He had an ill-word for every-one and was an evil-tongued, foul-mouthed, self-pleasing and dull-witted mannikin. He approved of no-one but himself. When I went from the Qūndūz country to near Dūshī (910 AH.-1503 AD.), separated Khusrau Shāh from his following and dismissed him, this person (*i.e.*, Walī) had come to Andar-āb and Sīr-āb, also in fear of the Aūzbegs. The Aīmāqs of those parts beat and robbed him[1] then, having let me know, came on to Kābul. Walī went to Shaibānī Khān who had his head struck off in the town of Samarkand.

Shaikh 'Abdu'l-lāh *Barlās*[2] was another; he had to wife one of the daughters of Shāh Sulṭān Muḥammad (*Badakhshī*) *i.e.*, the maternal aunt of Abā-bikr Mīrzā (*Mīrān-shāhī*) and of Sl. Maḥmūd Khān. He wore his tunic narrow and *pur shaqq*[3]; he was a kindly well-bred man.

Maḥmūd *Barlās* of the Barlāses of Nūndāk (Badakhshān) was another. He had been a beg also of Sl. Abū-sa'īd Mīrzā and had surrendered Karmān to him when the Mīrzā took the 'Irāq countries. When Abā-bikr Mīrzā (*Mīrān-shāhī*) came Fol. 30. against Ḥiṣār with Mazīd Beg Tarkhān and the Black Sheep Turkmāns, and Sl. Maḥmūd Mīrzā went off to his elder brother, Sl. Aḥmad Mīrzā in Samarkand, Maḥmūd *Barlās* did not surrender Ḥiṣār but held out manfully.[4] He was a poet and put a *dīwān* together.

(*i. Historical narrative resumed*).

When Sl. Maḥmūd Mīrzā died, Khusrau Shāh kept the event concealed and laid a long hand on the treasure. But

[1] This passage is made more clear by f. 120*b* and f. 125*b*.

[2] He is mentioned in 'Alī-sher *Nawā'ī's Majālis-i-nafā'is*; *see* B.M. Add. 7875, f. 278 and Rieu's Turkish Catalogue.

[3] ? full of splits or full handsome.

[4] This may have occurred after Abū-sa'īd Mīrzā's death whose son Abā-bikr was. *Cf.* f. 28. If so, over-brevity has obscured the statement.

how could such news be hidden? It spread through the town at once. That was a festive day for the Samarkand families; soldier and peasant, they uprose in tumult against Khusrau Shāh. Aḥmad Ḥājī Beg and the Tarkhānī begs put the rising down and turned Khusrau Shāh out of the town with an escort for Ḥiṣār.

As Sl. Maḥmūd Mīrzā himself after giving Ḥiṣār to Sl. Mas'ūd Mīrzā and Bukhārā to Bāī-sunghar Mīrzā, had dismissed both to their governments, neither was present when he died. The Ḥiṣār and Samarkand begs, after turning Khusrau Shāh out, agreed to send for Bāī-sunghar Mīrzā from Bukhārā, brought him to Samarkand and seated him on the throne. When he thus became supreme (*pādshāh*), he was 18 (lunar) years old.

At this crisis, Sl. Maḥmūd Khān (*Chaghatāī*), acting on the
Fol. 30*b*. word of Junaid *Barlās* and of some of the notables of Samarkand, led his army out to near Kān-bāī with desire to take that town. Bāī-sunghar Mīrzā, on his side, marched out in force. They fought near Kān-bāī. Ḥaidar *Kūkūldāsh*, the main pillar of the Mughūl army, led the Mughūl van. He and all his men dismounted and were pouring in flights of arrows (*shība*) when a large body of the mailed braves of Ḥiṣār and Samarkand made an impetuous charge and straightway laid them under their horses' feet. Their leader taken, the Mughūl army was put to rout without more fighting. Masses (*qālīn*) of Mughūls were wiped out; so many were beheaded in Bāī-sunghar Mīrzā's presence that his tent was three times shifted because of the number of the dead.

At this same crisis, Ibrāhīm *Sārū* entered the fort of Asfara, there read Bāī-sunghar Mīrzā's name in the *Khuṭba* and took up a position of hostility to me.

(*Author's note.*) Ibrāhīm *Sārū* is of the Mīnglīgh people;[1] he had served my father in various ways from his childhood but later on had been dismissed for some fault.

Fol. 31. The army rode out to crush this rebellion in the month of Sha'bān (May) and by the end of it, had dismounted round

[1] *mīnglīgh aïldīn dūr*, perhaps of those whose hereditary Command was a Thousand, the head of a Mīng (Pers. Hazāra), *i.e.* of the tenth of a *tūmān*.

Asfara. Our braves in the wantonness of enterprise, on the very day of arrival, took the new wall[1] that was in building outside the fort. That day Sayyid Qāsim, Lord of my Gate, outstripped the rest and got in with his sword; Sl. Aḥmad *Tambal* and Muḥammad-dost Ṭaghāī got theirs in also but Sayyid Qāsim won the Champion's Portion. He took it in Shāhrukhiya when I went to see my mother's brother, Sl. Maḥmūd Khān.

(*Author's note.*) The Championship Portion[2] is an ancient usage of the Mughūl horde. Whoever outdistanced his tribe and got in with his own sword, took the portion at every feast and entertainment.

My guardian, Khudāī-bīrdī Beg died in that first day's fighting, struck by a cross-bow arrow. As the assault was made without armour, several bare braves (*yīkīt yīlāng*)[3] perished and many were wounded. One of Ibrāhīm *Sārū's* cross-bowmen was an excellent shot; his equal had never been seen; he it was hit most of those wounded. When Asfara had been taken, he entered my service.

As the siege drew on, orders were given to construct head-strikes[4] in two or three places, to run mines and to make every effort to prepare appliances for taking the fort. The siege lasted 40 days; at last Ibrāhīm *Sārū* had no resource but, through the mediation of Khwāja Moulānā-i-qāẓī, to elect to serve me. In the month of Shawwāl (June 1495 AD.) he came out, with his sword and quiver hanging from his neck, waited on me and surrendered the fort. Fol. 31*b*.

Khujand for a considerable time had been dependent on 'Umar Shaikh Mīrzā's Court (*dīwān*) but of late had looked towards Sl. Aḥmad Mīrzā on account of the disturbance in the Farghāna government during the interregnum.[5] As the

[1] *qūrghān-nīng tāshīdā yāngī tām qūpārīb sālā dūr.* I understand, that what was taken was a new circumvallation in whole or in part. Such double walls are on record. *Cf.* Appendix A.

[2] *bahādurlūq aūlūsh*, an actual portion of food.

[3] *i.e.* either unmailed or actually naked.

[4] The old English noun *strike* expresses the purpose of the *sar-kob*. It is "an instrument for scraping off what rises above the top" (Webster, whose example is grain in a measure). The *sar-kob* is an erection of earth or wood, as high as the attacked walls, and it enabled besiegers to strike off heads appearing above the ramparts.

[5] *i.e.* the dislocation due to 'Umar Shaikh's death.

opportunity offered, a move against it also was now made. Mīr Mughūl's father, 'Abdu'l-wahhāb *Shaghāwal*[1] was in it; he surrendered without making any difficulty at once on our arrival.

Just then Sl. Maḥmūd Khān was in Shāhrukhiya. It has been said already that when Sl. Aḥmad Mīrzā came into Andijān (899 AH.), he also came and that he laid siege to Akhsī. It occurred to me that if since I was so close, I went and waited on him, he being, as it were, my father and my elder brother, and if bye-gone resentments were laid aside, it would be good hearing and seeing for far and near. So said, I went.

I waited on The Khān in the garden Ḥaidar *Kūkūldāsh* had made outside Shāhrukhiya. He was seated in a large four-
Fol. 32. doored tent set up in the middle of it. Having entered the tent, I knelt three times,[2] he for his part, rising to do me honour. We looked one another in the eyes;[3] and he returned to his seat. After I had kneeled, he called me to his side and shewed me much affection and friendliness. Two or three days later, I set off for Akhsī and Andijān by the Kīndīrlīk Pass.[4] At Akhsī I made the circuit of my Father's

[1] *Cf.* f. 13. The Ḥ.S. (ii, 274) places his son, Mīr Mughūl, in charge, but otherwise agrees with the B.N.

[2] *Cf.* Clavijo, Markham p. 132. Sir Charles Grandison bent the knee on occasions but illustrated MSS. *e.g.* the B.M. *Tawārīkh-i-guzīda Naṣrat-nāma* show that Bābur would kneel down on both knees. *Cf.* f. 123*b* for the fatigue of the genuflection.

[3] I have translated *kūrūshūb* thus because it appears to me that here and in other places, stress is laid by Bābur upon the mutual gaze as an episode of a ceremonious interview. The verb *kūrūshmak* is often rendered by the Persian translators as *daryāftan* and by the L. and E. Memoirs as *to embrace.* I have not found in the B.N. warrant for translating it as *to embrace; qūchūshmāq* is Bābur's word for this (f. 103). *Daryāftan*, taken as to grasp or see with the mind, to understand, well expresses mutual gaze and its sequel of mutual understanding. Sometimes of course, *kūrūsh*, the interview does not imply *kūrūsh*, the silent looking in the eyes with mutual understanding; it simply means *se voyer e.g.* f. 17. The point is thus dwelt upon because the frequent mention of an embrace gives a different impression of manners from that made by "interview" or words expressing mutual gaze.

[4] *dābān.* This word Réclus (vi, 171) quoting from Fedschenko, explains as a difficult rocky defile; *art*, again, as a dangerous gap at a high elevation; *bel*, as an easy low pass; and *kūtal*, as a broad opening between low hills. The explanation of *kūtal* does not hold good for Bābur's application of the word (f. 81*b*) to the Sara-tāq.

tomb. I left at the hour of the Friday Prayer (*i.e.*, about mid-day) and reached Andijān, by the Band-i-sālār Road between the Evening and Bedtime Prayers. This road *i.e.* the Band-i-sālār, people call a nine *yīghāch* road.[1]

One of the tribes of the wilds of Andijān is the Jīgrāk[2] a numerous people of five or six thousand households, dwelling in the mountains between Kāshghar and Farghāna. They have many horses and sheep and also numbers of yāks (*qūtās*), these hill-people keeping yāks instead of common cattle. As their mountains are border-fastnesses, they have a fashion of not paying tribute. An army was now sent against them under (Sayyid) Qāsim Beg in order that out of the tribute taken from them something might reach the soldiers. He took about 20,000 of their sheep and between 1000 and 1500 of their horses and shared all out to the men.

After its return from the Jīgrāk, the army set out for Aūrā-tīpā. Fol. 34. Formerly this was held by 'Umar Shaikh Mīrzā but it had gone out of hand in the year of his death and Sl. 'Alī Mīrzā was now in it on behalf of his elder brother, Bāī-sunghar Mīrzā. When Sl. 'Alī Mīrzā heard of our coming, he went off himself to the Macha hill-country, leaving his guardian, Shaikh Ẕū'n-nūn *Arghūn* behind. From half-way between Khujand and Aūrā-tīpā, Khalīfa[3] was sent as envoy to Shaikh Ẕū'n-nūn but that senseless mannikin, instead of giving him a plain answer, laid hands on him and ordered him to death. For Khalīfa to die cannot have been the Divine will; he escaped and came to me two or three days later, stripped bare and having suffered a hundred *tūmāns* (1,000,000) of hardships and fatigues. We went almost to Aūrā-tīpā but as, winter being near, people had carried away their corn and forage, after a few days we turned back for Andijān. After our retirement, The Khān's men moved on the place when the Aūrā-tīpā

[1] *Cf.* f. 4*b* and note. From Bābur's special mention of it, it would seem not to be the usual road.

[2] The spelling of this name is uncertain. Variants are many. Concerning the tribe *see* T.R. p. 165 n.

[3] Niẓāmu'd-dīn 'Alī *Barlās* : *see* Gul-badan's H.N. *s.n.* He served Bābur till the latter's death.

person[1] unable to make a stand, surrendered and came out. The Khān then gave it to Muḥammad Ḥusain *Kūrkān Dūghlāt* and in his hands it remained till 908 AH. (1503).[2]

[1] *i.e.* Ẕū'n-nūn or perhaps the garrison.

[2] *i.e.* down to Shaibānī's destruction of Chaghatāī rule in Tāshkīnt in 1503 AD.

901 AH.—SEP. 21ST. 1495 TO SEP. 9TH. 1496 AD.[1]

(a. Sulṭān Ḥusain Mīrzā's campaign against Khusrau Shāh).

In the winter of this year, Sl. Ḥusain Mīrzā led his army out of Khurāsān against Ḥiṣār and went to opposite Tīrmīẕ. Sl. Mas'ūd Mīrzā, for his part, brought an army (from Ḥiṣār) and sat down over against him in Tīrmīẕ. Khusrau Shāh strengthened himself in Qūndūz and to help Sl. Mas'ūd Mīrzā sent his younger brother, Walī. They (*i.e.*, the opposed forces) spent most of that winter on the river's banks, no crossing being effected. Sl. Ḥusain Mīrzā was a shrewd and experienced commander; he marched up the river,[2] his face set for Qūndūz and by this having put Sl. Mas'ūd Mīrzā off his guard, sent 'Abdu'l-laṭīf *Bakhshī* (pay-master) with 5 or 600 serviceable men, down the river to the Kilīf ferry. These crossed and had entrenched themselves on the other bank before Sl. Mas'ūd Mīrzā had heard of their movement. When he did hear of it, whether because of pressure put upon him by Bāqī *Chaghānīānī* to spite (his half-brother) Walī, or whether from his own want of heart, he did not march against those who had crossed but disregarding Walī's urgency, at once broke up his camp and turned for Ḥiṣār.[3]

Sl. Ḥusain Mīrzā crossed the river and then sent, (1) against Khusrau Shāh, Badī'u'z-zamān Mīrzā and Ibrāhīm Ḥusain Mīrzā with Muḥammad Walī Beg and Ẕū'n-nūn *Arghūn*, and Fol. 33b

[1] Elph. MS. f. 23; W.-i-B. I.O. 215 f. 26 and 217 f. 21; Mems. p. 35. Bābur's own affairs form a small part of this year's record; the rest is drawn from the H.S. which in its turn, uses Bābur's f. 34 and f. 37b. Each author words the shared material in his own style; one adding magniloquence, the other retracting to plain statement, indeed summarizing at times to obscurity. Each passes his own judgment on events, *e.g.* here Khwānd-amīr's is more favourable to Ḥusain Bāī-qarā's conduct of the Ḥiṣār campaign than Bābur's. *Cf.* H.S. ii, 256-60 and 274.

[2] This feint would take him from the Oxus.

[3] Tīrmīẕ to Ḥiṣār, 96m. (Réclus vi, 255).

(2) against Khutlān, Muẓaffar Ḥusain Mīrzā with Muḥammad *Barandūq Barlās.* He himself moved for Ḥiṣār.

When those in Ḥiṣār heard of his approach, they took their precautions; Sl. Mas'ūd Mīrzā did not judge it well to stay in the fort but went off up the Kām Rūd valley[1] and by way of Sara-tāq to his younger brother, Bāī-sunghar Mīrzā in Samarkand. Walī, for his part drew off to (his own district) Khutlān. Bāqī *Chaghānīānī*, Maḥmūd *Barlās* and Qūch Beg's father, Sl. Aḥmad strengthened the fort of Ḥiṣār. Ḥamza Sl. and Mahdī Sl. (*Aūzbeg*) who some years earlier had left Shaibānī Khān for (the late) Sl. Maḥmūd Mīrzā's service, now, in this dispersion, drew off with all their Aūzbegs, for Qarā-tīgīn. With them went Muḥammad *Dūghlāt*[2] and Sl. Ḥusain *Dūghlāt* and all the Mughūls located in the Ḥiṣār country.

Upon this Sl. Ḥusain Mīrzā sent Abū'l-muḥsin Mīrzā after Sl. Mas'ūd Mīrzā up the Kām Rūd valley. They were not strong enough for such work when they reached the defile.[3] There Mīrzā Beg *Fīringī-bāz*[4] got in his sword. In pursuit of Ḥamza Sl. into Qarā-tīgīn, Sl. Ḥusain Mīrzā sent Ibrāhīm Tarkhān and Yaq'ūb-i-ayūb. They overtook the sulṭāns and
Fol. 33. fought. The Mīrzā's detachment was defeated; most of his begs were unhorsed but all were allowed to go free.

(*b. Bābur's reception of the Aūzbeg sulṭāns.*)

As a result of this exodus, Ḥamza Sl. with his son, Mamāq Sl., and Mahdī Sl. and Muḥammad *Dūghlāt*, later known as *Ḥiṣārī* and his brother, Sl. Ḥusain *Dūghlāt* with the Aūzbegs dependent on the sulṭāns and the Mughūls who had been located in Ḥiṣār as (the late) Sl. Maḥmūd Mīrzā's retainers, came, after letting me know (their intention), and waited upon me in Ramẓān (May-June) at Andijān. According to the

[1] Ḥ.S. Wazr-āb valley. The usual route is up the Kām Rūd and over the Mūra pass to Sara-tāq. *Cf.* f. 81*b*.

[2] *i.e.* the Ḥiṣārī mentioned a few lines lower and on f. 99*b*. Nothing on f. 99*b* explains his cognomen.

[3] The road is difficult. *Cf.* f. 81*b*.

[4] Khwānd-amīr also singles out one man for praise, Sl. Maḥmūd *Mīr-i-ākhwur*; the two names probably represent one person. The sobriquet may refer to skill with a matchlock, to top-spinning (*firnagī-bāz*) or to some lost joke. (Ḥ.S. ii, 257.)

custom of Tīmūriya sulṭāns on such occasions, I had seated myself on a raised seat (*tūshāk*); when Ḥamza Sl. and Mamāq Sl. and Mahdī Sl. entered, I rose and went down to do them honour; we looked one another in the eyes and I placed them on my right, *bāghīsh dā*.[1] A number of Mughūls also came, under Muḥammad *Ḥiṣārī*; all elected for my service.

(c. Sl. Ḥusain Mīrzā's affairs resumed).

Sl. Ḥusain Mīrzā, on reaching Ḥiṣār, settled down at once to besiege it. There was no rest, day nor night, from the labours of mining and attack, of working catapults and mortars. Mines were run in four or five places. When one had gone well forward towards the Gate, the townsmen, countermining, struck it and forced smoke down on the Mīrzā's men; they, in turn, Fol. 34*b*. closed the hole, thus sent the smoke straight back and made the townsmen flee as from the very maw of death. In the end, the townsmen drove the besiegers out by pouring jar after jar of water in on them. Another day, a party dashed out from the town and drove off the Mīrzā's men from their own mine's mouth. Once the discharges from catapults and mortars in the Mīrzā's quarters on the north cracked a tower of the fort; it fell at the Bed-time Prayer; some of the Mīrzā's braves begged to assault at once but he refused, saying, "It is night." Before the shoot of the next day's dawn, the besieged had rebuilt the whole tower. That day too there was no assault; in fact, for the two to two and a half months of the siege, no attack was made except by keeping up the blockade,[2] by mining, rearing head-strikes,[3] and discharging stones.

[1] This pregnant phrase has been found difficult. It may express that Bābur assigned the sulṭāns places in their due precedence; that he seated them in a row; and that they sat cross-legged, as men of rank, and were not made, as inferiors, to kneel and sit back on their heels. Out of this last meaning, I infer comes the one given by dictionaries, "to sit at ease," since the cross-legged posture is less irksome than the genuflection, not to speak of the ease of mind produced by honour received. *Cf.* f. 18*b* and note on Aḥmad's posture; Redhouse *s.nn. bāghīsh* and *bāghdāsh*; and B.M. Tawārīkh-i-guzīda naṣrat-nāma, in the illustrations of which the chief personage, only, sits cross-legged.

[2] *siyāsat*. My translation is conjectural only.

[3] *sar-kob*. The old English noun *strike*, "an instrument for scraping off what appears above the top," expresses the purpose of the wall-high erections of wood or earth (*L. agger*) raised to reach what shewed above ramparts. *Cf.* Webster.

When Badī'u'z-zamān Mīrzā and whatever (*nī kīm*) troops had been sent with him against Khusrau Shāh, dismounted some 16 m. (3 to 4 *yīghāch*) below Qūndūz,[1] Khusrau Shāh arrayed whatever men (*nī kīm*) he had, marched out, halted one night on the way, formed up to fight and came down upon the Mīrzā and his men. The Khurāsānīs may not have been twice as many as his men but what question is there they were half
Fol. 35. as many more? None the less did such Mīrzās and such Commander-begs elect for prudence and remain in their entrenchments! Good and bad, small and great, Khusrau Shāh's force may have been of 4 or 5,000 men!

This was the one exploit of his life,—of this man who for the sake of this fleeting and unstable world and for the sake of shifting and faithless followers, chose such evil and such ill-repute, practised such tyranny and injustice, seized such wide lands, kept such hosts of retainers and followers,—latterly he led out between 20 and 30,000 and his countries and his districts (*parganāt*) exceeded those of his own ruler and that ruler's sons,[2] —for an exploit such as this his name and the names of his adherents were noised abroad for generalship and for this they were counted brave, while those timorous laggards, in the trenches, won the resounding fame of cowards.

Badī'u'z-zamān Mīrzā marched out from that camp and after a few stages reached the Alghū Mountain of Tāliqān[3] and there made halt. Khusrau Shāh, in Qūndūz, sent his brother, Walī, with serviceable men, to Ishkīmīsh, Fulūl and the hill-skirts thereabouts to annoy and harass the Mīrzā from outside also. Muḥibb-'alī, the armourer, (*qūrchī*) for his part, came down
Fol. 35*b*. (from Walī's Khutlān) to the bank of the Khutlān Water, met in with some of the Mīrzā's men there, unhorsed some, cut off a few heads and got away. In emulation of this, Sayyidīm 'Alī[4] the door-keeper, and his younger brother, Qulī Beg and

[1] Presumably lower down the Qūndūz Water.

[2] *aūz pādshāhī u mīrzālāridīn artīb.*

[3] *sic.* Ilai. MS.; Elph. MS., "near Tāliqān; some W.-i-B. MSS. "Great Garden." Gul-badan mentions a Tāliqān Garden. Perhaps the Mīrzā went so far east because, Ẕū'n-nūn being with him, he had Qandahār in mind. *Cf.* f. 42*b*.

[4] *i.e.* Sayyid Muḥammad 'Alī. *See* f. 15 n. to Sherīm. Khwāja Changā lies 14 m. below Tāliqān on the Tāliqān Water. (Erskine.)

Bihlūl-i-ayūb and a body of their men got to grips with the Khurāsānīs on the skirt of 'Ambar Koh, near Khwāja Changāl but, many Khurāsānīs coming up, Sayyidīm 'Alī and Bābā Beg's (son) Qulī Beg and others were unhorsed.

At the time these various news reached Sl. Ḥusain Mīrzā, his army was not without distress through the spring rains of Ḥiṣār; he therefore brought about a peace; Maḥmūd *Barlās* came out from those in the fort; Ḥājī Pīr the Taster went from those outside; the great commanders and what there was (*nī kīm*) of musicians and singers assembled and the Mīrzā took (Bega Begīm), the eldest[1] daughter of Sl. Maḥmūd Mīrzā by Khān-zāda Begīm, for Ḥaidar Mīrzā, his son by Pāyanda Begīm and through her the grandson of Sl. Abū-sa'īd Mīrzā. This done, he rose from before Ḥiṣār and set his face for Qūndūz.

At Qūndūz also Sl. Ḥusain Mīrzā made a few trenches and took up the besieger's position but by Badī'u'z-zamān Mīrzā's intervention peace at length was made, prisoners were exchanged and the Khurāsānīs retired. The twice-repeated[2] attacks made by Sl. Ḥusain Mīrzā on Khusrau Shāh and his unsuccessful retirements were the cause of Khusrau Shāh's Fol. 36. great rise and of action of his so much beyond his province.

When the Mīrzā reached Balkh, he, in the interests of Mā warā'u'n-nahr gave it to Badī'u'z-zamān Mīrzā, gave Badī'u'z-zamān Mīrzā's district of Astarābād to (a younger son), Muẓaffar Ḥusain Mīrzā and made both kneel at the same assembly, one for Balkh, the other for Astarābād. This offended Badī'u'z-zamān Mīrzā and led to years of rebellion and disturbance.[3]

(*d. Revolt of the Tarkhānīs in Samarkand*).

In Ramẓān of this same year, the Tarkhānīs revolted in Samarkand. Here is the story:—Bāī-sunghar Mīrzā was not so friendly and familiar with the begs and soldiers of Samarkand as he was with those of Ḥiṣār.[4] His favourite beg was Shaikh

[1] f. 27*b*, second.
[2] The first was *circa* 895 AH.-1490 AD. *Cf.* f. 27*b*.
[3] Bābur's wording suggests that their common homage was the cause of Badī'u'z-zamān's displeasure but *see* f. 41.
[4] The Mīrzā had grown up with Ḥiṣārīs. *Cf.* Ḥ.S. ii, 270.

'Abdu'l-lāh *Barlās*[1] whose sons were so intimate with the Mīrzā that it made a relation as of Lover and Beloved. These things displeased the Tarkhāns and the Samarkandī begs; Darwesh Muḥammad Tarkhān went from Bukhārā to Qarshī, brought Sl. 'Alī Mīrzā to Samarkand and raised him to be supreme. People then went to the New Garden where Bāī-
Fol. 36b. sunghar Mīrzā was, treated him like a prisoner, parted him from his following and took him to the citadel. There they seated both mīrzās in one place, thinking to send Bāī-sunghar Mīrzā to the Gūk Sarāī close to the Other Prayer. The Mīrzā, however, on plea of necessity, went into one of the palace-buildings on the east side of the Bū-stān Sarāī. Tarkhānīs stood outside the door and with him went in Muḥammad Qulī *Qūchīn* and Ḥasan, the sherbet-server. To be brief:—A gateway, leading out to the back, must have been bricked up for they broke down the obstacle at once. The Mīrzā got out of the citadel on the Kafshīr side, through the water-conduit (*āb-mūrī*), dropped himself from the rampart of the water-way (*dū-tahī*), and went to Khwājakī Khwāja's[2] house in Khwāja Kafshīr. When the Tarkhānīs, in waiting at the door, took the precaution of looking in, they found him gone. Next day the Tarkhānīs went in a large body to Khwājakī Khwāja's gate but the Khwāja said, "No!"[3] and did not give him up. Even they could not take him by force, the Khwāja's dignity was too great for them to be able to use force. A few days later, Khwāja Abu'l-makāram[4] and Aḥmad Ḥājī Beg and other begs, great and
Fol. 37. small, and soldiers and townsmen rose in a mass, fetched the Mīrzā away from the Khwāja's house and besieged Sl. 'Ali Mīrzā and the Tarkhāns in the citadel. They could not hold out for even a day; Muḥ. Mazīd Tarkhān went off through the Gate of the Four Roads for Bukhārā;

1 As the husband of one of the six Badakhshī Begīms, he was closely connected with local ruling houses. *See* T.R. p. 107.

2 *i.e.* Muḥammad 'Ubaidu'l-lāh the elder of *Aḥrārī's* two sons. d. 911 AH. *See Rashaḥāt-i-'ain-al-ḥayāt* (I.O. 633) f. 269-75; and *Khizinatu'l-aṣfiya* lith. ed. i, 597.

3 *Bū yūq tūr*, *i.e.* This is not to be.

4 d. 908 AH. He was not, it would seem, of the *Aḥrārī* family. His own had provided Pontiffs (*Shaikhu'l-islām*) for Samarkand through 400 years. *Cf. Shaibānī-nāma*, Vambéry, p. 106; also, for his character, p. 96.

Sl. 'Alī Mīrzā and Darwesh Muḥ. Tarkhān were made prisoner.

Bāī-sunghar Mīrzā was in Aḥmad Ḥājī Beg's house when people brought Darwesh Muḥammad Tarkhān in. He put him a few questions but got no good answer. In truth Darwesh Muḥammad's was a deed for which good answer could not be made. He was ordered to death. In his helplessness he clung to a pillar[1] of the house; would they let him go because he clung to a pillar? They made him reach his doom (*siyāsat*) and ordered Sl. 'Alī Mīrzā to the Gūk Sarāī there to have the fire-pencil drawn across his eyes.

(*Author's note.*) The Gūk Sarāī is one of Tīmūr Beg's great buildings in the citadel of Samarkand. It has this singular and special characterstic, if a Tīmūrid is to be seated on the throne, here he takes his seat; if one lose his head, coveting the throne, here he loses it; therefore the name Gūk Sarāī has a metaphorical sense (*kināyat*) and to say of any ruler's son, "They have taken him to the Gūk Sarāī," means, to death.[2]

To the Gūk Sarāī accordingly Sl. 'Alī Mīrzā was taken but when the fire-pencil was drawn across his eyes, whether by the surgeon's choice or by his inadvertence, no harm was done. Fol. 37*b*. This the Mīrzā did not reveal at once but went to Khwāja Yahya's house and a few days later, to the Tarkhāns in Bukhārā.

Through these occurrences, the sons of his Highness Khwāja 'Ubaidu'l-lāh became settled partisans, the elder (Muḥammad 'Ubaidu'l-lāh, Khwājakī Khwāja) becoming the spiritual guide of the elder prince, the younger (Yahya) of the younger. In a few days, Khwāja Yahya followed Sl. 'Alī Mīrzā to Bukhārā.

Bāī-sunghar Mīrzā led out his army against Bukhārā. On his approach, Sl. 'Alī Mīrzā came out of the town, arrayed for battle. There was little fighting; Victory being on the side of Sl. 'Alī Mīrzā, Bāī-sunghar Mīrzā sustained defeat. Aḥmad Ḥājī Beg and a number of good soldiers were taken; most of the men were put to death. Aḥmad Ḥājī Beg himself the slaves and slave-women of Darwesh Muḥammad Tarkhān, issuing out

[1] *i.e.* he claimed sanctuary.

[2] *Cf.* f. 45*b* and Pétis de la Croix's *Histoire de Chīngīz Khān* pp. 171 and 227. What Tīmūr's work on the Gūk Sarāī was is a question for archæologists.

of Bukhārā, put to a dishonourable death on the charge of their master's blood.

(*e. Bābur moves against Samarkand*).

These news reached us in Andijān in the month of Shawwāl (mid-June to mid-July) and as we (*act.* 14) coveted Samarkand, we got our men to horse. Moved by a like desire, Sl. Mas'ūd Mīrzā, his mind and Khusrau Shāh's mind set at ease by Sl.
Fol. 38. Ḥusain Mīrzā's[1] retirement, came over by way of Shahr-i-sabz. To reinforce him, Khusrau Shāh laid hands (*qāptī*) on his younger brother, Walī. We (three mīrzās) beleaguered the town from three sides during three or four months; then Khwāja Yahya came to me from Sl. 'Alī Mīrzā to mediate an agreement with a common aim. The matter was left at an interview arranged (*kūrūshmak*); I moved my force from Soghd to some 8m. below the town; Sl. 'Alī Mīrzā from his side, brought his own; from one bank, he, from the other, I crossed to the middle of[2] the Kohik water, each with four or five men; we just saw one another (*kūrūshūb*), asked each the other's welfare and went, he his way, I mine.

I there saw, in Khwāja Yahya's service, Mullā *Binā'ī* and Muḥammad Ṣāliḥ;[3] the latter I saw this once, the former was long in my service later on. After the interview (*kūrūshkān*) with Sl. 'Alī Mīrzā, as winter was near and as there was no great scarcity amongst the Samarkandīs, we retired, he to Bukhārā, I to Andijān.

Sl. Mas'ūd Mīrzā had a penchant for a daughter of Shaikh 'Abdu'l-lāh *Barlās*, she indeed was his object in coming to Samarkand. He took her, laid world-gripping ambition aside
Fol. 38*b*. and went back to Ḥiṣār.

When I was near Shīrāz and Kān-bāī, Mahdī Sl. deserted to Samarkand; Ḥamza Sl. went also from near Zamīn but with leave granted.

1 *i.e.* over the Aītmak Pass. *Cf.* f. 49.

2 Ilai. MS. *ārālīghīgha*. Elph. MS. *ārāl*, island.

3 *See* f. 179*b* for *Binā'ī*. Muḥammad Ṣāliḥ Mīrzā *Khwārizmī* is the author of the *Shaibānī-nāma*.

902 AH.—SEP. 9TH. 1496 TO AUG. 30TH. 1497 AD.[1]

(a. Bābur's second attempt on Samarkand.)

This winter, Bāī-sunghar Mīrzā's affairs were altogether in a good way. When 'Abdu'l-karīm *Ushrit* came on Sl. 'Alī Mīrzā's part to near Kūfīn, Mahdī Sl. led out a body of Bāī-sunghar Mīrzā's troops against him. The two commanders meeting exactly face to face, Mahdī Sl. pricked 'Abdu'l-karīm's horse with his Chirkas[2] sword so that it fell, and as 'Abdu'l-karīm was getting to his feet, struck off his hand at the wrist. Having taken him, they gave his men a good beating.

These (Aūzbeg) sulṭāns, seeing the affairs of Samarkand and the Gates of the (Tīmūrid) Mīrzās tottering to their fall, went off in good time (*āīrtā*) into the open country (?)[3] for Shaibānī.

Pleased[4] with their small success (over 'Abdu'l-karīm), the Samarkandīs drew an army out against Sl. 'Alī Mīrzā; Bāī-sunghar Mīrzā went to Sar-i-pul (Bridge-head), Sl. 'Alī Mīrzā to Khwāja Kārzūn. Meantime, Khwāja Abū'l-makāram, at the instigation of Khwāja Munīr of Aūsh, rode light against Bukhārā with Wais *Lāgharī* and Muḥammad Bāqir of the Andijān begs, and Qāsim *Dūldāī* and some of the Mīrzā's household. As the Bukhāriots took precautions when the invaders got near the town, they could make no progress. They therefore retired. Fol. 39.

[1] Elph. MS. f. 27; W.-i-B. I.O. 215 f. 30*b* and 217 f. 25; Mems. p. 42.

[2] *i.e.* Circassian. Muḥammad Ṣāliḥ (Sh.N. Vambéry p. 276 l. 58) speaks of other Aūzbegs using Chirkas swords.

[3] *aīrtā yāzīghā*. My translation is conjectural. *Aīrtā* implies *i.a.* foresight. *Yāzīghā* allows a pun at the expense of the sulṭāns; since it can be read both as *to the open country* and as *for their* (*next, aīrtā*) *misdeeds*. My impression is that they took the opportunity of being outside Samarkand with their men, to leave Bāī-sunghar and make for Shaibānī, then in Turkistān. Muḥammad Ṣāliḥ also marking the tottering Gate of Sl. 'Alī Mīrzā, left him now, also for Shaibānī. (Vambéry cap. xv.)

[4] *aūmāq*, to amuse a child in order to keep it from crying.

At the time when (last year) Sl. 'Alī Mīrzā and I had our interview, it had been settled[1] that this summer he should come from Bukhārā and I from Andijān to beleaguer Samarkand. To keep this tryst, I rode out in Ramẓān (May) from Andijān. Hearing when close to Yār Yīlāq, that the (two) Mīrzās were lying front to front, we sent Tūlūn Khwāja *Mūghūl*[2] ahead, with 2 or 300 scouting braves (*qāzāq yīkītlār*). Their approach giving Bāī-sunghar Mīrzā news of our advance, he at once broke up and retired in confusion. That same night our detachment overtook his rear, shot a mass (*qālīn*) of his men and brought in masses of spoil.

Two days later we reached Shīrāz. It belonged to Qāsim Beg *Dūldāī*; his *dārogha* (Sub-governor) could not hold it and surrendered.[3] It was given into Ibrāhīm *Sārū's* charge. After making there, next day, the Prayer of the Breaking of the Fast (*'Īdu'l-fiṭr*), we moved for Samarkand and dismounted in the reserve (*qūrūgh*) of Āb-i-yār (Water of Might). That day waited on me with 3 or 400 men, Qāsim *Dūldāī*,
Fol. 39b. Wais *Lāgharī*, Muḥammad Sīghal's grandson, Ḥasan,[4] and Sl. Muḥammad Wais. What they said was this: 'Bāī-sunghar Mīrzā came out and has gone back; we have left him therefore and are here for the *pādshāh's* service,' but it was known later that they must have left the Mīrzā at his request to defend Shīrāz, and that the Shīrāz affair having become what it was, they had nothing for it but to come to us.

When we dismounted at Qarā-būlāq, they brought in several Mughūls arrested because of senseless conduct to humble village elders coming in to us.[5] Qāsim Beg *Qūchīn* for discipline's

[1] *i.e.* with Khwāja Yahya presumably. *See* f. 38.

[2] This man is mentioned also in the *Tawārīkh-i-guzīda Nuṣratnāma* B.M. Or. 3222 f. 124*b*.

[3] H.S., on the last day of Ramẓān (June 28th. 1497 AD.).

[4] Muḥammad *Sīghal* appears to have been a marked man. I quote from the T.G.N.N. (*see supra*), f. 123*b* foot, the information that he was the grandson of Ya'qūb Beg. Zenker explains *Sīghalī* as the name of a Chaghatāī family. An *Ayūb-i-Ya'qūb Begchīk Mughūl* may be an uncle. See f. 43 for another grandson.

[5] *baẓ'ī kīrkān-kīnt-kīsākkā bāsh-sīz-qīlghān Mughūllārnī tūtūb.* I take the word *kīsāk* in this highly idiomatic sentence to be a diminutive of *kīs*, old person, on the analogy of *mīr, mīrāk, mard, mardak.* [The H.S. uses *Kīsāk* (ii, 261) as a proper noun.] The alliteration in *kāf* and the mighty adjective here are noticeable.

sake (*siyāsat*) had two or three of them cut to pieces. It was on this account he left me and went to Ḥiṣār four or five years later, in the guerilla times, (907 AH.) when I was going from the Macha country to The Khān.[1]

Marching from Qarā-būlāq, we crossed the river (*i.e.* the Zar-afshān) and dismounted near Yām.[2] On that same day, our men got to grips with Bāī-sunghar Mīrzā's at the head of the Avenue. Sl. Aḥmad *Tambal* was struck in the neck by a spear but not unhorsed. Khwājakī Mullā-i-ṣadr, Khwāja-i-kalān's eldest brother, was pierced in the nape of the neck[3] by an arrow and went straightway to God's mercy. An excellent soldier, my father before me had favoured him, making him Keeper of the Seal; he was a student of theology, had great Fol. 40 acquaintance with words and a good style; moreover he undertook hawking and rain-making with the jade-stone.

While we were at Yām, people, dealers and other, came out in crowds so that the camp became a bazar for buying and selling. One day, at the Other Prayer, suddenly, a general hubbub arose and all those Musalmān (traders) were plundered. Such however was the discipline of our army that an order to restore everything having been given, the first watch (*pahār*) of the next day had not passed before nothing, not a tag of cotton, not a broken needle's point, remained in the possession of any man of the force, all was back with its owners.

Marching from Yām, it was dismounted in Khān Yūrtī (The Khān's Camping Ground),[4] some 6 m. (3 *kuroh*) east of Samarkand. We lay there for 40 or 50 days. During the time, men from their side and from ours chopped at one another (*chāpqū-lāshtīlār*) several times in the Avenue. One day when Ibrāhīm *Begchīk* was chopping away there, he was cut on the face;

[1] Qāsim feared to go amongst the Mughūls lest he should meet retaliatory death. *Cf.* f. 99*b*.

[2] This appears from the context to be Yām (Jām) -bāī and not the Djouma (Jām) of the Fr. map of 1904, lying farther south. The Avenue named seems likely to be Tīmūr's of f. 45*b* and to be on the direct road for Khujand. *See* Schuyler i, 232.

[3] *būghān buyīnī*. W.-i-B. 215, *yān*, thigh, and 217 *gardan*, throat. I am in doubt as to the meaning of *būghān*; perhaps the two words stand for joint at the nape of the neck. Khwāja-i-kalān was one of seven brothers, six died in Bābur's service, he himself served till Bābur's death.

[4] *Cf.* f. 48.

thereafter people called him *Chāpūk* (*Balafré*). Another time, this also in the Avenue, at the Maghāk (Fosse) Bridge[1] Abū'l-qāsim (*Kohbur Chaghatāī*) got in with his mace. Once, again
Fol. 40b. in the Avenue, near the Mill-sluice, when Mīr Shāh *Qūchīn* also got in with his mace, they cut his neck almost half-through; most fortunately the great artery was not severed.

While we were in Khān Yūrtī, some in the fort sent the deceiving message,[2] 'Come you to-night to the Lovers' Cave side and we will give you the fort.' Under this idea, we went that night to the Maghāk Bridge and from there sent a party of good horse and foot to the rendezvous. Four or five of the household foot-soldiers had gone forward when the matter got wind. They were very active men; one, known as Ḥājī, had served me from my childhood; another people called Maḥmūd *Kūndūr-sangak*.[3] They were all killed.

While we lay in Khān Yūrtī, so many Samarkandīs came out that the camp became a town where everything looked for in a town was to be had. Meantime all the forts, Samarkand excepted, and the Highlands and the Lowlands were coming in to us. As in Aūrgūt, however, a fort on the skirt of the Shavdār (var. Shādwār) range, a party of men held fast[4], of necessity we moved out from Khān Yūrtī against them. They could not maintain themselves, and surrendered, making
Fol. 41. Khwāja-i-qāẓī their mediator. Having pardoned their offences against ourselves, we went back to beleaguer Samarkand.

(*b. Affairs of Sl. Ḥusain Mīrzā and his son, Badī'u'z-zamān Mīrzā.*)[6]

This year the mutual recriminations of Sl. Ḥusain Mīrzā and Badī'u'z-zamān Mīrzā led on to fighting; here are the par-

[1] Khorochkine (Radlov's *Réceuil d'Itinéraires* p. 241) mentions Pul-i-mougak, a great stone bridge thrown across a deep ravine, east of Samarkand. *For* Kūl-i-maghāk, deep pool, or pool of the fosse, *see* f. 48*b*.

[2] From Khwānd-amīr's differing account of this affair, it may be surmised that those sending the message were not treacherous; but the message itself was deceiving inasmuch as it did not lead Bābur to expect opposition. *Cf.* f. 43 and note.

[3] Of this nick-name several interpretations are allowed by the dictionaries.

[4] *See* Schuyler i, 268 for an account of this beautiful Highland village.

[5] Here Bābur takes up the thread, dropped on f. 36, of the affairs of the Khurāsānī mirzās. He draws on other sources than the H.S.; perhaps on

ticulars:—Last year, as has been mentioned, Badī'u'z-zamān Mīrzā and Muẓaffar Ḥusain Mīrzā had been made to kneel for Balkh and Astarābād. From that time till this, many envoys had come and gone, at last even 'Alī-sher Beg had gone but urge it as all did, Badī'u'z-zamān Mīrzā would not consent to give up Astarābād. 'The Mīrzā,' he said, 'assigned[1] it to my son, Muḥammad Mū'min Mīrzā at the time of his circumcision.' A conversation had one day between him and 'Alī-sher Beg testifies to his acuteness and to the sensibility of 'Alī-sher Beg's feelings. After saying many things of a private nature in the Mīrzā's ear, 'Alī-sher Beg added, 'Forget these matters.'[2] 'What matters?' rejoined the Mīrzā instantly 'Alī-sher Beg was much affected and cried a good deal.

At length the jarring words of this fatherly and filial discussion went so far that *his* father against his father, and *his* son against his son drew armies out for Balkh and Astarābād.[3]

Up (from Harāt) to the Pul-i-chirāgh meadow, below Garzawān,[4] went Sl. Ḥusain Mīrzā; down (from Balkh) came Fol. 41*b*. Badī'u'z-zamān Mīrzā. On the first day of Ramẓān (May 2nd.) Abū'l-muḥsin Mīrzā advanced, leading some of his father's light troops. There was nothing to call a battle; Badī'u'z-zamān Mīrzā was routed and of his braves masses were made prisoner. Sl. Ḥusain Mīrzā ordered that all prisoners should

---

his own memory, perhaps on information given by Khurāsānīs with him in Hindūstān *e.g.* Ḥusain's grandson. *See* f. 167*b*. *Cf.* Ḥ.S. ii, 261.

[1] *bāghishlāb tūr*. *Cf.* f. 34 note to *bāghish dā*.

[2] *Bū sozlār aūnūlūng*. Some W.-i-B. MSS., *Farāmosh bakunīd* for *nakunīd*, thus making the Mīrzā not acute but rude, and destroying the point of the story *i.e.* that the Mīrzā pretended so to have forgotten as to have an empty mind. Khwānd-amīr states that 'Alī-sher prevailed at first; his tears therefore may have been of joy at the success of his pacifying mission.

[3] *i.e.* B.Z.'s father, Ḥusain, against Mū'min's father, B.Z. and Ḥusain's son, Muẓaffar Ḥusain against B. Z.'s son Mū'min;—a veritable conundrum.

[4] Garzawān lies west of Balkh. Concerning Pul-i-chirāgh Col. Grodekoff's *Ride to Harāt* (Marvin p. 103 ff.) gives pertinent information. It has also a map showing the Pul-i-chirāgh meadow. The place stands at the mouth of a triply-bridged defile, but the name appears to mean Gate of the Lamp (*cf.* Gate of Tīmūr), and not Bridge of the Lamp, because the Ḥ.S. and also modern maps write *bīl* (*bel*), pass, where the Turkī text writes *pul*, bridge, narrows, pass.

The lamp of the name is one at the shrine of a saint, just at the mouth of the defile. It was alight when Col. Grodekoff passed in 1879 and to it, he says, the name is due now—as it presumably was 400 years ago and earlier.

be beheaded; this not here only but wherever he defeated a rebel son, he ordered the heads of all prisoners to be struck off. And why not? Right was with him. The (rebel) Mīrzās were so given over to vice and social pleasure that even when a general so skilful and experienced as their father was within half-a-day's journey of them, and when before the blessed month of Ramẓān, one night only remained, they busied themselves with wine and pleasure, without fear of their father, without dread of God. Certain it is that those so lost (*yūtkān*) will perish and that any hand can deal a blow at those thus going to perdition (*aūtkān*). During the several years of Badī'u'z-zamān Mīrzā's rule in Astarābād, his coterie and his following, his bare (*yālāng*) braves even, were in full splendour[4] and adornment. He had many gold and silver drinking-cups
Fol. 42. and utensils, much silken plenishing and countless tīpūchāq horses. He now lost everything. He hurled himself in his flight down a mountain track, leading to a precipitous fall. He himself got down the fall, with great difficulty, but many of his men perished there.[1]

After defeating Badī'u'z-zamān Mīrzā, Sl. Ḥusain Mīrzā moved on to Balkh. It was in charge of Shaikh 'Alī Ṭaghāī; he, not able to defend it, surrendered and made his submission. The Mīrzā gave Balkh to Ibrāhīm Ḥusain Mīrzā, left Muḥammad Walī Beg and Shāh Ḥusain, the page, with him and went back to Khurāsān.

Defeated and destitute, with his braves bare and his bare foot-soldiers[2], Badī'u'z-zamān Mīrzā drew off to Khusrau Shāh in Qūndūz. Khusrau Shāh, for his part, did him good service, such service indeed, such kindness with horses and camels, tents and pavilions and warlike equipment of all sorts, both for himself and those with him, that eye-witnesses said between this and his former equipment the only difference might be in the gold and silver vessels.

1 Khwānd-amīr heard from the Mīrzā on the spot, when later in his service, that he was let down the precipice by help of turban-sashes tied together.

2 *yīkit yīlāng u yāyāq yālīng*; a jingle made by due phonetic change of vowels; a play too on *yālāng*, which first means stripped *i.e.* robbed and next unmailed, perhaps sometimes bare-bodied in fight.

(*c. Dissension between Sl. Mas'ūd Mīrzā and Khusrau Shāh.*)

Ill-feeling and squabbles had arisen between Sl. Mas'ūd Mīrzā and Khusrau Shāh because of the injustices of the one and the self-magnifyings of the other. Now therefore Khusrau Shāh joined his brothers, Walī and Bāqī to Badī'u'z-zamān Mīrzā and sent the three against Ḥiṣār. They could not even get near the fort, in the outskirts swords were crossed once or twice; one day at the Bird-house[1] on the north of Ḥiṣār, Muḥibb-'alī, the armourer (*qūrchī*), outstripped his people and struck in well; he fell from his horse but at the moment of his capture, his men attacked and freed him. A few days later a somewhat compulsory peace was made and Khusrau Shāh's army retired. Fol. 42*b*

Shortly after this, Badī'u'z-zamān Mīrzā drew off by the mountain-road to Ẕū'n-nūn *Arghūn* and his son, Shujā' *Arghūn* in Qandahār and Zamīn-dāwar. Stingy and miserly as Ẕū'n-nūn was, he served the Mīrzā well, in one single present offering 40,000 sheep.

Amongst curious happenings of the time one was this: Wednesday was the day Sl. Ḥusain Mīrzā beat Badī'u'z-zamān Mīrzā; Wednesday was the day Muẓaffar Ḥusain Mīrzā beat Muḥammad Mū'min Mīrzā; Wednesday, more curious still, was the name of the man who unhorsed and took prisoner, Muḥammad Mū'min Mīrzā.[2]

1 *qūsh-khāna*. As the place was outside the walls, it may be a good hawking ground and not a falconry.

2 The H.S., mentions (ii, 222) a Sl. Aḥmad of Chār-shamba, a town mentioned *e.g.* by Grodekoff p. 123. It also spoils Bābur's coincidence by fixing Tuesday, Shab'ān 29th. for the battle. Perhaps the commencement of the Muḥammadan day at sunset, allows of both statements.

903 AH.—AUG. 30TH. 1497 TO AUG. 19TH. 1498 AD.[1]

(a. Resumed account of Bābur's second attempt on Samarkand.)

When we had dismounted in the Qulba (Plough) meadow,[2] behind the Bāgh-i-maidān (Garden of the plain), the Samarkandīs came out in great numbers to near Muḥammad Chap's
Fol. 43. Bridge. Our men were unprepared; and before they were ready, Bābā 'Alī's (son) Bābā Qulī had been unhorsed and taken into the fort. A few days later we moved to the top of Qulba, at the back of Kohik.[3] That day Sayyid Yūsuf,[4] having been sent out of the town, came to our camp and did me obeisance.

The Samarkandīs, fancying that our move from the one ground to the other meant, 'He has given it up,' came out, soldiers and townsmen in alliance (through the Turquoise Gate), as far as the Mīrzā's Bridge and, through the Shaikh-zāda's Gate, as far as Muḥammad Chap's. We ordered our braves to arm and ride out; they were strongly attacked from both sides, from Muḥammad Chap's Bridge and from the Mīrzā's, but God brought it right! our foes were beaten. Begs of the best and the boldest of braves our men unhorsed and brought in. Amongst them Ḥāfiẓ *Dūldāī's* (son) Muḥammad *Mīskīn*[5] was taken, after his index-finger had been struck off; Muḥammad Qāsim *Nabīra* also was unhorsed and brought in by his own younger brother, Ḥasan *Nabīra*.[6] There were many other such soldiers and known men. Of the town-

[1] Elph. MS. f. 30*b*; W.-i-B. I.O. 215 f. 34 and 217 f. 26*b*; Mems. p. 46. The abruptness of this opening is due to the interposition of Sl. Ḥusain M.'s affairs between Bābur's statement on f. 41 that he returned from Āūrgūt and this first of 903 AH. that on return he encamped in Qulba.

[2] *See* f. 48*b*.

[3] *i.e.* Chūpān-ātā; *see* f. 45 and note.

[4] *Aūghlāqchī*, the Grey Wolfer of f. 22.

[5] A sobriquet, the *suppliant* or perhaps something having connection with musk H.S. ii, 278, son of H.D.

[6] *i.e.* grandson (of Muḥammad Sīghal). *Cf.* f. 39.

rabble, were brought in Diwāna, the tunic-weaver and *Kāl-qāshūq*,[1] headlong leaders both, in brawl and tumult; they were ordered to death with torture in blood-retaliation for our foot-soldiers, killed at the Lovers' Cave.[2] This was a complete reverse for the Samarkandīs; they came out no more even when our men used to go to the very edge of the ditch and bring back their slaves and slave-women. Fol. 43*b*.

The Sun entered the Balance and cold descended on us.[3] I therefore summoned the begs admitted to counsel and it was decided, after discussion, that although the towns-people were so enfeebled that, by God's grace, we should take Samarkand, it might be to-day, it might be to-morrow, still, rather than suffer from cold in the open, we ought to rise from near it and go for winter-quarters into some fort, and that, even if we had to leave those quarters later on, this would be done without further trouble. As Khwāja Dīdār seemed a suitable fort, we marched there and having dismounted in the meadow lying before it, went in, fixed on sites for the winter-houses and covered shelters,[4] left overseers and inspectors of the work and returned to our camp in the meadow. There we lay during the few days before the winter-houses were finished.

Meantime Bāī-sunghar Mīrzā had sent again and again to ask help from Shaibānī Khān. On the morning of the very day on which, our quarters being ready, we had moved into Khwāja Dīdār, the Khān, having ridden light from Turkistān, stood over against our camping-ground. Our men were not all at hand; some, for winter-quarters, had gone to Khwāja Rabāṭī, some to Kabud, some to Shīrāz. None-the-less, we formed up those there were and rode out. Shaibānī Khān made no stand but drew off towards Samarkand. He went right up to the fort but because the affair had not gone as Fol. 44.

[1] This seeming sobriquet may show the man's trade. *Kāl* is a sort of biscuit; *qāshūq* may mean a spoon.

[2] The Ḥ.S. does not ascribe treachery to those inviting Bābur into Samarkand but attributes the murder of his men to others who fell on them when the plan of his admission became known. The choice here of "town-rabble" for retaliatory death supports the account of Ḥ.S. ii.

[3] "It was the end of September or beginning of October" (Erskine).

[4] *awī u kīpa yīrlār*. *Awī* is likely to represent *kibitkas*. For *kīpa yīr*, see Zenker p. 782.

Bāī-sunghar Mīrzā wished, did not get a good reception. He therefore turned back for Turkistān a few days later, in disappointment, with nothing done.

Bāī-sunghar Mīrzā had sustained a seven months' siege; his one hope had been in Shaibānī Khān; this he had lost and he now with 2 or 300 of his hungry suite, drew off from Samarkand, for Khusrau Shāh in Qūndūz.

When he was near Tīrmīẕ, at the Amū ferry, the Governor of Tīrmīẕ, Sayyid Ḥusain Akbar, kinsman and confidant both of Sl. Mas'ūd Mīrzā, heard of him and went out against him. The Mīrzā himself got across the river but Mīrīm Tarkhān was drowned and all the rest of his people were captured, together with his baggage and the camels loaded with his personal effects; even his page, Muḥammad Ṭāhir, falling into Sayyid Ḥusain Akbar's hands. Khusrau Shāh, for his part, looked kindly on the Mīrzā.

Fol. 44*b*. When the news of his departure reached us, we got to horse and started from Khwāja Dīdār for Samarkand. To give us honourable meeting on the road, were nobles and braves, one after another. It was on one of the last ten days of the first Rabī' (end of November 1497 AD.), that we entered the citadel and dismounted at the Bū-stān Sarāī. Thus, by God's favour, were the town and the country of Samarkand taken and occupied.

(*b. Description of Samarkand.*)[1]

Few towns in the whole habitable world are so pleasant as Samarkand. It is of the Fifth Climate and situated in lat. 40° 6′ and long. 99°.[2] The name of the town is Samarkand; its country people used to call Mā warā'u'n-nahr (Transoxania).

[1] Interesting reference may be made, amongst the many books on Samarkand, to Sharafu'd-dīn 'Alī *Yazdī's Ẓafar-nāma* Bib. Ind. ed. i, 300, 781, 799, 800 and ii, 6, 194, 596 etc.; to Ruy Gonzalves di Clavijo's *Embassy to Tīmūr* (Markham) cap. vi and vii; to Ujfalvy's *Turkistan* ii, 79 and Madame Ujfalvy's *De Paris à Samarcande* p. 161,—these two containing a plan of the town; to Schuyler's *Turkistan*; to Kostenko's *Turkistan Gazetteer* i, 345; to Réclus, vi, 270 and plan; and to a beautiful work of the St. Petersburg Archæological Society, *Les Mosquées de Samarcande*, of which the B.M. has a copy.

[2] This statement is confused in the Elp. and Ḥai. MSS. The second appears to give, by *abjad*, lat. 40′ 6″ and long. 99′. Mr. Erskine (p. 48) gives

They used to call it *Baldat-i-maḥfūẓa* because no foe laid hands on it with storm and sack.[1] It must have become [2] Musalmān in the time of the Commander of the Faithful, his Highness 'Usmān. Quṣam ibn 'Abbās, one of the Companions[3] must have gone there; his burial-place, known as the Tomb of Shāh-i-zinda (The Living Shāh, *i.e.*, Fāqīr) is outside the Iron Gate. Iskandar must have founded Samarkand. The Turk and Mughūl hordes call it Sīmīz-kīnt.[4] Tīmūr Beg made it his capital; no ruler so great will ever have made it a capital before (*qīlghān aīmās dūr*). I ordered people to pace round the ramparts of the walled-town; it came out at 10,000 steps.[5] Samarkandīs are all orthodox (*sunnī*), pure-in-the Faith, law-abiding and religious. The number of Leaders of Islām said to have arisen in Mā warā'u'n-nahr, since the days of his Highness the Prophet, are not known to have arisen in any other country.[6] From the Mātarīd suburb of Samarkand came Shaikh Abū'l-manṣūr, one of the Expositors of the Word.[7] Of the two sects of Expositors, the Mātarīdiyah Fol. 45.

---

lat. 39' 57" and long. 99' 16", noting that this is according to Ulūgh Beg's Tables and that the long. is calculated from Ferro. The Ency. Br. of 1910-11 gives lat. 39' 39" and long. 66' 45".

1 The enigmatical cognomen, Protected Town, is of early date; it is used *i.a.* by Ibn Batūta in the 14th. century. Bābur's tense refers it to the past. The town had frequently changed hands in historic times before he wrote. The name may be due to immunity from damage to the buildings in the town. Even Chīngīz Khān's capture (1222 AD.) left the place well-preserved and its lands cultivated, but it inflicted great loss of men. *Cf.* Schuyler i, 236 and his authorities, especially Bretschneider.

2 Here is a good example of Bābur's caution in narrative. He does not affirm that Samarkand became Musalmān, or (*infra*) that Quṣam ibn 'Abbās went, or that Alexander founded but in each case uses the presumptive past tense, resp. *būlghān dūr, bārghān dūr, bīnā qīlghān dūr*, thus showing that he repeats what may be inferred or presumed and not what he himself asserts.

3 *i.e.* of Muḥammad. See Ẓ.N. ii, 193.

4 *i.e.* Fat Village. His text misleading him, Mr. Erskine makes here the useful irrelevant note that Persians and Arabs call the place Samar-qand and Turks, Samar-kand, the former using *qaf* (q), the latter *kaf* (k). Both the Elph. and the Hai. MSS. write Samarqand.

For use of the name Fat Village, *see* Clavijo (Markham p. 170), Simesquinte, and Bretschneider's *Mediæval Geography* pp. 61, 64, 66 and 163.

5 *qadam*. Kostenko (i, 344) gives 9 m. as the circumference of the old walls and 1¾ m. as that of the citadel. *See* Mde. Ujfalvy p. 175 for a picture of the walls.

6 *Ma'lūm aīmās kīm mūncha paidā būlmīsh būlghāī*; an idiomatic phrase.

7 d. 333 AH. (944 AD.). *See* D'Herbélot art. Mātridī p. 572.

and the Ash'ariyah,[1] the first is named from this Shaikh Abū'l-manṣūr. Of Mā warā'u'n-nahr also was Khwāja Ismā'īl *Khartank*, the author of the *Ṣāḥiḥ-i-bukhārī*.[2] From the Farghāna district, Marghīnān—Farghāna, though at the limit of settled habitation, is included in Mā warā'u'n-nahr,—came the author of the *Hidāyat*,[3] a book than which few on Jurisprudence are more honoured in the sect of Abū Ḥanīfa.

On the east of Samarkand are Farghāna and Kāshghar; on the west, Bukhārā and Khwārizm; on the north, Tāshkīnt and Shāhrukhiya,—in books written Shāsh and Banākat; and on the south, Balkh and Tirmīz.

The Kohik Water flows along the north of Samarkand, at the distance of some 4 miles (2 *kuroh*); it is so-called because it comes out from under the upland of the Little Hill (*Kohik*)[4] lying between it and the town. The Dar-i-gham Water (canal) flows along the south, at the distance of some two miles (1 *sharī'*). This is a large and swift torrent,[5] indeed it is like a large river, cut off from the Kohik Water. All the gardens and suburbs and some of the *tūmāns* of Samarkand are cultivated by it. By the Kohik Water a stretch of from 30 to 40 *yīghāch*,[6] by road, is made habitable and cultivated, as far as Bukhārā

[1] *See* D'Herbélot art. Aschair p. 124.

[2] Abū 'Abdu'l-lāh bin Ismā'īlu'l-jausī b. 194 AH. d. 256 AH. (810-870 AD.). *See* D'Herbélot art. Bokhārī p. 191, art. Giorag p. 373, and art. Ṣāḥihu'l-bokhārī p. 722. He passed a short period, only, of his life in Khartank, a suburb of Samarkand.

[3] *Cf.* f. 3*b* and n. 1.

[4] This though 2475 ft. above the sea is only some 300 ft. above Samarkand. It is the Chūpān-ātā (Father of Shepherds) of maps and on it Tīmūr built a shrine to the local patron of shepherds. The Zar-afshān, or rather, its Qarā-sū arm, flows from the east of the Little Hill and turns round it to flow west. Bābur uses the name *Kohik Water* loosely; *e.g.* for the whole Zar-afshān when he speaks (*infra*) of cutting off the Dar-i-gham canal but for its southern arm only, the Qarā-sū in several places, and once, for the Dar-i-gham canal. *See* f. 49*b* and Kostenko i. 192.

[5] *rūd*. The Zar-afshān has a very rapid current. *See* Kostenko i. 196, and for the canal, i. 174. The name Dar-i-gham is used also for a musical note having charm to witch away grief; and also for a town noted for its wines.

[6] What this represents can only be guessed; perhaps 150 to 200 miles. Abū'l-fidā (Reinaud ii. 213) quotes Ibn Haukal as saying that from Bukhārā up to "Bottam" (this seems to be where the Zar-afshān emerges into the open land) is eight days' journey through an unbroken tangle of verdure and gardens.

and Qarā-kūl. Large as the river is, it is not too large for its dwellings and its culture; during three or four months of the year, indeed, its waters do not reach Bukhārā.[1] Grapes, melons, apples and pomegranates, all fruits indeed, are good in Samarkand; two are famous, its apple and its ṣāḥibī (grape).[2] Its winter is mightily cold; snow falls but not so much as in Kābul; in the heats its climate is good but not so good as Kābul's.

Fol. 45b.

In the town and suburbs of Samarkand are many fine buildings and gardens of Tīmūr Beg and Aūlūgh Beg Mīrzā.[3]

In the citadel,[4] Tīmūr Beg erected a very fine building, the great four-storeyed kiosque, known as the Gūk Sarāī.[5] In the walled-town, again, near the Iron Gate, he built a Friday Mosque[6] of stone (sangīn); on this worked many stone-cutters, brought from Hindūstān. Round its frontal arch is inscribed in letters large enough to be read two miles away, the Qu'rān verse, Wa az yerfaʽ Ibrāhīm al Qawāʽid alī akhara.[7] This also is a very fine building. Again, he laid out two gardens, on the

---

[1] See Schuyler i, 286 on the apportionment of water to Samarkand and Bukhārā.

[2] It is still grown in the Samarkand region, and in Mr. Erskine's time a grape of the same name was cultivated in Aurangābād of the Deccan.

[3] i.e. Shāhrukhī, Tīmūr's grandson, through Shāhrukh. It may be noted here that Bābur never gives Tīmūr any other title than Beg and that he styles all Tīmūrids, Mīrzā (Mīr-born).

[4] Mr. Erskine here points out the contradiction between the statements (1) of Ibn Haukal, writing, in 367 AH. (977 AD.), of Samarkand as having a citadel (ark), an outer-fort (qūrghān) and Gates in both circumvallations; and (2) of Sharafu'd-dīn Yazdī (Ẓ.N.) who mentions that when, in Tīmūr's day, the Getes besieged Samarkand, it had neither walls nor gates. See Ouseley's Ibn Haukal p. 253 ; Ẓ.N. Bib. Ind. ed. i, 109 and Pétis de la Croix's Ẓ.N. (Histoire de Tīmūr Beg) i, 91.

[5] Here still lies the Ascension Stone, the Gūk-tāsh, a block of greyish white marble. Concerning the date of the erection of the building and meaning of its name, see e.g. Pétis de la Croix's Histoire de Chingīz Khān p. 171 ; Mems. p. 40 note ; and Schuyler s.n.

[6] This seems to be the Bībī Khānīm Mosque. The author of Les Mosquées de Samarcande states that Tīmūr built Bībī Khānīm and the Gūr-i-amīr (Amīr's tomb); decorated Shāh-i-zinda and set up the Chūpān-ātā shrine. Cf. f 46 and note to Jahāngīr Mīrzā, as to the Gūr-i-amīr.

[7] Cap. II. Quoting from Sale's Qur'ān (i, 24) the verse is, " And Ibrāhīm and Ismāʽīl raised the foundations of the house, saying, ʽ Lord ! accept it from us, for Thou art he who hearest and knowest ; Lord ! make us also resigned to Thee, and show us Thy holy ceremonies, and be turned to us, for Thou art easy to be reconciled, and merciful.' "

east of the town, one, the more distant, the Bāgh-i-bulandī,[1] the other and nearer, the Bāgh-i-dilkushā.[2] From Dilkushā to the Turquoise Gate, he planted an Avenue of White Poplar,[3] and in the garden itself erected a great kiosque, painted inside
Fol. 46. with pictures of his battles in Hindūstān. He made another garden, known as the Naqsh-i-jahān (World's Picture), on the skirt of Kohik, above the Qarā-sū or, as people also call it, the Āb-i-raḥmat (Water-of-mercy) of Kān-i-gil.[4] It had gone to ruin when I saw it, nothing remaining of it except its name. His also are the Bāgh-i-chanār,[5] near the walls and below the town on the south,[6] also the Bāgh-i-shamāl (North Garden) and the Bāgh-i-bihisht (Garden of Paradise). His own tomb and those of his descendants who have ruled in Samarkand, are in a College, built at the exit (*chāqār*) of the walled-town, by Muḥammad Sulṭān Mīrzā, the son of Tīmūr Beg's son, Jahāngīr Mīrzā.[7]

Amongst Aūlūgh Beg Mīrzā's buildings inside the town are a College and a monastery (*Khānqāh*). The dome of the monastery is very large, few so large are shown in the world. Near these two buildings, he constructed an excellent Hot Bath (*ḥammām*) known as the Mīrzā's Bath; he had the pavements in this made of all sorts of stone (? mosaic); such

1 or, *buland*, Garden of the Height or High Garden. The Turkī texts have what can be read as *buldī* but the Ẓ.N. both when describing it (ii, 194) and elsewhere (*e.g.* ii, 596) writes *buland*. *Buldī* may be a clerical error for *bulandī*, the height, a name agreeing with the position of the garden.

2 In the Heart-expanding Garden, the Spanish Ambassadors had their first interview with Tīmūr. *See* Clavijo (Markham p. 130). Also the Ẓ.N. ii, 6 for an account of its construction.

3 Judging from the location of the gardens and of Bābur's camps, this appears to be the Avenue mentioned on f. 39*b* and f. 40.

4 *See infra* f. 48 and note.

5 The Plane-tree Garden. This seems to be Clavijo's *Bayginar*, laid out shortly before he saw it (Markham p. 136).

6 The citadel of Samarkand stands high; from it the ground slopes west and south; on these sides therefore gardens outside the walls would lie markedly below the outer-fort (*tāsh-qūrghān*). Here as elsewhere the second W.-i-B. reads *stone* for *outer* (*Cf.* index *s.n. tāsh*). For the making of the North garden *see* Ẓ.N. i, 799.

7 Tīmūr's eldest son, d. 805 AH. (1402 AD.), before his father, therefore. Bābur's wording suggests that in his day, the Gūr-i-amīr was known as the Madrāsa. *See* as to the buildings Ẓ.N. i, 713 and ii, 492, 595, 597, 705; Clavijo (Markham p. 164 and p. 166); and *Les Mosquées de Samarcande*.

another bath is not known in Khurāsān or in Samarkand.[1] Fol. 46*b*.
Again;—to the south of the College is his mosque, known as the Masjid-i-maqaṭa' (Carved Mosque) because its ceiling and its walls are all covered with *islīmī*[2] and Chinese pictures formed of segments of wood.[3] There is great discrepancy between the *qibla* of this mosque and that of the College; that of the mosque seems to have been fixed by astronomical observation.

Another of Aūlūgh Beg Mīrzā's fine buildings is an observatory, that is, an instrument for writing Astronomical Tables.[4] This stands three storeys high, on the skirt of the Kohik upland. By its means the Mīrzā worked out the Kūrkānī Tables, now used all over the world. Less work is done with any others. Before these were made, people used the Aīl-khānī Tables, put together at Marāgha, by Khwāja Naṣīr *Tūsī*,[5] in the time of Hulākū Khān. Hulākū Khān it is, people call *Aīl-khānī*.[6]

(*Author's note.*) Not more than seven or eight observatories seem to have been constructed in the world. Māmūm Khalīfa[7] (Caliph) made one with which the *Mamūmī* Tables were written. Batalmūs (Ptolemy) constructed another. Another was made, in Hindūstān, in the time of Rājā Vikramāditya *Hīndū*, in Ujjain and Dhar, that is, the Mālwa country, now known as Māndū. The Hindūs of Hindūstān use the Tables of this Observatory. They were put together 1,584 years ago.[8] Fol. 47.
Compared with others, they are somewhat defective.

---

1 Hindūstān would make a better climax here than Samarkand does.

2 These appear to be pictures or ornamentations of carved wood. Redhouse describes *islīmī* as a special kind of ornamentation in curved lines, similar to Chinese methods.

3 *i.e.* the Black Stone (*ka'ba*) at Makkah to which Musalmāns turn in prayer.

4 As ancient observatories were themselves the instruments of astronomical observation, Bābur's wording is correct. Aūlūgh Beg's great quadrant was 180 ft. high; Abū-muḥammad *Khujandī's* sextant had a radius of 58 ft. Jā'ī Singh made similar great instruments in Jā'īpūr, Dihlī has others. *Cf.* Greaves Misc. Works i, 50; Mems. p. 51 note; *Āīyīn-i-akbarī* (Jarrett) ii, 5 and note; Murray's Hand-book to Bengal p. 331; Indian Gazetteer xiii, 400.

5 b. 597 AH. d. 672 AH. (1201-1274 AD.). *See* D'Herbélot's art. Naṣīr-i-dīn p. 662; Abū'l-fidā (Reinaud, Introduction i, cxxxviii) and Beale's Biographical Dict. *s.n.*

6 a grandson of Chīngīz Khān, d. 663 AH. (1265 AD.). The cognomen *Aīl-khānī* (*Īl-khānī*) may mean Khān of the Tribe.

7 Harūnu'r-rashīd's second son; d. 218 AH. (833 AD.).

8 Mr. Erskine notes that this remark would seem to fix the date at which Bābur wrote it as 934 AH. (1527 AD.), that being the 1584th. year of the era of Vikramāditya, and therefore at three years before Bābur's death. (The Vikramāditya era begun 57 BC.)

Aūlūgh Beg Mīrzā again, made the garden known as the Bāgh-i-maidān (Garden of the Plain), on the skirt of the Kohik upland. In the middle of it he erected a fine building they call Chihil Sitūn (Forty Pillars). On both storeys are pillars, all of stone (*tāshdīn*).[1] Four turrets, like minarets, stand on its four corner-towers, the way up into them being through the towers. Everywhere there are stone pillars, some fluted, some twisted, some many-sided. On the four sides of the upper storey are open galleries enclosing a four-doored hall (*chār-dara*); their pillars also are all of stone. The raised floor of the building is all paved with stone.

He made a smaller garden, out beyond Chihil Sitūn and towards Kohik, also having a building in it. In the open gallery of this building he placed a great stone throne, some 14 or 15 yards (*qārī*) long, some 8 yards wide and perhaps 1 yard high. They brought a stone so large by a very long road.[2] There is a crack in the middle of it which people say must have come after it was brought here. In the same
Fol. 47*b*. garden he also built a four-doored hall, know as the Chīnī-khāna (Porcelain House) because its *īzāra*[3] are all of porcelain; he sent to China for the porcelain used in it. Inside the walls again, is an old building of his, known as the Masjid-i-laqlaqa (Mosque of the Echo). If anyone stamps on the ground under the middle of the dome of this mosque, the sound echoes back from the whole dome; it is a curious matter of which none know the secret.

In the time also of Sl. Aḥmad Mīrzā the great and lesser begs laid out many gardens, large and small.[4] For beauty, and air, and view, few will have equalled Darwesh Muḥammad Tarkhān's Chār-bāgh (Four Gardens).[5] It lies overlooking the whole of Qulba Meadow, on the slope below the Bāgh-i-

1 *Cf.* index *s.n. tāsh*.

2 This remark may refer to the 34 miles between the town and the quarries of its building stone. *See* f. 49 and note to Aītmāk Pass.

3 Steingass, any support for the back in sitting, a low wall in front of a house. *See* Vullers p. 148 and *Burhān-i-qāṭi'*; p. 119. Perhaps a *dado*.

4 *beg u begāt, bāgh u bāghcha.*

5 Four Gardens, a quadrilateral garden, laid out in four plots. The use of the name has now been extended for any well-arranged, large garden, especially one belonging to a ruler (Erskine).

maidān. Moreover it is arranged symmetrically, terrace above terrace, and is planted with beautiful *nārwān*[1] and cypresses and white poplar. A most agreeable sojourning place, its one defect is the want of a large stream.

Samarkand is a wonderfully beautified town. One of its specialities, perhaps found in few other places,[2] is that the different trades are not mixed up together in it but each has its own *bāzār*, a good sort of plan. Its bakers and its cooks are good. The best paper in the world is made there; the water for the paper-mortars[3] all comes from Kān-i-gil,[4] a meadow on the banks of the Qarā-sū (Blackwater) or Āb-i-raḥmat (Water of Mercy). Another article of Samarkand trade, carried to all sides and quarters, is cramoisy velvet. Fol. 48.

Excellent meadows lie round Samarkand. One is the famous Kān-i-gil, some 2 miles east and a little north of the town. The Qarā-sū or Āb-i-raḥmat flows through it, a stream (with driving power) for perhaps seven or eight mills. Some say the original name of the meadow must have been Kān-i-ābgīr (Mine of Quagmire) because the river is bordered by quagmire, but the histories all write Kān-i-gil (Mine of clay). It is an excellent meadow. The Samarkand sulṭans always made it their reserve,[5] going out to camp in it each year for a month or two.

[1] As two of the trees mentioned here are large, it may be right to translate *nārwān*, not by pomegranate, but as the hard-wood elm, Madame Ujfalvy's '*karagatche*' (p. 168 and p. 222). The name *qarā-yīghāch* (*karagatch*), dark tree, is given to trees other than this elm on account of their deep shadow.

[2] Now a common plan indeed! *See* Schuyler i, 173.

[3] *juwāz-i-kaghazlār* (*nīng*) *sū'ī*, *i.e.* the water of the paper-(pulping)-mortars. Owing to the omission from some MSS. of the word *sū*, water, *juwāz* has been mistaken for a kind of paper. *See* Mems. p. 52 and *Méms.* i, 102; A.Q.R. July 1910, p. 2, art. Paper-mills of Samarkand (H.B.); and Madame Ujfalvy p. 188. Kostenko, it is to be noted, does not include paper in his list (i, 346) of modern manufactures of Samarkand.

[4] Mine of mud or clay. My husband has given me support for reading *gil*, and not *gul*, rose;—(1) In two good MSS. of the W.-i-B. the word is pointed with *kasra*, *i.e.* as for *gil*, clay; and (2) when describing a feast held in the garden by Tīmūr, the Ẓ.N. says the mud-mine became a rose-mine, *shuda Kān-i-gil Kān-i-gul*. [Mr. Erskine refers here to Pétis de la Croix's *Histoire de Tīmūr Beg* (*i.e.* Ẓ.N.) i, 96 and ii, 133 and 421.]

[5] *qūrūgh*. Vullers, classing the word as Arabic, Zenker, classing it as Eastern Turkī, and Erskine (p. 42 n.) explain this as land reserved for the

Higher up (on the river) than Kān-i-gil and to the s.e. of it is a meadow some 4 miles east of the town, known as Khān Yūrtī (Khān's Camping-ground). The Qarā-sū flows through this meadow before entering Kān-i-gil. When it comes to Khān Yūrtī it curves back so far that it encloses, with a very narrow outlet, enough ground for a camp. Having noticed these advantages, we camped there for a time during the siege of Samarkand.[1]

Another meadow is the Būdana Qūrūgh (Quail Reserve), lying between Dil-kushā and the town. Another is the Kūl-i-maghāk (Meadow of the deep pool) at some 4 miles from the town. This also is a round[2] meadow. People call it Kul-i-maghāk meadow because there is a large pool on one side of it. Sl. 'Alī Mīrzā lay here during the siege, when I was in Khān Yūrtī. Another and smaller meadow is Qulba (Plough); it has Qulba Village and the Kohik Water on the north, the Bāgh-i-maidān and Darwesh Muḥammad Tarkhān's Chār-bāgh on the south, and the Kohik upland on the west.

Samarkand has good districts and *tūmāns*. Its largest district, and one that is its equal, is Bukhārā, 25 *yīghāch*[3] to the west. Bukhārā in its turn, has several *tūmāns*; it is a fine town; its fruits are many and good, its melons excellent; none in Mā warā'u'n-nahr matching them for quality and quantity. Although the Mīr Tīmūrī melon of Akhsī[4] is sweeter and more delicate than any Bukhārā melon, still in Bukhārā many kinds of melon are good and plentiful. The Bukhārā plum is famous; no other equals it. They skin it,[5] dry it and carry it from land to land with rarities (*tabarrūklār bīla*); it is an excellent laxative medicine. Fowls and geese are much

---

summer encampment of princes. Shaw (Voc. p. 155), deriving it from *qūrūmāq*, to frighten, explains it as a fenced field of growing grain.

[1] *Cf.* f. 40. There it is located at one *yīghāch* and here at 3 *kurohs* from the town.
[2] *ṭaur. Cf.* Zenker *s.n.* I understand it to lie, as Khān Yūrtī did, in a curve of the river.
[3] 162 m. by rail.
[4] *Cf.* f. 3.
[5] *tīrīsīnī sūīūb*. The verb *sūīmāk*, to despoil, seems to exclude the common plan of stoning the fruit. *Cf.* f. 3*b*, *dānasīnī alīp*, taking out the stones.

looked after (*parwārī*) in Bukhārā. Bukhārā wine is the strongest made in Mā warā'u'n-nahr; it was what I drank when drinking in those countries at Samarkand.[1]

Kesh is another district of Samarkand, 9 *yīghāch*[2] by road to the south of the town. A range called the Aītmāk Pass (*Dābān*)[3] lies between Samarkand and Kesh; from this are taken all the stones for building. Kesh is called also Shahr-i-sabz (Green-town) because its barren waste (*ṣahr*) and roofs and walls become beautifully green in spring. As it was Tīmūr Beg's birth-place, he tried hard to make it his capital. He erected noble buildings in it. To seat his own Court, he built a great arched hall and in this seated his Commander-begs and his Dīwān-begs, on his right and on his left. For those attending the Court, he built two smaller halls, and to seat petitioners to his Court, built quite small recesses on the four sides of the Court-house.[4] Few arches so fine can be shown in the world. It is said to be higher than the Kisrī Arch.[5] Tīmūr Beg also built in Kesh a college and a mausoleum, in which are the tombs of Jahāngīr Mīrzā and others of his descendants.[6] As Kesh did not offer the same facilities as Fol. 49*b*.

[1] *Mīn Samarkandtā aūl* (*or auwal*) *aīchkāndā Bukhārā chāghīrlār nī aīchār aīdīm.* These words have been understood to refer to Bābur's initial drinking of wine but this reading is negatived by his statement (f. 189) that he first drank wine in Harāt in 912 AH. I understand his meaning to be that the wine he drank in Samarkand was Bukhārā wine. The time cannot have been earlier than 917 AH. The two words *aūl aīchkāndā*, I read as parallel to *aūl* (*bāghrī qarā*) (f. 280) 'that drinking,' 'that bird,' *i.e.* of those other countries, not of Hindūstān where he wrote.

It may be noted that Bābur's word for wine, *chāghīr*, may not always represent wine of the grape but may include wine of the apple and pear (cider and perry), and other fruits. Cider, its name seeming to be a descendant of *chāghīr*, was introduced into England by Crusaders, its manufacture having been learned from Turks in Palestine.

[2] 48 m. 3 fur. by way of the Aītmāk Pass (mod. Takhta Qarachi), and, Réclus (vi, 256) Buz-gala-khāna, Goat-house.

[3] The name Aītmāk, to build, appears to be due to the stone quarries on the range. The pass-head is 34 m. from Samarkand and 3000 ft. above it. *See* Kostenko ii, 115 and Schuyler ii, 61 for details of the route.

[4] The description of this hall is difficult to translate. Clavijo (Markham 124) throws light on the small recesses. *Cf.* *Z*.N. i, 781 and 300 and Schuyler ii, 68.

[5] The Tāq-i-kisrī, below Bāghdād, is 105 ft. high, 84 ft. span and 150 ft. in depth (Erskine).

[6] *Cf.* f. 46. Bābur does not mention that Tīmūr's father was buried at Kesh. Clavijo (Markham p. 123) says it was Tīmūr's first intention to be buried near his father, in Kesh.

Samarkand for becoming a town and a capital, he at last made clear choice of Samarkand.

Another district is Qarshī, known also as Nashaf and Nakhshab.[1] Qarshī is a Mughūl name. In the Mughūl tongue they call a *kūr-khāna* Qarshī.[2] The name must have come in after the rule of Chīngīz Khān. Qarshī is somewhat scantily supplied with water; in spring it is very beautiful and its grain and melons are good. It lies 18 *yīghāch*[3] by road south and a little inclined to west of Samarkand. In the district a small bird, known as the *qīl-qūyīrūgh* and resembling the *bāghrī qarā*, is found in such countless numbers that it goes by the name of the Qarshī birdie (*murghak*).[4]

Khozār is another district; Karmīna another, lying between Samarkand and Bukhārā; Qarā-kūl another, 7 *yīghāch*[5] n.w. of Bukhārā and at the furthest limit of the water.

Samarkand has good *tūmāns*. One is Soghd with its dependencies. Its head Yār-yīlāq, its foot Bukhārā, there may be not one single *yīghāch* of earth without its village and its cultivated lands. So famous is it that the saying attributed to Tīmūr Beg, 'I have a garden 30 *yīghāch* long,[6] must have been spoken of Soghd. Another *tūmān* is Shāvdār (var. Shādwār), an excellent one adjoining the town-suburbs. On one side it has the range (Aītmāk Dābān), lying between Samarkand and
Fol. 50. Shahr-i-sabz, on the skirts of which are many of its villages. On the other side is the Kohik Water (*i.e.* the Dar-i-gham canal). There it lies! an excellent *tūmān*, with fine air, full of beauty, abounding in waters, its good things cheap. Observers of Egypt and Syria have not pointed out its match.

[1] Abū'l-fidā (Reinaud II, ii, 21) says that Nasaf is the Arabic and Nakhshab the local name for Qarshī. Ibn Haukal (Ouseley p. 260) writes Nakhshab.

[2] This word has been translated *burial-place* and *cimetière* but Qarshī means castle, or royal-residence. The Ẓ.N. (i, 111) says that Qarshī is an equivalent for Ar. *qaṣr*, palace, and was so called, from one built there by Qublāī Khān (d. 1294 AD.). Perhaps Bābur's word is connected with Gūrkhān, the title of sovereigns in Khutan, and means great or royal-house, *i.e.* palace.

[3] 94 m. 6½ fur. via Jām (Kostenko i, 115.)

[4] See Appendix B.

[5] some 34 m. (Kostenko i, 196). Schuyler mentions that he heard in Qarā-kūl a tradition that the district, in bye-gone days, was fertilized from the Sīr.

[6] *Cf.* f. 45.

Though Samarkand has other *tūmāns*, none rank with those enumerated; with so much, enough has been said.

Tīmūr Beg gave the government of Samarkand to his eldest son, Jahāngīr Mīrzā (in 776 AH.-1375 AD.); when Jahāngīr Mīrzā died (805 AH.-1403 AD.), he gave it to the Mīrzā's eldest son, Muḥammad Sulṭān-i-jahāngīr; when Muḥammad Sulṭān Mīrzā died, it went to Shāh-rukh Mīrzā, Tīmūr Beg's youngest son. Shāh-rukh Mīrzā gave the whole of Mā warā'u'n-nahr (in 872 AH.-1467 AD.) to his eldest son, Aūlūgh Beg Mīrzā. From him his own son, 'Abdu'l-laṭīf Mīrzā took it, (853 AH.-1449 AD.), for the sake of this five days' fleeting world martyring a father so full of years and knowledge.

The following chronogram gives the date of Aūlūgh Beg Mīrzā's death:—

> Aūlūgh Beg, an ocean of wisdom and science,
> The pillar of realm and religion,
> Sipped from the hand of 'Abbās, the mead of martyrdom,
> And the date of the death is '*Abbās kasht* ('Abbās slew).[1]

Though 'Abdu'l-laṭīf Mīrzā did not rule more than five or six months, the following couplet was current about him:—

> Ill does sovereignty befit the parricide;
> Should he rule, be it for no more than six months.[2]

This chronogram of the death of 'Abdu'l-laṭif Mīrzā is also well done:—

> 'Abdu'l-laṭif, in glory a Khusrau and Jamshīd, Fol. 50*b*.
> In his train a Farīdūn and Zardusht,
> Bābā Ḥusain slew on the Friday Eve,
> With an arrow. Write as its date, *Bābā Husain kasht* (Bābā Ḥusain slew).[3]

After 'Abdu'l-laṭīf Mīrzā's death, (Jumāda I, 22, 855 AH.-June 22nd. 1450 AD.), (his cousin) 'Abdu'l-lāh Mīrzā, the grandson of Shāh-rukh Mīrzā through Ibrāhīm Mīrzā, seated him-

1 By *abjad* the words '*Abbās kasht* yield 853. The date of the murder was Ramẓān 9, 853 AH. (Oct. 27th. 1449 AD.).

2 This couplet is quoted in the *Rauẓatu'ṣ-ṣafā* (lith. ed. vi, f. 234 foot) and in the Ḥ.S. ii, 44. It is said, in the R.Ṣ. to be by Niẓāmī and to refer to the killing by Shīrūya of his father, Khusrau Parwīz in 7 AH. (628 AD.). The Ḥ.S. says that 'Abdu'l-laṭīf constantly repeated the couplet, after he had murdered his father. [See also Daulat Shāh (Browne p. 356 and p. 366.) H.B.

3 By *abjad, Bābā Ḥusain kasht* yields 854. The death was on Rabī' I, 26, 854 AH. (May 9th. 1450 AD.). See R.Ṣ. vi, 235 for an account of this death.

self on the throne and ruled for 18 months to two years.[1] From him Sl. Abū-sa'īd Mīrzā took it (855 AH.-1451 AD.). He in his life-time gave it to his eldest son, Sl. Aḥmad Mīrzā; Sl. Aḥmad Mīrzā continued to rule it after his father's death (873 AH.-1469 AD.). On his death (899 AH.-1494 AD.) Sl. Maḥmūd Mīrzā was seated on the throne and on his death (900 AH.-1495 AD.) Bāī-sunghar Mīrzā. Bāī-sunghar Mīrzā was made prisoner for a few days, during the Tarkhān rebellion (901 AH.-1496 AD.), and his younger brother, Sl. 'Alī Mīrzā was seated on the throne, but Bāī-sunghar Mīrzā, as has been related in this history, took it again directly. From Bāī-sunghar Mīrzā I took it (903 AH.-1497 AD.). Further details will be learned from the ensuing history.

(*c. Bābur's rule in Samarkand.*)

When I was seated on the throne, I shewed the Samarkand begs precisely the same favour and kindness they had had before. I bestowed rank and favour also on the begs with me,
Fol. 51. to each according to his circumstances, the largest share falling to Sl. Aḥmad *Tambal;* he had been in the household begs' circle; I now raised him to that of the great begs.

We had taken the town after a seven months' hard siege. Things of one sort or other fell to our men when we got in. The whole country, with exception of Samarkand itself, had come in earlier either to me or to Sl. 'Alī Mīrzā and consequently had not been over-run. In any case however, what could have been taken from districts so long subjected to raid and rapine? The booty our men had taken, such as it was, came to an end. When we entered the town, it was in such distress that it needed seed-corn and money-advances; what place was this to take anything from? On these accounts our men suffered great privation. We ourselves could give them nothing. Moreover they yearned for their homes and, by ones and twos, set their faces for flight. The first to go was Bayān Qulī's (son) Khān Qulī; Ibrāhīm *Begchīk* was another; all the Mughūls went off and, a little later, Sl. Aḥmad *Tambal.*

Aūzūn Ḥasan counted himself a very sincere and faithful

[1] This overstates the time; dates shew 1 yr. 1 mth. and a few days.

friend of Khwāja-i-qāẓī; we therefore, to put a stop to these desertions, sent the Khwāja to him (in Andijān) so that they, in agreement, might punish some of the deserters and send others back to us. But that very Aūzūn Ḥasan, that traitor to his salt, may have been the stirrer-up of the whole trouble and the spur-to-evil of the deserters from Samarkand. Directly Sl. Aḥmad *Tambal* had gone, all the rest took up a wrong position. Fol. 51*b*

(d. Andijān demanded of Bābur by The Khān, and also for Jahāngīr Mīrzā.)

Although, during the years in which, coveting Samarkand, I had persistently led my army out, Sl. Maḥmūd Khān[1] had provided me with no help whatever, yet, now it had been taken, he wanted Andijān. Moreover, Aūzūn Ḥasan and Sl. Aḥmad *Tambal*, just when soldiers of ours and all the Mughūls had deserted to Andijān and Akhsī, wanted those two districts for Jahāngīr Mīrzā. For several reasons, those districts could not be given to them. One was, that though not promised to The Khān, yet he had asked for them and, as he persisted in asking, an agreement with him was necessary, if they were to be given to Jahāngīr Mīrzā. A further reason was that to ask for them just when deserters from us had fled to them, was very like a command. If the matter had been brought forward earlier, some way of tolerating a command might have been found. At Fol. 52. the moment, as the Mughūls and the Andijān army and several even of my household had gone to Andijān, I had with me in Samarkand, beg for beg, good and bad, somewhere about 1000 men.

When Aūzūn Ḥasan and Sl. Aḥmad *Tambal* did not get what they wanted, they invited all those timid fugitives to join them. Just such a happening, those timid people, for their own sakes, had been asking of God in their terror. Hereupon, Aūzūn Ḥasan and Sl. Aḥmad *Tambal*, becoming openly hostile and rebellious, led their army from Akhsī against Andijān.

Tūlūn Khwāja was a bold, dashing, eager brave of the Bārīn (Mughūls). My father had favoured him and he was still in favour, I myself having raised him to the rank of beg. In

[1] *i.e.* The Khān of the Mughūls, Bābur's uncle.

truth he deserved favour, a wonderfully bold and dashing brave! He, as being the man I favoured amongst the Mughūls, was sent (after them) when they began to desert from Samarkand, to counsel the clans and to chase fear from their hearts so that
I. 52b. they might not turn their heads to the wind.[1] Those two traitors however, those false guides, had so wrought on the clans that nothing availed, promise or entreaty, counsel or threat. Tūlūn Khwāja's march lay through Aīkī-sū-ārāsī,[2] known also as Rabāṭik-aūrchīnī. Aūzūn Ḥasan sent a skirmishing party against him; it found him off his guard, seized and killed him. This done, they took Jahāngīr Mīrzā and went to besiege Andijān.

(*e. Bābur loses Andijān.*)

In Andijān when my army rode out for Samarkand, I had left Aūzūn Ḥasan and 'Alī-dost Ṭaghāī (Ramẓān 902AH.-May 1497 AD.). Khwāja-i-qāẓī had gone there later on, and there too were many of my men from Samarkand. During the siege, the Khwāja, out of good-will to me, apportioned 18,000 of his own sheep to the garrison and to the families of the men still with me. While the siege was going on, letters kept coming to me from my mothers[3] and from the Khwāja, saying in effect, 'They are besieging us in this way; if at our cry of distress you do not come, things will go all to ruin. Samarkand was taken
Fol. 53. by the strength of Andijān; if Andijān is in your hands, God willing, Samarkand can be had again.' One after another came letters to this purport. Just then I was recovering from illness but, not having been able to take due care in the days of convalescence, I went all to pieces again and this time, became so very ill that for four days my speech was impeded and they

[1] Elph. MS. *aūrmāghāīlār*, might not turn; Ḥai. and Kehr's MSS. (*sar bā bād*) *birmāghāīlār*, might not give. Both metaphors seem drawn from the protective habit of man and beast of turning the back to a storm-wind.

[2] *i.e.* betwixt two waters, the Miyān-i-dū-āb of India. Here, it is the most fertile triangle of land in Turkistān (Réclus, vi, 199), enclosed by the eastern mountains, the Nārīn and the Qarā-sū; Rabāṭik-aūrchīnī, its alternative name, means Small Station sub-district. From the uses of *aūrchīn* I infer that it describes a district in which there is no considerable head-quarters fort.

[3] *i.e.* his own, Qūtlūq-nigār Khānīm and hers, Aīsān-daulat Begīm, with perhaps other widows of his father, probably Shāh Sulṭān Begīm.

used to drop water into my mouth with cotton. Those with me, begs and bare braves alike, despairing of my life, began each to take thought for himself. While I was in this condition, the begs, by an error of judgment, shewed me to a servant of Aūzūn Ḥasan's, a messenger come with wild proposals, and then dismissed him. In four or five days, I became somewhat better but still could not speak, in another few days, was myself again.

Such letters so anxious, so beseeching, coming from my mothers, that is from my own and hers, Aīsān-daulat Begīm, and from my teacher and spiritual guide, that is, Khwāja-i-maulānā-i-qāẓī, with what heart would a man not move? We left Samarkand for Andijān on a Saturday in Rajab (Feb.-March), when I had ruled 100 days in the town. It was Saturday again when we reached Khujand and on that day a person brought news from Andijān, that seven days before, that is on the very day we had left Samarkand, 'Alī-dost Ṭaghāī had surrendered Andijān. Fol. 53*b*.

These are the particulars;—The servant of Aūzūn Ḥasan who, after seeing me, was allowed to leave, had gone to Andijān and there said, 'The *pādshāh* cannot speak and they are dropping water into his mouth with cotton.' Having gone and made these assertions in the ordinary way, he took oath in 'Alī-dost Ṭaghāī's presence. 'Alī-dost Ṭaghāī was in the Khākān Gate. Becoming without footing through this matter, he invited the opposite party into the fort, made covenant and treaty with them, and surrendered Andijān. Of provisions and of fighting men, there was no lack whatever; the starting point of the surrender was the cowardice of that false and faithless manikin; what was told him, he made a pretext to put himself in the right.

When the enemy, after taking possession of Andijān, heard of my arrival in Khujand, they martyred Khwāja-i-maulānā-i-qāẓī by hanging him, with dishonour, in the Gate of the citadel. Fol. 54.
He had come to be known as Khwāja-maulānā-i-qāẓī but his own name was 'Abdu'l-lāh. On his father's side, his line went back to Shaikh Burhānu'd-dīn 'Alī *Qīlīch*, on his mother's to Sl. Aīlīk *Māẓī*. This family had come to be the Religious

Guides (*muqtadā*) and pontiff (*Shaikhu'l-islām*) and Judge (*qāẓī*) in the Farghāna country.[1] He was a disciple of his Highness 'Ubaidu'l-lāh (*Aḥrārī*) and from him had his upbringing. I have no doubt he was a saint (*walī*); what better witnesses to his sanctity than the fact that within a short time, no sign or trace remained of those active for his death? He was a wonderful man; it was not in him to be afraid; in no other man was seen such courage as his. This quality is a further witness to his sanctity. Other men, however bold, have anxieties and tremours; he had none. When they had killed him, they seized and plundered those connected with him, retainers and servants, tribesmen and followers.

In anxiety for Andijān, we had given Samarkand out of our hands; then heard we had lost Andijān. It was like the saying, 'In ignorance, made to leave this place, shut out from that' (*Ghafil az īn jā rānda, az ān jā mānda*). It was very hard and vexing to me; for why? never since I had ruled, had I been cut
Fol. 54*b*. off like this from my retainers and my country; never since I had known myself, had I known such annoyance and such hardship.

(*f. Bābur's action from Khujand as his base.*)

On our arrival in Khujand, certain hypocrites, not enduring to see Khalīfa in my Gate, had so wrought on Muḥammad Ḥusain Mīrzā *Dūghlāt* and others that he was dismissed towards Tāshkīnt. To Tāshkīnt also Qāsim Beg *Qūchīn* had been sent earlier, in order to ask The Khān's help for a move on Andijān. The Khān consented to give it and came himself by way of the Ahangarān Dale,[2] to the foot of the Kīndīrlīk Pass.[3] There I went also, from Khujand, and saw my Khān dādā.[4] We then crossed the pass and halted on the Akhsī side. The enemy for their part, gathered their men and went to Akhsī.

[1] *Cf.* f. 16 for almost verbatim statements.
[2] Blacksmith's Dale. *Ahangarān* appears corrupted in modern maps to *Angren*. *See* H.S. ii, 293 for Khwānd-amīr's wording of this episode.
[3] *Cf.* f. 1*b* and Kostenko i, 101.
[4] *i.e.* Khān Uncle (Mother's brother).

Just at that time, the people in Pāp[1] sent me word they had made fast the fort but, owing to something misleading in The Khān's advance, the enemy stormed and took it. Though The Khān had other good qualities and was in other ways businesslike, he was much without merit as a soldier and commander. Just when matters were at the point that if he made one more march, it was most probable the country would be had without fighting, at such a time! he gave ear to what the enemy said with alloy of deceit, spoke of peace and, as his messengers, sent them Khwāja Abū'l-makāram and his own Lord of the Gate, Beg *Tilba* (Fool), *Tambal's* elder brother. Fol 55.
To save themselves those others (*i.e.* Ḥasan and Tambal) mixed something true with what they fabled and agreed to give gifts and bribes either to The Khān or to his intermediaries. With this, The Khān retired.

As the families of most of my begs and household and braves were in Andijān, 7 or 800 of the great and lesser begs and bare braves, left us in despair of our taking the place. Of the begs were 'Alī-darwesh Beg, 'Alī-mazīd *Qūchīn*, Muḥammad Bāqir Beg, Shaikh 'Abdu'l-lāh, Lord of the Gate and Mīrīm *Lāgharī*. Of men choosing exile and hardship with me, there may have been, of good and bad, between 200 and 300. Of begs there were Qāsim *Qūchīn* Beg, Wais *Lāgharī* Beg, Ibrāhīm *Sārū Mīnglīgh* Beg, Shīrīm Ṭaghāī, Sayyidī Qarā Beg; and of my household, Mīr Shāh *Qūchīn*, Sayyid Qāsim *Jalāīr*, Lord of the Gate, Qāsim-'ajab, 'Alī-dost Ṭaghāī's (son) Muḥammad-dost, Muḥammad-'alī *Mubashir*,[2] Khudāī-bīrdī *Tūghchī Mughūl*, Yārīk Ṭaghāī, Bābā 'Alī's (son) Bābā Qulī, Pīr Wais, Shaikh Wais, Fol. 55*b*.
Yār-'alī *Balāl*,[3] Qāsim *Mīr Akhwūr* (Chief Equerry) and Ḥaidar *Rikābdār* (stirrup-holder).

It came very hard on me; I could not help crying a good deal. Back I went to Khujand and thither they sent me my

[1] n.w. of the Sang ferry over the Sīr.

[2] perhaps, messenger of good tidings.

[3] This man's family connections are interesting. He was 'Alī-shukr Beg *Bahārlū's* grandson, nephew therefore of Pāshā Begīm; through his son, Saif-'alī Beg, he was the grandfather of Bairām Khān-i-khānān and thus the g.g.f. of 'Abdu'r-raḥīm Mīrzā, the translator of the Second *Wāqi'āt-i-bāburī*. *See* Firishta lith. ed. p. 250.

mother and my grandmother and the families of some of the men with me.

That Ramẓān (April-May) we spent in Khujand, then mounted for Samarkand. We had already sent to ask The Khān's help; he assigned, to act with us against Samarkand, his son, Sl. Muḥammad (Sulṭānīm) Khānika and (his son's guardian) Aḥmad Beg with 4 or 5000 men and rode himself as far as Aūrā-tīpā. There I saw him and from there went on by way of Yār-yīlāq, past the Būrka-yīlāq Fort, the head-quarters of the sub-governor (*dārogha*) of the district. Sl. Muḥammad Sulṭān and Aḥmad Beg, riding light and by another road, got to Yār-yīlāq first but on their hearing that Shaibānī Khān was raiding Shīrāz and thereabouts, turned back. There was no help for it! Back I too had to go. Again I went to Khujand!

As there was in me ambition for rule and desire of conquest, I did not sit at gaze when once or twice an affair had made no progress. Now I myself, thinking to make another move for
Fol. 56. Andijān, went to ask The Khān's help. Over and above this, it was seven or eight years since I had seen Shāh Begīm[1] and other relations; they also were seen under the same pretext. After a few days, The Khān appointed Sayyid Muḥammad Ḥusain (*Dūghlāt*) and Ayūb *Begchik* and Jān-ḥasan *Bārīn* with 7 or 8000 men to help us. With this help we started, rode light, through Khujand without a halt, left Kand-i-badām on the left and so to Nasūkh, 9 or 10 *yīghāch* of road beyond Khujand and 3 *yīghāch* (12-18 m.) from Kand-i-badām, there set our ladders up and took the fort. It was the melon season; one kind grown here, known as Ismā'īl Shaikhī, has a yellow rind, feels like shagreen leather, has seeds like an apple's and flesh four fingers thick. It is a wonderfully delicate melon; no other such grows thereabout. Next day the Mughūl begs represented to me, 'Our fighting men are few; to what would holding this one fort lead on?' In truth they were right; of what use was it to make that fort fast and stay there? Back once more to Khujand!

[1] Bābur's (step-)grandmother, co-widow with Aīsān-daulat of Yūnas Khān and mother of Aḥmad and Maḥmud *Chaghatāī*.

(*f. Affairs of Khusrau Shāh and the Tīmūrid Mīrzās*).[1]

This year Khusrau Shāh, taking Bāī-sunghar Mīrzā with him, led his army (from Qūndūz) to Chaghānīān and with false and treacherous intent, sent this message to Ḥiṣār for Sl. Mas'ūd Mīrzā, 'Come, betake yourself to Samarkand; if Samarkand is taken, one Mīrzā may seat himself there, the other in Ḥiṣār.' Just at the time, the Mīrzā's begs and household were displeased with him, because he had shewn excessive favour to his father-in-law, Shaikh 'Abdu'l-lāh *Barlās* who from Bāī-sunghar Mīrzā had gone to him. Small district though Ḥiṣār is, the Mīrzā had made the Shaikh's allowance 1,000 *tūmāns* of *fulūs*[2] and had given him the whole of Khutlān in which were the holdings of many of the Mīrzā's begs and household. All this Shaikh 'Abdu'l-lāh had; he and his sons took also in whole and in part, the control of the Mīrzā's gate. Those angered began, one after the other, to desert to Bāī-sunghar Mīrzā. Fol. 56b.

By those words of false alloy, having put Sl. Mas'ūd Mīrzā off his guard, Khusrau Shāh and Bāī-sunghar Mīrzā moved light out of Chaghānīān, surrounded Ḥiṣār and, at beat of morning-drum, took possession of it. Sl. Mas'ūd Mīrzā was in Daulat Sarāī, a house his father had built in the suburbs. Not being able to get into the fort, he drew off towards Khutlān with Shaikh 'Abu'l-lāh *Barlās*, parted from him half-way, crossed the river at the Aūbāj ferry and betook himself to Sl. Ḥusain Mīrzā. Khusrau Shāh, having taken Ḥiṣār, set Bāī-sunghar Mīrzā on the throne, gave Khutlān to his own younger brother, Walī and rode a few days later, to lay siege to Balkh where, with many of his father's begs, was Ibrāhīm Ḥusain Mīrzā (*Bāī-qarā*). He sent Naẓar *Bahādur*, his chief retainer, on in advance with 3 or 400 men to near Balkh, and himself taking Bāī-sunghar Mīrzā with him, followed and laid the siege. Fol. 5.

1 Here the narrative picks up the thread of Khusrau Shāh's affairs, dropped on f. 44.

2 *ming tūmān fulūs*, *i.e.* a thousand sets-of-ten-thousand small copper coins. Mr. Erskine (Mems. p. 61) here has a note on coins. As here the *tūmān* does not seem to be a coin but a number, I do not reproduce it, valuable as it is *per se*.

Walī he sent off with a large force to besiege Shabarghān and raid and ravage thereabouts. Walī, for his part, not being able to lay close siege, sent his men off to plunder the clans and hordes of the Zardak Chūl, and they took him back over 100,000 sheep and some 3000 camels. He then came, plundering the Sān-chīrīk country on his way, and raiding and making captive the clans fortified in the hills, to join Khusrau Shāh before Balkh.

One day during the siege, Khusrau Shāh sent the Naẓar *Bahādur* already mentioned, to destroy the water-channels[1] of
Fol. 57*b*. Balkh. Out on him sallied Tīngrī-bīrdī *Samānchī*,[2] Sl. Ḥusain Mīrzā's favourite beg, with 70 or 80 men, struck him down, cut off his head, carried it off, and went back into the fort. A very bold sally, and he did a striking deed.

(*g. Affairs of Sl. Ḥusain Mīrzā and Badī'u'z-zamān Mīrzā.*)

This same year, Sl. Ḥusain Mīrzā led his army out to Bast and there encamped,[3] for the purpose of putting down Ẕū'n-nūn *Arghūn* and his son, Shāh Shujā', because they had become Badī'u'z-zamān Mīrzā's retainers, had given him a daughter of Ẕū'n-nūn in marriage and taken up a position hostile to himself. No corn for his army coming in from any quarter, it had begun to be distressed with hunger when the sub-governor of Bast surrendered. By help of the stores of Bast, the Mīrzā got back to Khurāsān.

Since such a great ruler as Sl. Ḥusain Mīrzā had twice led a splendid and well-appointed army out and twice retired, without taking Qūndūz, or Ḥiṣār or Qandahār, his sons and his begs waxed bold in revolt and rebellion. In the spring of this year, he sent a large army under Muḥammad Walī Beg to put down (his son) Muḥammad Ḥusain Mīrzā who, supreme in Astarābād, had taken up a position hostile to himself. While Sl. Ḥusain Mīrzā was still lying in the Nīshīn meadow (near

1 *āriqlār*; this the annotator of the Elph. MS. has changed to *āshliq* provisions, corn.

2 *Samān-chī* may mean Keeper of the Goods. Tīngrī-bīrdī, Theodore, is the purely Turkī form of the Khudāī-bīrdī, already met with several times in the B.N.

3 Bast (Bost) is on the left bank of the Halmand.

Harāt), he was surprised by Badī'u'z-zamān Mīrzā and Shāh Shujā' Beg (*Arghūn*). By unexpected good-fortune, he had been joined that very day by Sl. Mas'ūd Mīrzā, a refugee after bringing about the loss of Ḥiṣār,[1] and also rejoined by a force of his own returning from Astarābād. There was no question of fighting. Badī'u'z-zamān Mīrzā and Shāh Beg, brought face to face with these armies, took to flight. Fol. 58.

Sl. Ḥusain Mīrzā looked kindly on Sl. Mas'ūd Mīrzā, made him kneel as a son-in-law and gave him a place in his favour and affection. None-the-less Sl. Mas'ūd Mīrzā, at the instigation of Bāqī *Chaghānīānī*, who had come earlier into Sl. Ḥusain Mīrzā's service, started off on some pretext, without asking leave, and went from the presence of Sl. Ḥusain Mīrzā to that of Khusrau Shāh!

Khusrau Shāh had already invited and brought from Ḥiṣār, Bāī-sunghar Mīrzā; to him had gone Aūlūgh Beg Mīrzā's son,[2] Mīrān-shāh Mīrzā who, having gone amongst the Hazāra in rebellion against his father, had been unable to remain amongst them because of his own immoderate acts. Some short-sighted persons were themselves ready to kill these three (Tīmūrid) Mīrzās and to read Khusrau Shāh's name in the *khuṭba* but he himself did not think this combination desirable. The ungrateful manikin however, for the sake of gain in this five days' fleeting world,—it was not true to him nor will it be true to any man soever,—seized that Sl. Mas'ūd Mīrzā whom he had seen grow up in his charge from childhood, whose guardian he had been, and blinded him with the lancet. Fol. 58*b*.

Some of the Mīrzā's foster-brethren and friends of affection and old servants took him to Kesh intending to convey him to his (half)-brother Sl. 'Alī Mīrzā in Samarkand but as that party also (*i.e.* 'Alī's) became threatening, they fled with him, crossed the river at the Aūbāj ferry and went to Sl. Ḥusain Mīrzā.

[1] *Cf.* f. 56*b*.

[2] known as *Kābulī*. He was a son of Abū-sa'īd and thus an uncle of Bābur. He ruled Kābul and Ghaznī from a date previous to his father's death in 873 AH. (perhaps from the time 'Umar Shaikh was *not* sent there, in 870 AH. *See* f. 6*b*) to his death in 907 AH. Bābur was his virtual successor in Kābul, in 910 AH.

A hundred thousand curses light on him who planned and did a deed so horrible! Up to the very verge of Resurrection, let him who hears of this act of Khusrau Shāh, curse him; and may he who hearing, curses not, know cursing equally deserved!

This horrid deed done, Khusrau Shāh made Bāī-sunghar Mīrzā ruler in Ḥiṣār and dismissed him; Mīrān-shāh Mīrzā he despatched for Bāmīān with Sayyid Qāsim to help him.

904 AH.—AUG. 19TH. 1498 TO AUG. 8TH. 1499 AD.[1]

(*a. Bābur borrows Pashāghar and leaves Khujand.*)

Twice we had moved out of Khujand, once for Andijān, once for Samarkand, and twice we had gone back to it because our work was not opened out.[2] Khujand is a poor place; a man with 2 or 300 followers would have a hard time there; with what outlook would an ambitious man set himself down in it? Fol. 59.

As it was our wish to return to Samarkand, we sent people to confer with Muḥammad Ḥusain *Kūrkān Dūghlāt* in Aūrā-tīpā and to ask of him the loan for the winter of Pashāghar where we might sit till it was practicable to make a move on Samarkand. He consenting, I rode out from Khujand for Pashāghar.

(*Author's note on Pashāghar.*) Pashāghar is one of the villages of Yār-yīlāq; it had belonged to his Highness the Khwāja,[3] but during recent interregna,[4] it had become dependent on Muḥammad Ḥusain Mīrzā.

I had fever when we reached *Zamīn*, but spite of my fever we hurried off by the mountain road till we came over against Rabāṯ-i-khwāja, the head-quarters of the sub-governor of the Shavdār *tūmān*, where we hoped to take the garrison at unawares, set our ladders up and so get into the

[1] Elph. MS. f. 42; W.-i-B. I.O. 215 f. 47*b* and 217 f. 38; Mems. p. 63. Bābur here resumes his own story, interrupted on f. 56.

[2] *aīsh achīlmādī*, a phrase recurring on f. 59*b* foot. It appears to imply, of trust in Providence, what the English "The way was not opened," does. *Cf.* f. 60*b* for another example of trust, there clinching discussion whether to go or not to go to Marghīnān.

[3] *i.e. Aḥrārī*. He had been dead some 10 years The despoilment of his family is mentioned on f. 23*b*.

[4] *fatratlār*, here those due to the deaths of Aḥmad and Maḥmūd with their sequel of unstable government in Samarkand.

fort. We reached it at dawn, found its men on guard, turned back and rode without halt to Pashāghar. The pains and misery of fever notwithstanding, I had ridden 14 or 15 *yīghāch* (70 to 80 miles).

After a few days in Pashāghar, we appointed Ibrāhīm *Sārū*, Fol. 59*b*. Wais *Lāgharī*, Sherīm Ṭaghāī and some of the household and braves to make an expedition amongst the Yār-yīlāq forts and get them into our hands. Yār-yīlāq, at that time was Sayyid Yūsuf Beg's,[1] he having remained in Samarkand at the exodus and been much favoured by Sl. 'Ali Mīrzā. To manage the forts, Sayyid Yūsuf had sent his younger brother's son, Aḥmad-i-yūsuf, now[2] Governor of Sialkot, and Aḥmad-i-yūsuf was then in occupation. In the course of that winter, our begs and braves made the round, got possession of some of the forts peacefully, fought and took others, gained some by ruse and craft. In the whole of that district there is perhaps not a single village without its defences because of the Mughūls and the Aūzbegs. Meantime Sl. 'Alī Mīrzā became suspicious of Sayyid Yūsuf and his nephew on my account and dismissed both towards Khurāsān.

The winter passed in this sort of tug-of-war; with the on-coming heats,[3] they sent Khwāja Yaḥya to treat with me, while they, urged on by the (Samarkand) army, marched out to near Shīrāz and Kabud. I may have had 200 or 300 soldiers (*sipāhī*); powerful foes were on my every side; Fortune had Fol. 60. not favoured me when I turned to Andijān; when I put a hand out for Samarkand, no work was opened out. Of necessity, some sort of terms were made and I went back from Pashāghar.

Khujand is a poor place; one beg would have a hard time in it; there we and our families and following had been for half a

[1] *Aūghlāqchī*, the player of the kid-game, the gray-wolfer. Yār-yīlāq will have gone with the rest of Samarkand into 'Alī's hands in Rajab 903 AH. (March 1498). Contingent terms between him and Bābur will have been made; Yūsuf may have recognized some show of right under them, for allowing Bābur to occupy Yār-yīlāq.

[2] *i.e.* after 933 AH. *Cf.* f. 46*b* and note concerning the Bikramāditya era. See index *s.n.* Aḥmad-i-yūsuf and Ḥ.S. ii, 293.

[3] This plural, unless ironical, cannot be read as honouring 'Alī; Bābur uses the honorific plural most rarely and specially, *e.g.* for saintly persons, for The Khān and for elder women-kinsfolk.

year[1] and during the time the Musalmāns of the place had not been backward in bearing our charges and serving us to the best of their power. With what face could we go there again? and what, for his own part, could a man do there? 'To what home to go? For what gain to stay?'[2]

In the end and with the same anxieties and uncertainty, we went to the summer-pastures in the south of Aūrā-tīpā. There we spent some days in amazement at our position, not knowing where to go or where to stay, our heads in a whirl. On one of those days, Khwāja Abū'l-makāram came to see me, he like me, a wanderer, driven from his home.[3] He questioned us about our goings and stayings, about what had or had not been done and about our whole position. He was touched with compassion for our state and recited the *fātiḥa* for me before he left. I also was much touched; I pitied him.

(b. Bābur recovers Marghīnān.)

Near the Afternoon Prayer of that same day, a horseman appeared at the foot of the valley. He was a man named Yūl-chūq, presumably 'Ali-dost Ṭaghāī's own servant, and had been sent with this written message, 'Although many great misdeeds have had their rise in me, yet, if you will do me the Fol. 60*b*. favour and kindness of coming to me, I hope to purge my offences and remove my reproach, by giving you Marghīnān and by my future submission and single-minded service.'

Such news! coming on such despair and whirl-of-mind! Off we hurried, that very hour,—it was sun-set,—without reflecting, without a moment's delay, just as if for a sudden raid, straight for Marghīnān. From where we were to Marghīnān may have been 24 or 25 *yīghāch* of road.[4] Through that night it was rushed without delaying anywhere, and on

[1] *bīr yārīm yīl*. Dates shew this to mean six months. It appears a parallel expression to Pers. *hasht-yak*, one-eighth.

[2] Ḥ.S. ii, 293, in place of these two quotations, has a *misra'*,—*Na rāy ṣafar kardan u na rūy iqāmat*, (Nor resolve to march, nor face to stay).

[3] *i.e.* in Samarkand.

[4] Point to point, some 145 m. but much further by the road. Tang-āb seems likely to be one of the head-waters of Khwāja Bikargān-water. Thence the route would be by unfrequented hill-tracks, each man leading his second horse.

next day till at the Mid-day Prayer, halt was made at Tang-āb (Narrow-water), one of the villages of Khujand. There we cooled down our horses and gave them corn. We rode out again at beat of (twilight-) drum[1] and on through that night till shoot of dawn, and through the next day till sunset, and on through that night till, just before dawn, we were one *yīghāch* from Marghīnān. Here Wais Beg and others represented to me with some anxiety what sort of an evil-doer 'Ali-dost was. 'No-one,' they said, 'has come and gone, time and again, between him and us; no terms and compact have been made; trusting to what are we going?' In truth their fears were just! After waiting awhile to consult, we at last agreed that
Fol. 61. reasonable as anxiety was, it ought to have been earlier; that there we were after coming three nights and two days without rest or halt; in what horse or in what man was any strength left?—from where we were, how could return be made? and, if made, where were we to go?—that, having come so far, on we must, and that nothing happens without God's will. At this we left the matter and moved on, our trust set on Him.

At the Sunnat Prayer[2] we reached Fort Marghīnān. 'Alī-dost Ṭaghāī kept himself behind (*arqa*) the closed gate and asked for terms; these granted, he opened it. He did me obeisance between the (two) gates.[3] After seeing him, we dismounted at a suitable house in the walled-town. With me, great and small, were 240 men.

As Aūzūn Ḥasan and Tambal had been tyrannical and oppressive, all the clans of the country were asking for me. We therefore, after two or three days spent in Marghīnān, joined to Qāsim Beg over a hundred men of the Pashāgharīs, the new retainers of Marghīnān and of 'Alī-dost's following, and sent them to bring over to me, by force or fair words, such

1 *tūn yārīmī naqāra waqtīdā. Tūn yārīmī* seems to mean half-dark, twilight. Here it cannot mean mid-night since this would imply a halt of twelve hours and Bābur says no halt was made. The drum next following mid-day is the one beaten at sunset.

2 The voluntary prayer, offered when the sun has well risen, fits the context.

3 I understand that the obeisance was made in the Gate-house, betweer the inner and outer doors.

hill-people of the south of Andijān as the Ashpārī, Tūrūqshār, Chīkrāk and others roundabout. Ibrāhīm Sārū and Wais *Lāgharī* and Sayyidī Qarā were also sent out, to cross the Khujand-water and, by whatever means, to induce the people on that side to turn their eyes to me. Fol. 61*b*.

Aūzūn Ḥasan and Tambal, for their parts, gathered together what soldiers and Mughūls they had and called up the men accustomed to serve in the Andijān and Akhsī armies. Then, bringing Jahāngīr Mīrzā with them, they came to Sapān, a village 2m. east of Marghīnān, a few days after our arrival, and dismounted there with the intention of besieging Marghīnān. They advanced a day or two later, formed up to fight, as far as the suburbs. Though after the departure of the Commanders, Qāsim Beg. Ibrāhīm *Sārū* and Wais *Lāgharī*, few men were left with me, those there were formed up, sallied out and prevented the enemy from advancing beyond the suburbs. On that day, Page Khalīl, the turban-twister, went well forward and got his hand into the work. They had come; they could do nothing; on two other days they failed to get near the fort. Fol. 62.

When Qāsim Beg went into the hills on the south of Andijān, all the Ashpārī, Tūrūqshār, Chīkrāk, and the peasants and highland and lowland clans came in for us. When the Commanders, Ibrāhīm *Sārū* and Wais *Lāgharī*, crossed the river to the Akhsī side, Pāp and several other forts came in.

Aūzūn Ḥasan and Tambal being the heathenish and vicious tyrants they were, had inflicted great misery on the peasantry and clansmen. One of the chief men of Akhsī, Ḥasan-dīkcha by name,[1] gathered together his own following and a body of the Akhsī mob and rabble, black-bludgeoned[2] Aūzūn Ḥasan's and Tambal's men in the outer fort and drubbed them into the citadel. They then invited the Commanders, Ibrāhīm *Sārū*, Wais *Lāgharī* and Sayyidī Qarā and admitted them into the fort.

Sl. Maḥmūd Khān had appointed to help us, Ḥaidar *Kūkūldāsh's* (son) Banda-'alī and Ḥājī Ghāzī *Manghīt*,[3] the latter

[1] This seeming sobriquet may be due to eloquence or to good looks.

[2] *qarā tīyāq*. *Cf*. f. 63 where black bludgeons are used by a red rabble.

[3] He was head-man of his clan and again with Shaibānī in 909 AH. (Sh. N. Vambéry, p. 272). Erskine (p. 67) notes that the Manghīts are the modern Nogais.

just then a fugitive from 'Shaibānī Khān, and also the Bārīn *tūmān* with its begs. They arrived precisely at this time.

Fol. 62b. These news were altogether upsetting to Aūzūn Ḥasan; he at once started off his most favoured retainers and most serviceable braves to help his men in the citadel of Akhsī. His force reached the brow of the river at dawn. Our Commanders and the (Tāshkīnt) Mughūls had heard of its approach and had made some of their men strip their horses and cross the river (to the Andijān side). Aūzūn Ḥasan's men, in their haste, did not draw the ferry-boat up-stream;[1] they consequently went right away from the landing-place, could not cross for the fort and went down stream.[2] Here-upon, our men and the (Tāshkīnt) Mughūls began to ride bare-back into the water from both banks. Those in the boat could make no fight at all. Qārlūghāch (var. Qārbūghāch) *Bakhshī* (Pay-master) called one of Mughūl Beg's sons to him, took him by the hand, chopped at him and killed him. Of what use was it? The affair was past that! His act was the cause why most of those in the boat went to their death. Instantly our men seized them all (*arīq*) and killed all (but a few).[3] Of Aūzūn Ḥasan's confidants escaped Qārlūghāch *Bakhshī* and Khalīl *Dīwān* and Qāẓī *Ghulām*, the last getting off by pretending to be a slave (*ghulām*); and of his trusted braves, Sayyid 'Alī, now in trust in my own service,[4] and Ḥaidar-i-qulī and Qilka *Kāshgharī* escaped. Of his 70 or 80 men, no more than this

Fol. 63. same poor five or six got free.

On hearing of this affair, Aūzūn Ḥasan and Tambal, not being able to remain near Marghīnān, marched in haste and disorder for Andijān. There they had left Nāṣir Beg, the husband of Aūzūn Ḥasan's sister. He, if not Aūzūn Ḥasan's second, what question is there he was his third?[5] He was an

[1] *i.e.* in order to allow for the here very swift current. The H.S. varying a good deal in details from the B.N. gives the useful information that Aūzūn Ḥasan's men knew nothing of the coming of the Tāshkīnt Mughūls.

[2] *Cf.* f. 4b and App. A. as to the position of Akhsī.

[3] *bārīnī qīrdīlār.* After this statement the five exceptions are unexpected; Bābur's wording is somewhat confused here.

[4] *i.e.* in Hindūstān.

[5] Tambal would be the competitor for the second place.

experienced man, brave too; when he heard particulars, he knew their ground was lost, made Andijān fast and sent a man to me. They broke up in disaccord when they found the fort made fast against them; Aūzūn Ḥasan drew off to his wife in Akhsī, Tambal to his district of Aūsh. A few of Jahāngīr Mirzā's household and braves fled with him from Aūzūn Ḥasan and joined Tambal before he had reached Aūsh.

(*c. Bābur recovers Andijān.*)

Directly we heard that Andijān had been made fast against them, I rode out, at sun-rise, from Marghīnān and by mid-day was in Andijān.[1] There I saw Nāṣir Beg and his two sons, that is to say, Dost Beg and Mīrīm Beg, questioned them and uplifted their heads with hope of favour and kindness. In this way, by God's grace, my father's country, lost to me for two years, was regained and re-possessed, in the month Ẕū'l-qa'da of the date 904 (June 1498).[2] Fol. 63*b*.

Sl. Aḥmad Tambal, after being joined by Jahāngīr Mīrzā, drew away for Aūsh. On his entering the town, the red rabble (*qīzīl ayāq*) there, as in Akhsī, black-bludgeoned (*qarā tīyāq qīlīb*) and drubbed his men out, blow upon blow, then kept the fort for me and sent me a man. Jahāngīr and Tambal went off confounded, with a few followers only, and entered Aūzkīnt Fort.

Of Aūzūn Ḥasan news came that after failing to get into Andijān, he had gone to Akhsī and, it was understood, had entered the citadel. He had been head and chief in the rebellion; we therefore, on getting this news, without more than four or five days' delay in Andijān, set out for Akhsī. On our arrival, there was nothing for him to do but ask for peace and terms, and surrender the fort.

We stayed in Akhsī[3] a few days in order to settle its affairs

[1] 47 m. 4½ fur.

[2] Bābur had been about two lunar years absent from Andijān but his loss of rule was of under 16 months.

[3] A scribe's note entered here on the margin of the Ḥai. MS. is to the effect that certain words are not in the noble archetype (*nashka sharīf*); this supports other circumstances which make for the opinion that this Codex is a direct copy of Bābur's own MS. *See* Index s.n. Ḥai. MS. and JRAS 1906, p. 87.

and those of Kāsān and that country-side. We gave the Mughūls who had come in to help us, leave for return (to Tāshkīnt), then went back to Andijān, taking with us Aūzūn Ḥasan and his family and dependants. In Akhsī was left, for a time, Qāsim-i-'ajab (Wonderful Qāsim), formerly one of the household circle, now arrived at beg's rank.

(d. Renewed rebellion of the Mughūls.)

As terms had been made, Aūzūn Ḥasan, without hurt to life
Fol. 64. or goods, was allowed to go by the Qarā-tīgīn road for Ḥiṣār. A few of his retainers went with him, the rest parted from him and stayed behind. These were the men who in the throne-less times had captured and plundered various Musalmān dependants of my own and of the Khwāja. In agreement with several begs, their affair was left at this;—'This very band have been the captors and plunderers of our faithful Musalmān dependants;[1] what loyalty have they shown to their own (Mughūl) begs that they should be loyal to us? If we had them seized and stripped bare, where would be the wrong? and this especially because they might be going about, before our very eyes, riding our horses, wearing our coats, eating our sheep. Who could put up with that? If, out of humanity, they are not imprisoned and not plundered, they certainly ought to take it as a favour if they get off with the order to give back to our companions of the hard guerilla times, whatever goods of theirs are known to be here.'

In truth this seemed reasonable; our men were ordered to take what they knew to be theirs. Reasonable and just though the order was, (I now) understand that it was a little hasty.
Fol. 64b. With a worry like Jahāngīr seated at my side, there was no sense in frightening people in this way. In conquest and government, though many things may have an outside appearance of reason and justice, yet 100,000 reflections are right and necessary as to the bearings of each one of them. From this single incautious order of ours,[2] what troubles! what rebellions

[1] *Musalmān* here seems to indicate mental contrast with Pagan practices or neglect of Musalmān observances amongst Mughūls.

[2] *i.e.* of his advisors and himself.

arose! In the end this same ill-considered order was the cause of our second exile from Andijān. Now, through it, the Mughūls gave way to anxiety and fear, marched through Rabāṯik-aūrchīnī, that is, Aīkī-sū-ārāsī, for Aūzkīnt and sent a man to Taṃbal.

In my mother's service were 1500 to 2000 Mughūls from the horde; as many more had come from Ḥiṣār with Ḥamza Sl. and Mahdī Sl. and Muḥammad *Dūghlāt Ḥiṣārī*.[1] Mischief and devastation must always be expected from the Mughūl horde. Up to now[2] they have rebelled five times against me. It must not be understood that they rebelled through not getting on with me; they have done the same thing with their own Khāns, again and again. Sl. Qulī *Chūnāq*[3] brought me the news. His late father, Khudāī-bīrdī *Būqāq*[4] I had favoured amongst the Mughūls; he was himself with the (rebel) Mughūls Fol. 65. and he did well in thus leaving the horde and his own family to bring me the news. Well as he did then however, he, as will be told,[5] did a thing so shameful later on that it would hide a hundred such good deeds as this, if he had done them. His later action was the clear product of his Mughūl nature. When this news came, the begs, gathered for counsel, represented to me, 'This is a trifling matter; what need for the pādshāh to ride out? Let Qāsim Beg go with the begs and men assembled here.' So it was settled; they took it lightly; to do so must have been an error of judgment. Qāsim Beg led his force out that same day; Taṃbal meantime must have joined the Mughūls. Our men crossed the Aīlāīsh river[6] early next morning by the Yāsī-kījīt (Broad-crossing) and at once came face to

[1] *Cf.* f. 34.

[2] *circa* 933 AH. All the revolts chronicled by Bābur as made against himself were under Mughūl leadership. Long Ḥasan, Taṃbal and 'Alī-dost were all Mughūls. The worst was that of 914 AH. (1518 AD.) in which Qulī *Chūnāq* disgraced himself (T.R. p. 357).

[3] *Chūnāq* may indicate the loss of one ear.

[4] *Būqāq*, amongst other meanings, has that of *one who lies in ambush*.

[5] This remark has interest because it shews that (as Bābur planned to write more than is now with the B.N. MSS.) the first gap in the book (914 AH. to 925 AH.) is accidental. His own last illness is the probable cause of this gap. *Cf.* JRAS 1905, p. 744. Two other passages referring to unchronicled matters are one about the Bāgh-i-ṣafā (f. 224, and one about Sl. 'Alī Ṯaghāī (f. 242).

[6] I surmise Aīlāīsh to be a local name of the Qarā-daryā affluent of the Sīr.

face with the rebels. Well did they chop at one another (*chāpqūlāshūrlār*)! Qāsim Beg himself came face to face with Muḥammad *Arghūn* and did not desist from chopping at him in order to cut off his head.[1] Most of our braves exchanged
Fol. 65*b*. good blows but in the end were beaten. Qāsim Beg, 'Alī-dost Ṭaghāī, Ibrāhīm *Sārū*, Wais *Lāgharī*, Sayyidī Qarā and three or four more of our begs and household got away but most of the rest fell into the hands of the rebels. Amongst them were 'Alī-darwesh Beg and Mīrīm *Lāgharī* and (Sherīm ?) Ṭaghāī Beg's (son) Tūqā[2] and 'Alī-dost's son, Muḥammad-dost and Mīr Shāh *Qūchīn* and Mīrīm Dīwān.

Two braves chopped very well at one another; on our side, Samad, Ibrāhīm *Sārū's* younger brother, and on their side, Shāh-suwār, one of the Ḥiṣārī Mughūls. Shāh-suwār struck so that his sword drove through Samad's helm and seated itself well in his head; Samad, spite of his wound, struck so that his sword cut off Shāh-suwār's head a piece of bone as large as the palm of a hand. Shāh-suwār must have worn no helm; they trepanned his head and it healed; there was no one to trepan Samad's and in a few days, he departed simply through the wound.[3]

Amazingly unseasonable was this defeat, coming as it did just in the respite from guerilla fighting and just when we had regained the country. One of our great props, Qambar-'alī *Mughūl* (the Skinner) had gone to his district when Andijān
Fol. 66. was occupied and therefore was not with us.

(*e. Tambal attempts to take Andijān.*)

Having effected so much, Tambal, bringing Jāhāngīr Mīrzā with him, came to the east of Andijān and dismounted 2 miles off, in the meadow lying in front of the Hill of Pleasure ('Aīsh).[4]

[1] *aikī aūch naubat chāpqūlāb bāsh chīqārghalī qūīmās.* I cannot feel so sure as Mr. E. and M. de C. were that the man's head held fast, especially as for it to fall would make the better story.

[2] Tūqā appears to have been the son of a Ṭaghāī, perhaps of Sherīm; his name may imply blood-relationship.

[3] For the verb *awīmāq*, to trepan, *see* f. 67 note 5.

[4] The Fr. map of 1904 shews a hill suiting Bābur's location of this Hill of Pleasure.

Once or twice he advanced in battle-array, past Chihil-dukhterān[1] to the town side of the hill but, as our braves went out arrayed to fight, beyond the gardens and suburbs, he could not advance further and returned to the other side of the hill. On his first coming to those parts, he killed two of the begs he had captured, Mīrīm *Lāgharī* and Tūqā Beg. For nearly a month he lay round-about without effecting anything; after that he retired, his face set for Aūsh. Aūsh had been given to Ibrāhīm *Sārū* and his man in it now made it fast.

[1] A place near Kābul bears the same name; in both the name is explained by a legend that there Earth opened a refuge for forty menaced daughters.

905 AH. AUG. 8TH. 1499 TO JULY 28TH. 1500 AD.[1]

(*a. Bābur's campaign against Aḥmad Taṃbal Mughūl.*)

Commissaries were sent gallopping off at once, some to call up the horse and foot of the district-armies, others to urge return on Qaṃbar-'alī and whoever else was away in his own district, while energetic people were told off to get together mantelets (*tūra*), shovels, axes and the what-not of war-material and stores for the men already with us.

As soon as the horse and foot, called up from the various districts to join the army, and the soldiers and retainers who had been scattered to this and that side on their own affairs, were gathered together, I went out, on Muḥarram 18th. (August 25th.), putting my trust in God, to Ḥāfiẓ Beg's Four-
Fol. 66b. gardens and there stayed a few days in order to complete our equipment. This done, we formed up in array of right and left, centre and van, horse and foot, and started direct for Aūsh against our foe.

On approaching Aūsh, news was had that Taṃbal, unable to make stand in that neighbourhood, had drawn off to the north, to the Rabāṭ-i-sarhang sub-district, it was understood. That night we dismounted in Lāt-kīnt. Next day as we were passing through Aūsh, news came that Taṃbal was understood to have gone to Andijān. We, for our part, marched on as for Aūzkīnt, detaching raiders ahead to over-run those parts.[2] Our opponents went to Andijān and at night got into the ditch but being discovered by the garrison when they set their ladders up against the ramparts, could effect no more and retired. Our raiders

[1] Elph. MS. f. 47*b*; W.-i-B. I.O. 215 f. 53 and 217 f. 43; Mems. p. 70.

[2] From Andijān to Aūsh is a little over 33 miles. Taṃbal's road was east of Bābur's and placed him between Andijān and Aūzkīnt where was the force protecting his family.

retired also after over-running round about Aūzkīnt without getting into their hands anything worth their trouble.

Tambal had stationed his younger brother, Khalīl, with 200 or 300 men, in Mādū,[1] one of the forts of Aūsh, renowned in that centre (*ārā*) for its strength. We turned back (on the Aūzkīnt road) to assault it. It is exceedingly strong. Its northern face stands very high above the bed of a torrent; arrows shot from the bed might perhaps reach the ramparts. On this side is the water-thief,[2] made like a lane, with ramparts on both sides carried from the fort to the water. Towards the rising ground, on the other sides of the fort, there is a ditch. The torrent being so near, those occupying the fort had carried stones in from it as large as those for large mortars.[3] From no fort of its class we have ever attacked, have stones been thrown so large as those taken into Mādū. They dropped such a large one on 'Abdu'l-qāsim *Kohbur*, Kitta (Little) Beg's elder brother,[4] when he went up under the ramparts, that he spun head over heels and came rolling and rolling, without once getting to his feet, from that great height down to the foot of the glacis (*khāk-rez*). He did not trouble himself about it at all but just got on his horse and rode off. Again, a stone flung from the double water-way, hit Yār-'alī *Balāl* so hard on the head that in the end it had to be trepanned.[5] Many of our men perished by their stones. The assault began at dawn; the water-thief had been taken before breakfast-time;[6] fighting went on till evening; next morning, as they could not hold out after losing the water-thief, they asked for terms and came out. We took 60 or 70 or 80 men of Khalīl's command and sent them to Andijān for safe-keeping; as some of our begs and household were prisoners in their hands, the Mādū affair fell out very well.[7]

Fol. 67.

Fol. 67*b*

[1] mod. Mazy, on the main Aūsh-Kāshghar road.

[2] *āb-duzd*; de C. i, 144, *prise d'eau*.

[3] This simile seems the fruit of experience in Hindūstān. *See* f. 333, concerning Chānderi.

[4] These two Mughūls rebelled in 914 AH. with Sl. Qulī *Chūnāq* (T.R. *s.n.*).

[5] *awidī*. The head of Captain Dow, fractured at Chunār by a stone flung at it, was trepanned (*Saiyār-i-muta'akhirīn*, p. 577 and Irvine l.c. p. 283). Yār-'alī was alive in 910 AH. He seems to be the father of the great Bairām Khān-i-khānān of Akbar's reign.

[6] *chasht-gāh*; midway between sunrise and noon.

[7] *tauri*; because providing prisoners for exchange.

From there we went to Unjū-tūpa, one of the villages of Aūsh, and there dismounted. When Taṃbal retired from Andijān and went into the Rabāṭ-i-sarhang sub-district, he dismounted in a village called Āb-i-khān. Between him and me may have been one *yīghāch* (5 m.?). At such a time as this, Qaṃbar-'alī (the Skinner) on account of some sickness, went into Aūsh.

It was lain in Unjū-tūpa a month or forty days without a battle, but day after day our foragers and theirs got to grips. All through the time our camp was mightily well watched at night; a ditch was dug; where no ditch was, branches were set close together;[1] we also made our soldiers go out in their mail
Fol. 68. along the ditch. Spite of such watchfulness, a night-alarm was given every two or three days, and the cry to arms went up. One day when Sayyidī Beg Ṭaghāī had gone out with the foragers, the enemy came up suddenly in greater strength and took him prisoner right out of the middle of the fight.

(*b. Bāī-sunghar Mīrzā murdered by Khusrau Shāh.*)

Khusrau Shāh, having planned to lead an army against Balkh, in this same year invited Bāī-sunghar Mīrzā to go with him, brought him[2] to Qūndūz and rode out with him for Balkh. But when they reached the Aubāj ferry, that ungrateful infidel, Khusrau Shāh, in his aspiration to sovereignty,—and to what sort of sovereignty, pray, could such a no-body attain? a person of no merit, no birth, no lineage, no judgment, no magnanimity, no justice, no legal-mindedness,—laid hands on Bāī-sunghar Mīrzā with his begs, and bowstrung the Mīrzā. It was upon the 10th. of the month of Muḥarram (August 17th.) that he martyred that scion of sovereignty, so accomplished, so sweet-natured and so adorned by birth and lineage. He killed also a few of the Mīrzā's begs and household.

(*c. Bāī-sunghar Mīrzā's birth and descent.*)

He was born in 882 (1477 AD.), in the Ḥiṣār district. He was Sl. Maḥmūd Mīrzā's second son, younger than Sl. Mas'ud

[1] *shakh tūtūlūr idī*, perhaps a palisade.
[2] *i.e.* from Ḥiṣār where he had placed him in 903 AH.

M. and older than Sl. 'Alī M. and Sl. Ḥusain M. and Sl. Wais M. known as Khān Mīrzā. His mother was Pasha Begīm. Fol. 68*b*.

(*d. His appearance and characteristics.*)

He had large eyes, a fleshy face[1] and Turkmān features, was of middle height and altogether an elegant young man (*aet.* 22).

(*e. His qualities and manners.*)

He was just, humane, pleasant-natured and a most accomplished scion of sovreignty. His tutor, Sayyid Maḥmūd,[2] presumably was a Shī'a; through this he himself became infected by that heresy. People said that latterly, in Samarkand, he reverted from that evil belief to the pure Faith. He was much addicted to wine but on his non-drinking days, used to go through the Prayers.[3] He was moderate in gifts and liberality. He wrote the *naskh-ta'līq* character very well; in painting also his hand was not bad. He made 'Ādilī his pen-name and composed good verses but not sufficient to form a *dīwān*. Here is the opening couplet (*maṭla'*) of one of them[4];—

> Like a wavering shadow I fall here and there ;
> If not propped by a wall, I drop flat on the ground.

In such repute are his odes held in Samarkand, that they are to be found in most houses.

(*f. His battles.*)

He fought two ranged battles. One, fought when he was first seated on the throne (900 AH.-1495 AD.), was with Sl. Maḥmūd Khān[5] who, incited and stirred up by Sl. Junaid *Barlās* and others to desire Samarkand, drew an army out, Fol. 69. crossed the Āq-kutal and went to Rabāṭ-i-soghd and Kān-bāī. Bāī-sunghar Mīrzā went out from Samarkand, fought him near

[1] *qūba yūzlūq* (f. 6*b* and note 4). The Turkmān features would be a maternal inheritance.

[2] He is " Saifī Maulānā 'Arūzī " of Rieu's Pers. Cat. p. 525. *Cf.* H.S. ii, 341. His book, *'Arūz-i-saifī* has been translated by Blochmann and by Ranking.

[3] *namāz aūtār idī*. I understand some irony from this (de Meynard's Dict. *s.n. aūtmāq*).

[4] The *maṭla'* of poems serve as an index of first lines.

[5] *Cf.* f. 30.

Kān-bāī, beat him and beheaded 3 or 4000 Mughūls. In this fight died Ḥaidar *Kūkūldāsh*, the Khān's looser and binder (*ḥall u'aqdī*). His second battle was fought near Bukhārā with Sl. 'Alī Mīrzā (901 AH.-1496 AD.); in this he was beaten.[1]

(*g. His countries.*)

His father, Sl. Maḥmūd Mīrzā, gave him Bukhārā; when Sl. Maḥmūd M. died, his begs assembled and in agreement made Bāī-sunghar M. ruler in Samarkand. For a time, Bukhārā was included with Samarkand in his jurisdiction but it went out of his hands after the Tarkhān rebellion (901 AH.-1496 AD.). When he left Samarkand to go to Khusrau Shāh and I got possession of it (903 AH.-1497 AD.), Khusrau Shāh took Ḥiṣār and gave it to him.

(*h. Other details concerning him.*)

He left no child. He took a daughter of his paternal uncle, Sl. Khalīl Mīrzā, when he went to Khusrau Shāh; he had no other wife or concubine.

He never ruled with authority so independent that any beg was heard of as promoted by him to be his confidant; his begs
Fol. 69*b*. were just those of his father and his paternal uncle (Aḥmad).

(*i. Resumed account of Bābur's campaign against Tambal.*)

After Bāī-sunghar Mīrzā's death, Sl. Aḥmad *Qarāwal*,[2] the father of Qūch (Qūj) Beg, sent us word (of his intention) and came to us from Ḥiṣār through the Qarā-tīgīn country, together with his brethren, elder and younger, and their families and dependants. From Aūsh too came Qambar-'alī, risen from his sickness. Arriving, as it did, at such a moment, we took the providential help of Sl. Aḥmad and his party for a happy omen. Next day we formed up at dawn and moved direct upon our foe. He made no stand at Āb-i-khān but marched from his

[1] *Cf.* f. 37*b*.

[2] *i.e.* scout and in times of peace, huntsman. On the margin of the Elph. Codex here stands a note, mutilated in rebinding;—*Sl. Aḥmad pidr-i-Qūch Beg ast * * * pidr-i-Sher-afgan u Sher-afgan * * * u Sl. Ḥusain Khān * * * Qūch Beg ast. Hamesha * * * dar khāna Shaham Khān * * **.

ground, leaving many tents and blankets and things of the baggage for our men. We dismounted in his camp.

That evening Taṃbal, having Jahāngīr with him, turned our left and went to a village called Khūbān (var. Khūnān), some 3 *yīghāch* from us (15 m.?) and between us and Andijān. Next day we moved out against him, formed up with right and left, centre and van, our horses in their mail, our men in theirs, and with foot-soldiers, bearing mantelets, flung to the front. Our right was 'Alī-dost and his dependants, our left Ībrāhīm *Sārū*, Wais *Lāgharī*, Sayyidī Qarā, Muḥammad-'alī *Mubashir*, and Khwāja-i-kalān's elder brother, Kīchīk Beg, with several of Fol. 70. the household. In the left were inscribed[1] also Sl. Aḥmad *Qarāwal* and Qūch Beg with their brethren. With me in the centre was Qāsim Beg *Qūchīn*; in the van were Qaṃbar-'alī (the Skinner) and some of the household. When we reached Sāqā, a village two miles east of Khūbān, the enemy came out of Khūbān, arrayed to fight. We, for our part, moved on the faster. At the time of engaging, our foot-soldiers, provided how laboriously with the mantelets! were quite in the rear! By God's grace, there was no need of them; our left had got hands in with their right before they came up. Kīchīk Beg chopped away very well; next to him ranked Muḥammad 'Alī *Mubashir*. Not being able to bring equal zeal to oppose us, the enemy took to flight. The fighting did not reach the front of our van or right. Our men brought in many of their braves; we ordered the heads of all to be struck off. Favouring caution and good generalship, our begs, Qāsim Beg and, especially, 'Alī-dost did not think it advisable to send far in pursuit; for Fol. 70 this reason, many of their men did not fall into our hands. We dismounted right in Khūbān village. This was my first ranged battle; the Most High God, of His own favour and mercy, made it a day of victory and triumph. We accepted the omen.

On the next following day, my father's mother, my grandmother, Shāh Sulṭān Begīm[2] arrived from Andijān, thinking to beg off Jahāngīr Mīrzā if he had been taken.

[1] *pītīldī*; W.-i-B. *navishta shud*, words indicating the use by Bābur of a written record.

[2] *Cf.* f. 6*b* and note and f. 17 and note.

(*j. Bābur goes into winter-quarters in Between-the-two-rivers.*)

As it was now almost winter and no grain or fruits[1] remained in the open country, it was not thought desirable to move against (Taṃbal in) Aūzkīnt but return was made to Andijān. A few days later, it was settled after consultation, that for us to winter in the town would in no way hurt or hamper the enemy, rather that he would wax the stronger by it through raids and guerilla fighting; moreover on our own account, it was necessary that we should winter where our men would not become enfeebled through want of grain and where we could straiten the enemy by some sort of blockade. For these de-
Fol. 71. sirable ends we marched out of Andijān, meaning to winter near Armiyān and Nūsh-āb in the Rabāṭik-aūrchīnī, known also as Between-the-two-rivers. On arriving in the two villages above-mentioned, we prepared winter-quarters.

The hunting-grounds are good in that neighbourhood; in the jungle near the Aīlāīsh river is much *būghū-marāl*[2] and pig; the small scattered clumps of jungle are thick with hare and pheasant; and on the near rising-ground, are many foxes[3] of fine colour and swifter than those of any other place. While we were in those quarters, I used to ride hunting every two or three days; we would beat through the great jungle and hunt *būghū-marāl*, or we would wander about, making a circle round scattered clumps and flying our hawks at the pheasants. The pheasants are unlimited[4] there; pheasant-meat was abundant as long as we were in those quarters.

While we were there, Khudāī-bīrdī *Tūghchī*, then newly-favoured with beg's rank, fell on some of Taṃbal's raiders and brought in a few heads. Our braves went out also from Aūsh and Andijān and raided untiringly on the enemy, driving in his

[1] *tūlūk; i.e.* other food than grain. Fruit, fresh or preserved, being a principal constituent of food in Central Asia, *tūlūk* will include several, but chiefly melons. "Les melons constituent presque seuls vers le fin d'été, la nourriture des classes pauvres (Th. Radloff. l.c. p. 343).

[2] *Cf. f.* 6*b* and note.

[3] *tūlkī* var. *tūlkū*, the yellow fox. Following this word the Ḥai. MS. has *u dar kamīn dūr* instead of *u rangīn dūr*.

[4] *bī ḥadd*; with which I.O. 215 agrees but I.O. 217 adds *farbih*, fat, which is right in fact (f. 2*b*) but less pertinent here than an unlimited quantity.

herds of horses and much enfeebling him. If the whole winter had been passed in those quarters, the more probable thing is that he would have broken up simply without a fight. Fol. 71*b*

(k. Qambar-'alī again asks leave.)

It was at such a time, just when our foe was growing weak and helpless, that Qambar-'alī asked leave to go to his district. The more he was dissuaded by reminder of the probabilities of the position, the more stupidity he shewed. An amazingly fickle and veering manikin he was! It had to be! Leave for his district was given him. That district had been Khujand formerly but when Andijān was taken this last time, Asfara and Kand-i-badām were given him in addition. Amongst our begs, he was the one with large districts and many followers; no-one's land or following equalled his. We had been 40 or 50 days in those winter-quarters. At his recommendation, leave was given also to some of the clans in the army. We, for our part, went into Andijān.

(l. Sl. Maḥmūd Khān sends Mughūls to help Tambal.)

Both while we were in our winter-quarters and later on in Andijān, Tambal's people came and went unceasingly between him and The Khān in Tāshkīnt. His paternal uncle of the full-blood, Aḥmad Beg, was guardian of The Khān's son, Sl. Muḥammad Sl. and high in favour; his elder brother of the full-blood, Beg Tīlba (Fool), was The Khān's Lord of the Gate. After all the comings and goings, these two brought The Khān to the point of reinforcing Tambal. Beg Tīlba, leaving his wife and domestics and family in Tāshkīnt, came on ahead of the reinforcement and joined his younger brother, Tambal,—Beg Tīlba! who from his birth up had been in Mughūlistān, had grown up amongst Mughūls, had never entered a cultivated country or served the rulers of one, but from first to last had served The Khāns! Fol. 72.

Just then a wonderful (*'ajab*) thing happened;[1] Qāsim-i-'ajab (wonderful Qāsim) when he had been left for a time in Akhsī,

[1] Here a pun on *'ajab* may be read.

went out one day after a few marauders, crossed the Khujand-water by Bachrātā, met in with a few of Taṃbal's men and was made prisoner.

When Taṃbal heard that our army was disbanded and was assured of The Khān's help by the arrival of his brother, Beg Tīlba, who had talked with The Khān, he rode from Aūzkīnt into Between-the-two-rivers. Meantime safe news had come to us from Kāsān that The Khān had appointed his son, Sl. Muḥ. Khānika, commonly known as Sulṭānīm,[1] and Aḥmad Beg, with 5 or 6000 men, to help Taṃbal, that they had crossed by the Archa-kīnt road[2] and were laying siege to Kāsān. Hereupon we, without delay, without a glance at our absent men, just with those there were, in the hard cold of winter, put our Fol. 72b. trust in God and rode off by the Band-i-sālār road to oppose them. That night we stopped no-where; on we went through the darkness till, at dawn, we dismounted in Akhsī.[3] So mightily bitter was the cold that night that it bit the hands and feet of several men and swelled up the ears of many, each ear like an apple. We made no stay in Akhsī but leaving there Yārak Ṭaghāī, temporarily also, in Qāsim-i-'ajab's place, passed on for Kāsān. Two miles from Kāsān news came that on hearing of our approach, Aḥmad Beg and Sulṭānīm had hurried off in disorder.

(m. Bābur and Taṃbal again opposed.)

Taṃbal must have had news of our getting to horse for he had hurried to help his elder brother.[4] Somewhere between the two Prayers of the day,[5] his blackness[6] became visible towards Nū-kīnt. Astonished and perplexed by his elder brother's light departure and by our quick arrival, he stopped short. Said we, 'It is God has brought them in this fashion! here they have come with their horses' necks at full stretch;[7]

[1] *Cf.* f. 15, note to Ṭaghāī.
[2] Apparently not the usual Kīndīr-līk pass but one n.w. of Kāsān.
[3] A ride of at least 40 miles, followed by one of 20 to Kāsān.
[4] *Cf.* f. 72 and f. 72b. Tīlba would seem to have left Taṃbal.
[5] *Taṃbalnīng qarāsī.*
[6] *i.e.* the Other (Mid-afternoon) Prayer.
[7] *ātīning būīnīnī qātib. Qātmāq* has also the here-appropriate meaning of *to stiffen.*

if we join hands[1] and go out, and if God bring it right, not a man of them will get off.' But Wais *Lāgharī* and some others said, 'It is late in the day; even if we do not go out today, where can they go tomorrow? Wherever it is, we will meet them at dawn.' So they said, not thinking it well to make the joint effort there and then; so too the enemy, come so opportunely, broke up and got away without any hurt whatever. The (Turkī) proverb is, 'Who does not snatch at a chance, will worry himself about it till old age.' Fol. 73.

(Persian) couplet. Work must be snatched at betimes,
Vain is the slacker's mistimed work.

Seizing the advantage of a respite till the morrow, the enemy slipped away in the night, and without dismounting on the road, went into Fort Archīān. When a morrow's move against a foe was made, we found no foe; after him we went and, not thinking it well to lay close siege to Archīān, dismounted two miles off (one *shar'ī*) in Ghazna-namangān.[2] We were in camp there for 30 or 40 days, Taṃbal being in Fort Archīān. Every now and then a very few would go from our side and come from theirs, fling themselves on one another midway and return. They made one night-attack, rained arrows in on us and retired. As the camp was encircled by a ditch or by branches close-set, and as watch was kept, they could effect no more.

(n. Qaṃbar-'alī, the Skinner, again gives trouble.)

Two or three times while we lay in that camp, Qaṃbar-'alī, in ill-temper, was for going to his district; once he even had got to horse and started in a fume, but we sent several begs after him who, with much trouble, got him to turn back. Fol. 73b.

[1] *ailīk qūshmāq*, *i.e.* Bābur's men with the Kāsān garrison. But the two W.-i-B. write merely *dast burd* and *dast kardan*.

[2] The meaning of *Ghazna* here is uncertain. The Second W.-i-B. renders it by ar. *qaryat* but up to this point Bābur has not used *qaryat* for *village*. Ghazna-namangān cannot be modern Namangān. It was 2 m. from Archīān where Taṃbal was, and Bābur went to Bīshkhārān to be between Taṃbal and Machamī, coming from the south. Archīān and Ghazna-namangān seem both to have been n. or n.w. of Bishkārān (see maps).

It may be mentioned that at Archīān, in 909 AH. the two Chaghatāī Khāns and Bābur were defeated by Shaibānī.

(o. Further action against Tambal and an accommodation made.)

Meantime Sayyid Yūsuf of Macham had sent a man to Tambal and was looking towards him. He was the head-man of one of the two foot-hills of Andijān, Macham and Awīghūr. Latterly he had become known in my Gate, having outgrown the head-man and put on the beg, though no-one ever had made him a beg. He was a singularly hypocritical manikin, of no standing whatever. From our last taking of Andijān (June 1499) till then (Feb. 1500), he had revolted two or three times from Tambal and come to me, and two or three times had revolted from me and gone to Tambal. This was his last change of side. With him were many from the (Mughūl) horde and tribesmen and clansmen. 'Don't let him join Tambal,' we said and rode in between them. We got to Bīshkhārān with one night's halt. Tambal's men must have come earlier and entered the fort. A party of our begs, 'Alī-darwesh Beg and Qūch Beg, with his brothers, went close up to the Gate of
Fol. 74. Bīshkhārān and exchanged good blows with the enemy. Qūch Beg and his brothers did very well there, their hands getting in for most of the work. We dismounted on a height some two miles from Bīshkhārān; Tambal, having Jahāngīr with him, dismounted with the fort behind him.

Three or four days later, begs unfriendly to us, that is to say, 'Alī-dost and Qambar-'alī, the Skinner, with their followers and dependants, began to interpose with talk of peace. I and my well-wishers had no knowledge of a peace and we all[1] were utterly averse from the project. Those two manikins however were our two great begs; if we gave no ear to their words and if we did not make peace, other things from them were probable! It had to be! Peace was made in this fashion;—the districts on the Akhsī side of the Khujand-water were to depend on Jahāngīr, those on the Andijān side, on me; Aūzkīnt was to be left in my jurisdiction after they had removed their families from it; when the districts were settled and I and Jahāngīr had

[1] *bizlār*. The double plural is rare with Bābur; he writes *bīz*, we, when action is taken in common; he rarely uses *mīn*, I, with autocratic force; his phrasing is largely impersonal, *e.g.* with rare exceptions, he writes the impersonal passive verb.

made our agreement, we (*bīz*) should march together against Samarkand; and when I was in possession of Samarkand, Andijān was to be given to Jahāngīr. So the affair was settled. Fol. 74*b*.
Next day,—it was one of the last of Rajab, (end of Feb. 1500) Jahāngīr Mīrzā and Tambal came and did me obeisance; the terms and conditions were ratified as stated above; leave for Akhsī was given to Jahāngīr and I betook myself to Andijān.

On our arrival, Khalīl-of-Tambal and our whole band of prisoners were released; robes of honour were put on them and leave to go was given. They, in their turn, set free our begs and household, *viz.* the commanders[1] (Sherīm?) Ṭaghāī Beg, Muḥammad-dost, Mīr Shāh *Qūchīn*, Sayyidī Qarā Beg, Qāsim-i-'ajab, Mīr Wais, Mīrīm *Dīwān*, and those under them.

(p. The self-aggrandizement of 'Alī-dost Ṭaghāī.)

After our return to Andijān, 'Alī-dost's manners and behaviour changed entirely. He began to live ill with my companions of the guerilla days and times of hardship. First, he dismissed Khalīfa; next seized and plundered Ibrāhīm *Sārū* and Wais *Lāgharī*, and for no fault or cause deprived them of their districts and dismissed them. He entangled himself with Qāsim Beg and *he* was made to go; he openly declared, 'Khalīfa and Ibrāhīm are in sympathy about Khwāja-i-qāẓī; they will avenge him on me.'[2] His son, Muḥammad-dost set himself up on a regal footing, starting receptions and a public table and a Fol. 75.
Court and workshops, after the fashion of sulṭāns. Like father, like son, they set themselves up in this improper way because they had Tambal at their backs. No authority to restrain their unreasonable misdeeds was left to me; for why? Whatever their hearts desired, that they did because such a foe of mine as Tambal was their backer. The position was singularly delicate; not a word was said but many humiliations were endured from that father and that son alike.

[1] *bāshlīghlār.* Teufel was of opinion that this word is not used as a noun in the B.N. In this he is mistaken; it is so used frequently, as here, in apposition. *See* ZDMG, xxxvii, art. Bābur und Abū'l-faẓl.
[2] *Cf.* f. 54 foot.

(q. Bābur's first marriage.)

'Āyisha-sulṭān Begīm whom my father and hers, *i.e.* my uncle, Sl. Aḥmad Mīrzā had betrothed to me, came (this year) to Khujand[1] and I took her in the month of Sha'bān. Though I was not ill-disposed towards her, yet, this being my first marriage, out of modesty and bashfulness, I used to see her once in 10, 15 or 20 days. Later on when even my first inclination did not last, my bashfulness increased. Then my mother Khānīm used to send me, once a month or every 40
Fol. 75*b*. days, with driving and driving, dunnings and worryings.

(r. A personal episode and some verses by Bābur.)

In those leisurely days I discovered in myself a strange inclination, nay! as the verse says, 'I maddened and afflicted myself' for a boy in the camp-bazar, his very name, Bāburī, fitting in. Up till then I had had no inclination for any-one, indeed of love and desire, either by hear-say or experience, I had not heard, I had not talked. At that time I composed Persian couplets, one or two at a time; this is one of the them:—

> May none be as I, humbled and wretched and love-sick;
> No beloved as thou art to me, cruel and careless.

From time to time Bāburī used to come to my presence but out of modesty and bashfulness, I could never look straight at him; how then could I make conversation (*ikhtilāṭ*) and recital (*hikāyat*)? In my joy and agitation I could not thank him (for coming); how was it possible for me to reproach him with going away? What power had I to command the duty of service to myself?[2] One day, during that time of desire and passion when I was going with companions along a lane and suddenly met him face to face, I got into such a state of confusion that I almost went right off. To look straight at him
Fol. 76. or to put words together was impossible. With a hundred torments and shames, I went on. A (Persian) couplet of Muḥammad Ṣāliḥ's[3] came into my mind:—

[1] *Cf.* f. 20. She may have come from Samarkand and 'Alī's household or from Kesh and the Tarkhān households.

[2] *Cf.* f. 26 l. 2 for the same phrase

[3] He is the author of the *Shaibānī-nāma*.

I am abashed with shame when I see my friend ;
My companions look at me, I look the other way.

That couplet suited the case wonderfully well. In that frothing-up of desire and passion, and under that stress of youthful folly, I used to wander, bare-head, bare-foot, through street and lane, orchard and vineyard. I shewed civility neither to friend nor stranger, took no care for myself or others.

(*Turki*) Out of myself desire rushed me, unknowing
That this is so with the lover of a fairy-face.

Sometimes like the madmen, I used to wander alone over hill and plain; sometimes I betook myself to gardens and the suburbs, lane by lane. My wandering was not of my choice, not I decided whether to go or stay.

(*Turki*) Nor power to go was mine, nor power to stay ;
I was just what you made me, o thief of my heart.

(s. *Sl. 'Alī Mīrzā's quarrels with the Tarkhāns.*)

In this same year, Sl. 'Alī Mīrzā fell out with Muḥammad Mazīd Tarkhān for the following reasons;—The Tarkhāns had risen to over-much predominance and honour; Bāqī had taken the whole revenue of the Bukhārā Government and gave not a half-penny (*dāng*)[1] to any-one else; Muḥammad Mazīd, for his part, had control in Samarkand and took all its districts for his sons and dependants; a small sum only excepted, fixed by them, not a farthing (*fils*) from the town reached the Mīrzā by any channel. Sl. 'Alī Mīrzā was a grown man; how was he to tolerate such conduct as theirs? He and some of his household formed a design against Muḥ. Mazīd Tarkhān; the latter came to know of it and left the town with all his following and with whatever begs and other persons were in sympathy with him,[2] such as Sl. Ḥusain *Arghūn*, Pīr Aḥmad, Aūzūn Ḥasan's younger brother, Khwāja Ḥusain, Qarā *Barlās*, Ṣāliḥ Muḥammad[3] and some other begs and braves. Fol. 76*b*.

[1] *dāng* and *fils* (*infra*) are small copper coins.
[2] *Cf.* f. 25 l. 1 and note 1.
[3] Probably the poet again ; he had left Harāt and was in Samarkand (Sh. N. Vambéry, p. 34 l. 14).

At the time The Khān had joined to Khān Mīrzā a number of Mughūl begs with Muḥ. Ḥusain *Dūghlāt* and Aḥmad Beg, and had appointed them to act against Samarkand.[1] Khān Mīrzā's guardians were Ḥāfiẓ Beg *Dūldāī* and his son, Ṭāhir Beg; because of relationship to them, (Muḥ. Sīghal's) grandson, Ḥasan and Hindū Beg fled with several braves from Sl. 'Alī
Fol. 77. Mīrzā's presence to Khān Mīrzā's.

Muḥammad Mazīd Tarkhān invited Khān Mīrzā and the Mughūl army, moved to near Shavdār, there saw the Mīrzā and met the begs of the Mughūls. No small useful friendlinesses however, came out of the meeting between his begs and the Mughūls; the latter indeed seem to have thought of making him a prisoner. Of this he and his begs coming to know, separated themselves from the Mughūl army. As without him the Mughūls could make no stand, they retired. Here-upon, Sl. 'Alī Mīrzā hurried light out of Samarkand with a few men and caught them up where they had dismounted in Yār-yīlāq. They could not even fight but were routed and put to flight. This deed, done in his last days, was Sl. 'Alī Mīrzā's one good little affair.

Muḥ. Mazīd Tarkhān and his people, despairing both of the Mughūls and of these Mīrzās, sent Mīr Mughūl, son of 'Abdu'l-wahhāb *Shaghāwal*[2] to invite me (to Samarkand). Mīr Mughūl had already been in my service; he had risked his life in good accord with Khwāja-i-qāẓī during the siege of Andijān (903 AH.-1498 AD.).

This business hurt us also[3] and, as it was for that purpose we had made peace (with Jahāngīr), we resolved to move on Samarkand. We sent Mīr Mughūl off at once to give rendezvous[4]
Fol. 77b. to Jahāngīr Mīrzā and prepared to get to horse. We rode out

[1] From what follows, this Mughūl advance seems a sequel to a Tarkhān invitation.

[2] By omitting the word *Mīr* the Turkī text has caused confusion between this father and son (Index *s.nn.*).

[3] *bīz khūd kharāb bū mu'āmla aīdūk*. These words have been understood earlier, as referring to the abnormal state of Bābur's mind described under Sec. r. They better suit the affairs of Samarkand because Bābur is able to resolve on action and also because he here writes *bīz*, we, and not *mīn*, I as in Sec. r.

[4] For *būlghār*, rendezvous, *see* also f. 78 l. 2 fr. ft.

in the month of Ẕū'l-qa'da (June) and with two halts on the way, came to Qabā and there dismounted.[1] At the mid-afternoon Prayer of that day, news came that Taṃbal's brother, Khalīl had taken Aūsh by surprise.

The particulars are as follows;—As has been mentioned, Khalīl and those under him were set free when peace was made. Taṃbal then sent Khalīl to fetch away their wives and families from Aūzkīnt. He had gone and he went into the fort on this pretext. He kept saying untruthfully, 'We will go out today,' or 'We will go out tomorrow,' but he did not go. When we got to horse, he seized the chance of the emptiness of Aūsh to go by night and surprise it. For several reasons it was of no advantage for us to stay and entangle ourselves with him; we went straight on therefore. One reason was that as, for the purpose of making ready military equipment, all my men of name had scattered, heads of houses to their homes, we had no news of them because we had relied on the peace and were by this off our guard against the treachery and falsity of the other party. Another reason was that for some time, as has been Fol. 78.
said, the misconduct of our great begs, 'Alī-dost and Qaṃbar-'alī had been such that no confidence in them was left. A further reason was that the Samarkand begs, under Muḥ. Mazīd Tarkhān had sent Mīr Mughūl to invite us and, so long as a capital such as Samarkand stood there, what would incline a man to waste his days for a place like Andijān?

From Qabā we moved on to Marghīnān (20 m.). Marghīnān had been given to Qūch Beg's father, Sl. Aḥmad *Qarāwal*, and he was then in it. As he, owing to various ties and attachments, could not attach himself to me,[2] he stayed behind while his son, Qūch Beg and one or two of his brethren, older and younger, went with me.

Taking the road for Asfara, we dismounted in one of its villages, called Mahan. That night there came and joined us in Mahan, by splendid chance, just as if to a rendezvous, Qāsim Beg *Qūchīn* with his company, 'Alī-dost with his, and Sayyid

[1] 25 m. only; the halts were due probably to belated arrivals.
[2] Some of his ties would be those of old acquaintance in Ḥiṣār with 'Alī's father's begs, now with him in Samarkand.

Qāsim with a large body of braves. We rode from Mahan by the Khasbān (var. Yasān) plain, crossed the Chūpān (Shepherd)-bridge and so to Aūrā-tīpā.[1]

(t. Qambar-'alī punishes himself.)

Trusting to Tambal, Qambar-'alī went from his own district (Khujand) to Akhsī in order to discuss army-matters with him. Such an event happening,[2] Tambal laid hands on Qambar-'alī, marched against his district and carried him along. Here the (Turkī) proverb fits, 'Distrust your friend! he'll stuff your hide with straw.' While Qambar-'alī was being made to go to Khujand, he escaped on foot and after a hundred difficulties reached Aūrā-tīpā.

News came to us there that Shaibānī Khān had beaten Bāqī Tarkhān in Dabūsī and was moving on Bukhārā. We went on from Aūrā-tīpā, by way of Burka-yīlāq, to Sangzār[3] which the sub-governor surrendered. There we placed Qambar-'alī, as, after effecting his own capture and betrayal, he had come to us. We then passed on.

(u. Affairs of Samarkand and the end of 'Alī-dost.)

On our arrival in Khān-yūrtī, the Samarkand begs under Muḥ. Mazīd Tarkhān came and did me obeisance. Conference was held with them as to details for taking the town; they said, 'Khwāja Yaḥya also is wishing for the *pādshāh*;[4] with his consent the town may be had easily without fighting or disturbance.' The Khwāja did not say decidedly to our messengers that he had resolved to admit us to the town but at the same time, he said nothing likely to lead us to despair.

Leaving Khān-yūrtī, we moved to the bank of the Dar-i-gham (canal) and from there sent our librarian, Khwāja Muḥammad 'Alī to Khwāja Yaḥya. He brought word back, 'Let them come; we will give them the town.' Accordingly we rode from the Dar-i-gham straight for the town, at night-fall, but

---

[1] Point to point, some 90 m. but further by road.
[2] *Bū waqi' būlghāch,* manifestly ironical.
[3] Sangzār to Aūrā-tīpā, by way of the hills, some 50 miles.
[4] The Sh. N. Vambéry, p. 60, confirms this.

our plan came to nothing because Sl. Muḥammad *Dūldāī's* father, Sl. Maḥmūd had fled from our camp and given such information to (Sl. 'Alī's party) as put them on their guard. Back we went to the Dar-i-gham bank.

While I had been in Yār-yīlāq, one of my favoured begs, Ibrāhīm *Sārū* who had been plundered and driven off by 'Alī-dost,[1] came and did me obeisance, together with Muḥ. Yūsuf, the elder son of Sayyid Yūsuf (*Aūghlāqchī*). Coming in by ones and twos, old family servants and begs and some of the household gathered back to me there. All were enemies of 'Alī-dost; some he had driven away; others he had plundered; others again he had imprisoned. He became afraid. For why? Because with Tambal's backing, he had harassed and persecuted me and my well-wishers. As for me, my very nature sorted ill with the manikin's! From shame and fear, he could stay no longer with us; he asked leave; I took it as a personal favour; I gave it. On this leave, he and his son, Muḥammad-dost went to Tambal's presence. They became his intimates, Fol. 79*b*.
and from father and son alike, much evil and sedition issued. 'Alī-dost died a few years later from ulceration of the hand. Muḥammad-dost went amongst the Aūzbegs; that was not altogether bad but, after some treachery to his salt, he fled from them and went into the Andijān foot-hills.[2] There he stirred up much revolt and trouble. In the end he fell into the hands of Aūzbeg people and they blinded him. The meaning of 'The salt took his eyes,' is clear in his case.[3]

After giving this pair their leave, we sent Ghūrī *Barlās* toward Bukhārā for news. He brought word that Shaibānī Khān had taken Bukhārā and was on his way to Samarkand. Here-upon, seeing no advantage in staying in that neighbourhood, we set out for Kesh where, moreover, were the families of most of the Samarkand begs.

When we had been a few weeks there, news came that Sl. Alī Mīrzā had given Samarkand to Shaibānī Khān. The particulars are these;—The Mīrzā's mother, Zuhra Begī Āghā

[1] *Cf.* f. 74*b*.
[2] Macham and Awighūr, presumably.
[3] *gūzlār tūz tūtī, i.e.* he was blinded for some treachery to his hosts.

(*Aūzbeg*), in her ignorance and folly, had secretly written to
Fol. 80. Shaibānī Khān that if he would take her (to wife) her son should give him Samarkand and that when Shaibānī had taken (her son's) father's country, he should give her son a country.[1] Sayyid Yūsuf *Arghūn* must have known of this plan, indeed will have been the traitor inventing it.

1 Muḥ. Ṣāliḥ's well-informed account of this episode has much interest, filling out and, as by Shaibānī's Boswell, balancing Bābur's. Bābur is obscure about what country was to be given to 'Alī. Pāyanda-ḥasan paraphrases his brief words ;—Shaibānī was to be as a father to 'Alī and when he had taken 'Alī's father's *wilāyāt*, he was to give a country to 'Alī. It has been thought that the gift to 'Alī was to follow Shaibānī's recovery of his own ancestral camping-ground (*yūrt*) but this is negatived, I think, by the word, *wilāyat*, cultivated land.

906 AH.—JULY 28TH. 1500 TO JULY 17TH. 1501 AD.[1]

(a. Samarkand in the hands of the Aūzbegs.)

When, acting on that woman's promise, Shaibānī Khān went to Samarkand, he dismounted in the Garden of the Plain. About mid-day Sl. 'Alī Mīrzā went out to him through the Four-roads Gate, without a word to any of his begs or unmailed braves, without taking counsel with any-one soever and accompanied only by a few men of little consideration from his own close circle. The Khān, for his part, did not receive him very favourably; when they had seen one another, he seated him on his less honourable hand.[2] Khwāja Yaḥya, on hearing of the Mīrzā's departure, became very anxious but as he could find no remedy,[3] went out also. The Khān looked at him without rising and said a few words in which blame had part, but when the Khwāja rose to leave, showed him the respect of rising.

As soon as Khwāja 'Alī[4] Bāy's[5] son, Jān-'alī heard in Rabaṭ-

[1] Elp. MS. f. 57*b*; W.-i-B. I.O. 215 f. 63*b* and I.O. 217 f. 52; Mems. p. 82. Two contemporary works here supplement the B.N.; (1) the (*Tawārīkh-i-guzīda*) *Naṣrat-nāma*, dated 908 AH. (B.M. Turkī Or. 3222) of which Berezin's *Shaibānī-nāma* is an abridgment; (2) Muḥ. Ṣāliḥ Mīrzā's *Shaibānī-nāma* (Vambéry trs. cap. xix *et seq.*). The Ḥ.S. (Bomb. ed. p. 302, and Tehran ed. p. 384) is also useful.

[2] *i.e.* on his right. The Ḥ.S. ii, 302 represents that 'Alī was well-received. After Shaibāq had had Zuhra's overtures, he sent an envoy to 'Alī and Yaḥya; the first was not won over but the second fell in with his mother's scheme. This difference of view explains why 'Alī slipped away while Yaḥya was engaged in the Friday Mosque. It seems likely that mother and son alike expected their Aūzbeg blood to stand them in good stead with Shaibāq.

[3] He tried vainly to get the town defended. "Would to God Bābur Mīrzā were here!" he is reported as saying, by Muḥ. Ṣāliḥ.

[4] Perhaps it is for the play of words on 'Alī and 'Alī's life (*jān*) that this man makes his sole appearance here.

[5] *i.e.* rich man or merchant, but *Bī* (*infra*) is an equivalent of Beg.

i-khwāja of the Mīrzā's going to Shaibānī Khān, he also went. As for that calamitous woman who, in her folly, gave her son's
Fol. 80b. house and possessions to the winds in order to get herself a husband, Shaibānī Khān cared not one atom for her, indeed did not regard her as the equal of a mistress or a concubine.[1]

Confounded by his own act, Sl. 'Alī Mīrzā's repentance was extreme. Some of his close circle, after hearing particulars, planned for him to escape with them but to this he would not agree; his hour had come; he was not to be freed. He had dismounted in Tīmūr Sulṭān's quarters; three or four days later they killed him in Plough-meadow.[2] For a matter of this five-days' mortal life, he died with a bad name; having entered into a woman's affairs, he withdrew himself from the circle of men of good repute. Of such people's doings no more should be written; of acts so shameful, no more should be heard.

The Mīrzā having been killed, Shaibānī Khān sent Jān-'alī after his Mīrzā. He had apprehensions also about Khwāja Yaḥya and therefore dismissed him, with his two sons, Khwāja Muḥ. Zakarīya and Khwāja Bāqī, towards Khurāsān.[3] A few Aūzbegs followed them and near Khwāja Kārdzan martyred both the Khwāja and his two young sons. Though Shaibānī's
Fol. 81. words were, 'Not through me the Khwāja's affair! Qambar Bī and Kūpuk Bī did it,' this is worse than that! There is a proverb,[4] 'His excuse is worse than his fault,' for if begs, out of their own heads, start such deeds, unknown to their Khāns or Pādshāhs, what becomes of the authority of khānship and and sovereignty?

(b. Bābur leaves Kesh and crosses the Mūra pass.)

Since the Aūzbegs were in possession of Samarkand, we left Kesh and went in the direction of Ḥiṣār. With us started off

[1] Muḥ. Ṣāliḥ, invoking curses on such a mother, mentions that Zuhra was given to a person of her own sort.

[2] The Sh. N. and *Naṣrat-nāma* attempt to lift the blame of 'Alī's death from Shaibāq; the second saying that he fell into the Kohik-water when drunk.

[3] Harāt might be his destination but the H.S. names Makka. Some dismissals towards Khurāsān may imply pilgrimage to Meshhed.

[4] Used also by Bābur's daughter, Gul-badan (l.c. f. 31).

Muḥ. Mazīd Tārkhān and the Samarkand begs under his command, together with their wives and families and people, but when we dismounted in the Chultū meadow of Chaghāniān, they parted from us, went to Khusrau Shāh and became his retainers.

Cut off from our own abiding-town and country,[1] not knowing where (else) to go or where to stay, we were obliged to traverse the very heart of Khusrau Shāh's districts, spite of what measure of misery he had inflicted on the men of our dynasty!

One of our plans had been to go to my younger Khān dādā, *i.e.* Alacha Khān, by way of Qarā-tīgīn and the Alāī,[2] but this was not managed. Next we were for going up the valley of the Kām torrent and over the Sara-tāq pass (*dābān*). When we were near Nūndāk, a servant of Khusrau Shāh brought me one set of nine horses[3] and one of nine pieces of cloth. When we dismounted at the mouth of the Kām valley, Sher-'alī, the page, deserted to Khusrau Shāh's brother, Walī and, next day, Qūch Beg parted from us and went to Ḥiṣār.[4] Fol. 81*b*.

We entered the valley and made our way up it. On its steep and narrow roads and at its sharp and precipitous saddles[5] many horses and camels were left. Before we reached the Sara-tāq pass we had (in 25 m.) to make three or four night-halts. A pass! and what a pass! Never was such a steep and narrow pass seen; never were traversed such ravines and precipices. Those dangerous narrows and sudden falls, those perilous heights and knife-edge saddles, we got through with much difficulty and suffering, with countless hardships and miseries. Amongst the Fān mountains is a large lake (Iskandar); it is 2 miles in circumference, a beautiful lake and not devoid of marvels.[6]

[1] Cut off by alien lands and weary travel.

[2] The Pers. annotator of the Elph. Codex has changed Alāī to *wilāyat*, and *dābān* (pass) to *yān*, side. For the difficult route *see* Schuyler, i, 275, Kostenko, i, 129 and Rickmers, JRGS, 1907, art. Fan Valley.

[3] Amongst Turks and Mughūls, gifts were made by nines.

[4] Ḥiṣār was his earlier home.

[5] Many of these will have been climbed in order to get over places impassable at the river's level.

[6] Schuyler quotes a legend of the lake. He and Kostenko make it larger.

News came that Ibrāhīm Tarkhān had strengthened Fort Shīrāz and was seated in it; also that Qambar-'alī (the Skinner) and Abū'l-qāsim *Kohbur*, the latter not being able to stay in Khwāja Dīdār with the Aūzbegs in Samarkand,—had both come into Yār-yīlāq, strengthened its lower forts and occupied them.

Leaving Fān on our right, we moved on for Keshtūd. The head-man of Fān had a reputation for hospitality, generosity,
Fol. 82. serviceableness and kindness. He had given tribute of 70 or 80 horses to Sl. Mas'ūd Mīrzā at the time the Mīrzā, when Sl. Ḥusain Mīrzā made attack on Ḥisār, went through Fān on his way to his younger brother, Bāī-sunghar Mīrzā in Samarkand. He did like service to others. To me he sent one second-rate horse; moreover he did not wait on me himself. So it was! Those renowned for liberality became misers when they had to do with me, and the politeness of the polite was forgotten. Khusrau Shāh was celebrated for liberality and kindness; what service he did Badī'u'z-zamān Mīrzā has been mentioned; to Bāqī Tarkhān and other begs he shewed great generosity also. Twice I happened to pass through his country;[1] not to speak of courtesy shewn to my peers, what he shewed to my lowest servants he did not shew to me, indeed he shewed less regard for us than for them.

(*Turki*) Who, o my heart! has seen goodness from worldlings?
Look not for goodness from him who has none.

Under the impression that the Aūzbegs were in Keshtūd, we made an excursion to it, after passing Fān. Of itself it seemed
Fol. 82b. to have gone to ruin; no-one seemed to be occupying it. We went on to the bank of the Kohik-water (*Zar-afshān*) and there dismounted. From that place we sent a few begs under Qāsim *Qūchīn* to surprise Rabāṭ-i-khwāja; that done, we crossed the river by a bridge from opposite Yārī, went through Yārī and over the Shunqār-khāna (Falcons'-home) range into Yār-yīlāq. Our begs went to Rabāṭ-i-khwāja and had set up ladders when the men within came to know about them and

[1] The second occasion was when he crossed from Sūkh for Kābul in 910 AH. (fol. 120).

forced them to retire. As they could not take the fort, they rejoined us.

(*c. Bābur renews attack on Samarkand.*)

Qambar-'alī (the Skinner) was (still) holding Sangzār; he came and saw us; Abū'l-qāsim *Kohbur* and Ibrāhīm Tarkhān showed loyalty and attachment by sending efficient men for our service. We went into Asfīdik (var. Asfīndik), one of the Yār-yīlāq villages. At that time Shaibāq Khān lay near Khwāja Dīdār with 3 or 4000 Aūzbegs and as many more soldiers gathered in locally. He had given the Government of Samarkand to Jān-wafā, and Jan-wafā was then in the fort with 500 or 600 men. Ḥamza Sl. and Mahdī Sl. were lying near the fort, in the Quail-reserve. Our men, good and bad were 240. Fol. 83.

Having discussed the position with all my begs and unmailed braves, we left it at this;—that as Shaibānī Khān had taken possession of Samarkand so recently, the Samarkandīs would not be attached to him nor he to them; that if we made an effort at once, we might do the thing; that if we set ladders up and took the fort by surprise, the Samarkandīs would be for us; how should they not be? even if they gave us no help, they would not fight us for the Aūzbegs; and that Samarkand once in our hands, whatever was God's will, would happen.

Acting on this decision, we rode out of Yār-yīlāq after the Mid-day Prayer, and on through the dark till mid-night when we reached Khān-yūrtī. Here we had word that the Samarkandīs knew of our coming; for this reason we went no nearer to the town but made straight back from Khān-yūrtī. It was dawn when, after crossing the Kohik-water below Rabāṭ-i-khwāja, we were once more in Yār-yīlāq.

One day in Fort Asfīdik a household party was sitting in my presence; Dost-i-nāṣir and Nuyān[1] *Kūkūldāsh* and Khān-qulī-i-Karīm-dād and Shaikh Darwesh and Mīrīm-i-nāṣir were all there. Words were crossing from all sides when (I said), 'Come now! say when, if God bring it right, we shall take Fol. 83*b*.

[1] This name appears to indicate a Command of 10,000 (Bretschneider's *Mediaeval Researches*, i, 112).

Samarkand.' Some said, 'We shall take it in the heats.' It was then late in autumn. Others said, 'In a month,' 'Forty days,' 'Twenty days.' Nuyān *Kūkūldāsh* said, 'We shall take it in 14.' God shewed him right! we did take it in exactly 14 days.

Just at that time I had a wonderful dream;—His Highness Khwāja 'Ubaid'l-lāh (*Aḥrārī*) seemed to come; I seemed to go out to give him honourable meeting; he came in and seated himself; people seemed to lay a table-cloth before him, apparently without sufficient care and, on account of this, something seemed to come into his Highness Khwāja's mind. Mullā Bābā (? *Pashāgharī*) made me a sign; I signed back, 'Not through me! the table-layer is in fault!' The Khwāja understood and accepted the excuse.[1] When he rose, I escorted him out. In the hall of that house he took hold of either my right or left arm and lifted me up till one of my feet was off the ground, saying, in Turkī, 'Shaikh Maṣlaḥat has given (Samarkand.)'[2] I really took Samarkand a few days later.

(d. Bābur takes Samarkand by surprise.)

In two or three days move was made from Fort Asfīdik to Fort Wasmand. Although by our first approach, we had let
Fol. 84. our plan be known, we put our trust in God and made another expedition to Samarkand. It was after the Mid-day Prayer that we rode out of Fort Wasmand, Khwāja Abū'l-makāram accompanying us. By mid-night we reached the Deep-fosse-bridge in the Avenue. From there we sent forward a detachment of 70 or 80 good men who were to set up ladders opposite the Lovers'-cave, mount them and get inside, stand up to those in the Turquoise Gate, get possession of it and send a man

[1] It seems likely that the cloth was soiled. *Cf.* f. 25 and Hughes Dict. of Islām *s.n.* Eating.

[2] As, of the quoted speech, one word only, of three, is Turkī, others may have been dreamed. Shaikh Maṣlaḥat's tomb is in Khujand where Bābur had found refuge in 903 AH.; it had been circumambulated by Tīmūr in 790 AH. (1390 AD.) and is still honoured.

This account of a dream compares well for naturalness with that in the seemingly-spurious passage, entered with the Ilai. MS. on f. 118. For examination of the passage *see* JRAS, Jan. 1911, and App. D.

to me. Those braves went, set their ladders up opposite the Lovers'-cave, got in without making anyone aware, went to the Gate, attacked Fāẓil Tarkhān, chopped at him and his few retainers, killed them, broke the lock with an axe and opened the Gate. At that moment I came up and went in.

(Author's note on Fāẓil Tarkhān.) He was not one of those (Samarkand) Tarkhāns; he was a merchant-tarkhān of Turkistān. He had served Shaibānī Khān in Turkistān and had found favour with him.[1]

Abū'l-qāsim *Kohbur* himself had not come with us but had sent 30 or 40 of his retainers under his younger brother, Aḥmad-i-qāsim. No man of Ibrāhīm Tarkhān's was with us; his younger brother, Aḥmad Tarkhān came with a few retainers after I had entered the town and taken post in the Monastery. Fol. 84*b*.

The towns-people were still slumbering; a few traders peeped out of their shops, recognized me and put up prayers. When, a little later, the news spread through the town, there was rare delight and satisfaction for our men and the towns-folk. They killed the Aūzbegs in the lanes and gullies with clubs and stones like mad dogs; four or five hundred were killed in this fashion. Jān-wafā, the then governor, was living in Khwāja Yaḥya's house; he fled and got away to Shaibāq Khān.[2]

On entering the Turquoise Gate I went straight to the College and took post over the arch of the Monastery. There was a hubbub and shouting of 'Down! down!' till day-break. Some of the notables and traders, hearing what was happening, came joyfully to see me, bringing what food was ready and putting up prayers for me. At day-light we had news that the Aūzbegs were fighting in the Iron Gate where they had made themselves fast between the (outer and inner) doors. With 10, 15 or 20 men, I at once set off for the Gate but before I came up, the town-rabble, busy ransacking every corner of the newly-taken town for loot, had driven the Aūzbegs out through

1 He was made a Tarkhān by diploma of Shaibānī (Ḥ.S. ii, 306, l. 2).

2 Here the Ḥai. MS. begins to use the word *Shaibāq* in place of its previously uniform *Shaibānī*. As has been noted (f. 5*b* n. 2), the Elph. MS. writes *Shaibāq*. It may be therefore that a scribe has changed the earlier part of the Ḥai. MS. and that Bābur wrote *Shaibāq*. From this point my text will follow the double authority of the Elph. and Ḥai. MSS.

Fol. 85. it. Shaibāq Khān, on hearing what was happening, hurried at sun-rise to the Iron Gate with 100 or 140 men. His coming was a wonderful chance but, as has been said, my men were very few. Seeing that he could do nothing, he rode off at once. From the Iron Gate I went to the citadel and there dismounted, at the Bū-stān palace. Men of rank and consequence and various head-men came to me there, saw me and invoked blessings on me.

Samarkand for nearly 140 years had been the capital of our dynasty. An alien, and of what stamp! an Aūzbeg foe, had taken possession of it! It had slipped from our hands; God gave it again! plundered and ravaged, our own returned to us.

Sl. Ḥusain Mīrzā took Harāt[1] as we took Samarkand, by surprise, but to the experienced, and discerning, and just, it will be clear that between his affair and mine there are distinctions and differences, and that his capture and mine are things apart.

Firstly there is this;—He had ruled many years, passed through much experience and seen many affairs.

Secondly;—He had for opponent, Yādgār Muḥ. Nāṣir Mīrzā,
Fol. 85b. an inexperienced boy of 17 or 18.

Thirdly;—(Yādgār Mīrzā's) Head-equerry, Mīr 'Alī, a person well-acquainted with the particulars of the whole position, sent a man out from amongst Sl. Ḥusain Mīrzā's opponents to bring him to surprise them.

Fourthly;—His opponent was not in the fort but was in the Ravens'-garden. Moreover Yādgār Muḥ. Nāṣir Mīrzā and his followers are said to have been so prostrate with drink that three men only were in the Gate, they also drunk.

Fifthly;—he surprised and captured Harāt the first time he approached it.

On the other hand: firstly;—I was 19 when I took Samarkand.

Secondly;—I had as my opponent, such a man as Shaibāq Khān, of mature age and an eye-witness of many affairs.

[1] In 875 AH. (1470 AD.). Ḥusain was then 32 years old. Bābur might have compared his taking of Samarkand with Tīmūr's capture of Qarshī, also with 240 followers (Ẓ.N. i, 127). Firishta (lith. ed. p. 196) ascribes his omission to do so to reluctance to rank himself with his great ancestor.

Thirdly;—No-one came out of Samarkand to me; though the heart of its people was towards me, no-one could dream of coming, from dread of Shaibāq Khān.

Fourthly;—My foe was in the fort; not only was the fort taken but he was driven off.

Fifthly;—I had come once already; my opponent was on his guard about me. The second time we came, God brought it right! Samarkand was won.

In saying these things there is no desire to be-little the reputation of any man; the facts were as here stated. In Fol. 86. writing these things, there is no desire to magnify myself; the truth is set down.

The poets composed chronograms on the victory; this one remains in my memory;—Wisdom answered, 'Know that its date is the *Victory* (*Fatḥ*) *of Bābur Bahādur.*'

Samarkand being taken, Shavdār and Soghd and the *tūmāns* and nearer forts began, one after another, to return to us. From some their Aūzbeg commandants fled in fear and escaped; from others the inhabitants drove them and came in to us; in some they made them prisoner, and held the forts for us.

Just then the wives and families of Shaibāq Khān and his Aūzbegs arrived from Turkistān;[1] he was lying near Khwāja Dīdār and 'Alī-ābād but when he saw the forts and people returning to me, marched off towards Bukhārā. By God's grace, all the forts of Soghd and Miyān-kāl returned to me within three or four months. Over and above this, Bāqī Tarkhān seized this opportunity to occupy Qarshī; Khuzār and Qarshī (? Kesh) both went out of Aūzbeg hands; Qarā-kūl Fol. 86b. also was taken from them by people of Abū'l-muḥsin Mīrzā (*Bāī-qarā*), coming up from Merv. My affairs were in a very good way.

(e. Birth of Bābur's first child.)

After our departure (last year) from Andijān, my mothers and my wife and relations came, with a hundred difficulties and

[1] This arrival shews that Shaibānī expected to stay in Samarkand. He had been occupying Turkistān under The Chaghatāī Khān.

hardships, to Aūrātīpā. We now sent for them to Samarkand. Within a few days after their arrival, a daughter was born to me by 'Āyisha-sulṭān Begīm, my first wife, the daughter of Sl. Aḥmad Mīrzā. They named the child Fakhru'n-nisā' (Ornament of women); she was my first-born, I was 19. In a month or 40 days, she went to God's mercy.

(f. Bābur in Samarkand.)

On taking Samarkand, envoys and summoners were sent off at once, and sent again and again, with reiterated request for aid and reinforcement, to the khāns and sulṭāns and begs and marchers on every side. Some, though experienced men, made foolish refusal; others whose relations towards our family had been discourteous and unpleasant, were afraid for themselves and took no notice; others again, though they sent help, sent it insufficient. Each such case will be duly mentioned.

When Samarkand was taken the second time, 'Alī-sher Beg
Fol. 87. was alive. We exchanged letters once; on the back of mine to him I wrote one of my Turkī couplets. Before his reply reached me, separations (*tafarqa*) and disturbances (*ghūghā*) had happened.[1] Mullā Binā'ī had been taken iuto Shaibāq Khān's service when the latter took possession of Samarkand; he stayed with him until a few days after I took the place, when he came into the town to me. Qāsim Beg had his suspicions about him and consequently dismissed him towards Shahr-i-sabz but, as he was a man of parts, and as no fault of his came to light, I had him fetched back. He constantly presented me with odes (*qaṣīda u ghazal*). He brought me a song in the Nawā mode composed to my name and at the same time the following quatrain:—[2]

[1] 'Alī-sher died Jan. 3rd. 1501. It is not clear to what disturbances Bābur refers. He himself was at ease till after April 20th. 1502 and his defeat at Sar-i-pul. Possibly the reference is to the quarrels between Binā'ī and 'Alī-sher. *Cf.* Sām Mīrzā's Anthology, trs. S. de Saçy, *Notices et Extraits* iv, 287 *et seq.*

[2] I surmise a double play-of-words in this verse. One is on two rhyming words, *ghala* and *mallah* and is illustrated by rendering them as *oat* and *coat.* The other is on pointed and unpointed letters, *i.e.* *ghala* and *'ala.* We cannot find however a Persian word *'ala,* meaning garment.

No grain (*ghala*) have I by which I can be fed (*noshid*);
No rhyme of grain (*mallah*, nankeen) wherewith I can be clad (*poshid*);
The man who lacks both food and clothes,
In art or science where can he compete (*koshid*)?

In those days of respite, I had written one or two couplets but had not completed an ode. As an answer to Mullā Binā'ī I made up and set this poor little Turkī quatrain;—[1]

As is the wish of your heart, so shall it be (*būlghūsīdūr*);
For gift and stipend both an order shall be made (*buyurū'lghūsīdūr*);
I know the grain and its rhyme you write of;
The garments, you, your house, the corn shall fill (*tūlghūsīdūr*).

The Mullā in return wrote and presented a quatrain to me in which for his refrain, he took a rhyme to (the *tūlghūsīdūr* of) my last line and chose another rhyme;— Fol. 87*b*.

Mīrzā-of-mine, the Lord of sea and land shall be (*yīr būlghūsīdūr*);
His art and skill, world o'er, the evening tale shall be (*samar būlghūsīdūr*);
If gifts like these reward one rhyming (*or* pointless) word;
For words of sense, what guerdon will there be (*nīlār būlghūsīdūr*)?

Abū'l-barka, known as *Farāqi* (Parted), who just then had come to Samarkand from Shahr-i-sabz, said Binā'ī ought to have rhymed. He made this verse;—

Into Time's wrong to you quest shall be made (*sūrūlghūsīdūr*);
Your wish the Sulṭān's grace from Time shall ask (*qūlghūsīdūr*);
O Ganymede! our cups, ne'er filled as yet,
In this new Age, brimmed-up, filled full shall be (*tūlghūsīdūr*).

Though this winter our affairs were in a very good way and Shaibāq Khān's were on the wane, one or two occurrences were somewhat of a disservice; (1) the Merv men who had taken Qarā-kūl, could not be persuaded to stay there and it went back into the hands of the Aūzbegs; (2) Shaibāq Khān besieged Ibrāhīm Tarkhān's younger brother, Aḥmad in Dabūsī, stormed the place and made a general massacre of its inhabitants before the army we were collecting was ready to march.

With 240 proved men I had taken Samarkand; in the next five or six months, things so fell out by the favour of the Most High God, that, as will be told, we fought the arrayed battle of Sar-i-pul with a man like Shaibāq Khān. The help those Fol. 88.

[1] Bābur's refrain is *ghūsīdūr*, his rhymes *būl*, (*buyur*)*ūl* and *tūl*. Binā'ī makes *būlghūsīdūr* his refrain but his rhymes are not true *viz*. *yīr*, (*sa*)*mar* and *lār*.

round-about gave us was as follows;—From The Khān had come, with 4 or 5000 Bārīns, Ayūb *Begchīk* and Qashka Maḥmūd; from Jahāngīr Mīrzā had come Khalīl, Tambal's younger brother, with 100 or 200 men; not a man had come from Sl. Ḥusain Mīrzā, that experienced ruler, than whom none knew better the deeds and dealings of Shaibāq Khān; none came from Badī'u'z-zamān Mīrza; none from Khusrau Shāh because he, the author of what evil done,—as has been told,—to our dynasty! feared us more than he feared Shaibāq Khān.

(*g. Bābur defeated at Sar-i-pul.*)

I marched out of Samarkand, with the wish of fighting Shaibāq Khān, in the month of Shawwāl[1] and went to the New-garden where we lay four or five days for the convenience of gathering our men and completing our equipment. We took the precaution of fortifying our camp with ditch and branch. From the New-garden we advanced, march by march, to beyond Ṣar-i-pul (Bridge-head) and there dismounted.

Fol. 88*b*. Shaibāq Khān came from the opposite direction and dismounted at Khwāja Kārdzan, perhaps one *yīghāch* away (? 5 m.). We lay there for four or five days. Every day our people went from our side and his came from theirs and fell on one another. One day when they were in unusual force, there was much fighting but neither side had the advantage. Out of that engagement one of our men went rather hastily back into the entrenchments; he was using a standard; some said it was Sayyidī Qarā Beg's standard who really was a man of strong words but weak sword. Shaibāq Khān made one night-attack on us but could do nothing because the camp was protected by ditch and close-set branches. His men raised their war-cry, rained in arrows from outside the ditch and then retired.

In the work for the coming battle I exerted myself greatly and took all precautions; Qambar-'alī also did much. In Kesh lay Bāqī Tarkhān with 1000 to 2000 men, in a position to join us after a couple of days. In Diyūl, 4 *yīghāch* off

[1] Shawwāl 906 AH. began April 20th. 1501.

(? 20 m.), lay Sayyid Muḥ. Mīrzā *Dūghlāt*, bringing me 1000 to 2000 men from my Khān dādā; he would have joined me at dawn. With matters in this position, we hurried on the fight! Fol. 89.

> Who lays with haste his hand on the sword,
> Shall lift to his teeth the back-hand of regret.[1]

The reason I was so eager to engage was that on the day of battle, the Eight stars[2] were between the two armies; they would have been in the enemy's rear for 13 or 14 days if the fight had been deferred. I now understand that these considerations are worth nothing and that our haste was without reason.

As we wished to fight, we marched from our camp at dawn, we in our mail, our horses in theirs, formed up in array of right and left, centre and van. Our right was Ibrāhīm *Sārū*, Ibrāhīm Jānī, Abū'l-qāsim *Kohbur* and other begs. Our left was Muḥ. Mazīd Tarkhān, Ibrāhīm Tarkhān and other Samarkandī begs, also Sl. Ḥusain *Arghūn*, Qarā (Black) *Barlās*, Pīr Aḥmad and Khwāja Ḥusain. Qāsim Beg was (with me) in the centre and also several of my close circle and household. In the van were inscribed Qambar-'alī the Skinner, Banda-'alī, Khwāja 'Alī, Mīr Shāh *Qūchīn*, Sayyid Qāsim, Lord of the Gate,—Banda-'alī's younger brother Khaldar (mole-marked) and Ḥaidar-i-qāsim's son Qūch, together with all the good braves there were, and the rest of the household

Thus arrayed, we marched from our camp; the enemy, also in array, marched out from his. His right was Maḥmūd and Jānī and Tīmūr Sulṭāns; his left, Ḥamza and Mahdī and some other sulṭāns. When our two armies approached one another, he wheeled his right towards our rear. To meet this, I turned; this left our van,—in which had been inscribed what not of our best braves and tried swordsmen!—to our right and bared our front (*i.e.* the front of the centre). None-the-less we fought those who made the front-attack on us, turned them and forced them back on their own centre. So far did we carry it that some of Shaibāq Khān's old chiefs said to him, 'We must move off! It is past a stand.' He however held fast. His right beat our left, then wheeled (again) to our rear. Fol. 89*b*.

[1] From the *Bū-stān*, Graf ed. p. 55, l. 246.
[2] Sikiz Yïldūz. *See* Chardin's *Voyages*, v. 136 and Table; also Stanley Lane Poole's *Bābur*, p. 56.

(As has been said), the front of our centre was bare through our van's being left to the right. The enemy attacked us front and rear, raining in arrows on us. (Ayūb *Begchīk's*) Mughūl army, come for our help! was of no use in fighting; it set to work forthwith to unhorse and plunder our men. Not this Fol. 90. once only! This is always the way with those ill-omened Mughūls! If they win, they grab at booty; if they lose, they unhorse and pilfer their own side! We drove back the Aūzbegs who attacked our front by several vigorous assaults, but those who had wheeled to our rear came up and rained arrows on our standard. Falling on us in this way, from the front and from the rear, they made our men hurry off.

This same turning-movement is one of the great merits of Aūzbeg fighting; no battle of theirs is ever without it. Another merit of theirs is that they all, begs and retainers, from their front to their rear, ride, loose-rein at the gallop, shouting as they come and, in retiring, do not scatter but ride off, at the gallop, in a body.

Ten or fifteen men were left with me. The Kohik-water was close by,—the point of our right had rested on it. We made straight for it. It was the season when it comes down in flood. We rode right into it, man and horse in mail. It was just fordable for half-way over; after that it had to be swum. For more than an arrow's flight[1] we, man and mount in mail! made our horses swim and so got across. Once out of the water, we cut off the horse-armour and let it lie. By thus Fol. 90*b*. passing to the north bank of the river, we were free of our foes, but at once Mughūl wretches were the captors and pillagers of one after another of my friends. Ibrāhīm Tarkhān and some others, excellent braves all, were unhorsed and killed by Mughūls.[2] We moved along the north bank of the Kohik-river,

[1] In 1791 AD. Muḥ. Effendi shot 482 yards from a Turkish bow, before the R. Tox. S.; not a good shot, he declared. Longer ones are on record. *See* Payne-Gallwey's *Cross-bow* and AQR. 1911, H. Beveridge's *Oriental Cross-bows*.

[2] In the margin of the Elph. Codex, here, stands a Persian verse which appears more likely to be Humāyūn's than Bābur's. It is as follows:

Were the Mughūl race angels, they would be bad;
Written in gold, the name Mughūl would be bad;

recrossed it near Qulba, entered the town by the Shaikh-zāda's Gate and reached the citadel in the middle of the afternoon.

Begs of our greatest, braves of our best and many men perished in that fight. There died Ibrāhīm Tarkhān, Ibrāhīm *Sārū* and Ibrāhīm Jānī; oddly enough three great begs named Ibrāhīm perished. There died also Ḥaidar-i-qāsim's eldest son, Abū'l-qāsim *Kohbur*, and Khudāī-bīrdī *Tūghchī* and Khalīl, Tambal's younger brother, spoken of already several times. Many of our men fled in different directions; Muḥ. Mazīd Tarkhān went towards Qūndūz and Ḥiṣār for Khusrau Shāh. Fol. 91. Some of the household and of the braves, such as Karīm-dad-i-Khudāī-bīrdī *Turkmān* and Jānaka *Kūkūldāsh* and Mullā Bābā of Pashāghar got away to Aūrā-tīpā. Mullā Bābā at that time was not in my service but had gone out with me in a guest's fashion. Others again, did what Sherīm Ṭaghāī and his band did;—though he had come back with me into the town and though when consultation was had, he had agreed with the rest to make the fort fast, looking for life or death within it, yet spite of this, and although my mothers and sisters, elder and younger, stayed on in Samarkand, he sent off their wives and families to Aūrā-tīpā and remained himself with just a few men, all unencumbered. Not this once only! Whenever hard work had to be done, low and double-minded action was the thing to expect from him!

(h. Bābur besieged in Samarkand.)

Next day, I summoned Khwāja Abū'l-makāram, Qāsim and the other begs, the household and such of the braves as were admitted to our counsels, when after consultation, we resolved to make the fort fast and to look for life or death within it. I and Qāsim Beg with my close circle and household were the

---

Pluck not an ear from the Mughūl's corn-land,
What is sown with Mughūl seed will be bad.

This verse is written into the text of the First W.-i-B. (I.O. 215 f. 72) and is introduced by a scribe's statement that it is by *ān Ḥazrat*, much as notes known to be Humāyūn's are elsewhere attested in the Elph. Codex. It is not in the Ḥai. and Kehr's MSS. nor with, at least many, good copies of the Second W.-i-B.

reserve. For convenience in this I took up quarters in the middle of the town, in tents pitched on the roof of Aūlūgh Beg
Fol. 91b. Mīrzā's College. To other begs and braves posts were assigned in the Gates or on the ramparts of the walled-town.

Two or three days later, Shaibāq Khān dismounted at some distance from the fort. On this, the town-rabble came out of lanes and wards, in crowds, to the College gate, shouted good wishes for me and went out to fight in mob-fashion. Shaibāq Khān had got to horse but could not so much as approach the town. Several days went by in this fashion. The mob and rabble, knowing nothing of sword and arrow-wounds, never witnesses of the press and carnage of a stricken field, through these incidents, became bold and began to sally further and further out. If warned by the braves against going out so incautiously, they broke into reproach.

One day when Shaibāq Khān had directed his attack towards the Iron Gate, the mob, grown bold, went out, as usual, daringly and far. To cover their retreat, we sent several braves towards the Camel's-neck;[1] foster-brethren and some of the close household-circle, such as Nuyān *Kūkūldāsh*, Qul-naẓar (son of Sherīm ?) Ṭaghāī Beg, and Mazīd. An Aūzbeg or two
Fol. 92. put their horses at them and with Qul-naẓar swords were crossed. The rest of the Aūzbegs dismounted and brought their strength to bear on the rabble, hustled them off and rammed them in through the Iron Gate. Qūch Beg and Mīr Shāh *Qūchīn* had dismounted at the side of Khwāja Khiẓr's Mosque and were making a stand there. While the townsmen were being moved off by those on foot, a party of mounted Aūzbegs rode towards the Mosque. Qūch Beg came out when they drew near and exchanged good blows with them. He did distinguished work; all stood to watch. Our fugitives below were occupied only with their own escape; for them the time to shoot arrows and make a stand had gone by. I was shooting with a slur-bow[2] from above the Gate and some of my circle

1 This subterranean water-course, issuing in a flowing well (Erskine) gave its name to a bastion (Ḥ.S. ii, 300).

2 *nāwak*, a diminutive of *nāo*, a tube. It is described, in a MS. of Bābur's time, by Muḥ. Budhā'ī, and, in a second of later date, by Amīnu'd-dīn (AQR 1911, H.B.'s *Oriental Cross-bows*).

were shooting arrows (*aūq*). Our attack from above kept the enemy from advancing beyond the Mosque; from there he retired.

During the siege, the round of the ramparts was made each night; sometimes I went, sometimes Qāsim Beg, sometimes one of the household Begs. Though from the Turquoise to the Shaikh-zāda's Gate may be ridden, the rest of the way must be walked. When some men went the whole round on foot, it was dawn before they had finished.[1] Fol. 92*b*.

One day Shaibāq Khān attacked between the Iron Gate and the Shaikh-zāda's. I, as the reserve, went to the spot, without anxiety about the Bleaching-ground and Needle-makers' Gates. That day, (?) in a shooting wager (*aūq aūchīdā*), I made a good shot with a slur-bow, at a Centurion's horse.[2] It died at once (*aūq bārdī*) with the arrow (*aūq bīla*). They made such a vigorous attack this time that they got close under the ramparts. Busy with the fighting and the stress near the Iron Gate, we were entirely off our guard about the other side of the town. There, opposite the space between the Needle-makers' and Bleaching-ground Gates, the enemy had posted 7 or 800 good men in ambush, having with them 24 or 25 ladders so wide that two or three could mount abreast. These men came from their ambush when the attack near the Iron Gate, by occupying all our men, had left those other posts empty, and quickly set up their ladders between the two Gates, Fol. 93. just where a road leads from the ramparts to Muḥ. Mazīd Tarkhān's houses. That post was Qūch Beg's and Muḥammad-qulī *Qūchīn's*, with their detachment of braves, and they had their quarters in Muḥ. Mazīd's houses. In the Needle-makers' Gate was posted Qarā (Black) *Barlās*, in the Bleaching-ground Gate, Qūtlūq Khwāja *Kūkūldāsh* with Sherīm Ṭaghāī and his brethren, older and younger. As attack was being made on the other side of the town, the men attached to these posts were not on guard but had scattered to their quarters or to the

[1] Kostenko, i, 344, would make the rounds 9 m.

[2] *bīr yūz ātlīqning ātīnī nāwak aūqī bīla yakhshī atīm.* This has been read by Erskine as though *būz āt*, pale horse, and not *yūz ātlīq*, Centurion, were written. De. C. translates by Centurion and a marginal note of the Elph. Codex explains *yūz ātlīq* by *ṣad aspagī*.

bazar for necessary matters of service and servants' work. Only the begs were at their posts, with one or two of the populace. Qūch Beg and Mūhammad-qulī and Shāh Ṣufī and one other brave did very well and boldly. Some Aūzbegs were on the ramparts, some were coming up, when these four men arrived at a run, dealt them blow upon blow, and, by energetic drubbing, forced them all down and put them to flight. Qūch Beg did best; this was his out-standing and approved good deed; twice during this siege, he got his hand into the work. Qarā *Barlās* had been left alone in the Needle-makers' Gate; he also held out well to the end. Qūtlūq Khwāja and Qul-naẓar Mīrzā were also at their posts in the Bleaching-ground Gate; they held out well too, and charged the foe in his rear.

Another time Qāsim Beg led his braves out through the Fol. 93*b*. Needle-makers' Gate, pursued the Aūzbegs as far as Khwāja Kafsher, unhorsed some and returned with a few heads.

It was now the time of ripening rain but no-one brought new corn into the town. The long siege caused great privation to the towns-people;[1] it went so far that the poor and destitute began to eat the flesh of dogs and asses and, as there was little grain for the horses, people fed them on leaves. Experience shewed that the leaves best suiting were those of the mulberry and elm (*qarā-yīghāch*). Some people scraped dry wood and gave the shavings, damped, to their horses.

For three or four months Shaibāq Khān did not come near the fort but had it invested at some distance and himself moved round it from post to post. Once when our men were off their guard, at mid-night, the enemy came near to the Turquoise Fol. 94. Gate, beat his drums and flung his war-cry out. I was in the College, undressed. There was great trepidation and anxiety. After that they came night after night, disturbing us by drumming and shouting their war-cry.

Although envoys and messengers had been sent repeatedly to all sides and quarters, no help and reinforcement arrived from any-one. No-one had helped or reinforced me when I was in strength and power and had suffered no sort of defeat

1 The Sh. N. gives the reverse side of the picture, the plenty enjoyed by the besiegers.

or loss; on what score would any-one help me now? No hope in any-one whatever recommended us to prolong the siege. The old saying was that to hold a fort there must be a head, two hands and two legs, that is to say, the Commandant is the head; help and reinforcement coming from two quarters are the two arms and the food and water in the fort are the two legs. While we looked for help from those round about, their thoughts were elsewhere. That brave and experienced ruler, Sl. Ḥusain Mīrzā, gave us not even the help of an encouraging message, but none-the-less he sent Kamālu'd-dīn Ḥusain *Gāzurgāhī*[1] as an envoy to Shaibāq Khān.

(i. Taṃbal's proceedings in Farghāna.)[2]

(This year) Taṃbal marched from Andijān to near Bīshkīnt.[3] Aḥmad Beg and his party, thereupon, made The Khān move out against him. The two armies came face to face near Lak-lakān and the Tūrāk Four-gardens but separated without engaging. Sl. Maḥmūd was not a fighting man; now when opposed to Taṃbal, he shewed want of courage in word and deed. Aḥmad Beg was unpolished[4] but brave and well-meaning. In his very rough way, he said, 'What's the measure of this person, Taṃbal? that you are so tormented with fear and fright about him. If you are afraid to look at him, bandage your eyes before you go out to face him.' Fol. 94*b*.

[1] He may have been attached to the tomb of Khwāja 'Abdu'l-lāh *Anṣārī* in Harāt.

[2] The brusque entry here and elsewhere of *e.g.* Taṃbal's affairs, allows the inference that Bābur was quoting from perhaps a news-writer's, contemporary records. For a different view of Taṃbal, the Sh. N. cap. xxxiii should be read.

[3] Five-villages, on the main Khujand-Tāshkīnt road.

[4] *turk*, as on f. 28 of Khusrau Shāh.

907 AH.—JULY 17TH. 1501 TO JULY 7TH. 1502 AD.[1]

(*a. Surrender of Samarkand to Shaibānī.*)

The siege drew on to great length; no provisions and supplies came in from any quarter, no succour and reinforcement from any side. The soldiers and peasantry became hopeless and, by ones and twos, began to let themselves down outside[2] the walls and flee. On Shaibāq Khān's hearing of the distress in the town, he came and dismounted near the Lovers'-cave. I, in turn, went to Malik-muḥammad Mīrzā's dwellings in Low-lane, over against him. On one of those days, Khwāja Ḥusain's brother, Aūzūn Ḥasan[3] came into the town with 10 or 15 of his men,—he who, as has been told, had been the cause of Jahāngīr Mīrzā's rebellion, of my exodus from Samarkand (903 AH.—March 1498 AD.) and, again! of what an amount of sedition and
Fol. 95. disloyalty! That entry of his was a very bold act.[4]

The soldiery and townspeople became more and more distressed. Trusted men of my close circle began to let themselves down from the ramparts and get away; begs of known name and old family servants were amongst them, such as Pīr Wais, Shaikh Wais and Wais *Lāgharī*.[5] Of help from any side we utterly despaired; no hope was left in any quarter; our

[1] Elph. MS., f. 68*b*; W.-i-B. I.O. 215 f. 78 and 217 f. 61*b*; Mems. p. 97. The Kehr-Ilminsky text shews, in this year, a good example of its Persification and of Dr. Ilminsky's dealings with his difficult archetype by the help of the Memoirs.

[2] *tāshlāb*. The Sh. N. places these desertions as after four months of siege.

[3] It strikes one as strange to find Long Ḥasan described, as here, in terms of his younger brother. The singularity may be due to the fact that Ḥusain was with Bābur and may have invited Ḥasan. It may be noted here that Ḥusain seems likely to be that father-in-law of 'Umar Shaikh mentioned on f. 12*b* and 13*b*.

[4] This laudatory comment I find nowhere but in the Ḥai. Codex.

[5] There is some uncertainty about the names of those who left.

supplies and provisions were wretched, what there was was coming to an end; no more came in. Meantime Shaibāq Khān interjected talk of peace.[1] Little ear would have been given to his talk of peace, if there had been hope or food from any side. It had to be! a sort of peace was made and we took our departure from the town, by the Shaikh-zāda's Gate, somewhere about midnight.

(*b. Bābur leaves Samarkand.*)

I took my mother Khānīm out with me; two other women-folk went too, one was Bīshka (var. Peshka)-i-Khalīfa, the other, Mīnglīk *Kūkūldāsh*.[2] At this exodus, my elder sister, Khān-zāda Begīm fell into Shaibāq Khān's hands.[3] In the darkness of that night we lost our way[4] and wandered about amongst the main irrigation channels of Soghd. At shoot of dawn, after a hundred difficulties, we got past Khwāja Dīdār. At the Sunnat Prayer we scrambled up the rising-ground of Qarā-būgh. Fol. 95*b*.
From the north slope of Qarā-būgh we hurried on past the foot of Judūk village and dropped down into Yīlān-aūtī. On the road I raced with Qāsim Beg and Qambar-'alī (the Skinner); my horse was leading when I, thinking to look at theirs behind, twisted myself round; the girth may have slackened, for my saddle turned and I was thrown on my head to the ground. Although I at once got up and remounted, my brain did not steady till the evening; till then this world and what went on appeared to me like things felt and seen in a dream or fancy. Towards afternoon we dismounted in Yīlān-aūtī, there killed a

1 The Sh. N. is interesting here as giving an eye-witness' account of the surrender of the town and of the part played in the surrender by Khān-zāda's marriage (cap. xxxix).

2 The first seems likely to be a relation of Niẓāmu'd-dīn 'Alī Khalīfa; the second was Mole-marked, a foster-sister. The party numbered some 100 persons of whom Abū'l-makāram was one (Ḥ.S. ii, 310).

3 Bābur's brevity is misleading; his sister was not captured but married with her own and her mother's consent before attempt to leave the town was made. *Cf.* Gul-badan's H.N. f. 3*b* and Sh. N. Vambéry, p. 145.

4 The route taken avoided the main road for Dīzak; it can be traced by the physical features, mentioned by Bābur, on the Fr. map of 1904. The Sh. N. says the night was extraordinarily dark. Departure in blinding darkness and by unusual ways shews distrust of Shaibāq's safe-conduct suggesting that Yaḥyā's fate was in the minds of the fugitives.

horse, spitted and roasted its flesh, rested our horses awhile and rode on. Very weary, we reached Khalīla-village before the dawn and dismounted. From there it was gone on to Dīzak.

In Dīzak just then was Ḥāfiẓ Muḥ. *Dūldāī's* son, Ṭāhir. There, in Dīzak, were fat meats, loaves of fine flour, plenty of sweet melons and abundance of excellent grapes. From what privation we came to such plenty! From what stress to what repose!

From fear and hunger rest we won (*amānī tāptūq*);
A fresh world's new-born life we won (*jahānī tāptūq*).
Fol. 96. From out our minds, death's dread was chased (*rafa' būldī*);
From our men the hunger-pang kept back (*dafa' būldī*).[1]

Never in all our lives had we felt such relief! never in the whole course of them have we appreciated security and plenty so highly. Joy is best and more delightful when it follows sorrow, ease after toil. I have been transported four or five times from toil to rest and from hardship to ease.[2] This was the first. We were set free from the affliction of such a foe and from the pangs of hunger and had reached the repose of security and the relief of abundance.

(*c. Bābur in Dikh-kat.*)

After three or four days of rest in Dīzak, we set out for Aūrā tīpā. Pashāghar is a little[3] off the road but, as we had occupied it for some time (904 AH.), we made an excursion to it in passing by. In Pashāghar we chanced on one of Khānīm's old servants, a teacher[4] who had been left behind in Samarkand from want of a mount. We saw one another and on questioning her, I found she had come there on foot.

Khūb-nigār Khānīm, my mother Khānīm's younger sister[5]

1 The texts differ as to whether the last two lines are prose or verse. All four are in Turkī, but I surmise a clerical error in the refrain of the third, where *būlūb* is written for *būldī*.

2 The second was in 908 AH. (f. 18*b*); the third in 914 AH. (f. 216 *b*); the fourth is not described in the B.N.; it followed Bābur's defeat at Ghaj-dīwān in 918 AH. (Erskine's *History of India*, i, 325). He had a fifth, but of a different kind, when he survived poison in 933 AH. (f. 305).

3 Ḥai. MS. *qāqāsrāq*; Elph. MS. *yānasrāq*.

4 *ātūn*, one who instructs in reading, writing and embroidery. *Cf.* Gulbadan's H.N. f. 26. The distance walked may have been 70 or 80 m.

5 She was the wife of the then Governor of Aūrā-tīpā, Muḥ. Ḥusain *Dūghlāt*

already must have bidden this transitory world farewell; for they let Khānīm and me know of it in Aūrā-tīpā. My father's mother also must have died in Andijān; this too they let us Fol. 96 know in Aūrā-tīpā.[1] Since the death of my grandfather, Yūnas Khān (892 AH.), Khānīm had not seen her (step-)mother or her younger brother and sisters, that is to say, Shāh Begīm, Sl. Maḥmūd Khān, Sulṭān-nīgār Khānīm and Daulat-sulṭān Khānīm. The separation had lasted 13 or 14 years. To see these relations she now started for Tāshkīnt.

After consulting with Muḥ. Ḥusain Mīrzā, it was settled for us to winter in a place called Dikh-kat[2] one of the Aūrā-tīpā villages. There I deposited my impedimenta (*aūrūq*); then set out myself in order to visit Shāh Begīm and my Khān dādā and various relatives. I spent a few days in Tāshkīnt and waited on Shāh Begīm and my Khān dādā. My mother's elder full-sister, Mihr-nigār Khānīm[3] had come from Samarkand and was in Tāshkīnt. There my mother Kkānīm fell very ill; it was a very bad illness; she passed through mighty risks.

His Highness Khwājaka Khwāja, having managed to get out of Samarkand, had settled down in Far-kat; there I visited him. I had hoped my Khān dādā would shew me affection and kindness and would give me a country or a district (*pargana*). He did promise me Aūrā-tīpā but Muḥ. Ḥusain Mīrzā did not make it over, whether acting on his own account Fol. 97. or whether upon a hint from above, is not known. After spending a few days with him (in Aūrā-tīpā), I went on to Dikh-kat.

Dikh-kat is in the Aūrā-tīpā hill-tracts, below the range on the other side of which is the Macha[4] country. Its people, though Sārt, settled in a village, are, like Turks, herdsmen and

[1] It may be noted here that in speaking of these elder women Bābur uses the honorific plural, a form of rare occurrence except for such women, for saintly persons and exceptionally for The supreme Khān. For his father he has never used it.

[2] This name has several variants. The village lies, in a valley-bottom, on the Aq-sū and on a road. *See* Kostenko, i, 119.

[3] She had been divorced from Shaibānī in order to allow him to make legal marriage with her niece, Khān-zāda.

[4] Amongst the variants of this name, I select the modern one Macha is the upper valley of the Zar-afshān.

shepherds. Their sheep are reckoned at 40,000. We dismounted at the houses of the peasants in the village; I stayed in a head-man's house. He was old, 70 or 80, but his mother was still alive. She was a woman on whom much life had been bestowed for she was 111 years old. Some relation of hers may have gone, (as was said), with Tīmūr Beg's army to Hindūstān;[1] she had this in her mind and used to tell the tale. In Dikh-kat alone were 96 of her descendants, hers and her grandchildren, great-grandchildren and grandchildren's grandchildren. Counting in the dead, 200 of her descendants were reckoned up. Her grandchild's grandson was a strong young man of 25 or 26, with full black beard. While in Dikh-kat, I constantly made excursions amongst the mountains round
Fol. 97*b*. about. Generally I went bare-foot and, from doing this so much, my feet became so that rock and stone made no difference to them.[2] Once in one of these wanderings, a cow was seen, between the Afternoon and Evening prayers, going down by a narrow, ill-defined road. Said I, 'I wonder which way that road will be going; keep your eye on that cow; don't lose the cow till you know where the road comes out.' Khwāja Asadu'l-lāh made his joke, 'If the cow loses her way,' he said, 'what becomes of us?'

In the winter several of our soldiers asked for leave to Andijān because they could make no raids with us.[3] Qāsim Beg said, with much insistance, 'As these men are going, send something special of your own wear by them to Jahāngīr Mīrzā.' I sent my ermine cap. Again he urged, 'What harm would there be if you sent something for Tambal also?' Though I was very unwilling, yet as he urged it, I sent Tambal a large broad-sword which Nuyān *Kūkūldāsh* had had made for himself in Samarkand. This very sword it was which, as will

1 Tīmūr took Dihlī in 801 AH. (Dec. 1398), *i.e.* 103 solar and 106 lunar years earlier. The ancient dame would then have been under 5 years old. It is not surprising therefore that in repeating her story Bābur should use a tense betokening hear-say matter (*bārīb ikān dūr*).

2 The anecdote here following, has been analysed in JRAS 1908, p. 87, in order to show warrant for the opinion that parts of the Kehr-Ilminsky text are retranslations from the Persian W.-i-B.

3 Amongst those thus leaving seem to have been Qambar-'alī (f. 99*b*).

be told with the events of next year, came down on my own head![1]

A few days later, my grandmother, Aīsan-daulat Begīm, who, when I left Samarkand, had stayed behind, arrived in Dikh-kat with our families and baggage (*aūrūq*) and a few lean and hungry followers. Fol. 98.

(*d. Shaibāq Khān raids in The Khān's country.*)

That winter Shaibāq Khān crossed the Khujand river on the ice and plundered near Shāhrukhiya and Bīsh-kīnt. On hearing news of this, we gallopped off, not regarding the smallness of our numbers, and made for the villages below Khujand, opposite Hasht-yak (One-eighth). The cold was mightily bitter,[2] a wind not less than the Hā-darwesh[3] raging violently the whole time. So cold it was that during the two or three days we were in those parts, several men died of it. When, needing to make ablution, I went into an irrigation-channel, frozen along both banks but because of its swift current, not ice-bound in the middle, and bathed, dipping under 16 times, the cold of the water went quite through me. Next day we crossed the river on the ice from opposite Khaṣlār and went on through the dark to Bīsh-kīnt.[4] Shaibāq Khān, however, must have gone straight back after plundering the neighbourhood of Shāhrukhiya.

(*e. Death of Nuyān Kūkūldāsh.*)

Bīsh-kīnt, at that time, was held by Mullā Ḥaidar's son, 'Abdu'l-minān. A younger son, named Mūmin, a worthless and dissipated person, had come to my presence in Samarkand and had received all kindness from me. This sodomite, Mūmin, for what sort of quarrel between them is not known, cherished rancour against Nuyān *Kūkūldāsh*. At the time when we, having heard of the retirement of the Aūzbegs, sent a man to Fol. 98*b*.

[1] *Cf*. f. 107 foot.

[2] The Sh. N. speaks of the cold in that winter (Vambéry, p. 160). It was unusual for the Sīr to freeze in this part of its course (Sh. N. p. 172) where it is extremely rapid (Kostenko, i, 213).

[3] *Cf*. f. 4*b*.

[4] Point to point, some 50 miles.

The Khān and marched from Bīsh-kīnt to spend two or three days amongst the villages in the Blacksmith's-dale,[1] Mullā Ḥaidar's son, Mūmin invited Nuyān *Kūkūldāsh* and Aḥmad-i-qāsim and some others in order to return them hospitality received in Samarkand. When I left Bīsh-kīnt, therefore they stayed behind. Mūmin's entertainment to this party was given on the edge of a ravine (*jar*). Next day news was brought to us in Sām-sīrak, a village in the Blacksmith's-dale, that Nuyān was dead through falling when drunk into the ravine. We sent his own mother's brother, Ḥaq-naẓar and others, who searched out where he had fallen. They committed Nuyān to the earth in Bīsh-kīnt, and came back to me. They had found the body at the bottom of the ravine an arrow's flight from the place of the entertainment. Some suspected that Mūmin, nursing his trumpery rancour, had taken Nuyān's life. None knew the truth. His death made me strangely sad; for few men have I felt such grief; I wept unceasingly for a week or
Fol. 99. ten days. The chronogram of his death was found in *Nuyān is dead*.[2]

With the heats came the news that Shaibāq Khān was coming up into Aūrā-tīpā. Hereupon, as the land is level about Dikh-kat, we crossed the Āb-burdan pass into the Macha hill-country.[3] Āb-burdan is the last village of Macha; just below it a spring sends its water down (to the Zar-afshān); above the stream is included in Macha, below it depends on Palghar. There is a tomb at the spring-head. I had a rock at the side of the spring-head shaped (*qātīrīb*) and these three couplets inscribed on it;—

> I have heard that Jamshīd, the magnificent,
> Inscribed on a rock at a fountain-head[4]

---

1 *Āhangarān-julgasi*, a name narrowed on maps to Angren (valley).

2 *Faut shūd Nuyān*. The numerical value of these words is 907. Bābur when writing, looks back 26 years to the death of this friend.

3 Ab-burdan village is on the Zar-afshān; the pass is 11,200 ft. above the sea. Bābur's boundaries still hold good and the spring still flows. *See* Ujfalvy *l.c.* i. 14; Kostenko, i, 119 and 193; Rickmers, JRGS 1907, p. 358.

4 From the *Bū-stān* (Graf's ed. Vienna 1858, p. 561). The last couplet is also in the *Gulistān* (Platts' ed. p. 72). The Bombay lith. ed. of the *Bū-stān* explains (p. 39) that the "We" of the third couplet means Jamshīd and his predecessors who have rested by his fountain.

'Many men like us have taken breath at this fountain,
And have passed away in the twinkling of an eye;
We took the world by courage and might,
But we took it not with us to the tomb.'

There is a custom in that hill-country of cutting verses and things[1] on the rocks.

While we were in Macha, Mullā Hijrī,[2] the poet came from Ḥiṣār and waited on me. At that time I composed the following opening lines;—

Let your portrait flatter you never so much, than it you are more (*āndīn artūqsīn*);
Men call you their Life (*Jān*), than Life, without doubt, you are more (*jāndīn artūqsīn*).[3]

After plundering round about in Aūrā-tīpā, Shaibāq Khān retired.[4] While he was up there, we, disregarding the fewness of our men and their lack of arms, left our impedimenta (*aūrūq*) in Macha, crossed the Āb-burdan pass and went to Dikh-kat so that, gathered together close at hand, we might miss no chance on one of the next nights. He, however, retired straightway; we went back to Macha. Fol. 99b.

It passed through my mind that to wander from mountain to mountain, homeless and houseless, without country or abiding-place, had nothing to recommend it. 'Go you right off to The Khān,' I said to myself. Qāsim Beg was not willing for this move, apparently being uneasy because, as has been told, he had put Mughūls to death at Qarā-būlāq, by way of example. However much we urged it, it was not to be! He drew off for Ḥiṣār with all his brothers and his whole following. We for our part, crossed the Āb-burdan pass and set forward for The Khān's presence in Tāshkīnt.

[1] *nima*. The First W.-i-B. (I.O. 215 f. 81 l. 8) writes *tawārīkh*, annals.

[2] This may be the Khwāja Hijrī of the A.N. (index s.n.); and Badāyūnī's Ḥasan *Hijrī*, Bib. Ind. iii, 385; and Ethé's Pers. Cat. No. 793; and Bod. Cat. No. 189.

[3] The Ḥai. MS. points in the last line as though punning on Khān and Jān, but appears to be wrong.

[4] For an account of the waste of crops, the Sh. N. should be seen (p. 162 and 180).

(*f. Bābur with The Khān.*)

In the days when Taṃbal had drawn his army out and gone into the Blacksmith's-dale,[1] men at the top of his army, such as Muḥ. *Dūghlāt*, known as *Ḥiṣārī*, and his younger brother Ḥusain, and also Qaṃbar-'alī, the Skinner conspired to attempt his life. When he discovered this weighty matter, they, unable to remain with him, had gone to The Khān.

The Feast of Sacrifices ('Īd-i-qurbān) fell for us in Shāh-rukhiya (Ẕū'l-ḥijja 10th.—June 16th. 1502).

I had written a quatrain in an ordinary measure but was in some doubt about it, because at that time I had not studied
Fol. 100. poetic idiom so much as I have now done. The Khān was good-natured and also he wrote verses, though ones somewhat deficient in the requisites for odes. I presented my quatrain and I laid my doubts before him but got no reply so clear as to remove them. His study of poetic idiom appeared to have been somewhat scant. Here is the verse;—

> One hears no man recall another in trouble (*miḥnat-ta kīshī*);
> None speak of a man as glad in his exile (*ghurbat-ta kīshī*);
> My own heart has no joy in this exile;
> Called glad is no exile, man though he be (*albatta kīshī*).

Later on I came to know that in Turkī verse, for the purpose of rhyme, *ta* and *da* are interchangeable and also *ghain*, *qāf* and *kāf*.[2]

(*g. The acclaiming of the standards.*)

When, a few days later, The Khān heard that Taṃbal had gone up into Aūrā-tīpā, he got his army to horse and rode out from Tāshkīnt. Between Bīsh-kīnt and Sām-sīrak he formed up into array of right and left and saw the count[3] of his men.

[1] I think this refers to last year's move (f. 94 foot).

[2] In other words, the T. preposition, meaning E. in, at, *etc.* may be written with t or d, as *ta*(*tā*) or as *da*(*dā*). Also the one meaning E. towards, may be *gha*, *qa*, or *ka* (with long or short vowel).

[3] *dīm*, a word found difficult. It may be a derivative of root *de*, tell, and a noun with the meaning of English tale (number). The First W.-i-B. renders it by *san*, and by *san*, Abū'l-ghāzī expresses what Bābur's *dīm* expresses, the numbering of troops. It occurs thrice in the B.N. (here, on f. 183*b* and on f. 264*b*). In the Elphinstone Codex it has been written-over into *Ivīm*, once resembles *vīm* more than *dīm* and once is omitted. The L. and E. *Memoirs*

This done, the standards were acclaimed in Mughūl fashion.[1] The Khān dismounted and nine standards were set up in front of him. A Mughūl tied a long strip of white cloth to the thigh-bone (*aūrta aīlīk*) of a cow and took the other end in his hand. Three other long strips of white cloth were tied to the staves of three of the (nine) standards, just below the yak-tails, and their other ends were brought for The Khān to stand on one and for me and Sl. Muḥ. Khānika to stand each on one of the two others. The Mughūl who had hold of the strip of cloth fastened to the cow's leg, then said something in Mughūl while he looked at the standards and made signs towards them. The Khān and those present sprinkled *qumīz*[2] in the direction of the standards; hautbois and drums were sounded towards them;[3] the army flung the war-cry out three times towards them, mounted, cried it again and rode at the gallop round them. Fol. 100*b*.

Precisely as Chīngīz Khān laid down his rules, so the Mughūls still observe them. Each man has his place, just where his ancestors had it; right, right,—left, left,—centre, centre. The most reliable men go to the extreme points of the right and left. The Chīrās and Begchīk clans always demand to go to the point in the right.[4] At that time the Beg of the Chīrās tūmān was a very bold brave, Qāshka (Mole-marked) Maḥmud and the beg of the renowned Begchīk tūmān was Ayūb *Begchīk*. These two, disputing which should go out to the point, drew swords on one another. At last it seems to have been settled that one should take the highest place in the hunting-circle, the other, in the battle-array.

Next day after making the circle, it was hunted near Sām-

(p. 303) inserts what seems a gloss, saying that a whip or bow is used in the count, presumably held by the teller to 'keep his place' in the march past. The *Siyāsat-nāma* (Schefer, trs. p. 22) names the whip as used in numbering an army.

[1] The acclamation of the standards is depicted in B.M. W.-i-B. Or. 3714 f. 128*b*. One cloth is shewn tied to the off fore-leg of a live cow, above the knee, Bābur's word being *aūrtā aīlīk* (middle-hand).

[2] The libation was of fermented mares'-milk.

[3] *lit*. their one way.

[4] *Cf*. T.R. p. 308.

Fol. 101. sīrak; thence move was made to the Tūrāk Four-gardens. On that day and in that camp, I finished the first ode I ever finished. Its opening couplet is as follows;—

> Except my soul, no friend worth trust found I (*wafādār tāpmādīm*);
> Except my heart, no confidant found I (*asrār tāpmādīm*).

There were six couplets; every ode I finished later was written just on this plan.

The Khān moved, march by march, from Sām-sīrak to the bank of the Khujand-river. One day we crossed the water by way of an excursion, cooked food and made merry with the braves and pages. That day some-one stole the gold clasp of my girdle. Next day Bayān-qulī's Khān-qulī and Sl. Muḥ. Wais fled to Taṃbal. Every-one suspected them of that bad deed. Though this was not ascertained, Aḥmad-i-qāsim *Kohbur* asked leave and went away to Aūrā-tīpa. From that leave he did not return; he too went to Tambal.

908 AH.—JULY 7TH. 1502 TO JUNE 26TH. 1503 AD.[1]

(a. Bābur's poverty in Tāshkīnt.)

This move of The Khān's was rather unprofitable; to take no fort, to beat no foe, he went out and went back.

During my stay in Tāshkīnt, I endured much poverty and humiliation. No country or hope of one! Most of my retainers dispersed, those left, unable to move about with me because of their destitution! If I went to my Khān dādā's Gate,[2] I went sometimes with one man, sometimes with two. It was well he was no stranger but one of my own blood. Fol. 101*b*. After showing myself[3] in his presence, I used to go to Shāh Begīm's, entering her house, bareheaded and barefoot, just as if it were my own.

This uncertainty and want of house and home drove me at last to despair. Said I, 'It would be better to take my head[4] and go off than live in such misery; better to go as far as my feet can carry me than be seen of men in such poverty and humiliation. Having settled on China to go to, I resolved to take my head and get away. From my childhood up I had wished to visit China but had not been able to manage it because of ruling and attachments. Now sovereignty itself was gone! and my mother, for her part, was re-united to her (step)-mother and her younger brother. The hindrances to my journey had been removed; my anxiety for my mother was dispelled. I represented (to Shāh Begīm and The Khān) through Khwāja Abū'l-makāram that now such a foe as

1 Elph. MS. f. 74; W.-i-B. I.O. 215 f. 83 and 217 f. 66; Mems. p. 104.

2 It may be noted that Bābur calls his mother's brothers, not *taghāī* but *dādā* father. I have not met with an instance of his saying 'My taghāī' as he says 'My dādā.' *Cf.* index *s.n. taghāī*.

3 *kūrūnūsh qīlīb*, reflective from *kūrmak*, to see.

4 A rider's metaphor.

Shaibāq Khān had made his appearance, Mughūl and Turk[1] alike must guard against him; that thought about him must be taken while he had not well-mastered the (Aūzbeg) horde or grown very strong, for as they have said;—[2]

> To-day, while thou canst, quench the fire,
> Once ablaze it will burn up the world;
> Let thy foe not fix string to his bow,
> While an arrow of thine can pierce him;

that it was 20 or 25 years[3] since they had seen the Younger Khān (Aḥmad *Alacha*) and that I had never seen him; should I be able, if I went to him, not only to see him myself, but to bring about the meeting between him and them?

Fol. 102. Under this pretext I proposed to get out of those surroundings;[4] once in Mughūlistān and Turfān, my reins would be in my own hands, without check or anxiety. I put no-one in possession of my scheme. Why not? Because it was impossible for me to mention such a scheme to my mother, and also because it was with other expectations that the few of all ranks who had been my companions in exile and privation, had cut themselves off with me and with me suffered change of fortune. To speak to them also of such a scheme would be no pleasure.

The Khwāja, having laid my plan before Shāh Begīm and The Khān, understood them to consent to it but, later, it occurred to them that I might be asking leave a second time,[5] because of not receiving kindness. That touching their reputation, they delayed a little to give the leave.

(b. The Younger Khān comes to Tāshkīnt.)

At this crisis a man came from the Younger Khān to say that he was actually on his way. This brought my scheme to

1 As touching the misnomer, 'Mughūl dynasty' for the Tīmūrid rulers in Hindūstān, it may be noted that here, as Bābur is speaking to a Chaghatāi Mughūl, his 'Turk' is left to apply to himself.

2 Gulistān, cap. viii, Maxim 12 (Platts' ed. p. 147).

3 This backward count is to 890 AH. when Aḥmad fled from cultivated lands (T.R. p. 113).

4 It becomes clear that Aḥmad had already been asked to come to Tāshkīnt.

5 *Cf.* f. 96*b* for his first departure without help.

naught. When a second man announced his near approach, we all went out to give him honourable meeting, Shāh Begīm and his younger sisters, Sulṭān-nigār Khānīm and Daulat-sulṭān Khānīm, and I and Sl. Muḥ. Khānika and Khān Mīrzā (Wais).

Between Tāshkīnt and Sairām is a village called Yagha (var. Yaghma), with some smaller ones, where are the tombs of Father Abraham and Father Isaac. So far we went out. Knowing nothing exact about his coming,[1] I rode out for an Fol. 102b. excursion, with an easy mind. All at once, he descended on me, face to face. I went forward; when I stopped, he stopped. He was a good deal perturbed; perhaps he was thinking of dismounting in some fixed spot and there seated, of receiving me ceremoniously. There was no time for this; when we were near each other, I dismounted. He had not time even to dismount;[2] I bent the knee, went forward and saw him. Hurriedly and with agitation, he told Sl. Sa'īd Khān and Bābā Khān Sl. to dismount, bend the knee with (*bīla*) me and make my acquaintance.[3] Just these two of his sons had come with him; they may have been 13 or 14 years old. When I had seen them, we all mounted and went to Shāh Begīm's presence. After he had seen her and his sisters, and had renewed acquaintance, they all sat down and for half the night told one another particulars of their past and gone affairs.

Next day, my Younger Khān dādā bestowed on me arms of his own and one of his own special horses saddled, and a Mughūl head-to-foot dress,—a Mughūl cap,[4] a long coat of Chinese satin, with broidering of stitchery,[5] and Chinese

[1] Yagha (Yaghma) is not on the Fr. map of 1904, but suitably located is Turbat (Tomb) to which roads converge.

[2] Elph. MS. *tūshkūcha*; Ḥai. MS. *yūkūnchā*. The importance Aḥmad attached to ceremony can be inferred by the details given (f. 103) of his meeting with Maḥmūd.

[3] *kūrūshkāīlār*. *Cf.* Redhouse who gives no support for reading the verb *kūrmak* as meaning *to embrace*.

[4] *būrk*, a tall felt cap (Redhouse). In the adjective applied to the cap there are several variants. The Ḥai. MS. writes *muftūl*, solid or twisted. The Elph. MS. has *muftūn-lūq* which has been understood by Mr. Erskine to mean, gold-embroidered.

[5] The wording suggests that the decoration is in chain-stitch, pricked up and down through the stuff.

armour; in the old fashion, they had hung, on the left side, a haversack (*chantāī*) and an outer bag,[1] and three or four things such as women usually hang on their collars, perfume-holders and various receptacles;[2] in the same way, three or four things hung on the right side also.

Fol. 103. From there we went to Tāshkīnt. My Elder Khān dādā also had come out for the meeting, some 3 or 4 *yīghāch* (12 to 15 m.) along the road. He had had an awning set up in a chosen spot and was seated there. The Younger Khān went up directly in front of him; on getting near, fetched a circle, from right to left, round him; then dismounted before him. After advancing to the place of interview (*kūrūshūr yīr*), he nine times bent the knee; that done, went close and saw (his brother). The Elder Khān, in his turn, had risen when the Younger Khān drew near. They looked long at one another (*kūrūshtīlār*) and long stood in close embrace (*qūchūshūb*). The Younger Khān again bent the knee nine times when retiring, many times also on offering his gift; after that, he went and sat down.

All his men had adorned themselves in Mughūl fashion. There they were in Mughūl caps (*būrk*); long coats of Chinese satin, broidered with stitchery, Mughūl quivers and saddles of green shagreen-leather, and Mughūl horses adorned in a unique fashion. He had brought rather few men, over 1000 and under 2000 may-be. He was a man of singular manners, a mighty master of the sword, and brave. Amongst arms he preferred to trust to the sword. He used to say that of arms there are, the *shash-par*[3] (six-flanged mace), the *piyāzī* (rugged mace), the *kīstin*,[4] the *tabar-zīn* (saddle-hatchet) and the *bāltū* (battle-axe),

[1] *tāsh chantāī*. These words have been taken to mean whet-stone (*bilgū-tāsh*). I have found no authority for reading *tāsh* as whet-stone. Moreover to allow 'bag of the stone' to be read would require *tāsh* (*ning*) *chantāī-sī* in the text.

[2] lit. bag-like things. Some will have held spare bow-strings and archers' rings, and other articles of 'repairing kit.' With the gifts, it seems probable that the *gosha-gīr* (f. 107) was given.

[3] Vullers, *clava sex foliis*.

[4] Zenker, *casse-tête*. *Kīstin* would seem to be formed from the root, *kīs*, cutting, but M. de C. describes it as a ball attached by a strap or chain to a handle. *Sanglākh*, a sort of mace (*gurz*).

all, if they strike, work only with what of them first touches, but the sword, if it touch, works from point to hilt. He never parted with his keen-edged sword; it was either at his waist or to his hand. He was a little rustic and rough-of- Fol. 103*b*.
speech, through having grown up in an out-of-the-way place.

When, adorned in the way described, I went with him to The Khān, Khwāja Abū'l-makāram asked, 'Who is this honoured sulṭān?' and till I spoke, did not recognize me.

(*c. The Khāns march into Farghāna against Taṃbal.*)

Soon after returning to Tāshkīnt, The Khān led out an army for Andikān (Andijān) direct against Sl. Aḥmad *Taṃbal.*[1] He took the road over the Kīndīrlīk-pass and from Blacksmiths'-dale (Āhangarān-julgasī) sent the Younger Khān and me on in advance. After the pass had been crossed, we all met again near Zarqān (var. Zabarqān) of Karnān.

One day, near Karnān, they numbered their men[2] and reckoned them up to be 30,000. From ahead news began to come that Taṃbal also was collecting a force and going to Akhsī. After having consulted together, The Khāns decided to join some of their men to me, in order that I might cross the Khujand-water, and, marching by way of Aūsh and Aūzkīnt, turn Taṃbal's rear. Having so settled, they joined to me Ayūb *Begchīk* with his *tūmān*, Jān-ḥasan Bārīn (var. Nārīn) with his Bārīns, Muḥ. *Ḥiṣārī Dūghlāt*, Sl. Ḥusain *Dūghlāt* and Sl. Aḥmad Mīrzā *Dūghlāt*, not in command of the Dūghlāt *tūmān*,—and Qaṃbar-'alī Beg (the Skinner). The commandant (*darogha*) of their force was Sārīgh-bāsh (Yellow-head) Mīrza *Itārchī.*[3]

Leaving The Khāns in Karnān, we crossed the river on rafts near Sakan, traversed the Khūqān sub-district (*aūrchīn*), crushed Fol. 104.

1 The *Rauzatu'ṣ-ṣafā* states that The Khāns left Tāshkīnt on Muḥarram 15th (July 21st. 1502), in order to restore Bābur and expel Taṃbal (Erskine).

2 lit. saw the count (*dīm*). *Cf.* f. 100 and note concerning the count. Using a Persian substitute, the Kehr-Ilminsky text writes *san* (*kūrdīlār*).

3 Elph. MS. *aṃbārchī*, steward, for Itārchī, a tribal-name. The 'Mīrzā' and the rank of the army-begs are against supposing a steward in command. Here and just above, the texts write Mīrzā-i-Itārchī and Mīrzā-i-Dūghlāt, thus suggesting that in names not ending with a vowel, the *iẓāfat* is required for exact transliteration, *e.g.* Muḥammad-i-dūghlāt.

Qabā and by way of the Alāī sub-districts[1] descended suddenly on Aūsh. We reached it at dawn, unexpected; those in it could but surrender. Naturally the country-folk were wishing much for us, but they had not been able to find their means, both through dread of Tambal and through our remoteness. After we entered Aūsh, the hordes and the highland and lowland tribes of southern and eastern Andijān came in to us. The Aūzkīnt people also, willing to serve us, sent me a man and came in.

(*Author's note on Aūzkīnt.*) Aūzkīnt formerly must have been a capital of Farghāna;[2] it has an excellent fort and is situated on the boundary (of Farghāna).

The Marghīnānīs also came in after two or three days, having beaten and chased their commandant (*darogha*). Except Andijān, every fort south of the Khujand-water had now come in to us. Spite of the return in those days of so many forts, and spite of risings and revolt against him, Tambal did not yet come to his senses but sat down with an army of horse and foot, fortified with ditch and branch, to face The Khāns, between Karnān and Akhsī. Several times over there was a little fighting and pell-mell but without decided success to either side.

In the Andijān country (*wilāyat*), most of the tribes and hordes and the forts and all the districts had come in to me; naturally the Andijānīs also were wishing for me. They however could not find their means.

(*d. Bābur's attempt to enter Andijān frustrated by a mistake.*)

It occurred to me that if we went one night close to the town and sent a man in to discuss with the Khwāja[3] and notables, they might perhaps let us in somewhere. With this idea we rode out from Aūsh. By midnight we were opposite Forty-daughters (Chihil-dukhterān) 2 miles (one *kuroh*) from Andijān. From that place we sent Qambar-'alī Beg forward,

[1] *Alāī-līq aūrchīnī.* I understand the march to have been along the northern slope of the Little Alāī, south of Aūsh.

[2] As of Ālmāligh and Ālmātū (fol. 2*b*) Bābur reports a tradition with caution. The name Aūz-kīnt may be read to mean 'Own village,' independent, as *Aūz-beg*, Own-beg.

[3] He would be one of the hereditary Khwājas of Andijān (f. 16).

with some other begs, who were to discuss matters with the Khwāja after by some means or other getting a man into the fort. While waiting for their return, we sat on our horses, some of us patiently humped up, some wrapt away in dream, when suddenly, at about the third watch, there rose a war-cry[1] and a sound of drums. Sleepy and startled, ignorant whether the foe was many or few, my men, without looking to one another, took each his own road and turned for flight. There was no time for me to get at them; I went straight for the enemy. Only Mīr Shāh *Qūchīn* and Bābā Sher-zād (Tiger-whelp) and Nāṣir's Dost sprang forward; we four excepted, every man set his face for flight. I had gone a little way forward, when the enemy rode rapidly up, flung out his war-cry and poured arrows on us. One man, on a horse with a starred forehead,[2] came close to me; I shot at it; it rolled over and died. They made a little as if to retire. The three Fol. 105.
with me said, 'In this darkness it is not certain whether they are many or few; all our men have gone off; what harm could we four do them? Fighting must be when we have overtaken our run-aways and rallied them.' Off we hurried, got up with our men and beat and horse-whipped some of them, but, do what we would, they would not make a stand. Back the four of us went to shoot arrows at the foe. They drew a little back but when, after a discharge or two, they saw we were not more than three or four, they busied themselves in chasing and unhorsing my men. I went three or four times to try to rally my men but all in vain! They were not to be brought to order. Back I went with my three and kept the foe in check with our arrows. They pursued us two or three *kuroh* (4-6 m.), as far as the rising ground opposite Kharābūk and Pashāmūn. There we met Muḥ. 'Alī *Mubashir*. Said I, 'They are only few; let us stop and put our horses at them.' So we did. When we got up to them, they stood still.[3]

Our scattered braves gathered in from this side and that, but

[1] For several battle-cries *see* Th. Radloff's *Réceuils* etc. p. 322.

[2] *qāshqa ātlīq kīshī*. For a parallel phrase *see* f. 92*b*.

[3] Bābur does not explain how the imbroglio was cleared up; there must ave been a dramatic moment when this happened.

several very serviceable men, scattering in this attack, went right away to Aūsh.

The explanation of the affair seemed to be that some of Ayūb *Begchīk's* Mughūls had slipped away from Aūsh to raid near Andijān and, hearing the noise of our troop, came somewhat stealthily towards us; then there seems to have been confusion about the pass-word. The pass-words settled on for use during this movement of ours were Tāshkīnt and Sairām. If

Fol. 103b. (*Author's note on pass-words.*) Pass-words are of two kinds;—in each tribe there is one for use in the tribe, such as *Darwāna* or *Tūqqāi* or *Lūlū*;[1] and there is one for the use of the whole army. For a battle, two words are settled on as pass-words so that of two men meeting in the fight, one may give the one, the other give back the second, in order to distinguish friends from foes, own men from strangers.

Tāshkīnt were said, Sairām would be answered; if Sairām, Tāshkīnt. In this muddled affair, Khwāja Muḥ. 'Ali seems to have been somewhat in advance of our party and to have got bewildered,—he was a Sārt person,[2]—when the Mughūls came up saying, 'Tāshkīnt, Tāshkīnt,' for he gave them 'Tāshkīnt, Tāshkīnt,' as the counter-sign. Through this they took him for an enemy, raised their war-cry, beat their saddle-drums and poured arrows on us. It was through this we gave way, and through this false alarm were scattered! We went back to Aūsh.

(*e. Bābur again attempts Andijān.*)

Through the return to me of the forts and the highland and lowland clans, Tambal and his adherents lost heart and footing. His army and people in the next five or six days began to desert him and to flee to retired places and the open country.[3] Of his household some came and said, 'His affairs are nearly ruined; he will break up in three or four days, utterly ruined.' On hearing this, we rode for Andijān.

[1] *Darwāna* (a trap-door in a roof) has the variant *dur-dāna*, a single pearl; *tūqqāi* perhaps implies relationship; *lūlū* is a pearl, a wild cow etc.

[2] Ḥai. MS. *sāirt kishī*. Muḥ. 'Alī is likely to be the librarian (*cf.* index *s.n.*).

[3] Elph. MS. *ramāqgha u tūr-gā*; Ḥai. MS. *tārtātgha u tūr-gā*. Ilminsky gives no help, varying much here from the true text. The archetype of both MSS. must have been difficult to read.

Sl. Muḥ. *Galpuk*[1] was in Andijān,—the younger of Tambal's cadet brothers. We took the Mulberry-road and at the Mid-day Prayer came to the Khākān (canal), south of the town. A foraging-party was arranged; I followed it along Khākān to the skirt of 'Aīsh-hill. When our scouts brought word that Sl. Muḥ *Galpuk* had come out, with what men he had, beyond the suburbs and gardens to the skirt of 'Aīsh, I hurried to meet him, although our foragers were still scattered. He may have had over 500 men; we had more but many had scattered to forage. When we were face to face, his men and ours may have been in equal number. Without caring about order or array, down we rode on them, loose rein, at the gallop. When we got near, they could not stand; there was not so much fighting as the crossing of a few swords. My men followed them almost to the Khākān Gate, unhorsing one after another. Fol. 106.

It was at the Evening Prayer that, our foe outmastered, we reached Khwāja Kitta, on the outskirts of the suburbs. My idea was to go quickly right up to the Gate but Dost Beg's father, Nāṣir Beg and Qambar-'alī Beg, old and experienced begs both, represented to me, 'It is almost night; it would be ill-judged to go in a body into the fort in the dark; let us withdraw a little and dismount. What can they do to-morrow but surrender the place?' Yielding at once to the opinion of these experienced persons, we forthwith retired to the outskirts of the suburbs. If we had gone to the Gate, undoubtedly, Andijān would have come into our hands. Fol. 106b.

(f. Bābur surprised by Tambal.)

After crossing the Khākān-canal, we dismounted, near the Bed-time prayer, at the side of the village of Rabāṭ-i-zauraq (var. rūzaq). Although we knew that Tambal had broken camp and was on his way to Andijān, yet, with the negligence of inexperience, we dismounted on level ground close to the village, instead of where the defensive canal would have protected us.[2] There we lay down carelessly, without scouts or rear-ward.

[1] The Ḥai. MS.'s pointing allows the sobriquet to mean 'Butterfly.' His family lent itself to nick-names; in it three brothers were known respectively as Fat or Lubberly, Fool and, perhaps, Butterfly.

[2] *bīrk ārīgh*, doubly strong by its trench and its current.

At the top (*bāsh*) of the morning, just when men are in sweet sleep, Qambar-'alī Beg hurried past, shouting, 'Up with you! the enemy is here!' So much he said and went off without a moment's stay. It was my habit to lie down, even in times of peace, in my tunic; up I got instanter, put on sword and quiver and mounted. My standard-bearer had no time to adjust my standard,[1] he just mounted with it in his hand. There were ten or fifteen men with me when we started toward the enemy; after riding an arrow's flight, when we came up with his scouts, there may have been ten. Going rapidly forward, we overtook him, poured in arrows on him, over-mastered his foremost men and hurried them off. We followed them for another arrow's flight and came up with his centre where Sl. Aḥmad *Tambal* himself was, with as many as
Fol. 107. 100 men. He and another were standing in front of his array, as if keeping a Gate,[2] and were shouting, 'Strike, strike!' but his men, mostly, were sidling, as if asking themselves, 'Shall we run away? Shall we not?' By this time three were left with me; one was Nāṣir's Dost, another, Mīrzā Qulī *Kūkūldāsh*, the third, Khudāī-bīrdī *Turkmān's* Karīm-dād.[3] I shot off the arrow on my thumb,[4] aiming at Tambal's helm. When I put my hand into my quiver, there came out a quite new *gosha-gīr*[5]

1 I understand that time failed to set the standard in its usual rest. E. and de C. have understood that the yak-tail (*qūtās tūghī* f. 100) was apart from the staff and that time failed to adjust the two parts. The *tūgh* however is the whole standard; moreover if the tail were ever taken off at night from the staff, it would hardly be so treated in a mere bivouac.

2 *aīshiklik tūrlūq*, as on f. 113. I understand this to mean that the two men were as far from their followers as sentries at a Gate are posted outside the Gate.

3 So too 'Piero of Cosimo' and 'Lorenzo of Piero of the Medici.' *Cf.* the names of five men on f. 114.

4 *shashtīm*. The *shasht* (thumb) in archery is the thumb-shield used on the left hand, as the *zih-gīr* (string-grip), the archer's ring, is on the right-hand thumb.

It is useful to remember, when reading accounts of shooting with the Turkī (Turkish) bow, that the arrows (*aūq*) had notches so gripping the string that they kept in place until released with the string.

5 *sar-i-sabz gosha gīr*. The *gosha-gīr* is an implement for remedying the warp of a bow-tip and string-notch. For further particulars *see* Appendix C.

The term *sar-i-sabz*, lit. green-head, occurs in the sense of 'quite young' or 'new,' in the proverb, 'The red tongue loses the green head,' quoted in the *Ṭabaqāt-i-akbarī* account of Bābur's death. Applied here, it points to the *gosha-gīr* as part of the recent gift made by Aḥmad to Bābur.

given me by my Younger Khān dādā. It would have been vexing to throw it away but before I got it back into the quiver, there had been time to shoot, maybe, two or three arrows. When once more I had an arrow on the string, I went forward, my three men even holding back. One of those two in advance, Tambal seemingly,[1] moved forward also. The high-road was between us; I from my side, he, from his, got upon it and came face to face, in such a way that his right hand was towards me, mine towards him. His horse's mail excepted, he was fully accoutred; but for sword and quiver, I was unprotected. I shot off the arrow in my hand, adjusting for the attachment of his shield. With matters in this position, they shot my right leg through. I had on the cap of my helm;[2] Tambal chopped Fol. 107b so violently at my head that it lost all feeling under the blow. A large wound was made on my head, though not a thread of the cap was cut.[3] I had not bared[4] my sword; it was in the scabbard and I had no chance to draw it. Single-handed, I was alone amongst many foes. It was not a time to stand still; I turned rein. Down came a sword again; this time on my arrows. When I had gone 7 or 8 paces, those same three men rejoined me.[5] After using his sword on me, Tambal seems to have used it on Nāṣir's Dost. As far as an arrrow flies to the butt, the enemy followed us.

The Khākān-canal is a great main-channel, flowing in a deep cutting, not everywhere to be crossed. God brought it right! we came exactly opposite a low place where there was a passage over. Directly we had crossed, the horse Nāṣir's Dost was on, being somewhat weakly, fell down. We stopped and re-mounted him, then drew off for Aūsh, over the rising-ground

[1] *Tambal aīkāndūr.* By this tense I understand that Bābur was not at first sure of the identity of the pseudo-sentries, partly because of their distance, partly, it may be presumed, because of concealment of identity by armour.

[2] *dūwulgha būrkī; i.e.* the soft cap worn under the iron helm.

[3] Nūyān's sword dealt the blow (f. 97*b*). Gul-badan also tells the story (f. 77) à propos of a similar incident in Humāyūn's career. Bābur repeats the story on f. 234.

[4] *yāldāghlāmāī dūr aīdīm.* The Second W.-i-B. has taken this as from *yāltūrmāq*, to cause to glisten, and adds the gloss that the sword was rusty (I.O. 217 f. 70*b*).

[5] The text here seems to say that the three men were on foot, but this is negatived by the context.

between Farāghīna and Khirābūk. Out on the rise, Mazīd Ṭaghāī came up and joined us. An arrow had pierced his right leg also and though it had not gone through and come out again, he got to Aūsh with difficulty. The enemy unhorsed (*tūshūrdīlār*) good men of mine; Nāṣir Beg, Muḥ. 'Alī *Mubashir*, Khwāja Muḥ. 'Alī, Khusrau *Kūkūldāsh*, Na'man the page, all fell (to them, *tūshtīlār*), and also many unmailed braves.[1]

(*g. The Khāns move from Kāsān to Andijān.*)

The Khāns, closely following on Tambal, dismounted near Andijān,—the Elder at the side of the Reserve (*qūrūq*) in the Fol. 108. garden, known as Birds'-mill (*Qūsh-tīgīrmān*), belonging to my grandmother, Aīsān-daulat Begīm,—the Younger, near Bābā Tawakkul's Alms-house. Two days later I went from Aūsh and saw the Elder Khān in Birds'-mill. At that interview, he simply gave over to the Younger Khān the places which had come in to me. He made some such excuse as that for our advantage, he had brought the Younger Khān, how far! because such a foe as Shaibāq Khān had taken Samarkand and was waxing greater; that the Younger Khān had there no lands whatever, his own being far away; and that the country under Andijān, on the south of the Khujand-water, must be given him to encamp in. He promised me the country under Akhsī, on the north of the Khujand-water. He said that after taking a firm grip of that country (Farghāna), they would move, take Samarkand, give it to me and then the whole of the Farghāna country was to be the Younger Khān's. These words seem to have been meant to deceive me, since there is no knowing what they would have done when they had attained their object. It had to be however! willy-nilly, I agreed.

When, leaving him, I was on my way to the Younger Khān's presence, Qambar-'alī, known as the Skinner, joined me in a friendly way and said, 'Do you see? They have taken the whole of the country just become yours. There is no opening

1 Amongst the various uses of the verb *tūshmak*, to descend in any way, the B.N. does not allow of 'falling (death) in battle.' When I made the index of the Hai. MS. facsimile, this was not known to me; I therefore erroneously entered the men enumerated here as killed at this time.

for you through them. You have in your hands Aūsh, Marghīnān, Aūzkīnt and the cultivated land and the tribes and the hordes; go you to Aūsh; make that fort fast; send a man to Tambal, make peace with him, then strike at the Mughūl and drive him out. After that, divide the districts into an elder and a younger brother's shares.' 'Would that be right?' said I. 'The Khāns are my blood relations; better serve them than rule for Tambal.' He saw that his words had made no impression, so turned back, sorry he had spoken. I went on to see my Younger Khān Dādā. At our first interview, I had come upon him without announcement and he had no time to dismount, so it was all rather unceremonious. This time I got even nearer perhaps, and he ran out as far as the end of the tent-ropes. I was walking with some difficulty because of the wound in my leg. We met and renewed acquaintance; then he said, 'You are talked about as a hero, my young brother!' took my arm and led me into his tent. The tents pitched were rather small and through his having grown up in an out-of-the-way place, he let the one he sat in be neglected; it was like a raider's, melons, grapes, saddlery, every sort of thing, in his sitting-tent. I went from his presence straight back to my own camp and there he sent his Mughūl surgeon to examine my wound. Mughūls call a surgeon also a *bakhshī*; this one was called Ātākā Bakhshī.[1] Fol. 108b.

He was a very skilful surgeon; if a man's brains had come out, he would cure it, and any sort of wound in an artery he easily healed. For some wounds his remedy was in form of a plaister, for some medicines had to be taken. He ordered a bandage tied on[2] the wound in my leg and put no seton in; once he made me eat something like a fibrous root (*yīldīz*). He told me himself, 'A certain man had his leg broken in the slender part and the bone was shattered for the breadth of the hand. I cut the flesh open and took the bits of bone out. Where they had been, I put a remedy in powder-form. That Fol. 109.

[1] Elph. MS. *yakhshī*. Zenker explains *bakhshī* (pay-master) as meaning also a Court-physician.

[2] The Ilai. Elph. and Kehr's MS. all have *pūchqāq tāqmāq* or it may be *pūhqāq tāqmāq*. T. *būkhāq* means bandage, *pūchāq*, rind of fruit, but the word clear in the three Turkī MSS. means, skin of a fox's leg.

remedy simply became bone where there had been bone before.' He told many strange and marvellous things such as surgeons in cultivated lands cannot match.

Three or four days later, Qambar-'alī, afraid on account of what he had said to me, fled (to Tambal) in Andijān. A few days later, The Khāns joined to me Ayūb *Begchīk* with his *tūmān*, and Jān-ḥasan *Bārīn* with the Bārīn *tūmān* and, as their army-beg, Sārīgh-bāsh Mīrzā,—1000 to 2000 men in all, and sent us towards Akhsī.

(*h. Bābur's expedition to Akhsī.*)

Shaikh Bāyazīd, a younger brother of Tambal, was in Akhsī; Shahbāz *Qārlūq* was in Kāsān. At the time, Shahbāz was lying before Nū-kīnt fort; crossing the Khujand-water opposite Bīkhrātā, we hurried to fall upon him there. When, a little

Fol. 109*b*. before dawn, we were nearing the place, the begs represented to me that as the man would have had news of us, it was advisable not to go on in broken array. We moved on therefore with less speed. Shahbāz may have been really unaware of us until we were quite close; then getting to know of it, he fled into the fort. It often happens so! Once having said, 'The enemy is on guard!' it is easily fancied true and the chance of action is lost. In short, the experience of such things is that no effort or exertion must be omitted, once the chance for action comes. After-repentance is useless. There was a little fighting round the fort at dawn but we delivered no serious attack.

For the convenience of foraging, we moved from Nū-kīnt towards the hills in the direction of Bīshkhārān. Seizing his opportunity, Shahbāz *Qārlūq* abandoned Nū-kīnt and returned to Kāsān. We went back and occupied Nū-kīnt. During those days, the army several times went out and over-ran all sides and quarters. Once they over-ran the villages of Akhsī, once those of Kāsān. Shahbāz and Long Ḥasan's adopted son, Mīrīm came out of Kāsān to fight; they fought, were beaten, and there Mīrīm died.

(*i. The affairs of Pāp.*)

Pāp is a strong fort belonging to Akhsī. The Pāpīs made it fast and sent a man to me. We accordingly sent Sayyid Qāsim with a few braves to occupy it. They crossed the river (*daryā*) opposite the upper villages of Akhsī and went into Pāp.[1] Fol. 110.
A few days later, Sayyid Qāsim did an astonishing thing. There were at the time with Shaikh Bāyazīd in Akhsi, Ibrāhīm *Chāpūk* (Slash-face) Ṭaghāī,[2] Aḥmad-of-qāsim *Kohbur*, and Qāsim Khitika (?) *Arghūn*. To these Shaikh Bāyazīd joins 200 serviceable braves and one night sends them to surprise Pāp. Sayyid Qāsim must have lain down carelessly to sleep, without setting a watch. They reach the fort, set ladders up, get up on the Gate, let the drawbridge down and, when 70 or 80 good men in mail are inside, goes the news to Sayyid Qāsim! Drowsy with sleep, he gets into his vest (*kūnglāk*), goes out, with five or six of his men, charges the enemy and drives them out with blow upon blow. He cut off a few heads and sent to me. Though such a careless lying down was bad leadership, yet, with so few, just by force of drubbing, to chase off such a mass of men in mail was very brave indeed.

Meantime The Khāns were busy with the siege of Andijān but the garrison would not let them get near it. The Andijān braves used to make sallies and blows would be exchanged.

(*j. Bābur invited into Akhsī.*)

Shaikh Bāyazīd now began to send persons to us from Akhsī to testify to well-wishing and pressingly invite us to Akhsī. His object was to separate me from The Khāns, by any artifice, because without me, they had no standing-ground. Fol. 110*b*
His invitation may have been given after agreeing with his elder brother, Tambal that if I were separated from The Khāns, it might be possible, in my presence, to come to some arrange-

[1] The *daryā* here mentioned seems to be the Kāsān-water ; the route taken from Bīshkhārān to Pāp is shewn on the Fr. map to lead past modern Tūpa-qūrghān. Pāp is not marked, but was, I think, at the cross-roads east of Touss (Karnān).

[2] Presumably Jahāngīr's.

ment with them. We gave The Khāns a hint of the invitation. They said, 'Go! and by whatever means, lay hands on Shaikh Bāyazīd.' It was not my habit to cheat and play false; here above all places, when promises would have been made, how was I to break them? It occurred to me however, that if we could get into Akhsī, we might be able, by using all available means, to detach Shaikh Bāyazīd from Taṃbal, when he might take my side or something might turn up to favour my fortunes. We, in our turn, sent a man to him; compact was made, he invited us into Akhsī and when we went, came out to meet us, bringing my younger brother, Nāṣir Mīrzā with him. Then he took us into the town, gave us ground to camp in (*yūrt*) and to me one of my father's houses in the outer fort[1] where I dismounted.

(*k. Taṃbal asks help of Shaibāq Khān.*)

Taṃbal had sent his elder brother, Beg Tīlba, to Shaibāq Khān with proffer of service and invitation to enter Farghāna. At this very time Shaibāq Khān's answer arrived; 'I will come,' he wrote. On hearing this, The Khāns were all upset; they could sit no longer before Andijān and rose from before it.

Fol. 111.
The Younger Khān himself had a reputation for justice and orthodoxy, but his Mughūls, stationed, contrary to the expectations of the towns-people, in Aūsh, Marghīnān and other places,—places that had come in to me,—began to behave ill and oppressively. When The Khāns had broken up from before Andijān, the Aūshīs and Marghīnānīs, rising in tumult, seized the Mughūls in their forts, plundered and beat them, drove them out and pursued them.

The Khāns did not cross the Khujand-water (for the Kīndīrlīk-pass) but left the country by way of Marghīnān and Kand-i-badām and crossed it at Khujand, Taṃbal pursuing them as far as Marghīnān. We had had much uncertainty; we had not had much confidence in their making any stand, yet for us to go away, without clear reason, and leave them, would not have looked well.

[1] Here his father was killed (f. 6b). *Cf.* App. A.

(l. Bābur attempts to defend Akhsī.)

Early one morning, when I was in the Hot-bath, Jahāngīr Mīrzā came into Akhsī, from Marghīnān, a fugitive from Taṃbal. We saw one another, Shaikh Bāyazīd also being present, agitated and afraid. The Mīrzā and Ibrāhīm Beg said, 'Shaikh Bāyazīd must be made prisoner and we must get the citadel into our hands.' In good sooth, the proposal was wise. Said I, 'Promise has been made; how can we break it?' Shaikh Bāyazīd went into the citadel. Men ought to have been posted on the bridge; not even there did we post any-one! These blunders were the fruit of inexperience. At the top of the morning came Taṃbal himself with 2 or 3000 men in mail, crossed the bridge and went into the citadel. To begin with I had had rather few men; when I first went into Akhsī some had been sent to other forts and some had been made commandants and summoners all round. Left with me in Akhsī may have been something over 100 men. We Fol. 111b. had got to horse with these and were posting braves at the top of one lane after another and making ready for the fight, when Shaikh Bāyazīd and Qaṃbar-'alī (the Skinner), and Muḥammad-dost[1] came gallopping from Taṃbal with talk of peace.

After posting those told off for the fight, each in his appointed place, I dismounted at my father's tomb for a conference, in which I invited Jahāngīr Mīrzā to join. Muḥammad-dost went back to Taṃbal but Qaṃbar-'alī and Shaikh Bāyazīd were present. We sat in the south porch of the tomb and were in consultation when the Mīrzā, who must have settled beforehand with Ibrāhīm *Chāpūk* to lay hands on those other two, said in my ear, 'They must be made prisoner.' Said I, 'Don't hurry! matters are past making prisoners. See here! with terms made, the affair might be coaxed into something. For why? Not only are they many and we few, but they with their strength are in the citadel, we with our weakness, in the outer fort.' Shaikh Bāyazīd and Qaṃbar-'alī both being present, Jahāngīr Mīrzā looked at Ibrāhīm Beg and made him a sign to refrain. Whether he misunderstood to the contrary

[1] 'Alī-dost's son (f. 79b).

or whether he pretended to misunderstand, is not known; suddenly he did the ill-deed of seizing Shaikh Bāyazīd. Braves
Fol. 112. closing in from all sides, flung those two to the ground. Through this the affair was taken past adjustment; we gave them into charge and got to horse for the coming fight.

One side of the town was put into Jahāngīr Mīrzā's charge; as his men were few, I told off some of mine to reinforce him. I went first to his side and posted men for the fight, then to other parts of the town. There is a somewhat level, open space in the middle of Akhsī; I had posted a party of braves there and gone on when a large body of the enemy, mounted and on foot, bore down upon them, drove them from their post and forced them into a narrow lane. Just then I came up (the lane), gallopped my horse at them, and scattered them in flight. While I was thus driving them out from the lane into the flat, and had got my sword to work, they shot my horse in the leg; it stumbled and threw me there amongst them. I got up quickly and shot one arrow off. My squire, Kahil (lazy) had a weakly pony; he got off and led it to me. Mounting this, I started for another lane-head. Sl. Muḥ. Wais noticed the weakness of my mount, dismounted and led me his own. I mounted that horse. Just then, Qāsim Beg's son, Qambar-'alī came, wounded, from Jahāngīr Mīrzā and said the Mīrzā had
Fol. 112b. been attacked some time before, driven off in panic, and had gone right away. We were thunderstruck! At the same moment arrived Sayyid Qāsim, the commandant of Pāp! His was a most unseasonable visit, since at such a crisis it was well to have such a strong fort in our hands. Said I to Ibrāhīm Beg, 'What's to be done now?' He was slightly wounded; whether because of this or because of stupefaction, he could give no useful answer. My idea was to get across the bridge, destroy it and make for Andijān. Bābā Sher-zād did very well here. 'We will storm out at the gate and get away at once,' he said. At his word, we set off for the Gate. Khwāja Mīr Mīrān also spoke boldly at that crisis. In one of the lanes, Sayyid Qāsim and Nāṣir's Dost chopped away at Bāqī *Khīz*,[1] I being in front with Ibrāhīm Beg and Mīrzā Qulī *Kūkūldāsh*.

[1] The sobriquet *Khīz* may mean Leaper, or Impetuous.

As we came opposite the Gate, we saw Shaikh Bāyazīd, wearing his pull-over shirt[1] above his vest, coming in with three or four horsemen. He must have been put into the charge of Jahāngīr's men in the morning when, against my will, he was made prisoner, and they must have carried him off when they got away. They had thought it would be well to kill him; they set him free alive. He had been released just when I chanced upon him in the Gate. I drew and shot off the arrow on my thumb; it grazed his neck, a good shot! He came confusedly in at the Gate, turned to the right and fled down a lane. We followed him instantly. Mīrzā Qulī *Kūkūldāsh* got at one man with his rugged-mace and went on. Another man took Fol. 113. aim at Ibrāhīm Beg, but when the Beg shouted 'Hāī! Hāī!' let him pass and shot me in the arm-pit, from as near as a man on guard at a Gate. Two plates of my Qālmāq mail were cut; he took to flight and I shot after him. Next I shot at a man running away along the ramparts, adjusting for his cap against the battlements; he left his cap nailed on the wall and went off, gathering his turban-sash together in his hand. Then again,—a man was in flight alongside me in the lane down which Shaikh Bāyazīd had gone. I pricked the back of his head with my sword; he bent over from his horse till he leaned against the wall of the lane, but he kept his seat and with some trouble, made good his flight. When we had driven all the enemy's men from the Gate, we took possession of it but the affair was past discussion because they, in the citadel, were 2000 or 3000, we, in the outer fort, 100 or 200. Moreover they had chased off Jahāngīr Mīrzā, as long before as it takes milk to boil, and with him had gone half my men. This notwithstanding, we sent a man, while we were in the Gate, to say to him, 'If you are near at hand, come, let us attack again.' But the matter had gone past that! Ibrāhīm Beg, either because his horse was really weak or because of his wound, said, 'My horse is done.' On this, Sulaimān, one of Muḥ. 'Alī's *Mubashir's* servants, did a plucky thing, for with matters Fol. 113 as they were and none constraining him, while we were wait-

[1] *kūilāk*; syn. *kūnglāk*, a shirt not opening at the breast. It will have been a short garment since the under-vest was visible.

ing in the Gate, he dismounted and gave his horse to Ibrāhīm Beg. Kīchīk (little) 'Alī, now the Governor of Koel,[1] also shewed courage while we were in the Gate; he was a retainer of Sl. Muḥ. Wais and twice did well, here and in Aūsh. We delayed in the Gate till those sent to Jahāngīr Mīrzā came back and said he had gone off long before. It was too late to stay there; off we flung; it was ill-judged to have stayed as long as we did. Twenty or thirty men were with me. Just as we hustled out of the Gate, a number of armed men[2] came right down upon us, reaching the town-side of the drawbridge just as we had crossed. Banda-'alī, the maternal grandfather of Qāsim Beg's son, Ḥamza, called out to Ibrāhīm Beg, 'You are always boasting of your zeal! Let's take to our swords!' 'What hinders? Come along!' said Ibrāhīm Beg, from beside me. The senseless fellows were for displaying their zeal at a time of such disaster! Ill-timed zeal! That was no time to make stand or delay! We went off quickly, the enemy following and unhorsing our men.

(*m. Bābur a fugitive before Tambal's men.*)

When we were passing Meadow-dome (Gumbaz-i-chaman), two miles out of Akhsī, Ibrāhīm Beg called out to me. Looking
Fol. 114. back, I saw a page of Shaikh Bāyazīd's striking at him and turned rein, but Bayān-qulī's Khān-qulī, said at my side, 'This is a bad time for going back,' seized my rein and pushed ahead. Many of our men had been unhorsed before we reached Sang, 4 miles (2 *shar'ī*) out of Akhsī.[3] Seeing no pursuers at Sang, we

[1] *i.e.* when Bābur was writing in Hindūstān. Exactly at what date he made this entry is not sure. 'Alī was in Koel in 933 AH. (f. 315) and then taken prisoner, but Bābur does not say he was killed,—as he well might say of a marked man, and, as the captor was himself taken shortly after, 'Alī may have been released, and may have been in Koel again. So that the statement 'now in Koel' may refer to a time later than his capture. The interest of the point is in its relation to the date of composition of the *Bābur-nāma*.

No record of 'Alī's bravery in Aūsh has been preserved. The reference here made to it may indicate something attempted in 908 AH. after Bābur's adventure in Karnān (f. 118*b*) or in 909 AH. from Sūkh. *Cf.* Translator's note f. 118*b*.

[2] *aūpchīnlīk*. Vambéry, *gepanzert*; Shaw, four horse-shoes and their nails; Steingass, *aūpcha-khāna*, a guard-house.

[3] Sang is a ferry-station (Kostenko, i, 213). Pāp may well have been regretted (f. 109*b* and f. 112*b*)! The well-marked features of the French map of 1904 allows Bābur's flight to be followed.

passed it by and turned straight up its water. In this position of our affairs there were eight men of us;—Nāṣir's Dost, Qāsim Beg's Qambar-'alī, Bayān-qulī's Khān-qulī, Mīrzā Qulī *Kūkūldāsh*, Nāṣir's Shāham, Sayyidī Qarā's 'Abdu'l-qadūs, Khwāja Ḥusainī and myself, the eighth. Turning up the stream, we found, in the broad valley, a good little road, far from the beaten track. We made straight up the valley, leaving the stream on the right, reached its waterless part and, near the Afternoon Prayer, got up out of it to level land. When we looked across the plain, we saw a blackness on it, far away. I made my party take cover and myself had gone to look out from higher ground, when a number of men came at a gallop up the hill behind us. Without waiting to know whether they were many or few, we mounted and rode off. There were 20 or 25; we, as has been said, were eight. If we had known their number at first, we should have made a good stand against them but we thought they would not be pursuing us, unless they had good support behind. A Fol. 114*b*. fleeing foe, even if he be many, cannot face a few pursuers, for as the saying is, '*Hāī* is enough for the beaten ranks.'[1]

Khān-qulī said, 'This will never do! They will take us all. From amongst the horses there are, you take two good ones and go quickly on with Mīrzā Qulī *Kūkūldāsh*, each with a led horse. May-be you will get away.' He did not speak ill; as there was no fighting to hand, there was a chance of safety in doing as he said, but it really would not have looked well to leave any man alone, without a horse, amongst his foes. In the end they all dropped off, one by one, of themselves. My horse was a little tired; Khān-qulī dismounted and gave me his; I jumped off at once and mounted his, he mine. Just then they unhorsed Sayyidī Qarā's 'Abdu'l-qadūs and Nāṣir's Shāham who had fallen behind. Khān-qulī also was left. It was no time to profer help or defence; on it was gone, at the full speed of our mounts. The horses began to flag; Dost Beg's failed and stopped. Mine began to tire; Qambar-'alī got off

[1] In the Turkī text this saying is in Persian; in the Kehr-Ilminsky, in Turkī, as though it had gone over with its Persian context of the W.-i-B. from which the K.-I. text here is believed to be a translation.

and gave me his; I mounted his, he mine. He was left. Khwāja Ḥusainī was a lame man; he turned aside to the higher ground. I was left with Mīrzā Qulī *Kūkūldāsh*. Our
Fol. 115. horses could not possibly gallop, they trotted. His began to flag. Said I, 'What will become of me, if you fall behind? Come along! let's live or die together.' Several times I looked back at him; at last he said, 'My horse is done! It can't go on. Never mind me! You go on, perhaps you will get away.' It was a miserable position for me; he remained behind, I was alone.

Two of the enemy were in sight, one Bābā of Sairām, the other Banda-'alī. They gained on me; my horse was done; the mountains were still 2 miles (1 *kuroh*) off. A pile of rock was in my path. Thought I to myself, 'My horse is worn out and the hills are still somewhat far away; which way should I go? In my quiver are at least 20 arrows; should I dismount and shoot them off from this pile of rock?' Then again, I thought I might reach the hills and once there, stick a few arrows in my belt and scramble up. I had a good deal of confidence in my feet and went on, with this plan in mind. My horse could not possibly trot; the two men came within arrow's reach.
Fol. 115*b*. For my own sake sparing my arrows, I did not shoot; they, out of caution, came no nearer. By sunset I was near the hills. Suddenly they called out, 'Where are you going in this fashion? Jahāngīr Mīrzā has been brought in a prisoner; Nāṣir Mīrzā also is in their hands.' I made no reply and went on towards the hills. When a good distance further had been gone, they spoke again, this time more respectfully, dismounting to speak. I gave no ear to them but went on up a glen till, at the Bed-time prayer, I reached a rock as big as a house. Going behind it, I saw there were places to be jumped, where no horse could go. They dismounted again and began to speak like servants and courteously. Said they, 'Where are you going in this fashion, without a road and in the dark? Sl. Aḥmad Tambal will make you *pādshāh*.' They swore this. Said I, 'My mind is not easy as to that. I cannot go to him.
Fol 110. If you think to do me timely service, years may pass before you have such another chance. Guide me to a road by which

I can go to The Khān's presence. If you will do this, I will shew you favour and kindness greater than your heart's-desire. If you will not do it, go back the way you came; that also would be to serve me well.' Said they, 'Would to God we had never come! But since we are here, after following you in the way we have done, how can we go back from you? If you will not go with us, we are at your service, wherever you go.' Said I, 'Swear that you speak the truth.' They, for their part, made solemn oath upon the Holy Book.

I at once confided in them and said, 'People have shewn me a road through a broad valley, somewhere near this glen; take me to it.' Spite of their oath, my trust in them was not so complete but that I gave them the lead and followed. After 2 to 4 miles (1-2 *kuroh*), we came to the bed of a torrent. 'This will not be the road for the broad valley,' I said. They drew back, saying, 'That road is a long way ahead,' but it really must have been the one we were on and they have been concealing the fact, in order to deceive me. About half through the night, we reached another stream. This time they said, 'We have been negligent; it now seems to us that the road through the broad valley is behind.' Said I, 'What is to be done?' Said they, 'The Ghawā road is certainly in front; by it people cross for Far-kat.[1] They guided me for that and we went on till in Fol. 116*b*.
the third watch of the night we reached the Karnān gully which comes down from Ghawā. Here Bābā Sairāmī said, 'Stay here a little while I look along the Ghawā road.' He came back after a time and said, 'Some men have gone along that road, led by one wearing a Mughūl cap; there is no going that way.' I took alarm at these words. There I was, at dawn, in the middle of the cultivated land, far from the road I wanted to take. Said I, 'Guide me to where I can hide to-day, and tonight when you will have laid hands on something for the horses, lead me to cross the Khujand-water and along its further bank.' Said they, 'Over there, on the upland, there might be hiding.'

Banda-'alī was Commandant in Karnān. 'There is no doing without food for ourselves or our horses;' he said, 'let me go

[1] *Cf.* f. 96*b* and Fr. Map for route over the Kīndīr-tau.

into Karnān and bring what I can find.' We stopped 2 miles (1 *kuroh*) out of Karnān; he went on. He was a long time away; near dawn there was no sign of him. The day had shot when he hurried up, bringing three loaves of bread but no corn for the horses. Each of us putting a loaf into the breast of his tunic, we went quickly up the rise, tethered our horses there in the open valley and went to higher ground, each to keep watch

Fol. 117. Near mid-day, Ahmad the Falconer went along the Ghawā road for Akhsī. I thought of calling to him and of saying, with promise and fair word, 'You take those horses,' for they had had a day and a night's strain and struggle, without corn, and were utterly done. But then again, we were a little uneasy as we did not entirely trust him. We decided that, as the men Babā Sairāmī had seen on the road would be in Karnān that night, the two with me should fetch one of their horses for each of us, and that then we should go each his own way.

At mid-day, a something glittering was seen on a horse, as far away as eye can reach. We were not able to make out at all what it was. It must have been Muḥ. Bāqir Beg himself; he had been with us in Akhsī and when we got out and scattered, he must have come this way and have been moving then to a hiding-place.[1]

Banda-'alī and Bābā Sairāmī said, 'The horses have had no corn for two days and two nights; let us go down into the dale and put them there to graze.' Accordingly we rode down and put them to the grass. At the Afternoon Prayer, a horseman passed along the rising-ground where we had been. We recognized him for Qādīr-bīrdī, the head-man of Ghawā. 'Call him,' I said. They called; he came. After questioning him, and speaking to him of favour and kindness, and giving him promise and fair word, I sent him to bring rope, and a grass-hook, and an axe, and material for crossing water,[2] and corn

Fol. 117*b*. for the horses, and food and, if it were possible, other horses. We made tryst with him for that same spot at the Bed-time Prayer.

[1] This account of Muḥ. Bāqir reads like one given later to Bābur; he may have had some part in Bābur's rescue (*cf.* Translator's Note to f. 118*b*).

[2] Perhaps reeds for a raft. Sh. N. p. 258, *Sāl aūchūn bār qāmīsh*, reeds are there also for rafts.

Near the Evening Prayer, a horseman passed from the direction of Karnān for Ghawā. 'Who are you?' we asked. He made some reply. He must have been Muḥ. Bāqir Beg himself, on his way from where we had seen him earlier, going at night-fall to some other hiding-place, but he so changed his voice that, though he had been years with me, I did not know it. It would have been well if I had recognized him and he had joined me. His passing caused much anxiety and alarm; tryst could not be kept with Qādir-bīrdī of Ghawā. Banda-'alī said, 'There are retired gardens in the suburbs of Karnān where no one will suspect us of being; let us go there and send to Qādir-bīrdī and have him brought there.' With this idea, we mounted and went to the Karnān suburbs. It was winter and very cold. They found a worn, coarse sheepskin coat and brought it to me; I put it on. They brought me a bowl of millet-porridge; I ate it and was wonderfully refreshed. 'Have you sent off the man to Qādir-bīrdī?' said I to Banda-'alī. 'I have sent,' he said. But those luckless, clownish mannikins seem to have agreed together to send the man to Tambal in Akhsī!

We went into a house and for awhile my eyes closed in sleep. Those mannikins artfully said to me, 'You must not bestir yourself to leave Karnān till there is news of Qādīr-bīrdī but this house is right amongst the suburbs; on the outskirts the orchards are empty; no-one will suspect if we go Fol. 118.
there.' Accordingly we mounted at mid-night and went to a distant orchard. Bābā Sairāmī kept watch from the roof of a house. Near mid-day he came down and said, 'Commandant Yūsuf is coming.' Great fear fell upon me! 'Find out,' I said, 'whether he comes because he knows about me.' He went and after some exchange of words, came back and said, 'He says he met a foot-soldier in the Gate of Akhsī who said to him, "The pādshāh is in such a place," that he told no-one, put the man with Walī the Treasurer whom he had made prisoner in the fight, and then gallopped off here.' Said I, 'How does it strike you?' 'They are all your servants,' he said, 'you must go. What else can you do? They will make you their ruler.' Said I, 'After such rebellion and fighting,

with what confidence could I go?' We were saying this, when Yūsuf knelt before me, saying, 'Why should it be hidden? Sl. Aḥmad Tambal has no news of you, but Shaikh Bāyazīd has and he sent me here.' On hearing this, my state of mind was miserable indeed, for well is it understood that nothing in the world is worse than fear for one's life. 'Tell the truth!' I said, 'if the affair is likely to go on to worse, I will make
118*b*. ablution.' Yūsuf swore oaths, but who would trust them? I knew the helplessness of my position. I rose and went to a corner of the garden, saying to myself, 'If a man live a hundred years or a thousand years, at the last nothing . . .'[1]

TRANSLATOR'S NOTE.

Friends are likely to have rescued Bābur from his dangerous isolation. His presence in Karnān was known both in Ghawā and in Akhsī; Muḥ. Bāqir Beg was at hand (f. 117); some of those he had dropped in his flight would follow him when their horses had had rest; Jahāngīr was somewhere north of the river with the half of Bābur's former force (f. 112); The Khāns with their long-extended line of march, may have been on the main road through or near Karnān. If Yūsuf took Bābur as a prisoner along the Akhsī road, there were these various chances of his meeting friends.

His danger was evaded; he joined his uncles and was with them, leading 1000 men (Sh. N. p. 268), when they were defeated at Archīān just before or in the season of Cancer, *i.e. circa* June (T. R. p. 164). What he was doing between the winter cold of Karnān (f. 117*b*) and June might have been

1 Here the Turkī text breaks off, as it might through loss of pages, causing a blank of narrative extending over some 16 months. *Cf.* App. D. for a passage, supposedly spurious, found with the Ḥaidarābād Codex and the Kehr-Ilminsky text, purporting to tell how Bābur was rescued from the risk in which the lacuna here leaves him.

known from his lost pages. Muḥ. Ṣāliḥ writes at length of one affair falling within the time,—Jahāngīr's occupation of Khujand, its siege and its capture by Shaibānī. This capture will have occurred considerably more than a month before the defeat of The Khāns (Sh. N. p. 230).

It is not easy to decide in what month of 908 AH. they went into Farghāna or how long their campaign lasted. Bābur chronicles a series of occurrences, previous to the march of the army, which must have filled some time. The road over the Kīndīrlīk-pass was taken, one closed in Bābur's time (f. 1*b*) though now open through the winter. Looking at the rapidity of his own movements in Farghāna, it seems likely that the pass was crossed after and not before its closed time. If so, the campaign may have covered 4 or 5 months. Muḥ. Ṣāliḥ's account of Shaibāq's operations strengthens this view. News that Aḥmad had joined Maḥmūd in Tāshkīnt (f. 102) went to Shaibānī in Khusrau Shāh's territories; he saw his interests in Samarkand threatened by this combination of the Chaghatāī brothers to restore Bābur in Farghāna, came north therefore in order to help Taṃbal. He then waited a month in Samarkand (Sh. N. p. 230), besieged Jahāngīr, went back and stayed in Samarkand long enough to give his retainers time to equip for a year's campaigning (l. c. p. 244) then went to Akhsī and so to Archīān.

Bābur's statement (f. 110*b*) that The Khāns went from Andijān to the Khujand-crossing over the Sīr attracts attention because this they might have done if they had meant to leave Farghāna by Mīrzā-rabāṭ but they are next heard of as at Akhsī. Why did they make that great détour? Why not have crossed opposite Akhsī or at Sang? Or if they had thought of retiring, what turned them east again? Did they place Jahāngīr in Khujand? Bābur's missing pages would have answered these questions no doubt. It was useful for them to encamp where they did, east of Akhsī, because they there had near them a road by which reinforcement could come from Kāshghar or retreat be made. The Akhsī people told Shaibānī that he could easily overcome The Khāns if he went without warning, and if they had not withdrawn by the Kulja road (Sh. N. p. 262). By that road the few men who went with Aḥmad to Tāshkīnt (f. 103) may have been augmented to the force, enumerated as his in the battle by Muḥ. Ṣāliḥ (Sh. N. cap. LIII.).

When The Khāns were captured, Bābur escaped and made 'for Mughūlistān,' a vague direction seeming here to mean Tāshkīnt, but, finding his road blocked, in obedience to orders from Shaibāq that he and Abū'l-makāram were to be captured, he turned back and, by unfrequented ways, went into the hill-country of Sūkh and Huṣhīār. There he spent about a year in great misery (f. 14 and Ḥ. S. ii, 318). Of the wretchedness of the time Ḥaidar also writes. If anything was attempted in Farghāna in the course of those months, record of it has been lost with Bābur's missing pages. He was not only homeless and poor, but shut in by enemies. Only the loyalty or kindness of the hill-tribes can have saved him and his few followers. His mother was with him; so also were the families of his men. How Qūtlūq-nigār contrived to join him from Tāshkīnt, though historically a small matter, is one he would chronicle. What had happened there after the Mughūl defeat, was that the horde had marched away for Kāshghar while Shāh Begīm remained in charge of her daughters with whom the Aūzbeg chiefs intended to contract alliance. Shaibānī's orders for her stay and for the general exodus were communicated to her by her son, The Khān, in what Muḥ. Ṣāliḥ, quoting its purport, describes as a right beautiful letter (p. 296).

By some means Qūtlūq-nigār joined Bābur, perhaps helped by the circumstance that her daughter, Khān-zāda was Shaibāq's wife. She spent at least some part of those hard months with him, when his fortunes were at their lowest ebb. A move becoming imperative, the ragged and destitute company started in mid-June 1504 (Muḥ. 910 AH.) on that perilous mountain journey to which Ḥaidar applies the Prophet's dictum, 'Travel is a foretaste of Hell,' but of which the end was the establishment of a Tīmūrid dynasty in Hindūstān. To look down the years from the destitute Bābur to Akbar, Shāh-jahān and Aurangzīb is to see a great stream of human life flow from its source in his resolve to win upward, his quenchless courage and his abounding vitality. Not yet 22, the sport of older men's intrigues, he had been tempered by failure, privation and dangers.

He left Sūkh intending to go to Sl. Ḥusain Mīrzā in Khurāsān but he changed this plan for one taking him to Kābul where a Tīmūrid might claim to dispossess the Arghūns, then holding it since the death, in 907 AH. of his uncle, Aūlūgh Beg Mīrzā *Kābulī*.

THE MEMOIRS OF BABUR

SECTION II. KĀBUL[1]

910 AH.—JUNE 14TH 1504 TO JUNE 4TH 1505 AD.[2]

(*a. Bābur leaves Farghāna.*)

In the month of Muḥarram, after leaving the Farghāna country intending to go to Khurāsān, I dismounted at Aīlāk-yīlāq,[3] one of the summer pastures of Ḥiṣār. In this camp I entered my 23rd year, and applied the razor to my face.[4] Those who, hoping in me, went with me into exile, were, small and great, between 2 and 300; they were almost all on foot, had walking-staves in their hands, brogues [5] on their feet, and long coats [6] on Haidarābād MS. Fol. 120.

[1] As in the Farghāna Section, so here, reliance is on the Elphinstone and Haidarābād MSS. The Kehr-Ilminsky text still appears to be a retranslation from the *Wāqi'āt-i-bāburī* and verbally departs much from the true text; moreover, in this Section it has been helped out, where its archetype was illegible or has lost fragmentary passages, from the Leyden and Erskine *Memoirs*. It may be mentioned, as between the First and the Second *Wāqi'āt-i-bāburī*, that several obscure passages in this Section are more explicit in the First (Pāyanda-ḥasan's) than in its successor ('Abdu-r-raḥīm's).

[2] Elph. MS. f. 90*b*; W.-i-B. I.O. 215, f. 96*b* and 217, f. 79; Mems. p. 127. "In 1504 AD. Ferdinand the Catholic drove the French out of Naples" (Erskine). In England, Henry VII was pushing forward a commercial treaty, the *Intercursus malus*, with the Flemings and growing in wealth by the exactions of Empson and Dudley.

[3] presumably the pastures of the "Ilak" Valley. The route from Sūkh would be over the 'Alā'u'd-dīn-pass, into the Qīzīl-sū valley, down to Ab-i-garm and on to the Aīlāq-valley, Khwāja 'Imād, the Kāfirnigān, Qabādīān, and Aūbāj on the Amū. See T.R. p. 175 and Farghāna Section, p. 184, as to the character of the journey.

[4] Amongst the Turkī tribes, the time of first applying the razor to the face is celebrated by a great entertainment. Bābur's miserable circumstances would not admit of this (Erskine).

The text is ambiguous here, reading either that Sūkh was left or that Aīlāq-yīlāq was reached in Muḥarram. As the birthday was on the 8th, the journey very arduous and, for a party mostly on foot, slow, it seems safest to suppose that the start was made from Sūkh at the end of 909 AH. and not in Muḥarram, 910 AH.

[5] *chārūq*, rough boots of untanned leather, formed like a moccasin with the lower leather drawn up round the foot; they are worn by Khirghiz mountaineers and caravan-men on journeys (Shaw).

[6] *chāpān*, the ordinary garment of Central Asia (Shaw).

their shoulders. So destitute were we that we had but two tents (*chādar*) amongst us; my own used to be pitched for my mother, and they set an *ālāchūq* at each stage for me to sit in.[1]

Though we had started with the intention of going into Khurāsān, yet with things as they were[2] something was hoped for from the Ḥiṣār country and Khusrau Shāh's retainers. Every few days some-one would come in from the country or a tribe or the (Mughūl) horde, whose words made it probable that we had growing ground for hope. Just then Mullā Bābā of Pashāghar came back, who had been our envoy to Khusrau Shāh; from Khusrau Shāh he brought nothing likely to please, but he did from the tribes and the horde.

Fol. 120*b*. Three or four marches beyond Aīlāk, when halt was made at a place near Ḥiṣār called Khwāja 'Imād, Muḥibb-'alī, the Armourer, came to me from Khusrau Shāh. Through Khusrau Shāh's territories I have twice happened to pass;[3] renowned though he was for kindness and liberality, he neither time showed me the humanity he had shown to the meanest of men.

As we were hoping something from the country and the tribes, we made delay at every stage. At this critical point Sherīm Ṭaghāī, than whom no man of mine was greater, thought of leaving me because he was not keen to go into Khurāsān. He had sent all his family off and stayed himself unencumbered, when after the defeat at Sar-i-pul (906 AH.) I went back to defend Samarkand; he was a bit of a coward and he did this sort of thing several times over.

(b. Bābur joined by one of Khusrau Shāh's kinsmen.)

After we reached Qabādīān, a younger brother of Khusrau Shāh, Bāqī *Chaghānīānī*, whose holdings were Chaghānīān,[4] Shahr-i-ṣafā and Tīrmīz, sent the *khatīb*[5] of Qarshī to me to

[1] The *ālāchūq*, a tent of flexible poles, covered with felt, may be the *khargāh* (kibitka); Persian *chādar* seems to represent Turkī *āq awī*, white house.

[2] *i.e.* with Khusrau's power shaken by Aūzbeg attack, made in the winter of 909 AH. (*Shaibānī-nāma* cap. lviii).

[3] Cf. ff. 81 and 81*b*. The armourer's station was low for an envoy to Bābur, the superior in birth of the armourer's master.

[4] var. Chaqānīān and Saghānīān. The name formerly described the whole of the Ḥiṣār territory (Erskine).

[5] the preacher by whom the *Khuṭba* is read (Erskine).

express his good wishes and his desire for alliance, and, after we had crossed the Amū at the Aūbāj-ferry, he came himself to wait on me. By his wish we moved down the river to opposite Tīrmīẕ, where, without fear [or, without going over himself],[1] he had their families [2] and their goods brought across to join us. This done, we set out together for Kāhmard and Bāmīān, then held by his son [3] Aḥmad-i-qāsim, the son of Khusrau Shāh's sister. Our plan was to leave the households (*awī-aīl*) safe in Fort Ajar of the Kāhmard-valley and to take action wherever Fol. 121. action might seem well. At Aībak, Yār-'alī Balāl,[4] who had fled from Khusrau Shāh, joined us with several braves; he had been with me before, and had made good use of his sword several times in my presence, but was parted from me in the recent throneless times [5] and had gone to Khusrau Shāh. He represented to me that the Mughūls in Khusrau Shāh's service wished me well. Moreover, Qaṃbar-'alī Beg, known also as Qaṃbar-'alī *Silākh* (Skinner), fled to me after we reached the Zindān-valley.[6]

(*c. Occurrences in Kāhmard.*)

We reached Kāhmard with three or four marches and deposited our households and families in Ajar. While we stayed there, Jahāngīr Mīrzā married (Aī Begīm) the daughter of Sl. Maḥmūd Mīrzā and Khān-zāda Begīm, who had been set aside for him during the lifetime of the Mīrzās.[7]

Meantime Bāqī Beg urged it upon me, again and again, that two rulers in one country, or two chiefs in one army are a source of faction and disorder—a foundation of dissension and ruin.

[1] *bī bāqī* or *bī Bāqī*; perhaps a play of words with the double meaning expressed in the above translation.

[2] Amongst these were widows and children of Bābur's uncle, Maḥmūd (f. 27*b*).

[3] *aūghūl*. As being the son of Khusrau's sister, Aḥmad was nephew to Bāqī; there may be in the text a scribe's slip from one *aūghūl* to another, and the real statement be that Aḥmad was the son of Bāqī's son, Muḥ. Qāsim, which would account for his name Aḥmad-i-qāsim.

[4] Cf. f. 67.

[5] Bābur's loss of rule in Farghāna and Samarkand.

[6] about 7 miles south of Aībak, on the road to Sar-i-tāgh (mountain-head, Erskine).

[7] *viz.* the respective fathers, Maḥmūd and 'Umar Shaikh. The arrangement was made in 895 AH. (1490 AD.).

"For they have said, 'Ten darwīshes can sleep under one blanket, but two kings cannot find room in one clime.'

> If a man of God eat half a loaf,
> He gives the other to a darwīsh;
> Let a king grip the rule of a clime,
> He dreams of another to grip." [1]

Bāqī Beg urged further that Khusrau Shāh's retainers and followers would be coming in that day or the next to take service with the Pādshāh (*i.e.* Bābur); that there were such
Fol. 121*b*. sedition-mongers with them as the sons of Ayūb *Begchīk*, besides other who had been the stirrers and spurs to disloyalty amongst their Mīrzās,[2] and that if, at this point, Jahāngīr Mīrzā were dismissed, on good and friendly terms, for Khurāsān, it would remove a source of later repentance. Urge it as he would, however, I did not accept his suggestion, because it is against my nature to do an injury to my brethren, older or younger,[3] or to any kinsman soever, even when something untoward has happened. Though formerly between Jahāngīr Mīrzā and me, resentments and recriminations had occurred about our rule and retainers, yet there was nothing whatever then to arouse anger against him; he had come out of that country (*i.e.* Farghāna) with me and was behaving like a blood-relation and a servant. But in the end it was just as Bāqī Beg predicted;—those tempters to disloyalty, that is to say, Ayūb's Yūsuf and Ayūb's Bihlūl, left me for Jahāngīr Mīrzā, took up a hostile and mutinous position, parted him from me, and conveyed him into Khurāsān.

(d. Co-operation invited against Shaibāq Khān.)

In those days came letters from Sl. Ḥusain Mīrzā, long and far-fetched letters which are still in my possession and in that
Fol. 122. of others, written to Badī'u'z-zamān Mīrzā, myself, Khusrau Shāh and Ẕū'n-nūn Beg, all to the same purport, as follows:—"When the three brothers, Sl. Maḥmūd Mīrzā, Sl. Aḥmad Mīrzā, and Aūlūgh Beg Mīrzā, joined together and advanced

[1] *Gulistān* cap. i, story 3. Part of this quotation is used again on f. 183.
[2] Maḥmūd's sons under whom Bāqī had served.
[3] Uncles of all degrees are included as elder brethren, cousins of all degrees, as younger ones.

against me, I defended the bank of the Murgh-āb [1] in such a way that they retired without being able to effect anything. Now if the Aūzbegs advance, I might myself guard the bank of the Murgh-āb again; let Badī'u'z-zamān Mīrzā leave men to defend the forts of Balkh, Shibarghān, and Andikhūd while he himself guards Girzawān, the Zang-valley, and the hill-country thereabouts." As he had heard of my being in those parts, he wrote to me also, "Do you make fast Kāhmard, Ajar, and that hill-tract; let Khusrau Shāh place trusty men in Ḥiṣār and Qūndūz; let his younger brother Walī make fast Badakhshān and the Khutlān hills; then the Aūzbeg will retire, able to do nothing."

These letters threw us into despair;—for why? Because at that time there was in Tīmūr Beg's territory (*yūrt*) no ruler so great as Sl. Ḥusain Mīrzā, whether by his years, armed strength, or dominions; it was to be expected, therefore, that envoys would go, treading on each other's heels, with clear and sharp orders, such as, "Arrange for so many boats at the Tīrmīz, Fol. 122*b*. Kilīf, and Kīrkī ferries," "Get any quantity of bridge material together," and "Well watch the ferries above Tūqūz-aūlūm," [2] so that men whose spirit years of Aūzbeg oppression had broken, might be cheered to hope again.[3] But how could hope live in tribe or horde when a great ruler like Sl. Ḥusain Mīrzā, sitting in the place of Tīmūr Beg, spoke, not of marching forth to meet the enemy, but only of defence against his attack?

When we had deposited in Ajar what had come with us of hungry train (*aj aūrūq*) and household (*awī-aīl*), together with the families of Bāqī Beg, his son, Muḥ. Qāsim, his soldiers and his tribesmen, with all their goods, we moved out with our men.

[1] presumably the ferries; perhaps the one on the main road from the north-east which crosses the river at Fort Murgh-āb.

[2] Nine deaths, perhaps where the Amū is split into nine channels at the place where Mīrzā Khān's son Sulaimān later met his rebel grandson-Shāh-rukh (*Tabaqāt-i-akbarī*, Elliot & Dowson, v, 392, and A.N. Bib. Ind., 3rd ed., 441). Tūqūz-aūlūm is too far up the river to be Arnold's "shorn and parcelled Oxus".

[3] Shaibāq himself had gone down from Samarkand in 908 AH. and in 909 AH. and so permanently located his troops as to have sent their families to them. In 909 AH. he drove Khusrau into the mountains of Badakhshān, but did not occupy Qūndūz; thither Khusrau returned and there stayed till now, when Shaibāq again came south (fol. 123). See Sh. N. cap. lviii *et seq.*

(e. Increase of Bābur's following.)

One man after another came in from Khusrau Shāh's Mughūls and said, "We of the Mughūl horde, desiring the royal welfare, have drawn off from Ṭāīkhān (Ṭālīkān) towards Ishkīmīsh and Fūlūl. Let the Pādshāh advance as fast as possible, for the greater part of Khusrau Shāh's force has broken up and is ready to take service with him." Just then news arrived that Shaibāq Khān, after taking Andijān,[1] was getting to horse again against Ḥiṣār and Qūndūz. On hearing
Fol. 123. this, Khusrau Shāh, unable to stay in Qūndūz, marched out with all the men he had, and took the road for Kābul. No sooner had he left than his old servant, the able and trusted Mullā Muḥammad *Turkistānī* made Qūndūz fast for Shaibāq Khān.

Three or four thousand heads-of-houses in the Mughūl horde, former dependants of Khusrau Shāh, brought their families and joined us when, going by way of Sham-tū, we were near the Qīzīl-sū.[2]

(f. Qambar-'alī, the Skinner, dismissed.)

Qambar-'alī Beg's foolish talk has been mentioned several times already; his manners were displeasing to Bāqī Beg; to gratify Bāqī Beg, he was dismissed. Thereafter his son, 'Abdu'l-shukūr, was in Jahāngīr Mīrzā's service.

(g. Khusrau Shāh waits on Bābur.)

Khusrau Shāh was much upset when he heard that the Mughūl horde had joined me; seeing nothing better to do for himself, he sent his son-in-law, Ayūb's Yaq'ūb, to make profession of well-wishing and submission to me, and respectfully to represent that he would enter my service if I would make terms and compact with him. His offer was accepted, because Bāqī *Chaghāniānī* was a man of weight, and, however steady in his favourable disposition to me, did not overlook his brother's side in this matter. Compact was made that Khusrau

[1] From Tambal, to put down whom he had quitted his army near Balkh (Sh. N. cap. lix).
[2] This, one of the many Red-rivers, flows from near Kāhmard and joins the Andar-āb water near Dūshī.

Shāh's life should be safe, and that whatever amount of his goods he selected, should not be refused him. After giving Yaq'ūb leave to go, we marched down the Qīzīl-sū and dismounted near to where it joins the water of Andar-āb. Fol. 123*b*.

Next day, one in the middle of the First Rabī' (end of August, 1504 AD.), riding light, I crossed the Andar-āb water and took my seat under a large plane-tree near Dūshī, and thither came Khusrau Shāh, in pomp and splendour, with a great company of men. According to rule and custom, he dismounted some way off and then made his approach. Three times he knelt when we saw one another, three times also on taking leave; he knelt once when asking after my welfare, once again when he offered his tribute, and he did the same with Jahāngīr Mīrzā and with Mīrza Khān (Wais). That sluggish old mannikin who through so many years had just pleased himself, lacking of sovereignty one thing only, namely, to read the *Khuṭba* in his own name, now knelt 25 or 26 times in succession, and came and went till he was so wearied out that he tottered forward. His many years of begship and authority vanished from his view. When we had seen one another and he had offered his gift, I desired him to be seated. We stayed in that place for one or two *garīs*,[1] exchanging tale and talk. His conversation was vapid and empty, presumably because he was a coward and false to his salt. Two things he said were extraordinary for the time when, under his eyes, his trusty and trusted retainers were becoming mine, and when his affairs had reached the point that he, the sovereign-aping mannikin, had had to come, willy-nilly, abased and unhonoured, to what sort Fol. 124 of an interview! One of the things he said was this:—When condoled with for the desertion of his men, he replied, "Those very servants have four times left me and returned." The other was said when I had asked him where his brother Walī would cross the Amū and when he would arrive. "If he find a ford, he will soon be here, but when waters rise, fords change; the (Persian) proverb has it, 'The waters have carried down the fords.'" These words God brought to his tongue in that hour of the flowing away of his own authority and following!

[1] A *garī* is twenty-four minutes.

After sitting a *garī* or two, I mounted and rode back to camp, he for his part returning to his halting-place. On that day his begs, with their servants, great and small, good and bad, and tribe after tribe began to desert him and come, with their families, to me. Between the two Prayers of the next afternoon not a man remained in his presence.

"Say,—O God! who possessest the kingdom! Thou givest it to whom Thou wilt and Thou takest it from whom Thou wilt! In Thy hand is good, for Thou art almighty."[1]

Wonderful is His power! This man, once master of 20 or 30,000 retainers, once owning Sl. Maḥmūd's dominions from Qaḥlūgha,—known also as the Iron-gate,—to the range of
Fol. 124*b*. Hindū-kush, whose old mannikin of a tax-gatherer, Ḥasan *Barlās* by name, had made us march, had made us halt, with all the tax-gatherer's roughness, from Aīlāk to Aūbāj,[2] that man He so abased and so bereft of power that, with no blow struck, no sound made, he stood, without command over servants, goods, or life, in the presence of a band of 200 or 300 men, defeated and destitute as we were.

In the evening of the day on which we had seen Khusrau Shāh and gone back to camp, Mīrzā Khān came to my presence and demanded vengeance on him for the blood of his brothers.[3] Many of us were at one with him, for truly it is right, both by Law and common justice, that such men should get their deserts, but, as terms had been made, Khusrau Shāh was let go free. An order was given that he should be allowed to take whatever of his goods he could convey; accordingly he loaded up, on three or four strings of mules and camels, all jewels, gold, silver, and precious things he had, and took them with him.[4] Sherīm Ṭaghāī was told off to escort him, who after setting Khusrau Shāh on his road for Khurāsān, by way of Ghūrī and Dahānah, was to go to Kāhmard and bring the families after us to Kābul.

[1] Qorān, *Surat* iii, verse 25; Sale's Qorān, ed. 1825, i, 56.
[2] Cf. f. 82.
[3] *viz.* Bāī-sanghar, bowstrung, and Mas'ūd, blinded.
[4] Muḥ. Ṣāliḥ is florid over the rubies of Badakhshān he says Bābur took from Khusrau, but Ḥaidar says Bābur not only had Khusrau's property, treasure, and horses returned to him, but refused all gifts Khusrau offered. "This is one trait out of a thousand in the Emperor's character." Ḥaidar mentions, too, the then lack of necessaries under which Bābur suffered (Sh. N., cap. lxiii, and T.R. p. 176).

(*h. Bābur marches for Kābul.*)

Marching from that camp for Kābul, we dismounted in Khwāja Zaid.

On that day, Ḥamza Bī *Mangfīt*,[1] at the head of Aūzbeg raiders, was over-running round about Dūshī. Sayyid Qāsim, the Lord of the Gate, and Aḥmad-i-qāsim *Kohbur* were sent Fol. 125. with several braves against him; they got up with him, beat his Aūzbegs well, cut off and brought in a few heads.

In this camp all the armour (*jība*) of Khusrau Shāh's armoury was shared out. There may have been as many as 7 or 800 coats-of-mail (*joshan*) and horse accoutrements (*kūhah*);[2] these were the one thing he left behind; many pieces of porcelain also fell into our hands, but, these excepted, there was nothing worth looking at.

With four or five marches we reached Ghūr-bund, and there dismounted in Ushtur-shahr. We got news there that Muqīm's chief beg, Sherak (var. Sherka) *Arghūn*, was lying along the Bārān, having led an army out, not through hearing of me, but to hinder 'Abdu'r-razzāq Mīrzā from passing along the Panjhīr-road, he having fled from Kābul[3] and being then amongst the Tarkalānī Afghāns towards Lamghān. On hearing this we marched forward, starting in the afternoon and pressing on through the dark till, with the dawn, we surmounted the Hūpīān-pass.[4]

I had never seen Suhail;[5] when I came out of the pass I saw a star, bright and low. "May not that be Suhail?" said I. Said they, "It is Suhail." Bāqī *Chaghānīānī* recited this couplet;—[6]

> "How far dost thou shine, O Suhail, and where dost thou rise?
> A sign of good luck is thine eye to the man on whom it may light."

---

[1] Cf. T.R. p. 134 n. and 374 n.

[2] *Jība*, so often used to describe the quilted corselet, seems to have here a wider meaning, since the *jība-khāna* contained both *joshan* and *kūhah*, *i.e.* coats-of-mail and horse-mail with accoutrements. It can have been only from this source that Bābur's men obtained the horse-mail of f. 127.

[3] He succeeded his father, Aūlūgh Beg *Kābulī*, in 907 AH.; his youth led to the usurpation of his authority by Sherīm Ẕikr, one of his begs; but the other begs put Sherīm to death. During the subsequent confusions Muḥ. Muqīm *Arghūn*, in 908 AH., got possession of Kābul and married a sister of 'Abdu'r-razzāq. Things were in this state when Bābur entered the country in 910 AH. (Erskine).

[4] var. Ūpīān, a few miles north of Chārikār.

[5] Suhail (Canopus) is a most conspicuous star in Afghānistān; it gives its name to the south, which is never called Janūb but Suhail; the rising of Suhail marks one of their seasons (Erskine). The honour attaching to this star is due to its seeming to rise out of Arabia Felix.

[6] The lines are in the Preface to the *Anwār-i-suhailī* (Lights of Canopus).

The Sun was a spear's-length high[1] when we reached the foot of the Sanjid (Jujube)-valley and dismounted. Our scouting
Fol. 125b. braves fell in with Sherak below the Qarā-bāgh,[2] near Aīkarī-yār, and straightway got to grips with him. After a little of some sort of fighting, our men took the upper hand, hurried their adversaries off, unhorsed 70–80 serviceable braves and brought them in. We gave Sherak his life and he took service with us.

(*i. Death of Walī of Khusrau.*)

The various clans and tribes whom Khusrau Shāh, without troubling himself about them, had left in Qūndūz, and also the Mughūl horde, were in five or six bodies (*būlāk*). One of those belonging to Badakhshān,—it was the Rūstā-hazāra,—came, with Sayyidīm 'Alī *darbān*,[3] across the Panjhīr-pass to this camp, did me obeisance and took service with me. Another body came under Ayūb's Yūsuf and Ayūb's Bihlūl; it also took service with me. Another came from Khutlān, under Khusrau Shāh's younger brother, Walī; another, consisting of the (Mughūl) tribesmen (*aīmāq*) who had been located in Yīlānchaq, Nikdiri (?), and the Qūndūz country, came also. The last-named two came by Andar-āb and Sar-i-āb,[4] meaning to cross by the Panjhīr-pass; at Sar-i-āb the tribesmen were ahead; Walī came up behind; they held the road, fought and beat him. He himself fled to the Aūzbegs,[5] and Shaibāq Khān had his head struck off in the Square (*Chār-sū*) of Samarkand; his followers, beaten and plundered, came on with the tribesmen, and like these, took service with me. With them came Sayyid
Fol. 126. Yūsuf Beg (the Grey-wolfer).

(*j. Kābul gained.*)

From that camp we marched to the Āq-sarāī meadow of the Qarā-bāgh and there dismounted. Khusrau Shāh's people were

1 "Die Kirghis-qazzāq drücken die Sonnen-höhe in Piken aus" (von Schwarz, p. 124).

2 presumably, dark with shade, as in *qarā-yīghāch*, the hard-wood elm (f. 47*b* and note to *narwān*).

3 *i.e.* Sayyid Muḥammad 'Alī, the door-ward. These *būlāks* seem likely to have been groups of 1,000 fighting-men (Turki *Mīng*).

4 In-the-water and Water-head.

5 Walī went from his defeat to Khwāst; wrote to Maḥmūd *Aūzbeg* in Qūndūz to ask protection; was fetched to Qūndūz by Muḥ Ṣāliḥ, the author of the *Shaibānī-nāma*, and forwarded from Qūndūz to Samarkand (Sh. N. cap. lxiii). Cf. f. 29*b*.

well practised in oppression and violence; they tyrannized over one after another till at last I had up one of Sayyidīm 'Alī's good braves to my Gate[1] and there beaten for forcibly taking a jar of oil. There and then he just died under the blows; his example kept the rest down.

We took counsel in that camp whether or not to go at once against Kābul. Sayyid Yūsuf and some others thought that, as winter was near, our first move should be into Lamghān, from which place action could be taken as advantage offered. Bāqī Beg and some others saw it good to move on Kābul at once; this plan was adopted; we marched forward and dismounted in Ābā-qūrūq.

My mother and the belongings left behind in Kāhmard rejoined us at Ābā-qūrūq. They had been in great danger, the particulars of which are these:—Sherīm Ṭaghāī had gone to set Khusrau Shāh on his way for Khurāsān, and this done, was to fetch the families from Kāhmard. When he reached Dahānah, he found he was not his own master; Khusrau Shāh went on with him into Kāhmard, where was his sister's son, Aḥmad-i-qāsim. These two took up an altogether wrong Fol. 126*b*. position towards the families in Kāhmard. Hereupon a number of Bāqī Beg's Mughūls, who were with the families, arranged secretly with Sherīm Ṭaghāī to lay hands on Khusrau Shāh and Aḥmad-i-qāsim. The two heard of it, fled along the Kāhmard-valley on the Ajar side[2] and made for Khurāsān. To bring this about was really what Sherīm Ṭaghāī and the Mughūls wanted. Set free from their fear of Khusrau Shāh by his flight, those in charge of the families got them out of Ajar, but when they reached Kāhmard, the Sāqānchī (var. Asīqanchī) tribe blocked the road, like an enemy, and plundered the families of most of Bāqī Beg's men.[3] They made prisoner Qul-i-bāyazīd's little son, Tīzak; he came into Kābul three or four years later. The plundered and unhappy families crossed by the Qībchāq-pass, as we had done, and they rejoined us in Ābā-qūrūq.

1 *i.e.* where justice was administered, at this time, outside Bābur's tent.
2 They would pass Ajar and make for the main road over the Dandān-shikan Pass.
3 The clansmen may have obeyed Aḥmad's orders in thus holding up the families.

Leaving that camp we went, with one night's halt, to the Chālāk-meadow, and there dismounted. After counsel taken, it was decided to lay siege to Kābul, and we marched forward. With what men of the centre there were, I dismounted between Ḥaidar *Tāqī s*[1] garden and the tomb of Qul-i-bāyazīd, the Taster (*bakāwal*):[2] Jahāngīr Mīrzā, with the men of the right, Fol. 127. dismounted in my great Four-gardens (*Chār-bāgh*), Nāṣir Mīrzā, with the left, in the meadow of Qūtlūq-qadam's tomb. People of ours went repeatedly to confer with Muqīm; they sometimes brought excuses back, sometimes words making for agreement. His tactics were the sequel of his dispatch, directly after Sherak's defeat, of a courier to his father and elder brother (in Qandahār); he made delays because he was hoping in them.

One day our centre, right, and left were ordered to put on their mail and their horses' mail, to go close to the town, and to display their equipment so as to strike terror on those within. Jahāngīr Mīrzā and the right went straight forward by the Kūcha-bāgh;[3] I, with the centre, because there was water, went along the side of Qūtlūq-qadam's tomb to a mound facing the rising-ground;[4] the van collected above Qūtlūq-qadam's bridge,—at that time, however, there was no bridge. When the braves, showing themselves off, galloped close up to the Curriers'-gate,[5] a few who had come out through it fled in again without making any stand. A crowd of Kābulīs who had come out to see the sight raised a great dust when they ran away from the high slope of the glacis of the citadel (*i.e.* Bālā-ḥiṣār). A number of pits had been dug up the rise Fol. 127*b*. between the bridge and the gate, and hidden under sticks and rubbish; Sl. Qulī *Chūnāq* and several others were thrown as they galloped over them. A few braves of the right exchanged sword-cuts with those who came out of the town, in amongst

[1] The name may be from Turkī *tāq*, a horse-shoe, but I.O. 215 f. 102 writes Persian *naqīb*, the servant who announces arriving guests.

[2] Here, as immediately below, when mentioning the Chār-bāgh and the tomb of Qūtlūq-qadam, Bābur uses names acquired by the places at a subsequent date. In 910 AH. the Taster was alive; the Chār-bāgh was bought by Bābur in 911 AH., and Qūtlūq-qadam fought at Kānwāha in 933 AH.

[3] The Kūcha-bāgh is still a garden about 4 miles from Kābul on the north-west and divided from it by a low hill-pass. There is still a bridge on the way (Erskine).

[4] Presumably that on which the Bālā-ḥiṣār stood, the glacis of a few lines further.

[5] Cf. f. 130.

the lanes and gardens, but as there was no order to engage, having done so much, they retired.

Those in the fort becoming much perturbed, Muqīm made offer through the begs, to submit and surrender the town. Bāqī Beg his mediator, he came and waited on me when all fear was chased from his mind by our entire kindness and favour. It was settled that next day he should march out with retainers and following, goods and effects, and should make the town over to us. Having in mind the good practice Khusrau Shāh's retainers had had in indiscipline and longhandedness, we appointed Jahāngīr Mīrzā and Nāṣir Mīrzā with the great and household begs, to escort Muqīm's family out of Kābul[1] and to bring out Muqīm himself with his various dependants, goods and effects. Camping-ground was assigned to him at Tīpa.[2] When the Mīrzās and the Begs went at dawn to the Gate, they saw much mobbing and tumult of the common people, so they sent me a man to say, "Unless you come yourself, there will be no holding these people in." In the end I got to horse, had two or three persons shot, two or three cut in pieces, and so stamped the rising down. Muqīm and his belongings then got out, safe and sound, and they betook themselves to Tīpa. Fol. 128.

It was in the last ten days of the Second Rabī' (Oct. 1504 AD.)[3] that without a fight, without an effort, by Almighty God's bounty and mercy, I obtained and made subject to me Kābul and Ghaznī and their dependent districts.

DESCRIPTION OF KĀBUL[4]

The Kābul country is situated in the Fourth climate and in the midst of cultivated lands.[5] On the east it has the

[1] One of Muqīm's wives was a Tīmūrid, Bābur's first-cousin, the daughter of Aūlūgh Beg *Kābulī*; another was Bībī Zarīf Khātūn, the mother of that Māh-chūchūq, whose anger at her marriage to Bābur's faithful Qāsim Kūkūldāsh has filled some pages of history (Gulbadan's H.N. *s.n.* Māh-chūchūq and Erskine's B. and H. i, 348).

[2] Some 9m. north of Kābul on the road to Āq-sarāī.

[3] The Ḥai. MS. (only) writes First Rabī but the Second better suits the near approach of winter.

[4] Elph. MS. fol. 97; W.-i-B. I.O. 215 f. 102*b* and 217 f. 85; Mems. p. 136. Useful books of the early 19th century, many of them referring to the *Bābur-nāma*, are Conolly's *Travels*, Wood's *Journey*, Elphinstone's *Caubul*, Burnes' *Cabool*, Masson's *Narrative*, Lord's and Leech's articles in JASB 1838 and in Burnes' *Reports* (India Office Library), Broadfoot's *Report* in RGS Supp. Papers vol. I.

[5] f. 1*b* where Farghāna is said to be on the limit of cultivation.

Lamghānāt,[1] Parashāwar (Pashāwar), Hash(t)-nagar and some of the countries of Hindūstān. On the west it has the mountain region in which are Karnūd (?) and Ghūr, now the refuge and dwelling-places of the Hazāra and Nikdīrī (var. Nikudārī) tribes. On the north, separated from it by the range of Hindū-kush, it has the Qūndūz and Andar-āb countries. On the south, it has Farmūl, Naghr (var. Naghz), Bannū and Afghānistān.[2]

(*a. Town and environs of Kābul.*)

The Kābul district itself is of small extent, has its greatest length from east to west, and is girt round by mountains. Its walled-town connects with one of these, rather a low one known as Shāh-of-Kābul because at some time a (Hindū) Shāh of Kābul built a residence on its summit.[3] Shāh-of-Kābul begins at the Dūrrīn narrows and ends at those of Dih-i-yaq'ūb[4]; it may be 4 miles (2 *shar'ī*) round; its skirt is covered with gardens fertilized from a canal which was brought along the hill-slope in the time of my paternal uncle, Aūlūgh Beg Mīrzā by his guardian, Wais Atāka.[5] The water of this canal comes to an end in a retired corner, a quarter known as Kul-kīna[6]

[1] f. 131*b*. To find these *tūmāns* here classed with what was not part of Kābul suggest a clerical omission of "beyond" or "east of" (Lamghānāt). It may be more correct to write Lāmghānāt, since the first syllable may be *lām*, fort. The modern form Laghmān is not used in the *Bābur-nāma*, nor, it may be added is Paghmān for Pamghān.

[2] It will be observed that Bābur limits the name Afghānistān to the countries inhabited by Afghān tribesmen; they are chiefly those south of the road from Kābul to Pashāwar (Erskine). See Vigne, p. 102, for a boundary between the Afghāns and Khurāsān.

[3] Al-birūnī's *Indika* writes of both Turk and Hindū-shāhī Kings of Kābul. See Raverty's *Notes* p. 62 and Stein's *Shāhī Kings of Kābul*. The mountain is 7592 ft. above the sea, some 1800 ft. therefore above the town.

[4] The Kābul-river enters the Chār-dih plain by the Dīh-i-yaq'ūb narrows, and leaves it by those of Dūrrīn. Cf. *S.A. War*, Plan p. 288 and Plan of action at Chār-āsiyā (Four-mills), the second shewing an off-take which may be Wais Ātāka's canal. See Vigne, p. 163 and Raverty's *Notes* pp. 69 and 689.

[5] This, the Bālā-jūī (upper-canal) was a four-mill stream and in Masson's time, as now, supplied water to the gardens round Bābur's tomb. Masson found in Kābul honoured descendants of Wais Ātāka (ii, 240).

[6] But for a, perhaps negligible, shortening of its first vowel, this form of the name would describe the normal end of an irrigation canal, a little pool, but other forms with other meanings are open to choice, *e.g.* small hamlet (Pers. *kul*), or some compound containing Pers. *gul*, a rose, in its plain or metaphorical senses. Jarrett's *Āyīn-i-akbarī* writes Gul-kīnah, little rose (?). Masson (ii, 236) mentions a similar pleasure-resort, Sanjī-tāq.

where much debauchery has gone on. About this place it sometimes used to be said, in jesting parody of Khwāja Ḥāfiẓ[1], —"Ah! the happy, thoughtless time when, with our names in ill-repute, we lived days of days at Kul-kīna!" Fol. 128b.

East of Shāh-of-Kabūl and south of the walled-town lies a large pool[2] about a 2 miles [*shar'ī*] round. From the town side of the mountain three smallish springs issue, two near Kul-kīna; Khwāja Shamū's[3] tomb is at the head of one; Khwāja Khiẓr's Qadam-gāh[4] at the head of another, and the third is at a place known as Khwāja Raushānāī, over against Khwāja 'Abdu'ṣ-ṣamad. On a detached rock of a spur of Shāh-of-Kābul, known as 'Uqābain,[5] stands the citadel of Kābul with the great walled-town at its north end, lying high in excellent air, and overlooking the large pool already mentioned, and also three meadows, namely, Siyāh-sang (Black-rock), Sūng-qūrghān (Fort-back), and Chālāk (Highwayman?),—a most beautiful outlook when the meadows are green. The north-wind does not fail Kābul in the heats; people call it the Parwān-wind[6]; it makes a delightful temperature in the windowed houses on the northern part of the citadel. In praise of the citadel of Kābul, Mullā Muḥammad *Ṭālib Mu'ammāī* (the Riddler)[7]

[1] The original ode, with which the parody agrees in rhyme and refrain, is in the *Dīwān, s.l. Dāl* (Brockhaus ed. 1854, i, 62 and lith. ed. p. 96). See Wilberforce Clarke's literal translation i, 286 (H.B.). A marginal note to the Ḥaidarābād Codex gives what appears to be a variant of one of the rhymes of the parody.

[2] *aūlūgh kūl*; some 3 m. round in Erskine's time; mapped as a swamp in *S.A. War* p. 288.

[3] A marginal note to the Ḥai. Codex explains this name to be an abbreviation of Khwāja Shamsū'd-dīn *Jān-bāz* (or *Jahān-bāz*; Masson, ii, 279 and iii, 93).

[4] *i.e.* the place made holy by an impress of saintly foot-steps.

[5] Two eagles or, Two poles, used for punishment. Vigne's illustration (p. 161) clearly shows the spur and the detached rock. Erskine (p. 137 n.) says that 'Uqābain seems to be the hill, known in his day as 'Ashiqān-i-'ārifān, which connects with Bābur Bādshāh. See Raverty's *Notes* p. 68.

[6] During most of the year this wind rushes through the Hindū-kush (Parwān)-pass; it checks the migration of the birds (f. 142), and it may be the cause of the deposit of the Running-sands (Burnes, p. 158). Cf. Wood, p. 124.

[7] He was Badī'u'z-zamān's *Ṣadr* before serving Bābur; he died in 918 AH. (1512 AD.), in the battle of Kūl-i-malik where 'Ubaidu'l-lāh *Aūzbeg* defeated Bābur. He may be identical with Mīr Ḥusain the Riddler of f. 181, but seems not to be Mullā Muḥ. *Badakhshī*, also a Riddler, because the *Ḥabību's-siyār* (ii, 343 and 344) gives this man a separate notice. Those interested in enigmas can find one made by Ṭālib on the name Yaḥya (H.S. ii, 344). Sharafu'd-dīn 'Alī *Yazdī*, the author of the *Ẓafar-nāma*, wrote a book about a novel kind of these puzzles (T.R. p. 84).

Fol. 129. used to recite this couplet, composed on Badī'u'z-zamān Mīrzā's name:—

> Drink wine in the castle of Kābul and send the cup round without pause;
> For Kābul is mountain, is river, is city, is lowland in one.[1]

(*b. Kābul as a trading-town.*)

Just as 'Arabs call every place outside 'Arab (Arabia), 'Ajam, so Hindūstānīs call every place outside Hindūstān, Khurāsān. There are two trade-marts on the land-route between Hindūstān and Khurāsān; one is Kābul, the other, Qandahār. To Kābul caravans come from Kāshghar,[2] Farghāna, Turkistān, Samarkand, Bukhārā, Balkh, Ḥiṣār and Badakhshān. To Qandahār they come from Khurāsān. Kābul is an excellent trading-centre; if merchants went to Khīta or to Rūm,[3] they might make no higher profit. Down to Kābul every year come 7, 8, or 10,000 horses and up to it, from Hindūstān, come every year caravans of 10, 15 or 20,000 heads-of-houses, bringing slaves (*barda*), white cloth, sugar-candy, refined and common sugars, and aromatic roots. Many a trader is not content with a profit of 30 or 40 on 10.[4] In Kābul can be had the products of Khurāsān, Rūm, 'Irāq and Chīn (China); while it is Hindūstān's own market.

(*c. Products and climate of Kābul.*)

In the country of Kābul, there are hot and cold districts close to one another. In one day, a man may go out of the town of Kābul to where snow never falls, or he may go, in two sidereal
Fol. 129b. hours, to where it never thaws, unless when the heats are such that it cannot possibly lie.

Fruits of hot and cold climates are to be had in the districts near the town. Amongst those of the cold climate, there are had in the town the grape, pomegranate, apricot, apple, quince,

[1] The original couplet is as follows:—

> *Bakhūr dar arg-i Kābul mai, bagardān kāsa pāy dar pāy,*
> *Kah ham koh ast, u ham daryā, u ham shahr ast, u ham ṣaḥrā'.*

What Ṭālib's words may be inferred to conceal is the opinion that like Badī'u'z-zamān and like the meaning of his name, Kābul is the Wonder-of-the-world. (Cf. M. Garçin de Tassy's *Rhétorique* [p. 165], for *ces combinaisons énigmatiques.*)

[2] All MSS. do not mention Kāshghar.

[3] Khīta (Cathay) is Northern China; Chīn (*infra*) is China; Rūm is Turkey and particularly the provinces near Trebizond (Erskine).

[4] 300% to 400% (Erskine).

pear, peach, plum, *sinjid*, almond and walnut.[1] I had cuttings of the *ālū-bālū* [2] brought there and planted; they grew and have done well. Of fruits of the hot climate people bring into the town;—from the Lamghānāt, the orange, citron, *amlūk* (*diospyrus lotus*), and sugar-cane; this last I had had brought and planted there;[3]—from Nijr-'au (Nijr-water), they bring the *jīl-ghūza*,[4] and, from the hill-tracts, much honey. Bee-hives are in use; it is only from towards Ghaznī, that no honey comes.

The rhubarb [5] of the Kābul district is good, its quinces and plums very good, so too its *badrang*;[6] it grows an excellent grape, known as the water-grape.[7] Kābul wines are heady, those of the Khwāja Khāwand Sa'īd hill-skirt being famous for their strength; at this time however I can only repeat the praise of others about them:—[8]

> The flavour of the wine a drinker knows;
> What chance have sober men to know it?

Kābul is not fertile in grain, a four or five-fold return is reckoned good there; nor are its melons first-rate, but they are not altogether bad when grown from Khurāsān seed.

It has a very pleasant climate; if the world has another so pleasant, it is not known. Even in the heats, one cannot sleep

[1] Persian *sinjid*, Brandis, *elæagnus hortensis*; Erskine (Mems. p. 138) jujube, presumably the *zizyphus jujuba* of Speede, Supplement p. 86. Turkī *yāngāq*, walnut, has several variants, of which the most marked is *yānghkāq*. For a good account of Kābul fruits *see* Masson, ii, 230.

[2] a kind of plum (?). It seems unlikely to be a cherry since Bābur does not mention cherries as good in his old dominions, and Firminger (p. 244) makes against it as introduced from India. Steingass explains *alū-bālū* by "sour-cherry, an armaryllа"; if sour, is it the Morello cherry?

[3] The sugar-cane was seen in abundance in Lan-po (Lamghān) by a Chinese pilgrim (Beale, p. 90); Bābur's introduction of it may have been into his own garden only in Nīngnahār (f. 132*b*).

[4] *i.e.* the seeds of *pinus Gerardiana*.

[5] *rawāshlār*. The green leaf-stalks (*chūkrī*) of *ribes rheum* are taken into Kābul in mid-April from the Pamghān-hills; a week later they are followed by the blanched and tended *rawāsh* (Masson, ii, 7). *See* Gul-badan's H.N. trs. p. 188, Vigne, p. 100 and 107, Masson, ii, 230, Conolly, i, 213.

[6] a large green fruit, shaped something like a citron; also a large sort of cucumber (Erskine).

[7] The *ṣāḥibī*, a grape praised by Bābur amongst Samarkandī fruits, grows in Koh-dāman; another well-known grape of Kābul is the long stoneless *ḥusainī*, brought by Afghān traders into Hindūstān in round, flat boxes of poplar wood (Vigne, p. 172).

[8] An allusion, presumably, to the renouncement of wine made by Bābur and some of his followers in 933 AH. (1527 AD. f. 312). He may have had 'Umar *Khayyām's* quatrain in mind. "Wine's power is known to wine-bibbers alone" (Whinfield's 2nd ed. 1901, No. 164).

at night without a fur-coat.[1] Although the snow in most places lies deep in winter, the cold is not excessive; whereas in Fol. 130. Samarkand and Tabrīz, both, like Kābul, noted for their pleasant climate, the cold is extreme.

(*d. Meadows of Kābul.*)

There are good meadows on the four sides of Kābul. An excellent one, Sūng-qūrghān, is some 4 miles (2 *kuroh*) to the north-east; it has grass fit for horses and few mosquitos. To the north-west is the Chālāk meadow, some 2 miles (1 *shar'ī*) away, a large one but in it mosquitos greatly trouble the horses. On the west is the Dūrrīn, in fact there are two, Tīpa and Qūsh-nādir (var. nāwar),—if two are counted here, there would be five in all. Each of these is about 2 miles from the town; both are small, have grass good for horses, and no mosquitos; Kābul has no others so good. On the east is the Siyāh-sang meadow with Qūtlūq-qadam's tomb[2] between it and the Currier's-gate; it is not worth much because, in the heats, it swarms with mosquitos. Kamarī[3] meadow adjoins it; counting this in, the meadows of Kābul would be six, but they are always spoken of as four.

(*e. Mountain-passes into Kābul.*)

The country of Kābul is a fastness hard for a foreign foe to make his way into.

The Hindū-kush mountains, which separate Kabul from Balkh, Qūndūz and Badakhshān, are crossed by seven roads.[4] Three

[1] *pūstīn*, usually of sheep-skin. For the wide range of temperature at Kābul in 24 hours, *see* Ency. Brtt. art. Afghānistān. The winters also vary much in severity (Burnes, p. 273).

[2] Index *s.n.* As he fought at Kānwāha, he will have been buried after March 1527 AD.; this entry therefore will have been made later. The Curriers'-gate is the later Lahor-gate (Masson, ii, 259).

[3] Index *s.n.*

[4] For lists of the Hindū-kush passes *see* Leech's Report VII; Yule's *Introductory Essay* to Wood's *Journey* 2nd ed.; PRGS 1879, Markham's art. p. 121.

The highest *cols* on the passes here enumerated by Bābur are,—Khawāk 11,640 ft.—Tūl, height not known,—Pārandī 15,984 ft.—Bāj-gāh (Toll-place) 12,000 ft.—Wallān (Saints) 15,100 ft.—Chahār-dār (Four-doors) 18,900 ft. and Shibr-tū 9800 ft. In considering the labour of their ascent and descent, the general high level, north and south of them, should be borne in mind; *e.g.* Chārikār (Chār-yak-kār) stands 5200 ft. and Kābul itself at 5780 ft. above the sea.

of these lead out of Panjhīr (Panj-sher), *viz.* Khawāk, the uppermost, Ṭūl, the next lower, and Bāzārak.[1] Of the passes on them, the one on the Ṭūl road is the best, but the road itself is rather the longest whence, seemingly, it is called Ṭūl. Bāzārak is the most direct; like Ṭūl, it leads over into Sar-i-āb; as it passes through Pārandī, local people call its main pass, the Pārandī. Another road leads up through Parwān; it has seven minor passes, known as Haft-bacha (Seven-younglings), between Parwān and its main pass (Bāj-gāh). It is joined at its main pass by two roads from Andar-āb, which go on to Parwān by it. This is a road full of difficulties. Out of Ghūr-bund, again, three roads lead over. The one next to Parwān, known as the Yāngī-yūl pass (New-road), goes through Wālīān to Khinjan; next above this is the Qīpchāq road, crossing to where the water of Andar-āb meets the Sūrkh-āb (Qīzīl-sū); this also is an excellent road; and the third leads over the Shibr-tū pass;[2] those crossing by this in the heats take their way by Bāmīān and Saighān, but those crossing by it in winter, go on by Āb-dara (Water-valley).[3] Shibr-tū excepted, all the Hindū-kush roads are closed for three or four months in winter,[4] because no road through a valley-bottom is passable when the waters are high. If any-one thinks to cross the Hindū-kush at that time, over the mountains instead of through a valley-bottom, his journey is hard indeed. The time to cross is during the three or four autumn months when the snow is less and the waters are low. Whether on the mountains or in the valley-bottoms, Kāfir highwaymen are not few.

Fol. 130*b*. Fol. 131.

The road from Kābul into Khurāsān passes through Qandahār; it is quite level, without a pass.

[1] *i.e.* the hollow, long, and small-bāzār roads respectively. Panjhīr is explained by Hindūs to be Panj-sher, the five lion-sons of Pandu (Masson, iii, 168).

[2] Shibr is a Hazāra district between the head of the Ghūr-bund valley and Bāmīān. It does not seem to be correct to omit the *tū* from the name of the pass. Persian *tū*, turn, twist (syn. *pīch*) occurs in other names of local passes; to read it here as a *turn* agrees with what is said of Shibr-tū pass as not crossing but turning the Hindū-kush (Cunningham). Lord uses the same wording about the Ḥājī-ghāt (var. -kāk etc.) traverse of the same spur, which "turns the extremity of the Hindū-kush". *See* Cunningham's *Ancient Geography*, i, 25; Lord's *Ghūr-bund* (JASB 1838 p. 528), Masson, iii, 169 and Leech's *Report* VII.

[3] Perhaps through Jālmīsh into Saighān.

[4] *i.e.* they are closed.

Four roads leads into Kābul from the Hindūstān side; one by rather a low pass through the Khaibar mountains, another by way of Bangash, another by way of Naghr (var. Naghz),[1] and another through Farmūl;[2] the passes being low also in the three last-named. These roads are all reached from three ferries over the Sind. Those who take the Nīl-āb[3] ferry, come on through the Lamghānāt.[4] In winter, however, people ford the Sind-water (at Hāru) above its junction with the Kābul-water,[5] and ford this also. In most of my expeditions into Hindūstān, I crossed those fords, but this last time (932 AH.—1525 AD.), when I came, defeated Sl. Ibrāhīm and conquered the country, I crossed by boat at Nīl-āb. Except at the one place mentioned above, the Sind-water can be crossed only by boat. Those again, who cross at Dīn-kot[6] go on through Bangash. Those crossing at Chaupāra, if they take the Farmūl road, go on to Ghaznī, or, if they go by the Dasht, go on to Qandahār.[7]

[1] It was unknown in Mr. Erskine's day (Mems. p. 140). Several of the routes in Raverty's *Notes* (p. 92 etc.) allow it to be located as on the Īrī-āb, near to or identical with Bāghzān, 35 *kurohs* (70 m.) s.s.e. of Kābul.

[2] Farmūl, about the situation of which Mr. Erskine was in doubt, is now marked in maps, Ūrghūn being its principal village.

[3] 15 miles below Atak (Erskine). Mr. Erskine notes that he found no warrant, previous to Abū'l-faẓl's, for calling the Indus the Nīl-āb, and that to find one would solve an ancient geographical difficulty. This difficulty, my husband suggests, was Alexander's supposition that the Indus was the Nile. In books grouping round the *Bābur-nāma*, the name Nīl-āb is not applied to the Indus, but to the ferry-station on that river, said to owe its name to a spring of azure water on its eastern side. (Cf. Afẓal Khān *Khattak*, R.'s *Notes* p. 447.)

I find the name Nīl-āb applied to the Kābul-river:—1. to its Arghandī affluent (Cunningham. p. 17, Map); 2. through its boatman class, the Nīl-ābīs of Lālpūra, Jalālābād and Kūnār (G. of I. 1907, art. Kābul); 3. inferentially to it as a tributary of the Indus (D'Herbélot); 4. to it near its confluence with the grey, silt-laden Indus, as blue by contrast (Sayyid Ghulām-i-muḥammad, R.'s *Notes* p. 34). (For Nīl-āb (Naulibis?) in Ghūr-bund *see* Cunningham, p. 32 and Masson, iii, 169.)

[4] By one of two routes perhaps,—either by the Khaibar-Nīngnahār-Jagdālīk road, or along the north bank of the Kābul-river, through Goshṭa to the crossing where, in 1879, the 10th Hussars met with disaster. *See S.A. War*, Map 2 and p. 63; Leech's *Reports* II and IV (Fords of the Indus); and R.'s *Notes* p. 44.

[5] Hāru, Leech's Harroon, apparently, 10 m. above Atak. The text might be read to mean that both rivers were forded near their confluence, but, finding no warrant for supposing the Kābul-river fordable below Jalālābād, I have guided the translation accordingly; this may be wrong and may conceal a change in the river.

[6] known also as Dhān-kot and as Mu'aẓẓam-nagar (*Ma'āṣiru'l-'umrā* i, 249 and A.N. trs. H.B. index *s.n.* Dhān-kot). It was on the east bank of the Indus, probably near modern Kālā-bāgh, and was washed away not before 956 AH. (1549 AD. H. Beveridge).

[7] Chaupāra seems, from f. 148*b*, to be the Chapari of Survey Map 1889. Bābur's *Dasht* is modern Dāman.

(f. Inhabitants of Kābul.)

There are many differing tribes in the Kābul country; in its dales and plains are Turks and clansmen[1] and 'Arabs; in its town and in many villages, Sārts; out in the districts and also in villages are the Pashāī, Parājī, Tājīk, Bīrkī and Afghān tribes. In the western mountains are the Hazāra and Nikdīrī tribes, some of whom speak the Mughūlī tongue. In the north-eastern mountains are the places of the Kāfirs, such as Kitūr (Gawār?) and Gibrik. To the south are the places of the Afghān tribes. Fol. 131*b*.

Eleven or twelve tongues are spoken in Kābul,—'Arabī, Persian, Turkī, Mughūlī, Hindī, Afghānī, Pashāī, Parājī, Gibrī, Bīrkī and Lamghānī. If there be another country with so many differing tribes and such a diversity of tongues, it is not known.

(e. Sub-divisions of the Kābul country.)

The [Kābul] country has fourteen *tūmāns*.[2]

Bajaur, Sawād and Hash-nagar may at one time have been dependencies of Kābul, but they now have no resemblance to cultivated countries (*wilāyāt*), some lying desolate because of the Afghāns, others being now subject to them.

In the east of the country of Kābul is the Lamghānāt, 5 *tūmāns* and 2 *bulūks* of cultivated lands.[3] The largest of these is Nīngnahār, sometimes written Nagarahār in the histories.[4] Its *dārogha's* residence is in Adīnapūr,[5] some 13 *yīghāch* east of Kābul by a very bad and tiresome road, going in three or four places over small hill-passes, and in three or four others, through Fol. 132.

[1] *aīmāq*, used usually of Mughūls, I think. It may be noted that Lieutenant Leech compiled a vocabulary of the tongue of the Mughūl Aīmāq in Qandahār and Harāt (JASB 1838, p. 785).

[2] The *Āyīn-i-akbarī* account of Kābul both uses and supplements the *Bābur-nāma.*

[3] *viz.* 'Alī-shang, Alangār and Mandrāwar (the Lamghānāt proper), Nīngnahār (with its *bulūk*, Kāma), Kūnār-with-Nūr-gal, (and the two *bulūks* of Nūr-valley and Chaghān-sarāī).

[4] *See* Appendix E, *On Nagarahāra.*

[5] The name Adīnapūr is held to be descended from ancient Udyānapūra (Garden-town); its ancestral form however was applied to Nagarahāra, apparently, in the Bārān-Sūrkh-rūd *dū-āb*, and not to Bābur's *dārogha's* seat. The Sūrkh-rūd's deltaic mouth was a land of gardens; when Masson visited Adīnapūr he went from Bālā-bāgh (High-garden); this appears to stand where Bābur locates his Bāgh-i-wafā, but he was shown a garden he took to be this one of Bābur's, a mile higher up the Sūrkh-rūd. A later ruler made the Chār-bāgh of maps. It may be mentioned that Bālā-bāgh has become in some maps Rozābād (Garden-town). *See* Masson, i, 182 and iii, 186; R.'s *Notes*; and Wilson's *Ariana Antiqua*, Masson's art.

narrows.[1] So long as there was no cultivation along it, the Khirilchī and other Afghān thieves used to make it their beat, but it has become safe[2] since I had it peopled at Qarā-tū,[3] below Qūrūq-sāī. The hot and cold climates are separated on this road by the pass of Bādām-chashma (Almond-spring); on its Kābul side snow falls, none at Qūrūq-sāī, towards the Lamghānāt.[4] After descending this pass, another world comes into view, other trees, other plants (or grasses), other animals, and other manners and customs of men. Nīngnahār is nine torrents (*tūqūz-rūd*).[5] It grows good crops of rice and corn, excellent and abundant oranges, citrons and pomegranates. In 914 AH. (1508–9 AD.) I laid out the Four-gardens, known as the Bāgh-i-wafā (Garden-of-fidelity), on a rising-ground, facing south and having the Sūrkh-rūd between it and Fort Adīnapūr.[6] There oranges, citrons and pomegranates grow in abundance. The year I defeated Pahār Khān and took Lāhor and Dipālpūr,[7] I had plantains (bananas) brought and planted there; they did very well. The year before I had had sugar-cane planted there; it also did well; some of it was sent to Bukhārā and Badakhshān.[8] The garden lies high, has running-water close at hand, and a mild winter
Fol. 132*b*. climate. In the middle of it, a one-mill stream flows constantly past the little hill on which are the four garden-plots. In the south-west part of it there is a reservoir, 10 by 10,[9] round which

[1] One of these *tangī* is now a literary asset in Mr. Kipling's *My Lord the Elephant.* Bābur's 13 y. represent some 82 miles; on f. 137*b* the Kābul-Ghaznī road of 14 y. represents some 85; in each case the *yīghāch* works out at over six miles (Index *s.n.* *yīghāch* and Vigne, p. 454). Sayyid Ghulām-i-muḥammad traces this route minutely (R.'s *Notes* pp. 57, 59).

[2] Masson was shewn "Chaghatai castles", attributed to Bābur (iii, 174).

[3] Dark-turn, perhaps, as in Shibr-tū, Jāl-tū, *etc.* (f. 130*b* and note to Shibr-tū).

[4] f. 145 where the change is described in identical words, as seen south of the Jagdālīk-pass. The Bādām-chashma pass appears to be a traverse of the eastern rampart of the Tīzīn-valley.

[5] Appendix E, *On Nagarahāra.*

[6] No record exists of the actual laying-out of the garden; the work may have been put in hand during the Mahmand expedition of 914 AH. (f. 216); the name given to it suggests a gathering there of loyalists when the stress was over of the bad Mughūl rebellion of that year (f. 216*b* where the narrative breaks off abruptly in 914 AH. and is followed by a gap down to 925 AH.–1519 AD.).

[7] No annals of 930 AH. are known to exist; from Ṣafar 926 AH. to 932 AH. (Jan. 1520–Nov. 1525 AD.) there is a lacuna. Accounts of the expedition are given by Khāfī Khān, i, 47 and Firishta, lith. ed. p. 202.

[8] Presumably to his son, Humāyūn, then governor in Badakhshān; Bukhārā also was under Bābur's rule.

[9] here, *qārī*, yards. The dimensions 10 by 10, are those enjoined for places of ablution.

are orange-trees and a few pomegranates, the whole encircled by a trefoil-meadow. This is the best part of the garden, a most beautiful sight when the oranges take colour. Truly that garden is admirably situated!

The Safed-koh runs along the south of Nīngnahār, dividing it from Bangash; no riding-road crosses it; nine torrents (*tūqūz-rūd*) issue from it.[1] It is called Safed-koh[2] because its snow never lessens; none falls in the lower parts of its valleys, a half-day's journey from the snow-line. Many places along it have an excellent climate; its waters are cold and need no ice.

The Sūrkh-rūd flows along the south of Adīnapūr. The fort stands on a height having a straight fall to the river of some 130 ft. (40–50 *qārī*) and isolated from the mountain behind it on the north; it is very strongly placed. That mountain runs between Nīngnahār and Lamghān[3]; on its head snow falls when it snows Fol. 133
in Kābul, so Lamghānīs know when it has snowed in the town.

In going from Kābul into the Lamghānāt,[4]—if people come by Qūrūq-sāī, one road goes on through the Dīrī-pass, crosses the Bārān-water at Būlān, and so on into the Lamghānāt,—another goes through Qarā-tū, below Qūrūq-sāī, crosses the Bārān-water at Aūlūgh-nūr (Great-rock?), and goes into Lamghān by the pass of Bād-i-pīch.[5] If however people come by Nijr-aū, they traverse Badr-aū (Tag-aū), and Qarā-nakariq (?), and go on through the pass of Bād-i-pīch.

[1] Presumably those of the *tūqūz-rūd*, *supra*. Cf. Appendix E, *On Nagarahāra*.

[2] White-mountain; Pushtū Spīn-ghur (or ghar).

[3] *i.e.* the Lamghānāt proper. The range is variously named; in (Persian) Siyāh-koh (Black-mountain), which like Turkī Qarā-tāgh may mean non-snowy; by Tājīks, Bāgh-i-ātāka (Foster-father's garden); by Afghāns, Kanda-ghur, and by Lamghānīs Koh-i-būlān,—Kanda and Būlān both being ferry-stations below it (Masson, iii, 189; also the Times Nov. 20th 1912 for a cognate illustration of diverse naming).

[4] A comment made here by Mr. Erskine on changes of name is still appropriate, but some seeming changes may well be due to varied selection of land-marks. Of the three routes next described in the text, one crosses as for Mandrāwar; the second, as for 'Alī-shang, a little below the outfall of the Tīzīn-water; the third may take off from the route, between Kābul and Tag-aū, marked in Col. Tanner's map (PRGS 1881 p. 180). Cf. R's Route 11; and for Aūlūgh-nūr, Appendix F, *On the name Nūr*.

[5] The name of this pass has several variants. Its second component, whatever its form, is usually taken to mean *pass*, but to read it here as pass would be redundant, since Bābur writes "pass (*kūtal*) of Bād-i-pīch". Pīch occurs as a place name both east (Pīch) and west (Pīchghān) of the *kūtal*, but what would suit the bitter and even fatal winds of the pass would be to read the name as Whirling-wind (*bād-i-pīch*). Another explanation suggests itself from finding a considerable number of pass-names such as Shibr-tū, Jāl-tū, Qarā-tū, in which *tū* is a synonym of *pīch*, turn, twist; thus Bād-i-pīch may be the local form of Bād-tū, Windy-turn.

Although Nīngnahār is one of the five *tūmāns* of the Lamghān *tūmān* the name Lamghānāt applies strictly only to the three (mentioned below).

One of the three is the 'Alī-shang *tūmān*, to the north of which are fastness-mountains, connecting with Hindū-kush and inhabited by Kāfirs only. What of Kāfiristān lies nearest to 'Alī-shang, is Mīl out of which its torrent issues. The tomb of Lord Lām,[1] father of his Reverence the prophet Nuḥ (Noah), is in this *tūmān*. In some histories he is called Lamak and Lamakān. Some people are observed often to change *kāf* for *ghain* (*k* for *gh*); it would seem to be on this account that the country is called Lamghān.

The second is Alangār. The part of Kāfiristān nearest to it is Gawār (Kawār), out of which its torrent issues (the Gau or Kau). This torrent joins that of 'Alī-shang and flows with it

Fol. 133*b*. into the Bārān-water, below Mandrāwar, which is the third *tūmān* of the Lamghānāt.

Of the two *bulūks* of Lamghān one is the Nūr-valley.[2] This is a place (*yīr*) without a second[3]; its fort is on a beak (*tūmshūq*) of rock in the mouth of the valley, and has a torrent on each side; its rice is grown on steep terraces, and it can be traversed by one road only.[4] It has the orange, citron and other fruits of hot climates in abundance, a few dates even. Trees cover the banks of both the torrents below the fort; many are *amlūk*, the fruit of which some Turks call *qarā-yīmīsh*;[5] here they are many, but none have been seen elsewhere. The valley grows grapes also, all trained on trees.[6] Its wines are those of Lamghān that have reputation. Two sorts of grapes are grown,

[1] *See* Masson, iii, 197 and 289. Both in Pashāī and Lamghānī, *lām* means fort.

[2] *See* Appendix F, *On the name Dara-i-nūr.*

[3] *ghair mukarrar.* Bābur may allude to the remarkable change men have wrought in the valley-bottom (Appendix F, for Col. Tanner's account of the valley).

[4] f. 154.

[5] *diospyrus lotus*, the European date-plum, supposed to be one of the fruits eaten by the Lotophagi. It is purple, has bloom and is of the size of a pigeon's egg or a cherry. See Watts' *Economic Products of India*; Brandis' *Forest Trees*, Illustrations; and Speede's *Indian Hand-book.*

[6] As in Lombardy, perhaps; in Luhūgur vines are clipped into standards; in most other places in Afghānistān they are planted in deep trenches and allowed to run over the intervening ridges or over wooden framework. In the narrow Khūlm-valley they are trained up poplars so as to secure them the maximum of sun. *See* Wood's *Report* VI p. 27; Bellew's *Afghānistān* p. 175 and *Mems.* p. 142 note.

the *arah-tāshī* and the *sūhān-tāshī*;[1] the first are yellowish, the second, full-rea of fine colour. The first make the more cheering wine, but it must be said that neither wine equals its reputation for cheer. High up in one of its glens, apes (*maimūn*) are found, none below. Those people (*i.e.* Nūrīs) used to keep swine but they have given it up in our time.[2]

Another *tūmān* of Lamghān is Kūnār-with-Nūr-gal. It lies somewhat out-of-the-way, remote from the Lamghānāt, with its borders in amongst the Kāfir lands; on these accounts its people give in tribute rather little of what they have. The Chaghān- Fol. 134. sarāī water enters it from the north-east, passes on into the *bulūk* of Kāma, there joins the Bārān-water and with that flows east.

Mīr Sayyid 'Alī *Hamadānī*,[3]—God's mercy on him!—coming here as he journeyed, died 2 miles (1 *shar'ī*) above Kūnār. His disciples carried his body to Khutlān. A shrine was erected at the honoured place of his death, of which I made the circuit when I came and took Chaghān-sarāī in 920 AH.[4]

The orange, citron and coriander[5] abound in this *tūmān*. Strong wines are brought down into it from Kāfiristān.

A strange thing is told there, one seeming impossible, but one told to us again and again. All through the hill-country above Multa-kundī, *viz.* in Kūnār, Nūr-gal, Bajaur, Sawād and

(*Author's note to Multa-kundī.*) As Multa-kundī is known the lower part of the *tūmān* of Kūnār-with-Nūr-gal; what is below (*i.e.* on the river) belongs to the valley of Nūr and to Atar.[6]

---

[1] Appendix G, *On the names of two Nūrī wines.*

[2] This practice Bābur viewed with disgust, the hog being an impure animal according to Muḥammadan Law (Erskine).

[3] The *Khazīnatu'l-aṣfiyā* (ii, 293) explains how it came about that this saint, one honoured in Kashmīr, was buried in Khutlān. He died in Hazāra (Paklī) and there the Paklī Sulṭān wished to have him buried, but his disciples, for some unspecified reason, wished to bury him in Khutlān. In order to decide the matter they invited the Sultān to remove the bier with the corpse upon it. It could not be stirred from its place. When, however a single one of the disciples tried to move it, he alone was able to lift it, and to bear it away on his head. Hence the burial in Khutlān. The death occurred in 786 AH. (1384 AD.). A point of interest in this legend is that, like the one to follow, concerning dead women, it shews belief in the living activities of the dead.

[4] The MSS. vary between 920 and 925 AH.—neither date seems correct. As the annals of 925 AH. begin in Muḥarram, with Bābur to the east of Bājaur, we surmise that the Chaghān-sarāī affair may have occurred on his way thither, and at the end of 924 AH.

[5] *karanj, coriandrum sativum.*

[6] some 20–24 m. north of Jalālābād. The name Multa-kundī may refer to the Rām-kundī range, or mean Lower district, or mean Below Kundī. *See* Biddulph's *Khowārī Dialect s.n* under; R.'s *Notes* p. 108 and *Dict. s.n. kund*; Masson, i, 209.

thereabouts, it is commonly said that when a woman dies and has been laid on a bier, she, if she has not been an ill-doer, gives the bearers such a shake when they lift the bier by its four sides, that against their will and hindrance, her corpse falls to the ground; but, if she has done ill, no movement occurs. This was heard not only from Kūnārīs but, again and again, in Bajaur,
Fol. 134*b*. Sawād and the whole hill-tract. Ḥaidar-'alī *Bajaurī*,—a sulṭān who governed Bajaur well,—when his mother died, did not weep, or betake himself to lamentation, or put on black, but said, "Go! lay her on the bier! if she move not, I will have her burned."[1] They laid her on the bier; the desired movement followed; when he heard that this was so, he put on black and betook himself to lamentation.

Another *bulūk* is Chaghān-sarāī,[2] a single village with little land, in the mouth of Kāfiristān; its people, though Muṣalmān, mix with the Kāfirs and, consequently, follow their customs.[3] A great torrent (the Kūnār) comes down to it from the north-east from behind Bajaur, and a smaller one, called Pīch, comes down out of Kāfiristān. Strong yellowish wines are had there, not in any way resembling those of the Nūr-valley, however. The village has no grapes or vineyards of its own; its wines are all brought from up the Kāfiristān-water and from Pīch-i-kāfiristānī.

The Pīch Kāfirs came to help the villagers when I took the place. Wine is so commonly used there that every Kāfir has his leathern wine-bag (*khīg*) at his neck, and drinks wine instead of water.[4]

[1] *i.e.* treat her corpse as that of an infidel (Erskine).

[2] It would suit the position of this village if its name were found to link to the Turkī verb *chaqmāq*, to go out, because it lies in the mouth of a defile (Dahānah-i-koh, Mountain-mouth) through which the road for Kāfiristān goes out past the village. A not-infrequent explanation of the name to mean White-house, Āq-sarāī, may well be questioned. *Chaghān*, white, is Mughūlī and it would be less probable for a Mughūlī than for a Turkī name to establish itself. Another explanation may lie in the tribe name Chugānī. The two forms *chaghān* and *chaghār* may well be due to the common local interchange in speech of *n* with *r*. (For Dahānah-i-koh *see* [some] maps and Raverty's Bājaur routes.)

[3] Nīmchas, presumably,—half-bred in custom, perhaps in blood—; and not improbably, converted Kāfirs. It is useful to remember that Kāfiristān was once bounded, west and south, by the Bārān-water.

[4] Kāfir wine is mostly poor, thin and, even so, usually diluted with water. When kept two or three years, however, it becomes clear and sometimes strong. Sir G. S. Robertson never saw a Kāfir drunk (*Kāfirs of the Hindū-kush*, p. 591).

Kāma, again, though not a separate district but dependent on Nīngnahār, is also called a *bulūk*.[1] Fol. 135.

Nijr-aū[2] is another *tūmān*. It lies north of Kābul, in the Kohistān, with mountains behind it inhabited solely by Kāfirs; it is a quite sequestered place. It grows grapes and fruits in abundance. Its people make much wine but, they boil it. They fatten many fowls in winter, are wine-bibbers, do not pray, have no scruples and are Kāfir-like.[3]

In the Nijr-aū mountains is an abundance of *archa*, *jīlghūza*, *bīlūt* and *khanjak*.[4] The first-named three do not grow above Nigr-aū but they grow lower, and are amongst the trees of Hindūstān. *Jīlghūza*-wood is all the lamp the people have; it burns like a candle and is very remarkable. The flying-squirrel[5] is found in these mountains, an animal larger than a bat and having a curtain (*parda*), like a bat's wing, between its arms and legs. People often brought one in; it is said to fly, downward from one tree to another, as far as a *giz* flies;[6] I myself have never seen one fly. Once we put one to a tree; it clambered up directly and got away, but, when people went after it, it spread its wings and came down, without hurt, as if it had flown. Another of the curiosities of the Nijr-aū mountains is the *lūkha* (var. *lūja*) bird, called also *bū-qalamūn* (chameleon) because, between head and tail, it has four or five changing colours, resplendent like a pigeon's throat.[7] It is about as large as the

[1] Kāma might have classed better under Nīngnahār of which it was a dependency.

[2] *i.e.* water-of-Nijr; so too, Badr-aū and Tag-aū. Nijr-aū has seven-valleys (JASB 1838 p. 329 and Burnes' *Report X*). Sayyid Ghulām-i-muhammad mentions that Bābur established a frontier-post between Nijr-aū and Kāfiristān which in his own day was still maintained. He was an envoy of Warren Hastings to Tīmūr Shāh *Sadozī* (R.'s *Notes* p. 36 and p. 142).

[3] *Kāfirwash*; they were Kāfirs converted to Muhammadanism.

[4] *Archa*, if not inclusive, meaning conifer, may represent *juniperus excelsa*, this being the common local conifer. The other trees of the list are *pinus Gerardiana* (Brandis, p. 69c), *quercus bīlūt*, the holm-oak, and *pistacia mutica* or *khanjak*, a tree yielding mastic.

[5] *rūba-i-parwān*, *pteromys inornatus*, the large, red flying-squirrel (Blandford's *Fauna of British India*, *Mammalia*, p. 363).

[6] The *giz* is a short-flight arrow used for shooting small birds etc. Descending flights of squirrels have been ascertained as 60 yards, one, a record, of 80 (Blandford).

[7] Apparently *tetrogallus himalayensis*, the Himalayan snow-cock (Blandford, iv, 143). Burnes (*Cabool* p. 163) describes the *kabg-i-darī* as the *rara avis* of the Kābul Kohistān, somewhat less than a turkey, and of the *chikor* (partridge) species. It was procured for him first in Ghūr-bund, but, when snow has fallen, it could be had nearer Kābul. Bābur's *bū-qalamūn* may have come into his vocabulary, either as a survival direct from Greek occupation of Kābul and Panj-āb, or through Arabic writings. PRGS 1879 p. 251, Kaye's art. and JASB 1838 p. 863, Hodgson's art.

kabg-i-darī and seems to be the *kabg-i-darī* of Hindūstān.[1] People tell this wonderful thing about it :—When the birds, at
Fol. 135*b*. the on-set of winter, descend to the hill-skirts, if they come over a vineyard, they can fly no further and are taken.[2] There is a kind of rat in Nijr-aū, known as the musk-rat, which smells of musk ; I however have never seen it.[3]

Panjhīr (Panj-sher) is another *tūmān* ; it lies close to Kāfiristān, along the Panjhir road, and is the thoroughfare of Kāfir highwaymen who also, being so near, take tax of it. They have gone through it, killing a mass of persons, and doing very evil deeds, since I came this last time and conquered Hindūstān (932 AH.-1526 AD.).[4]

Another is the *tūmān* of Ghūr-bund. In those countries they call a *kūtal* (*koh* ?) a *bund* ;[5] they go towards Ghūr by this pass (*kūtal*) ; apparently it is for this reason that they have called (the *tūmān* ?) Ghūr-bund. The Hazāra hold the heads of its valleys.[6] It has few villages and little revenue can be raised from it. There are said to be mines of silver and lapis lazuli in its mountains.

Again, there are the villages on the skirts of the (Hindū-kush) mountains,[7] with Mīta-kacha and Parwān at their head, and

1 Bartavelle's *Greek-partridge*, *tetrao-* or *perdrix-rufus* [f. 279 and Mems. p. 320 n.].

2 A similar story is told of some fields near Whitby :—"These wild geese, which in winter fly in great flocks to the lakes and rivers unfrozen in the southern parts, to the great amazement of every-one, fall suddenly down upon the ground when they are in flight over certain neighbouring fields thereabouts ; a relation I should not have made, if I had not received it from several credible men." See *Notes to Marmion* p. xlvi (Erskine) ; Scott's *Poems*, Black's ed. 1880, vii, 104.

3 Are we to infer from this that the musk-rat (*Crocidura cærulea*, Lydekker, p. 626) was not so common in Hindūstān in the age of Bābur as it has now become ? He was not a careless observer (Erskine).

4 Index *s.n.* *Bābur-nāma*, date of composition ; also f. 131.

5 In the absence of examples of *bund* to mean *kūtal*, and the presence "in those countries" of many in which *bund* means *koh*, it looks as though a clerical error had here written *kūtal* for *koh*. But on the other hand, the wording of the next passage shows just the confusion an author's unrevised draft might shew if a place were, as this is, both a *tūmān* and a *kūtal* (*i.e.* a steady rise to a traverse). My impression is that the name Ghūr-bund applies to the embanking spur at the head of the valley-*tūmān*, across which roads lead to Ghūrī and Ghūr (PRGS 1879, Maps ; Leech's Report VII ; and Wood's VI).

6 So too when, because of them, Leech and Lord turned back, *re infectâ*.

7 It will be noticed that these villages are not classed in any *tūmān* ; they include places "rich without parallel" in agricultural products, and level lands on which towns have risen and fallen, one being Alexandria ad Caucasum. They cannot have been part of the unremunerative Ghūr-bund *tūmān* ; from their place of mention in Bābur's list of *tūmāns*, they may have been part of the Kābul *tūmān* (f. 178), as was Koh-dāman (Burnes' *Cabool* p. 154 ; Haughton's *Charikar* p. 73 ; and Cunningham's *Ancient History*, i, 18).

Dūr-nāma [1] at their foot, 12 or 13 in all. They are fruit-bearing villages, and they grow cheering wines, those of Khwāja Khāwand Sa'īd being reputed the strongest roundabouts. The villages all lie on the foot-hills; some pay taxes but not all are taxable because they lie so far back in the mountains.

Between the foot-hills and the Bārān-water are two detached stretches of level land, one known as *Kurrat-tāziyān*,[2] the other as *Dasht-i-shaikh* (Shaikh's-plain). As the green grass of the millet [3] grows well there, they are the resort of Turks and (Mughūl) clans (*aīmāq*). Fol. 136.

Tulips of many colours cover these foot-hills; I once counted them up; it came out at 32 or 33 different sorts. We named one the Rose-scented, because its perfume was a little like that of the red rose; it grows by itself on Shaikh's-plain, here and nowhere else. The Hundred-leaved tulip is another; this grows, also by itself, at the outlet of the Ghūr-bund narrows, on the hill-skirt below Parwān. A low hill known as Khwāja-i-reg-rawān (Khwāja-of-the-running-sand), divides the afore-named two pieces of level land; it has, from top to foot, a strip of sand from which people say the sound of nagarets and tambours issues in the heats.[4]

Again, there are the villages depending on Kābul itself. South-west from the town are great snow mountains [5] where snow falls on snow, and where few may be the years when, falling, it does not light on last year's snow. It is fetched, 12 miles may-be, from these mountains, to cool the drinking water when ice-houses in Kābul are empty. Like the Bāmiān mountains,

[1] Dūr-namāī, seen from afar (Masson, iii, 152) is not marked on the Survey Maps; Masson, Vigne and Haughton locate it. Bābur's "head" and "foot" here indicate status and not location.

[2] Mems. p. 146 and *Mêms.* i, 297, Arabs' encampment and *Cellule des Arabes*. Perhaps the name may refer to uses of the level land and good pasture by horse *qāfilas*, since *Kurra* is written with *tashdīd* in the Ḥaidarābād Codex, as in *kurra-tāz*, a horse-breaker. Or the *tāziyān* may be the fruit of a legend, commonly told, that the saint of the neighbouring Running-sands was an Arabian.

[3] Presumably this is the grass of the millet, the growth before the ear, on which grazing is allowed (Elphinstone, i, 400; Burnes, p. 237).

[4] Wood, p. 115; Masson, iii, 167; Burnes, p. 157 and JASB 1838 p. 324 with illustration; Vigne, pp. 219, 223; Lord, JASB 1838 p. 537; *Cathay and the way thither*, Hakluyt Society vol. I. p. xx, para. 49; *History of Musical Sands*, C. Carus-Wilson.

[5] *West* might be more exact, since some of the group are a little north, others a little south of the latitude of Kābul.

these are fastnesses. Out of them issue the Harmand (Halmand), Sind, Dūghāba of Qūndūz, and Balkh-āb,[1] so that in a single day, a man might drink of the water of each of these four rivers.

It is on the skirt of one of these ranges (Pamghān) that most of the villages dependent on Kābul lie.[2] Masses of grapes ripen in their vineyards and they grow every sort of fruit in abundance. No-one of them equals Istālīf or Astarghach; these must be the
Fol. 136*b*. two which Aūlūgh Beg Mīrzā used to call his Khurāsān and Samarkand. Pamghān is another of the best, not ranking in fruit and grapes with those two others, but beyond comparison with them in climate. The Pamghān mountains are a snowy range. Few villages match Istālīf, with vineyards and fine orchards on both sides of its great torrent, with waters needing no ice, cold and, mostly, pure. Of its Great garden Aūlūgh Beg Mīrzā had taken forcible possession; I took it over, after paying its price to the owners. There is a pleasant halting-place outside it, under great planes, green, shady and beautiful. A one-mill stream, having trees on both banks, flows constantly through the middle of the garden; formerly its course was zig-zag and irregular; I had it made straight and orderly; so the place became very beautiful. Between the village and the valley-bottom, from 4 to 6 miles down the slope, is a spring, known as Khwāja Sih-yārān (Three-friends), round which three sorts of tree grow. A group of planes gives pleasant shade above it; holm-
Fol. 137. oak (*quercus bilūt*) grows in masses on the slope at its sides,—these two oaklands (*bilūtistān*) excepted, no holm-oak grows in the mountains of western Kābul,—and the Judas-tree (*arghwān*)[3] is much cultivated in front of it, that is towards the level ground, —cultivated there and nowhere else. People say the three different sorts of tree were a gift made by three saints,[4] whence

[1] Affluents and not true sources in some cases (Col. Holdich's *Gates of India*, *s.n.* Koh-i-bābā; and PRGS 1879, maps pp. 80 and 160).

[2] The Pamghān range. These are the villages every traveller celebrates. Masson's and Vigne's illustrations depict them well.

[3] *Cercis siliquastrum*, the Judas-tree. Even in 1842 it was sparingly found near Kābul, adorning a few tombs, one Bābur's own. It had been brought from Sih-yārān where, as also at Chārikār, (Chār-yak-kār) it was still abundant and still a gorgeous sight. It is there a tree, as at Kew, and not a bush, as in most English gardens (Masson, ii, 9; Elphinstone, i, 194; and for the tree near Harāt, f. 191 n. to Ṣafar).

[4] Khwāja Maudūd of Chisht, Khwāja Khāwand Sa'īd and the Khwāja of the Running-sands (Elph. MS. f. 104*b*, marginal note).

Running-sands (Elph. MS. f. 104*b*, marginal note).

its name. I ordered that the spring should be enclosed in mortared stone-work, 10 by 10, and that a symmetrical, right-angled platform should be built on each of its sides so as to overlook the whole field of Judas-trees. If, the world over, there is a place to match this when the *arghwāns* are in full bloom, I do not know it. The yellow *arghwān* grows plentifully there also, the red and the yellow flowering at the same time.[1]

In order to bring water to a large round seat which I had built on the hillside and planted round with willows, I had a channel dug across the slope from a half-mill stream, constantly flowing in a valley to the south-west of Sih-yārān. The date of cutting this channel was found in *jūī-khūsh* (kindly channel).[2]

Another of the *tūmāns* of Kābul is Luhūgur (mod. Logar). Its one large village is Chīrkh from which were his Reverence Maulānā Ya'qūb and Mullā-zāda 'Uṣmān.[3] Khwāja Aḥmad and Khwāja Yūnas were from Sajāwand, another of its villages. Chīrkh has many gardens, but there are none in any other village of Luhūgur. Its people are Aūghān-shāl, a term common in Kābul, seeming to be a mispronouncement of Aūghān-sha'ār.[4] Fol. 137*b*

Again, there is the *wilāyat*, or, as some say, *tūmān* of Ghaznī, said to have been [5] the capital of Sabuk-tīgīn, Sl. Maḥmūd and their descendants. Many write it Ghaznīn. It is said also to have been the seat of government of Shihābu'd-dīn *Ghūrī*,[6] styled Mu'izzu'd-dīn in the *Tabaqāt-i-nāṣirī* and also some of the histories of Hind.

Ghaznī is known also as Zābulistān; it belongs to the Third climate. Some hold that Qandahār is a part of it. It lies 14 *yīghāch* (south-) west of Kābul; those leaving it at dawn, may reach Kābul between the Two Prayers (*i.e.* in the afternoon);

[1] The yellow-flowered plant is not *cercis siliquastrum* but one called *mahaka* (?) in Persian, a shrubby plant with pea-like blossoms, common in the plains of Persia, Bilūchistān and Kābul (Masson, iii, 9 and Vigne, p. 216).

[2] The numerical value of these words gives 925 (Erskine). F. 246*b et seq.* for the expedition.

[3] f. 178. I.O. MS. No. 724, *Haft-iqlīm* f. 135 (Ethé, p. 402); Rieu, pp. 21*a*, 1058*b*.

[4] of Afghān habit. The same term is applied (f. 139*b*) to the Zurmutīs; it may be explained in both places by Bābur's statement that Zurmutīs grow corn, but do not cultivate gardens or orchards.

[5] *aīkān dūr.* Sabuk-tīgīn, d. 387 AH.-997 AD., was the father of Sl. Maḥmūd *Ghaznawī*, d. 421 AH.-1030 AD.

[6] d. 602 AH.-1206 AD.

whereas the 13 *yīghāch* between Adīnapūr and Kābul can never be done in one day, because of the difficulties of the road.

Ghaznī has little cultivated land. Its torrent, a four-mill or five-mill stream may-be, makes the town habitable and fertilizes four or five villages; three or four others are cultivated from under-ground water-courses (*kārez*). Ghaznī grapes are better than those of Kābul; its melons are more abundant; its apples
Fol. 138. are very good, and are carried to Hindūstān. Agriculture is very laborious in Ghaznī because, whatever the quality of the soil, it must be newly top-dressed every year; it gives a better return, however, than Kābul. Ghaznī grows madder; the entire crop goes to Hindūstān and yields excellent profit to the growers. In the open-country of Ghaznī dwell Hazāra and Afghāns. Compared with Kābul, it is always a cheap place. Its people hold to the Ḥanafī faith, are good, orthodox Muṣalmāns, many keep a three months' fast,[1] and their wives and children live modestly secluded.

One of the eminent men of Ghaznī was Mullā 'Abdu'r-raḥmān, a learned man and always a learner (*dars*), a most orthodox, pious and virtuous person; he left this world the same year as Nāṣir Mīrzā (921 AH.-1515 AD.). Sl. Maḥmūd's tomb is in the suburb called Rauẓa,[2] from which the best grapes come; there also are the tombs of his descendants, Sl. Mas'ūd and Sl. Ibrāhīm. Ghaznī has many blessed tombs. The year[3] I took Kābul and Ghaznī, over-ran Kohāt, the plain of Bannū and lands of the Afghāns, and went on to Ghaznī by way of Dūkī (Dūgī) and Āb-istāda, people told me there was a tomb, in a village of Ghaznī, which moved when a benediction on the Prophet was
Fol. 138*b*. pronounced over it. We went to see it. In the end I discovered that the movement was a trick, presumably of the servants at the tomb, who had put a sort of platform above it which moved when pushed, so that, to those on it, the tomb seemed to move, just as the shore does to those passing in a boat. I ordered the

[1] Some Musalmāns fast through the months of Rajab, Sha'bān and Ramẓān; Muḥammadans fast only by day; the night is often given to feasting (Erskine).

[2] The Garden; the tombs of more eminent Muṣalmāns are generally in gardens (Erskine). See Vigne's illustrations, pp. 133, 266.

[3] *i.e.* the year now in writing. The account of the expedition, Bābur's first into Hindūstān, begins on f. 145.

scaffold destroyed and a dome built over the tomb; also I forbad the servants, with threats, ever to bring about the movement again.

Ghaznī is a very humble place; strange indeed it is that rulers in whose hands were Hindūstān and Khurāsānāt,[1] should have chosen it for their capital. In the Sulṭān's (Maḥmūd's) time there may have been three or four dams in the country; one he made, some three *yīghāch* (18 m.?) up the Ghaznī-water to the north; it was about 40–50 *qārī* (yards) high and some 300 long; through it the stored waters were let out as required.[2] It was destroyed by 'Alāu'u'd-dīn *Jahān-soz Ghūrī* when he conquered the country (550 AH.-1152 AD.), burned and ruined the tombs of several descendants of Sl. Maḥmūd, sacked and burned the town, in short, left undone no tittle of murder and rapine. Since Fol. 139.
that time, the Sulṭān's dam has lain in ruins, but, through God's favour, there is hope that it may become of use again, by means of the money which was sent, in Khwāja Kalān's hand, in the year Hindūstān was conquered (932 AH.-1526 AD.).[3] The Sakhan-dam is another, 2 or 3 *yīghāch* (12–18 m.), may-be, on the east of the town; it has long been in ruins, indeed is past repair. There is a dam in working order at Sar-i-dih (Village-head).

In books it is written that there is in Ghaznī a spring such that, if dirt and foul matter be thrown into it, a tempest gets up instantly, with a blizzard of rain and wind. It has been seen said also in one of the histories that Sabuk-tīgīn, when besieged by the Rāī (Jāī-pāl) of Hind, ordered dirt and foulness to be thrown into the spring, by this aroused, in an instant, a tempest with blizzard of rain and snow, and, by this device, drove off his foe.[4] Though we made many enquiries, no intimation of the spring's existence was given us.

In these countries Ghaznī and Khwārizm are noted for cold, in the same way that Sulṭānīā and Tabrīz are in the two 'Irāqs and Azarbāījān.

[1] *i.e.* the countries groupable as Khurāsān.
[2] For picture and account of the dam, *see* Vigne, pp. 138, 202.
[3] f. 295*b*.
[4] The legend is told in numerous books with varying location of the spring. One narrator, Zakarīyā *Qazwīnī*, reverses the parts, making Jāī-pāl employ the ruse; hence Leyden's note (Mems. p. 150; E. and D.'s *History of India* ii, 20, 182 and iv, 162; for historical information, R.'s *Notes* p. 320). The date of the events is shortly after 378 AH.-988 AD.

Zurmut is another *tūmān*, some 12–13 *yīghāch* south of Kābul and 7–8 south-east of Ghaznī.[1] Its *dārogha's* head-quarters are
Fol. 139*b*. in Gīrdīz; there most houses are three or four storeys high. It does not want for strength, and gave Nāṣir Mīrzā trouble when it went into hostility to him. Its people are Aūghān-shāl; they grow corn but have neither vineyards nor orchards. The tomb of Shaikh Muḥammad *Muṣalmān* is at a spring, high on the skirt of a mountain, known as Barakistān, in the south of the *tūmān*.

Farmūl is another *tūmān*,[2] a humble place, growing not bad apples which are carried into Hindūstān. Of Farmūl were the Shaikh-zādas, descendants of Shaikh Muḥammad *Muṣalmān*, who were so much in favour during the Afghān period in Hindūstān.

Bangash is another *tūmān*.[3] All round about it are Afghān highwaymen, such as the Khūgīānī, Khirilchī, Tūrī and Landar. Lying out-of-the-way, as it does, its people do not pay taxes willingly. There has been no time to bring it to obedience; greater tasks have fallen to me,—the conquests of Qandahār, Balkh, Badakhshān and Hindūstān! But, God willing! when I get the chance, I most assuredly will take order with those Bangash thieves.

One of the *bulūks* of Kābul is Ālā-sāī,[4] 4 to 6 miles (2–3 *shar'ī*) east of Nijr-aū. The direct road into it from Nijr-aū leads, at a place called Kūra, through the quite small pass which in that locality separates the hot and cold climates. Through this pass the birds migrate at the change of the seasons, and at those times many are taken by the people of Pīchghān, one of the dependencies of Nijr-aū, in the following manner:—
Fol. 140. From distance to distance near the mouth of the pass, they make hiding-places for the bird-catchers. They fasten one corner of a net five or six yards away, and weight the lower side to the

[1] R.'s *Notes s.n.* Zurmut.

[2] The question of the origin of the Farmūlī has been written of by several writers; perhaps they were Turks of Persia, Turks and Tājīks.

[3] This completes the list of the 14 *tūmāns* of Kābul, *viz.* Nīngnahār, 'Alī-shang, Alangār, Mandrāwar, Kūnār-with-Nūr-gal, Nijr-aū, Panjhīr, Ghūr-bund, Koh-dāman (with Kohistān?), Luhūgur (of the Kābul *tūmān*), Ghaznī, Zurmut, Farmūl and Bangash.

[4] Between Nijr-aū and Tag-aū (Masson, iii, 165). Mr. Erskine notes that Bābur reckoned it in the hot climate but that the change of climate takes place further east, between 'Alī-shang and Aūzbīn (*i.e.* the valley next eastwards from Tag-aū).

ground with stones. Along the other side of the net, for half its width, they fasten a stick some 3 to 4 yards long. The hidden bird-catcher holds this stick and by it, when the birds approach, lifts up the net to its full height. The birds then go into the net of themselves. Sometimes so many are taken by this contrivance that there is not time to cut their throats.[1]

Though the Ālā-sāī pomegranates are not first-rate, they have local reputation because none are better there-abouts; they are carried into Hindūstān. Grapes also do not grow badly, and the wines of Ālā-sāī are better and stronger than those of Nijr-aū.

Badr-aū (Tag-aū) is another *bulūk*; it runs with Ālā-sāī, grows no fruit, and for cultivators has corn-growing Kāfirs.[2]

(*f. Tribesmen of Kābul.*)

Just as Turks and (Mughūl) clans (*aīmāq*) dwell in the open country of Khurāsān and Samarkand, so in Kābul do the Hazāra and Afghāns. Of the Hazāra, the most widely-scattered are the Sulṭān-mas'ūdi Hazāra, of Afghāns, the Mahmand.

(*g. Revenue of Kābul.*)

The revenues of Kābul, whether from the cultivated lands or from tolls (*tamghā*) or from dwellers in the open country, amount to 8 *laks* of *shāhrukhīs*.[3] Fol. 140*b*.

(*h. The mountain-tracts of Kābul.*)

Where the mountains of Andar-āb, Khwāst,[4] and the Badakhshānāt have conifers (*archa*), many springs and gentle slopes, those of eastern Kābul have grass (*aūt*), grass like a beautiful floor, on hill, slope and dale. For the most part it is *būta-kāh* grass (*aūt*), very suitable for horses. In the Andijān country they talk of *būta-kāh*, but why they do so was not known (to me?); in Kābul it was heard-say to be because the grass comes

[1] *būghūzlārīghā furṣat būlmās*; *i.e.* to kill them in the lawful manner, while pronouncing the *Bi'smi'llāh*.

[2] This completes the *bulūks* of Kābul *viz.* Badr-aū (Tag-aū), Nūr-valley, Chaghān-sarāī, Kāma and Ālā-sāī.

[3] The *rūpī* being equal to 2½ *shāhrukhīs*, the *shāhrukhī* may be taken at 10*d.* thus making the total revenue only £33,333 6*s.* 8*d.* See *Āyīn-i-akbarī* ii, 169 (Erskine).

[4] *sic* in all B.N. MSS. Most maps print Khost. Muḥ. Ṣāliḥ says of Khwāst, 'Who sees it, would call it a Hell" (Vambéry, p. 361).

up in tufts (*būta, būta*).[1] The alps of these mountains are like those of Ḥiṣār, Khutlān, Farghāna, Samarkand and Mughūlistān,—all these being alike in mountain and alp, though the alps of Farghāna and Mughūlistān are beyond comparison with the rest.

From all these the mountains of Nijr-aū, the Lamghānāt and Sawād differ in having masses of cypresses,[2] holm-oak, olive and mastic (*khanjak*); their grass also is different,—it is dense, it is tall, it is good neither for horse nor sheep. Although these mountains are not so high as those already described, indeed they look to be low, none-the-less, they are strongholds; what to the eye is even slope, really is hard rock on which it is impossible to ride. Many of the beasts and birds of Hindūstān
Fol. 141. are found amongst them, such as the parrot, *mīna*, peacock and *lūja* (*lūkha*), the ape, *nīl-gāu* and hog-deer (*kūta-pāī*);[3] some found there are not found even in Hindūstān.

The mountains to the west of Kābul are also all of one sort, those of the Zindān-valley, the Ṣūf-valley, Garzawān and Gharjistān (Gharchastān).[4] Their meadows are mostly in the dales; they have not the same sweep of grass on slope and top as some of those described have; nor have they masses of trees; they have, however, grass suiting horses. On their flat tops, where all the crops are grown, there is ground where a horse can gallop. They have masses of *kīyik*.[5] Their valley-bottoms are strongholds, mostly precipitous and inaccessible from above. It is remarkable that, whereas other mountains have their fastnesses in their high places, these have theirs below.

Of one sort again are the mountains of Ghūr, Karnūd (var. Kuzūd) and Hazāra; their meadows are in their dales; their trees are few, not even the *archa* being there;[6] their grass is fit

[1] Bābur's statement about this fodder is not easy to translate; he must have seen grass grow in tufts, and must have known the Persian word *būta* (bush). Perhaps *kāh* should be read to mean plant, not grass. Would Wood's *bootr* fit in, a small furze bush, very plentiful near Bāmīān? (Wood's Report VI, p. 23; and for regional grasses, Aitchison's *Botany of the Afghān Delimitation Commission*, p. 122.)

[2] *nāzū*, perhaps *cupressus torulosa* (Brandis, p. 693).

[3] f. 276.

[4] A laborious geographical note of Mr. Erskine's is here regretfully left behind, as now needless (Mems. p. 152).

[5] Here, mainly wild-sheep and wild-goats, including *mār-khwār*.

[6] Perhaps, no conifers; perhaps none of those of the contrasted hill-tract.

for horses and for the masses of sheep they keep. They differ from those last described in this, their strong places are not below.

The mountains (south-east of Kābul) of Khwāja Ismā'īl, Dasht, Dūgī (Dūkī)[1] and Afghānistān are all alike; all low, scant of vegetation, short of water, treeless, ugly and good-for-nothing. Their people take after them, just as has been said, *Tīng būlmā-* Fol. 141*b* *ghūncha tūsh būlmās.*[2] Likely enough the world has few mountains so useless and disgusting.

(*h. Fire-wood of Kābul.*)

The snow-fall being so heavy in Kābul, it is fortunate that excellent fire-wood is had near by. Given one day to fetch it, wood can be had of the *khanjak* (mastic), *bīlūt* (holm-oak), *bādāmcha* (small-almond) and *qarqand.*[3] Of these *khanjak* wood is the best; it burns with flame and nice smell, makes plenty of hot ashes and does well even if sappy. Holm-oak is also first-rate fire-wood, blazing less than mastic but, like it, making a hot fire with plenty of hot ashes, and nice smell. It has the peculiarity in burning that when its leafy branches are set alight, they fire up with amazing sound, blazing and crackling from bottom to top. It is good fun to burn it. The wood of the small-almond is the most plentiful and commonly-used, but it does not make a lasting fire. The *qarqand* is quite a low shrub, thorny, and burning sappy or dry; it is the fuel of the Ghaznī people.

(*i. Fauna of Kābul.*)

The cultivated lands of Kābul lie between mountains which are like great dams[4] to the flat valley-bottoms in which most villages and peopled places are. On these mountains *kīyik* and

[1] While here *dasht* (plain) represents the eastern skirt of the Mehtar Sulaimān range, *dūkī* or *dūgī* (desert) seems to stand for the hill tracts on the west of it, and not, as on f. 152, for the place there specified.

[2] Mems. p. 152, "A narrow place is large to the narrow-minded"; *Méms.* i, 311, "Ce qui n'est pas trop large, ne reste pas vide." Literally, "So long as heights are not equal, there is no vis-à-vis," or, if *tāng* be read for *tīng*, "No dawn, no noon," *i.e.* no effect without a cause.

[3] I have not lighted on this name in botanical books or explained by dictionaries. Perhaps it is a Cis-oxanian name for the *sax-aol* of Transoxania. As its uses are enumerated by some travellers, it might be *Haloxylon ammodendron*, *ta-ghaz etc.* and *sax-aol* (Aitchison, p. 102).

[4] f. 135*b* note to Ghūr-bund.

āhū[1] are scarce. Across them, between its summer and winter quarters, the dun sheep,[2] the *arqārghalcha*, have their regular track,[3] to which braves go out with dogs and birds[4] to take them. Fol. 142. Towards Khūrd-kābul and the Sūrkh-rūd there is wild-ass, but there are no white *kīyik* at all; Ghaznī has both and in few other places are white *kīyik* found in such good condition.[5]

In the heats the fowling-grounds of Kābul are crowded. The birds take their way along the Bārān-water. For why? It is because the river has mountains along it, east and west, and a great Hindū-kush pass in a line with it, by which the birds must cross since there is no other near.[6] They cannot cross when the north wind blows, or if there is even a little cloud on Hindū-kush; at such times they alight on the level lands of the Bārān-water and are taken in great numbers by the local people. Towards the end of winter, dense flocks of mallards (*aūrdūq*) reach the banks of the Bārān in very good condition. Follow these the cranes and herons,[7] great birds, in large flocks and countless numbers.

(*j. Bird-catching.*)

Along the Bārān people take masses of cranes (*tūrna*) with the cord; masses of *aūqār*, *qarqara* and *qūṭān* also.[8] This

[1] I understand that wild-goats, wild-sheep and deer (*āhū*) were not localized, but that the dun-sheep migrated through.. Antelope (*āhū*) was scarce in Elphinstone's time.

[2] *qīzīl kīyik* which, taken with its alternative name, *arqārghalcha*, allows it to be the dun-sheep of Wood's *Journey* p. 241. From its second name it may be *Ovis amnon* (*Raos*), or *O. argalī*.

[3] *tusqāwal*, var. *tutqāwal*, *tuṣaqāwal* and *tūshqāwal*, a word which has given trouble to scribes and translators. As a sporting-term it is equivalent to *shikār-i-nihilam*; in one or other of its forms I find it explained as *Weg-hüter*, *Fahnen-hüter*, *Zahl-meister*, *Schlucht*, *Gefahrlicher-weg* and *Schmaler-weg*. It recurs in the B.N. on f. 197*b* l. 5 and l. 6 and there might mean either a narrow road or a *Weg-hüter*. If its Turkī root be *tūs*, the act of stopping, all the above meanings can follow, but there may be two separate roots, the second, *tūsh*, the act of descent (JRAS 1900 p. 137, H. Beveridge's art. *On the word nihilam*).

[4] *qūshlīk*, *aītlīk*. Elphinstone writes (i, 191) of the excellent greyhounds and hawking birds of the region; here the bird may be the *charkh*, which works with the dogs, fastening on the head of the game (Von Schwarz, p. 117, for the same use of eagles).

[5] An antelope resembling the usual one of Hindūstān is common south of Ghaznī (Vigne, p. 110); what is not found may be some classes of wild-sheep, frequent further north, at higher elevation, and in places more familiar to Bābur.

[6] The Parwān or Hindū-kush pass, concerning the winds of which *see* f. 128.

[7] *tūrnā u qarqara*; the second of which is the Hindī *būglā*, heron, *egret ardea gazetta*, the furnisher of the aigrette of commerce.

[8] The *aūqār* is *ardea cinerea*, the grey heron; the *qarqara* is *ardea gazetta*, the egret. *Qūṭān* is explained in the Elph. Codex (f. 110) by *khawāsil*, goldfinch, but the context concerns large birds; Scully (Shaw's Voc.) has *qodan*, water-hen, which suits better.

method of bird-catching is unique. They twist a cord as long as the arrow's[1] flight, tie the arrow at one end and a *bīldūrga*[2] at the other, and wind it up, from the arrow-end, on a piece of wood, span-long and wrist-thick, right up to the *bīldūrga*. They Fol. 142*b*. then pull out the piece of wood, leaving just the hole it was in. The *bīldūrga* being held fast in the hand, the arrow is shot off[3] towards the coming flock. If the cord twist round a neck or wing, it brings the bird down. On the Bārān everyone takes birds in this way; it is difficult; it must be done on rainy nights, because on such nights the birds do not alight, but fly continually and fly low till dawn, in fear of ravening beasts of prey. Through the night the flowing river is their road, its moving water showing through the dark; then it is, while they come and go, up and down the river, that the cord is shot. One night I shot it; it broke in drawing in; both bird and cord were brought in to me next day. By this device Bārān people catch the many herons from which they take the turban-aigrettes sent from Kābul for sale in Khurāsān.

Of bird-catchers there is also the band of slave-fowlers, two or three hundred households, whom some descendant of Tīmūr Beg made migrate from near Multān to the Bārān.[4] Bird-catching Fol. 143. is their trade; they dig tanks, set decoy-birds[5] on them, put a net over the middle, and in this way take all sorts of birds. Not fowlers only catch birds, but every dweller on the Bārān does it, whether by shooting the cord, setting the springe, or in various other ways.

(*k. Fishing.*)

The fish of the Bārān migrate at the same seasons as birds. At those times many are netted, and many are taken on wattles

[1] *giz*, the short-flight arrow.

[2] a small, round-headed nail with which a whip-handle is decorated (Vambery). Such a stud would keep the cord from slipping through the fingers and would not check the arrow-release.

[3] It has been understood (Mems. p. 158 and *Méms.* i, 313) that the arrow was flung by hand but if this were so, something heavier than the *giz* would carry the cord better, since it certainly would be difficult to direct a missile so light as an arrow without the added energy of the bow. The arrow itself will often have found its billet in the closely-flying flock; the cord would retrieve the bird. The verb used in the text is *aītmāq*, the one common to express the discharge of arrows *etc.*

[4] For Tīmūrids who may have immigrated the fowlers *see* Raverty's *Notes* p. 579 and his Appendix p. 22.

[5] *milwāh*; this has been read by all earlier translators, and also by the Persian annotator of the Elph. Codex, to mean *shākh*, bough. For decoy-ducks *see* Bellew's *Notes on Afghānistān* p. 404.

(*chīgh*) fixed in the water. In autumn when the plant known as *wild-ass-tail*[1] has come to maturity, flowered and seeded, people take 10–20 loads (of seed?) and 20–30 of green branches (*gūk-shībāk*) to some head of water, break it up small and cast it in. Then going into the water, they can at once pick up drugged fish. At some convenient place lower down, in a hole below a fall, they will have fixed before-hand a wattle of finger-thick willow-withes, making it firm by piling stones on its sides. The water goes rushing and dashing through the wattle, but leaves on it any fish that may have come floating down. This way of catching fish is practised in Gul-bahār, Parwān and Istālīf.

Fol. 143*b*. Fish are had in winter in the Lamghānāt by this curious device:—People dig a pit to the depth of a house, in the bed of a stream, below a fall, line it with stones like a cooking-place, and build up stones round it above, leaving one opening only, under water. Except by this one opening, the fish have no inlet or outlet, but the water finds its way through the stones. This makes a sort of fish-pond from which, when wanted in winter, fish can be taken, 30–40 together. Except at the opening, left where convenient, the sides of the fish-pond are made fast with rice-straw, kept in place by stones. A piece of wicker-work is pulled into the said opening by its edges, gathered together, and into this a second piece, (a tube,) is inserted, fitting it at the mouth but reaching half-way into it only.[2] The fish go through the smaller piece into the larger one, out from which they cannot get. The second narrows towards its inner mouth, its pointed ends being drawn so close that the fish, once entered, cannot
Fol. 144. turn, but must go on, one by one, into the larger piece. Out of that they cannot return because of the pointed ends of the inner, narrow mouth. The wicker-work fixed and the rice-straw making the pond fast, whatever fish are inside can be taken out;[3] any also which, trying to escape may have gone into the wicker-work,

[1] *qūlān qūyirūghī*. Amongst the many plants used to drug fish I have not found this one mentioned. *Khār-zāhra* and *khār-fāq* approach it in verbal meaning; the first describes colocynth, the second, wild rue. See Watts' *Economic Products of India* iii, 366 and Bellew's *Notes* pp. 182, 471 and 478.

[2] Much trouble would have been spared to himself and his translators, if Bābur had known a lobster-pot.

[3] The fish, it is to be inferred, came down the fall into the pond.

are taken in it, because they have no way out. This method of catching fish we have seen nowhere else.[1]

HISTORICAL NARRATIVE RESUMED.[2]

(a. Departure of Muqīm and allotment of lands.)

A few days after the taking of Kābul, Muqīm asked leave to set off for Qandahār. As he had come out of the town on terms and conditions, he was allowed to go to his father (Ẕu'n-nūn) and his elder brother (Shāh Beg), with all his various people, his goods and his valuables, safe and sound.

Directly he had gone, the Kābul-country was shared out to the Mīrzās and the guest-begs.[3] To Jahāngīr Mīrzā was given Ghaznī with its dependencies and appurtenancies ; to Nāṣir Mīrzā, the Nīngnahār *tūmān*, Mandrāwar, Nūr-valley, Kūnār, Nūr-gal (Rock-village?) and Chīghān-sarāī. To some of the begs who had been with us in the guerilla-times and had come to Kābul with us, were given villages, fief-fashion.[4] *Wilāyat* Fol. 144*b*. itself was not given at all.[5] It was not only then that I looked with more favour on guest-begs and stranger-begs than I did on old servants and Andijānīs ; this I have always done whenever the Most High God has shown me His favour ; yet it is remarkable that, spite of this, people have blamed me constantly as though I had favoured none but old servants and Andijānīs. There is a proverb, (Turkī) "What will a foe not say? what enters not into dream?" and (Persian) "A town-gate can be shut, a foe's mouth never."

[1] Burnes and Vigne describe a fall 20 miles from Kābul, at "Tangī Gharoi", [below where the Tag-aū joins the Bārān-water,] to which in their day, Kābulīs went out for the amusement of catching fish as they try to leap up the fall. Were these migrants seeking upper waters or were they captives in a fish-pond?

[2] Elph. MS. f. 111 ; W.-i-B. I.O. 215 f. 116*b* and 217 f. 97*b* ; Mems. p. 155 ; *Mems.* i. 318.

[3] *mihmān-beglār*, an expression first used by Bābur here, and due, presumably, to accessions from Khusrau Shāh's following. A parallel case is given in Max Müller's *Science of Language* i, 348 ed. 1871, "Turkmān tribes . . . . call themselves, not subjects, but guests of the Uzbeg Khāns."

[4] *tiyūl-dīk* in all the Turkī MSS. Ilminsky, de Courteille and Zenker, *yitūl-dīk*, Turkī, a fief.

[5] *Wilāyat khūd hech bīrīlmādī* ; W.-i-B. 215 f. 116*b*, *Wilāyat dāda na shuda* and 217 f. 97*b*, *Wilāyat khūd hech dāda na shud.* By this I understand that he kept the lands of Kābul itself in his own hands. He mentions (f. 350) and Gul-badan mentions (H.N. f. 40*b*) his resolve so to keep Kābul. I think he kept not only the fort but all lands constituting the Kābul *tūmān* (f. 135*b* and note).

(b. A levy in grain.)

Many clans and hordes had come from Samarkand, Ḥiṣār and Qūndūz into the Kābul-country. Kābul is a small country; it is also of the sword, not of the pen;[1] to take in money from it for all these tribesmen was impossible. It therefore seemed advisable to take in grain, provision for the families of these clans so that their men could ride on forays with the army. Accordingly it was decided to levy 30,000 ass-loads[2] of grain on Kābul, Ghaznī and their dependencies; we knew nothing at that time about the harvests and incomings; the impost was excessive, and under it the country suffered very grievously.

In those days I devised the Bāburī script.[3]

(c. Foray on the Hazāra.)

A large tribute in horses and sheep had been laid on the Sulṭān Mas'ūdī Hazāras;[4] word came a few days after collectors Fol. 145. had gone to receive it, that the Hazāras were refractory and would not give their goods. As these same tribesmen had before that come down on the Ghaznī and Gīrdīz roads, we got to horse, meaning to take them by surprise. Riding by the Maidān-road, we crossed the Nirkh-pass[5] by night and at the Morning-prayer fell upon them near Jāl-tū (var. Chā-tū). The incursion was not what was wished.[6] We came back by the Tunnel-rock (Sang-i-sūrākh); Jahāngīr Mīrzā (there?) took leave for Ghaznī. On our reaching Kābul, Yār-i-ḥusain, son of Daryā Khān, coming in from Bhīra, waited on me.[7]

[1] *Saifī dūr, qalamī almās, i.e.* tax is taken by force, not paid on a written assessment.

[2] *khar-wār*, about 700 lbs Averdupois (Erskine). Cf. *Āyīn-i-akbarī* (Jarrett, ii, 394).

[3] Niẓāmu'd-dīn Aḥmad and Badāyūnī both mention this script and say that in it Bābur transcribed a copy of the Qorān for presentation to Makka. Badāyūnī says it was unknown in his day, the reign of Akbar (*Ṭabaqāt-i-akbarī*, lith. ed. p. 193, and *Muntakhabu'l-tawārīkh* Bib. Ind. ed. iii, 273).

[4] Bābur's route, taken with one given by Raverty (*Notes* p. 691), allows these Hazāras, about whose location Mr. Erskine was uncertain, to be located between the Takht-pass (Arghandī-Maidān-Unai road), on their east, and the Sang-lākh mountains, on their west.

[5] The Takht-pass, one on which from times immemorial, toll (*nirkh*) has been taken.

[6] *khāṭir-khwāh chāpīlmādī*, which perhaps implies mutual discontent, Bābur's with his gains, the Hazāras' with their losses. As the second Persian translation omits the negative, the Memoirs does the same.

[7] Bhīra being in Shāhpūr, this Khān's *daryā* will be the Jehlam.

(d. Bābur's first start for Hindūstān.)

When, a few days later, the army had been mustered, persons acquainted with the country were summoned and questioned about its every side and quarter. Some advised a march to the Plain (Dasht);[1] some approved of Bangash; some wished to go into Hindūstān. The discussion found settlement in a move on Hindūstān.

It was in the month of Sha'bān (910 AH.–Jan. 1505 AD.), the Sun being in Aquarius, that we rode out of Kābul for Hindūstān. We took the road by Bādām-chashma and Jagdālīk and reached Adīnapūr in six marches. Till that time I had never seen a hot country or the Hindūstān border-land. In Nīngnahār[2] another world came to view,—other grasses, other trees, other animals, other birds, and other manners and customs of clan and horde. We were amazed, and truly there was ground for amaze. Fol. 145*b*.

Nāṣir Mīrzā, who had gone earlier to his district, waited on me in Adīnapūr. We made some delay in Adīnapūr in order to let the men from behind join us, also a contingent from the clans which had come with us into Kābul and were wintering in the Lamghānāt.[3] All having joined us, we marched to below Jūī-shāhī and dismounted at Qūsh-gumbaz.[4] There Nāṣir Mīrzā asked for leave to stay behind, saying he would follow in a few days after making some sort of provision for his dependants and followers. Marching on from Qūsh-gumbaz, when we dismounted at Hot-spring (Garm-chashma), a head-man of the Gāgīānī was brought in, a *Fajjī*,[5] presumably with his caravan. We took him with us to point out the roads. Crossing Khaibar in a march or two, we dismounted at Jām.[6]

[1] Bābur uses Persian *dasht* and Hindī *dūkī*, plain and hill, for the tracts east and west of Mehtar Sulaimān. The first, *dasht*, stands for Dāman (skirt) and Dara-i-jāt, the second, *dūkī*, indefinitely for the broken lands west of the main range, but also, in one instance for the Dūkī [Dūgī] district of Qandahār, as will be noted.

[2] f. 132. The Jagdālīk-pass for centuries has separated the districts of Kābul and Nīngnahār. Forster (*Travels* ii, 68), making the journey the reverse way, was sensible of the climatic change some 3m. east of Gandamak. Cf. Wood's *Report* I. p. 6.

[3] These are they whose families Nāṣir Mīrzā shepherded out of Kābul later (f. 154, f. 155).

[4] Bird's-dome, opposite the mouth of the Kūnār-water (*S.A. War*, Map p. 64).

[5] This word is variously pointed and is uncertain. Mr. Erskine adopted "Pekhi", but, on the whole, it may be best to read, here and on f. 146, Ar. *fajj* or pers. *paj*, mountain or pass. To do so shews the guide to be one located in the Khaibar-pass, a *Fajjī* or *Pajī*.

[6] mod. Jām-rūd (Jām-torrent), presumably.

Tales had been told us about Gūr-khattrī;[1] it was said to be a holy place of the Jogīs and Hindūs who come from long distances to shave their heads and beards there. I rode out at once from Jām to visit Bīgrām,[2] saw its great tree,[3] and all the country round, but, much as we enquired about Gūr-khattrī, our guide, one Malik Bū-sa'īd *Kamarī*,[4] would say nothing
Fol. 146. about it. When we were almost back in camp, however, he told Khwāja Muḥammad-amīn that it was in Bīgrām and that he had said nothing about it because of its confined cells and narrow passages. The Khwāja, having there and then abused him, repeated to us what he had said, but we could not go back because the road was long and the day far spent.

(*e. Move against Kohāt.*)

Whether to cross the water of Sind, or where else to go, was discussed in that camp.[5] Bāqī *Chaghānīānī* represented that it seemed we might go, without crossing the river and with one night's halt, to a place called Kohāt where were many rich tribesmen; moreover he brought Kābulīs forward who represented the matter just as he had done. We had never heard of the place, but, as he, my man in great authority, saw it good to go to Kohāt and had brought forward support of his recommendation,—this being so! we broke up our plan of crossing the Sind-water into Hindūstān, marched from Jām, forded the Bāra-water, and dismounted not far from the pass (*dābān*) through the Muḥammad-mountain (*fajj*). At the time the Gāgīānī Afghāns were located in Parashawār but, in dread of our army, had drawn off to the skirt-hills. One of their head-men, coming into this camp, did me obeisance; we took him, as

[1] G. of I. xx, 125 and Cunningham's *Ancient History* i, 80. Bābur saw the place in 925 AH. (f. 232*b*).

[2] Cunningham, p. 29. Four ancient sites, not far removed from one another, bear this name, Bīgrām, *viz.* those near Hūpīān, Kābul, Jalālābād and Pashāwar.

[3] Cunningham, i, 79.

[4] Perhaps a native of Kamarī on the Indus, but *kamarī* is a word of diverse application (index *s.n.*).

[5] The annals of this campaign to the eastward shew that Bābur was little of a free agent; that many acts of his own were merciful; that he sets down the barbarity of others as it was, according to his plan of writing (f. 86); and that he had with him undisciplined robbers of Khusrau Shāh's former following. He cannot be taken as having power to command or control the acts of those, his guest-begs and their following, who dictated his movements in this disastrous journey, one worse than a defeat, says Ḥaidar Mīrzā.

well as the Fajjī, with us, so that, between them, they might point out the roads. We left that camp at midnight, crossed Muḥammad-fajj at day-rise[1] and by breakfast-time descended on Kohāt. Much cattle and buffalo fell to our men; many Afghāns were taken but I had them all collected and set them free. In the Kohāt houses corn was found without limit. Our foragers raided as far as the Sind-river (*daryā*), rejoining us after one night's halt. As what Bāqī *Chaghāniānī* had led us to expect did not come to hand, he grew rather ashamed of his scheme. Fol. 146*b*

When our foragers were back and after two nights in Kohāt, we took counsel together as to what would be our next good move, and we decided to over-run the Afghāns of Bangash and the Bannū neighbourhood, then to go back to Kābul, either through Naghr (Bāghzān ?), or by the Farmūl-road (Tochī-valley ?).

In Kohāt, Daryā Khān's son, Yār-i-ḥusain, who had waited on me in Kābul made petition, saying, "If royal orders were given me for the Dilazāk,[2] the Yūsuf-zāī, and the Gāgīānī, these would not go far from my orders if I called up the Pādshāh's swords on the other side of the water of Sind."[3] The farmān he petitioned for being given, he was allowed to go from Kohāt.

(f. March to Thāl.)

Marching out of Kohāt, we took the Hangū-road for Bangash. Fol. 147.
Between Kohāt and Hangū that road runs through a valley shut in on either hand by the mountains. When we entered this valley, the Afghāns of Kohāt and thereabouts who were gathered on both hill-skirts, raised their war-cry with great clamour. Our then guide, Malik Bū-sa'īd *Kamarī* was well-acquainted with the Afghān locations; he represented that further on there was a detached hill on our right, where, if the Afghāns came down to it from the hill-skirt, we might surround and take them. God brought it right! The Afghāns, on reaching the place, did come down. We ordered one party of braves to seize the neck of land between that hill and the mountains, others to move along

[1] For the route here *see* Masson, i, 117 and Colquhoun's *With the Kuram Field-force* p. 48.
[2] The Hai. MS. writes this Dilah-zāk.
[3] *i.e.* raised a force in Bābur's name. He took advantage of this *farmān* in 911 AH. to kill Bāqī *Chaghāniānī* (f. 159*b*-160)

its sides, so that under attack made from all sides at once, the Afghāns might be made to reach their doom. Against the all-round assault, they could not even fight; a hundred or two were taken, some were brought in alive but of most, the heads only were brought. We had been told that when Afghāns are powerless to resist, they go before their foe with grass between their teeth, this being as much as to say, "I am your cow."[1] Here
Fol. 147b. we saw this custom; Afghāns unable to make resistance, came before us with grass between their teeth. Those our men had brought in as prisoners were ordered to be beheaded and a pillar of their heads was set up in our camp.[2]

Next day we marched forward and dismounted at Hangū, where local Afghāns had made a *sangur* on a hill. I first heard the word *sangur* after coming to Kābul where people describe fortifying themselves on a hill as making a *sangur*. Our men went straight up, broke into it and cut off a hundred or two of insolent Afghān heads. There also a pillar of heads was set up.

From Hangū we marched, with one night's halt, to Tīl (Thāl),[3] below Bangash; there also our men went out and raided the Afghāns near-by; some of them however turned back rather lightly from a *sangur*.[4]

(*g. Across country into Bannū.*)

On leaving Tīl (Thāl) we went, without a road, right down a steep descent, on through out-of-the-way narrows, halted one night, and next day came down into Bannū,[5] man, horse and camel all worn out with fatigue and with most of the booty in cattle left on the way. The frequented road must have been a few miles to our right; the one we came by did not seem

[1] Of the Yūsuf-zāī and Ranjīt-sīngh, Masson says, (i, 141) "The miserable, hunted wretches threw themselves on the ground, and placing a blade or tuft of grass in their mouths, cried out, "I am your cow." This act and explanation, which would have saved them from an orthodox Hindū, had no effect with the infuriated Sikhs." This form of supplication is at least as old as the days of Firdausī (Erskine, p. 159 n.). The *Bahār-i-'ajam* is quoted by Vullers as saying that in India, suppliants take straw in the mouth to indicate that they are blanched and yellow from fear.

[2] This barbarous custom has always prevailed amongst the Tartar conquerors of Asia (Erskine). For examples under Tīmūr *see* Raverty's *Notes* p. 137.

[3] For a good description of the road from Kohāt to Thāl *see* Bellew's *Mission* p. 104.

[4] F. 88b has the same phrase about the doubtful courage of one Sayyidī Qarā.

[5] Not to the mod. town of Bannū, [that having been begun only in 1848 AD.] but wherever their wrong road brought them out into the Bannū amphitheatre. The Survey Map of 1868, No. 15, shews the physical features of the wrong route.

a riding-road at all; it was understood to be called the Gosfand-liyār (Sheep-road),—*liyār* being Afghānī for a road,—because sometimes shepherds and herdsmen take their flocks and herds by it through those narrows. Most of our men regarded our being brought down by that left-hand road as an ill-design of Malik Bū-sa'īd *Kamarī*.[1] Fol. 148.

(*h. Bannū and the 'Īsa-khail country.*)

The Bannū lands lie, a dead level, immediately outside the Bangash and Naghr hills, these being to their north. The Bangash torrent (the Kūrām) comes down into Bannū and fertilizes its lands. South(-east) of them are Chaupāra and the water of Sind; to their east is Dīn-kot; (south-)west is the Plain (Dasht), known also as Bāzār and Tāq.[2] The Bannū lands are cultivated by the Kurānī, Kīwī, Sūr, 'Īsa-khail and Nīā-zāī of the Afghān tribesmen.

After dismounting in Bannū, we heard that the tribesmen in the Plain (Dasht) were for resisting and were entrenching themselves on a hill to the north. A force headed by Jahāngīr Mīrzā, went against what seemed to be the Kīwī *sangur*, took it at once, made general slaughter, cut off and brought in many heads. Much white cloth fell into (their) hands. In Bannū also a pillar of heads was set up. After the *sangur* had been taken, the Kīwī head-man, Shādī Khān, came to my presence, with grass between his teeth, and did me obeisance. I pardoned all the prisoners.

After we had over-run Kohāt, it had been decided that Bangash and Bannū should be over-run, and return to Kābul Fol. 148*b*. made through Naghr or through Farmūl. But when Bannū had been over-run, persons knowing the country represented that the Plain was close by, with its good roads and many people; so it was settled to over-run the Plain and to return to Kābul afterwards by way of Farmūl.[3]

[1] Perhaps he connived at recovery of cattle by those raided already.

[2] Tāq is the Tank of Maps; Bāzār was s.w. of it. Tank for Tāq looks to be a variant due to nasal utterance (Vigne, p. 77, p. 203 and Map; and, as bearing on the nasal, *in loco*, Appendix E).

[3] If return had been made after over-running Bannū, it would have been made by the Tochī-valley and so through Farmūl; if after over-running the Plain, Bābur's details shew that the westward turn was meant to be by the Gūmāl-valley and one of

Marching next day, we dismounted at an 'Īsa-khail village on that same water (the Kūrām) but, as the villagers had gone into the Chaupāra hills on hearing of us, we left it and dismounted on the skirt of Chaupāra. Our foragers went from there into the hills, destroyed the 'Īsa-khail *sangur* and came back with sheep, herds and cloth. That night the 'Īsa-khail made an attack on us but, as good watch was kept all through these operations, they could do nothing. So cautious were we that at night our right and left, centre and van were just in the way they had dismounted, each according to its place in battle, each prepared for its own post; with men on foot all round the camp, at an arrow's distance from the tents. Every night the army was posted in this way and every night three or four of my household

Fol. 149. made the rounds with torches, each in his turn. I for my part made the round once each night. Those not at their posts had their noses slit and were led round through the army. Jahāngīr Mīrzā was the right wing, with Bāqī *Chaghānīānī*, Sherīm Taghāī, Sayyid Ḥusain Akbar, and other begs. Mīrzā Khān was the left wing, with 'Abdu'r-razzāq Mīrzā, Qāsim Beg and other begs. In the centre there were no great begs, all were household-begs. Sayyid Qāsim Lord-of-the-gate, was the van, with Bābā Aūghūlī, Allāh-bīrdī (var. Allāh-qulī Purān), and some other begs. The army was in six divisions, each of which had its day and night on guard.

Marching from that hill-skirt, our faces set west, we dismounted on a waterless plain (*qūl*) between Bannū and the Plain. The soldiers got water here for themselves, their herds and so on, by digging down, from one to one-and-a-half yards, into the dry water-course, when water came. Not here only did this happen for all the rivers of Hindūstān have the peculiarity that water is safe to be found by digging down from one to one-and-a-half yards in their beds. It is a wonderful provision of God that where, except for the great rivers, there are no running-waters,[1] water should be so placed within reach in dry water-courses.

two routes out of it, still to Farmūl; but the extended march southward to near Dara-i-Ghazī Khān made the westward turn be taken through the valley opening at Sakhī-sawār.

[1] This will mean, none of the artificial runlets familiar where Bābur had lived before getting to know Hindūstān.

We left that dry channel next morning. Some of our men, riding light, reached villages of the Plain in the afternoon, raided a few, and brought back flocks, cloth and horses bred for trade.[1] Pack-animals and camels and also the braves we had outdistanced, kept coming into camp all through that night till dawn and on till that morrow's noon. During our stay there, the foragers brought in from villages in the Plain, masses of sheep and cattle, and, from Afghān traders met on the roads, white cloths, aromatic roots, sugars, *tīpūchāqs*, and horses bred for trade. Hindī (var. Mindī) *Mughūl* unhorsed Khwāja Khiẓr *Lūhānī*, a well-known and respected Afghān merchant, cutting off and bringing in his head. Once when Sherīm Ṭaghāī went in the rear of the foragers, an Afghān faced him on the road and struck off his index-finger. Fol. 149*b*.

(*i. Return made for Kābul.*)

Two roads were heard of as leading from where we were to Ghaznī; one was the Tunnel-rock (Sang-i-sūrākh) road, passing Birk (Barak) and going on to Farmūl; the other was one along the Gūmāl, which also comes out at Farmūl but without touching Birk (Barak).[2] As during our stay in the Plain rain had fallen incessantly, the Gūmāl was so swollen that it would have been difficult to cross at the ford we came to; moreover persons well-acquainted with the roads, represented that going by the Gūmāl road, this torrent must be crossed several times, that this was always difficult when the waters were so high and that there was always uncertainty on the Gūmāl road. Nothing was settled then as to which of these two roads to take; I expected it to be settled next day when, after the drum of departure had sounded, Fol. 150.
we talked it over as we went.[3] It was the 'Īd-i-fitr (March 7th 1505 AD.); while I was engaged in the ablutions due for the breaking of the fast, Jahāngīr Mīrzā and the begs discussed the

[1] *sauda-āt*, perhaps, pack-ponies, perhaps, bred for sale and not for own use. Burnes observes that in 1837 Lūhānī merchants carried precisely the same articles of trade as in Bābur's day, 332 years earlier (*Report* IX p. 99).

[2] Mr. Erskine thought it probable that the first of these routes went through Kanigūram, and the second through the Ghwālirī-pass and along the Gūmāl. *Birk*, fastness, would seem an appropriate name for Kanigūram, but, if Bābur meant to go to Ghaznī, he would be off the ordinary Gūmāl-Ghaznī route in going through Farmūl (Aūrgūn). Raverty's *Notes* give much useful detail about these routes, drawn from native sources. For Barak (Birk) *see Notes* pp. 88, 89; Vigne, p. 102.

[3] From this it would seem that the alternative roads were approached by one in common.

question of the roads. Some-one said that if we were to turn the bill[1] of the Mehtar Sulaimān range, this lying between the Plain and the Hill-country (*desht u dūkī*),[2] we should get a level road though it might make the difference of a few marches. For this they decided and moved off; before my ablutions were finished the whole army had taken the road and most of it was across the Gūmāl. Not a man of us had ever seen the road; no-one knew whether it was long or short; we started off just on a rumoured word!

The Prayer of the 'Id was made on the bank of the Gūmāl. That year New-year's Day[3] fell close to the 'Id-i-fitr, there being only a few days between; on their approximation I composed the following (Turkī) ode:—

> Glad is the Bairām-moon for him who sees both the face of the Moon and the Moon-face of his friend;
> Sad is the Bairām-moon for me, far away from thy face and from thee.[4]
>
> O Bābur! dream of your luck when your Feast is the meeting, your New-year the face;
> For better than that could not be with a hundred New-years and Bairāms.

After crossing the Gūmāl torrent, we took our way along the skirt of the hills, our faces set south. A mile or two further on,
Fol. 150*b*. some death-devoted Afghāns shewed themselves on the lower edge of the hill-slope. Loose rein, off we went for them; most of them fled but some made foolish stand on rocky-piles[5] of the foot-hills. One took post on a single rock seeming to have a precipice on the further side of it, so that he had not even a way of escape. Sl. Qulī *Chūnāq* (One-eared), all in his mail as he was, got up, slashed at, and took him. This was one of Sl. Qulī's deeds done under my own eyes, which led to his favour and promotion.[6] At another pile of rock, when Qūtlūq-qadam exchanged blows with an Afghān, they grappled and came down

[1] *tūmshūq*, a bird's bill, used here, as in Selsey-bill, for the naze (nose), or snout, the last spur, of a range.

[2] Here these words may be common nouns.

[3] Nū-roz, the feast of the old Persian New-year (Erskine); it is the day on which the Sun enters Aries.

[4] In the [Turkī] Elph. and Ḥai. MSS. and in some Persian ones, there is a space left here as though to indicate a known omission.

[5] *kamarī*, sometimes a cattle-enclosure, which may serve as a *sangur*. The word may stand in one place of its *Bābur-nāma* uses for Gum-rāhī (R.'s *Notes s.n.* Gum-rāhān).

[6] Index *s.n.*

together, a straight fall of 10 to 12 yards; in the end Qūtlūq-qadam cut off and brought in his man's head. Kūpūk Beg got hand-on-collar with an Afghān at another hill; both rolled down to the bottom; that head also was brought in. All Afghāns taken prisoner were set free.

Marching south through the Plain, and closely skirting Mehtar Sulaimān, we came, with three nights' halt, to a small township, called Bīlah, on the Sind-water and dependent on Multān.[1] The villagers crossed the water, mostly taking to their boats, but some flung themselves in to cross. Some were seen standing on an island in front of Bīlah. Most of our men, man and horse in mail, plunged in and crossed to the island; some were carried down, one being Qul-i-arūk (thin slave), one of my servants, another the head tent-pitcher, another Jahāngīr Mīrzā's servant, Qāītmās *Turkmān*.[2] Cloth and things of the baggage (*partaldīk nīma*) fell to our men. The villagers all crossed by boat to the further side of the river; once there, some of them, trusting to the broad water, began to make play with their swords. Qul-i-bāyazīd, the taster, one of our men who had crossed to the island, stripped himself and his horse and, right in front of them, plunged by himself into the river. The water on that side of the island may have been twice or thrice as wide as on ours. He swum his horse straight for them till, an arrow's-flight away, he came to a shallow where his weight must have been up-borne, the water being as high as the saddle-flap. There he stayed for as long as milk takes to boil; no-one supported him from behind; he had not a chance of support. He made a dash at them; they shot a few arrows at him but, this not checking him, they took to flight. To swim such a river as the Sind, alone, bare on a bare-backed horse, no-one behind him, and to chase off a foe and occupy his ground, was a mightily bold deed! He having driven the enemy off, other soldiers went over who returned with cloth and droves of various sorts. Qul-i-bāyazīd had already his place in my favour and kindness on account of his good service, and of courage several times shewn; from the cook's office I had raised him to the royal taster's; this time, as

Fol. 151.

Fol. 151*b*.

[1] Vigne, p. 241.
[2] This name can be translated "He turns not back" or "He stops not".

will be told, I took up a position full of bounty, favour and promotion,—in truth he was worthy of honour and advancement.

Two other marches were made down the Sind-water. Our men, by perpetually gallopping off on raids, had knocked up their horses; usually what they took, cattle mostly, was not worth the gallop; sometimes indeed in the Plain there had been sheep, sometimes one sort of cloth or other, but, the Plain left behind, nothing was had but cattle. A mere servant would bring in 3 or 400 head during our marches along the Sind-water, but every march many more would be left on the road than they brought in.

(*j. The westward march.*)

Having made three more marches[1] close along the Sind, we left it when we came opposite Pīr Kānū's tomb.[2] Going to the tomb, we there dismounted. Some of our soldiers having injured
Fol. 152. several of those in attendance on it, I had them cut to pieces. It is a tomb on the skirt of one of the Mehtar Sulaimān mountains and held in much honour in Hindūstān.

Marching on from Pīr Kānū, we dismounted in the (Pawat) pass; next again in the bed of a torrent in Dūkī.[3] After we left this camp there were brought in as many as 20 to 30 followers of a retainer of Shāh Beg, Fāẓil *Kūkūldāsh*, the dārogha of Sīwī. They had been sent to reconnoitre us but, as at that time, we were not on bad terms with Shāh Beg, we let them go, with horse and arms. After one night's halt, we reached Chūtīālī, a village of Dūkī.

Although our men had constantly gallopped off to raid, both before we reached the Sind-water and all along its baṇk, they had not left horses behind, because there had been plenty of green food and corn. When, however, we left the river and set our faces for Pīr Kānū, not even green food was to be had; a little land under green crop might be found every two or three

[1] *i.e.* five from Bilah.

[2] Raverty gives the saint's name as Pīr Kānūn (Ar. *kānūn*, listened to). It is the well-known Sakhī-sarwār, honoured by Hindūs and Muḥammadans. (G. of I., xxi, 390; R.'s *Notes* p. 11 and p. 12 and JASB 1855; Calcutta Review 1875, Macauliffe's art. *On the fair at Sakhi-sarwar*; Leech's *Report* VII, for the route; *Khazīnatu 'l-aṣfiyā* iv, 245.)

[3] This seems to be the sub-district of Qandahār, Dūkī or Dūgī.

marches, but of horse-corn, none. So, beyond the camps mentioned, there began the leaving of horses behind. After passing Chūtīālī, my own felt-tent[1] had to be left from want of baggage-beasts. One night at that time, it rained so much, that water stood knee-deep in my tent (*chădăr*); I watched the night out till dawn, uncomfortably sitting on a pile of blankets.

(*k. Bāqi Chaghānīānī s treachery.*)

A few marches further on came Jahāngīr Mīrzā, saying, "I have a private word for you." When we were in private, he said, "Bāqī *Chaghānīānī* came and said to me, 'You make the Pādshāh cross the water of Sind with 7, 8, 10 persons, then make yourself Pādshāh.'" Said I, "What others are heard of as consulting with him?" Said he, "It was but a moment ago Bāqī Beg spoke to me; I know no more." Said I, "Find out who the others are; likely enough Sayyid Ḥusain Akbar and Sl. 'Alī the page are in it, as well as Khusrau Shāh's begs and braves." Here the Mīrzā really behaved very well and like a blood-relation; what he now did was the counterpart of what I had done in Kāhmard,[2] in this same ill-fated mannikin's other scheme of treachery.[3] Fol. 152*b*.

On dismounting after the next march, I made Jahāngīr Mīrzā lead a body of well-mounted men to raid the Aūghāns (Afghāns) of that neighbourhood.

Many men's horses were now left behind in each camping-ground, the day coming when as many as 2 or 300 were left. Braves of the first rank went on foot; Sayyid Maḥmūd *Aūghlāqchī*, one of the best of the household-braves, left his horses behind and walked. In this state as to horses we went all the rest of the way to Ghaznī.

Three or four marches further on, Jahāngīr Mīrzā plundered some Afghāns and brought in a few sheep. Fol. 153.

(*l. The Āb-i-istāda.*)

When, with a few more marches, we reached the Standing-water (*Āb-i-istāda*) a wonderfully large sheet of water presented

[1] *khar-gāh*, a folding tent on lattice frame-work, perhaps a *khibitka*.
[2] It may be more correct to write Kāh-mard, as the Ḥai. MS. does and to understand in the name a reference to the grass(*kāh*)-yielding capacity of the place.
[3] f. 121.

itself to view; the level lands on its further side could not be seen at all; its water seemed to join the sky; the higher land and the mountains of that further side looked to hang between Heaven and Earth, as in a mirage. The waters there gathered are said to be those of the spring-rain floods of the Kattawāz-plain, the Zurmut-valley, and the Qarā-bāgh meadow of the Ghaznī-torrent,—floods of the spring-rains, and the over-plus[1] of the summer-rise of streams.

When within two miles of the Āb-i-istāda, we saw a wonderful thing,—something as red as the rose of the dawn kept shewing and vanishing between the sky and the water. It kept coming and going. When we got quite close we learned that what seemed the cause were flocks of geese,[2] not 10,000, not 20,000 in a flock, but geese innumerable which, when the mass of birds flapped their wings in flight, sometimes shewed red feathers, sometimes not. Not only was this bird there in countless numbers, but birds of every sort. Eggs lay in masses on the shore. When two Afghāns, come there to collect eggs, saw us,
Fol. 153*b*. they went into the water half a *kuroh* (a mile). Some of our men following, brought them back. As far as they went the water was of one depth, up to a horse's belly; it seemed not to lie in a hollow, the country being flat.

We dismounted at the torrent coming down to the Āb-i-istāda from the plain of Kattawāz. The several other times we have passed it, we have found a dry channel with no water whatever,[3] but this time, there was so much water, from the spring-rains, that no ford could be found. The water was not very broad but very deep. Horses and camels were made to swim it; some of the baggage was hauled over with ropes. Having got across, we went on through Old Nānī and Sar-i-dih to Ghaznī where for a few days Jahāngīr Mīrzā was our host, setting food before us and offering his tribute.

[1] This may mean, what irrigation has not used.

[2] Mr. Erskine notes that the description would lead us to imagine a flock of flamingoes. Masson found the lake filled with red-legged, white fowl (i, 262); these and also what Bābur saw, may have been the China-goose which has body and neck white, head and tail russet (Bellew's *Mission* p. 402). Broadfoot seems to have visited the lake when migrants were few, and through this to have been led to adverse comment on Bābur's accuracy (p. 350).

[3] The usual dryness of the bed may have resulted from the irrigation of much land some 12 miles from Ghaznī.

(*m. Return to Kābul.*)

That year most waters came down in flood. No ford was found through the water of Dih-i-yaq'ūb.[1] For this reason we went straight on to Kamarī, through the Sajāwand-pass. At Kamarī I had a boat fashioned in a pool, brought and set on the Dih-i-yaq'ūb-water in front of Kamarī. In this all our people were put over.

We reached Kābul in the month of Ẕū'l-ḥijja (May 1505 AD.).[2] A few days earlier Sayyid Yūsuf *Aūghlāqchī* had gone to God's mercy through the pains of colic. Fol. 154.

(*n. Misconduct of Nāṣir Mīrzā.*)

It has been mentioned that at Qūsh-gumbaz, Nāṣir Mīrzā asked leave to stay behind, saying that he would follow in a few days after taking something from his district for his retainers and followers.[3] But having left us, he sent a force against the people of Nūr-valley, they having done something a little refractory. The difficulty of moving in that valley owing to the strong position of its fort and the rice-cultivation of its lands, has already been described.[4] The Mīrzā's commander, Faẓlī, in ground so impracticable and in that one-road tract, instead of safe-guarding his men, scattered them to forage. Out came the valesmen, drove the foragers off, made it impossible to the rest to keep their ground, killed some, captured a mass of others and of horses,—precisely what would happen to any army chancing to be under such a person as Faẓlī! Whether because of this affair, or whether from want of heart, the Mīrzā did not follow us at all; he stayed behind.

Moreover Ayūb's sons, Yūsuf and Bahlūl (Begchīk), more seditious, silly and arrogant persons than whom there may not exist,—to whom I had given, to Yūsuf Alangār, to Bahlūl 'Alī-shang, they like Nāṣir Mīrzā, were to have taken something from Fol. 154b. their districts and to have come on with him, but, he not coming,

[1] This is the Luhūgur (Logar) water, knee-deep in winter at the ford but spreading in flood with the spring-rains. Bābur, not being able to cross it for the direct roads into Kābul, kept on along its left bank, crossing it eventually at the Kamarī of maps, s.e. of Kābul.

[2] This disastrous expedition, full of privation and loss, had occupied some four months (T.R. p. 201).

[3] f. 145b. [4] f. 133b and Appendix F.

neither did they. All that winter they were the companions of his cups and social pleasures. They also over-ran the Tarkalānī Afghāns in it.[1] With the on-coming heats, the Mīrzā made march off the families of the clans, outside-tribes and hordes who had wintered in Nīngnahār and the Lamghānāt, driving them like sheep before him, with all their goods, as far as the Bārān-water.[2]

(*o. Affairs of Badakhshān.*)

While Nāṣir Mīrzā was in camp on the Bārān-water, he heard that the Badakhshīs were united against the Aūzbegs and had killed some of them.

Here are the particulars:—When Shaibāq Khān had given Qūndūz to Qambar Bī and gone himself to Khwārizm[3]; Qambar Bī, in order to conciliate the Badakhshīs, sent them a son of Muḥammad-i-makhdūmī, Maḥmūd by name, but Mubārak Shāh, —whose ancestors are heard of as begs of the Badakhshān Shāhs,—having uplifted his own head, and cut off Maḥmūd's and those of some Aūzbegs, made himself fast in the fort once known as Shāf-tiwār but re-named by him Qila'-i-ẓafar. Moreover, in Rustāq Muḥammad *qūrchī*, an armourer of Khusrau Shāh, then occupying Khamalangān, slew Shaibāq Khān's *ṣadr* and some Aūzbegs and made that place fast. Zubair of Rāgh, again,
Fol. 155. whose forefathers also will have been begs of the Badakhshān Shāhs, uprose in Rāgh.[4] Jahāngīr *Turkmān*, again, a servant of Khusrau Shāh's Walī, collected some of the fugitive soldiers and tribesmen Walī had left behind, and with them withdrew into a fastness.[5]

Nāṣir Mīrzā, hearing these various items of news and spurred on by the instigation of a few silly, short-sighted persons to covet Badakhshān, marched along the Shibr-tū and Āb-dara road, driving like sheep before him the families of the men who had come into Kābul from the other side of the Amū.[6]

[1] They were located in Mandrāwar in 926 AH. (f. 251).
[2] This was done, manifestly, with the design of drawing after the families their fighting men, then away with Bābur.
[3] f. 163. Shaibāq Khān besieged Chīn Ṣūfī, Sl. Ḥusain Mīrzā's man in Khwārizm (T.R. p. 204; *Shaibānī-nāma*, Vambéry, Table of Contents and note 89).
[4] Survey Map 1889, Sadda. The Rāgh-water flows n.w. into the Oxus (Amū).
[5] *birk*, a mountain stronghold; cf. f. 149*b* note to Birk (Barak).
[6] They were thus driven on from the Bārān-water (f. 154*b*).

(*p. Affairs of Khusrau Shāh.*)

At the time Khusrau Shāh and Aḥmad-i-qāsim were in flight from Ājar for Khurāsān,[1] they meeting in with Badī'u'z-zamān Mīrzā and Ẕū'n-nūn Beg, all went on together to the presence of Sl. Ḥusain Mīrzā in Herī. All had long been foes of his; all had behaved unmannerly to him; what brands had they not set on his heart! Yet all now went to him in their distress, and all went through me. For it is not likely they would have seen him if I had not made Khusrau Shāh helpless by parting him from his following, and if I had not taken Kābul from Ẕū'n'nūn's son, Muqīm. Badī'u'z-zamān Mīrzā himself was as dough in the Fol. 155*b*. hands of the rest; beyond their word he could not go. Sl. Ḥusain Mīrzā took up a gracious attitude towards one and all, mentioned no-one's misdeeds, even made them gifts.

Shortly after their arrival Khusrau Shāh asked for leave to go to his own country, saying, "If I go, I shall get it all into my hands." As he had reached Herī without equipment and without resources, they finessed a little about his leave. He became importunate. Muḥammad Barandūq retorted roundly on him with, "When you had 30,000 men behind you and the whole country in your hands, what did you effect against the Aūzbeg? What will you do now with your 500 men and the Aūzbegs in possession?" He added a little good advice in a few sensible words, but all was in vain because the fated hour of Khusrau Shāh's death was near. Leave was at last given because of his importunity; Khusrau Shāh with his 3 or 400 followers, went straight into the borders of Dahānah. There as Nāṣir Mīrzā had just gone across, these two met.

Now the Badakhshī chiefs had invited only the Mīrzā; they had not invited Khusrau Shāh. Try as the Mīrzā did to persuade Khusrau Shāh to go into the hill-country,[2] the latter, quite understanding the whole time, would not consent to go, his own idea being that if he marched under the Mīrzā, he would get the Fol. 156. country into his own hands. In the end, unable to agree, each of them, near Ishkīmīsh, arrayed his following, put on mail, drew out to fight, and—departed. Nāṣir Mīrzā went on for Badakhshān; Khusrau Shāh after collecting a disorderly rabble, good and bad

[1] f. 126*b*.

[2] Ḥiṣār, presumably.

of some 1,000 persons, went, with the intention of laying siege to Qūndūz, to Khwāja Chār-tāq, one or two *yīghāch* outside it.

(*q. Death of Khusrau Shāh.*)

At the time Shaibāq Khān, after overcoming Sulṭān Aḥmad *Tambal* and Andijān, made a move on Ḥiṣār, his Honour Khusrau Shāh[1] flung away his country (Qūndūz and Ḥiṣār) without a blow struck, and saved himself. Thereupon Shaibāq Khān went to Ḥiṣār in which were Sherīm the page and a few good braves. *They* did not surrender Ḥiṣār, though their honourable beg had flung *his* country away and gone off; they made Ḥiṣār fast. The siege of Ḥiṣār Shaibāq Khān entrusted to Ḥamza Sl. and Mahdī Sulṭān,[2] went to Qūndūz, gave Qūndūz to his younger brother, Maḥmūd Sulṭān and betook himself without delay to Khwārizm against Chīn Ṣūfī. But as, before he reached Samarkand on his way to Khwārizm, he heard of the death in Qūndūz of his brother, Maḥmūd Sulṭān, he gave that place to Qambar Bī of Marv.[3]

Qambar Bī was in Qūndūz when Khusrau Shāh went against it; he at once sent off galloppers to summon Ḥamza Sl. and the
Fol. 156*b*. others Shaibāq Khān had left behind. Ḥamza Sl. came himself as far as the *sarāī* on the Amū bank where he put his sons and begs in command of a force which went direct against Khusrau Shāh. There was neither fight nor flight for that fat, little man; Ḥamza Sulṭān's men unhorsed him, killed his sister's son, Aḥmad-i-qāsim, Sherīm the page and several good braves. Him they took into Qūndūz, there struck his head off and from there sent it to Shaibāq Khān in Khwārizm.[4]

(*r. Conduct in Kābul of Khusrau Shāh's retainers.*)

Just as Khusrau Shāh had said they would do, his former retainers and followers, no sooner than he marched against

[1] Here "His Honour" translates Bābur's clearly ironical honorific plural.

[2] These two sulṭāns, almost always mentioned in alliance, may be Tīmūrids by maternal descent (Index *s.nn.*). So far I have found no direct statement of their parentage. My husband has shewn me what may be one indication of it, *viz.* that two of the uncles of Shaibāq Khān (whose kinsmen the sulṭāns seem to be), Qūj-kūnjī and Sīūnjak, were sons of a daughter of the Tīmūrid Aūlūgh Beg *Samarkandī* (Ḥ.S. ii, 318). *See* Vambéry's *Bukhārā* p. 248 note.

[3] For the deaths of Tambal and Maḥmūd, mentioned in the above summary of Shaibāq Khān's actions, *see* the *Shaibānī-nāma*, Vambéry, p. 323.

[4] Ḥ.S. ii, 323, for Khusrau Shāh's character and death.

Qūndūz, changed in their demeanour to me,[1] most of them marching off to near Khwāja-i-riwāj.[2] The greater number of the men in my service had been in his. The Mughūls behaved well, taking up a position of adherence to me.[3] On all this the news of Khusrau Shāh's death fell like water on fire; it put his men out.

[1] f. 124.

[2] Khwāja-of-the-rhubarb, presumably a shrine near rhubarb-grounds (f. 129*b*).

[3] *yakshī bārdīlār*, lit. went well, a common expression in the *Bābur-nāma*, of which the reverse statement is *yamānlīk bīla bārdī* (f. 163). Some Persian MSS. make the Mughūls disloyal but this is not only in opposition to the Turkī text, it is a redundant statement since if disloyal, they are included in Bābur's previous statement, as being Khusrau Shāh's retainers. What might call for comment in Mughūls would be loyalty to Bābur.

911 AH.—JUNE 4TH 1505 TO MAY 24TH 1506 AD.[1]

(*a. Death of Qūtlūq-nigār Khānīm.*)

In the month of Muḥarram my mother had fever. Blood was let without effect and a Khurāsānī doctor, known as Sayyid Ṭabīb, in accordance with the Khurāsān practice, gave her water-melon, but her time to die must have come, for on the
Fol. 157. Ṣaturday after six days of illness, she went to God's mercy.

On Sunday I and Qāsim Kūkūldāsh conveyed her to the New-year's Garden on the mountain-skirt[2] where Aūlūgh Beg Mīrzā had built a house, and there, with the permission of his heirs,[3] we committed her to the earth. While we were mourning for her, people let me know about (the death of) my younger Khān *dādā* Alacha Khān, and my grandmother Aīsān-daulat Begīm.[4] Close upon Khānīm's Fortieth[5] arrived from Khurāsān Shāh Begīm the mother of the Khāns, together with my maternal-aunt Mihr-nigār Khānīm, formerly of Sl. Aḥmad Mīrzā's *ḥaram*, and Muḥammad Ḥusain *Kūrkān Dūghlāt*.[6] Lament broke out afresh ; the bitterness of these partings was extreme. When the mourning-rites had been observed, food and victuals set out for the poor and destitute, the Qorān recited, and prayers offered for the departed souls, we steadied ourselves and all took heart again.

(*b. A futile start for Qandahār.*)

When set free from these momentous duties, we got an army to horse for Qandahār under the strong insistance of Bāqī

[1] Elph. MS. f. 121*b* : W.-i-B. I.O. 215 f. 126 and 217 f. 106*b* ; Mems. p. 169.

[2] *tāgh-dāmanasī*, presumably the Koh-dāman, and the garden will thus be the one of f. 136*b*.

[3] If these heirs were descendants of Aūlūgh Beg M. one would be at hand in 'Abdu'r-razzāq, then a boy, and another, a daughter, was the wife of Muqīm *Arghūn*. As Mr. Erskine notes, Musalmāns are most scrupulous not to bury their dead in ground gained by violence or wrong.

[4] The news of Aḥmad's death was belated ; he died some 13 months earlier, in the end of 909 AH. and in Eastern Turkistān. Perhaps details now arrived.

[5] *i.e.* the fortieth day of mourning, when alms are given.

[6] Of those arriving, the first would find her step-daughter dead, the second her sister, the third, his late wife's sister (T.R. p. 196).

Chaghāniānī. At the start I went to Qūsh-nādir (var. nāwar) where on dismounting I got fever. It was a strange sort of illness for whenever with much trouble I had been awakened, my eyes closed again in sleep. In four or five days I got quite well.

(*c. An earthquake.*)

At that time there was a great earthquake[1] such that most of the ramparts of forts and the walls of gardens fell down; houses were levelled to the ground in towns and villages and many persons lay dead beneath them. Every house fell in Paghmān- Fol. 157*b*.
village, and 70 to 80 strong heads-of-houses lay dead under their walls. Between Pagh-mān and Beg-tūt[2] a piece of ground, a good stone-throw[3] wide may-be, slid down as far as an arrow's-flight; where it had slid springs appeared. On the road between Istarghach and Maidān the ground was so broken up for 6 to 8 *yīghāch* (36–48 m.) that in some places it rose as high as an elephant, in others sank as deep; here and there people were sucked in. When the Earth quaked, dust rose from the tops of the mountains. Nūru'l-lāh the *ṭambourchī*[4] had been playing before me; he had two instruments with him and at the moment of the quake had both in his hands; so out of his own control was he that the two knocked against each other. Jahāngīr Mīrzā was in the porch of an upper-room at a house built by Aūlūgh Beg Mīrzā in Tīpa; when the Earth quaked, he let himself down and was not hurt, but the roof fell on some-one with him in that upper-room, presumably one of his own circle; that this person was not hurt in the least must have been solely through God's mercy. In Tīpa most of the houses were levelled to the ground. The Earth quaked 33 times on the first day, and for a month afterwards used to quake two or three times in the 24 hours. The begs and soldiers having been

[1] This will be the earthquake felt in Agra on Ṣafar 3rd 911 AH. (July 5th 1505 AD. Erskine's *History of India* i, 229 note). Cf. Elliot and Dowson, iv, 465 and v, 99.

[2] Raverty's *Notes* p. 690.

[3] *bīr kitta tāsh ātīmī*; var. *bāsh ātīmī*. If *tāsh* be right, the reference will probably be to the throw of a catapult.

[4] Here almost certainly, a drummer, because there were two tambours and because also Bābur uses *'aūdī* & *ghachakī* for the other meanings of *ṭambourchi*, lutanist and guitarist. The word has found its way, as *tambourgi*, into Childe Harold's Pilgrimage (Canto ii, lxxii. H. B.).

ordered to repair the breaches made in the towers and ramparts Fol. 158. of the fort (Kābul), everything was made good again in 20 days or a month by their industry and energy.

(*d. Campaign against Qalāt-i-ghilzāī.*)

Owing to my illness and to the earthquake, our plan of going to Qandahār had fallen somewhat into the background. The illness left behind and the fort repaired, it was taken up again. We were undecided at the time we dismounted below Shniz[1] whether to go to Qandahār, or to over-run the hills and plains. Jahāngīr Mīrzā and the begs having assembled, counsel was taken and the matter found settlement in a move on Qalāt. On this move Jahāngīr Mīrzā and Bāqī *Chaghāniānī* insisted strongly.

At Tāzī[2] there was word that Sher-i-'alī the page with Kīchīk Bāqī *Diwāna* and others had thoughts of desertion; all were arrested; Sher-i-'alī was put to death because he had given clear signs of disloyalty and misdoing both while in my service and not in mine, in this country and in that country.[3] The others were let go with loss of horse and arms.

On arriving at Qalāt we attacked at once and from all sides, without our mail and without siege-appliances. As has been mentioned in this History, Kīchīk Khwāja, the elder brother of Khwāja Kalān, was a most daring brave; he had used his sword Fol. 158*b*. in my presence several times; he now clambered up the south-west tower of Qalāt, was pricked in the eye with a spear when almost up, and died of the wound two or three days after the place was taken. Here that Kīchīk Bāqī *Dīwāna* who had been arrested when about to desert with Sher-i-'alī the page, expiated his baseness by being killed with a stone when he went under the ramparts. One or two other men died also. Fighting of this sort went on till the Afternoon Prayer when, just as our men were worn-out with the struggle and labour, those in the fort asked for peace and made surrender. Qalāt had been given by Ẕū'n-nūn *Arghūn* to Muqīm, and in it now were Muqīm's retainers, Farrukh *Arghūn* and Qarā *Bīlūt* (Afghān). When they came out with their swords and quivers hanging round

[1] Kābul-Ghaznī road (R.'s *Notes* index *s.n.*).
[2] var. Yārī. Tāzī is on the Ghaznī-Qalāt-i-ghilzāī road (R.'s *Notes*, Appendix p. 46).
[3] *i.e.* in Kābul and in the Trans-Himalayan country.

their necks, we forgave their offences.[1] It was not my wish to reduce this high family[2] to great straits; for why? Because if we did so when such a foe as the Aūzbeg was at our side, what would be said by those of far and near, who saw and heard?

As the move on Qalāt had been made under the insistance of Jahāngīr Mīrzā and Bāqī *Chaghānīānī*, it was now made over to the Mīrzā's charge. He would not accept it; Bāqī also could give no good answer in the matter. So, after such a storming and assaulting of Qalāt, its capture was useless.

We went back to Kābul after over-running the Afghāns of Sawā-sang and Ālā-tāgh on the south of Qalāt. Fol. 159.

The night we dismounted at Kābul I went into the fort; my tent and stable being in the Chār-bāgh, a Khirilchī thief going into the garden, fetched out and took away a bay horse of mine with its accoutrements, and my *khachar*.[3]

(*e. Death of Bāqī Chaghānīānī.*)

From the time Bāqī *Chaghānīanī* joined me on the Amū-bank, no man of mine had had more trust and authority.[4] If a word were said, if an act were done, that word was his word, that act, his act. Spite of this, he had not done me fitting service, nor had he shewn me due civility. Quite the contrary! he had done things bad and unmannerly. Mean he was, miserly and malicious, ill-tongued, envious and cross-natured. So miserly was he that although when he left Tīrmīẕ, with his family and possessions, he may have owned 30 to 40,000 sheep, and although those masses of sheep used to pass in front of us at every camping-ground, he did not give a single one to our bare

[1] These will be those against Bābur's suzerainty done by their defence of Qalāt for Muqīm.

[2] *tabaqa*, dynasty. By using this word Bābur shews recognition of high birth. It is noticeable that he usually writes of an Arghūn chief either simply as "Beg" or without a title. This does not appear to imply admission of equality, since he styles even his brothers and sisters Mīrzā and Begīm; nor does it shew familiarity of intercourse, since none seems to have existed between him and Ẕū'n-nūn or Muqīm. That he did not admit equality is shewn on f. 208. The T.R. styles Ẕū'n-nūn "Mīrzā", a title by which, as also by Shāh, his descendants are found styled (A.-i-a. Blochmann, *s.n.*).

[3] Turkī *khachar* is a camel or mule used for carrying personal effects. The word has been read by some scribes as *khanjar*, dagger.

[4] In 910 AH. he had induced Bābur to come to Kābul instead of going into Khurāsān (H.S. iii, 319); in the same year he dictated the march to Kohāt, and the rest of that disastrous travel. His real name was not Bāqī but Muḥammad Bāqir (Ḥ.S. iii, 311).

braves, tortured as they were by the pangs of hunger; at last in Kāh-mard, he gave 50!

Spite of acknowledging me for his chief (*pādshāh*), he had nagarets beaten at his own Gate. He was sincere to none, had regard for none. What revenue there is from Kābul (town) comes from the *tamghā*[1]; the whole of this he had, together
Fol. 159*b*. with the *dārogha*-ship in Kābul and Panjhīr, the Gadai (var. Kidī) Hazāra, and *kūshlūk*[2] and control of the Gate.[3] With all this favour and finding, he was not in the least content; quite the reverse! What medley of mischief he planned has been told; we had taken not the smallest notice of any of it, nor had we cast it in his face. He was always asking for leave, affecting scruple at making the request. We used to acknowledge the scruple and excuse ourselves from giving the leave. This would put him down for a few days; then he would ask again. He went too far with his affected scruple and his takings of leave! Sick were we too of his conduct and his character. We gave the leave; he repented asking for it and began to agitate against it, but all in vain! He got written down and sent to me, "His Highness made compact not to call me to account till nine[4] misdeeds had issued from me." I answered with a reminder of eleven successive faults and sent this to him through Mullā Bābā of Pashāghar. He submitted and was allowed to go towards Hindūstān, taking his family and possessions. A few of his retainers escorted him through Khaibar and returned; he joined Bāqī *Gāgiānī's* caravan and crossed at Nīl-āb.

Daryā Khān's son, Yār-i-ḥusain was then in Kacha-kot,[5] having drawn into his service, on the warrant of the *farmān* taken from me in Kohāt, a few Afghāns of the Dilazāk (var. Dilah-zāk) and Yūsuf-zāī and also a few Jats and Gujūrs.[6] With these he beat the roads, taking toll with might and main.

[1] These transit or custom duties are so called because the dutiable articles are stamped with a *tamghā*, a wooden stamp.

[2] Perhaps this word is an equivalent of Persian *goshī*, a tax on cattle and beasts of burden.

[3] Bāqī was one only and not the head of the Lords of the Gate.

[4] The choice of the number nine, links on presumably to the mystic value attached to it *e.g.* Tarkhāns had nine privileges; gifts were made by nines.

[5] It is near Ḥasan-abdāl (A. i-A. Jarrett, ii, 324).

[6] For the *farmān*, f. 146*b*; for Gujūrs, G. of I.

Hearing about Bāqī, he blocked the road, made the whole party prisoner, killed Bāqī and took his wife. Fol. 160.

We ourselves had let Bāqī go without injuring him, but his own misdeeds rose up against him; his own acts defeated him.

> Leave thou to Fate the man who does thee wrong;
> For Fate is an avenging servitor.

(*f. Attack on the Turkmān Hazāras.*)

That winter we just sat in the Chār-bāgh till snow had fallen once or twice.

The Turkmān Hazāras, since we came into Kābul, had done a variety of insolent things and had robbed on the roads. We thought therefore of over-running them, went into the town to Aūlūgh Beg Mīrzā's house at the Būstān-sarāī, and thence rode out in the month of Sha'bān (Feb. 1506 AD.).

We raided a few Hazāras at Janglīk, at the mouth of the Dara-i-khūsh (Happy-valley).[1] Some were in a cave near the valley-mouth, hiding perhaps. Shaikh Darwīsh Kūkūldāsh went

(*Author's note on Shaikh Darwīsh.*) He had been with me in the guerilla-times, was Master-armourer (*qūr-begī*), drew a strong bow and shot a good shaft.

incautiously right (*auq*) up to the cave-mouth, was shot (*aūqlāb*) in the nipple by a Hazāra inside and died there and then (*aūq*).[2]

As most of the Turkmān Hazāras seemed to be wintering inside the Dara-i-khūsh, we marched against them.

The valley is shut in,[3] by a mile-long gully stretching inwards from its mouth. The road engirdles the mountain, having a straight fall of some 50 to 60 yards below it and above it a precipice. Horsemen go along it in single-file. We passed the gully and went on through the day till between the Two Prayers (3 p.m.) without meeting a single person. Having spent the night somewhere, we found a fat camel[4] belonging to the Hazāras, had it killed, made part of its flesh into *kabābs*[5] and Fol. 160*b*.

[1] var. Khwesh. Its water flows into the Ghūr-bund stream; it seems to be the Dara-i-Turkmān of Stanford and the Survey Maps both of which mark Janglīk. For Hazāra turbulence, f. 135*b* and note.

[2] The repetition of *aūq* in this sentence can hardly be accidental.

[3] *taur* [*dara*], which I take to be Turkī, round, complete.

[4] Three MSS. of the Turkī text write *bīr sīmīzlūq tīwah*; but the two Persian translations have *yak shuturlūq farbīh*, a *shuturlūq* being a baggage-camel with little hair (Erskine).

[5] *brochettes*, meat cut into large mouthfuls, spitted and roasted.

cooked part in a ewer (*aftāb*). Such good camel-flesh had never been tasted; some could not tell it from mutton.

Next day we marched on for the Hazāra winter-camp. At the first watch (9 a.m.) a man came from ahead, saying that the Hazāras had blocked a ford in front with branches, checked our men and were fighting. That winter the snow lay very deep; to move was difficult except on the road. The swampy meadows (*tuk-āb*) along the stream were all frozen; the stream could only be crossed from the road because of snow and ice. The Hazāras had cut many branches, put them at the exit from the water and were fighting in the valley-bottom with horse and foot or raining
Fol. 161. arrows down from either side.

Muḥammad 'Alī *Mubashshir*[1] Beg one of our most daring braves, newly promoted to the rank of beg and well worthy of favour, went along the branch-blocked road without his mail, was shot in the belly and instantly surrendered his life. As we had gone forward in haste, most of us were not in mail. Shaft after shaft flew by and fell; with each one Yūsuf's Aḥmad said anxiously, "Bare[2] like this you go into it! I have seen two arrows go close to your head!" Said I, "Don't fear! Many as good arrows as these have flown past my head!" So much said, Qāsim Beg, his men in full accoutrement,[3] found a ford on our right and crossed. Before their charge the Hazāras could make no stand; they fled, swiftly pursued and unhorsed one after the other by those just up with them.

In guerdon for this feat Bangash was given to Qāsim Beg. Ḥātim the armourer having been not bad in the affair, was promoted to Shaikh Darwīsh's office of *qūr-begī*. Bābā Qulī's Kīpik (*sic*) also went well forward in it, so we entrusted Muḥ. 'Alī *Mubashshir's* office to him.

Sl. Qulī *Chūnāq* (one-eared) started in pursuit of the Hazāras but there was no getting out of the hollow because of the snow.
Fol. 161*b*. For my own part I just went with these braves.

Near the Hazāra winter-camp we found many sheep and herds of horses. I myself collected as many as 4 to 500 sheep

[1] Perhaps he was officially an announcer; the word means also bearer of good news.
[2] *yīlāng*, without mail, as in the common phrase *yigīt yīlāng*, a bare brave.
[3] *aūpchīn*, of horse and man (f. 113*b* and note).

and from 20 to 25 horses. Sl. Qulī *Chūnāq* and two or three of my personal servants were with me. I have ridden in a raid twice[1]; this was the first time; the other was when, coming in from Khurāsān (912 AH.), we raided these same Turkmān Hazāras. Our foragers brought in masses of sheep and horses. The Hazāra wives and their little children had gone off up the snowy slopes and stayed there; we were rather idle and it was getting late in the day; so we turned back and dismounted in their very dwellings. Deep indeed was the snow that winter! Off the road it was up to a horse's *qāptāl*,[2] so deep that the night-watch was in the saddle all through till shoot of dawn.

Going out of the valley, we spent the next night just inside the mouth, in the Hazāra winter-quarters. Marching from there, we dismounted at Janglīk. At Janglīk Yārak Ṭaghāī and other late-comers were ordered to take the Hazāras who had killed Shaikh Darwīsh and who, luckless and death-doomed, seemed still to be in the cave. Yārak Ṭaghāī and his band by sending smoke into the cave, took 70 to 80 Hazāras who mostly died by the sword.

(*g. Collection of the Nijr-aū tribute.*)

On the way back from the Hazāra expedition we went to the Āī-tūghdī neighbourhood below Bārān[3] in order to collect the revenue of Nijr-aū. Jahāngīr Mīrzā, come up from Ghaznī, Fol. 162.
waited on me there. At that time, on Ramẓān 13th (Feb. 7th) such sciatic-pain attacked me that for 40 days some-one had to turn me over from one side to the other.

Of the (seven) valleys of the Nijr-water the Pīchkān-valley,—and of the villages in the Pīchkān-valley Ghain,—and of Ghain its head-man Ḥusain *Ghainī* in particular, together with his elder and younger brethren, were known and notorious for obstinacy and daring. On this account a force was sent under Jahāngīr Mīrzā, Qāsim Beg going too, which went to Sar-i-tūp (Hill-top), stormed and took a *sangur* and made a few meet their doom.

[1] Manifestly Bābur means that he twice actually helped to collect the booty.

[2] This is that part of a horse covered by the two side-pieces of a Turkī saddle, from which the side-arch springs on either side (Shaw).

[3] *Bārān-nīng ayāghī.* Except the river I have found nothing called Bārān; the village marked Baian on the French Map would suit the position; it is n.e. of Chār-yak-kār (f. 184*b* note).

Because of the sciatic pain, people made a sort of litter for me in which they carried me along the bank of the Bārān and into the town to the Būstān-sarāī. There I stayed for a few days; before that trouble was over a boil came out on my left cheek; this was lanced and for it I also took a purge. When relieved, I went out into the Chār-bāgh.

(*h. Misconduct of Jahāngīr Mīrzā.*)

At the time Jahāngīr Mīrzā waited on me, Ayūb's sons Yūsuf and Buhlūl, who were in his service, had taken up a strifeful and seditious attitude towards me; so the Mīrzā was not found to be what he had been earlier. In a few days he marched out of Tīpa in his mail,[1] hurried back to Ghaznī, there took Nānī, killed some of its people and plundered all.
Fol. 162*b*. After that he marched off with whatever men he had, through the Hazāras,[2] his face set for Bāmīān. God knows that nothing had been done by me or my dependants to give him ground for anger or reproach! What was heard of later on as perhaps explaining his going off in the way he did, was this;—When Qāsim Beg went with other begs, to give him honouring meeting as he came up from Ghaznī, the Mīrzā threw a falcon off at a quail. Just as the falcon, getting close, put out its pounce to seize the quail, the quail dropped to the ground. Hereupon shouts and cries, "Taken! is it taken?" Said Qāsim Beg, "Who looses the foe in his grip?" Their misunderstanding of this was their sole reason for going off, but they backed themselves on one or two other worse and weaker old cronish matters.[3] After doing in Ghaznī what has been mentioned, they drew off through the Hazāras to the Mughūl

[1] *i.e.* prepared to fight.

[2] For the Hazāra (Turkī, Mīng) on the Mīrzā's road *see* Raverty's routes from Ghaznī to the north. An account given by the *Tārīkh-i-rashīdī* (p. 196) of Jahāngīr's doings is confused; its parenthetical "(at the same time)" can hardly be correct. Jahāngīr left Ghaznī now, (911 AH.), as Bābur left Kābul in 912 AH. without knowledge of Ḥusain's death (911 AH.). Bābur had heard it (f. 183*b*) before Jahāngīr joined him (912 AH.); after their meeting they went on together to Herī. The petition of which the T.R. speaks as made by Jahāngīr to Bābur, that he might go into Khurāsān and help the Bāī-qarā Mīrzās must have been made after the meeting of the two at Ṣaf-hill (f. 184*b*).

[3] The plurals *they* and *their* of the preceding sentence stand no doubt for the Mīrzā, Yūsuf and Buhlūl who all had such punishment due as would lead them to hear threat in Qāsim's words now when all were within Bābur's pounce.

clans.[1] These clans at that time had left Nāṣir Mīrzā but had not joined the Aūzbeg, and were in Yāī, Astar-āb and the summer-pastures thereabouts.

(*i. Sl. Ḥusain Mīrzā calls up help against Shaibāq Khān.*)

Sl. Ḥusain Mīrzā, having resolved to repel Shaibāq Khān, summoned all his sons; me too he summoned, sending to me Sayyid Afẓal, son of Sayyid 'Alī *Khwāb-bīn* (Seer-of-dreams). It was right on several grounds for us to start for Khurāsān. One ground was that when a great ruler, sitting, as Sl. Ḥusain Mīrzā sat, in Tīmūr Beg's place, had resolved to act against such a foe as Shaibāq Khān and had called up many men and had summoned his sons and his begs, if there were some who went on foot it was for us to go if on our heads! if some took the bludgeon, we would take the stone! A second ground was that, since Jahāngīr Mīrzā had gone to such lengths and had behaved so badly,[2] we had either to dispel his resentment or to repel his attack. Fol. 163.

(*j. Chīn Ṣūfī's death.*)

This year Shaibāq Khān took Khwārizm after besieging Chīn Sūfī in it for ten months. There had been a mass of fighting during the siege; many were the bold deeds done by the Khwārizmī braves; nothing soever did they leave undone. Again and again their shooting was such that their arrows pierced shield and cuirass, sometimes the two cuirasses.[3] For ten months they sustained that siege without hope in any quarter. A few bare braves then lost heart, entered into talk with the Aūzbeg and were in the act of letting him up into the fort when Chīn Ṣūfī had the news and went to the spot. Just as he was beating and forcing down the Aūzbegs, his own page, in a discharge of arrows, shot him from behind. No man was left to fight; the Aūzbegs took Khwārizm. God's mercy on

[1] These are the *aīmāqs* from which the fighting-men went east with Bābur in 910 AH. and the families in which Nāṣir shepherded across Hindu-kush (f. 154 and f. 155).

[2] *yamānlīk bīla bārdī*; cf. f. 156*b* and n. for its opposite, *yakhshī bārdīlār*; and T.R. p. 196.

[3] One might be of mail, the other of wadded cloth.

Chīn Ṣūfī, who never for one moment ceased to stake his life

Fol. 163b. for his chief![1]

Shaibāq Khān entrusted Khwārizm to Kūpuk (*sic*) Bī and went back to Samarkand.

(*k. Death of Sultān Ḥusain Mīrzā.*)

Sl. Ḥusain Mīrzā having led his army out against Shaibāq Khān as far as Bābā Ilāhī[2] went to God's mercy, in the month of Ẕū'l-ḥijja (Ẕū'l-ḥijja 11th 911 AH.—May 5th 1506 AD.).

SULṬĀN ḤUSAIN MĪRZĀ AND HIS COURT.[3]

(*a.*) *His birth and descent.*

He was born in Herī (Harāt), in (Muḥarram) 842 (AH.—June–July, 1438 AD.) in Shāhrukh Mīrzā's time[4] and was the son of Manṣūr Mīrzā, son of Bāī-qara Mīrza, son of 'Umar Shaikh Mīrzā, son of Amīr Tīmūr. Manṣūr Mīrzā and Bāī-qarā Mīrzā never reigned.

His mother was Fīrūza Begīm, a (great-)grandchild (*nabīra*) of Tīmūr Beg; through her he became a grandchild of Mīrān-shāh also.[5] He was of high birth on both sides, a ruler of royal

[1] Chīn Ṣūfī was Ḥusain *Bāī-qarā's* man (T.R. p. 204). His arduous defence, faithfulness and abandonment recall the instance of a later time when also a long road stretched between the man and the help that failed him. But the Mīrzā was old, his military strength was, admittedly, sapped by ease; hence his elder Khartum, his neglect of his Gordon.

It should be noted that no mention of the page's fatal arrow is made by the *Shaibānī-nāma* (Vambéry, p. 442), or by the *Tārīkh-i-rashīdī* (p. 204). Chīn Ṣūfī's death was on the 21st of the Second Rabī 911 AH. (Aug. 22nd 1505 AD.).

[2] This may be the "Baboulei" of the French Map of 1904, on the Herī-Kushk-Marūchāq road.

[3] Elph. MS. f. 127; W.-i-B. I.O. 215 f. 132 and 217 f. 111*b*; Mems. p. 175; *Méms.* i, 364.

That Bābur should have given his laborious account of the Court of Herī seems due both to loyalty to a great Tīmūrid, seated in Tīmūr Beg's place (f. 122*b*), and to his own interest, as a man-of-letters and connoisseur in excellence, in that ruler's galaxy of talent. His account here opening is not complete; its sources are various; they include the *Ḥabību's-siyār* and what he will have learned himself in Herī or from members of the Bāī-qarā family, knowledgeable women some of them, who were with him in Hindūstān. The narrow scope of my notes shews that they attempt no more than to indicate further sources of information and to clear up a few obscurities.

[4] Tīmūr's youngest son, d. 850 AH. (1446 AD.). Cf. Ḥ.S. iii, 203. The use in this sentence of Amīr and not Beg as Tīmūr's title is, up to this point, unique in the *Bābur-nāma*; it may be a scribe's error.

[5] Fīrūza's paternal line of descent was as follows:—Fīrūza, daughter of Sl. Ḥusain *Qānjūt*, son of Ākā Begīm, daughter of Tīmūr. Her maternal descent was:—Fīrūza, d. of Qūtlūq-sulṭān Begīm, d. of Mīrān-shāh, s. of Tīmūr. She died Muḥ. 24th 874 AH. (July 25th 1489 AD. Ḥ.S. iii, 218).

lineage.[1] Of the marriage (of Manṣūr with Fīrūza) were born two sons and two daughters, namely, Bāī-qarā Mīrzā and Sl. Ḥusain Mīrzā, Ākā Begīm and another daughter, Badka Begīm whom Aḥmad Khān took.[2]

Bāī-qarā Mīrzā was older than Sl. Ḥusain Mīrzā; he was his younger brother's retainer but used not to be present as head of the Court;[3] except in Court, he used to share his brother's divan (*tūshak*). He was given Balkh by his younger brother and was its Commandant for several years. He had three sons, Sl. Muḥammad Mīrzā, Sl. Wais Mīrzā and Sl. Iskandar Mīrzā.[4]

Ākā Begīm was older than the Mīrzā; she was taken by Sl. Aḥmad Mīrzā,[5] a grandson (*nabīra*) of Mīrān-shāh; by him she had a son (Muḥammad Sulṭān Mīrzā), known as Kīchīk (Little) Mīrzā, who at first was in his maternal-uncle's service, but later on gave up soldiering to occupy himself with letters. He is said to have become very learned and also to have taste in verse.[6] Here is a Persian quatrain of his:— Fol. 164.

For long on a life of devotion I plumed me,
As one of the band of the abstinent ranged me;
Where when Love came was devotion? denial?
By the mercy of God it is I have proved me!

---

[1] "No-one in the world had such parentage", writes Khwānd-amīr, after detailing the Tīmūrid, Chīngīz-khānid, and other noted strains meeting in Ḥusain *Bāī-qarā* (H.S. iii, 204).

[2] The Elph. MS. gives the Begīm no name; Badī'u'l-jamāl is correct (H.S. iii, 242). The curious "Badka" needs explanation. It seems probable that Bābur left one of his blanks for later filling-in; the natural run of his sentence here is "Ākā B. and Badī'u'l-jamāl B." and not the detail, which follows in its due place, about the marriage with Aḥmad.

[3] *Dīwān bāshīdā ḥāẓir būlmās aīdī*; the sense of which may be that Bāī-qarā did not sit where the premier retainer usually sat at the head of the Court (Pers. trs. *sar-i-dīwān*).

[4] From this Wais and Sl. Ḥusain M.'s daughter Sulṭānīm (f. 167*b*) were descended the Bāī-qarā Mīrzās who gave Akbar so much trouble.

[5] As this man might be mistaken for Bābur's uncle (*q.v.*) of the same name, it may be well to set down his parentage. He was a s. of Mīrzā Sayyidī Aḥmad, s. of Mīrān-shāh, s. of Tīmūr (H.S. iii, 217, 241). I have not found mention elsewhere of "Aḥmad s. of Mīrān-shāh"; the *sayyidī* in his style points to a sayyida mother. He was Governor of Herī for a time, for Sl. H.M.; 'Alī-sher has notices of him and of his son, Kīchīk Mīrzā (*Journal Asiatique* xvii, 293, M. Belin's art. where may be seen notices of many other men mentioned by Bābur).

[6] He collected and thus preserved 'Alī-sher's earlier poems (Rieu's Pers. Cat. p. 294). Mu'inu'd-dīn al Zamji writes respectfully of his being worthy of credence in some Egyptian matters with which he became acquainted in twice passing through that country on his Pilgrimage (*Journal Asiatique* xvi, 476, de Meynard's article).

This quatrain recalls one by the Mullā.[1] Kīchīk Mīrzā made the circuit of the *ka'ba* towards the end of his life.

Badka (Badī'u'l-jamāl) Begīm also was older[2] than the Mīrzā. She was given in the guerilla times to Aḥmad Khān of Ḥājī-tarkhān;[3] by him she had two sons (Sl. Maḥmūd Khān and Bahādur Sl.) who went to Herī and were in the Mīrzā's service.

(*b.*) *His appearance and habits.*

He was slant-eyed (*qīyik güslüq*) and lion-bodied, being slender from the waist downwards. Even when old and white-bearded, he wore silken garments of fine red and green. He used to wear either the black lambskin cap (*būrk*) or the *qālpāq*,[4] but on a Feast-day would sometimes set up a little three-fold turban, wound broad and badly,[5] stick a heron's plume in it and so go to Prayers.

When he first took Herī, he thought of reciting the names of
Fol. 164*b*. the Twelve Imāms in the *khuṭba*,[6] but 'Alī-sher Beg and others prevented it; thereafter all his important acts were done in accordance with orthodox law. He could not perform the Prayers on account of a trouble in the joints,[7] and he kept no fasts. He was lively and pleasant, rather immoderate in temper, and with words that matched his temper. He shewed great respect for the law in several weighty matters; he once surrendered to the Avengers of blood a son of his own who had

[1] Kīchīk M.'s quatrain is a mere plagiarism of Jāmī's which I am indebted to my husband for locating as in the *Dīwān* I.O. MS. 47 p. 47; B.M. Add. 7774 p. 290; and Add. 7775 p. 285. M. Belin interprets the verse as an expression of the rise of the average good man to mystical rapture, not as his lapse from abstinence to indulgence (l.c. xvii, 296 and notes).

[2] Elph. MS. *younger* but Ḥai. MS. *older* in which it is supported by the "also" (*ham*) of the sentence.

[3] modern Astrakhan. Ḥusain's guerilla wars were those through which he cut his way to the throne of Herī. This begīm was married first to Pīr Budāgh Sl. (Ḥ.S. iii, 242); he dying, she was married by Aḥmad, presumably by levirate custom (*yīnkālīk*; f. 12 and note). By Aḥmad she had a daughter, styled Khān-zāda Begīm whose affairs find comment on f. 206 and Ḥ.S. iii, 359. (The details of this note negative a suggestion of mine that Badka was the Rābī'a-sulṭān of f. 168 (Gul-badan, App. *s. nn.*).)

[4] This is a felt wide-awake worn by travellers in hot weather (Shaw); the Turkmān bonnet (Erskine).

[5] Ḥai. MS. *yamānlīk*, badly, but Elph. MS. *namāyan*, whence Erskine's *showy*.

[6] This was a proof that he was then a Shī'a (Erskine).

[7] The word *perform* may be excused in speaking of Musalmān prayers because they involve ceremonial bendings and prostrations (Erskine).

killed a man, and had him taken to the Judgment-gate (*Dāru'l-qaẓā*). He was abstinent for six or seven years after he took the throne; later on he degraded himself to drink. During the almost 40 years of his rule [1] in Khurāsān, there may not have been one single day on which he did not drink after the Mid-day prayer; earlier than that however he did not drink. What happened with his sons, the soldiers and the town was that every-one pursued vice and pleasure to excess. Bold and daring he was! Time and again he got to work with his own sword, getting his own hand in wherever he arrayed to fight; no man of Tīmūr Beg's line has been known to match him in the slashing of swords. He had a leaning to poetry and even put a *dīwān* together, writing in Turkī with Ḥusainī for his pen-name.[2] Many couplets in his *dīwān* are not bad; it is however in one and the same metre throughout. Great ruler though he was, Fol. 165. both by the length of his reign (*yāsh*) and the breadth of his dominions, he yet, like little people kept fighting-rams, flew pigeons and fought cocks.

(*c.*) *His wars and encounters.*[3]

He swam the Gurgān-water[4] in his guerilla days and gave a party of Aūzbegs a good beating.

Again,—with 60 men he fell on 3000 under Pay-master Muḥammad 'Alī, sent ahead by Sl. Abū-sa'īd Mīrzā, and gave them a downright good beating (868 AH.). This was his one fine, out-standing feat-of-arms.[5]

Again,—he fought and beat Sl. Mahmūd Mīrzā near Astarābād (865 AH.).[6]

[1] If Bābur's 40 include rule in Herī only, it over-states, since Yādgār died in 875 AH. and Ḥusain in 911 AH. while the intervening 36 years include the 5 or 6 temperate ones. If the 40 count from 861 AH. when Ḥusain began to rule in Merv, it under-states. It is a round number, apparently.

[2] Relying on the Ilminsky text, Dr. Rieu was led into the mistake of writing that Bābur gave Ḥusain the wrong pen-name, *i.e.* Ḥusain, and not Ḥusainī (Turk. Cat. p. 256).

[3] Daulat-shāh says that as he is not able to enumerate all Ḥusain's feats-of-arms, he, Turkmān fashion, offers a gift of Nine. The Nine differ from those of Bābur's list in some dates; they are also records of victory only (Browne, p. 521; *Not. et Extr.* iv, 262, de Saçy's article).

[4] Wolves'-water, a river and its town at the s.e. corner of the Caspian, the ancient boundary between Russia and Persia. The name varies a good deal in MSS.

[5] The battle was at Tarshīz; Abū-sa'īd was ruling in Herī; Daulat-shāh (l.c. p. 523) gives 90 and 10,000 as the numbers of the opposed forces!

[6] f. 26*b* and note; Ḥ.S. iii, 209; Daulat-shāh p. 523.

Again,—this also in Astarābād, he fought and beat Sa'īdlīq Sa'īd, son of Ḥusain *Turkmān* (873 AH. ?).

Again,—after taking the throne (of Herī in Ramẓān 873 AH.—March 1469 AD.), he fought and beat Yādgār-i-muḥammad Mīrzā at Chanārān (874 AH.).[1]

Again,—coming swiftly[2] from the Murgh-āb bridge-head (Sar-i-pul), he fell suddenly on Yādgār-i-muḥammad Mīrzā where he lay drunk in the Ravens'-garden (875 AH.), a victory which kept all Khurāsān quiet.

Again,—he fought and beat Sl. Maḥmūd Mīrzā at Chīkmān-sarāī in the neighbourhood of Andikhūd and Shibrghān (876 AH.).[3]

Again,—he fell suddenly on Abā-bikr Mīrzā[4] after that Mīrzā, joined by the Black-sheep Turkmāns, had come out of 'Irāq, beaten Aūlūgh Beg Mīrzā (*Kābulī*) in Takāna and Khimār (var. Ḥimār), taken Kābul, left it because of turmoil in 'Irāq, crossed Khaibar, gone on to Khūsh-āb and Multān, on again to Fol. 165*b*. Sīwī,[5] thence to Karmān and, unable to stay there, had entered the Khurāsān country (884 AH.).[6]

Again,—he defeated his son Badī'u'z-zamān Mīrzā at Pul-i-chirāgh (902 AH.); he also defeated his sons Abū'l-muḥsin Mīrzā and Kūpuk (Round-shouldered) Mīrzā at Ḥalwā-spring (904 AH.).[7]

Again,—he went to Qūndūz, laid siege to it, could not take it, and retired; he laid siege to Ḥiṣār, could not take that either, and rose from before it (901 AH.); he went into Ẕū'n-nūn's country, was given Bast by its *dārogha*, did no more and retired (903 AH.).[8] A ruler so great and so brave, after resolving royally on these three movements, just retired with nothing done!

[1] The loser was the last Shāhrukhī ruler. Chanārān (variants) is near Abīward, Anwarī's birth-place (Ḥ.S. iii, 218; D.S. p. 527).

[2] f. 85. D.S. (p. 540) and the Ḥ.S. (iii, 223) dwell on Ḥusain's speed through three continuous days and nights.

[3] f. 26; Ḥ.S. iii, 227; D.S. p. 532.

[4] Abū-sa'īd's son by a Badakhshī Begīm (T.R. p. 108); he became his father's Governor in Badakhshān and married Ḥusain *Bāī-qarā's* daughter Begīm Sultān at a date after 873 AH. (f. 168 and note; Ḥ.S. iii, 196, 229, 234–37; D.S. p. 535).

[5] f. 152.

[6] Abā-bikr was defeated and put to death at the end of Rajab 884 AH.-Oct. 1479 AD. after flight before Ḥusain across the Gurgān-water (Ḥ.S. iii, 196 and 237 but D.S. p. 539, Ṣafar 885 AH.).

[7] f. 41, Pul-i-chirāgh; for Halwā-spring, H.S. iii, 283 and Rieu's Pers. Cat. p. 443.

[8] f. 33 (p. 57) and f. 57*b*.

Again,—he fought his son Badī'u'z-zamān Mīrzā in the Nīshīn-meadow, who had come there with Ẕū'n-nūn's son, Shāh Beg (903 AH.). In that affair were these curious coincidences:—The Mīrzā's force will have been small, most of his men being in Astarābād; on the very day of the fight, one force rejoined him coming back from Astarābād, and Sl. Mas'ūd Mīrzā arrived to join Sl. Ḥusain Mīrzā after letting Bāī-sunghar Mīrzā take Ḥiṣār, and Ḥaidar Mīrzā came back from reconnoitring Badī'u'z-zamān Mīrzā at Sabzawār.

(*d.*) *His countries.*

His country was Khurāsān, with Balkh to the east, Bistām and Damghān to the west, Khwārizm to the north, Qandahār and Sīstān to the south. When he once had in his hands such a town as Herī, his only affair, by day and by night, was with comfort and pleasure; nor was there a man of his either who did not take his ease. It followed of course that, as he no longer tolerated the hardships and fatigue of conquest and soldiering, his retainers and his territories dwindled instead of increasing right down to the time of his departure.[1] Fol. 166.

(*e.*) *His children.*

Fourteen sons and eleven daughters were born to him.[2] The oldest of all his children was Badī'u'z-zamān Mīrzā; (Bega Begīm) a daughter of Sl. Sanjar of Marv, was his mother.

Shāh-i-gharīb Mīrzā was another; he had a stoop (*būkūrī*) though ill to the eye, he was of good character; though weak of body, he was powerful of pen. He even put a *dīwān* together, using Gharbatī (Lowliness) for his pen-name and writing both Turkī and Persian verse. Here is a couplet of his:—

> Seeing a peri-face as I passed, I became its fool;
> Not knowing what was its name, where was its home.

For a time he was his father's Governor in Herī. He died before his father, leaving no child.

[1] In commenting thus Bābur will have had in mind what he best knew, Ḥusain's futile movements at Qūndūz and Ḥiṣār

[2] *qālīb aīdī*; if *qālīb* be taken as Turkī, survived or remained, it would not apply here since many of Ḥusain's children predeceased him; Ar. *qālab* would suit, meaning *begotten, born*.

There are discrepancies between Bābur's details here and Khwānd-amīr's scattered through the *Ḥabību's-siyār*, concerning Ḥusain's family.

Muẓaffar-i-ḥusain Mīrzā was another; he was his father's favourite son, but though this favourite, had neither accomplishments nor character. It was Sl. Ḥusain Mīrzā's over-fondness for this son that led his other sons into rebellion. The mother of Shāh-i-gharīb Mīrzā and of Muẓaffar-i-ḥusain Mīrzā was Fol. 166b. Khadīja Begīm, a former mistress of Sl. Abū-sa'īd Mīrzā by whom she had had a daughter also, known as Āq (Fair) Begīm.

Two other sons were Abū'l-ḥusain Mīrzā and Kūpuk (var. Kīpik) Mīrzā whose name was Muḥammad Muḥsin Mīrzā; their mother was Laṭīf-sulṭān Āghācha.

Abū-turāb Mīrzā was another. From his early years he had an excellent reputation. When the news of his father's increased illness[1] reached him and other news of other kinds also, he fled with his younger brother Muḥammad-i-ḥusain Mīrzā into 'Irāq,[2] and there abandoned soldiering to lead the darwish-life; nothing further has been heard about him.[3] His son Sohrāb was in my service when I took Ḥiṣār after having beaten the sulṭāns led by Ḥamza Sl. and Mahdī Sl. (917 AH.—1511 AD.); he was blind of one eye and of wretchedly bad aspect; his disposition matched even his ill-looks. Owing to some immoderate act (*bī i'tidāl*), he could not stay with me, so went off. For some of his immoderate doings, Nijm Ṣānī put him to death near Astarābād.[4]

Muḥammad-i-ḥusain Mīrzā was another. He must have been shut up (*bund*) with Shāh Ismā'īl at some place in 'Irāq and have become his disciple;[5] he became a rank heretic later on and became this although his father and brethren, older and younger, were all orthodox. He died in Astarābād, still on the same wrong road, still with the same absurd opinions. A good deal is heard about his courage and heroism, but no deed of his

[1] *bī ḥuẓūrī*, which may mean aversion due to Khadīja Begīm's malevolence.

[2] Some of the several goings into 'Irāq chronicled by Bābur point to refuge taken with Tīmūrids, descendants of Khalīl and 'Umar, sons of Mīrān-shāh (Lane-Poole's *Muhammadan Dynasties*, Table of the Tīmūrids).

[3] He died before his father (Ḥ.S. iii, 327).

[4] He will have been killed previous to Ramẓān 3rd 918 AH. (Nov. 12th, 1512 AD.), the date of the battle of Ghaj-dawān when Nijm Ṣānī died.

[5] The *bund* here may not imply that both were in prison, but that they were bound in close company, allowing Ismā'īl, a fervent Shī'a, to convert the Mīrzā.

stands out as worthy of record. He may have been poetically-disposed; here is a couplet of his:—

> Grimed with dust, from tracking what game dost thou come?
> Steeped in sweat, from whose heart of flame dost thou come?

Farīdūn-i-ḥusain Mīrzā was another. He drew a very strong bow and shot a first-rate shaft; people say his cross-bow (*kamān-i-guroha*) may have been 40 *bātmāns.*[1] He himself was very brave but he had no luck in war; he was beaten wherever he fought. He and his younger brother Ibn-i-ḥusain Mīrzā were defeated at Rabāṭ-i-dūzd (var. Dudūr) by Tīmūr Sl. and 'Ubaid Sl. leading Shaibāq Khān's advance (913 AH.?), but he had done good things there.[2] In Dāmghān he and Muḥammad-i-zamān Mīrzā[3] fell into the hands of Shaibāq Khān who, killing neither, let both go free. Farīdūn-i-ḥusain Mīrzā went later on to Qalāt[4] where Shāh Muḥammad *Diwāna* had made himself fast; there when the Aūzbegs took the place, he was captured and killed. The three sons last-named were by Mīnglī Bībī Āghācha, Sl. Ḥusain Mīrzā's Aūzbeg mistress. Fol. 167.

Ḥaidar Mīrzā was another; his mother Payānda-sulṭān Begīm was a daughter of Sl. Abū-sa'īd Mīrzā. Ḥaidar Mīrzā was Governor of Balkh and Mashhad for some time during his father's life. For him his father, when besieging Ḥiṣār (901 AH.) took (Bega Begīm) a daughter of Sl. Maḥmūd Mīrzā and Khān-zāda Begīm; this done, he rose from before Ḥiṣār. One daughter only[5] was born of that marriage; she was named Shād (Joy)

[1] The *bātmān* is a Turkish weight of 13lbs (Meninsky) or 15lbs (Wollaston). The weight seems likely to refer to the strength demanded for rounding the bow (*kamān guroha-sī*) *i.e.* as much strength as to lift 40 *bātmāns.* Rounding or bending might stand for stringing or drawing. The meaning can hardly be one of the weight of the cross-bow itself. Erskine read *gūrdehieh* for *guroha* (p. 180) and translated by "double-stringed bow"; de Courteille (i, 373) read *guirdhiyeh*, *arrondi*, *circulaire*, in this following Ilminsky who may have followed Erskine. The Elph. and Ḥai. MSS. and the first W.-i-B. (I.O. 215 f. 113*b*) have *kamān guroha-sī*; the second W.-i-B. omits the passage, in the MSS. I have seen.

[2] *yakhshīlār bārīb tūr*; lit. good things went (on); cf. f. 156*b* and note.

[3] Badī'u'z-zamān's son, drowned at Chausa in 946 AH. (1539 AD.) A.N. (H. Beveridge, i, 344).

[4] Qalāt-i-nādirī, in Khurāsān, the birth-place of Nādir Shāh (T.R. p. 209).

[5] *bīr gīna qīz*, which on f. 86*b* can fitly be read to mean daughterling, *Töchterchen*, *fillette*, but here and *i.a.* f. 168, must have another meaning than diminutive and may be an equivalent of German *Stück* and mean *one only.* Gul-badan gives an account of Shād's manly pursuits (H.N. f. 25*b*).

Begīm and given to 'Ādil Sl.[1] when she came to Kābul later on. Ḥaidar Mīrzā departed from the world in his father's life-time.

Fol. 167b. Muḥammad Ma'ṣūm Mīrzā was another. He had Qandahār given to him and, as was fitting with this, a daughter of Aūlūgh Beg Mīrzā, (Bega Begīm), was set aside for him; when she went to Herī (902 AH.), Sl. Ḥusain Mīrzā made a splendid feast, setting up a great *chār-ṭāq* for it.[2] Though Qandahār was given to Muḥ. Ma'ṣūm Mīrzā, he had neither power nor influence there, since, if black were done, or if white were done, the act was Shāh Beg *Arghūn's*. On this account the Mīrzā left Qandahār and went into Khurāsān. He died before his father.

Farrukh-i-ḥusain Mīrzā was another. Brief life was granted to him; he bade farewell to the world before his younger brother Ibrāhīm-i-ḥusain Mīrzā.

[1] He was the son of Mahdī Sl. (f. 320b) and the father of 'Āqil Sl. *Aūzbeg* (A.N. index *s.n.*). Several matters suggest that these men were of the Shabān Aūzbegs who intermarried with Ḥusain *Bāī-qarā's* family and some of whom went to Bābur in Hindūstān. One such matter is that Kābul was the refuge of dispossessed Harātīs, after the Aūzbeg conquest; that there 'Āqil married Shād *Bāī-qarā* and that 'Ādil went on to Bābur. Moreover Khāfī Khān makes a statement which (if correct) would allow 'Ādil's father Mahdī to be a grandson of Ḥusain *Bāī-qarā*; this statement is that when Bābur defeated the Aūzbegs in 916 AH. (1510 AD.), he freed from their captivity two sons (descendants) of his paternal uncle, named Mahdī Sl. and Sulṭān Mīrzā. [Leaving the authenticity of the statement aside for a moment, it will be observed that this incident is of the same date and place as another well-vouched for, namely that Bābur then and there killed Mahdī Sl. *Aūzbeg* and Ḥamza Sl. *Aūzbeg* after defeating them.] What makes in favour of Khāfī Khān's correctness is, not only that Bābur's foe Mahdī is not known to have had a son 'Ādil, but also that his "Sulṭān Mīrzā" is not a style so certainly suiting Ḥamza as it does a Shabān sulṭān, one whose father was a Shabān sulṭān, and whose mother was a Mīrzā's daughter. Moreover this point of identification is pressed by the correctness, according to oriental statement of relationship, of Khāfī Khān's "paternal uncle" (of Bābur), because this precisely suits Sl. Ḥusain Mīrzā with whose family these Shabān sulṭāns allied themselves. On the other hand it must be said that Khāfī Khān's statement is not in the English text of the *Tārīkh-i-rashīdī*, the book on which he mostly relies at this period, nor is it in my husband's MS. [a copy from the Rampūr Codex]; and to this must be added the verbal objection that a modicum of rhetoric allows a death to be described both in Turkī and Persian, as a release from the captivity of a sinner's own acts (f. 160). Still Khāfī Khān may be right; his statement may yet be found in some other MS. of the T.R. or some different source; it is one a scribe copying the T.R. might be led to omit by reason of its coincidences. The killing and the release may both be right; 'Ādil's Mahdī may be the Shabān sulṭān inference makes him seem. This little *crux* presses home the need of much attention to the *lacunae* in the *Bābur-nāma*, since in them are lost some exits and some entries of Bābur's *dramatis personae*, pertinently, mention of the death of Mahdī with Ḥamza in 916 AH., and possibly also that of 'Ādil's Mahdī's release.

[2] A *chār-ṭāq* may be a large tent rising into four domes or having four porches.

Ibrāhīm-i-ḥusain Mīrzā was another. They say his disposition was not bad; he died before his father from bibbing and bibbing Herī wines.

Ibn-i-ḥusain Mīrzā and Muḥ. Qāsim Mīrzā were others;[1] their story will follow. Pāpā Āghācha was the mother of the five sons last-named.

Of all the Mīrzā's daughters, Sulṭānīm Begīm was the oldest. She had no brother or sister of the full-blood. Her mother, known as Chūlī (Desert) Begīm, was a daughter of one of the Aẕāq begs. Sulṭānīm Begīm had great acquaintance with words (*soz bīlūr aīdī*); she was never at fault for a word. Her father sent her out[2] to Sl. Wais Mīrzā, the middle son of his own elder brother Bāī-qarā Mīrzā; she had a son and a daughter by him; the daughter was sent out to Aīsān-qulī Sl. younger brother of Yīlī-bārs of the Shabān sulṭāns;[3] the son is that Muḥammad Sl. Mīrzā to whom I have given the Qanaūj district.[4] At that same date Sulṭānīm Begīm, when on her way with her grandson from Kābul to Hindūstān, went to God's mercy at Nīl-āb. Her various people turned back, taking her bones; her grandson came on.[5] Fol. 168.

Four daughters were by Payānda-sulṭān Begīm. Āq Begīm, the oldest, was sent out to Muḥammad Qāsim *Arlāt*, a grandson of Bega Begīm the younger sister of Bābur Mīrzā;[6] there was one daughter (*bīr gīna qīz*), known as Qarā-gūz (Dark-eyed) Begīm, whom Nāṣir Mīrzā (*Mīrān-shāhī*) took. Kīchīk Begīm was the second; for her Sl. Mas'ūd Mīrzā had great desire but, try as he would, Payānda-sulṭān Begīm, having an aversion for him, would not give her to him;[7] she sent Kīchīk Begīm out afterwards

[1] Ḥ.S. iii, 367.

[2] This phrase, common but not always selected, suggests unwillingness to leave the paternal roof.

[3] Abū'l-ghāzī's *History of the Mughūls*, Désmaisons, p. 207.

[4] The appointment was made in 933 AH. (1527 AD.) and seems to have been held still in 934 AH. (ff. 329, 332).

[5] This grandson may have been a child travelling with his father's household, perhaps Aūlūgh Mīrzā, the oldest son of Muḥammad Sulṭān Mīrzā (A. A. Blochmann, p. 461). No mention is made here of Sulṭānīm Begīm's marriage with 'Abdu'l-bāqī Mīrzā (f. 175).

[6] Abū'l-qāsim Bābur *Shāhrukhī* presumably.

[7] The time may have been 902 AH. when Mas'ūd took his sister Bega Begīm to Herī for her marriage with Ḥaidar (Ḥ.S. iii, 260).

to Mullā Khwāja of the line of Sayyid Ātā.[1] Her third and fourth daughters Bega Begīm and Āghā Begīm, she gave to Bābur Mīrzā and Murād Mīrzā the sons of her younger sister, Rābī'a-sulṭān Begīm.[2]

Two other daughters of the Mīrzā were by Mīnglī Bībī Āghācha. They gave the elder one, Bairam-sulṭān Begīm to Sayyid 'Abdu'l-lāh, one of the sayyids of Andikhūd who was a grandson of Bāī-qarā Mīrzā[3] through a daughter. A son of this marriage, Sayyid Barka[4] was in my service when Samarkand was taken (917 AH.–1511 AD.); he went to Aūrganj later and there made claim to rule; the Red-heads[5] killed him in Astarābād. Mīnglī Bībī's second daughter was Fāṭima-sulṭān Begīm; her they gave to Yādgār(-i-farrukh) Mīrzā of Tīmūr Beg's line.[6]

Three daughters[7] were by Pāpā Āghācha. Of these the oldest, Sulṭān-nizhād Begīm was made to go out to Iskandar Mīrzā, youngest son of Sl. Ḥusain Mīrzā's elder brother Bāī-qarā Mīrzā. The second, (Sa'ādat-bakht, known as) Begīm Sulṭān, was given to Sl. Mas'ūd Mīrzā after his blinding.[8] By Sl. Mas'ūd

Fol. 168*b*.

[1] Khwāja Aḥmad *Yāsawī*, known as Khwāja Ātā, founder of the Yāsawī religious order.

[2] Not finding mention of a daughter of Abū-sa'īd named Rābī'a-sulṭān, I think she may be the daughter styled Āq Begīm who is No. 3 in Gul-badan's guest-list for the Mystic Feast.

[3] This man I take to be Ḥusain's grandfather and not brother, both because 'Abdu'l-lāh was of Ḥusain's and his brother's generation, and also because of the absence here of Bābur's usual defining words "elder brother" (of Sl. Ḥusain Mīrzā). In this I have to differ from Dr. Rieu (Pers. Cat. p. 152).

[4] So-named after his ancestor Sayyid Barka whose body was exhumed from Andikhūd for reburial in Samarkand, by Tīmūr's wish and there laid in such a position that Tīmūr's body was at its feet (*Ẓafar-nāma* ii, 719; Ḥ.S. iii, 82). (For the above interesting detail I am indebted to my husband.)

[5] *Qizil-bāsh*, Persians wearing red badges or caps to distinguish them as Persians.

[6] Yādgār-i-farrukh *Mīrān-shāhī* (Ḥ.S. iii, 327). He may have been one of those Mīrān-shāhīs of 'Irāq from whom came Ākā's and Sulṭānīm's husbands, Aḥmad and 'Abdu'l-bāqī (ff. 164, 175*b*).

[7] This should be four (f. 169*b*). The Ḥ.S. (iii, 327) also names three only when giving Pāpā Āghācha's daughters (the omission linking it with the B.N.), but elsewhere (iii, 229) it gives an account of a fourth girl's marriage; this fourth is needed to make up the total of 11 daughters. Bābur's and Khwānd-amīr's details of Pāpā Āghācha's quartette are defective; the following may be a more correct list:—(1) Begīm Sulṭān (a frequent title), married to Abā-bikr *Mīrān-shāhī* (who died 884 AH.) and seeming too old to be the one [No. 3] who married Mas'ūd (Ḥ.S. iii, 229); (2) Sulṭān-nizhād, married to Iskandar *Bāī-qarā*; (3) Sa'ādat-bakht also known as Begīm Sulṭān, married to Mas'ūd *Mīrān-shāhī* (Ḥ.S. iii, 327); (4) Manauwar-sulṭān, married to a son of Aūlūgh Beg *Kābulī* (Ḥ.S. iii, 327).

[8] This "after" seems to contradict the statement (f. 58) that Mas'ūd was made to kneel as a son-in-law (*kūyādlīk-kā yūkūndūrūb*) at a date previous to his blinding, but the seeming contradiction may be explained by considering the following details;

Mīrzā she had one daughter and one son. The daughter was brought up by Apāq Begīm of Sl. Ḥusain Mīrzā's *ḥaram*; from Herī she came to Kābul and was there given to Sayyid Mīrzā Apāq.[1] (Sa'ādat-bakht) Begīm Sulṭān after the Aūzbeg killed her husband, set out for the *ka'ba* with her son.[2] News has just come (*circa* 934 AH.) that they have been heard of as in Makka and that the boy is becoming a bit of a great personage.[3] Pāpā Āghācha's third daughter was given to a sayyid of Andikhūd, generally known as Sayyid Mīrzā.[4]

Another of the Mīrzā's daughters, 'Āyisha-sulṭān Begīm was by a mistress, Zubaida Āghācha the grand-daughter of Ḥusain-i-Shaikh Tīmūr.[5] They gave her to Qāsim Sl. of the Shabān sulṭāns; she had by him a son, named Qāsim-i-ḥusain Sl. who came to serve me in Hindūstān, was in the Holy Battle with Rānā Sangā, and was given Badāyūn.[6] When Qāsim Sl. died, (his widow) 'Āyisha-sulṭān Begīm was taken by Būrān Sl. one of his relations,[7] by whom she had a son, named 'Abdu'l-lāh Sl. now serving me and though young, not doing badly.

(*f. His wives and concubines.*)

The wife he first took was Bega Sulṭān Begīm, a daughter of Sl. Sanjar of Marv. She was the mother of Badī'u'z-zamān Mīrzā. She was very cross-tempered and made the Mīrzā endure

he left Herī hastily (f. 58), went to Khusrau Shāh and was blinded by him,—all in the last two months of 903 AH. (1498 AD.), after the kneeling on Ẕū'l-qa'da 3rd, (June 23rd) in the Ravens'-garden. Here what Bābur says is that the Begīm was given (*bīrib*) after the blinding, the inference allowed being that though Mas'ūd had kneeled before the blinding, she had remained in her father's house till his return after the blinding.

[1] The first W.-i-B. writes "Apāq Begīm" (I.O. 215 f. 136) which would allow Sayyid Mīrzā to be a kinsman of Apāq Begīm, wife of Ḥusain *Bāī-qarā*.

[2] This brief summary conveys the impression that the Begīm went on her pilgrimage shortly after Mas'ūd's death (913 AH. ?), but may be wrong :—After Mas'ūd's murder, by one Bīmāsh Mīrzā, *dārogha* of Sarakhs, at Shaibāq Khān's order, she was married by Bīmāsh M. (Ḥ.S. iii, 278). How long after this she went to Makka is not said; it was about 934 AH. when Bābur heard of her as there.

[3] This clause is in the Ḥai. MS. but not in the Elph. MS. (f. 131), or Kehr's (Ilminsky, p. 210), or in either Persian translation. The boy may have been 17 or 18.

[4] This appears a mistake (f. 168 foot, and note on Pāpā's daughters).

[5] f. 171*b*.

[6] 933 AH.-1527 AD. (f. 329).

[7] Presumably this was a *yīnkālīk* marriage; it differs from some of those chronicled and also from a levirate marriage in not being made with a childless wife. (Cf. index *s.n. yīnkālīk.*)

much wretchedness, until driven at last to despair, he set himself
Fol. 169. free by divorcing her. What was he to do? Right was with him.[1]

A bad wife in a good man's house
Makes this world already his hell.[2]

God preserve every Musalmān from this misfortune! Would that not a single cross or ill-tempered wife were left in the world!

Chūlī Begīm was another; she was a daughter of the Azāq begs and was the mother of Sulṭānīm Begīm.

Shahr-bānū Begīm was another; she was Sl. Abū-sa'īd Mīrzā's daughter, taken after Sl. Ḥusain Mīrzā took the throne (873 AH.). When the Mīrzā's other ladies got out of their litters and mounted horses, at the battle of Chīkmān, Shahr-bānū Begīm, putting her trust in her younger brother (Sl. Maḥmūd M.), did not leave her litter, did not mount a horse;[3] people told the Mīrzā of this, so he divorced her and took her younger sister Payānda-sulṭān Begīm. When the Aūzbegs took Khurāsān (913 AH.), Payānda-sulṭān Begīm went into 'Irāq, and in 'Irāq she died in great misery.

Khadīja Begīm was another.[4] She had been a mistress of Sl. Abū-sa'īd Mīrzā and by him had had a daughter, Āq Begīm; after his defeat (873 AH.–1468 AD.) she betook herself to Herī where Sl. Ḥusain Mīrzā took her, made her a great favourite, and promoted her to the rank of Begīm. Very dominant indeed she became later on; she it was wrought Muḥ. Mūmin Mīrzā's death;[5] she in chief it was caused Sl. Ḥusain Mīrzā's sons to rebel against him. She took herself for a sensible woman but was a silly chatterer, may also have been a heretic. Of her were
Fol. 169b. born Shāh-i-gharīb Mīrzā and Muẓaffar-i-ḥusain Mīrzā.

Apāq Begīm was another;[6] she had no children; that Pāpā Āghācha the Mīrzā made such a favourite of was her foster-sister.

[1] Khwānd-amīr says that Bega Begīm was jealous, died of grief at her divorce, and was buried in a College, of her own erection, in 893 AH. (1488 AD. Ḥ.S. iii, 245).

[2] *Gulistān* Cap. II, Story 31 (Platts, p. 114).

[3] *i.e.* did not get ready to ride off if her husband were beaten by her brother (f. 11 and note to Ḥabība).

[4] Khadīja Begī Āghā (Ḥ.S. ii, 230 and iii, 327); she would be promoted probably after Shāh-i-gharīb's birth.

[5] He was a son of Badī'u'z-zamān.

[6] It is singular that this honoured woman's parentage is not mentioned; if it be right on f. 168b (*q.v.* with note) to read Sayyid Mīrzā of Apāq Begīm, she may be a sayyida of Andikhūd.

Being childless, Apāq Begīm brought up as her own the children of Pāpā Āghācha. She nursed the Mīrzā admirably when he was ill; none of his other wives could nurse as she did. The year I came into Hindūstān (932 AH.)[1] she came into Kābul from Herī and I shewed her all the honour and respect I could. While I was besieging Chandīrī (934 AH.) news came that in Kābul she had fulfilled God's will.[2]

One of the Mīrzā's mistresses was Laṭīf-sulṭān Āghācha of the Chār-shamba people[3]; she became the mother of Abū'l-muḥsin Mīrzā and Kūpuk (or Kīpik) Mīrza (*i.e.* Muḥammad Muḥsin).

Another mistress was Mīnglī Bībī Āghācha,[4] an Aūzbeg and one of Shahr-bānū Begīm's various people. She became the mother of Abū-turāb Mīrzā, Muḥammad-i-ḥusain Mīrzā, Farīdūn-i-ḥusain Mīrzā and of two daughters.

Pāpā Āghācha, the foster-sister of Apāq Begīm was another mistress. The Mīrzā saw her, looked on her with favour, took her and, as has been mentioned, she became the mother of five of his sons and four of his daughters.[5]

Begī Sulṭān Āghācha was another mistress; she had no child. There were also many concubines and mistresses held in little respect; those enumerated were the respected wives and mistresses of Sl. Ḥusain Mīrzā.

Strange indeed it is that of the 14 sons born to a ruler so great as Sl. Ḥusain Mīrzā, one governing too in such a town as Herī, three only were born in legal marriage.[6] In him, in his sons, and in his tribes and hordes vice and debauchery were Fol. 170. extremely prevalent. What shews this point precisely is that of the many sons born to his dynasty not a sign or trace was left

[1] As Bābur left Kābul on Ṣafar 1st (Nov. 17th 1525 AD.), the Begīm must have arrived in Muḥarram 932 AH. (Oct. 18th to Nov. 17th).

[2] f. 333. As Chandīrī was besieged in Rabī'u'l-ākhar 934 AH. this passage shews that, as a minimum estimate, what remains of Bābur's composed narrative (*i.e.* down to f. 216*b*) was written after that date (Jan. 1528).

[3] *Chār-shambalār*. Mention of another inhabitant of this place with the odd name, Wednesday (Chār-shamba), is made on f. 42*b*.

[4] Mole-marked Lady; most MSS. style her Bī but Ḥ.S. iii, 327, writes Bībī; it varies also by calling her a Turk. She was a purchased slave of Shahr-bānū's and was given to the Mīrzā by Shahr-bānū at the time of her own marriage with him.

[5] As noted already, f. 168*b* enumerates three only.

[6] The three were almost certainly Badī'u'z-zamān, Ḥaidar, son of a Tīmūrid mother, and Muẓaffar-i-ḥuṣain, born after his mother had been legally married.

in seven or eight years, excepting only Muḥammad-i-zamān Mīrzā.[1]

(*g. His amīrs.*)

There was Muḥammad Baranduq *Barlās*, descending from Chākū *Barlās* as follows,—Muḥammad Baranduq, son of 'Alī, son of Baranduq, son of Jahān-shāh, son of Chākū *Barlās*.[2] He had been a beg of Bābur Mīrzā's presence; later on Sl. Abū-sa'īd Mīrzā favoured him, gave him Kābul conjointly with Jahāngīr *Barlās*, and made him Aūlūgh Beg Mīrzā's guardian. After the death of Sl. Abū-sa'īd Mīrzā, Aūlūgh Beg Mīrzā formed designs against the two Barlās; they got to know this, kept tight hold of him, made the tribes and hordes march,[3] moved as for Qūndūz; and when up on Hindū-kush, courteously compelled Aūlūgh Beg Mīrzā to start back for Kābul, they themselves going on to Sl. Ḥusain Mīrzā in Khurāsān, who, in his turn, shewed them great favour. Muḥammad Baranduq was remarkably intelligent, a very leaderlike man indeed! He was extravagantly fond of a hawk; so much so, they say, that if a hawk of his had strayed or had died, he would ask, taking the names of his sons on his lips, what it would have mattered if such or such a son had died or had broken his neck, rather than this or that bird had died or had strayed.

Muẓaffar *Barlās* was another.[4] He had been with the Mīrzā in the guerilla fighting and, for some cause unknown, had received extreme favour. In such honour was he in those guerilla days that the compact was for the Mīrzā to take four *dāng* (sixths)
Fol. 170*b*. of any country conquered, and for him to take two *dāng*. A strange compact indeed! How could it be right to make even a faithful servant a co-partner in rule? Not even a younger

[1] Seven sons predeceased him:—Farrukh, Shāh-i-gharīb, Muḥ. Ma'ṣūm, Ḥaidar, Ibrāhīm-i-ḥusain, Muḥ. Ḥusain and Abū-turāb. So too five daughters:—Āq, Bega, Āghā, Kīchīk and Fāṭima-sulṭān Begīms. So too four wives:—Bega-sulṭān and Chūlī Begīms, Zubaida and Laṭīf-sulṭān Āghāchas (Ḥ.S. iii, 327).

[2] Chākū, a Barlās, as was Tīmūr, was one of Tīmūr's noted men.

At this point some hand not the scribe's has entered on the margin of the Ḥai. MS. the descendants of Muḥ. Baranduq down into Akbar's reign:—Muḥ. Farīdūn, bin Muḥ. Qulī Khān, bin Mīrzā 'Alī, bin Muḥ. Baranduq *Barlās*. Of these Farīdūn and Muḥ. Qulī are amīrs of the *Āyīn-i-akbarī* list (Blochmann, pp. 341, 342; Ḥ.S. iii, 233).

[3] Enforced marches of Mughūls and other nomads are mentioned also on f. 154*b* and f. 155.

[4] Ḥ.S. iii, 228, 233, 235.

brother or a son obtains such a pact; how then should a beg?[1] When the Mīrzā had possession of the throne, he repented the compact, but his repentance was of no avail; that muddy-minded mannikin, favoured so much already, made growing assumption to rule. The Mīrzā acted without judgment; people say Muzaffar *Barlās* was poisoned in the end.[2] God knows the truth!

'Alī-sher *Nawā'i* was another, the Mīrzā's friend rather than his beg. They had been learners together in childhood and even then are said to have been close friends. It is not known for what offence Sl. Abū-sa'īd Mīrzā drove 'Alī-sher Beg from Herī; he then went to Samarkand where he was protected and supported by Aḥmad Ḥājī Beg during the several years of his stay.[3] He was noted for refinement of manner; people fancied this due to the pride of high fortune but it may not have been so, it may have been innate, since it was equally noticeable also in Samarkand.[4] 'Alī-sher Beg had no match. For as long as verse has been written in the Turkī tongue, no-one has written so much or so well as he. He wrote six books of poems (*maṣnawī*), five of them answering to the Quintet (*Khamsah*),[5] the sixth, entitled the *Lisānu't-ṭair* (Tongue of the birds), was in the same metre as the *Manṭiqu't-ṭair* (Speech of the birds).[6] He put together four *dīwāns* (collections) of odes, bearing the names, *Curiosities of Childhood, Marvels of Youth, Wonders of Manhood* and *Advantages of Age.*[7] There are good quatrains of his also. Some others of his compositions rank below those Fol. 171.
mentioned; amongst them is a collection of his letters, imitating that of Maulānā 'Abdu'r-raḥmān *Jāmī* and aiming at gathering together every letter on any topic he had ever written to any person. He wrote also the *Mīzānu'l-aūzān* (Measure of measures) on prosody; it is very worthless; he has made mistake in it about the metres of four out of twenty-four

[1] *beg kīshī*, beg-person.
[2] Khwānd-amīr says he died a natural death (Ḥ.S. iii, 235).
[3] f. 21. For a fuller account of Nawā'i, *J. Asiatique* xvii, 175, M. Belin's article.
[4] *i.e.* when he was poor and a beg's dependant. He went back to Herī at Sl. Ḥusain M.'s request in 873 AH.
[5] Nizāmī's (Rieu's Pers. Cat. s.n.).
[6] Farīdu'd-dīn-'aṭṭar's (Rieu l.c. and Ency. Br.).
[7] *Gharā'ibu'ṣ-ṣighar, Nawādiru'sh-shahāb, Badā'i'u'l-wasaṭ* and *Fawā'idu'l-kibr.*

quatrains, while about other measures he has made mistake such as any-one who has given attention to prosody, will understand. He put a Persian *dīwān* together also, Fānī (transitory) being his pen-name for Persian verse.[1] Some couplets in it are not bad but for the most part it is flat and poor. In music also he composed good things (*nīma*), some excellent airs and preludes (*nakhsh u peshrau*). No such patron and protector of men of parts and accomplishments is known, nor has one such been heard of as ever appearing. It was through his instruction and support that Master (Ustād) Qul-i-muḥammad the lutanist, Shaikhī the flautist, and Ḥusain the lutanist, famous performers all, rose to eminence and renown. It was through his effort and supervision that Master Bih-zād and Shāh Muẓaffar became so distinguished in painting. Few are heard of as having helped to lay the good foundation for future excellence he helped to lay. He had neither son nor daughter, wife or family; he let the world pass by, alone and unencumbered. At first he was Keeper of the Seal; in middle-life he became a beg and for a time was Commandant in Astarābād; later on he forsook soldiering. He took nothing from the Mīrzā, on the contrary, he each year
Fol. 171*b*. offered considerable gifts. When the Mīrzā was returning from the Astarābād campaign, 'Alī-sher Beg went out to give him meeting; they saw one another but before 'Alī-sher Beg should have risen to leave, his condition became such that he could not rise. He was lifted up and carried away; the doctors could not tell what was wrong; he went to God's mercy next day,[2] one of his own couplets suiting his case:—

I was felled by a stroke out of their ken and mine;
What, in such evils, can doctors avail?

Aḥmad the son of Tawakkal *Barlās* was another;[3] for a time he held Qandahār.

Walī Beg was another; he was of Ḥājī Saifu'd-dīn Beg's line,[4] and had been one of the Mīrzā's father's (Manṣūr's) great

[1] Every Persian poet has a *takhalluṣ* (pen-name) which he introduces into the last couplet of each ode (Erskine).
[2] The death occurred in the First Jumāda 906 AH. (Dec. 1500 AD.).
[3] Niẓāmu'd-dīn Aḥmad bin Tawakkal *Barlās* (Ḥ.S. iii, 229).
[4] This may be that uncle of Tīmūr who made the Ḥaj (T.R. p. 48, quoting the *Ẓafar-nāma*).

begs.[1] Short life was granted to him after the Mīrzā took the throne (973 AH.); he died directly afterwards. He was orthodox and made the Prayers, was rough (*turk*) and sincere.

Ḥusain of Shaikh Tīmūr was another; he had been favoured and raised to the rank of beg[2] by Bābur Mīrzā.

Nuyān Beg was another. He was a Sayyid of Tīrmīẕ on his father's side; on his mother's he was related both to Sl. Abū-sa'īd Mīrzā and to Sl. Ḥusain Mīrzā.[3] Sl. Abū-sa'īd Mīrzā had favoured him; he was the beg honoured in Sl. Aḥmad Mīrzā's presence and he met with very great favour when he went to Sl. Ḥusain Mīrzā's. He was a bragging, easy-going, wine-bibbing, jolly person. Through being in his father's service,[4] Ḥasan of Ya'qūb used to be called also Nuyān's Ḥasan.

Jahāngīr *Barlās* was another.[5] For a time he shared the Kābul command with Muḥammad Barandūq *Barlās*, later on Fol. 172. went to Sl. Ḥusain Mīrzā's presence and received very great favour. His movements and poses (*ḥarakāt u sakanāt*) were graceful and charming; he was also a man of pleasant temper. As he knew the rules of hunting and hawking, in those matters the Mīrzā gave him chief charge. He was a favourite of Badī'u'z-zamān Mīrzā and, bearing that Mīrzā's friendliness in mind, used to praise him.

Mīrzā Aḥmad of 'Alī *Farsī Barlās* was another. Though he wrote no verse, he knew what was poetry. He was a gay-hearted, elegant person, one by himself.

'Abdu'l-khalīq Beg was another. Fīrūz Shāh, Shāhrukh Mīrzā's

[1] Some MSS. omit the word "father" here but to read it obviates the difficulty of calling Walī a great beg of Sl. Ḥusain Mīrzā although he died when that mīrzā took the throne (973 AH.) and although no leading place is allotted to him in Bābur's list of Herī begs. Here as in other parts of Bābur's account of Herī, the texts vary much whether Turkī or Persian, *e.g.* the Elph. MS. appears to call Walī a blockhead (*dūnkūz dūr*), the Ḥai. MS. writing *n:kūz dūr* (?).

[2] He had been Bābur *Shāhrukhī's yasāwal* (Court-attendant), had fought against Ḥusain for Yādgār-i-muḥammad and had given a daughter to Ḥusain (Ḥ.S. iii, 206, 228, 230-32; D.S. in *Not. et Ex.* de Saçy p. 265).

[3] f. 29*b*.

[4] *Sic*, Elph. MS. and both Pers. trss. but the Ḥai. MS. omits "father". To read it, however, suits the circumstance that Ḥasan of Ya'qūb was not with Ḥusain and in Harāt but was connected with Maḥmūd *Mīrānshāhī* and Tīrmīẕ (f. 24). Nuyān is not a personal name but is a title; it implies good-birth; all uses of it I have seen are for members of the religious family of Tīrmīẕ.

[5] He was the son of Ibrāhīm *Barlās* and a Badakhshī begīm (T.R. p. 108).

greatly favoured beg, was his grandfather;[1] hence people called him Fīrūz Shāh's 'Abdu'l-khalīq. He held Khwārizm for a time.

Ibrāhīm *Dūldāī* was another. He had good knowledge of revenue matters and the conduct of public business; his work was that of a second Muḥ. Barandūq.

Ẕū'n-nūn *Arghūn* was another.[2] He was a brave man, using his sword well in Sl. Abū-sa'īd Mīrzā's presence and later on getting his hand into the work whatever the fight. As to his courage there was no question at all, but he was a bit of a fool. After he left our (*Mīrān-shāhī*) Mīrzās to go to Sl. Ḥusain Mīrzā, the Mīrzā gave him Ghūr and the Nikdīrīs. He did
Fol. 172b. excellent work in those parts with 70 to 80 men, with so few beating masses and masses of Hazāras and Nikdīrīs; he had not his match for keeping those tribes in order. After a while Zamīn-dāwar was given to him. His son Shāh-i-shujā' *Arghūn* used to move about with him and even in childhood used to chop away with his sword. The Mīrzā favoured Shāh-i-shujā' and, somewhat against Ẕū'n-nūn Beg's wishes, joined him with his father in the government of Qandahār. Later on this father and son made dissension between that father and that son,[3] and stirred up much commotion. After I had overcome Khusrau Shāh and parted his retainers from him, and after I had taken Kābul from Ẕū'n-nūn *Arghūn*'s son Muqīm, Ẕū'n-nūn Beg and Khusrau Shāh both went, in their helplessness, to see Sl. Ḥusain Mīrzā. Ẕū'n-nūn *Arghūn* grew greater after the Mīrzā's death when they gave him the districts of the Herī Koh-dāman, such as Aūba (Ubeh) and Chachcharān.[4] He was made Lord of Badī'u'z-zamān Mīrzā's Gate[5] and Muḥammad Barandūq *Barlās* Lord of Muẕaffar-i-ḥusain Mīrzā's, when the two Mīrzās became

[1] He will have been therefore a collateral of Daulat-shāh whose relation to Fīrūz-shāh is thus expressed by Nawā'i:—*Mīr Daulat-shāh Fīrūz-shāh Beg-nīng 'amm-zāda-sī Amīr 'Alā'u'd-daula Isfārayīnī-nīng aūghūlī dur*, *i.e.* Mīr Daulat-shāh was the son of Fīrūz-shāh Beg's paternal uncle's son, Amīr 'Alā'u'd-daula *Isfārayīnī*. Thus, Fīrūz-shāh and Isfārayīnī were first cousins; Daulat-shāh and 'Abdu'l-khalīq's father were second cousins; while Daulat-shāh and Fīrūz-shāh were first cousins, once removed (Rieu's Pers. Cat. p. 534; Browne's D.S. English preface p. 14 and its reference to the Pers. preface).

[2] *Tarkhān-nāma*, E. & D.'s *History of India* i, 303; Ḥ.S. iii, 227.

[3] f. 41 and note.

[4] Both places are in the valley of the Herī-rūd.

[5] Badī'u'z-zamān married a daughter of Ẕū'n-nūn; she died in 911 AH. (E. & D. i, 305; Ḥ.S. iii, 324).

joint-rulers in Herī. Brave though he was, he was a little crazed and shallow-pated; if he had not been so, would he have accepted flattery as he did? would he have made himself so contemptible? Here are the details of the matter:—While he was so dominant and so trusted in Herī, a few shaikhs and mullās went to him and said, "The Spheres are holding commerce with us; you are to be styled *Hizabru'l-lāh* (Lion of God); you will overcome the Aūzbeg." Fully accepting this flattery, he put his *fūṭa* (bathing-cloth) round his neck [1] and gave thanks. Then, after Shaibāq Khān, coming against the Mīrzās, had beaten them one Fol. 173. by one near Bādghīs, Ẕū'n-nūn *Arghūn* met him face to face near Qarā-rabāṭ and, relying on that promise, stood up against him with 100 to 150 men. A mass of Aūzbegs came up, overcame them and hustled them off; he himself was taken and put to death.[2] He was orthodox and no neglecter of the Prayers, indeed made the extra ones. He was mad for chess; he played it according to his own fancy and, if others play with one hand, he played with both.[3] Avarice and stinginess ruled in his character.

Darwīsh-i-'alī Beg was another,[4] the younger full-brother of 'Alī-sher Beg. He had the Balkh Command for a time and there did good beg-like things, but he was a muddle-head and somewhat wanting in merit. He was dismissed from the Balkh Command because his muddle-headedness had hampered the Mīrzā in his first campaign against Qūndūz and Ḥiṣār. He came to my presence when I went to Qūndūz in 916 AH. (1510 AD.), brutalized and stupefied, far from capable begship and out-side peaceful home-life. Such favour as he had had, he appears to have had for 'Alī-sher Beg's sake.

Mughūl Beg was another. He was Governor of Herī for a time, later on was given Astarābād, and from there fled to Ya'qūb Beg in 'Irāq. He was of amorous disposition [5] and an incessant dicer.

[1] This indicates, both amongst Musalmāns and Hindūs, obedience and submission. Several instances occur in Macculloch's *Bengali Household Stories*.

[2] T.R. p. 205.

[3] This is an idiom expressive of great keenness (Erskine).

[4] Ḥ.S. iii, 250, *kitābdār*, librarian; so too Ḥai. MS. f. 174*b*.

[5] *mutaiyam* (f. 7*b* and note). Mīr Mughūl Beg was put to death for treachery in 'Irāq (Ḥ.S. iii, 227, 248).

Sayyid Badr (Full-moon) was another, a very strong man, Fol. 173b. graceful in his movements and singularly well-mannered. He danced wonderfully well, doing one dance quite unique and seeming to be his own invention.[1] His whole service was with the Mīrzā whose comrade he was in wine and social pleasure.

Islīm *Barlās* was another, a plain (*turk*) person who understood hawking well and did some things to perfection. Drawing a bow of 30 to 40 *bātmāns* strength,[2] he would make his shaft pass right through the target (*takhta*). In the gallop from the head of the *qabaq-maidān*,[3] he would loosen his bow, string it again, and then hit the gourd (*qabaq*). He would tie his string-grip (*zih-gīr*) to the one end of a string from 1 to 1½ yards long, fasten the other end to a tree, let his shaft fly, and shoot through the string-grip while it revolved.[4] Many such remarkable feats he did. He served the Mīrzā continuously and was at every social gathering.

Sl. Junaid *Barlās* was another;[5] in his latter days he went to Sl. Aḥmad Mīrzā's presence.[6] He is the father of the Sl. Junaid *Barlās* on whom at the present time[7] the joint-government of Jaunpūr depends.

Shaikh Abū-sa'īd Khān *Dar-miyān* (In-between) was another. It is not known whether he got the name of Dar-miyān because he took a horse to the Mīrzā *in the middle* of a fight, or whether because he put himself *in between* the Mīrzā and some-one designing on his life.[8]

[1] Bābur speaks as an eye-witness (f. 187b). For a single combat of Sayyid Badr, Ḥ.S. iii, 233.

[2] f. 157 and note to *bātmān*.

[3] A level field in which a gourd (*qabaq*) is set on a pole for an archer's mark to be hit in passing at the gallop (f. 18b and note).

[4] Or possibly during the gallop the archer turned in the saddle and shot backwards.

[5] Junaid was the father of Niẓāmu'd-dīn 'Alī, Bābur's Khalīfa (Vice-gerent). That Khalīfa was of a religious house on his mother's side may be inferred from his being styled both Sayyid and Khwāja neither of which titles could have come from his Turkī father. His mother may have been a sayyida of one of the religious families of Marghīnān (f. 18 and note), since Khalīfa's son Muḥibb-i-'alī writes his father's name "Niẓāmu'd-dīn 'Alī *Marghīlānī*" (*Marghīnānī*) in the Preface of his *Book on Sport* (Rieu's Pers. Cat. p. 485).

[6] This northward migration would take the family into touch with Bābur's in Samarkand and Farghāna.

[7] He was left in charge of Jaunpūr in Rabī' I, 933 AH. (Jan. 1527 AD.) but exchanged for Chunār in Ramẓān 935 AH. (June 1529 AD.); so that for the writing of this part of the *Bābur-nāma* we have the major and minor limits of Jan. 1527 and June 1529.

[8] Ḥ.S. iii, 227.

Bih-būd Beg was another. He had served in the pages' circle (*chuhra jīrgasī*) during the guerilla times and gave such satisfaction by his service that the Mīrzā did him the favour of putting his name on the stamp (*tamghā*) and the coin (*sikka*).[1] Fol. 174.

Shaikhīm Beg was another.[2] People used to call him Shaikhīm *Suhailī* because Suhailī was his pen-name. He wrote all sorts of verse, bringing in terrifying words and mental images. Here is a couplet of his :—

> In the anguish of my nights, the whirlpool of my sighs engulphs the firmament;
> Like a dragon, the torrent of my tears swallows the quarters of the world.

Well-known it is that when he once recited that couplet in Maulānā 'Abdu'r-raḥmān *Jāmī's* presence, the honoured Mullā asked him whether he was reciting verse or frightening people. He put a *dīwān* together; *masnawīs* of his are also in existence.

Muḥammad-i-walī Beg was another, the son of the Walī Beg already mentioned. Latterly he became one of the Mīrzā's great begs but, great beg though he was, he never neglected his service and used to recline (*yāstānīb*) day and night in the Gate. Through doing this, his free meals and open table were always set just outside the Gate. Quite certainly a man who was so constantly in waiting, *would* receive the favour he received! It is an evil noticeable today that effort must be made before the man, dubbed Beg because he has five or six of the bald and blind at his back, can be got into the Gate at all! Where this sort of service is, it must be to their own misfortune! Muḥammad-i-walī Beg's public table and free meals were good; he kept his servants neat and well-dressed and with his own hands gave Fol. 174b ample portion to the poor and destitute, but he was foul-mouthed and evil-spoken. He and also Darwīsh-i-'alī the librarian were in my service when I took Samarkand in 917 AH. (Oct. 1511 AD.); he was palsied then; his talk lacked salt; his former claim to favour was gone. His assiduous waiting appears to have been the cause of his promotion.

[1] *See* Appendix H, *On the counter-mark Bih-būd on coins.*

[2] Niẓāmu'd-dīn Amīr Shaikh Aḥmadu's-suhailī was surnamed Suhailī through a *fāl* (augury) taken by his spiritual guide, Kamālu'd-dīn Ḥusain *Gāzur-gāhī*; it was he induced Ḥusain *Kashifī* to produce his *Anwār-i-suhailī* (Lights of Canopus) (f. 125 and note; Rieu's Pers. Cat. p. 756; and for a couplet of his, H.S. iii, 242 l. 10).

Bābā 'Alī the Lord of the Gate was another. First, 'Alī-sher Beg showed him favour; next, because of his courage, the Mīrzā took him into service, made him Lord of the Gate, and promoted him to be a beg. One of his sons is serving me now (*circa* 934 AH.), that Yūnas of 'Alī who is a beg, a confidant, and of my household. He will often be mentioned.[1]

Badru'd-dīn (Full-moon of the Faith) was another. He had been in the service of Sl. Abū-sa'īd Mīrzā's Chief Justice Mīrak 'Abdu'r-raḥīm; it is said he was very nimble and sure-footed, a man who could leap over seven horses at once. He and Bābā 'Alī were close companions.

Ḥasan of 'Alī *Jalāīr* was another. His original name was Ḥusain *Jalāīr* but he came to be called 'Alī's Hasan.[2] His father 'Alī *Jalāīr* must have been favoured and made a beg by Bābur Mīrzā; no man was greater later on when Yādgār-i-muḥammad M. took Herī. Ḥasan-i-'alī was Sl. Ḥusain Mīrzā's *Qūsh-begī*.[3] He made Ṭufailī (Uninvited-guest) his pen-name; wrote good odes and was the Master of this art in his day. He wrote odes on my name when he came to my presence at the time I took Samarkand in 917 AH. (1511 AD.). Impudent (*bī bāk*) and
Fol. 175. prodigal he was, a keeper of catamites, a constant dicer and draught-player.

Khwāja 'Abdu'l-lāh *Marwārīd* (Pearl)[4] was another; he was at first Chief Justice but later on became one of the Mīrzā's favourite household-begs. He was full of accomplishments; on the dulcimer he had no equal, and he invented the shake on the dulcimer; he wrote in several scripts, most beautifully in the *ta'līq*; he composed admirable letters, wrote good verse, with Bayānī for his pen-name, and was a pleasant companion. Compared with his other accomplishments, his verse ranks low, but he knew what was poetry. Vicious and shameless, he became

[1] Index *s.n.*

[2] Did the change complete an analogy between 'Alī *Jalāīr* and his (perhaps) elder son with 'Alī Khalīfa and his elder son Ḥasan?

[3] The Qūsh-begī is, in Central Asia, a high official who acts for an absent ruler (Shaw); he does not appear to be the Falconer, for whom Bābur's name is Qūshchī (f. 15 n.).

[4] He received this sobriquet because when he returned from an embassy to the Persian Gulf, he brought, from Bahrein, to his Tīmūrid master a gift of royal pearls (Sām Mīrzā). For an account of Marwārīd *see* Rieu's Pers. Cat. p. 1094 and (*re* portrait) p. 787.

the captive of a sinful disease through his vicious excesses, outlived his hands and feet, tasted the agonies of varied torture for several years, and departed from the world under that affliction.[1]

Sayyid Muḥammad-i-aūrūs was another; he was the son of that Aūrūs (Russian?) *Arghūn* who, when Sl. Abū-sa'īd Mīrzā took the throne, was his beg in chief authority. At that time there were excellent archer-braves; one of the most distinguished was Sayyid Muḥammad-i-aūrūs. His bow strong, his shaft long, he must have been a bold (*yūrak*) shot and a good one. He was Commandant in Andikhūd for some time.

Mīr (Qambar-i-)'alī the Master of the Horse was another. He it was who, by sending a man to Sl. Ḥusain Mīrzā, brought him down on the defenceless Yādgār-i-muḥammad Mīrzā.

Sayyid Ḥasan *Aūghlāqchī* was another, a son of Sayyid *Aūghlāqchī* and a younger brother of Sayyid Yūsuf Beg.[2] He was the father of a capable and accomplished son, named Mīrzā Farrukh. He had come to my presence before I took Samarkand in 917 AH. (1511 AD.). Though he had written little verse, he wrote fairly; he understood the astrolabe and astronomy well, was excellent company, his talk good too, but he was rather a bad drinker (*bad shrāb*). He died in the fight at Ghaj-dawān.[3] Fol. 175*b*.

Tīngrī-bīrdī the storekeeper (*sāmānchī*) was another; he was a plain (*turk*), bold, sword-slashing brave. As has been said, he charged out of the Gate of Balkh on Khusrau Shāh's great retainer Naẓar Bahādur and overcame him (903 AH.).

There were a few Turkmān braves also who were received with great favour when they came to the Mīrzā's presence. One of the first to come was 'Alī Khān *Bāyandar*.[4] Asad Beg and Taham-tan (Strong-bodied) Beg were others, an elder and younger brother these; Badī'u'z-zamān Mīrzā took Taham-tan Beg's daughter and by her had Muḥammad-i-zamān Mīrzā. Mīr 'Umar Beg was another; later on he was in Badī'u'z-zamān Mīrzā's service; he was a brave, plain, excellent person. His

[1] Sām Mīrzā specifies this affliction as *ābla-i-farang*, thus making what may be one of the earliest Oriental references to *morbus gallicus* [as de Saçy here translates the name], the foreign or European pox, the "French disease of Shakespeare" (H. B.).

[2] Index *s.n.* Yūsuf.

[3] Ramẓān 3rd 918 AH.-Nov. 12th 1512.

[4] *i.e.* of the White-sheep Turkmāns.

son, Abū'l-fatḥ by name, came from 'Irāq to my presence, a very soft, unsteady and feeble person; such a son from such a father!

Of those who came into Khurāsān after Shāh Ismā'īl took 'Irāq and Azarbāījān (*circa* 906 AH.–1500 AD.), one was 'Abdu'l-bāqī Mīrzā of Tīmūr Beg's line. He was a Mīrān-shāhī[1] whose ancestors will have gone long before into those parts, put thought
Fol. 176. of sovereignty out of their heads, served those ruling there, and from them have received favour. That Tīmūr 'Uṣmān who was the great, trusted beg of Ya'qūb Beg (*White-sheep Turkmān*) and who had once even thought of sending against Khurāsān the mass of men he had gathered to himself, must have been this 'Abdu'l-bāqī Mīrzā's paternal-uncle. Sl. Ḥusain Mīrzā took 'Abdu'l-bāqī Mīrzā at once into favour, making him a son-in-law by giving him Sulṭānīm Begīm, the mother of Muḥammad Sl. Mīrzā.[2] Another late-comer was Murād Beg *Bāyandarī.*

(*h. His Chief Justices* (*ṣadūr*).)

One was Mīr Sar-i-barahna (Bare-head)[3]; he was from a village in Andijān and appears to have made claim to be a sayyid (*mutasayyid*). He was a very agreeable companion, pleasant of temper and speech. His were the judgment and rulings that carried weight amongst men of letters and poets of Khurāsān. He wasted his time by composing, in imitation of the story of Amīr Ḥamza,[4] a work which is one long, far-fetched lie, opposed to sense and nature.

Kamālu'd-dīn Ḥusain *Gāzur-gāhī*[5] was another. Though not a Ṣūfī, he was mystical.[6] Such mystics as he will have

[1] His paternal line was, 'Abdu'l-bāqī, son of 'Uṣmān, son of Sayyidī Aḥmad, son of Mīrān-shāh. His mother's people were begs of the White-sheep (Ḥ.S. iii, 290).

[2] Sulṭānīm had married Wais (f. 157) not later than 895 or 896 AH. (Ḥ.S. iii, 253); she married 'Abdu'l-bāqī in 908 AH. (1502–3 AD.).

[3] Sayyid Shamsu'd-dīn Muḥammad, Mīr Sayyid *Sar-i-barahna* owed his sobriquet of Bare-head to love-sick wanderings of his youth (Ḥ.S. iii, 328). The Ḥ.S. it is clear, recognizes him as a sayyid.

[4] Rieu's Pers. Cat. p. 760; it is immensely long and "filled with tales that shock all probability" (Erskine).

[5] f. 94 and note. Sl. Ḥusain M. made him curator of Anṣārī's shrine, an officer represented, presumably, by Col. Yate's "Mīr of Gāzur-gāh", and he became Chief Justice in 904 AH. (1498–99 AD.). *See* Ḥ.S. iii, 330 and 340; JASB 1887, art. *On the city of Harāt* (C. E. Yate) p. 85.

[6] *mutasauwif*, perhaps meaning not a professed Ṣūfī.

gathered in 'Alī-sher Beg's presence and there have gone into their raptures and ecstacies. Kamālu'd-dīn will have been better-born than most of them; his promotion will have been due to his good birth, since he had no other merit to speak of.[1] A production of his exists, under the name *Majālisu'l-'ushshāq* (Assemblies of lovers), the authorship of which he ascribes (in its preface) to Sl. Ḥusain Mīrzā.[2] It is mostly a lie and a tasteless lie. He has written such irreverent things in it that some Fol. 176*b*. of them cast doubt upon his orthodoxy; for example, he represents the Prophets,—Peace be on them,—and Saints as subject to earthly passion, and gives to each a minion and a mistress. Another and singularly absurd thing is that, although in his preface he says, "This is Sl. Ḥusain Mīrzā's own written word and literary composition," he, never-the-less, enters, in the body of the book, "All by the sub-signed author", at the head of odes and verses well-known to be his own. It was his flattery gave Ẕū'n-nūn *Arghūn* the title Lion of God.

(*i. His wazīrs.*)

One was Majdu'd-dīn Muḥammad, son of Khwāja Pīr Aḥmad of Khwāf, the one man (*yak-qalam*) of Shāhrukh Mīrzā's Finance-office.[3] In Sl. Ḥusain Mīrzā's Finance-office there was not at first proper order or method; waste and extravagance resulted; the peasant did not prosper, and the soldier was not satisfied. Once while Majdu'd-dīn Muḥammad was still *parwānchī*[4] and styled Mīrak (Little Mīr), it became a matter of importance to the Mīrzā to have some money; when he asked the Finance-officials for it, they said none had been collected and that there was none. Majdu'd-dīn Muḥammad must have heard this and have smiled, for the Mīrzā asked him why he smiled; privacy was made and he told Mīrzā what was in his mind.

[1] He was of high birth on both sides, of religious houses of Ṯabas and Nishāpūr (D.S. pp. 161, 163).

[2] In agreement with its preface, Dr. Rieu entered the book as written by Sl. Ḥusain Mīrzā; in his Addenda, however, he quotes Bābur as the authority for its being by Gāzur-gāhī; Khwānd-amīr's authority can be added to Bābur's (Ḥ.S. 340; Pers. Cat. pp. 351, 1085).

[3] *Dīwān*. The Wazīr is a sort of Minister of Finance; the Dīwān is the office of revenue receipts and issues (Erskine).

[4] a secretary who writes out royal orders (Ḥ.S. iii, 244).

Said he, "If the honoured Mīrzā will pledge himself to strengthen
Fol. 177. my hands by not opposing my orders, it shall so be before long that the country shall prosper, the peasant be content, the soldier well-off, and the Treasury full." The Mīrzā for his part gave the pledge desired, put Majdu'd-dīn Muḥammad in authority throughout Khurāsān, and entrusted all public business to him. He in his turn by using all possible diligence and effort, before long had made soldier and peasant grateful and content, filled the Treasury to abundance, and made the districts habitable and cultivated. He did all this however in face of opposition from the begs and men high in place, all being led by 'Alī-sher Beg, all out of temper with what Majdu'd-dīn Muḥammad had effected. By their effort and evil suggestion he was arrested and dismissed.[1] In succession to him Niẓāmu'l-mulk of Khwāf was made Dīwān but in a short time they got him arrested also, and him they got put to death.[2] They then brought Khwāja Afẓal out of 'Irāq and made him Dīwān; he had just been made a beg when I came to Kābul (910 AH.), and he also impressed the Seal in Dīwān.

Khwāja 'Atā[3] was another; although, unlike those already mentioned, he was not in high office or Finance-minister (*dīwān*) nothing was settled without his concurrence the whole Khurasānāt over. He was a pious, praying, upright (*mutadaiyin*) person; he must have been diligent in business also.

[1] Count von Noer's words about a cognate reform of later date suit this man's work, it also was "a bar to the defraudment of the Crown, a stumbling-block in the path of avaricious chiefs" (*Emperor Akbar* trs. i, 11). The opposition made by 'Alī-sher to reform so clearly to Ḥusain's gain and to Ḥusain's begs' loss, stirs the question, "What was the source of his own income?" Up to 873 AH. he was for some years the dependant of Aḥmad Ḥājī Beg; he took nothing from the Mīrzā, but gave to him; he must have spent much in benefactions. The question may have presented itself to M. Belin for he observes, "'Alī-sher qui sans doute, à son retour de l'exil, recouvra l'héritage de ses pères, et depuis occupa de hautes positions dans le gouvernement de son pays, avait acquis une grande fortune" (*J. Asiatique* xvii, 227). While not contradicting M. Belin's view that vested property such as can be described as "paternal inheritance", may have passed from father to son, even in those days of fugitive prosperity and changing appointments, one cannot but infer, from Nawā'ī's opposition to Majdu'd-dīn, that he, like the rest, took a partial view of the "rights" of the cultivator.

[2] This was in 903 AH. after some 20 years of service (Ḥ.S. iii, 231; Ethé I.O. Cat. p. 252).

[3] Amīr Jamālu'd-dīn 'Atā'u'l-lāh, known also as Jamālu'd-dīn Ḥusain, wrote a *History of Muhammad* (Ḥ.S. iii, 345; Rieu's Pers. Cat. p. 147 & (a correction) p. 1081).

(*j. Others of the Court.*)

Those enumerated were Sl. Ḥusain Mīrzā's retainers and followers.[1] His was a wonderful Age; in it Khurāsān, and Herī above all, was full of learned and matchless men. Whatever the work a man took up, he aimed and aspired at bringing that work to perfection. One such man was Maulānā 'Abdu'r-raḥmān *Jāmī*, who was unrivalled in his day for esoteric and exoteric knowledge. Famous indeed are his poems! The Mullā's dignity it is out of my power to describe; it has occurred to me merely to mention his honoured name and one atom of his excellence, as a benediction and good omen for this part of my humble book. Fol. 177b.

Shaikhu'l-islām Saifu'd-dīn Aḥmad was another. He was of the line of that Mullā Sa'du'd-dīn (Mas'ūd) *Taftazānī*[2] whose descendants from his time downwards have given the Shaikhu'l-islām to Khurāsān. He was a very learned man, admirably versed in the Arabian sciences[3] and the Traditions, most God-fearing and orthodox. Himself a Shafi'ī,[4] he was tolerant of all the sects. People say he never once in 70 years omitted the Congregational Prayer. He was martyred when Shāh Ismā'īl took Herī (916 AH.); there now remains no man of his honoured line.[5]

Maulānā Shaikh Ḥusain was another; he is mentioned here, although his first appearance and his promotion were under Sl. Abū-sa'īd Mīrzā, because he was living still under Sl. Ḥusain Mīrzā. Being well-versed in the sciences of philosophy, logic and rhetoric, he was able to find much meaning in a few words and to bring it out opportunely in conversation. Being very intimate and influential with Sl. Abū-sa'īd Mīrzā, he took part in all momentous affairs of the Mīrzā's dominions; there was Fol. 178.

[1] Amongst noticeable omissions from Bābur's list of Herī celebrities are Mīr Khwānd Shāh ("Mirkhond"), his grandson Khwānd-amīr, Ḥusain *Kashifī* and Muinu'd-dīn al Zamjī, author of a *History of Harāt* which was finished in 897 AH.

[2] Sa'du'd-dīn Mas'ūd, son of 'Umar, was a native of Taft in Yazd, whence his cognomen (Bahār-i-'ajam); he died in 792 AH.-1390 AD. (Ḥ.S. iii, 59, 343; T.R. p. 236; Rieu's Pers. Cat. pp. 352, 453).

[3] These are those connected with grammar and rhetoric (Erskine).

[4] This is one of the four principal sects of Muhammadanism (Erskine).

[5] T.R. p. 235, for Shāh Ismā'īl's murders in Herī.

no better *muḥtasib*[1]; this will have been why he was so much trusted. Because he had been an intimate of that Mīrzā, the incomparable man was treated with insult in Sl. Ḥusain Mīrzā's time.

Mullā-zāda Mullā 'Uṣmān was another. He was a native of Chīrkh, in the Luhūgur *tūmān* of the *tūmān* of Kābul[2] and was called the Born Mullā (*Mullā-zāda*) because in Aūlūgh Beg Mīrzā's time he used to give lessons when 14 years old. He went to Herī on his way from Samarkand to make the circuit of the *ka'ba*, was there stopped, and made to remain by Sl. Ḥusain Mīrzā. He was very learned, the most so of his time. People say he was nearing the rank of Ijtihād[3] but he did not reach it. It is said of him that he once asked, "How should a person forget a thing heard?" A strong memory he must have had!

Mīr Jamālu'd-dīn the Traditionalist[4] was another. He had no equal in Khurāsān for knowledge of the Muḥammadan Traditions. He was advanced in years and is still alive (934 to 937 AH.).

Mīr Murtāẓ was another. He was well-versed in the sciences Fol. 178*b*. of philosophy and metaphysics; he was called *murtāẓ* (ascetic) because he fasted a great deal. He was madly fond of chess, so much so that if he had met two players, he would hold one by the skirt while he played his game out with the other, as much as to say, "Don't go!"

Mīr Mas'ūd of Sherwān was another.[5]

Mīr 'Abdu'l-ghafūr of Lār was another. Disciple and pupil both of Maulānā 'Abdu'r-raḥmān *Jāmī*, he had read aloud most of the Mullā's poems (*maṣnawī*) in his presence, and wrote a plain exposition of the *Nafaḥāt*.[6] He had good acquaintance

[1] Superintendent of Police, who examines weights, measures and provisions, also prevents gambling, drinking and so on.

[2] f. 137.

[3] The rank of Mujtahid, which is not bestowed by any individual or class of men but which is the result of slow and imperceptible opinion, finally prevailing and universally acknowledged, is one of the greatest peculiarities of the religion of Persia. The Mujtahid is supposed to be elevated above human fears and human enjoyments, and to have a certain degree of infallibility and inspiration. He is consulted with reverence and awe. There is not always a Mujtahid necessarily existing. *See* Kaempfer, *Amoenitates Exoticae* (Erskine).

[4] *muḥaddaṣ*, one versed in the traditional sayings and actions of Muḥammad.

[5] Ḥ.S. iii, 340.

[6] B.M. Or. 218 (Rieu's Pers. Cat. p. 350). The Commentary was made in order to explain the *Nafaḥāt* to Jāmī's son.

with the exoteric sciences, and in the esoteric ones also was very successful. He was a curiously casual and unceremonious person; no person styled Mullā by any-one soever was debarred from submitting a (Qorān) chapter to him for exposition; moreover whatever the place in which he heard there was a darwīsh, he had no rest till he had reached that darwīsh's presence. He was ill when I was in Khurāsān (912 AH.); I went to enquire for him where he lay in the Mullā's College,[1] after I had made the circuit of the Mullā's tomb. He died a few days later, of that same illness.

Mīr 'Atā'u'l-lāh of Mashhad was another.[2] He knew the Arabian sciences well and also wrote a Persian treatise on rhyme. That treatise is well-done but it has the defect that he brings into it, as his examples, couplets of his own and, assuming them Fol. 179.
to be correct, prefixes to each, "As must be observed in the following couplet by your slave" (*banda*). Several rivals of his find deserved comment in this treatise. He wrote another on the curiosities of verse, entitled *Badāi'u's-sanāi*; a very well-written treatise. He may have swerved from the Faith.

Qāẓī Ikhtiyār was another. He was an excellent Qāẓī and wrote a treatise in Persian on Jurisprudence, an admirable treatise; he also, in order to give elucidation (*iqtibās*), made a collection of homonymous verses from the Qorān. He came with Muḥammad-i-yūsuf to see me at the time I met the Mīrzās on the Murgh-āb (912 AH.). Talk turning on the Bāburī script,[3] he asked me about it, letter by letter; I wrote it out, letter by letter; he went through it, letter by letter, and having learned its plan, wrote something in it there and then.

Mīr Muḥammad-i-yūsuf was another; he was a pupil of the Shaikhu'l-islām[4] and afterwards was advanced to his place. In some assemblies he, in others, Qāẓī Ikhtiyār took the higher place. Towards the end of his life he was so infatuated

[1] He was buried by the Mullā's side.

[2] Amīr Burhānu'd-dīn 'Atā'u'l-lāh bin Maḥmūdu'l-ḥusainī was born in Nishāpūr but known as Mashhadī because he retired to that holy spot after becoming blind.

[3] f. 144*b* and note. Qāẓī Ikhtiyāru'd-dīn Ḥasan (Ḥ.S. iii, 347) appears to be the Khwāja Ikhtiyār of the *Āyīn-i-akbarī*, and, if so, will have taken professional interest in the script, since Abū'l-faẓl describes him as a distinguished calligrapher in Sl. Ḥusain M.'s presence (Blochmann, p. 101).

[4] Saifu'd-dīn (Sword of the Faith) Aḥmad, presumably.

with soldiering and military command, that except of those two tasks, what could be learned from his conversation? what known from his pen? Though he failed in both, those two ambitions ended by giving to the winds his goods and his life, his house and his home. He may have been a Shī'a.

(*k. The Poets.*)

Fol. 179*b*. The all-surpassing head of the poet-band was Maulānā 'Abdu'r-raḥmān *Jāmī*. Others were Shaikhīm Suhailī and Ḥasan of 'Alī *Jalāīr*[1] whose names have been mentioned already as in the circle of the Mīrzā's begs and household.

Āṣafī was another,[2] he taking Āṣafī for his pen-name because he was a wazīr's son. His verse does not want for grace or sentiment, but has no merit through passion and ecstacy. He himself made the claim, "I have never packed up (*būlmādī*) my odes to make the oasis (*wādī*) of a collection."[3] This was affectation, his younger brothers and his intimates having collected his odes. He wrote little else but odes. He waited on me when I went into Khurāsān (912 AH.).

Banā'i was another; he was a native of Herī and took such a pen-name (Banā'i) on account of his father Ustād Muḥammad *Sabz-banā*.[4] His odes have grace and ecstacy. One poem (*maṣnawī*) of his on the topic of fruits, is in the *mutaqārib* measure;[5] it is random and not worked up. Another short poem is in the *khafīf* measure, so also is a longer one finished towards the end of his life. He will have known nothing of music in his young days and 'Alī-sher Beg seems to have taunted him about it, so one winter when the Mīrzā, taking 'Alī-sher Beg

[1] A sister of his, Apāq Bega, the wife of 'Alī-sher's brother Darwīsh-i-'alī *kitābdār*, is included as a poet in the *Biography of Ladies* (Sprenger's Cat. p. 11). Amongst the 20 women named one is a wife of Shaibāq Khān, another a daughter of Hilālī.

[2] He was the son of Khw. Ni'amatu'l-lāh, one of Sl. Abū-sa'īd M.'s wazīrs. When dying *aet.* 70 (923 AH.), he made this chronogram on his own death, "With 70 steps he measured the road to eternity." The name Āsaf, so frequent amongst wazīrs, is that of Solomon's wazīr.

[3] Other interpretations are open; *wādī*, taken as *river*, might refer to the going on from one poem to another, the stream of verse; or it might be taken as *desert*, with disparagement of collections.

[4] Maulānā Jamālu'd-dīn *Banā'i* was the son of a *sabz-banā*, an architect, a good builder.

[5] Steingass's Dictionary allows convenient reference for examples of metres.

with him, went to winter in Merv, Banā'i stayed behind in Herī and so applied himself to study music that before the heats he had composed several works. These he played and sang, airs with variations, when the Mīrzā came back to Herī in the heats. Fol. 180.
All amazed, 'Alī-sher Beg praised him. His musical compositions are perfect; one was an air known as *Nuh-rang* (Nine modulations), and having both the theme (*tūkānash*) and the variation (*yīla*) on the note called *rāst* (?). Banā'i was 'Alī-sher Beg's rival; it will have been on this account he was so much ill-treated. When at last he could bear it no longer, he went into Āzarbāījān and 'Irāq to the presence of Ya'qūb Beg; he did not remain however in those parts after Ya'qūb Beg's death (896 AH.–1491 AD.) but went back to Herī, just the same with his jokes and retorts. Here is one of them:—'Alī-sher at a chess-party in stretching his leg touched Banā'i on the hinder-parts and said jestingly, "It is the sad nuisance of Herī that a man can't stretch his leg without its touching a poet's backside." "Nor draw it up again," retorted Banā'i.[1] In the end the upshot of his jesting was that he had to leave Herī again; he went then to Samarkand.[2] A great many good new things used to be made for 'Alī-sher Beg, so whenever any-one produced a novelty, he called it 'Alī-sher's in order to give it credit and vogue.[3] Some things were called after him in compliment *e.g.* because when he had ear-ache, he wrapped his head up in one of the blue triangular kerchiefs women tie over their heads in winter, that kerchief was called 'Alī-sher's comforter. Then again, Banā'i when he had decided to leave Herī, ordered a quite new kind of pad for his ass and Fol. 180b.
dubbed it 'Alī-sher's.

1 Other jokes made by *Banā'i* at the expense of Nawā'i are recorded in the various sources.

2 Bābur saw Banā'i in Samarkand at the end of 901 AH. (1496 AD. f. 38).

Here Dr. Leyden's translation ends; one other fragment which he translated will be found under the year 925 AH. (Erskine). This statement allows attention to be drawn to the inequality of the shares of the work done for the Memoirs of 1826 by Leyden and by Erskine. It is just to Mr. Erskine, but a justice he did not claim, to point out that Dr. Leyden's share is slight both in amount and in quality; his essential contribution was the initial stimulus he gave to the great labours of his collaborator.

3 So of Lope de Vega (b. 1562; d. 1635 AD.), "It became a common proverb to praise a good thing by calling it *a Lope*, so that jewels, diamonds, pictures, *etc.* were raised into esteem by calling them his" (Montalvan in Ticknor's *Spanish Literature* ii, 270).

Maulāṇā Saifī of Bukhārā was another;[1] he was a Mullā complete[2] who in proof of his mullā-ship used to give a list of the books he had read. He put two *dīwāns* together, one being for the use of tradesmen (*ḥarfa-kar*), and he also wrote many fables. That he wrote no *maṣnawī* is shewn by the following quatrain:—

Though the *maṣnawī* be the orthodox verse,
I know the ode has Divine command;
Five couplets that charm the heart
I know to outmatch the Two Quintets.[3]

A Persian prosody he wrote is at once brief and prolix, brief in the sense of omitting things that should be included, and prolix in the sense that plain and simple matters are detailed down to the diacritical points, down even to their Arabic points.[4] He is said to have been a great drinker, a bad drinker, and a mightily strong-fisted man.

'Abdu'l-lāh the *maṣnawī*-writer was another.[5] He was from Jām and was the Mullā's sister's son. Hātifī was his pen-name. He wrote poems (*maṣnawī*) in emulation of the Two Quintets,[6] and called them *Haft-manẓar* (Seven-faces) in imitation of the *Haft-paikar* (Seven-faces). In emulation of the *Sikandar-nāma* he composed the *Tīmūr-nāma*. His most renowned *maṣnawī* is *Laila and Majnūn*, but its reputation is greater than its charm.

Mīr Ḥusain the Enigmatist[7] was another. He seems to have had no equal in making riddles, to have given his whole time to it, and to have been a curiously humble, disconsolate (*nā-murād*)
Fol. 181. and harmless (*bī-bad*) person.

Mīr Muḥammad *Badakhshī* of Ishkīmīsh was another. As Ishkīmīsh is not in Badakhshān, it is odd he should have made it

[1] Maulānā Saifī, known as 'Arūẓī from his mastery in prosody (Rieu's Pers. Cat. p. 525).
[2] Here pedantry will be implied in the mullahood.
[3] *Khamsatīn* (*infra* f. 180*b* and note).
[4] This appears to mean that not only the sparse diacritical pointing common in writing Persian was dealt with but also the fuller Arabic.
[5] He is best known by his pen-name Hātifī. The B.M. and I.O. have several of his books.
[6] *Khamsatīn*. Hātifī regarded himself as the successor of Niẓāmī and Khusrau; this, taken with Bābur's use of the word *Khamsatīn* on f. 7 and here, and Saifī's just above, leads to the opinion that the *Khamsatīn* of the *Bābur-nāma* are always those of Niẓāmī and Khusrau, *the* Two Quintets (Rieu's Pers. Cat. p. 653).
[7] Maulānā Mīr Kamālu'd-dīn Ḥusain of Nishāpūr (Rieu l.c. index s.n.; Ethé's I.O. Cat. pp. 433 and 1134).

his pen-name. His verse does not rank with that of the poets previously mentioned,[1] and though he wrote a treatise on riddles, his riddles are not first-rate. He was a very pleasant companion; he waited on me in Samarkand (917 AH.).

Yūsuf the wonderful (*badī*)[2] was another. He was from the Farghāna country; his odes are said not to be bad.

Āhī was another, a good ode-writer, latterly in Ibn-i-ḥusain Mīrzā's service, and *ṣāḥib-i-dīwān*.[3]

Muḥammad *Ṣāliḥ* was another.[4] His odes are tasty but better-flavoured than correct. There is Turkī verse of his also, not badly written. He went to Shaibāq Khān later on and found complete favour. He wrote a Turkī poem (*maṣnawī*), named from Shaibāq Khān, in the *raml masaddas majnūn* measure, that is to say the metre of the *Subḥat*.[5] It is feeble and flat; Muḥammad *Ṣāliḥ*'s reader soon ceases to believe in him.[6] Here is one of his good couplets:—

> A fat man (Tambal) has gained the land of Farghāna,
> Making Farghāna the house of the fat-man (Tambal-khāna).

Farghāna is known also as Tambal-khāna.[7] I do not know whether the above couplet is found in the *maṣnawī* mentioned.

[1] One of his couplets on good and bad fortune is striking; "The fortune of men is like a sand-glass; one hour up, the next down." *See* D'Herbélot in his article (Erskine).

[2] Ḥ.S. iii, 336; Rieu's Pers. Cat. p. 1089.

[3] Āhī (sighing) was with Shāh-i-gharīb before Ibn-i-ḥusain and to him dedicated his *dīwān*. The words *ṣāḥib-i-dīwān* seem likely to be used here with double meaning *i.e.* to express authorship and finance office. Though Bābur has made frequent mention of authorship of a *dīwān* and of office in the *Dīwān*, he has not used these words hitherto in either sense; there may be a play of words here.

[4] Muḥammad *Ṣāliḥ* Mīrzā *Khwārizmī*, author of the *Shaibānī-nāma* which manifestly is the poem (*maṣnawī*) mentioned below. This has been published with a German translation by Professor Vambéry and has been edited with Russian notes by Mr. Platon Melioransky (Rieu's Turkish Cat. p. 74; Ḥ.S. iii, 301).

[5] Jāmī's *Subḥatu'l-abrār* (Rosary of the righteous).

[6] The reference may be to things said by Muḥ. *Ṣāliḥ* the untruth of which was known to Bābur through his own part in the events. A crying instance of misrepresentation is Ṣāliḥ's assertion, in rhetorical phrase, that Bābur took booty in jewels from Khusrau Shāh; other instances concern the affairs of The Khāns and of Bābur in Transoxiana (f. 124*b* and index *s.nn.* Aḥmad and Maḥmūd *Chaghatāī etc.*; T.R. index *s.nn.*).

[7] The name Fat-land (Tambal-khāna) has its parallel in Fat-village (Sīmīz-kīnt) a name of Samarkand; in both cases the nick-name is accounted for by the fertility of irrigated lands. We have not been able to find the above-quoted couplet in the *Shaibānī-nāma* (Vambéry); needless to say, the pun is on the nick-name [*tambal*, fat] of Sl. Aḥmad *Tambal*.

Muḥammad *Ṣāliḥ* was a very wicked, tyrannical and heartless person.[1]

Maulānā Shāh Ḥusain *Kāmī*[2] was another. There are not-bad verses of his; he wrote odes, and also seems to have put a *dīwān* together.

Hilālī (New-moon) was another; he is still alive.[3] Correct and graceful though his odes are, they make little impression. There is a *dīwān* of his;[4] and there is also the poem (*maṣnawī*) in the
Fol. 181*b*. *khafīf* measure, entitled *Shāh and Darwīsh* of which, fair though many couplets are, the basis and purport are hollow and bad. Ancient poets when writing of love and the lover, have represented the lover as a man and the beloved as a woman; but Hilālī has made the lover a darwīsh, the beloved a king, with the result that the couplets containing the king's acts and words set him forth as shameless and abominable. It is an extreme effrontery in Hilālī that for a poem's sake he should describe a young man and that young man a king, as resembling the shameless and immoral.[5] It is heard-said that Hilālī had a very retentive memory, and that he had by heart 30 or 40,000 couplets, and the greater part of the Two Quintets,—all most useful for the minutiae of prosody and the art of verse.

Ahlī[6] was another; he was of the common people (*'āmī*), wrote verse not bad, even produced a *dīwān*.

[1] Muḥ. Ṣāliḥ does not show well in his book; he is sometimes coarse, gloats over spoil whether in human captives or goods, and, his good-birth not-forbidding, is a servile flatterer. Bābur's word "heartless" is just; it must have had sharp prompting from Ṣāliḥ's rejoicing in the downfall of The Khāns, Bābur's uncles.

[2] the Longer (Ḥ.S. iii, 349).

[3] Maulānā Badru'd-dīn (Full-moon of the Faith) whose pen-name was Hilālī, was of Astarābād. It may be noted that two dates of his death are found, 936 and 939 AH. the first given by de Saçy, the second by Rieu, and that the second seems to be correct (*Not. et Extr.* p. 285; Pers. Cat. p. 656; Hammer's *Geschichte* p. 368).

[4] B.M. Add. 7783.

[5] Opinions differ as to the character of this work:—Bābur's is uncompromising; von Hammer (p. 369) describes it as "*ein romantisches Gedicht, welches eine sentimentale Männerliebe behandelt*"; Sprenger (p. 427), as a mystical *maṣnawī* (poem); Rieu finds no spiritual symbolism in it and condemns it (Pers. Cat. p. 656 and, quoting the above passage of Bābur, p. 1090); Ethé, who has translated it, takes it to be mystical and symbolic (I.O. Cat. p. 783).

[6] Of four writers using the pen-name Ahlī (Of-the-people), *viz.* those of Turān, Shīrāz, Tarshīz (in Khurāsān), and 'Irāq, the one noticed here seems to be he of Tarshīz. Ahlī of Tarshīz was the son of a locally-known pious father and became a Superintendent of the Mint; Bābur's *'āmī* may refer to Ahlī's first patrons, tanners and shoe-makers by writing for whom he earned his living (Sprenger, p. 319). Erskine read *'ummī*, meaning that Ahlī could neither read nor write; de Courteille that he was *un homme du commun*.

(*l. Artists.*)

Of fine pen-men there were many; the one standing-out in *nakhsh ta'līq* was Sl. 'Alī of Mashhad[1] who copied many books for the Mīrzā and for 'Alī-sher Beg, writing daily 30 couplets for the first, 20 for the second.

Of the painters, one was Bih-zād.[2] His work was very dainty but he did not draw beardless faces well; he used greatly to lengthen the double chin (*ghab-ghab*); bearded faces he drew admirably.

Shāh Muzaffar was another; he painted dainty portraits, representing the hair very daintily.[3] Short life was granted him; he left the world when on his upward way to fame. Fol. 182

Of musicians, as has been said, no-one played the dulcimer so well as Khwāja 'Abdu'l-lāh *Marwārīd.*

Qul-i-muhammad the lutanist (*'aūdī*) was another; he also played the guitar (*ghichak*) beautifully and added three strings to it. For many and good preludes (*peshrau*) he had not his equal amongst composers or performers, but this is only true of his preludes.

Shaikhī the flautist (*nāyī*) was another; it is said he played also the lute and the guitar, and that he had played the flute from his 12th or 13th year. He once produced a wonderful air on the flute, at one of Badī'u'z-zamān Mīrzā's assemblies; Qul-i-muhammad could not reproduce it on the guitar, so declared this a worthless instrument; Shaikhī *Nāyī* at once took the guitar from Qul-i-muhammad's hands and played the air on it, well and in perfect tune. They say he was so expert in music that having once heard an air, he was able to say, "This or that is the tune of so-and-so's or so-and-so's flute."[4] He composed few works; one or two airs are heard of.

Shāh Qulī the guitar-player was another; he was of 'Irāq, came into Khurāsān, practised playing, and succeeded. He composed many airs, preludes and works (*nakhsh, peshrau u aīshlār*).

[1] He was an occasional poet (H.S. iii, 350 and iv, 118; Rieu's Pers. Cat. p. 531; Ethé's I.O. Cat. p. 428).

[2] Ustād Kamālu'd-dīn Bih-zād (well-born; H.S. iii, 350). Work of his is reproduced in Dr. Martin's *Painting and Painters of Persia* of 1913 AD.

[3] This sentence is not in the Elph. MS.

[4] Perhaps he could reproduce tunes heard and say where heard.

Ḥusain the lutanist was another; he composed and played with taste; he would twist the strings of his lute into one and play on that. His fault was affectation about playing. He Fol. 182*b*. made a fuss once when Shaibāq Khān ordered him to play, and not only played badly but on a worthless instrument he had brought in place of his own. The Khān saw through him at once and ordered him to be well beaten on the neck, there and then. This was the one good action Shaibāq Khān did in the world; it was well-done truly! a worse chastisement is the due of such affected mannikins!

Ghulām-i-shādī (Slave of Festivity), the son of Shādī the reciter, was another of the musicians. Though he performed, he did it less well than those of the circle just described. There are excellent themes (*ṣūt*) and beautiful airs (*nakhsh*) of his; no-one in his day composed such airs and themes. In the end Shaibāq Khān sent him to the Qāzān Khān, Muḥammad Amīn; no further news has been heard of him.

Mīr Azū was another composer, not a performer; he produced few works but those few were in good taste.

Banā'i was also a musical composer; there are excellent airs and themes of his.

An unrivalled man was the wrestler Muḥammad Bū-sa'īd; he was foremost amongst the wrestlers, wrote verse too, composed themes and airs, one excellent air of his being in *chār-gāh* (four-time),—and he was pleasant company. It is extraordinary that such accomplishments as his should be combined with wrestling.[1]

HISTORICAL NARRATIVE RESUMED.

(*a. Burial of Sl. Ḥusain Mīrzā.*)

At the time Sl. Ḥusain Mīrzā took his departure from the world, there were present of the Mīrzās only Badī'u'z-zamān Mīrzā and Muẓaffar-i-ḥusain Mīrzā. The latter had been his father's favourite son; his leading beg was Muḥammad Barandūq *Barlās*; his mother Khadīja Begīm had been the Mīrzā's most

[1] M. Belin quotes quatrains exchanged by 'Alī-sher and this man (*J. Asiatique* xvii. 199).

influential wife; and to him the Mīrzā's people had gathered. Fol. 183. For these reasons Badī'u'z-zamān Mīrzā had anxieties and thought of not coming,[1] but Muẓaffar-i-ḥusain Mīrzā and Muḥammad Barandūq Beg themselves rode out, dispelled his fears and brought him in.

Sl. Ḥusain Mīrzā was carried into Herī and there buried in his own College with royal rites and ceremonies.

(b. A dual succession.)

At this crisis Ẕū'n-nūn Beg was also present. He, Muḥ. Barandūq Beg, the late Mīrzā's begs and those of the two (young) Mīrzās having assembled, decided to make the two Mīrzās joint-rulers in Herī. Ẕū'n-nūn Beg was to have control in Badī'u'z-zamān Mīrzā's Gate, Muḥ. Barandūq Beg, in Muẓaffar-i-ḥusain Mīrzā's. Shaikh 'Alī Ṭaghāī was to be *dārogha* in Herī for the first, Yūsuf-i-'alī for the second. Theirs was a strange plan! Partnership in rule is a thing unheard of; against it stand Shaikh Sa'dī's words in the Gulistān:—"Ten darwishes sleep under a blanket (*gilīm*); two kings find no room in a clime" (*aqlīm*).[2]

[1] *i.e.* from his own camp to Bābā Ilāhī.

[2] f. 121 has a fuller quotation. On the dual succession, *see* T.R. p. 196.

912 AH.—MAY 24TH 1506 TO MAY 13TH 1507 AD.[1]

(*a. Bābur starts to join Sl. Ḥusain Mīrzā.*)

In the month of Muḥarram we set out by way of Ghūr-bund
Fol. 183*b*. and Shibr-tū to oppose the Aūzbeg.

As Jahāngīr Mīrzā had gone out of the country in some sort of displeasure, we said, "There might come much mischief and trouble if he drew the clans (*aīmāq*) to himself;" and "What trouble might come of it!" and, "First let's get the clans in hand!" So said, we hurried forward, riding light and leaving the baggage (*aūrūq*) at Ushtur-shahr in charge of Walī the treasurer and Daulat-qadam of the scouts. That day we reached Fort Ẓaḥāq; from there we crossed the pass of the Little-dome (Gumbazak-kūtal), trampled through Sāīghān, went over the Dandān-shikan pass and dismounted in the meadow of Kāhmard. From Kāhmard we sent Sayyid Afẓal the Seer-of-dreams (*Khwāb-bīn*) and Sl. Muḥammad *Dūldāī* to Sl. Ḥusain Mīrzā with a letter giving the particulars of our start from Kābul.[2]

Jahāngīr Mīrzā must have lagged on the road, for when he got opposite Bāmīān and went with 20 or 30 persons to visit it, he saw near it the tents of our people left with the baggage. Thinking we were there, he and his party hurried back to their camp and, without an eye to anything, without regard for their own people marching in the rear, made off for Yaka-aūlāng.[3]

(*b. Action of Shaibāq Khān.*)

When Shaibāq Khān had laid siege to Balkh, in which was Sl. Qul-i-nachāq,[4] he sent two or three sulṭāns with 3 or 4000 men to overrun Badakhshān. At the time Mubārak Shāh and

[1] Elph. MS. f. 144; W.-i-B. I.O. 215 f. 148*b* and 217 f. 125*b*; Mems. p. 199.

[2] News of Ḥusain's death in 911 AH. (f. 163*b*) did not reach Bābur till 912 AH. (f. 184*b*).

[3] Lone-meadow (f. 195*b*). Jahāngīr will have come over the 'Irāq-pass, Bābur's baggage-convoy, by Shibr-tū. Cf. T.R. p. 199 for Bābur and Jahāngīr at this time.

[4] Servant-of-the-mace; but perhaps, Qilinj-chāq, swords-man.

Zubair had again joined Nāṣir Mīrzā, spite of former resentments and bickerings, and they all were lying at Shakdān, below Kishm and east of the Kishm-water. Moving through the night, one body of Aūzbegs crossed that water at the top of the morning and advanced on the Mīrzā; he at once drew off to rising-ground, mustered his force, sounded trumpets, met and overcame them. Behind the Aūzbegs was the Kishm-water in flood, many were drowned in it, a mass of them died by arrow and sword, more were made prisoner. Another body of Aūzbegs, sent against Mubārak Shāh and Zubair where they lay, higher up the water and nearer Kishm, made them retire to the rising-ground. Of this the Mīrzā heard; when he had beaten off his own assailants, he moved against theirs. So did the Kohistān begs, gathered with horse and foot, still higher up the river. Unable to make stand against this attack, the Aūzbegs fled, but of this body also a mass died by sword, arrow, and water. In all some 1000 to 1500 may have died. This was Nāṣir Mīrzā's one good success; a man of his brought us news about it while we were in the dale of Kāhmard. Fol. 184.

(*c. Bābur moves on into Khurāsān.*)

While we were in Kāhmard, our army fetched corn from Ghūrī and Dahāna. There too we had letters from Sayyid Afẓal and Sl. Muḥammad *Dūldāī* whom we had sent into Khurāsān; their news was of Sl. Ḥusain Mīrzā's death. Fol. 184*b*.

This news notwithstanding, we set forward for Khurāsān; though there were other grounds for doing this, what decided us was anxious thought for the reputation of this (Tīmūrid) dynasty. We went up the trough (*aīchī*) of the Ājar-valley, on over Tūp and Mandaghān, crossed the Balkh-water and came out on Ṣāf-hill. Hearing there that Aūzbegs were overrunning Sān and Chār-yak,[1] we sent a force under Qāsim Beg against them; he got up with them, beat them well, cut many heads off, and returned.

We lay a few days in the meadow of Ṣāf-hill, waiting for news of Jahāngīr Mīrzā and the clans (*aīmāq*) to whom persons

[1] One of four, a fourth. Chār-yak may be a component of the name of the well-known place, n. of Kābul, "Chārikār"; but also the *Chār* in it may be Hindūstānī and refer to the permits-to-pass after tolls paid, given to caravans halted there for taxation. Raverty writes it Chārīākār.

had been sent. We hunted once, those hills being very full of wild sheep and goats (*kiyīk*). All the clans came in and waited on me within a few days; it was to me they came; they had not gone to Jahāngīr Mīrzā though he had sent men often enough to them, once sending even 'Imādu'd-dīn Mas'ūd. He himself was forced to come at last; he saw me at the foot of the valley when I came down off Ṣāf-hill. Being anxious about Khurāsān, we neither paid him attention nor took thought for the clans, but went right on through Gurzwān, Almār, Qaiṣār, Chīchīk-tū, and Fakhru'd-dīn's-death (*aūlūm*) into the Bām-
Fol. 185. valley, one of the dependencies of Bādghīs.

The world being full of divisions,[1] things were being taken from country and people with the long arm; we ourselves began to take something, by laying an impost on the Turks and clans of those parts, in two or three months taking perhaps 300 ***tūmāns*** of ***kipkī***.[2]

(*d. Coalition of the Khurāsān Mīrzās.*)

A few days before our arrival (in Bām-valley?) some of the Khurāsān light troops and of Ẕū'n-nūn Beg's men had well beaten Aūzbeg raiders in Pand-dih (Panj-dih?) and Marūchāq, killing a mass of men.[3]

Badī'u'z-zamān Mīrzā and Muẓaffar-i-ḥusain Mīrzā with Muḥammad Barandūq *Barlās*, Ẕū'n-nūn *Arghūn* and his son Shāh Beg resolved to move on Shaibāq Khān, then besieging Sl. Qul-i-nachāq (?) in Balkh. Accordingly they summoned all Sl. Ḥusain Mīrzā's sons, and got out of Herī to effect their purpose. At Chihil-dukhtarān Abū'l-muḥsin M. joined them from Marv; Ibn-i-ḥusain M. followed, coming up from Tūn and Qāīn. Kūpuk (Kīpik) M. was in Mashhad; often though they sent to him, he behaved unmanly, spoke senseless words, and did not come. Between him and Muẓaffar Mīrzā, there was jealousy; when Muẓaffar M. was made (joint-)ruler, he said, "How should *I* go to *his* presence?" Through this disgusting jealousy he did

[1] Amongst the disruptions of the time was that of the Khānate of Qībchāq (Erskine).

[2] The nearest approach to *kipkī* we have found in Dictionaries is *kupaki*, which comes close to the Russian *copeck*. Erskine notes that the *casbeke* is an oval copper coin (Tavernier, p. 121); and that a *tūmān* is a myriad (10,000). *Cf.* Manucci (Irvine), i, 78 and iv, 417 note; Chardin iv, 278.

[3] Muḥarram 912 AH.–June 1506 AD. (Ḥ.S. iii, 353).

not come now, even at this crisis when all his brethren, older and younger, were assembling in concord, resolute against such a foe as Shaibāq Khān. Kūpuk M. laid his own absence to rivalry, but everybody else laid it to his cowardice. One word! In this world acts such as his outlive the man; if a man have any share of intelligence, why try to be ill-spoken of after death? if he be ambitious, why not try so to act that, he gone, men will praise him? In the honourable mention of their names, wise men find a second life! Fol. 185*b*.

Envoys from the Mīrzās came to me also, Mūh. Barandūq *Barlās* himself following them. As for me, what was to hinder my going? It was for that very purpose I had travelled one or two hundred *yīghāch* (500–600 miles)! I at once started with Muḥ. Barandūq Beg for Murgh-āb[1] where the Mīrzās were lying.

(*e. Bābur meets the Mīrzās.*)

The meeting with the Mīrzās was on Monday the 8th of the latter Jumāda (Oct. 26th 1506 AH.). Abū'l-muḥsin Mīrzā came out a mile to meet me; we approached one another; on my side, I dismounted, on his side, he; we advanced, saw one another and remounted. Near the camp Muẓaffar Mīrzā and Ibn-i-ḥusain Mīrzā met us; they, being younger than Abū'l-muḥsin Mīrzā ought to have come out further than he to meet me.[2] Their dilatoriness may not have been due to pride, but to heaviness after wine; their negligence may have been no slight on me, but due to their own social pleasures. On this Muẓaffar Mīrzā laid stress;[3] we two saw one another without dismounting, so did Ibn-i-ḥusain Mīrzā and I. We rode on together and, in an amazing crowd and press, dismounted at Badī'u'z-zamān Mīrzā's Gate. Such was the throng that some were lifted off the ground for three or four steps together, while others, wishing for some reason to get out, were carried, willy-nilly, four or five steps the other way. Fol. 186.

[1] I take Murgh-āb here to be the fortified place at the crossing of the river by the main n.e. road; Bābur when in Dara-i-bām was on a tributary of the Murgh-āb. Khwānd-amīr records that the information of his approach was hailed in the Mīrzās' camp as good news (H.S. iii, 354).

[2] Bābur gives the Mīrzās precedence by age, ignoring Muẓaffar's position as joint-ruler.

[3] *mubālgha qīldī*; perhaps he laid stress on their excuse; perhaps did more than was ceremonially incumbent on him.

We reached Badī'u'z-zamān Mīrzā's Audience-tent. It had been agreed that I, on entering, should bend the knee (*yūkūnghāī*) once, that the Mīrzā should rise and advance to the edge of the estrade,[1] and that we should see one another there. I went in, bent the knee once, and was going right forward; the Mīrzā rose rather languidly and advanced rather slowly; Qāsim Beg, as he was my well-wisher and held my reputation as his own, gave my girdle a tug; I understood, moved more slowly, and so the meeting was on the appointed spot.

Four divans (*tūshuk*) had been placed in the tent. Always in the Mīrzā's tents one side was like a gate-way[2] and at the edge of this gate-way he always sat. A divan was set there now
Fol. 186*b*. on which he and Muzaffar Mīrzā sat together. Abū'l-muḥsin, Mīrzā and I sat on another, set in the right-hand place of honour (*tūr*). On another, to Badī'u'z-zamān Mīrzā's left, sat Ibn-i-ḥusain Mīrzā with Qāsim Sl. *Aūzbeg*, a son-in-law of the late Mīrzā and father of Qāsim-i-ḥusain Sulṭān. To my right and below my divan was one on which sat Jahāngīr Mīrzā and 'Abdu'r-razzāq Mīrzā. To the left of Qāsim Sl. and Ibn-i-ḥusain Mīrzā, but a good deal lower, were Muḥ. Barandūq Beg, Ẕū'n-nūn Beg and Qāsim Beg.

Although this was not a social gathering, cooked viands were brought in, drinkables[3] were set with the food, and near them gold and silver cups. Our forefathers through a long space of time, had respected the Chīngīz-tūrā (ordinance), doing nothing opposed to it, whether in assembly or Court, in sittings-down

[1] *'irq*, to which estrade answers in its sense of a carpet on which stands a raised seat.

[2] Perhaps it was a recess, resembling a gate-way (W.-i-B. I.O. 215 f. 151 and 217 f. 127*b*). The impression conveyed by Bābur's words here to the artist who in B.M. Or. 3714, has depicted the scene, is that there was a vestibule opening into the tent by a door and that the Mīrzā sat near that door. It must be said however that the illustration does not closely follow the text, in some known details.

[3] *shīra*, fruit-syrups, sherbets. Bābur's word for wine is *chāghīr* (*q.v.* index) and this reception being public, wine could hardly have been offered in Sunnī Herī. Bābur's strictures can apply to the vessels of precious metal he mentions, these being forbidden to Musalmāns; from his reference to the Tūra it would appear to repeat the same injunctions. Bābur broke up such vessels before the battle of Kanwāha (f. 315). Shāh-i-jahān did the same; when sent by his father Jahāngīr to reconquer the Deccan (1030 AH.–1621 AD.) he asked permission to follow the example of his ancestor Bābur, renounced wine, poured his stock into the Chambal, broke up his cups and gave the fragments to the poor (*'Amal-i-ṣāliḥ*, ; Hughes' *Dict. of Islām* quoting the *Hidāyah* and *Mishkāt*, *s.nn.* Drinkables, Drinking-vessels, and Gold; Lane's *Modern Egyptians* p. 125 n.).

or risings-up. Though it has not Divine authority so that a man obeys it of necessity, still good rules of conduct must be obeyed by whom-soever they are left; just in the same way that, if a forefather have done ill, his ill must be changed for good.

After the meal I rode from the Mīrzā's camp some 2 miles to our own dismounting-place. Fol. 187.

(*f. Bābur claims due respect.*)

At my second visit Badī'u'z-zamān Mīrzā shewed me less respect than at my first. I therefore had it said to Muḥ. Barandūq Beg and to Ẕū'n-nūn Beg that, small though my age was (*aet.* 24), my place of honour was large; that I had seated myself twice on the throne of our forefathers in Samarkand by blow straight-dealt; and that to be laggard in shewing me respect was unreasonable, since it was for this (Tīmūrid) dynasty's sake I had thus fought and striven with that alien foe. This said, and as it was reasonable, they admitted their mistake at once and shewed the respect claimed.

(*g. Bābur's temperance.*)

There was a wine-party (*chāghīr-majlisī*) once when I went after the Mid-day Prayer to Badī'u'z-zamān Mīrzā's presence. At that time I drank no wine. The party was altogether elegant; every sort of relish to wine (*gazak*) was set out on the napery, with brochettes of fowl and goose, and all sorts of viands. The Mīrzā's entertainments were much renowned; truly was this one free from the pang of thirst (*bī ghall*), reposeful and tranquil. I was at two or three of his wine-parties while we were on the bank of the Murgh-āb; once it was known I did not drink, no pressure to do so was put on me.

I went to one wine-party of Muẕaffar Mīrzā's. Ḥusain of 'Alī *Jalāīr* and Mīr Badr were both there, they being in his service. When Mīr Badr had had enough (*kaifīyat*), he danced, Fol. 187*b*. and danced well what seemed to be his own invention.

(*h. Comments on the Mīrzās.*)

Three months it took the Mīrzās to get out of Herī, agree amongst themselves, collect troops, and reach Murgh-āb.

Meantime Sl. Qul-i-nachāq (?), reduced to extremity, had surrendered Balkh to the Aūzbeg but that Aūzbeg, hearing of our alliance against him, had hurried back to Samarkand. The Mīrzās were good enough as company and in social matters, in conversation and parties, but they were strangers to war, strategy, equipment, bold fight and encounter.

(*i. Winter plans.*)

While we were on the Murgh-āb, news came that Ḥaq-naẓīr *Chapā* (var. Ḥiān) was over-running the neighbourhood of Chīchīk-tū with 4 or 500 men. All the Mīrzās there present, do what they would, could not manage to send a light troop against those raiders! It is 10 *yīghāch* (50–55 m.) from Murgh-āb to Chīchīk-tū. I asked the work; they, with a thought for their own reputation, would not give it to me.

The year being almost at an end when Shaibāq Khān retired, the Mīrzās decided to winter where it was convenient and to reassemble next summer in order to repel their foe.

They pressed me to winter in Khurāsān, but this not one of my well-wishers saw it good for me to do because, while Kābul and Ghaznī were full of a turbulent and ill-conducted medley of Fol. 188. people and hordes, Turks, Mughūls, clans and nomads (*aīmāq u aḥsham*), Afghāns and Hazāra, the roads between us and that not yet desirably subjected country of Kābul were, one, the mountain-road, a month's journey even without delay through snow or other cause,—the other, the low-country road, a journey of 40 or 50 days.

Consequently we excused ourselves to the Mīrzās, but they would accept no excuse and, for all our pleas, only urged the more. In the end Badī'u'z-zamān Mīrzā, Abū'l-muḥsin Mīrzā and Muẓaffar Mīrzā themselves rode to my tent and urged me to stay the winter. It was impossible to refuse men of such ruling position, come in person to press us to stay on. Besides this, the whole habitable world has not such a town as Herī had become under Sl. Ḥusain Mīrzā, whose orders and efforts had increased its splendour and beauty as ten to one, rather, as twenty to one. As I greatly wished to stay, I consented to do so.

Abū'l-muḥsin M. went to Marv, his own district; Ibn-i-ḥusain M. went to his, Tūn and Qāīn; Badī'u'z-zamān M. and Muẓaffar M. set off for Herī; I followed them a few days later, taking the road by Chihil-dukhtarān and Tāsh-rabāṭ.[1]

(j. Bābur visits the Begīms in Herī.)

All the Begīms, *i.e.* my paternal-aunt Pāyanda-sulṭān Begīm, Khadīja Begīm, Apāq Begīm, and my other paternal-aunt Begīms, daughters of Sl. Abū-sa'īd Mīrzā,[2] were gathered together, at the time I went to see them, in Sl. Ḥusain Mīrzā's College at his Mausoleum. Having bent the knee with *(yūkūnūb bīla)* Pāyanda-sulṭān Begīm first of all, I had an interview with her; next, not bending the knee,[3] I had an interview with Apāq Begīm; next, having bent the knee with Khadīja Begīm, I had an interview with her. After sitting there for some time during recitation of the Qorān,[4] we went to the South College where Khadīja Begīm's tents had been set up and where food was placed before us. After partaking of this, we went to Pāyanda-sulṭān Begīm's tents and there spent the night. Fol. 188*b*

The New-year's Garden was given us first for a camping-ground; there our camp was arranged; and there I spent the night of the day following my visit to the Begīms, but as I did not find it a convenient place, 'Alī-sher Beg's residence was

[1] This may be the Rabāṭ-i-sanghī of some maps, on a near road between the "Forty-daughters" and Harāt; or Bābur may have gone out of his direct way to visit Rabāṭ-i-sang-bast, a renowned halting place at the Carfax of the Herī-Ṭūs and Nishāpūr-Mashhad roads, built by one Arslān *Jazāla* who lies buried near, and rebuilt with great magnificence by 'Alī-sher *Nawā'ī* (Daulat-shāh, Browne, p. 176).

[2] The wording here is confusing to those lacking family details. The paternal-aunt begīms can be Pāyanda-sulṭān (named), Khadīja-sulṭān, Apāq-sulṭān, and Fakhr-jahān Begīms, all daughters of Abū-sa'īd. The Apāq Begīm named above (also on f. 168*b q.v.*) does not now seem to me to be Abū-sa'īd's daughter (Gul-badan, trs. Bio. App.).

[3] *yūkūnmāī*. Unless all copies I have seen reproduce a primary clerical mistake of Bābur's, the change of salutation indicated by there being no kneeling with Apāq Begīm, points to a *nuance* of etiquette. Of the verb *yūkūnmāk* it may be noted that it both describes the ceremonious attitude of intercourse, *i.e.* kneeling and sitting back on both heels (Shaw), and also the kneeling on meeting. From Bābur's phrase *Begīm bīla yūkūnūb* [having kneeled with], it appears that each of those meeting made the genuflection; I have not found the phrase used of other meetings; it is not the one used when a junior or a man of less degree meets a senior or superior in rank (*e.g.* Khusrau and Bābur f. 123, or Bābur and Badī'u'z-zamān f. 186).

[4] Musalmāns employ a set of readers who succeed one another in reading (reciting) the Qorān at the tombs of their men of eminence. This reading is sometimes continued day and night. The readers are paid by the rent of lands or other funds assigned for the purpose (Erskine).

assigned to me, where I was as long as I stayed in Herī, every few days shewing myself in Badī'u'z-zamān Mīrzā's presence in the World-adorning Garden.

(*k. The Mīrzās entertain Bābur in Herī.*)

A few days after Muẓaffar Mīrzā had settled down in the White-garden, he invited me to his quarters; Khadīja Begīm was also there, and with me went Jahāngīr Mīrzā. When we had eaten a meal in the Begīm's presence,[1] Muẓaffar Mīrzā took me to where there was a wine-party, in the Ṭarab-khāna (Joy-house) built by Bābur Mīrzā, a sweet little abode, a smallish, two-storeyed house in the middle of a smallish garden. Great pains have been taken with its upper storey; this has a retreat (*ḥujra*) in each of its four corners, the space between each two retreats being like a *shāh-nīshīn*[2]; in between these retreats and *shāh-nīshīns* is one large room on all sides of which are pictures which, although Bābur Mīrzā built the house, were commanded by Abū-sa'īd Mīrzā and depict his own wars and encounters.

Two divans had been set in the north *shāh-nīshīn*, facing each other, and with their sides turned to the north. On one Muẓaffar Mīrzā and I sat, on the other Sl. Mas'ūd Mīrzā[3] and Jahāngīr Mīrzā. We being guests, Muẓaffar Mīrzā gave me place above himself. The social cups were filled, the cup-bearers ordered to carry them to the guests; the guests drank down the mere wine as if it were water-of-life; when it mounted to their heads, the party waxed warm.

They thought to make me also drink and to draw me into their own circle. Though up till then I had not committed the sin of wine-drinking[4] and known the cheering sensation of comfortable drunkenness, I was inclined to drink wine and my heart was drawn to cross that stream (*wāda*). I had had no inclination for wine in my childhood; I knew nothing of its cheer and pleasure. If, as sometimes, my father pressed wine

---

[1] A suspicion that Khadīja put poison in Jahāngīr's wine may refer to this occasion (T.R. p. 199).
[2] These are *jharokha-i-darsān*, windows or balconies from which a ruler shews himself to the people.
[3] Mas'ūd was then blind.
[4] Bābur first drank wine not earlier than 917 AH. (f. 49 and note), therefore when nearing 30.

on me, I excused myself; I did not commit the sin. After he died, Khwāja Qāẓī's right guidance kept me guiltless; as at that time I abstained from forbidden viands, what room was there for the sin of wine? Later on when, with the young man's lusts and at the prompting of sensual passion, desire for wine arose, there was no-one to press it on me, no-one indeed aware of my leaning towards it; so that, inclined for it though my heart was, it was difficult of myself to do such a thing, one thitherto undone. It crossed my mind now, when the Mīrzās were so pressing and when too we were in a town so refined as Herī, "Where should I drink if not here? here where all the chattels and utensils of luxury and comfort are gathered and in use." So saying to myself, I resolved to drink wine; I determined to cross that stream; but it occurred to me that as I had not taken wine in Badī'u'z-zamān Mīrzā's house or from his hand, who was to me as an elder brother, things might find way into his mind if I took wine in his younger brother's house and from his hand. Having so said to myself, I mentioned my doubt and difficulty. Said they, "Both the excuse and the obstacle are reasonable," pressed me no more to drink then but settled that when I was in company with both Mīrzās, I should drink under the insistance of both. Fol. 189b.

Amongst the musicians present at this party were Ḥāfiẓ Ḥājī, Jalālu'd-dīn Maḥmūd the flautist, and Ghulām *shādī*'s younger brother, Ghulām *bacha* the Jews'-harpist. Ḥāfiẓ Ḥājī sang well, as Herī people sing, quietly, delicately, and in tune. With Jahāngīr Mīrzā was a Samarkandī singer Mīr Jān whose singing was always loud, harsh and out-of-tune. The Mīrzā, having had enough, ordered him to sing; he did so, loudly, harshly and without taste. Khurāsānīs have quite refined manners; if, under this singing, one did stop his ears, the face of another put question, not one could stop the singer, out of consideration for the Mīrzā. Fol. 190.

After the Evening Prayer we left the Ṭarab-khāna for a new house in Muẓaffar Mīrzā's winter-quarters. There Yūsuf-i-'alī danced in the drunken time, and being, as he was, a master in music, danced well. The party waxed very warm there. Muẓaffar Mīrzā gave me a sword-belt, a lambskin surtout, and a grey *tīpūchāq* (horse). Jānak recited in Turkī. Two slaves of the Mīrzā's, known as Big-moon and Little-moon, did offensive, drunken tricks in the drunken time. The party was warm till night when those assembled scattered, I, however, staying the night in that house.

Qāsim Beg getting to hear that I had been pressed to drink wine, sent some-one to Ẕū'n-nūn Beg with advice for him and for Muẕaffar Mīrzā, given in very plain words; the result was Fol. 190*b*. that the Mīrzās entirely ceased to press wine upon me.

Badī'u'z-zamān Mīrzā, hearing that Muẕaffar M. had entertained me, asked me to a party arranged in the Maqauwī-khāna of the World-adorning Garden. He asked also some of my close circle [1] and some of our braves. Those about me could never drink (openly) on my own account; if they ever did drink, they did it perhaps once in 40 days, with doorstrap fast and under a hundred fears. Such as these were now invited; here too they drank with a hundred precautions, sometimes calling off my attention, sometimes making a screen of their hands, notwithstanding that I had given them permission to follow common custom, because this party was given by one standing to me as a father or elder brother. People brought in weeping-willows . . . [2]

At this party they set a roast goose before me but as I was no carver or disjointer of birds, I left it alone. "Do you not like it?" inquired the Mīrzā. Said I, "I am a poor carver." On this he at once disjointed the bird and set it again before Fol. 191. me. In such matters he had no match. At the end of the party he gave me an enamelled waist-dagger, a *chār-qāb*,[3] and a *tīpūchāq*.

(*l. Bābur sees the sights of Herī.*)

Every day of the time I was in Herī I rode out to see a new sight; my guide in these excursions was Yūsuf-i-'alī Kūkūldāsh; wherever we dismounted, he set food before me. Except Sl.

[1] *aīchkīlār*, French, *intérieur*.

[2] The obscure passage following here is discussed in Appendix I, *On the weeping-willows of* f. 190*b*.

[3] Here this may well be a gold-embroidered garment.

Ḥusain Mīrzā's Almshouse, not one famous spot, maybe, was left unseen in those 40 days.

I saw the Gāzur-gāh,[1] 'Alī-sher's Bāghcha (Little-garden), the Paper-mortars,[2] Takht-astāna (Royal-residence), Pul-i-gāh, Kahad-stān,[3] Naẓar-gāh-garden, Ni'matābād (Pleasure-place), Gāzur-gāh Avenue, Sl. Aḥmad Mīrzā's Ḥaẓirat,[4] Takht-i-safar,[5] Takht-i-nawā'ī, Takht-i-barkar, Takht-i-Ḥājī Beg, Takht-i-Bahā'-u'd-dīn 'Umar, Takht-i-Shaikh Zainu'd-dīn, Maulānā 'Abdu'r-raḥmān *Jāmī*'s honoured shrine and tomb,[6] Namāz-gāh-i-mukhtār,[7] the Fish-pond,[8] Sāq-i-sulaimān,[9] Bulūrī (Crystal) which originally may have been Abū'l-walīd,[10] Imām Fakhr,[11] Avenue-garden, Mīrzā's Colleges and tomb, Guhār-shād Begīm's College, tomb,[12] and Congregational Mosque, the Ravens'-garden,

[1] This, the tomb of Khwāja 'Abdu'l-lāh *Anṣarī* (d. 481 AH.) stands some 2m. north of Herī. Bābur mentions one of its numerous attendants of his day, Kamālu'd-dīn Ḥusain *Gāzur-gāhī*. Mohan Lall describes it as he saw it in 1831; says the original name of the locality was Kār-zār-gāh, place-of-battle; and, as perhaps his most interesting detail, mentions that Jalālu'd-dīn *Rūmī's Masnawī* was recited every morning near the tomb and that people fainted during the invocation (*Travels in the Panj-āb* etc. p. 252). Colonel Yate has described the tomb as he saw it some 50 years later (JASB 1887); and explains the name Gāzur-gāh (lit. bleaching-place) by the following words of an inscription there found; "His tomb (Anṣarī's) is a washing-place (*gāzur-gāh*) wherein the cloud of the Divine forgiveness washes white the black records of men" (p. 88 and p. 102).

[2] *juāz-i-kaghazlār* (f. 47*b* and note).

[3] The *Ḥabību's-siyār* and Ḥai. MS. write this name with medial "round *hā*"; this allows it to be Kahad-stān, a running-place, race-course. Khwānd-amīr and Daulat-shāh call it a meadow (*aūlāng*); the latter speaks of a feast as held there; it was Shaibānī's head-quarters when he took Harāt.

[4] *var.* Khatīra; either an enclosure (*qūrūq*?) or a fine and lofty building.

[5] This may have been a usual halting-place on a journey (*safar*) north. It was built by Ḥusain *Bāī-qarā*, overlooked hills and fields covered with *arghwān* (f. 137*b*) and seems once to have been a Paradise (Mohan Lall, p. 256).

[6] Jāmī's tomb was in the 'Īd-gah of Herī (Ḥ.S. ii, 337), which appears to be the Muṣalla (Praying-place) demolished by Amīr 'Abdu'r-raḥmān in the 19th century. Col. Yate was shewn a tomb in the Muṣalla said to be Jāmī's and agreeing in the age, 81, given on it, with Jāmī's at death, but he found a *crux* in the inscription (pp. 99, 106).

[7] This may be the Muṣalla (Yate, p. 98).

[8] This place is located by the Ḥ.S. at 5 *farsakh* from Herī (de Meynard at 25 *kilomètres*). It appears to be rather an abyss or fissure than a pond, a crack from the sides of which water trickles into a small bason in which dwells a mysterious fish, the beholding of which allows the attainment of desires. The story recalls Wordsworth's undying fish of Bow-scale Tarn. (Cf. Ḥ.S. Bomb. ed. ii, *Khatmat* p. 20 and de Meynard, *Journal Asiatique* xvi, 480 and note.)

[9] This is on maps to the north of Herī.

[10] d. 232 AH. (847 AD.). *See* Yate, p. 93.

[11] Imām Fakhru'd-dīn *Razī* (de Meynard, *Journal Asiatique* xvi, 481).

[12] d. 861 AH.–1457 AD. Guhār-shād was the wife of Tīmūr's son Shāhrukh. *See* Mohan Lall, p. 257 and Yate, p. 98.

New-garden, Zubaida-garden,[1] Sl. Abū-sa'īd Mīrzā's White-house
Fol. 191*b*. outside the 'Irāq-gate, Pūrān,[2] the Archer's-seat, Chargh (hawk)-meadow, Amīr Wāḥid,[3] Mālān-bridge,[4] Khwāja-tāq,[5] White-garden, Ṭarab-khāna, Bāgh-i-jahān-ārā, Kūshk,[6] Maqauwī-khāna, Lily-house, Twelve-towers, the great tank to the north of Jahān-ārā and the four dwellings on its four sides, the five Fort-gates, *viz.* the Malik, 'Irāq, Fīrūzābād, Khūsh[7] and Qībchāq Gates, Chār-sū, Shaikhu'l-islām's College, Maliks' Congregational Mosque, Town-garden, Badī'u'z-zamān Mīrzā's College on the bank of the Anjīl-canal, 'Alī-sher Beg's dwellings where we resided and which people call Unsīya (Ease), his tomb and mosque which they call Qudsīya (Holy), his College and Almshouse which they call Khalāṣīya and Akhlāṣīya (Freedom and Sincerity), his Hot-bath and Hospital which they call Ṣafā'iya and Shafā'īya. All these I visited in that space of time.

(*m. Bābur engages Ma'ṣūma-sulṭān in marriage.*)

It must have been before those throneless times[8] that Ḥabība-sulṭān Begīm, the mother of Sl. Aḥmad Mīrzā's youngest daughter Ma'ṣūma-sulṭān Begīm, brought her daughter into Herī. One day when I was visiting my Ākā, Ma'ṣūma-sulṭān Begīm came there with her mother and at once felt arise in her a great inclination towards me. Private messengers having been sent, my Ākā and my Yīnkā, as I used to call Pāyanda-sulṭān Begīm
Fol. 192. and Ḥabība-sulṭān Begīm, settled between them that the latter should bring her daughter after me to Kābul.[9]

[1] This Marigold-garden may be named after Hārūnu'r-rashīd's wife Zubaida.

[2] This will be the place n. of Herī from which Maulānā Jalālu'd-dīn *Pūrānī* (d. 862 AH.) took his cognomen, as also Shaikh Jamālu'd-dīn Abū-sa'īd *Pūrān* (f. 206) who was visited there by Sl. Ḥusain Mīrzā, ill-treated by Shaibānī (f. 206), left Herī for Qandahār, and there died, through the fall of a roof, in 921 AH. (Ḥ.S. iii, 345; *Khazīnatu'l-aṣfiya* ii, 321).

[3] His tomb is dated 35 or 37 AH. (656 or 658 AD.; Yate, p. 94).

[4] Mālān was a name of the Herī-rūd (*Journal Asiatique* xvi, 476, 511; Mohan Lall, p. 279; Ferrier, p. 261; *etc.*).

[5] Yate, p. 94.

[6] The position of this building between the Khūsh and Qībchāq Gates (de Meynard, l.c. p. 475) is the probable explanation of the variant, noted just below, of Kushk for Khūsh as the name of the Gate. The *Tārīkh-i-rashīdī* (p. 429), mentions this kiosk in its list of the noted ones of the world.

[7] var. Kushk (de Meynard, l.c. p. 472).

[8] The reference here is, presumably, to Bābur's own losses of Samarkand and Andijān.

[9] Ākā or Āgā is used of elder relations; a *yīnkā* or *yīngā* is the wife of an uncle or elder brother; here it represents the widow of Bābur's uncle Aḥmad *Mīrān-shāhī*. From it is formed the word *yīnkālīk*, levirate.

(n. Bābur leaves Khurāsān.)

Very pressingly had Muḥ. Barandūq Beg and Ẕū'n-nūn *Arghūn* said, "Winter here:" but they had given me no winter-quarters nor had they made any winter-arrangements for me. Winter came on; snow fell on the mountains between us and Kābul; anxiety grew about Kābul; no winter-quarters were offered, no arrangements made! As we could not speak out, of necessity we left Herī!

On the pretext of finding winter-quarters, we got out of the town on the 7th day of the month of Sha'bān (Dec. 24th 1506 AD.), and went to near Bādghīs. Such were our slowness and our tarryings that the Ramẓān-moon was seen a few marches only beyond the Langar of Mīr Ghiyāṣ.[1] Of our braves who were absent on various affairs, some joined us, some followed us into Kābul 20 days or a month later, some stayed in Herī and took service with the Mīrzās. One of these last was Sayyidīm 'Alī the gate-ward, who became Badī'u'z-zamān Mīrzā's retainer. To no servant of Khusrau Shāh had I shewn so much favour as to him; he had been given Ghaznī when Jahāngīr Mīrzā abandoned it, and in it when he came away with the army, had left his younger brother Dost-i-anjū (?) Shaikh. There were in truth Fol. 192*b*. no better men amongst Khusrau Shāh's retainers than this man Sayyidīm 'Alī the gate-ward and Muḥibb-i-'alī the armourer. Sayyidīm was of excellent nature and manners, a bold swordsman, a singularly competent and methodical man. His house was never without company and assembly; he was greatly generous, had wit and charm, a variety of talk and story, and was a sweet-natured, good-humoured, ingenious, fun-loving person. His fault was that he practised vice and pederasty. He may have swerved from the Faith; may also have been a hypocrite in his dealings; some of what seemed double-dealing people attributed to his jokes, but, still, there must have been a something![2] When Badī'u'z-zamān Mīrzā had let Shaibāq Khān take Herī and had gone to Shāh Beg (*Arghūn*), he had Sayyidīm 'Alī thrown into the Harmand because of his double-dealing words

[1] The almshouse or convent was founded here in Tīmūr's reign (de Meynard, l.c. p. 500).

[2] *i.e.* No smoke without fire.

spoken between the Mīrzā and Shāh Beg. Muḥibb-i-'alī's story will come into the narrative of events hereafter to be written.

(*o. A perilous mountain-journey.*)

From the Langar of Mīr Ghiyāṣ we had ourselves guided past the border-villages of Gharjistān to Chach-charān.[1] From the almshouse to Gharjistān was an unbroken sheet of snow; it was deeper further on; near Chach-charān itself it was above the horses' knees. Chach-charān depended on Ẕū'n-nūn *Arghūn*; his retainer Mīr Jān-aīrdī was in it now; from him we took, on payment, the whole of Ẕū'n-nūn Beg's store of provisions. A march or two further on, the snow was very deep, being above
Fol. 193. the stirrup, indeed in many places the horses' feet did not touch the ground.

We had consulted at the Langar of Mīr Ghiyāṣ which road to take for return to Kābul; most of us agreed in saying, "It is winter, the mountain-road is difficult and dangerous; the Qandahār road, though a little longer, is safe and easy." Qāsim Beg said, "That road is long; you will go by this one." As he made much dispute, we took the mountain-road.

Our guide was a Pashāī named Pīr Sulṭān (Old sultan?). Whether it was through old age, whether from want of heart, whether because of the deep snow, he lost the road and could not guide us. As we were on this route under the insistance of Qāsim Beg, he and his sons, for his name's sake, dismounted, trampled the snow down, found the road again and took the lead. One day the snow was so deep and the way so uncertain that we could not go on; there being no help for it, back we turned, dismounted where there was fuel, picked out 60 or 70 good men and sent them down the valley in our tracks to fetch any one soever of the Hazāra, wintering in the valley-bottom, who might shew us the road. That place could not be left till our men returned three or four days later. They brought no
Fol. 193*b*. guide; once more we sent Sulṭān *Pashāī* ahead and, putting our

[1] This name may be due to the splashing of water. A Langar which may be that of Mīr Ghiyāṣ, is shewn in maps in the Bām valley; from it into the Herī-rūd valley Bābur's route may well have been the track from that Langar which, passing the villages on the southern border of Gharjistān, goes to Ahangarān.

trust in God, again took the road by which we had come back from where it was lost. Much misery and hardship were endured in those few days, more than at any time of my life. In that stress I composed the following opening couplet :—

> Is there one cruel turn of Fortune's wheel unseen of me?
> Is there a pang, a grief my wounded heart has missed?

We went on for nearly a week, trampling down the snow and not getting forward more than two or three miles a day. I was one of the snow-stampers, with 10 or 15 of my household, Qāsim Beg, his sons Tīngrī-bīrdī and Qambar-i-'alī and two or three of their retainers. These mentioned used to go forward for 7 or 8 yards, stamping the snow down and at each step sinking to the waist or the breast. After a few steps the leading man would stand still, exhausted by the labour, and another would go forward. By the time 10, 15, 20, men on foot had stamped the snow down, it became so that a horse might be led over it. A horse would be led, would sink to the stirrups, could do no more than 10 or 12 steps, and would be drawn aside to let another go on. After we, 10, 15, 20, men had stamped down the snow and had led horses forward in this fashion, very serviceable Fol. 194. braves and men of renowned name would enter the beaten track, hanging their heads. It was not a time to urge or compel! the man with will and hardihood for such tasks does them by his own request! Stamping the snow down in this way, we got out of that afflicting place (*ānjūkān yīr*) in three or four days to a cave known as the Khawāl-i-qūtī (Blessed-cave), below the Zirrīn-pass.

That night the snow fell in such an amazing blizzard of cutting wind that every man feared for his life. The storm had become extremely violent by the time we reached the *khawāl*, as people in those parts call a mountain-cave (*ghar*) or hollow (*khāwāk*). We dismounted at its mouth. Deep snow! a one-man road! and even on that stamped-down and trampled road, pitfalls for horses! the days at their shortest! The first arrivals reached the cave by daylight; others kept coming in from the Evening Prayer till the Bed-time one; later than that people dismounted wherever they happened to be; dawn shot with many still in the saddle.

The cave seeming to be rather small, I took a shovel and shovelled out a place near its mouth, the size of a sitting-mat
Fol. 194*b*. (*takiya-namad*), digging it out breast-high but even then not reaching the ground. This made me a little shelter from the wind when I sat right down in it. I did not go into the cave though people kept saying, "Come inside," because this was in my mind, "Some of my men in snow and storm, I in the comfort of a warm house! the whole horde (*aūlūs*) outside in misery and pain, I inside sleeping at ease! That would be far from a man's act, quite another matter than comradeship! Whatever hardship and wretchedness there is, I will face; what strong men stand, I will stand; for, as the Persian proverb says, to die with friends is a nuptial." Till the Bed-time Prayer I sat through that blizzard of snow and wind in the dug-out, the snow-fall being such that my head, back, and ears were overlaid four hands thick. The cold of that night affected my ears. At the Bed-time Prayer some-one, looking more carefully at the cave, shouted out, "It is a very roomy cave with place for every-body." On hearing this I shook off my roofing of snow and, asking the braves near to come also, went inside. There was room for 50 or 60! People brought out their rations, cold meat, parched grain, whatever they had. From such cold and tumult to a place so warm, cosy and quiet![1]

Next day the snow and wind having ceased, we made an early start and we got to the pass by again stamping down
Fol. 195. a road in the snow. The proper road seems to make a détour up the flank of the mountain and to go over higher up, by what is understood to be called the Zirrīn-pass. Instead of taking that road, we went straight up the valley-bottom (*qūl*).[2] It was night before we reached the further side of the (Bakkak-)pass; we spent the night there in the mouth of the valley, a night of

[1] This escape ought to have been included in the list of Bābur's transportations from risk to safety given in my note to f. 96.

[2] The right and wrong roads are shewn by the Indian Survey and French Military maps. The right road turns off from the wrong one, at Daulat-yār, to the right, and mounts diagonally along the south rampart of the Herī-rūd valley, to the Zirrīn-pass, which lies above the Bakkak-pass and carries the regular road for Yaka-aūlāng. It must be said, however, that we are not told whether Yaka-aūlāng was Qāsim Beg's objective; the direct road for Kābul from the Herī-rūd valley is not over the Zirrīn-pass but goes from Daulat-yār by "Āq-zarat", and the southern flank of Koh-i-bābā (bābār) to the Unai-pass (Holdich's *Gates of India* p. 262).

mighty cold, got through with great distress and suffering. Many a man had his hands and feet frost-bitten; that night's cold took both Kīpa's feet, both Sīūndūk *Turkmān*'s hands, both Āhī's feet. Early next morning we moved down the valley; putting our trust in God, we went straight down, by bad slopes and sudden falls, knowing and seeing it could not be the right way. It was the Evening Prayer when we got out of that valley. No long-memoried old man knew that any-one had been heard of as crossing that pass with the snow so deep, or indeed that it had ever entered the heart of man to cross it at that time of year. Though for a few days we had suffered greatly through the depth of the snow, yet its depth, in the end, enabled us to reach our destination. For why? How otherwise should we have traversed those pathless slopes and sudden falls? Fol. 195*b*.

All ill, all good in the count, is gain if looked at aright!

The Yaka-aūlāng people at once heard of our arrival and our dismounting; followed, warm houses, fat sheep, grass and horse-corn, water without stint, ample wood and dried dung for fires! To escape from such snow and cold to such a village, to such warm dwellings, was comfort those will understand who have had our trials, relief known to those who have felt our hardships. We tarried one day in Yaka-aūlāng, happy-of-heart and easy-of-mind; marched 2 *yīghāch* (10–12 m.) next day and dismounted. The day following was the Ramẓān Feast[1]; we went on through Bāmīān, crossed by Shibr-tū and dismounted before reaching Janglīk.

(*p. Second raid on the Turkmān Hazāras.*)

The Turkmān Hazāras with their wives and little children must have made their winter-quarters just upon our road[2]; they had no word about us; when we got in amongst their cattle-pens and tents (*alāchūq*) two or three groups of these went to ruin and plunder, the people themselves drawing off with their little children and abandoning houses and goods. News was Fol. 196.
brought from ahead that, at a place where there were narrows,

[1] *circa* Feb. 14th 1507, Bābur's 24th birthday.

[2] The Hazāras appear to have been wintering outside their own valley, on the Ghūr-bund road, in wait for travellers [*cf.* T.R. p. 197]. They have been perennial highwaymen on the only pass to the north not closed entirely in winter.

a body of Hazaras was shooting arrows, holding up part of the army, and letting no-one pass. We, hurrying on, arrived to find no narrows at all; a few Hazāras were shooting from a naze, standing in a body on the hill[1] like very good soldiers.[2]

They saw the blackness of the foe;
Stood idle-handed and amazed;
I arriving, went swift that way,
Pressed on with shout, "Move on! move on!"
I wanted to hurry my men on,
To make them stand up to the foe.
With a "Hurry up!" to my men,
I went on to the front.
Not a man gave ear to my words.
I had no armour nor horse-mail nor arms,
I had but my arrows and quiver.
I went, the rest, maybe all of them, stood,
Stood still as if slain by the foe!
Your servant you take that you may have use
Of his arms, of his life, the whole time;
Not that the servant stand still
While the beg makes advance to the front;
Not that the servant take rest
While his beg is making the rounds.
From no such a servant will come
Speed, or use in your Gate, or zest for your food.
At last I charged forward myself,
Fol. 196*b*. Herding the foe up the hill;
Seeing me go, my men also moved,
Leaving their terrors behind.
With me they swift spread over the slope,
Moving on without heed to the shaft;
Sometimes on foot, mounted sometimes,
Boldly we ever moved on,
Still from the hill poured the shafts.
Our strength seen, the foe took to flight.
We got out on the hill; we drove the Hazāras,
Drove them like deer by valley and ridge;
We shot those wretches like deer;
We shared out the booty in goods and in sheep;
The Turkmān Hazāras' kinsfolk we took;
We made captive their people of sorts (*qarā*);
We laid hands on their men of renown;
Their wives and their children we took.

[1] The Ghūr-bund valley is open in this part; the Hazāras may have been p on the naze near the narrows leading into the Janglīk and their own side valleys

[2] Although the verses following here in the text are with the Turkī Codices, ' cannot but be felt as to their authenticity. They do not fit verbally to the sen... they follow; they are a unique departure from Bābur's plain prose narrative and nothing in the small Hazāra affair shews cause for such departure; they differ from his usual topics in their bombast and comment on his men (*cf.* f. 194 for comment on shirking begs). They appear in the 2nd Persian translation (217 f. 134) in Turkī followed by a prose Persian rendering (*khalāṣa*). They are not with the 1st Pers. trs. (215 f. 159), the text of which runs on with a plain prose account suiting the size of the affair, as follows:—"The braves, seeing their (the Hazāras) good soldiering, had stopped surprised; wishing to hurry them I went swiftly past them, shouting 'Move on!

I myself collected a few of the Hazāras' sheep, gave them into Yārak Ṯaghāī's charge, and went to the front. By ridge and valley, driving horses and sheep before us, we went to Tīmūr Beg's Langar and there dismounted. Fourteen or fifteen Hazāra thieves had fallen into our hands; I had thought of having them put to death when we next dismounted, with various torture, as a warning to all highwaymen and robbers, but Qāsim Beg came across them on the road and, with mis- Fol. 197.
timed compassion, set them free.

> To do good to the bad is one and the same
> As the doing of ill to the good;
> On brackish soil no spikenard grows,
> Waste no seed of toil upon it.[1]

Out of compassion the rest of the prisoners were released also.

(*j. Disloyalty in Kābul.*)

News came while we were raiding the Turkmān Hazāras, that Muḥammad Ḥusain Mīrzā *Dūghlāt* and Sl. Sanjar *Barlās* had drawn over to themselves the Mughūls left in Kābul, declared Mīrzā Khān (Wais) supreme (*pādshāh*), laid siege to the fort and spread a report that Badī'u'z-zamān Mīrzā and Muẕaffar Mīrzā had sent me, a prisoner, to Fort Ikhtiyāru'd-dīn, now known as Ālā-qūrghān.

In command of the Kābul-fort there had been left Mullā Bābā of Pashāghar, Khalīfa, Muḥibb-i-'alī the armourer, Aḥmad-i-yūsuf and Aḥmad-i-qāsim. They did well, made the fort fast, strengthened it, and kept watch.

(*k. Bābur's advance to Kābul.*)

From Tīmūr Beg's Langar we sent Qāsim Beg's servant, Muḥ. of Andijān, a *Tūqbāī*, to the Kābul begs, with written details of our arrival and of the following arrangements :—" When we

move on!' They paid me no attention. When, in order to help, I myself attacked, dismounting and going up the hill, they shewed courage and emulation in following. Getting to the top of the pass, we drove that band off, killing many, capturing others, making their families prisoner and plundering their goods." This is followed by "I myself collected" *etc.* as in the Turkī text after the verse. It will be seen that the above extract is not a translation of the verse; no translator or even summariser would be likely to omit so much of his original. It is just a suitably plain account of a trivial matter.

[1] *Gulistān* Cap. I. Story 4.

are out of the Ghūr-bund narrows,[1] we will fall on them suddenly; let our signal to you be the fire we will light directly we have passed Minār-hill; do you in reply light one in the citadel, on
Fol. 197*b*. the old Kūshk (kiosk)," now the Treasury, "so that we may be sure you know of our coming. We will come up from our side; you come out from yours; neglect nothing your hands can find to do!" This having been put into writing, Muḥammad *Andijānī* was sent off.

Riding next dawn from the Langar, we dismounted over against Ushtur-shahr. Early next morning we passed the Ghūr-bund narrows, dismounted at Bridge-head, there watered and rested our horses, and at the Mid-day Prayer set forward again. Till we reached the *tūtqāwal*,[2] there was no snow, beyond that, the further we went the deeper the snow. The cold between Ẕamma-yakhshī and Minār was such as we had rarely felt in our lives.

We sent on Aḥmad the messenger (*yāsāwal*) and Qarā Aḥmad *yūrūnchī*[3] to say to the begs, "Here we are at the time promised; be ready! be bold!" After crossing Minār-hill[4] and dismounting on its skirt, helpless with cold, we lit fires to warm ourselves. It was not time to light the signal-fire; we just lit these because we were helpless in that mighty cold. Near shoot of dawn we rode on from Minār-hill; between it and Kābul the snow was up to the horses' knees and had hardened, so off the road to move was difficult. Riding single-file the whole way, we got to Kābul
Fol 198. in good time undiscovered.[5] Before we were at Bībī Māh-rūī (Lady Moon-face), the blaze of fire on the citadel let us know that the begs were looking out.

(*l. Attack made on the rebels.*)

On reaching Sayyid Qāsim's bridge, Sherīm Ṭaghāī and the men of the right were sent towards Mullā Bābā's bridge, while

[1] Bābur seems to have left the Ghūr-bund valley, perhaps pursuing the Hazāras towards Janglīk, and to have come "by ridge and valley" back into it for Ushtur-shahr. I have not located Tīmūr Beg's Langar. As has been noted already (*q.v.* index) the Ghūr-bund narrows are at the lower end of the valley; they have been surmised to be the fissured rampart of an ancient lake.

[2] Here this may represent a guard- or toll-house (Index *s.n.*).

[3] As *yūrūn* is a patch, the bearer of the sobriquet might be Black Aḥmad the repairing-tailor.

[4] *Second Afghān War*, Map of Kābul and its environs.

[5] I understand that the arrival undiscovered was a result of riding in single-file and thus shewing no black mass.

we of the left and centre took the Bābā Lūlī road. Where Khalīfa's garden now is, there was then a smallish garden made by Aūlūgh Beg Mīrzā for a Langar (almshouse); none of its trees or shrubs were left but its enclosing wall was there. In this garden Mīrzā Khān was seated, Muḥ. Ḥusain Mīrzā being in Aūlūgh Beg Mīrzā's great Bāgh-i-bihisht. I had gone as far along the lane of Mullā Bābā's garden as the burial-ground when four men met us who had hurried forward into Mīrzā Khān's quarters, been beaten, and forced to turn back. One of the four was Sayyid Qāsim Lord of the Gate, another was Qāsim Beg's son Qaṃbar-i-'alī, another was Sher-qulī the scout, another was Sl. Aḥmad *Mughūl* one of Sher-qulī's band. These four, without a "God forbid!" (*taḥāshī*) had gone right into Mīrzā Khān's quarters; thereupon he, hearing an uproar, had mounted and got away. Abū'l-ḥasan the armourer's younger brother even, Muḥ. Ḥusain by name, had taken service with Mīrzā Khān; he had slashed at Sher-qulī, Fol. 198*b*. one of those four, thrown him down, and was just striking his head off, when Sher-qulī freed himself. Those four, tasters of the sword, tasters of the arrow, wounded one and all, came pelting back on us to the place mentioned.

Our horsemen, jammed in the narrow lane, were standing still, unable to move forward or back. Said I to the braves near, "Get off and force a road". Off got Nāṣir's Dost, Khwāja Muḥammad 'Alī the librarian, Bābā Sher-zād (Tiger-whelp), Shāh Maḥmūd and others, pushed forward and at once cleared the way. The enemy took to flight.

We had looked for the begs to come out from the Fort but they could not come in time for the work; they only dropped in, by ones and twos, after we had made the enemy scurry off. Aḥmad-i-yūsuf had come from them before I went into the Chār-bāgh where Mīrzā Khān had been; he went in with me, but we both turned back when we saw the Mīrzā had gone off. Coming in at the garden-gate was Dost of Sar-i-pul, a foot-soldier I had promoted for his boldness to be Kotwāl and had left in Kābul; he made straight for me, sword in hand. I had my cuirass on but had not fastened the *gharīcha*[1] nor had I put on Fol. 199.

[1] or *gharbīcha*, which Mr. Erskine explains to be the four plates of mail, made to cover the back, front and sides; the *jība* would thus be the wadded under-coat to which they are attached.

my helm. Whether he did not recognize me because of change wrought by cold and snow, or whether because of the flurry of the fight, though I shouted "Hāī Dost! hāī Dost!" and though Aḥmad-i-yūsuf also shouted, he, without a "God forbid!" brought down his sword on my unprotected arm. Only by God's grace can it have been that not a hairbreadth of harm was done to me.

> If a sword shook the Earth from her place,
> Not a vein would it cut till God wills.

It was through the virtue of a prayer I had repeated that the Great God averted this danger and turned this evil aside. That prayer was as follows :—

> "O my God! Thou art my Creator; except Thee there is no God. On Thee do I repose my trust; Thou art the Lord of the mighty throne. What God wills comes to pass; and what he does not will comes not to pass; and there is no power or strength but through the high and exalted God; and, of a truth, in all things God is almighty; and verily He comprehends all things by his knowledge, and has taken account of everything. O my Creator! as I sincerely trust in Thee, do Thou seize by the forelock all evil proceeding from within myself, and all evil coming from without, and all evil proceeding from every man who can be the occasion of evil, and all such evil as can proceed from any living thing, and remove them far from me; since, of a truth, Thou art the Lord of the exalted throne!"[1]

On leaving that garden we went to Muḥ. Ḥusain Mīrzā's quarters in the Bāgh-i-bihisht, but he had fled and gone off to hide himself. Seven or eight men stood in a breach of the Fol. 199*b*. garden-wall; I spurred at them; they could not stand; they fled; I got up with them and cut at one with my sword; he rolled over in such a way that I fancied his head was off, passed on and went away; it seems he was Mīrzā Khān's foster-brother, Tūlik Kūkūldāsh and that my sword fell on his shoulder.

At the gate of Muḥ. Ḥusain Mīrzā's quarters, a Mughūl I recognized for one of my own servants, drew his bow and aimed at my face from a place on the roof as near me as a gate-ward stands to a Gate. People on all sides shouted, "Hāi! hāi! it is the Pādshāh." He changed his aim, shot off his arrow and ran away. The affair was beyond the shooting of arrows! His Mīrzā, his leaders, had run away or been taken; why was he shooting?

[1] This prayer is composed of extracts from the Qorān (*Mém.* i, 454 note); it is reproduced as it stands in Mr. Erskine's wording (p. 216).

There they brought Sl. Sanjar *Barlās*, led in by a rope round his neck; he even, to whom I had given the Nīngnahār *tūmān*, had had his part in the mutiny! Greatly agitated, he kept crying out, "Hāi! what fault is in me?" Said I, "Can there be one clearer than that you are higher than the purpose and counsels of this crew?"[1] But as he was the sister's son of my Khān *dādā's* mother, Shāh Begīm, I gave the order, "Do not lead him with such dishonour; it is not death."

On leaving that place, I sent Aḥmad-i-qasim *Kohbur*, one of the begs of the Fort, with a few braves, in pursuit of Mīrzā Khān. Fol. 200.

(*m. Bābur's dealings with disloyal women.*)

When I left the Bāgh-i-bihisht, I went to visit Shāh Begīm and (Mihr-nigār) Khānīm who had settled themselves in tents by the side of the garden.

As townspeople and black-bludgeoners had raised a riot, and were putting hands out to pillage property and to catch persons in corners and outside places, I sent men, to beat the rabble off, and had it herded right away.[2]

Shāh Begīm and Khānīm were seated in one tent. I dismounted at the usual distance, approached with my former deference and courtesy, and had an interview with them. They were extremely agitated, upset, and ashamed; could neither excuse themselves reasonably[3] nor make the enquiries of affection. I had not expected this (disloyalty) of them; it was not as though that party, evil as was the position it had taken up, consisted of persons who would not give ear to the words of Shāh Begīm and Khānīm; Mīrzā Khān was the begīm's grandson, in her presence night and day; if she had not fallen in with the affair, she could have kept him with her.

[1] Bābur's reference may well be to Sanjar's birth as well as to his being the holder of Nīngnahār. Sanjar's father had been thought worthy to mate with one of the six Badakhshī begīms whose line traced back to Alexander (T.R. p. 107); and his father was a Barlās, seemingly of high family.

[2] It may be inferred that what was done was for the protection of the two women.

[3] Not a bad case could have been made out for now putting a Tīmūrid in Bābur's place in Kābul; *viz.* that he was believed captive in Herī and that Mīrzā Khān was an effective *locum tenens* against the Arghūns. Ḥaidar sets down what in his eyes pleaded excuse for his father Muḥ. Ḥusain (T.R. p. 198).

Twice over when fickle Fortune and discordant Fate had parted
Fol. 200b. me from throne and country, retainer and following, I, and my mother with me, had taken refuge with them and had had no kindness soever from them. At that time my younger brother (*i.e.* cousin) Mīrzā Khān and his mother Sulṯān-nigār Khānīm held valuable cultivated districts; yet my mother and I,—to leave all question of a district aside,—were not made possessors of a single village or a few yoke of plough-oxen.[1] Was my mother not Yūnas Khān's daughter? was I not his grandson?

In my days of plenty I have given from my hand what matched the blood-relationship and the position of whatsoever member of that (Chaghatāī) dynasty chanced down upon me. For example, when the honoured Shāh Begīm came to me, I gave her Pamghān, one of the best places in Kābul, and failed in no sort of filial duty and service towards her. Again, when Sl. Sa'īd Khān, Khān in Kāshghar, came [914 AH.] with five or six naked followers on foot, I looked upon him as an honoured guest and gave him Mandrāwar of the Lamghān *tūmāns*. Beyond this also, when Shāh Ismā'īl had killed Shaibāq Khān in Marv and I crossed over to Qūndūz (916 AH.—1511 AD.), the Andijānīs, some driving their (Aūzbeg) *dāroghas* out, some making their places fast, turned their eyes to me and sent me a man; at that time I trusted those old family servants to that same Sl. Sa'īd Khān, gave him a force, made him Khān and sped him forth. Again, down to the present time (*circa* 934 AH.) I have not looked upon any member of that family who has come to me, in any other light than as a blood-relation. For example, there
Fol. 201. are now in my service Chīn-tīmūr Sulṯān; Aīsān-tīmūr Sulṯān, Tūkhtā-būghā Sulṯān, and Bābā Sulṯān;[2] on one and all of these I have looked with more favour than on blood-relations of my own.

I do not write this in order to make complaint; I have written the plain truth. I do not set these matters down in order to make known my own deserts; I have set down exactly what has happened. In this History I have held firmly to it that the truth should be reached in every matter, and that every

[1] *qūsh*, not even a little plough-land being given (*chand qulba dihya*, 215 f. 162).
[2] They were sons of Sl. Aḥmad Khān *Chaghatāī*.

act should be recorded precisely as it occurred. From this it follows of necessity that I have set down of good and bad whatever is known, concerning father and elder brother, kinsman and stranger; of them all I have set down carefully the known virtues and defects. Let the reader accept my excuse; let the reader pass on from the place of severity!

(*n. Letters of victory.*)

Rising from that place and going to the Chār-bāgh where Mīrzā Khān had been, we sent letters of victory to all the countries, clans, and retainers. This done, I rode to the citadel.

(*o. Arrest of rebel leaders.*)

Muḥammad Ḥusain Mīrzā in his terror having run away into Khānīm's bedding-room and got himself fastened up in a bundle of bedding, we appointed Mīrīm *Dīwān* with other begs of the fort, to take control in those dwellings, capture, and bring him in. Mīrīm *Dīwān* said some plain rough words at Khānīm's Fol. 201*b*. gate, by some means or other found the Mīrzā, and brought him before me in the citadel. I rose at once to receive the Mīrzā with my usual deference, not even shewing too harsh a face. If I had had that Muḥ. Ḥusain M. cut in pieces, there was the ground for it that he had had part in base and shameful action, started and spurred on mutiny and treason. Death he deserved with one after another of varied pain and torture, but because there had come to be various connexion between us, his very sons and daughters being by my own mother's sister Khūb-nigār Khānīm, I kept this just claim in mind, let him go free, and permitted him to set out towards Khurāsān. The cowardly ingrate then forgot altogether the good I did him by the gift of his life; he blamed and slandered me to Shaibāq Khān. Little time passed, however, before the Khān gave him his deserts by death.

Leave thou to Fate the man who does thee wrong,
For Fate is an avenging servitor.[1]

---

[1] f. 160.

Aḥmad-i-qāsim *Kohbur* and the party of braves sent in pursuit of Mīrzā Khān, overtook him in the low hills of Qargha-yīlāq, not able even to run away, without heart or force to stir a finger!
Fol. 202. They took him, and brought him to where I sat in the north-east porch of the old Çourt-house. Said I to him, "Come! let's have a look at one another" (*kūrūshālīng*), but twice before he could bend the knee and come forward, he fell down through agitation. When we had looked at one another, I placed him by my side to give him heart, and I drank first of the sherbet brought in, in order to remove his fears.[1]

As those who had joined him, soldiers, peasants, Mughūls and Chaghatāīs,[2] were in suspense, we simply ordered him to remain for a few days in his elder sister's house; but a few days later he was allowed to set out for Khurāsān[3] because those mentioned above were somewhat uncertain and it did not seem well for him to stay in Kābul.

(p. Excursion to Koh-dāman.)

After letting those two go, we made an excursion to Bārān, Chāsh-tūpa, and the skirt of Gul-i-bahār.[4] More beautiful in

[1] Ḥaidar's opinion of Bābur at this crisis is of the more account that his own father was one of the rebels let go to the mercy of the "avenging servitor". When he writes of Bābur, as being, at a time so provoking, gay, generous, affectionate, simple and gentle, he sets before us insight and temper in tune with Kipling's "If . . ."

[2] Bābur's distinction, made here and elsewhere, between Chaghatāī and Mughūl touches the old topic of the right or wrong of the term "Mughūl dynasty". What he, as also Ḥaidar, allows said is that if Bābur were to describe his mother in tribal terms, he would say she was half-Chaghatāī, half-Mughūl; and that if he so described himself, he would say he was half-Tīmūrid-Turk, half-Chaghatāī. He might have called the dynasty he founded in India Turkī, might have called it Tīmūriya; he would never have called it Mughūl, after his maternal grandmother.

Ḥaidar, with imperfect classification, divides Chīngīz Khān's "Mughūl horde" into Mughūls and Chaghatāīs and of this Chaghatāī offtake says that none remained in 953 AH. (1547 AD.) except the rulers, *i.e.* sons of Sl. Aḥmad Khan (T.R. 148). Manifestly there was a body of Chaghatāīs with Bābur and there appear to have been many near his day in the Herī region,—'Alī-sher *Nawā'ī* the best known.

Bābur supplies directions for naming his dynasty when, as several times, he claims to rule in Hindūstān where the "Turk" had ruled (f. 233*b*, f. 224*b*, f. 225). To call his dynasty Mughūl seems to blot out the centuries, something as we should do by calling the English Teutons. If there is to be such blotting-out, Abū'l-ghāzī would allow us, by his tables of Turk descent, to go further, to the primal source of all the tribes concerned, to Turk, son of Japhet. This traditional descent is another argument against "Mughūl dynasty."

[3] They went to Qandahār and there suffered great privation.

[4] Bārān seems likely to be the Baian of some maps. Gul-i-bahār is higher up on the Panjhīr road. Chāsh-tūpa will have been near-by; its name might mean *Hill of the heap of winnowed-corn.*

Spring than any part even of Kābul are the open-lands of Bārān, the plain of Chāsh-tūpa, and the skirt of Gul-i-bahār. Many sorts of tulip bloom there; when I had them counted once, it came out at 34 different kinds as [has been said].[1] This couplet has been written in praise of these places,—

> Kābul in Spring is an Eden of verdure and blossom;
> Matchless in Kābul the Spring of Gul-i-bahār and Bārān.

On this excursion I finished the ode,—

> My heart, like the bud of the red, red rose,
> Lies fold within fold aflame; Fol. 202b.
> Would the breath of even a myriad Springs
> Blow my heart's bud to a rose?

In truth, few places are quite equal to these for spring-excursions, for hawking (*qūsh sālmāq*) or bird-shooting (*qūsh ātmāq*), as has been briefly mentioned in the praise and description of the Kābul and Ghaznī country.

(*q. Nāṣir Mīrzā expelled from Badakhshān.*)

This year the begs of Badakhshān *i.e.* Muḥammad the armourer, Mubārak Shāh, Zubair and Jahāngīr, grew angry and mutinous because of the misconduct of Nāṣir Mīrzā and some of those he cherished. Coming to an agreement together, they drew out an army of horse and foot, arrayed it on the level lands by the Kūkcha-water, and moved towards Yaftal and Rāgh, to near Khamchān, by way of the lower hills. The Mīrzā and his inexperienced begs, in their thoughtless and unobservant fashion, came out to fight them just in those lower hills. The battle-field was uneven ground; the Badakhshīs had a dense mass of men on foot who stood firm under repeated charges by the Mīrzā's horse, and returned such attack that the horsemen fled, unable to keep their ground. Having beaten the Mīrzā, the Badakhshīs plundered his dependants and connexions.

Beaten and stripped bare, he and his close circle took the road through Ishkīmīsh and Nārīn to Kīlā-gāhī, from there followed the Qīzīl-sū up, got out on the Āb-dara road, crossed at Shibr-tū, and so came to Kābul, he with 70 or 80 followers, worn-out, naked and famished.

[1] f. 136.

That was a marvellous sign of the Divine might! Two or three years earlier the Mīrzā had left the Kābul country like a
Fol. 203. foe, driving tribes and hordes like sheep before him, reached Badakhshān and made fast its forts and valley-strongholds. With what fancy in his mind had he marched out?[1] Now he was back, hanging the head of shame for those earlier misdeeds, humbled and distraught about that breach with me!

My face shewed him no sort of displeasure; I made kind enquiry about himself, and brought him out of his confusion.

[1] Answer; Visions of his father's sway.

913 AH.—MAY 13TH 1507 TO MAY 2ND 1508 AD.[1]

(a. Raid on the Ghiljī Afghāns.)

We had ridden out of Kābul with the intention of over-running the Ghiljī;[2] when we dismounted at Sar-i-dih news was brought that a mass of Mahmands (Afghāns) was lying in Masht and Sih-kāna one *yīghāch* (*circa* 5 m.) away from us.[3] Our begs and braves agreed in saying, "The Mahmands must be over-run", but I said, "Would it be right to turn aside and raid our own peasants instead of doing what we set out to do? It cannot be."

Riding at night from Sar-i-dih, we crossed the plain of Kattawāz in the dark, a quite black night, one level stretch of land, no mountain or rising-ground in sight, no known road or track, not a man able to lead us! In the end I took the lead. I had been in those parts several times before; drawing inferences from those times, I took the Pole-star on my right shoulder-blade[4] and, with some anxiety, moved on. God brought it right! We went straight to the Qīāq-tū and the Aūlābā-tū torrent, that is to say, straight for Khwāja Ismā'īl *Sirītī* where the Ghiljīs were lying, the road to which crosses the torrent named. Dismounting near the torrent, we let ourselves and our horses sleep a little, Fol. 203*b* took breath, and bestirred ourselves at shoot of dawn. The Sun was up before we got out of those low hills and valley-bottoms to the plain on which the Ghiljī lay with a good *yīghāch*[5] of

[1] Elph. MS. f. 161; W.-i-B. I.O. 215 f. 164 and 217 f. 139*b*; Mems. p. 220.

[2] The narrative indicates the location of the tribe, the modern Ghilzāī or Ghilzī.

[3] Sih-kāna lies s.e. of Shorkach, and near Kharbīn. Sar-i-dih is about 25 or 30 miles s. of Ghaznī (Erskine). A name suiting the pastoral wealth of the tribe *viz.* Mesh-khail, Sheep-tribe, is shewn on maps somewhat s. from Kharbīn. Cf. Steingass *s.n.* Masht.

[4] *yāghrūn*, whence *yāghrūnchī*, a diviner by help of the shoulder-blades of sheep. The defacer of the Elphinstone Codex has changed *yāghrūn* to *yān*, side, thus making Bābur turn his side and not his half-back to the north, altering his direction, and missing what looks like a jesting reference to his own divination of the road. The Pole Star was seen, presumably, before the night became quite black.

[5] From the subsequent details of distance done, this must have been one of those good *yīghāch* of perhaps 5–6 miles, that are estimated by the ease of travel on level lands (Index *s.v. yīghāch*).

road between them and us; once out on the plain we could see their blackness, either their own or from the smoke of their fires.

Whether bitten by their own whim,[1] or whether wanting to hurry, the whole army streamed off at the gallop (*chāpqūn qūīdīlār*); off galloped I after them and, by shooting an arrow now at a man, now at a horse, checked them after a *kuroh* or two (3 m. ?). It is very difficult indeed to check 5 or 6000 braves galloping loose-rein! God brought it right! They were checked! When we had gone about one *shar'ī* (2 m.) further, always with the Afghān blackness in sight, the raid[2] was allowed. Masses of sheep fell to us, more than in any other raid.

After we had dismounted and made the spoils turn back,[3] one body of Afghāns after another came down into the plain, provoking a fight. Some of the begs and of the household went against one body and killed every man; Nāṣir Mīrzā did the same with another, and a pillar of Afghān heads was set up. An arrow pierced the foot of that foot-soldier Dost the Kotwāl who has been mentioned already;[4] when we reached Kābul, he died.

Marching from Khwāja Ismā'īl, we dismounted once more at Aūlābā-tū. Some of the begs and of my own household were ordered to go forward and carefully separate off the Fifth (*Khums*) of the enemy's spoils. By way of favour, we did not
Fol. 204. take the Fifth from Qāsim Beg and some others.[5] From what

[1] I am uncertain about the form of the word translated by "whim". The Elph. and Ḥai. Codices read *khūd d:lma* (altered in the first to *y:lma*); Ilminsky (p. 257) reads *khūd l:ma* (de C. ii, 2 and note); Erskine has been misled by the Persian translation (215 f. 164*b* and 217 f. 139*b*). Whether *khūd-dilma* should be read, with the sense of "out of their own hearts" (spontaneously), or whether *khūd-yalma*, own pace (Turkī, *yalma*, pace) the contrast made by Bābur appears to be between an unpremeditated gallop and one premeditated for haste. Persian *dalama*, tarantula, also suggests itself.

[2] *chāpqūn*, which is the word translated by gallop throughout the previous passage. The Turkī verb *chāpmāq* is one of those words-of-all-work for which it is difficult to find a single English equivalent. The verb *qūīmāq* is another; in its two occurrences here the first may be a metaphor from the pouring of molten metal; the second expresses that permission to gallop off for the raid without which to raid was forbidden. The root-notion of *qūīmāq* seems to be letting-go, that of *chāpmāq*, rapid motion.

[3] *i.e.* on the raiders' own road for Kābul. [4] f. 198*b*.

[5] The Fifth taken was manifestly at the ruler's disposition. In at least two places when dependants send gifts to Bābur the word [*tassaduq*] used might be rendered as "gifts for the poor". Does this mean that the *pādshāh* in receiving this stands in the place of the Imām of the Qorān injunction which orders one-fifth of spoil to be given to the Imām for the poor, orphans, and travellers,—four-fifths being reserved for the troops? (Qorān, Sale's ed. 1825, i, 212 and Hidāyat, Book ix).

was written down,[1] the Fifth came out at 16,000, that is to say, this 16,000 was the fifth of 80,000 sheep; no question however but that with those lost and those not asked for, a *lak* (100,000) of sheep had been taken.

(*b. A hunting-circle.*)

Next day when we had ridden from that camp, a hunting-circle was formed on the plain of Kattawāz where deer (*kiyīk*)[2] and wild-ass are always plentiful and always fat. Masses went into the ring; masses were killed. During the hunt I galloped after a wild-ass, on getting near shot one arrow, shot another, but did not bring it down, it only running more slowly for the two wounds. Spurring forwards and getting into position[3] quite close to it, I chopped at the nape of its neck behind the ears, and cut through the wind-pipe; it stopped, turned over and died. My sword cut well! The wild-ass was surprisingly fat. Its rib may have been a little under one yard in length. Sherīm Ṭaghāī and other observers of *kiyīk* in Mughūlistān said with surprise, "Even in Mughūlistān we have seen few *kiyīk* so fat!" I shot another wild-ass; most of the wild-asses and deer brought down in that hunt were fat, but not one of them was so fat as the one I first killed.

Turning back from that raid, we went to Kābul and there dismounted.

(*c. Shaibāq Khān moves against Khurāsān.*)

Shaibāq Khān had got an army to horse at the end of last year, meaning to go from Samarkand against Khurāsān, his Fol. 204*b*. march out being somewhat hastened by the coming to him of a servant of that vile traitor to his salt, Shāh Manṣūr the Paymaster, then in Andikhūd. When the Khān was approaching Andikhūd, that vile wretch said, "I have sent a man to the Aūzbeg," relied on this, adorned himself, stuck up an aigrette on his head, and went out, bearing gift and tribute. On this the leaderless[4] Aūzbegs poured down on him from all sides, and

[1] This may be the sum of the separate items of sheep entered in account-books by the commissaries.

[2] Here this comprehensive word will stand for deer, these being plentiful in the region.

[3] Three Turkī MSS. write *ṣighīnib*, but the Elph. MS. has had this changed to *yītib*, having reached.

[4] *bāsh-sīz*, lit. without head, doubtless a pun on Aūz-beg (own beg, leaderless). B.M. Or. 3714 shows an artist's conception of this *tart-part*.

turned upside down (*tart-part*) the blockhead, his offering and his people of all sorts.

(*d. Irresolution of the Khurāsān Mīrzās.*)

Badī'u'z-zamān Mīrzā, Muzaffar Mīrzā, Muḥ. Barandūq *Barlās* and Zū'n-nūn *Arghūn* were all lying with their army in Bābā Khākī,[1] not decided to fight, not settled to make (Herī) fort fast, there they sat, confounded, vague, uncertain what to do. Muḥammad Barandūq *Barlās* was a knowledgeable man; he kept saying, "You let Muzaffar Mīrzā and me make the fort fast; let Badī'u'z-zamān Mīrzā and Zū'n-nūn Beg go into the mountains near Herī and gather in Sl. 'Alī *Arghūn* from Sīstān and Zamīn-dāwar, Shāh Beg and Muqīm from Qandahār with all their armies, and let them collect also what there is of Nikdīrī and Hazāra force; this done, let them make a swift and telling move. The enemy would find it difficult to go into the mountains, and could not come against the (Herī) fort because
Fol. 205. he would be afraid of the army outside." He said well, his plan was practical.

Brave though Zū'n-nūn *Arghūn* was, he was mean, a lover-of-goods, far from businesslike or judicious, rather shallow-pated, and a bit of a fool. As has been mentioned,[2] when that elder and that younger brother became joint-rulers in Herī, he had chief authority in Badī'u'z-zamān Mīrzā's presence. He was not willing now for Muḥ. Barandūq Beg to remain inside Herī town; being the lover-of-goods he was, he wanted to be there himself. But he could not make this seem one and the same thing![3] Is there a better sign of his shallow-pate and craze than that he degraded himself and became contemptible by accepting the lies and flattery of rogues and sycophants? Here are the particulars[4]:—While he was so dominant and trusted in Herī, certain Shaikhs and Mullās went to him and said, "The Spheres are holding commerce with us; you are styled *Hizabru'l-lāh* (Lion of God); you will overcome the Aūzbeg." Believing

[1] Bābā Khākī is a fine valley, some 13 *yīghāch* e. of Herī (f. 13) where the Herī sultāns reside in the heats (*J. Asiatique* xvi, 501, de Meynard's article; H.S. iii, 356).
[2] f. 172*b*.
[3] *aūkhshātā almādī*. This is one of many passages which Ilminsky indicates he has made good by help of the Memoirs (p. 261; *Mémoires* ii, 6).
[4] They are given also on f. 172.

these words, he put his bathing-cloth round his neck and gave thanks. It was through this he did not accept Muḥammad Barandūq Beg's sensible counsel, did not strengthen the works (*aīsh*) of the fort, get ready fighting equipment, set scout or rearward to warn of the foe's approach, or plan out such method of array that, should the foe appear, his men would fight with ready heart.

(*e. Shaibāq Khān takes Herī.*)

Shaibāq Khān passed through Murgh-āb to near Sīr-kāī[1] in the month of Muḥarram (913 AH. May–June 1507 AD.). When the Mīrzās heard of it, they were altogether upset, could not act, collect troops, array those they had. Dreamers, they moved through a dream![2] Ẕū'n-nūn *Arghūn*, made glorious by that flattery, went out to Qarā-rabāṭ, with 100 to 150 men, to face 40,000 to 50,000 Aūzbegs: a mass of these coming up, hustled his off, took him, killed him and cut off his head.[3] Fol. 205b.

In Fort Ikhtiyāru'd-dīn, it is known as Ālā-qūrghān,[4] were the Mīrzās' mothers, elder and younger sisters, wives and treasure. The Mīrzās reached the town at night, let their horses rest till midnight, slept, and at dawn flung forth again. They could not think about strengthening the fort; in the respite and crack of time there was, they just ran away,[5] leaving mother, sister, wife and little child to Aūzbeg captivity.

What there was of Sl. Ḥusain Mīrzā's *ḥaram*, Pāyanda-sulṭān Begīm and Khadīja Begīm at the head of it, was inside Ālā-qūrghān; there too were the *ḥarams* of Badī'u'z-zamān

[1] This may be Sirakhs or Sirakhsh (Erskine).

[2] *Tūshlīq tūshdīn yūrdī bīrūrlār.* At least two meanings can be given to these words. Circumstances seem to exclude the one in which the Memoirs (p. 222) and *Mémoires* (ii, 7) have taken them here, *viz.* "each man went off to shift for himself", and "chacun s'en alla de son côté et s'enfuit comme il put", because Ẕū'n-nūn did not go off, and the Mīrzās broke up after his defeat. I therefore suggest another reading, one prompted by the Mīrzās' vague fancies and dreams of what they might do, but did not.

[3] The encounter was between "Belāq-i-marāl and Rabāṭ-i-'alī-sher, near Bādghīs" (Raverty's *Notes* p. 580). For particulars of the taking of Herī *see* Ḥ.S. iii, 353.

[4] One may be the book-name, the second the name in common use, and due to the colour of the buildings. But Bābur may be making an ironical jest, and nickname the fort by a word referring to the defilement (*ālā*) of Aūzbeg possession. (Cf. Ḥ.S. iii, 359.)

[5] Mr. Erskine notes that Badī'u'z-zamān took refuge with Shāh Ismā'īl *Ṣafawī* who gave him Tabrīz. When the Turkish Emperor Sālim took Tabrīz in 920 AH. (1514 AD.), he was taken prisoner and carried to Constantinople, where he died in 923 AH. (1517 AD.).

Mīrzā[1] and Muẓaffar Mīrzā with their little children, treasure, and households (*biyutāt*). What was desirable for making the fort fast had not been done; even braves to reinforce it had not arrived. 'Āshiq-i-muḥammad *Arghūn*, the younger brother of Mazīd Beg, had fled from the army on foot and gone into it; Fol. 206. in it was also Amīr 'Umar Beg's son 'Alī Khān (*Turkmān*); Shaikh 'Abdu'l-lāh the taster was there; Mīrzā Beg *Kāī-khusraūī* was there; and Mīrak *Gūr* (or *Kūr*) the Dīwān was there.

When Shaibāq Khān arrived two or three days later; the Shaikhu'l-islām and notables went out to him with the keys of the outer-fort. That same 'Āshiq-i-muḥammad held Ālā-qūrghān for 16 or 17 days; then a mine, run from the horse-market outside, was fired and brought a tower down; the garrison lost heart, could hold out no longer, so let the fort be taken.

(*f. Shaibāq Khān in Herī.*)

Shaibāq Khān, after taking Herī,[2] behaved badly not only to the wives and children of its rulers but to every person soever. For the sake of this five-days' fleeting world, he earned himself a bad name. His first improper act and deed in Herī was that, for the sake of this rotten world (*chirk dunyā*), he caused Khadīja Begīm various miseries, through letting the vile wretch Pay-master Shāh Manṣūr get hold of her to loot. Then he let 'Abdu'l-wahhāb *Mughūl* take to loot a person so saintly and so revered as Shaikh Pūrān, and each one of Shaikh Pūrān's children be taken by a separate person. He let the band of poets be seized by Mullā Banā'ī, a matter about which this verse is well-known in Khurāsān:—

> Except 'Abdu'l-lāh the stupid fool (*kīr-khar*),
> Not a poet to-day sees the colour of gold;
> From the poets' band Banā'ī would get gold,
> All he will get is *kīr-khar*.[3]

Fol. 206*b*.

---

[1] In the fort were his wife Kābulī Begīm, d. of Aūlūgh Beg M. *Kābulī* and Ruqaiya Āghā, known as the Nightingale. A young daughter of the Mīrzā, named the Rose-bud (Chūchak), had died just before the siege. After the surrender of the fort, Kābulī Begīm was married by Mīrzā Kūkūldāsh (perhaps 'Āshiq-i-muḥammad *Arghūn*); Ruqaiya by Tīmūr Sl. *Aūzbeg* (Ḥ.S. iii, 359).

[2] The *Khuṭba* was first read for Shaibāq Khān in Herī on Friday Muḥarram 15th 913 AH. (May 27th 1507 AD.).

[3] There is a Persian phrase used when a man engages in an unprofitable undertaking *Kīr-i-khar gerift, i.e. Asini nervum deprehendet* (Erskine). The Ḥ.S. does not

Directly he had possession of Herī, Shaibāq Khān married and took Muẓaffar Mīrzā's wife, Khān-zāda Khānīm, without regard to the running-out of the legal term.[1] His own illiteracy not forbidding, he instructed in the exposition of the Qoran, Qāẓī Ikhtiyār and Muḥammad Mīr Yūsuf, two of the celebrated and highly-skilled mullās of Herī; he took a pen and corrected the hand-writing of Mullā Sl. 'Alī of Mashhad and the drawing of Bih-zād; and every few days, when he had composed some tasteless couplet, he would have it read from the pulpit, hung in the Chār-sū [Square], and for it accept the offerings of the towns-people![2] Spite of his early-rising, his not neglecting the Five Prayers, and his fair knowledge of the art of reciting the Qorān, there issued from him many an act and deed as absurd, as impudent, and as heathenish as those just named

(*g. Death of two Mīrzās.*)

Ten or fifteen days after he had possession of Herī, Shaibāq Khān came from Kahd-stān[3] to Pul-i-sālār. From that place he sent Tīmūr Sl. and 'Ubaid Sl. with the army there present, against Abū'l-muḥsin Mīrzā and Kūpuk (Kīpik) Mīrzā then seated carelessly in Mashhad. The two Mīrzās had thought at one time of making Qalāt[4] fast; at another, this after they had had news of the approach of the Aūzbeg, they were for moving on Shaibāq Khān himself, by forced marches and along a different

mention Banā'ī as fleecing the poets but has much to say about one Maulānā 'Abdu'r-raḥīm a Turkistānī favoured by Shaibānī, whose victim Khwānd-amīr was, amongst many others. Not infrequently where Bābur and Khwānd-amīr state the same fact, they accompany it by varied details, as here (H.S. iii, 358, 360).

[1] '*adat.* Muḥammadan Law fixes a term after widowhood or divorce within which re-marriage is unlawful. Light is thrown upon this re-marriage by H.S. iii, 359. The passage, a somewhat rhetorical one, gives the following details:—"On coming into Herī on Muḥarram 11th, Shaibānī at once set about gathering in the property of the Tīmūrids. He had the wives and daughters of the former rulers brought before him. The great lady Khān-zāda Begīm (f. 163*b*) who was daughter of Aḥmad Khān, niece of Sl. Ḥusain Mīrzā, and wife of Muẓaffar Mīrzā, shewed herself pleased in his presence. Desiring to marry him, she said Muẓaffar M. had divorced her two years before. Trustworthy persons gave evidence to the same effect, so she was united to Shaibānī in accordance with the glorious Law. Mihr-angez Begīm, Muẓaffar M.'s daughter, was married to 'Ubaidu'llāh Sl. (*Aūzbeg*); the rest of the chaste ladies having been sent back into the city, Shaibānī resumed his search for property." Manifestly Bābur did not believe in the divorce Khwānd-amīr thus records.

[2] A sarcasm this on the acceptance of literary honour from the illiterate.

[3] f. 191 and note; Pul-i-sālār may be an irrigation-dam.

[4] Qalāt-i-nādirī, the birth-place of Nādir Shāh, n. of Mashhad and standing on very strong ground (Erskine).

road,[1]—which might have turned out an amazingly good idea! But while they sit still there in Mashhad with nothing decided, the Sulṭāns arrive by forced marches. The Mīrzās for their part
Fol. 207. array and go out; Abū'l-muḥsin Mīrzā is quickly overcome and routed; Kūpuk Mīrzā charges his brother's assailants with somewhat few men; him too they carry off; both brothers are dismounted and seated in one place; after an embrace (*qūchūsh*), they kiss farewell; Abū'l-muḥsin shews some want of courage; in Kūpuk Mirza it all makes no change at all. The heads of both are sent to Shaibāq Khān in Pul-i-sālār.

(*h. Bābur marches for Qandahār.*)

In those days Shāh Beg and his younger brother Muḥammad Muqīm, being afraid of Shaibāq Khān, sent one envoy after another to me with dutiful letters (*'arz-dāsht*), giving sign of amity and good-wishes. Muqīm, in a letter of his own, explicitly invited me. For us to look on at the Aūzbeg over-running the whole country, was not seemly; and as by letters and envoys, Shāh Beg and Muqīm had given me invitation, there remained little doubt they would wait upon me.[2] When all begs and counsellors had been consulted, the matter was left at this:—We were to get an army to horse, join the Arghūn begs and decide in accord and agreement with them, whether to move into Khurāsān or elsewhere as might seem good.

(*i. In Ghaznī and Qalāt-i-ghilzāī.*)

Ḥabība-sulṭān Begīm, my aunt (*yīnkā*) as I used to call her, met us in Ghaznī, having come from Herī, according to arrangement, in order to bring her daughter Maṣ'ūma-sulṭān Begīm.
Fol. 207*b*. With the honoured Begīm came Khusrau Kūkūldāsh, Sl. Qulī *Chūnāq* (One-eared) and Gadāī *Balāl* who had returned to me

[1] This is likely to be the road passing through the Carfax of Rabāṭ-i-sangbast, described by Daulat-shāh (Browne, p. 176).

[2] This will mean that the Arghūns would acknowledge his suzerainty; Ḥaidar Mīrzā however says that Shāh Beg had higher views (T.R. p. 202). There had been earlier negociations between Ẕū'n-nūn with Badī'u'z-zamān and Bābur which may have led to the abandonment of Bābur's expedition in 911 AD. (f. 158; Ḥ.S. iii, 323; Raverty's account (*Notes* p. 581–2) of Bābur's dealings with the Arghūn chiefs needs revision).

after flight from Herī, first to Ibn-i-ḥusain Mīrzā then to Abū'l-muḥsin Mīrzā,[1] with neither of whom they could remain.

In Qalāt the army came upon a mass of Hindūstān traders, come there to traffic and, as it seemed, unable to go on. The general opinion about them was that people who, at a time of such hostilities, are coming into an enemy's country [2] must be plundered. With this however I did not agree; said I, "What is the traders' offence? If we, looking to God's pleasure, leave such scrapings of gain aside, the Most High God will apportion our reward. It is now just as it was a short time back when we rode out to raid the Ghiljī; many of you then were of one mind to raid the Mahmand Afghāns, their sheep and goods, their wives and families, just because they were within five miles of you! Then as now I did not agree with you. On the very next day the Most High God apportioned you more sheep belonging to Afghān enemies, than had ever before fallen to the share of the army." Something by way of *peshkash* (offering) was taken from each trader when we dismounted on the other side of Qalāt.

(*j. Further march south.*)

Beyond Qalāt two Mīrzās joined us, fleeing from Qandahār. One was Mīrzā Khān (Wais) who had been allowed to go into Khurāsān after his defeat at Kābul. The other was 'Abdu'r-razzāq Mīrzā who had stayed on in Khurāsān when I left. With them came and waited on me the mother of Jahāngīr Mīrzā's son Pīr-i-muḥammad, a grandson of Pahār Mīrzā.[3] Fol. 208.

(*k. Behaviour of the Arghūn chiefs.*)

When we sent persons and letters to Shāh Beg and Muqīm, saying, "Here we are at your word; a stranger-foe like the

[1] They will have gone first to Tūn or Qāīn, thence to Mashhad, and seem likely to have joined the Begīm after cross-cutting to avoid Herī.

[2] *yāghī wilāyatī-ghā kilādūrghān.* There may have been an accumulation of caravans on their way to Herāt, checked in Qalāt by news of the Aūzbeg conquest.

[3] Jahāngīr's son, thus brought by his mother, will have been an infant; his father had gone back last year with Bābur by the mountain road and had been left, sick and travelling in a litter, with the baggage when Bābur hurried on to Kābul at the news of the mutiny against him (f. 197); he must have died shortly afterwards, seemingly between the departure of the two rebels from Kābul (f. 201*b*–202) and the march out for Qandahār. Doubtless his widow now brought her child to claim his uncle Bābur's protection.

Aūzbeg has taken Khurāsān; come! let us settle, in concert and amity, what will be for the general good," they returned a rude and ill-mannered answer, going back from the dutiful letters they had written and from the invitations they had given. One of their incivilities was that Shāh Beg stamped his letter to me in the middle of its reverse, where begs seal if writing to begs, where indeed a great beg seals if writing to one of the lower circle.[1] But for such ill-manners and his rude answers, his affair would never have gone so far as it did, for, as they say,—

A strife-stirring word will accomplish the downfall of an ancient line.

By these their headstrong acts they gave to the winds house, family, and the hoards of 30 to 40 years.

One day while we were near Shahr-i-ṣafā [2] a false alarm being given in the very heart of the camp, the whole army was made to arm and mount. At the time I was occupied with a bath
Fol. 208*b*. and purification; the begs were much flurried; I mounted when I was ready; as the alarm was false, it died away after a time.

March by march we moved on to Guzar.[3] There we tried again to discuss with the Arghūns but, paying no attention to us, they maintained the same obstinate and perverse attitude. Certain well-wishers who knew the local land and water, represented to me, that the head of the torrents (*rūdlār*) which come down to Qandahār, being towards Bābā Ḥasan Abdāl and Khalishak,[4] a move ought to be made in that direction, in order

[1] Persians pay great attention in their correspondence not only to the style but to the kind of paper on which a letter is written, the place of signature, the place of the seal, and the situation of the address. Chardin gives some curious information on the subject (Erskine). Bābur marks the distinction of rank he drew between the Arghūn chiefs and himself when he calls their letter to him, *'arẓ-dāsht*, his to them *khaṭṭ*. His claim to suzerainty over those chiefs is shewn by Ḥaidar Mīrzā to be based on his accession to Tīmūrid headship through the downfall of the Bāī-qarās, who had been the acknowledged suzerains of the Arghūns now repudiating Bābur's claim. Cf. Erskine's *History of India* i, cap. 3.

[2] on the main road, some 40 miles east of Qandahār.

[3] var. Kūr or Kawar. If the word mean *ford*, this might well be the one across the Tarnak carrying the road to Qarā (maps). Here Bābur seems to have left the main road along the Tarnak, by which the British approach was made in 1880 A.D., for one crossing west into the valley of the Argand-āb.

[4] Bābā Ḥasan *Abdāl* is the Bābā Walī of maps. The same saint has given his name here, and also to his shrine east of Atak where he is known as Bābā Walī of Qandahār. The torrents mentioned are irrigation off-takes from the Argand-āb, which river flows between Bābā Walī and Khalishak. Shāh Beg's force was south of the torrents (cf. Murghān-koh on S.A.W. map).

to cut off (*yīqmāq*) all those torrents.[1] Leaving the matter there, we next day made our men put on their mail, arrayed in right and left, and marched for Qandahār.

(*l. Battle of Qandahār.*)

Shāh Beg and Muqīm had seated themselves under an awning which was set in front of the naze of the Qandahār-hill where I am now having a rock-residence cut out.[2] Muqīm's men pushed forward amongst the trees to rather near us. Ṭūfān *Arghūn* had fled to us when we were near Shahr-i-ṣafā; he now betook himself alone close up to the Arghūn array to where one named 'Ashaqu'l-lāh was advancing rather fast leading 7 or 8 men. Alone, Ṭūfān *Arghūn* faced him, slashed swords with him, unhorsed him, cut off his head and brought it to me as we were passing Sang-i-lakhshak;[3] an omen we accepted! Not thinking it well to fight where we were, amongst suburbs and trees, we went on along the skirt of the hill. Just as we had settled on ground for the camp, in a meadow on the Qandahār side of the torrent,[4] opposite Khalishak, and were dismounting, Sher Qulī the scout hurried up and represented that the enemy was arrayed to fight and on the move towards us. Fol. 209.

As on our march from Qalāt the army had suffered much from hunger and thirst, most of the soldiers on getting near Khalishak scattered up and down for sheep and cattle, grain

[1] The narrative and plans of *Second Afghan War* (Murray 1908) illustrate Bābur's movements and show most of the places he names. The end of the 280 mile march, from Kābul to within sight of Qandahār, will have stirred in the General of 1507 what it stirred in the General of 1880. Lord Roberts speaking in May 1913 in Glasgow on the rapid progress of the movement for National Service thus spoke:—"A memory comes over me which turns misgiving into hope and apprehension into confidence. It is the memory of the morning when, accompanied by two of Scotland's most famous regiments, the Seaforths and the Gordons, at the end of a long and arduous march, *I saw in the distance the walls and minarets of Qandahar, and knew that the end of a great resolve and a great task was near.*"

[2] *mīn tāsh 'imārat qāzdūrghān tūmshūghī-nīng alīdā*; 215 f. 168*b*, *'imārātī kah az sang yak pāra farmūda būdīm*; 217 f. 143*b*, *jāy kah man 'imāratī sākhtam*; Mems. p. 226, where I have built a palace; *Mém*s. ii, 15, *l'endroit même où j'ai bâti un palais*. All the above translations lose the sense of *qāzdūrghān*, am causing to dig out, to quarry stone. Perhaps for coolness' sake the dwelling was cut out in the living rock. That the place is south-west of the main *ariqs*, near Murghān-koh or on it, Bābur's narrative allows. Cf. Appendix J.

[3] *sic*, Hai. MS. There are two Lakhshas, Little Lakhsha, a mile west of Qandahār, and Great Lakhsha, about a mile s.w. of Old Qandahār, 5 or 6 m. from the modern one (Erskine).

[4] This will be the main irrigation channel taken off from the Argand-āb (Maps).

and eatables. Without looking to collect them, we galloped off. Our force may have been 2000 in all, but perhaps not over 1000 were in the battle because those mentioned as scattering up and down could not rejoin in time to fight.

Though our men were few I had them organized and posted on a first-rate plan and method; I had never arrayed them before by such a good one. For my immediate command (*khāṣa tābīn*) I had selected braves from whose hands comes work [1] and had inscribed them by tens and fifties, each ten and each fifty under a leader who knew the post in the right or left of the centre for his ten or his fifty, knew the work of each in the battle, and was there on the observant watch; so that, after mounting, the right and left, right and left hands, right and left sides, charged right and left without the trouble of arraying them or the need of a *tawāchī*.[2]

Fol. 209*b*. (*Author's note on his terminology.*) Although *barānghār*, *aūng qūl*, *aūng yān* and *aūng* (right wing, right hand, right side and right) all have the same meaning, I have applied them in different senses in order to vary terms and mark distinctions. As, in the battle-array, the (Ar.) *maimana* and *maisara* *i.e.* what people call (Turkī) *barānghār* and *jawānghār* (r. and l. wings) are not included in the (Ar.) *qalb*, *i.e.* what people call (T.) *ghūl* (centre), so it is in arraying the centre itself. Taking the array of the centre only, its (Ar.) *yamīn* and *yasār* (r. and l.) are called (by me) *aūng qūl* and *sūl qūl* (r. and l. hands). Again,—the (Ar.) *khāṣa tābīn* (royal troop) in the centre has its *yamīn* and *yasār* which are called (by me) *aūng yān* and *sūl yān* (r. and l. sides, T. *yān*). Again,—in the *khāṣa tābīn* there is the (T.) *būī* (*nīng*) *tīkīnī* (close circle); its *yamīn* and *yasār* are called *sūng* and *sūl*. In the Turkī tongue they call one single thing a *būī*,[3] but that is not the *būī* meant here; what is meant here is close (*yāqīn*).

The right wing (*barānghār*) was Mīrzā Khān (Wais), Sherīm Ṭaghāī, Yārak Ṭaghāī with his elder and younger brethren, Chilma *Mughūl*, Ayūb Beg, Muḥammad Beg, Ibrāhīm Beg, 'Alī Sayyid *Mughūl* with his Mughūls, Sl. Qulī *chuhra*, Khudā-bakhsh and Abū'l-ḥasan with his elder and younger brethren.

The left (*jawānghār*) was 'Abdu'r-razzāq Mīrzā, Qāsim Beg, Tīngrī-bīrdī, Qambar-i-'alī, Aḥmad *Aīlchī-būghā*, Ghūrī *Barlās*, Sayyid Ḥusain Akbar, and Mīr Shāh *Qūchīn*.

[1] *tamām aīlīkīdīn—aīsh-kīlūr yīkītlār*, an idiomatic phrase used of 'Alī-dost (f. 14*b* and n.), not easy to express by a single English adjective.

[2] The *tawāchī* was a sort of adjutant who attended to the order of the troops and carried orders from the general (Erskine). The difficult passage following gives the Turkī terms Bābur selected to represent Arabic military ones.

[3] Ar. *aḥad* (*Āyīn-i-akbarī*, Blochmann, index *s.n.*). The word *būī* recurs in the text on f. 210.

The advance (*aïrāwal*) was Nāṣir Mīrzā, Sayyid Qāsim Lord of the Gate, Muḥibb-i-'alī the armourer, Pāpā Aūghulī (Pāpā's son ?), Allāh-wairan *Turkmān*, Sher Qulī *Mughūl* the scout with his elder and younger brethren, and Muḥammad 'Alī.

In the centre (*ghūl*), on my right hand, were Qāsim Kūkūldāsh, Khusrau Kūkūldāsh, Sl. Muḥammad *Dūldāī*, Shāh Maḥmūd the secretary, Qūl-i-bāyazīd the taster, and Kamāl the sherbet-server; on my left were Khwāja Muḥammad 'Alī, Nāṣir's Dost, Nāṣir's Mīrīm, Bābā Sher-zād, Khān-qulī, Walī the treasurer, Qūtlūq-qadam the scout, Maqsūd the water-bearer (*sū-chī*), and Bābā Shaikh. Those in the centre were all of my household; there were no great begs; not one of those enumerated had reached the rank of beg. Those inscribed in this *būī*[1] were Sher Beg, Ḥātim the Armoury-master, Kūpuk, Qulī Bābā, Abū'l-ḥasan the armourer;—of the Mughūls, Aūrūs (Russian) 'Alī Sayyid,[2] Darwīsh-i-'alī Sayyid, Khūsh-kīldī, Chilma, Dost-kīldī, Chilma *Tāghchī*, Dāmāchī, Mindī;—of the Turkmāns, Manṣūr, Rustam-i-'alī with his elder and younger brother, and Shāh Naẓir and Sīūndūk. Fol. 210.

The enemy was in two divisions, one under Shāh Shujā' *Arghūn*, known as Shāh Beg and hereafter to be written of simply as Shāh Beg, the other under his younger brother Muqīm.

Some estimated the dark mass of Arghūns[3] at 6 or 7000 men; no question whatever but that Shāh Beg's own men in mail were 4 or 5000. He faced our right, Muqīm with a force smaller may-be than his brother's, faced our left. Muqīm made a mightily strong attack on our left, that is on Qāsim Beg from whom two or three persons came before fighting began, to ask for reinforcement; we however could not detach a man because in front of us also the enemy was very strong. We made our onset without any delay; the enemy fell suddenly on our van, Fol. 210*b*. turned it back and rammed it on our centre. When we, after a discharge of arrows, advanced, they, who also had been

[1] *i.e.* the *būī tīkīnī* of f. 209*b*, the *khāṣa tābīn*, close circle.

[2] As Mughūls seem unlikely to be descendants of Muḥammad, perhaps the title Sayyid in some Mughūl names here, may be a translation of a Mughūl one meaning Chief.

[3] *Arghūn-nīng qarāsī*, a frequent phrase.

shooting for a time, seemed likely to make a stand (*tūkhtaghāndīk*). Some-one, shouting to his men, came forward towards me, dismounted and was for adjusting his arrow, but he could do nothing because we moved on without stay. He remounted and rode off; it may have been Shāh Beg himself. During the fight Pīrī Beg *Turkmān* and 4 or 5 of his brethren turned their faces from the foe and, turban in hand,[1] came over to us.

(*Author's note on Pīrī Beg.*) This Pīrī Beg was one of those Turkmāns who came [into Herī] with the Turkmān Begs led by 'Abdu'l-bāqī Mīrzā and Murād Beg, after Shāh Ismā'īl vanquished the Bāyandar sulṭāns and seized the 'Irāq countries.[2]

Our right was the first to overcome the foe; it made him hurry off. Its extreme point had gone pricking (*sānjīlīb*)[3] as far as where I have now laid out a garden. Our left extended as far as the great tree-tangled[4] irrigation-channels, a good way below Bābā Ḥasan Abdāl. Muqīm was opposite it, its numbers very small compared with his. God brought it right! Between it and Muqīm were three or four of the tree-tangled water-channels going on to Qandahār;[5] it held the crossing-place and allowed no passage; small body though it was, it made splendid stand
Fol. 211. and kept its ground. Ḥalwāchī Tarkhān[6] slashed away in the water with Tīngrī-bīrdī and Qambar-i-'alī. Qambar-i-'alī was wounded; an arrow stuck in Qāsim Beg's forehead, another struck Ghūrī *Barlās* above the eyebrow and came out above his cheek.[7]

We meantime, after putting our adversary to flight, had crossed those same channels towards the naze of Murghān-koh (Birds'-hill). Some-one on a grey *tīpūchāq* was going backwards and forwards irresolutely along the hill-skirt, while we

[1] in sign of submission.
[2] f. 176. It was in 908 AH. [1502 AD.].
[3] This word seems to be from *sānjmāq*, to prick or stab; and here to have the military sense of *prick*, *viz.* riding forth. The Second Pers. trs. (217 f. 144*b*) translates it by *ghauta khūrda raft*, went tasting a plunge under water (215 f. 170; Muḥ. *Shīrāzī*'s lith. ed. p. 133). Erskine (p. 228), as his Persian source dictates, makes the men sink into the soft ground; de Courteille varies much (ii, 21).
[4] Ar. *akhmail*, so translated under the known presence of trees; it may also imply soft ground (Lane p. 813 col. b) but soft ground does not suit the purpose of *arīqs* (channels), the carrying on of water to the town.
[5] The S.A.W. map is useful here.
[6] That he had a following may be inferred.
[7] Ḥai. MS. *qāchār*; Ilminsky, p. 268; and both Pers. trss. *rukhsār* or *rukhsāra* (f. 25 and note to *qāchār*).

were getting across; I likened him to Shāh Beg; seemingly it was he.

Our men having beaten their opponents, all went off to pursue and unhorse them. Remained with me eleven to count, 'Abdu'l-lāh the librarian being one. Muqīm was still keeping his ground and fighting. Without a glance at the fewness of our men, we had the nagarets sounded and, putting our trust in God, moved with face set for Muqīm.

(Turkī) For few or for many God is full strength;
No man has might in His Court.

(Arabic) How often, God willing it, a small force has vanquished a large one!

Learning from the nagarets that we were approaching, Muqīm forgot his fixed plan and took the road of flight. God brought it right!

After putting our foe to flight, we moved for Qandahār and dismounted in Farrukh-zād Beg's Chār-bāgh, of which at this time not a trace remains!

(*m. Bābur enters Qandahār.*) Fol. 211*b*.

Shāh Beg and Muqīm could not get into Qandahār when they took to flight; Shāh Beg went towards Shāl and Mastūng (Quetta), Muqīm towards Zamīn-dāwar. They left no-one able to make the fort fast. Aḥmad 'Alī Tarkhān was in it together with other elder and younger brethren of Qulī Beg *Arghūn* whose attachment and good-feeling for me were known. After parley they asked protection for the families of their elder and younger brethren; their request was granted and all mentioned were encompassed with favour. They then opened the Māshūr-gate of the town; with leaderless men in mind, no other was opened. At that gate were posted Sherīm Ṭaghāī and Yārīm Beg. I went in with a few of the household, charged the leaderless men and had two or three put to death by way of example.[1]

(*n. The spoils of Qandahār.*)

I got to Muqīm's treasury first, that being in the outer-fort; 'Abdu'r-razzāq Mīrzā must have been quicker than I, for he was

[1] So in the Turkī MSS. and the first Pers. trs. (215 f. 170*b*). The second Pers. trs. (217 f. 145*b*) has a gloss of *ātqū u tika*; this consequently Erskine follows (p. 229) and adds a note explaining the punishment. Ilminsky has the gloss also (p. 269), thus indicating Persian and English influence.

just dismounting there when I arrived; I gave him a few things from it. I put Dost-i-nāṣir Beg, Qul-i-bāyazīd the taster and, of pay-masters, Muḥammad *bakhshī* in charge of it, then passed on into the citadel and posted Khwāja Muḥammad 'Alī, Shāh Maḥmūd and, of the pay-masters, Ṭaghāī Shāh *bakhshī* in charge of Shāh Beg's treasury.

Nāṣir's Mīrīm and Maqṣūd the sherbet-server were sent to keep the house of Ẕū'n-nūn's *Dīwān* Mīr Jān for Nāṣir Mīrzā; for Mīrzā Khān was kept Shaikh Abū-sa'īd *Tarkhānī's*; for 'Abdu'r-razzāq Mīrzā . . . . 's.[1]

Fol. 212. Such masses of white money had never been seen in those countries; no-one indeed was to be heard of who had seen so much. That night, when we ourselves stayed in the citadel, Shāh Beg's slave Saṃbhal was captured and brought in. Though he was then Shāh Beg's intimate, he had not yet received his later favour.[2] I had him given into some-one's charge but as good watch was not kept, he was allowed to escape. Next day I went back to my camp in Farrukh-zād Beg's Chār-bāgh.

I gave the Qandahār country to Nāṣir Mīrzā. After the treasure had been got into order, loaded up and started off, he took the loads of white *tankas* off a string of camels (*i.e.* 7 beasts) at the citadel-treasury, and kept them. I did not demand them back; I just gave them to him.

On leaving Qandahār, we dismounted in the Qūsh-khāna meadow. After setting the army forward, I had gone for an excursion, so I got into camp rather late. It was another camp! not to be recognized! Excellent *tīpūchāqs*, strings and strings of he-camels, she-camels, and mules, bearing saddle-bags (*khurzīn*) of silken stuffs and cloth,—tents of scarlet (cloth) and velvet, all sorts of awnings, every kind of work-shop, ass-load after ass-load of chests! The goods of the elder and younger (Arghūn) brethren had been kept in separate treasuries; out of each had come chest upon chest, bale upon bale of stuffs and

[1] No MS. gives the missing name.

[2] The later favour mentioned was due to Saṃbhal's laborious release of his master from Aūzbeg captivity in 917 AH. (1511 AD.) of which Erskine quotes a full account from the *Tārīkh-i-sind* (History of India i, 345).

clothes-in-wear (*artmāq artmāq*), sack upon sack of white *tankas*. In *aūtāgh* and *chādar* (lattice-tent and pole-tent) was much spoil for every man soever; many sheep also had been taken but sheep were less cared about!

I made over to Qāsim Beg Muqīm's retainers in Qalāt, under Qūj *Arghūn* and Tāju'd-dīn Maḥmūd, with their goods and effects. Qāsim Beg was a knowing person; he saw it unadvisable for us to stay long near Qandahār, so, by talking and talking, worrying and worrying, he got us to march off. As has been said, I had bestowed Qandahār on Nāṣir Mīrzā; he was given leave to go there; we started for Kābul. Fol. 212*b*.

There had been no chance of portioning out the spoils while we were near Qandahār; it was done at Qarā-bāgh where we delayed two or three days. To count the coins being difficult, they were apportioned by weighing them in scales. Begs of all ranks, retainers and household (*tābīn*) loaded up ass-load after ass-load of sacks full of white *tankas*, and took them away for their own subsistence and the pay of their soldiers.

We went back to Kābul with masses of goods and treasure, great honour and reputation.

(*o. Bābur's marriage with Ma'ṣūma-sulṭān.*)

After this return to Kābul I concluded alliance (*'aqd qīldīm*) with Sl. Aḥmad Mīrzā's daughter Ma'ṣūma-sulṭān Begīm whom I had asked in marriage at Khurāsān, and had had brought from there.

(*p. Shaibāq Khān before Qandahār.*)

A few days later a servant of Nāṣir Mīrzā brought the news that Shaibāq Khān had come and laid siege to Qandahār. That Muqīm had fled to Zamīn-dāwar has been said already; from there he went on and saw Shaibāq Khān. From Shāh Beg also one person after another had gone to Shaibāq Khān. At the instigation and petition of these two, the Khān came swiftly down on Qandahār by the mountain road,[1] thinking to find me there. This was the very thing that experienced person Fol. 213.

[1] Presumably he went by Sabzār, Daulatābād, and Washīr.

Earlier on Muḥibb-i-'alī the armourer had told Khalīfa and Mullā Bābā once or twice of their assemblies, and both had given me a hint, but the thing seeming incredible, it had had no attention. One night, towards the Bed-time Prayer, when I was sitting in the Audience-hall of the Chār-bāgh, Mūsa Khwāja, coming swiftly up with another man, said in my ear, "The Mughūls are really rebelling! We do not know for certain whether they have got 'Abdu'r-razzāq M. to join them. They have not settled to rise to-night." I feigned disregard and a little later went towards the *ḥarams* which at the time were in the Yūrūnchqa-garden [1] and the Bāgh-i-khilwat, but after page, servitor and messenger (*yasāwal*) had turned back on getting
Fol. 216b. near them, I went with the chief-slave towards the town, and on along the ditch. I had gone as far as the Iron-gate when Khwāja Muḥ. 'Alī [2] met me, he coming by the *bāzār* road from the opposite direction. He joined me . . . . . . of the porch of the Hot-bath (*ḥammām*) . . . . .[3]

if the Aūzbeg attacked it; for its safety and his own he may have relied, and Bābur also in appointing him, upon influence his Arghūn connections could use. For these, one was Muqim his brother-in-law, had accepted Shaibānī's suzerainty after being defeated in Qandahār by Bābur. It suited them better no doubt to have the younger Mīrzā rather than Bābur in Kābul; the latter's return thither will have disappointed them and the Mīrzā; they, as will be instanced later, stood ready to invade his lands when he moved East; they seem likely to have promoted the present Mughūl uprising. In the battle which put this down, the Mīrzā was captured; Bābur pardoned him; but he having rebelled again, was then put to death.

[1] Bāgh-i-yūrūnchqā may be an equivalent of Bāgh-i-safar, and the place be one of waiting "up to" (*ūnchqā*) the journey (*yūr*). *Yūrūnchqā* also means *clover* (De Courteille).

[2] He seems to have been a brother or uncle of Humāyūn's mother Māhīm (Index; A.N. trs. i, 492 and note).

[3] In all MSS. the text breaks off abruptly here, as it does on f. 118*b* as though through loss of pages, and a blank of narrative follows. Before the later gap of f. 251*b* however the last sentence is complete.

to Shāh Begīm[1] and with her approval. He was allowed to go and the honoured Begīm herself started off with him. My honoured maternal-aunt Mihr-nigār Khānīm also wished to go to Badakhshān, notwithstanding that it was more seemly for her to be with me, a blood-relation; but whatever objection was made, she was not to be dissuaded; she also betook[2] herself to Badakhshān.

(s. Bābur's second start for Hindūstān.)

Under our plan of going to Hindūstān, we marched out of Kābul in the month of the first Jumāda (September 1507 AD.), taking the road through Little Kābul and going down by Sūrkh-rabāṭ to Qūrūq-sāī.

The Afghāns belonging between Kābul and Lamghān (Ning-nahār) are thieves and abettors of thieves even in quiet times; for just such a happening as this they had prayed in vain. Said they, "He has abandoned Kābul", and multiplied their misdeeds by ten, changing their very merits for faults. To such Fol. 214 lengths did things go that on the morning we marched from Jagdālīk, the Afghāns located between it and Lamghān, such as the Khiẓr-khail, Shimū-khail, Khirilchī and Khūgīanī, thought of blocking the pass, arrayed on the mountain to the north, and advancing with sound of tambour and flourish of sword, began to shew themselves off. On our mounting I ordered our men to move along the mountain-side, each man from where he had dismounted;[3] off they set at the gallop up every ridge and every valley of the saddle.[4] The Afghāns stood awhile, but could not let even one arrow fly,[5] and betook themselves to flight. While I was on the mountain during the pursuit, I shot one in the hand as he was running back below me. That arrow-stricken man and a few others were brought in; some were put to death by impalement, as an example.

[1] ff. 10*b*, 11*b*. Ḥaidar M. writes, "Shāh Begīm laid claim to Badakhshān, saying, "It has been our hereditary kingdom for 3000 years; though I, being a woman, cannot myself attain sovereignty, yet my grandson Mīrzā Khān can hold it" (T.R. p. 203).

[2] *tībrādīlār.* The agitation of mind connoted, with movement, by this verb may well have been, here, doubt of Bābur's power to protect.

[3] *tūshlūq tūshdīn tāghghā yūrūkāīlār.* Cf. 205*b* for the same phrase, with supposedly different meaning.

[4] *qāngshār* lit. ridge of the nose.

[5] *bīr aūq ham qūīā-ālmādīlār* (f. 203*b* note to *chāpqūn*).

We dismounted over against the Adīnapūr-fort in the Nīngnahār *tūmān*.

(*t. A raid for winter stores.*)

Up till then we had taken no thought where to camp, where to go, where to stay; we had just marched up and down, camping in fresh places, while waiting for news.[1] It was late in the autumn; most lowlanders had carried in their rice. People knowing the local land and water represented that the Mīl Kāfirs up the water of the 'Alīshang *tūmān* grow great quantities of rice, so that we might be able to collect winter supplies from them for the army. Accordingly we rode out of the Nīngnahār dale (*julga*), crossed (the Bārān-water) at Sāī-kal, and went swiftly as far as the Pūr-amīn (easeful) valley.
Fol. 214*b*. There the soldiers took a mass of rice. The rice-fields were all at the bottom of the hills. The people fled but some Kāfirs went to their death. A few of our braves had been sent to a look-out (*sar-kūb*)[2] on a naze of the Pūr-anīm valley; when they were returning to us, the Kāfirs rushed from the hill above, shooting at them. They overtook Qāsim Beg's son-in-law Pūrān, chopped at him with an axe, and were just taking him when some of the braves went back, brought strength to bear, drove them off and got Pūrān away. After one night spent in the Kāfirs' rice-fields, we returned to camp with a mass of provisions collected.

(*u. Marriage of Muqīm's daughter.*)

While we were near Mandrāwar in those days, an alliance was concluded between Muqīm's daughter Māh-chūchūk, now married to Shāh Ḥasan *Arghūn*, and Qāsim Kūkūldāsh.[3]

[1] This will have been news both of Shaibāq Khān and of Mīrzā Khān. The Pers. trss. vary here (215 f. 173 and 217 f. 148).

[2] Index *s.n.*

[3] Māh-chūchūk can hardly have been married against her will to Qāsim. Her mother regarded the alliance as a family indignity; appealed to Shāh Beg and compassed a rescue from Kābul while Bābur and Qāsim were north of the Oxus [*circa* 916 AH.]. Māh-chūchūk quitted Kābul after much hesitation, due partly to reluctance to leave her husband and her infant of 18 months, [Nāhīd Begīm,] partly to dread less family honour might require her death (Erskine's *History*, i, 348 and Gul-badan's *Humāyūn-nāma*).

(v. Abandonment of the Hindūstān project.)

As it was not found desirable to go on into Hindūstān, I sent Mullā Bābā of Pashāghar back to Kābul with a few braves. Meantime I marched from near Mandrāwar to Atar and Shīwa and lay there for a few days. From Atar I visited Kūnār and Nūr-gal; from Kūnār I went back to camp on a raft; it was the first time I had sat on one; it pleased me much, and the raft came into common use thereafter.

(w. Shaibāq Khān retires from Qandahār.)

In those same days Mullā Bābā of Farkat came from Nāṣir Mīrzā with news in detail that Shaibāq Khān, after taking the outer-fort of Qandahār, had not been able to take the citadel but had retired; also that the Mīrzā, on various accounts, had left Qandahār and gone to Ghaznī.

Shaibāq Khān's arrival before Qandahār, within a few days of our own departure, had taken the garrison by surprise, and they had not been able to make fast the outer-fort. He ran mines several times round about the citadel and made several assaults. The place was about to be lost. At that anxious time Khwāja Muḥ. Amīn, Khwāja Dost Khāwand, Muḥ. 'Alī, a foot-soldier, and Shāmī (Syrian ?) let themselves down from the walls and got away. Just as those in the citadel were about to surrender in despair, Shaibāq Khān interposed words of peace and uprose from before the place. Why he rose was this:— It appears that before he went there, he had sent his *haram* to Nīrah-tū,[1] and that in Nīrah-tū some-one lifted up his head and got command in the fort; the Khān therefore made a sort of peace and retired from Qandahār. Fol. 215.

(x. Bābur returns to Kābul.)

Mid-winter though it was we went back to Kābul by the Bād-i-pīch road. I ordered the date of that transit and that crossing of the pass to be cut on a stone above Bād-i-pīch;[2] Ḥāfiẓ Mīrak wrote the inscription, Ustād Shāh Muhammad did the cutting, not well though, through haste.

[1] Erskine gives the fort the alternative name "Kaliūn", locates it in the Bādghīs district east of Herī, and quotes from Abū'l-ghāzī in describing its strong position (*History* i, 282). H.S. Tīrah-tū.

[2] f. 133 and note. Abū'l-faẓl mentions that the inscription was to be seen in his time.

I bestowed Ghaznī on Nāṣir Mīrzā and gave 'Abdu'r-razzāq Mīrzā the Nīngnahār *tūmān* with Mandrāwar, Nūr-valley, Kūnār and Nūr-gal.[1]

(y. Bābur styles himself Pādshāh.)

Up to that date people had styled Tīmūr Beg's descendants *Mīrzā*, even when they were ruling; now I ordered that people should style me *Pādshāh*.[2]

(z. Birth of Bābur's first son.)

At the end of this year, on Tuesday the 4th day of the month of Ẕū'l-qa'da (March 6th 1506 AD.), the Sun being in Pisces
Fol. 215b. (*Ḥūt*), Humāyūn was born in the citadel of Kābul. The date of his birth was found by the poet Maulānā Masnadī in the words *Sulṭān Humāyūn Khān*,[3] and a minor poet of Kābul found it in *Shāh-i-fīrūz-qadr* (Shāh of victorious might). A few days later he received the name Humāyūn; when he was five or six days old, I went out to the Chār-bāgh where was had the feast of his nativity. All the begs, small and great, brought gifts; such a mass of white *tankas* was heaped up as had never been seen before. It was a first-rate feast!

[1] This fief ranks in value next to the Kābul *tūmān*.

[2] Various gleanings suggest motives for Bābur's assertion of supremacy at this particular time. He was the only Tīmūrid ruler and man of achievement; he filled Ḥusain *Bāī-qarā*'s place of Tīmūrid headship; his actions through a long period show that he aimed at filling Tīmūr Beg's. There were those who did not admit his suzerainty,—Tīmūrids who had rebelled, Mughūls who had helped them, and who would also have helped Sa'īd Khān *Chaghatāī*, if he had not refused to be treacherous to a benefactor; there were also the Arghūns, Chīngīz-khānids of high pretensions. In old times the Mughūl Khāqāns were *pādshāh* (supreme); Pādshāh is recorded in history as the style of at least Sātūq-būghra Khān Pādshāh Ghāzī; no Tīmūrid had been lifted by his style above all Mīrzās. When however Tīmūrids had the upper hand, Bābur's Tīmūrid grandfather Abū-sa'īd asserted his *de facto* supremacy over Bābur's Chaghatāī grandfather Yūnas (T.R. p. 83). For Bābur to re-assert that supremacy by assuming the Khāqān's style was highly opportune at this moment. To be Bābur Supreme was to declare over-lordship above Chaghatāī and Mughūl, as well as over all Mīrzās. It was done when his sky had cleared; Mīrzā Khān's rebellion was scotched; the Arghūns were defeated; he was the stronger for their lost possessions; his Aūzbeg foe had removed to a less ominous distance; and Kābul was once more his own.

Gul-badan writes as if the birth of his first-born son Humāyūn were a part of the uplift in her father's style, but his narrative does not support her in this, since the order of events forbids.

[3] The "Khān" in Humāyūn's title may be drawn from his mother's family, since it does not come from Bābur. To whose family Māhīm belonged we have not been able to discover. It is one of the remarkable omissions of Bābur, Gul-badan and Abū'l-faẓl that they do not give her father's name. The topic of her family is discussed in my Biographical Appendix to Gul-badan's *Humāyūn-nāma* and will be taken up again, here, in a final Appendix on Bābur's family.

914 AH.—MAY 2ND 1508 TO APRIL 21ST 1509 AD.[1]

This spring a body of Mahmand Afghāns was over-run near Muqur.[2]

(*a. A Mughūl rebellion.*)

A few days after our return from that raid, Qūj Beg, Faqīr-i-'alī, Karīm-dād and Bābā *chuhra* were thinking about deserting, but their design becoming known, people were sent who took them below Astarghach. As good-for-nothing words of theirs had been reported to me, even during Jahāngīr M.'s life-time,[3] I ordered that they should be put to death at the top of the *bāzār*. They had been taken to the place; the ropes had been fixed; and they were about to be hanged when Qāsim Beg sent Khalīfa to me with an urgent entreaty that I would pardon their offences. To please him I gave them their lives, but I ordered them kept in custody.

What there was of Khusrau Shāh's retainers from Ḥiṣār and Qūndūz, together with the head-men of the Mughūls, Chilma, Fol. 216.
'Alī Sayyid,[4] Sakma (?), Sher-qulī and Aīkū-sālam (?), and also Khusrau Shāh's favourite Chaghatāī retainers under Sl. 'Alī *chuhra* and Khudabakhsh, with also 2 or 3000 serviceable Turkmān braves led by Sīūndūk and Shāh Naẓar,[5] the whole of these, after consultation, took up a bad position towards me. They were all seated in front of Khwāja Riwāj, from the Sūng-qūrghān meadow to the Chālāk; 'Abdu'r-razzāq Mīrzā, come in from Nīng-nahār, being in Dih-i-afghān.[6]

[1] Elph. MS. f. 172*b*; W.-i-B. I.O. 215 f. 174*b* and 217 f. 148*b*; Mems. p. 234.

[2] on the head-waters of the Tarnak (R.'s *Notes* App. p. 34).

[3] Bābur has made no direct mention of his half-brother's death (f. 208 and n. to Mīrzā)..

[4] This may be Darwesh-i-'alī of f. 210; the Sayyid in his title may merely mean chief, since he was a Mughūl.

[5] Several of these mutineers had fought for Bābur at Qandahār.

[6] It may be useful to recapitulate this Mīrzā's position:—In the previous year he had been left in charge of Kābul when Bābur went eastward in dread of Shaibānī, and, so left, occupied his hereditary place. He cannot have hoped to hold Kābul

Earlier on Muḥibb-i-'alī the armourer had told Khalīfa and Mullā Bābā once or twice of their assemblies, and both had given me a hint, but the thing seeming incredible, it had had no attention. One night, towards the Bed-time Prayer, when I was sitting in the Audience-hall of the Chār-bāgh, Mūsa Khwāja, coming swiftly up with another man, said in my ear, "The Mughūls are really rebelling! We do not know for certain whether they have got 'Abdu'r-razzāq M. to join them. They have not settled to rise to-night." I feigned disregard and a little later went towards the *ḥarams* which at the time were in the Yūrūnchqa-garden [1] and the Bāgh-i-khilwat, but after page, servitor and messenger (*yasāwal*) had turned back on getting
Fol. 216*b*. near them, I went with the chief-slave towards the town, and on along the ditch. I had gone as far as the Iron-gate when Khwāja Muḥ. 'Alī [2] met me, he coming by the *bāzār* road from the opposite direction. He joined me . . . . . . of the porch of the Hot-bath (*ḥammām*) . . . . . .[3]

if the Aūzbeg attacked it; for its safety and his own he may have relied, and Bābur also in appointing him, upon influence his Arghūn connections could use. For these, one was Muqim his brother-in-law, had accepted Shaibānī's suzerainty after being defeated in Qandahār by Bābur. It suited them better no doubt to have the younger Mīrzā rather than Bābur in Kābul; the latter's return thither will have disappointed them and the Mīrzā; they, as will be instanced later, stood ready to invade his lands when he moved East; they seem likely to have promoted the present Mughūl uprising. In the battle which put this down, the Mīrzā was captured; Bābur pardoned him; but he having rebelled again, was then put to death.

[1] Bāgh-i-yūrūnchqā may be an equivalent of Bāgh-i-safar, and the place be one of waiting "up to" (*ūnchqā*) the journey (*yūr*). *Yūrūnchqā* also means *clover* (De Courteille).

[2] He seems to have been a brother or uncle of Humāyūn's mother Māhīm (Index; A.N. trs. i, 492 and note).

[3] In all MSS. the text breaks off abruptly here, as it does on f. 118*b* as though through loss of pages, and a blank of narrative follows. Before the later gap of f. 251*b* however the last sentence is complete.

TRANSLATOR'S NOTE ON 914 TO 925 AH.—1508 TO 1519 AD.

From several references made in the *Bābur-nāma* and from a passage in Gul-badan's *Humāyūn-nāma* (f. 15), it is inferrible that Bābur was composing the annals of 914 AH. not long before his last illness and death.[1]

Before the diary of 925 AH. (1519 AD.) takes up the broken thread of his autobiography, there is a *lacuna* of narrative extending over nearly eleven years. The break was not intended, several references in the *Bābur-nāma* shewing Bābur's purpose to describe events of the unchronicled years.[2] Mr. Erskine, in the Leyden and Erskine *Memoirs*, carried Bābur's biography through the major *lacunæ*, but without first-hand help from the best sources, the *Ḥabību's-siyar* and *Tārīkh-i-rashīdī*. He had not the help of the first even in his *History of India*. M. de Courteille working as a translator only, made no attempt to fill the gaps.

Bābur's biography has yet to be completed; much time is demanded by the task, not only in order to exhaust known sources and seek others further afield, but to weigh and balance the contradictory statements of writers deep-sundered in sympathy and outlook. To strike such a balance is essential when dealing with the events of 914 to 920 AH. because in those years Bābur had part in an embittered conflict between Sunnī and Shī'a. What I offer below, as a stop-gap, is a mere summary of events, mainly based on material not used by Mr. Erskine, with a few comments prompted by acquaintance with Bāburiana.

USEFUL SOURCES

Compared with what Bābur could have told of this most interesting period of his life, the yield of the sources is scant,

[1] Index *s.n. Bābur-nāma*, date of composition and gaps.
[2] *ibid.*

a natural sequel from the fact that no one of them had his biography for its main theme, still less had his own action in crises of enforced ambiguity.

Of all known sources the best are Khwānd-amīr's *Ḥabību's-siyar* and Ḥaidar Mīrzā *Dūghlāt's Tārīkh-i-rashīdī*. The first was finished nominally in 930 AH. (1524–5 AD.), seven years therefore before Bābur's death, but it received much addition of matter concerning Bābur after its author went to Hindūstān in 934 AH. (f. 339). Its fourth part, a life of Shāh Ismā'īl *Ṣafawī* is especially valuable for the years of this *lacuna*. Ḥaidar's book was finished under Humāyūn in 953 AH. (1547 AD.), when its author had reigned five years in Kashmīr. It is the most valuable of all the sources for those interested in Bābur himself, both because of Ḥaidar's excellence as a biographer, and through his close acquaintance with Bābur's family. From his eleventh to his thirteenth year he lived under Bābur's protection, followed this by 19 years service under Sa'īd Khān, the cousin of both, in Kāshghar, and after that Khān's death, went to Bābur's sons Kāmrān and Humāyūn in Hindūstān.

A work issuing from a Sunnī Aūzbeg centre, Faẓl bin Ruzbahān *Isfahānī's Sūlūku'l-mulūk*, has a Preface of special value, as shewing one view of what it writes of as the spread of heresy in Māwarā'u'n-nahr through Bābur's invasions. The book itself is a Treatise on Musalmān Law, and was prepared by order of 'Ubaidu'l-lāh Khān *Aūzbeg* for his help in fulfilling a vow he had made, before attacking Bābur in 918 AH., at the shrine of Khwāja Aḥmad *Yasawī* [in Ḥaẓrat Turkistān], that, if he were victorious, he would conform exactly with the divine Law and uphold it in Māwarā'u'n-nahr (Rieu's Pers. Cat. ii, 448).

The *Tārīkh-i Ḥājī Muḥammad 'Ārif Qandahārī* appears, from the frequent use Firishta made of it, to be a useful source, both because its author was a native of Qandahār, a place much occupying Bābur's activities, and because he was a servant of Bairām Khān-i-khānān, whose assassination under Akbar he witnessed.[1] Unfortunately, though his life of Akbar survives

[1] Jumāda I, 14th 968 AH.—Jan. 31st 1561 AD. Concerning the book *see* Elliot and Dowson's *History of India* vi, 572 and JRAS 1901 p. 76, H. Beveridge's art. *On Persian MSS. in Indian Libraries*.

no copy is now known of the section of his General History which deals with Bābur's.

An early source is Yahya *Kazwīnī's Lubbu't-tawārīkh*, written in 948 AH. (1541 AD.), but brief only in the Bābur period. It issued from a Shī'a source, being commanded by Shāh Ismā'īl *Ṣafawī*'s son Bahrām.

Another work issuing also from a *Ṣafawī* centre is Mīr Sikandar's *Tārīkh-i-'ālam-arāī*, a history of Shāh 'Abbas I, with an introduction treating of his predecessors which was completed in 1025 AH. (1616 AD.). Its interest lies in its outlook on Bābur's dealings with Shāh Ismā'īl.

A later source, brief only, is Firishta's *Tārīkh-i-firishta*, finished under Jahāngīr in the first quarter of the 17th century.

Mr. Erskine makes frequent reference to Kh(w)āfī Khān's *Tārīkh*, a secondary authority however, written under Aurangzīb, mainly based on Firishta's work, and merely summarizing Bābur's period. References to detached incidents of the period are found in Shaikh 'Abdu'l-qādir's *Tārīkh-i-badāyūnī* and Mīr Ma'ṣūm's *Tārīkh-i-sind.*

EVENTS OF THE UNCHRONICLED YEARS

914 AH.—MAY 2ND 1508 TO APRIL 21ST 1509 AD.

The mutiny, of which an account begins in the text, was crushed by the victory of 500 loyalists over 3,000 rebels, one factor of success being Bābur's defeat in single combat of five champions of his adversaries.[1] The disturbance was not of long duration; Kābul was tranquil in Sha'bān (November) when Sl. Sa'īd Khān *Chaghatāī*, then 21, arrived there seeking his cousin's protection, after defeat by his brother Manṣūr at Almātū, escape from death, commanded by Shaibānī, in Farghāna, a winter journey through Qarā-tīgīn to Mīrzā Khān in Qilā'-i-ẓafar, refusal of an offer to put him in that feeble Mīrzā's place, and so on to Kābul, where he came a destitute fugitive and

[1] The T.R. gives the names of two only of the champions but Firishta, writing much later gives all five; we surmise that he found his five in the book of which copies are not now known, the *Tārīkh-i Muḥ. 'Ārif Qandahārī*. Firishta's five are 'Alī *shab-kūr* (night-blind), 'Alī *Sīstānī*, Naẓar Bahādur *Aūzbeg*, Ya'qūb *tez-jang* (swift in fight), and Aūzbeg Bahādur. Ḥaidar's two names vary in the MSS. of the T.R. but represent the first two of Firishta's list.

enjoyed a freedom from care never known by him before (f. 200*b*; T.R. p. 226). The year was fatal to his family and to Ḥaidar's; in it Shaibānī murdered Sl. Maḥmūd Khān and his six sons, Muḥammad Ḥusain Mīrzā and other Dūghlāt sulṭāns.

915 AH.—APRIL 21ST 1509 TO APRIL 11TH 1510 AD.

In this year hostilities began between Shāh Ismā'īl *Ṣafawī* and Muḥ. Shaibānī Khān *Aūzbeg*, news of which must have excited keen interest in Kābul.

In it occurred also what was in itself a minor matter of a child's safety, but became of historical importance, namely, the beginning of personal acquaintance between Bābur and his sympathetic biographer Ḥaidar Mīrzā *Dūghlāt.* Ḥaidar, like Sa'īd, came a fugitive to the protection of a kinsman; he was then eleven, had been saved by servants from the death commanded by Shaibānī, conveyed to Mīrzā Khān in Badakhshān, thence sent for by Bābur to the greater security of Kābul (f. 11; Index *s.n.*; T.R. p. 227).

916 AH.—APRIL 11TH 1510 TO MARCH 31ST 1510 AD.

a. News of the battle of Merv.

Over half of this year passed quietly in Kābul; Ramẓān (December) brought from Mīrzā Khān (Wais) the stirring news that Ismā'īl had defeated Shaibānī near Merv.[1] "It is not known," wrote the Mīrzā, "whether Shāhī Beg Khān has been killed or not. All the Aūzbegs have crossed the Amū. Amīr Aūrūs, who was in Qūndūz, has fled. About 20,000 Mughūls, who left the Aūzbeg at Merv, have come to Qūndūz. I have come there." He then invited Bābur to join him and with him to try for the recovery of their ancestral territories (T.R. p. 237).

[1] There are curious differences of statement about the date of Shaibānī's death, possibly through confusion between this and the day on which preliminary fighting began near Merv. Ḥaidar's way of expressing the date carries weight by its precision, he giving *roz-i-shakk* of Ramẓān, *i.e.* a day of which there was doubt whether it was the last of Sha'bān or the first of Ramẓān (Lane, *yauma'u'l-shakk*). As the sources support Friday for the day of the week and on a Friday in the year 915 AH. fell the 29th of Sha'bān, the date of Shaibānī's death seems to be Friday Sha'bān 29th 915 AH. (Friday December 2nd 1510 AD.).

b. Bābur's campaign in Transoxiana begun.

The Mīrzā's letter was brought over passes blocked by snow; Bābur, with all possible speed, took the one winter-route through Āb-dara, kept the Ramẓān Feast in Bāmīān, and reached Qūndūz in Shawwāl (Jan. 1511 AD.). Ḥaidar's detail about the Feast seems likely to have been recorded because he had read Bābur's own remark, made in Ramẓān 933 AH. (June 1527) that up to that date, when he kept it in Sīkrī, he had not since his eleventh year kept it twice in the same place (f. 330).

c. Mughūl affairs.

Outside Qūndūz lay the Mughūls mentioned by Mīrzā Khān as come from Merv and so mentioned, presumably, as a possible reinforcement. They had been servants of Bābur's uncles Maḥmūd and Aḥmad, and when Shaibānī defeated those Khāns at Akhsī in 908 AH., had been compelled by him to migrate into Khurāsān to places remote from Mughūlistān. Many of them had served in Kāshghar; none had served a Tīmūrid Mīrzā. Set free by Shaibānī's death, they had come east, a Khān-less 20,000 of armed and fully equipped men and they were there, as Ḥaidar says, in their strength while of Chaghatāīs there were not more than 5,000. They now, and with them the Mughūls from Kābul, used the opportunity offering for return to a more congenial location and leadership, by the presence in Qūndūz of a legitimate Khāqān and the clearance in Andijān, a threshold of Mughūlistān, of its Aūzbeg governors (f. 200*b*) The chiefs of both bodies of Mughūls, Sherīm Taghāī at the head of one, Ayūb *Begchīk* of the other, proffered the Mughūl Khānship to Sa'īd with offer to set Bābur aside, perhaps to kill him. It is improbable that in making their offer they contemplated locating themselves in the confined country of Kābul; what they seem to have wished was what Bābur gave, Sa'īd for their Khāqān and permission to go north with him.

Sa'īd, in words worth reading, rejected their offer to injure Bābur, doing so on the grounds of right and gratitude, but, the two men agreeing that it was now expedient for them to part, asked to be sent to act for Bābur where their friendship could be maintained for their common welfare. The matter was settled by Bābur's sending him into Andijān in response to an urgent petition for help there just arrived from Ḥaidar's uncle. He "was made Khān" and started forth in the following year, on Ṣafar 14th 917 AH. (May 13th 1511 AD.); with him went most of the Mughūls but not all, since even of those from Merv, Ayūb *Begchīk* and others are found mentioned on several later occasions as being with Bābur.

Bābur's phrase "I made him Khān" (f. 200*b*) recalls his earlier mention of what seems to be the same appointment (f. 10*b*), made by Abū-sa'īd of Yūnas as Khān of the Mughūls; in each case the meaning seems to be that the Tīmūrid Mīrzā made the Chaghatāī Khān Khāqān of the Mughūls.

d. First attempt on Ḥiṣār.

After spending a short time in Qūndūz, Bābur moved for Ḥiṣār in which were the Aūzbeg sulṭāns Mahdī and Ḥamza. They came out into Wakhsh to meet him but, owing to an imbroglio, there was no encounter and each side retired (T.R. p. 238).

e. Intercourse between Bābur and Ismā'īl Ṣafawī.

While Bābur was now in Qūndūz his sister Khān-zāda arrived there, safe-returned under escort of the Shāh's troops, after the death in the battle of Merv of her successive husbands Shaibānī and Sayyid Hādī, and with her came an envoy from Ismā'īl proffering friendship, civilities calculated to arouse a hope of Persian help in Bābur. To acknowledge his courtesies, Bābur sent Mīrzā Khān with thanks and gifts; Ḥaidar says that the Mīrzā also conveyed protestations of good faith and a request for military assistance. He was well received and his request for help was granted; that it was granted under hard conditions then stated later occurrences shew.

917 AH.—MARCH 31ST 1511 TO MARCH 19TH 1512 AD.

a. Second attempt on Ḥiṣār.

In this year Bābur moved again on Ḥiṣār. He took post, where once his forbear Tīmūr had wrought out success against great odds, at the Pul-i-sangīn (Stone-bridge) on the Sūrkh-āb, and lay there[1] a month awaiting reinforcement. The Aūzbeg sulṭans faced him on the other side of the river, they too, presumably, awaiting reinforcement. They moved when they felt themselves strong enough to attack, whether by addition to their own numbers, whether by learning that Bābur had not largely increased his own. Concerning the second alternative it is open to surmise that he hoped for larger reinforcement than he obtained; he appears to have left Qūndūz before the return of Mīrzā Khān from his embassy to Ismā'īl, to have expected Persian reinforcement with the Mīrzā, and at Pul-i-sangīn, where the Mīrzā joined him in time to fight, to have been strengthened by the Mīrzā's own following, and few, if any, foreign auxiliaries. These surmises are supported by what Khwānd-amīr relates of the conditions [specified later] on which the Shāh's main contingent was despatched and by his shewing that it did not start until after the Shāh had had news of the battle at Pul-i-sangīn.

At the end of the month of waiting, the Aūzbegs one morning swam the Sūrkh-āb below the bridge; in the afternoon of the same day, Bābur retired to better ground amongst the mountain fastnesses of a local Āb-dara. In the desperate encounter which followed the Aūzbegs were utterly routed with great loss in men; they were pursued to Darband-i-ahanīn (Iron-gate) on the Ḥiṣār border, on their way to join a great force assembled at Qarshī under Kūchūm Khān, Shaibānī's successor as Aūzbeg Khāqān. The battle is admirably described by Ḥaidar, who was then a boy of 12 with keen eye watching his own first fight, and that fight with foes who had made him the last male survivor of his line. In the evening of the victory Mahdī, Ḥamza and Ḥamza's son Mamak were brought before Bābur who, says Ḥaidar, did to them what they had done to the Mughūl Khāqāns and Chaghatāī Sulṭāns, that is, he retaliated in blood for the blood of many kinsmen.

b. Persian reinforcement.

After the battle Bābur went to near Ḥiṣār, was there joined by many local tribesmen, and, some time later, by a large body of Ismā'īl's troops under Aḥmad Beg *Ṣafawī*, 'Alī Khān *Istiljū* and Shāhrukh Sl. *Afshār*, Ismā'īl's seal-keeper. The following particulars, given by Khwānd-amīr, about the despatch of this contingent help to fix the order of occurrences, and throw light on the price paid by Bābur for his auxiliaries. He announced his victory over Mahdī and Ḥamza to the Shāh, and at the same time promised that if he reconquered the rest of Trans-oxiana by the Shāh's help, he would read his name in the *khuṭba*, stamp it on coins together with those of the Twelve Imāms, and work to destroy the power of the Aūzbegs. These undertakings look like a response to a demand; such conditions cannot have been proffered; their acceptance must have been compelled. Khwānd-amīr says that when Ismā'īl fully understood the purport of Bābur's letter, [by which would seem to be meant, when he knew that his conditions of help were accepted,] he despatched the troops under the three Commanders named above.

The Persian chiefs advised a move direct on Bukhārā and Samarkand; and with this Bābur's councillors concurred, they saying, according to Ḥaidar, that Bukhārā was then empty of troops and full of fools. 'Ubaid Khān had thrown himself into Qarshī; it was settled not to attack him but to pass on and encamp a stage beyond the town. This was done; then scout followed scout, bringing news that he had come out of Qarshī and was hurrying to Bukhārā, his own fief. Instant and swift pursuit followed him up the 100 miles of caravan-road, into Bukhārā, and on beyond, sweeping him and his garrison, plundered as they fled, into the open land of Turkistān. Many sulṭāns had collected in Samarkand, some no doubt being, like Tīmūr its governor, fugitives escaped from Pul-i-sangīn. Dismayed by Bābur's second success, they scattered into Turkistān, thus leaving him an open road.

c. *Samarkand re-occupied and relations with Ismā'īl Ṣafawī.*

He must now have hoped to be able to dispense with his dangerous colleagues, for he dismissed them when he reached Bukhārā, with gifts and thanks for their services. It is Ḥaidar, himself present, who fixes Bukhārā as the place of the dismissal (T.R. p. 246).

From Bukhārā Bābur went to Samarkand. It was mid-Rajab 917 AH. (October 1511 AD.), some ten months after leaving Kābul, and after 9 years of absence, that he re-entered the town, itself gay with decoration for his welcome, amidst the acclaim of its people.[1]

Eight months were to prove his impotence to keep it against the forces ranged against him,—Aūzbeg strength in arms compacted by Sunnī zeal, Sunnī hatred of a Shī'a's suzerainty intensified by dread lest that potent Shī'a should resolve to perpetuate his dominance. Both as a Sunnī and as one who had not owned a suzerain, the position was unpleasant for Bābur. That his alliance with Ismā'īl was dangerous he will have known, as also that his risks grew as Transoxiana was over-spread by news of Ismā'īl's fanatical barbarism to pious and learned Sunnīs, notably in Herī. He manifested desire for release both now and later,—now when he not only dismissed his Persian helpers but so behaved to the Shāh's envoy Muḥammad Jān,—he was Najm Ṣānī's Lord of the Gate,—that the envoy felt neglect and made report of Bābur as arrogant, in opposition, and unwilling to fulfil his compact,—later when he eagerly attempted success unaided against 'Ubaid Khān, and was then worsted. It illustrates the Shāh's view of his suzerain relation to Bābur that on hearing Muḥammad Jān's report, he ordered Najm Ṣānī to bring the offender to order.

Meantime the Shāh's conditions seem to have been carried out in Samarkand and Bābur's subservience clearly shewn.[2] Of this there are the indications,—that Bābur had promised and was a man of his word; that Sunnī irritation against him waxed and did not wane as it might have done without food to nourish it; that Bābur knew himself impotent against the Aūzbegs unless he had foreign aid, expected attack, knew it was preparing; that he would hear of Muḥammad Jān's report and of Najm Ṣānī's commission against himself. Honesty, policy and necessity

[1] If my reading be correct of the Turkī passage concerning wines drunk by Bābur which I have noted on f. 49 (*in loco* p. 83 n. 1), it was during this occupation of Kābul that Bābur first broke the Law against stimulants.

[2] Mr. R. S. Poole found a coin which he took to be one struck in obedience to Bābur's compact with the Shāh (B.M.Cat. of the coins of Persian Shāhs 1887, pp. xxiv *et seq.*; T.R. p. 246 n.).

combined to enforce the fulfilment of his agreement. What were the precise terms of that agreement beyond the two as to the *khuṭba* and the coins, it needs close study of the wording of the sources to decide, lest metaphor be taken for fact. Great passions,—ambition, religious fervour, sectarian bigotry and fear confronted him.. His problem was greater than that of Henry of Navarre and of Napoleon in Egypt; they had but to seem what secured their acceptance; he had to put on a guise that brought him hate.

Khān-zāda was not the only member of Bābur's family who now rejoined him after marriage with an Aūzbeg. His half-sister Yādgār-sulṭān had fallen to the share of Ḥamza Sulṭān's son 'Abdu'l-laṭīf in 908 AH. when Shaibānī defeated the Khāns near Akhsī. Now that her half-brother had defeated her husband's family, she returned to her own people (f. 9).

918 AH.—MARCH 19TH 1512 TO MARCH 9TH 1513 AD.

a. Return of the Aūzbegs.

Emboldened by the departure of the Persian troops, the Aūzbegs, in the spring of the year, came out of Turkistān, their main attack being directed on Tāshkīnt, then held for Bābur.[1] 'Ubaid Khān moved for Bukhārā. He had prefaced his march by vowing that, if successful, he would thenceforth strictly observe Musalmān Law. The vow was made in Ḥaẓrat Turkistān at the shrine of Khwāja Aḥmad *Yasawī*, a saint revered in Central Asia through many centuries; he had died about 1120 AD.; Tīmūr had made pilgrimage to his tomb, in 1397 AD., and then had founded the mosque still dominating the town, still the pilgrim's land-mark.[2] 'Ubaid's vow, like Bābur's of 933 AH., was one of return to obedience. Both men took oath in the Ghāzī's mood, Bābur's set against the Hindū whom he saw as a heathen, 'Ubaid's set against Bābur whom he saw as a heretic.

[1] It was held by Aḥmad-i-qāsim *Kohbur* and is referred to on f. 234*b*, as one occasion of those in which Dost Beg distinguished himself.

[2] Schuyler's *Turkistān* has a good account and picture of the mosque. 'Ubaid's vow is referred to in my earlier mention of the *Sūlūku'l-mulūk*. It may be noted here that this MS. supports the spelling *Bābur* by making the second syllable rhyme to *pūr*, as against the form *Bābar*.

b. Bābur's defeat at Kul-i-malik.

In Ṣafar (April–May) 'Ubaid moved swiftly down and attacked the Bukhārā neighbourhood. Bābur went from Samarkand to meet him. Several details of what followed, not given by Ḥaidar and, in one particular, contradicting him, are given by Khwānd-amīr. The statement in which the two historians contradict one another is Ḥaidar's that 'Ubaid had 3000 men only, Bābur 40,000. Several considerations give to Khwānd-amīr's opposed statement that Bābur's force was small, the semblance of being nearer the fact. Ḥaidar, it may be said, did not go out on this campaign; he was ill in Samarkand and continued ill there for some time; Khwānd-amīr's details have the well-informed air of things learned at first-hand, perhaps from some-one in Hindūstān after 934 AH.

Matters which make against Bābur's having a large effective force at Kul-i-malik, and favour Khwānd-amīr's statement about the affair are these :—'Ubaid must have formed some estimate of what he had to meet, and he brought 3000 men. Where could Bābur have obtained 40,000 men worth reckoning in a fight? In several times of crisis his own immediate and ever-faithful troop is put at 500; as his cause was now unpopular, local accretions may have been few. Some Mughūls from Merv and from Kābul were near Samarkand (T.R. pp. 263, 265); most were with Sa'īd in Andijān; but however many Mughūls may have been in his neighbourhood, none could be counted on as resolute for his success. If too, he had had more than a small effective force, would he not have tried to hold Samarkand with the remnant of defeat until Persian help arrived? All things considered, there is ground for accepting Khwānd-amīr's statement that Bābur met 'Ubaid with a small force.

Following his account therefore :—Bābur in his excess of daring, marched to put the Aūzbeg down with a small force only, against the advice of the prudent, of whom Muḥammad Mazīd Tarkhān was one, who all said it was wrong to go out unprepared and without reinforcement. Paying them no attention, Bābur marched for Bukhārā, was rendered still more daring by news had when he neared it, that the enemy had retired some stages, and followed him up almost to his camp. 'Ubaid was in great force; many Aūzbegs perished but, in the end, they were victors and Bābur was compelled to take refuge in Bukhārā. The encounter took place near Kul-i-malik (King's-lake) in Safar 918 AH. (April–May 1512 AD.).

c. Bābur leaves Samarkand.

It was not possible to maintain a footing in Samarkand; Bābur therefore collected his family and train[1] and betook himself to Ḥiṣār. There went with him on this expedition Māhīm and her children Humāyūn, Mihr-jahān and Bārbūl,—the motherless Ma'ṣūma,—Gul-rukh with her son Kāmrān (Gul-badan f. 7). I have not found any account of his route; Ḥaidar gives no details about the journey; he did not travel with Bābur, being still invalided in Samarkand. Perhaps the absence of information is a sign that the Aūzbegs had not yet appeared on the direct road for Ḥiṣār. A local tradition however would make Bābur go round through Farghāna. He certainly might have gone into Farghāna hoping to co-operate with Sa'īd Khān; Tāshkīnt was still holding out under Aḥmad-i-qāsim *Kohbur* and it is clear that all activity in Bābur's force had not been quenched because during the Tāshkīnt siege, Dost Beg broke through the enemy's ranks and made his way into the town. Sairām held out longer than Tāshkīnt. Of any such move by Bābur into Andijān the only hint received is given by what may be a mere legend.[2]

[1] *aūrūq.* Bābur refers to this exodus on f. *12b* when writing of Daulat-sulṭān Khānīm.

[2] It is one recorded with some variation, in Niyāz Muḥammad *Khukandī's Tārīkh-i-shāhrukhī* (Kazan, 1885) and Nalivkine's *Khānate of Khokand* (p. 63). It says that when Bābur in 918 AH. (1512 AD.) left Samarkand after defeat by the Aūzbegs, one of his wives, Sayyida Āfāq who accompanied him in his flight, gave birth to a son in the desert which lies between Khujand and Kand-i-badām; that Bābur, not daring to tarry and the infant being too young to make the impending journey, left it under some bushes with his own girdle round it in which were things of price; that the child was found by local people and in allusion to the valuables amongst which it lay, called Altūn bīshik (golden cradle); that it received other names and was best known in later life as Khudāyān Sulṭān. He is said to have spent most of his life in Akhsī; to have had a son Tīngrī-yār; and to have died in 952 AH. (1545 AD.). His grandson Yār-i-muḥammad is said to have gone to India to relations who was descendants of Bābur (JASB 1905 p. 137 H. Beveridge's art. *The Emperor Bābur*). What is against the truth of this tradition is that Gul-badan mentions no such wife as Sayyida Āfāq. Māhīm however seems to have belonged to a religious family, might therefore be styled Sayyida, and, as Bābur mentions (f. 220), had several children who did not live (a child left a. this infant was, might if not heard of, be supposed dead). There is this opening allowed for considering the tradition.

d. Bābur in Ḥiṣār.

After experiencing such gains and such losses, Bābur was still under 30 years of age.

The Aūzbegs, after his departure, re-occupied Bukhārā and Samarkand without harm done to the towns-people, and a few weeks later, in Jumāda I (July–August) followed him to Ḥiṣār. Meantime he with Mīrzā Khān's help, had so closed the streets of the town by massive earth-works that the sulṭāns were convinced its defenders were ready to spend the last drop of their blood in holding it, and therefore retired without attack.[1] Some sources give as their reason for retirement that Bābur had been reinforced from Balkh; Bairām Beg, it is true, had sent a force but one of 300 men only; so few cannot have alarmed except as the harbinger of more. Greater precision as to dates would shew whether they can have heard of Najm S̤ānī's army advancing by way of Balkh.

e. Qarshī and Ghaj-davān.

Meantime Najm S̤ānī, having with him some 11,000 men, had started on his corrective mission against Bābur. When he reached the Khurāsān frontier, he heard of the defeat at Kul-i-malik and the flight to Ḥiṣār, gathered other troops from Harāt and elsewhere, and advanced to Balkh. He stayed there for 20 days with Bairām Beg, perhaps occupied, in part, by communications with the Shāh and Bābur. From the latter repeated request for help is said to have come; help was given, some sources say without the Shāh's permission. A rendezvous was fixed, Najm S̤ānī marched to Tīrmīẕ, there crossed the Amū and in Rajab (Sep.–Oct.) encamped near the Darband-i-ahanīn. On Bābur's approach through the Chak-chaq pass, he paid him the civility of going several miles out from his camp to give him honouring reception.

Advancing thence for Bukhārā, the combined armies took Khuzār and moved on to Qarshī. This town Bābur wished to pass by, as it had been passed by on his previous march for Bukhārā; each time perhaps he wished to spare its people,

[1] Bābur refers to this on f. 265.

formerly his subjects, whom he desired to rule again, and who are reputed to have been mostly his fellow Turks. Najm Ṣānī refused to pass on; he said Qarshī must be taken because it was 'Ubaidu'l-lāh Khān's nest; in it was 'Ubaid's uncle Shaikhīm Mīrzā; it was captured; the Aūzbeg garrison was put to the sword and, spite of Bābur's earnest entreaties, all the towns-people, 15,000 persons it is said, down to the "suckling and decrepit", were massacred. Amongst the victims was Banā'ī who happened to be within it. This action roused the utmost anger against Najm Ṣānī; it disgusted Bābur, not only through its merciless slaughter but because it made clear the disregard in which he was held by his magnificent fellow-general.

From murdered Qarshī Najm Ṣānī advanced for Bukhārā. On getting within a few miles of it, he heard that an Aūzbeg force was approaching under Tīmūr and Abū-sa'īd, presumably from Samarkand therefore. He sent Bairām Beg to attack them; they drew off to the north and threw themselves into Ghaj-davān, the combined armies following them. This move placed Najm Ṣānī across the Zar-afshān, on the border of the desert with which the Aūzbegs were familiar, and with 'Ubaid on his flank in Bukhārā.

As to what followed the sources vary; they are brief; they differ less in statement of the same occurrence than in their choice of details to record; as Mr. Erskine observes their varying stories are not incompatible. Their widest difference is a statement of time but the two periods named, one a few days, the other four months, may not be meant to apply to the same event. Four months the siege is said to have lasted; this could not have been said if it had been a few days only. The siege seems to have been of some duration.

At first there were minor engagements, ending with varying success; provisions and provender became scarce; Najm Ṣānī's officers urged retirement, so too did Bābur. He would listen to none of them. At length 'Ubaid Khān rode out from Bukhārā at the head of excellent troops; he joined the Ghaj-davān garrison and the united Aūzbegs posted themselves in the suburbs where walled lanes and gardens narrowed the field and lessened Najm Ṣānī's advantage in numbers. On Tuesday

Ramẓān 3rd (Nov. 12th)[1] a battle was fought in which his army was routed and he himself slain.

f. Bābur and Yār-i-aḥmad Najm Sānī.

Some writers say that Najm S̤ānī's men did not fight well; it must be remembered that they may have been weakened by privation and that they had wished to retire. Of Bābur it is said that he, who was the reserve, did not fight at all; it is difficult to see good cause why, under all the circumstances, he should risk the loss of his men. It seems likely that Ḥaidar's strong language about this defeat would suit Bābur's temper also. "The victorious breezes of Islām overturned the banners of the schismatics. . . . Most of them perished on the field; the rents made by the sword at Qarshī were sewn up at Ghaj-davān by the arrow-stitches of vengeance. Najm S̤ānī and all the Turkmān amīrs were sent to hell."

The belief that Bābur had failed Najm S̤ānī persisted at the Persian Court, for his inaction was made a reproach to his son Humāyūn in 951 AH. (1544 AD.), when Humāyūn was a refugee with Ismā'īl's son T̤ahmāsp. Badāyūnī tells a story which, with great inaccuracy of name and place, represents the view taken at that time. The part of the anecdote pertinent here is that Bābur on the eve of the battle at Ghaj-davān, shot an arrow into the Aūzbeg camp which carried the following couplet, expressive of his ill-will to the Shāh and perhaps also of his rejection of the Shī'a guise he himself had worn.

> I made the Shāh's Najm road-stuff for the Aūzbegs;
> If fault has been mine, I have now cleansed the road.[2]

g. The Mughūls attack Bābur.

On his second return to Ḥiṣār Bābur was subjected to great danger by a sudden attack made upon him by the Mughūls where he lay at night in his camp outside the town. Firishta says, but without particulars of their offence, that Bābur had reproached

[1] The *Lubbu't-tawārīkh* would fix Ramẓān 7th.

[2] Mr. Erskine's quotation of the Persian original of the couplet differs from that which I have translated (*History of India* ii, 326; *Tārīkh-i-badāyūnī* Bib. Ind. ed. f. 444). Perhaps in the latter a pun is made on Najm as the leader's name and as meaning *fortune*; if so it points the more directly at the Shāh. The second line is quoted by Badāyūnī on his f. 362 also.

them for their misconduct; the absence of detail connecting the affair with the defeat just sustained, leads to the supposition that their misdeeds were a part of the tyranny over the country-people punished later by 'Ubaidu'l-lāh Khān. Roused from his sleep by the noise of his guards' resistance to the Mughūl attack, Bābur escaped with difficulty and without a single attendant[1] into the fort. The conspirators plundered his camp and withdrew to Qarā-tīgīn. He was in no position to oppose them, left a few men in Ḥiṣār and went to Mīrzā Khān in Qūndūz.

After he left, Ḥiṣār endured a desolating famine, a phenomenal snowfall and the ravages of the Mughūls. 'Ubaid Khān avenged Bābur on the horde; hearing of their excesses, he encamped outside the position they had taken up in Wakhsh defended by river, hills and snow, waited till a road thawed, then fell upon them and avenged the year's misery they had inflicted on the Ḥiṣārīs. Ḥaidar says of them that it was their villainy lost Ḥiṣār to Bābur and gained it for the Aūzbeg.[2]

These Mughūls had for chiefs men who when Sa'īd went to Andijān, elected to stay with Bābur. One of the three named by Ḥaidar was Ayūb *Begchīk.* He repented his disloyalty; when he lay dying some two years later (920 AH.) in Yāngī-ḥiṣār, he told Sa'īd Khān who visited him, that what was "lacerating his bowels and killing him with remorse", was his faithlessness to Bābur in Ḥiṣār, the oath he had broken at the instigation of those "hogs and bears", the Mughūl chiefs (T.R. p. 315).

In this year but before the Mughūl treachery to Bābur, Ḥaidar left him, starting in Rajab (Sep.–Oct.) to Sa'īd in Andijān and thus making a beginning of his 19 years spell of service.

919 AH.—MARCH 9TH 1513 TO FEB. 26TH 1514 AD.

Bābur may have spent this year in Khishm (Ḥ.S. iii, 372). During two or three months of it, he had one of the Shāh's

[1] Some translators make Bābur go "naked" into the fort but, on his own authority (f. 106*b*), it seems safer to understand what others say, that he went stripped of attendance, because it was always his habit even in times of peace to lie down in his tunic; much more would he have done so at such a crisis of his affairs as this of his flight to Ḥiṣār.

[2] Haidar gives a graphic account of the misconduct of the horde and of their punishment (T.R. p. 261–3).

retainers in his service, Khwāja Kamālu'd-dīn Maḥmūd, who had fled from Ghaj-davān to Balkh, heard there that the Balkhīs favoured an Aūzbeg chief whose coming was announced, and therefore went to Bābur. In Jumāda II (August), hearing that the Aūzbeg sultan had left Balkh, he returned there but was not admitted because the Balkhīs feared reprisals for their welcome to the Aūzbeg, a fear which may indicate that he had taken some considerable reinforcement to Bābur. He went on into Khurāsān and was there killed; Balkh was recaptured for the Shāh by Deo Sulṭān, a removal from Aūzbeg possession which helps to explain how Bābur came to be there in 923 AH.

920 AH.—FEB. 26TH 1514 TO FEB. 15TH 1515 AD.

Ḥaidar writes of Bābur as though he were in Qūnduz this year (TR. p. 263), says that he suffered the greatest misery and want, bore it with his accustomed courtesy and patience but, at last, despairing of success in recovering Ḥiṣār, went back to Kābul. Now it seems to be that he made the stay in Khwāst to which he refers later (f. 241*b*) and during which his daughter Gul-rang was born, as Gul-badan's chronicle allows known.

It was at the end of the year, after the privation of winter therefore, that he reached Kābul. When he re-occupied Samarkand in 917 AH., he had given Kābul to his half-brother Nāṣir Mīrzā; the Mīrzā received him now with warm welcome and protestations of devotion and respect, spoke of having guarded Kābul for him and asked permission to return to his own old fief Ghaznī. His behaviour made a deep impression on Bābur; it would be felt as a humane touch on the sore of failure.

921 AH.—FEB. 15TH 1515 TO FEB. 5TH 1516 AD.

a. Rebellion of chiefs in Ghaznī.

Nāṣir Mīrzā died shortly after (*dar hamān ayyām*) his return to Ghaznī. Disputes then arose amongst the various commanders who were in Ghaznī; Sherīm Ṭaghāī was one of them and the main strength of the tumult was given by the Mughūls. Many others were however involved in it, even such an old servant as Bābā of Pashāghar taking part (f. 234*b*; T.R. p. 356). Ḥaidar did not know precisely the cause of the dispute, or shew why it should have turned against Bābur, since he attributes it to possession taken by Satan of the brains of the chiefs and a consequent access of vain-glory and wickedness. Possibly some question of succession to Nāṣir arose. Dost Beg distinguished himself in the regular battle which ensued; Qāsim Beg's son Qambar-i-'alī hurried down from Qūndūz and also did his good part to win it for Bābur. Many of the rioters were killed, others fled to Kāshghar. Sherīm Ṭaghāī was one of the latter; as Sa'īd Khān gave him no welcome, he could not stay there; he fell back on the much injured Bābur who, says Ḥaidar, showed him his usual benevolence, turned his eyes from his offences and looked only at his past services until he died shortly afterwards (T.R. p. 357).[1]

922 AH.—FEB. 5TH 1516 TO JAN. 24TH 1517 AD.

This year may have been spent in and near Kābul in the quiet promoted by the dispersion of the Mughūls.

In this year was born Bābur's son Muḥammad known as *'Askarī* from his being born in camp. He was the son of Gulrukh *Begchīk* and full-brother of Kāmrān.

923 AH.—JAN. 24TH 1517 TO JAN. 13TH 1518 AD.

a. Bābur visits Balkh.

Khwānd-amīr is the authority for the little that is known of Bābur's action in this year (Ḥ.S. iii, 367 *et seq.*). It is connected with the doings of Badī'u'z-zamān *Bāī-qarā's* son Muḥammad-i-zamān. This Mīrzā had had great wanderings, during a part of which Khwānd-amīr was with him. In 920 AH. he was in Shāh Ismā'īl's service and in Balkh, but was not able to keep it. Bābur invited him to Kābul,—the date of invitation will have been later therefore than Bābur's return there at the end of 920 AH. The Mīrzā was on his way but was dissuaded from going into Kābul by Mahdī Khwāja and went instead into

[1] One of the mutineers named as in this affair (T.R. p. 257) was Sl. Qulī *chūnāq*, a circumstance attracting attention by its bearing on the cause of the *lacunae* in the *Bābur-nāma*, inasmuch as Bābur, writing at the end of his life, expresses (f. 65) his intention to tell of this man's future misdeeds. These misdeeds may have been also at Ḥiṣār and in the attack there made on Bābur; they are known from Ḥaidar to have been done at Ghaznī; both times fall within this present gap. Hence it is clear that Bābur meant to write of the events falling in the gap of 914 AH. onwards.

Ghurjistān. Bābur was angered by his non-arrival and pursued him in order to punish him but did not succeed in reaching Ghurjistān and went back to Kābul by way of Fīrūz-koh and Ghūr. The Mīrzā was captured eventually and sent to Kābul. Bābur treated him with kindness, after a few months gave him his daughter Ma'ṣūma in marriage, and sent him to Balkh. He appears to have been still in Balkh when Khwānd-amīr was writing of the above occurrences in 929 AH. The marriage took place either at the end of 923 or beginning of 924 AH. The Mīrzā was then 21, Ma'ṣūma 9; she almost certainly did not then go to Balkh. At some time in 923 AH. Bābur is said by Khwānd-amīr to have visited that town.[1]

b. Attempt on Qandahār.

In this year Bābur marched for Qandahār but the move ended peacefully, because a way was opened for gifts and terms by an illness which befell him when he was near the town.

The *Tārīkh-i-sind* gives what purports to be Shāh Beg's explanation of Bābur's repeated attempts on Qandahār. He said these had been made and would be made because Bābur had not forgiven Muqīm for taking Kābul 14 years earlier from the Tīmūrid 'Abdu'r-razzāq; that this had brought him to Qandahār in 913 AH., this had made him then take away Māh-chuchak, Muqīm's daughter; that there were now (923 AH.) many unemployed Mīrzās in Kābul for whom posts could not be found in regions where the Persians and Aūzbegs were dominant; that an outlet for their ambitions and for Bābur's own would be sought against the weaker opponent he himself was.

Bābur's decision to attack in this year is said to have been taken while Shāh Beg was still a prisoner of Shāh Ismā'īl in the Harāt country; he must have been released meantime by the admirable patience of his slave Sambhal.

924 AH.—JAN. 13TH 1518 TO JAN. 3RD 1519 AD.

In this year Shāh Beg's son Shāh Ḥasan came to Bābur after quarrel with his father. He stayed some two years, and during

[1] In 925 AH. (ff. 227 and 238) mention is made of courtesies exchanged between Bābur and Muḥammad-i-zamān in Balkh. The Mīrzā was with Bābur later on in Hindūstān.

that time was married to Khalīfa's daughter Gul-barg (Rose-leaf). His return to Qandahār will have taken place shortly before Bābur's campaign of 926 A.H. against it, a renewed effort which resulted in possession on Shawwāl 13th 928 AH. (Sep. 6th 1522 AD.).[1]

In this year began the campaign in the north-east territories of Kābul, an account of which is carried on in the diary of 925 AH. It would seem that in the present year Chaghān-sarāī was captured, and also the fortress at the head of the valley of Bābā-qarā, belonging to Ḥaidar-i-'alī *Bajaurī* (f. 216*b*).[2]

[1] Mīr Ma'ṣūm's *Tārīkh-i-sind* is the chief authority for Bābur's action after 913 AH. against Shāh Beg in Qandahār; its translation, made in 1846 by Major Malet, shews some manifestly wrong dates; they appear also in the B.M. MS. of the work

[2] f. 216*b* and note to "Monday".

View from above Babur's Grave and Shah-Jahan's Mosque.

to face p. 367]

925 AH.—JAN. 3RD TO DEC. 23RD 1519 AD.[1]

(*a. Bābur takes the fort of Bajaur.*)

(*Jan. 3rd*) On Monday[2] the first day of the month of Muḥarram, there was a violent earthquake in the lower part of the dale (*julga*) of Chandāwal,[3] which lasted nearly half an astronomical hour.

(*Jan. 4th*) Marching at dawn from that camp with the intention of attacking the fort of Bajaur,[4] we dismounted near it and sent a trusty man of the Dilazāk[5] Afghāns to advise its

[1] Elph. MS. f. 173*b*; W.-i-B. I.O. 215 f. 178 and 217 f. 149; Mems. p. 246. The whole of the Ḥijra year is included in 1519 AD. (Erskine). What follows here and completes the Kābul section of the *Bābur-nāma* is a diary of a little over 13 months' length, supplemented by matter of later entry. The product has the character of a draft, awaiting revision to harmonize it in style and, partly, in topic with the composed narrative that breaks off under 914 AH.; for the diary, written some 11 years earlier than that composed narrative, varies, as it would be expected *à priori* to vary, in style and topic from the terse, lucid and idiomatic output of Bābur's literary maturity. A good many obscure words and phrases in it, several new from Bābur's pen, have opposed difficulty to scribes and translators. Interesting as such *minutiae* are to a close observer of Turkī and of Bābur's diction, comment on all would be tedious; a few will be found noted, as also will such details as fix the date of entry for supplementary matter.

[2] Here Mr. Erskine notes that Dr. Leyden's translation begins again; it broke off on f. 180*b*, and finally ends on f. 223*b*.

[3] This name is often found transliterated as Chandul or [mod.] Jandul but the Ḥai. MS. supports Raverty's opinion that Chandāwal is correct.

The year 925 AH. opens with Bābur far from Kābul and east of the Khahr (fort) he is about to attack. Afghān and other sources allow surmise of his route to that position; he may have come down into the Chandāwal-valley, first, from taking Chaghān-sarāī (f. 124, f. 134 and n.), and, secondly, from taking the Gibrī stronghold of Ḥaidar-i-'alī *Bajaurī* which stood at the head of the Bābā Qarā-valley. The latter surmise is supported by the romantic tales of Afghān chroniclers which at this date bring into history Bābur's Afghān wife, Bībī Mubāraka (f. 220*b* and note; Mems. p. 250 n.; and Appendix K, *An Afghān legend*). (It must be observed here that R.'s *Notes* (pp. 117, 128) confuse the two sieges, *viz.* of the Gibrī fort in 924 AH. and of the Khahr of Bajaur in 925 AH.)

[4] Raverty lays stress on the circumstance that the fort Bābur now attacks has never been known as Bajaur, but always simply as Khahr, the fort (the Arabic name for the place being, he says, plain *Shahr*); just as the main stream is called simply Rūd (the torrent). The name Khahr is still used, as modern maps shew. There are indeed two neighbouring places known simply as Khahr (Fort), *i.e.* one at the mouth of the "Mahmand-valley" of modern campaigns, the other near the Malakand (Fincastle's map).

[5] This word the Ḥai. MS. writes, *passim*, Dilah-zāk.

sulṭān [1] and people to take up a position of service (*qullūq*) and surrender the fort. Not accepting this counsel, that stupid and ill-fated band sent back a wild answer, where-upon the army was ordered to make ready mantelets, ladders and other appliances for taking a fort. For this purpose a day's (*Jan. 5th*) halt was made on that same ground.

(*Jan. 6th*) On Thursday the 4th of Muḥarram, orders were given that the army should put on mail, arm and get to horse; [2] that the left wing should move swiftly to the upper side of the fort, cross the water at the water-entry,[3] and dismount on the
Fol. 217. north side of the fort; that the centre, not taking the way across the water, should dismount in the rough, up-and-down land to the north-west of the fort; and that the right should dismount to the west of the lower gate. While the begs of the left under Dost Beg were dismounting, after crossing the water, a hundred to a hundred and fifty men on foot came out of the fort, shooting arrows. The begs, shooting in their turn, advanced till they had forced those men back to the foot of the ramparts, Mullā 'Abdu'l-malūk of Khwāst, like a madman,[4] going up right under them on his horse. There and then the fort would have been taken if the ladders and mantelets had been ready, and if it had not been so late in the day. Mullā Tirik-i-'alī [5] and a servant of Tīngrī-bīrdī crossed swords with the enemy; each overcame his man, cut off and brought in his head; for this each was promised a reward.

As the Bajaurīs had never before seen matchlocks (*tufang*) they at first took no care about them, indeed they made fun when they heard the report and answered it by unseemly

[1] Either Ḥaidar-i-'alī himself or his nephew, the latter more probably, since no name is mentioned.

[2] Looking at the position assigned by maps to Khahr, in the *dū-āb* of the Charmanga-water and the Rūd of Bajaur, it may be that Bābur's left moved along the east bank of the first-named stream and crossed it into the *dū-āb*, while his centre went direct to its post, along the west side of the fort.

[3] *sū-kīrīshī*; to interpret which needs local knowledge; it might mean where water entered the fort, or where water disembogued from narrows, or, perhaps, where water is entered for a ford. (The verb *kīrmāk* occurs on f. 154*b* and f. 227 to describe water coming down in spate.)

[4] *dīwānawār*, perhaps a jest on a sobriquet earned before this exploit, perhaps the cause of the man's later sobriquet *dīwāna* (f. 245*b*).

[5] Text, t:r:k, read by Erskine and de Courteille as Turk; it might however be a Turkī component in Jān-i-'alī or Muḥibb-i-'alī. (Cf. Zenker *s.n. tirik.*)

gestures. On that day[1] Ustād 'Alī-qulī shot at and brought down five men with his matchlock; Walī the Treasurer, for his part, brought down two; other matchlockmen were also very active in firing and did well, shooting through shield, through cuirass, through *kusarū*,[2] and bringing down one man after another. Perhaps 7, 8, or 10 Bajaurīs had fallen to the matchlock-fire (*ẓarb*) before night. After that it so became that not a head could be put out because of the fire. The order was given, "It is night; let the army retire, and at dawn, if the appliances are ready, let them swarm up into the fort." Fol. 217*b*.

(*Jan. 7th*) At the first dawn of light (*farẓ waqt*) on Friday the 5th of Muḥarram, orders were given that, when the battle-nagarets had sounded, the army should advance, each man from his place to his appointed post (*yīrlīk yīrdīn*) and should swarm up. The left and centre advanced from their ground with mantelets in place all along their lines, fixed their ladders, and swarmed up them. The whole left hand of the centre, under Khalīfa, Shāh Ḥasan *Arghūn* and Yūsuf's Aḥmad, was ordered to reinforce the left wing. Dost Beg's men went forward to the foot of the north-eastern tower of the fort, and busied themselves in undermining and bringing it down. Ustād 'Alī-qulī was there also; he shot very well on that day with his matchlock, and he twice fired off the *firingī*.[3] Walī the Treasurer also brought down a man with his matchlock. Malik 'Alī *quṭnī*[4] was first up a ladder of all the men from the left hand of the centre,

[1] *aūshūl gūnī*, which contrasts with the frequent *aūshbū gūnī* (this same day, today) of manifestly diary entries; it may indicate that the full account of the siege is a later supplement.

[2] This puzzling word might mean cow-horn (*kau-sarū*) and stand for the common horn trumpet. Erskine and de Courteille have read it as *gau-sar*, the first explaining it as *cow-head*, surmised to be a protection for matchlockmen when loading; the second, as *justaucorps de cuir*. That the word is baffling is shewn by its omission in I.O. 215 (f. 178*b*), in 217 (f. 149*b*) and in Muḥ. *Shīrāzī*'s lith. ed. (p. 137).

[3] or *farangī*. Much has been written concerning the early use of gun-powder in the East. There is, however, no well-authenticated fact to prove the existence of anything like artillery there, till it was introduced from Europe. Bābur here, and in other places (f. 267) calls his larger ordnance Firingī, a proof that they were then regarded as owing their origin to Europe. The Turks, in consequence of their constant intercourse with the nations of the West, have always excelled all the other Orientals in the use of artillery; and, when heavy cannon were first used in India, Europeans or Turks were engaged to serve them (Erskine). It is owing no doubt to the preceding gap in his writings that we are deprived of Bābur's account of his own introduction to fire-arms. *See* E. & D.'s *History of India*, vi, Appendix *On the early use of gun-powder in India*.

[4] var. *quṭbī*, *qūchīnī*.

and there was busy with fight and blow. At the post of the centre, Muḥ. 'Alī *Jang-jang*[1] and his younger brother Nau-roz got up, each by a different ladder, and made lance and sword to touch. Bābā the waiting man (*yasāwal*), getting up by another ladder, occupied himself in breaking down the fort-wall with his
Fol. 218. axe. Most of our braves went well forward, shooting off dense flights of arrows and not letting the enemy put out a head; others made themselves desperately busy in breaching and pulling down the fort, caring naught for the enemy's fight and blow, giving no eye to his arrows and stones. By breakfast-time Dost Beg's men had undermined and breached the north-east— tower, got in and put the foe to flight. The men of the ce got in up the ladders by the same time, but those (*aūl*) oth were first (*awwal?*) in.[2] By the favour and pleasure of t High God, this strong and mighty fort was taken in two three astronomical hours! Matching the fort were the utt struggle and effort of our braves; distinguish themselves the did, and won the name and fame of heroes.

As the Bajaurīs were rebels and at enmity with the people of Islām, and as, by reason of the heathenish and hostile customs prevailing in their midst, the very name of Islām was rooted out from their tribe, they were put to general massacre and their wives and children were made captive. At a guess more than 3000 men went to their death; as the fight did not reach to the eastern side of the fort, a few got away there.

The fort taken, we entered and inspected it. On the walls, in houses, streets and alleys, the dead lay, in what numbers! Comers and goers to and fro were passing over the bodies.
Fol. 218*b*. Returning from our inspection, we sat down in the Bajaur sulṭān's residence. The country of Bajaur we bestowed on Khwāja Kalān,[3] assigning a large number of braves to reinforce him. At the Evening Prayer we went back to camp.

[1] This sobriquet might mean "ever a fighter", or an "argle-bargler", or a brass shilling (Zenker), or (if written *jing-jing*) that the man was visaged like the bearded reeding (Scully in Shaw's Vocabulary). The *Ṭabaqāt-i-akbarī* includes a Mīrak Khān *Jang-jang* in its list of Akbar's Commanders.

[2] *ghūl-dīn* (*awwal*) *aūl qūrghān-gha chīqtī*. I suggest to supply *awwal*, first, on the warrant of Bābur's later statement (f. 234*b*) that Dost was first in.

[3] He was a son of Maulānā Muḥ. *Ṣadr*, one of the chief men of 'Umar-shaikh M.'s Court; he had six brothers, all of whom spent their lives in Bābur's service, to whom, if we may believe Abū'l-faẓl, they were distantly related (Erskine).

(*b. Movements in Bajaur.*)

(*Jan. 8th*) Marching at dawn (Muḥ. 6th), we dismounted by the spring[1] of Bābā Qarā in the dale of Bajaur. At Khwāja Kalān's request the prisoners remaining were pardoned their offences, reunited to their wives and children, and given leave to go, but several sulṭāns and of the most stubborn were made to reach their doom of death. Some heads of sulṭāns and of others were sent to Kābul with the news of success; some also to Badakhshān, Qūndūz and Balkh with the letters-of-victory.

Shāh Manṣūr *Yūsuf-zāī*,—he was with us as an envoy from his tribe,—[2] was an eye-witness of the victory and general massacre. We allowed him to leave after putting a coat (*tūn*) on him and after writing orders with threats to the Yūsuf-zāī.

(*Jan. 11th*) With mind easy about the important affairs of the Bajaur fort, we marched, on Tuesday the 9th of Muḥarram, one *kuroh* (2 m.) down the dale of Bajaur and ordered that a tower of heads should be set up on the rising-ground.

(*Jan. 12th*) On Wednesday the 10th of Muḥarram, we rode out to visit the Bajaur fort. There was a wine-party in Khwāja Kalān's house,[3] several goat-skins of wine having been brought

[1] Bābur now returns towards the east, down the Rūd. The *chashma* by which he encamped, would seem to be near the mouth of the valley of Bābā Qarā, one 30 miles long; it may have been, anglicé, a spring [not that of the main stream of the long valley], but the word may be used as it seems to be of the water supplying the Bāgh-i-ṣafā (f. 224), *i.e.* to denote the first considerable gathering-place of small head-waters. It will be observed a few lines further on that this same valley seems to be meant by "Khwāja Khiẓr".

[2] He will have joined Bābur previous to Muḥarram 925 AH.

[3] This statement, the first we have, that Bābur has broken Musalmān Law against stimulants (f. 49 and n.), is followed by many others more explicit, jotting down where and what and sometimes why he drank, in a way which arrests attention and asks some other explanation than that it is an unabashed record of conviviality such conceivably as a non-Musalmān might write. Bābur is now 37 years old; he had obeyed the Law till past early manhood; he wished to return to obedience at 40; he frequently mentions his lapses by a word which can be translated as "commitment of sin" (*irtqāb*); one gathers that he did not at any time disobey with easy conscience. Does it explain his singular record,—one made in what amongst ourselves would be regarded as a private diary,—that his sins were created by Law? Had he a balance of reparation in his thoughts?

Detaching into their separate class as excesses, all his instances of confessed drunkenness, there remains much in his record which, seen from a non-Musalmān point of view, is venial; *e.g.* his *ṣubūḥī* appears to be the "morning" of the Scot, the *Morgen-trank* of the Teuton; his afternoon cup, in the open air usually, may have been no worse than the sober glass of beer or local wine of modern Continental Europe. Many of these legal sins of his record were interludes in the day's long ride, stirrup-cups some of them, all in a period of strenuous physical activity. Many of his

down by Kāfirs neighbouring on Bajaur. All wine and fruit had in Bajaur comes from adjacent parts of Kāfiristān.

Fol. 219.

(*Jan. 13th*) We spent the night there and after inspecting the towers and ramparts of the fort early in the morning (Muḥ. 11th), I mounted and went back to camp.

(*Jan. 14th*) Marching at dawn (Muḥ. 12th), we dismounted on the bank of the Khwāja Khiẓr torrent.[1]

(*Jan. 15th*) Marching thence, we dismounted (Muḥ. 13th) on the bank of the Chandāwal torrent. Here all those inscribed in the Bajaur reinforcement, were ordered to leave.

(*Jan. 16th*) On Sunday the 14th of Muḥarram, a standard was bestowed on Khwāja Kalān and leave given him for Bajaur. A few days after I had let him go, the following little verse having come into my head, it was written down and sent to him :—[2]

> Not such the pact and bargain betwixt my friend and me,
> At length the tooth of parting, unpacted grief for me !
> Against caprice of Fortune, what weapons (*chāra*) arm the man ?
> At length by force of arms (*ba jaur*) my friend is snatched from me !

(*Jan. 19th*) On Wednesday the 17th of Muḥarram, Sl. 'Alā'u'd-dīn of Sawād, the rival (*mu'āriẓ*) of Sl. Wais of Sawād,[3] came and waited on me.

records are collective and are phrased impersonally ; they mention that there was drinking, drunkenness even, but they give details sometimes such as only a sober observer could include.

Bābur names a few men as drunkards, a few as entirely obedient ; most of his men seem not to have obeyed the Law and may have been "temperate drinkers" ; they effected work, Bābur amongst them, which habitual drunkards could not have compassed. Spite of all he writes of his worst excesses, it must be just to remember his Musalmān conscience, and also the distorting power of a fictitious sin. Though he broke the law binding all men against excess, and this on several confessed occasions, his rule may have been no worse than that of the ordinarily temperate Western. It cannot but lighten judgment that his recorded lapses from Law were often prompted by the bounty and splendour of Nature ; were committed amidst the falling petals of fruit-blossom, the flaming fire of autumn leaves, where the eye rested on the *arghwān* or the orange grove, the coloured harvest of corn or vine.

[1] As Mr. Erskine observes, there seems to be no valley except that of Bābā Qarā, between the Khahr and the Chandāwal-valley ; "Khwāja Khiẓr" and "Bābā Qarā" may be one and the same valley.

[2] Time and ingenuity would be needed to bring over into English all the quips of this verse. The most obvious pun is, of course, that on Bajaur as the compelling cause (*ba jaur*) of the parting ; others may be meant on *guzīd* and *gazīd*, on *sazīd* and *chāra*. The verse would provide the holiday amusement of extracting from it two justifiable translations.

[3] His possessions extended from the river of Sawād to Bārāmūla ; he was expelled from them by the Yūsuf-zāī (Erskine).

(*Jan. 20th*) On Thursday the 18th of the month, we hunted the hill between Bajaur and Chandāwal.[1] There the *būghū-marāl*[2] have become quite black, except for the tail which is of another colour; lower down, in Hindūstān, they seem to become black all over.[3] Today a *sārīq-qūsh*[4] was taken; that was black all over, its very eyes being black! Today an eagle (*būrkūt*)[5] took a deer (*kīyīk*).

Corn being somewhat scarce in the army, we went into the Kahrāj-valley, and took some. Fol. 219*b*.

(*Jan. 21st*) On Friday (Muḥ. 19th) we marched for Sawād, with the intention of attacking the Yūsuf-zāī Afghāns, and dismounted in between[6] the water of Panj-kūra and the united waters of Chandāwal and Bajaur. Shāh Manṣūr *Yūsuf-zāī* had brought a few well-flavoured and quite intoxicating confections (*kamālī*); making one of them into three, I ate one portion, Gadāī Ṭaghāī another, 'Abdu'l-lāh the librarian another. It produced remarkable intoxication; so much so that at the Evening Prayer when the begs gathered for counsel, I was not able to go out. A strange thing it was! If in these days[7] I ate the whole of such a confection, I doubt if it would produce half as much intoxication.

c. An impost laid on Kahrāj.)

(*Jan. 22nd*) Marching from that ground, (Muh. 20th), we dismounted over against Kahrāj, at the mouth of the valleys of Kahrāj and Peshgrām.[8] Snow fell ankle-deep while we were on that ground; it would seem to be rare for snow to fall thereabouts, for people were much surprised. In agreement with

[1] This will be the naze of the n.e. rampart of the Bābā Qarā valley.

[2] f. 4 and note; f. 276. Bābur seems to use the name for several varieties of deer.

[3] There is here, perhaps, a jesting allusion to the darkening of complexion amongst the inhabitants of countries from west to east, from Highlands to Indian plains.

[4] In Dr. E. D. Ross' *Polyglot list of birds* the *sārīgh*(*sārīq*)-*qūsh* is said to frequent fields of ripening grain; this suggests to translate its name as Thief-bird.

[5] *Aquila chrysaetus*, the hunting eagle.

[6] This *ārālīgh* might be identified with the "Miankalai" of maps (since Soghd, lying between two arms of the Zar-afshān is known also as Mīānkal), but Raverty explains the Bajaur Miankalai to mean Village of the holy men (*mīān*).

[7] After 933 AH. presumably, when final work on the B.N. was in progress.

[8] Mr. Erskine notes that Pesh-grām lies north of Mahyar (on the Chandāwal-water), and that he has not found Kahrāj (or Kohrāj). Judging from Bābur's next movements, the two valleys he names may be those in succession east of Chandāwal.

Sl. Wais of Sawād there was laid on the Kahrāj people an impost of 4000 ass-loads of rice for the use of the army, and he himself was sent to collect it. Never before had those rude mountaineers borne such a burden; they could not give (all) the grain and were brought to ruin.

(*cc. Raid on Panj-kūra.*)

(*Jan. 25th*) On Tuesday the 23rd of Muḥarram an army was
Fol. 220. sent under Hindū Beg to raid Panj-kūra. Panj-kūra lies more than half-way up the mountain;[1] to reach its villages a person must go for nearly a *kuroh* (2 m.) through a pass. The people had fled and got away; our men brought a few beasts of sorts, and masses of corn from their houses.

(*Jan. 26th*) Next day (Muḥ. 24th) Qūj Beg was put at the head of a force and sent out to raid.

(*Jan. 27th*) On Thursday the 25th of the month, we dismounted at the village of Māndīsh, in the trough of the Kahrāj-valley, for the purpose of getting corn for the army.

(*d. Māhīm's adoption of Dil-dār's unborn child.*)

(*Jan. 28th*) Several children born of Humāyūn's mother had not lived. Hind-āl was not yet born.[2] While we were in those parts, came a letter from Māhīm in which she wrote, "Whether it be a boy, whether it be a girl, is my luck and chance; give it to me; I will declare it my child and will take charge of it." On Friday the 26th of the month, we being still on that ground, Yūsuf-i-'alī the stirrup-holder was sent off to Kābul with letters[3] bestowing Hind-āl, not yet born, on Māhīm.

[1] There is hardly any level ground in the cleft of the Panj-kūra (R.'s *Notes* p. 193); the villages are perched high on the sides of the valley. The pass leading to them may be Katgola (Fincastle's Map).

[2] This account of Hind-āl's adoption is sufficiently confused to explain why a note, made apparently by Humāyūn, should have been appended to it (Appendix L, *On Hind-āl's adoption*). The confusion reminds the reader that he has before him a sort of memorandum only, diary jottings, apt to be allusive and abbreviated. The expected child was Dil-dār's; Māhīm, using her right as principal wife, asked for it to be given to her. That the babe in question is here called Hind-āl shews that at least part of this account of his adoption was added after the birth and naming (f. 227).

[3] One would be, no doubt, for Dil-dār's own information. She then had no son but had two daughters, Gul-rang and Gul-chihra. News of Hind-āl's birth reached Bābur in Bhīra, some six weeks later (f. 227).

(*dd. Construction of a stone platform.*)

While we were still on that same ground in the Māndīsh-country, I had a platform made with stones (*tāsh bīla*) on a height in the middle of the valley, so large that it held the tents of the advance-camp. All the household and soldiers carried the stones for it, one by one like ants.

(*e. Bābur's marriage with his Afghān wife, Bībī Mubāraka.*)

In order to conciliate the Yūsuf-zāī horde, I had asked for a daughter of one of my well-wishers, Malik Sulaimān Shāh's son Malik Shāh Manṣūr, at the time he came to me as envoy Fol. 220*b*. from the Yūsuf-zāī Afghāns.[1]

While we were on this ground news came that his daughter[2] was on her way with the Yūsuf-zāī tribute. At the Evening Prayer there was a wine-party to which Sl. 'Alā'u'd-dīn (of Sawād) was invited and at which he was given a seat and special dress of honour (*khilcat-i-khāṣa*).

(*Jan. 30th*) On Sunday the 28th, we marched from that valley. Shāh Manṣūr's younger brother Ṭāūs (Handsome) Khān brought the above-mentioned daughter of his brother to our ground after we had dismounted.

(*f. Repopulation of the fort of Bajaur.*)

For the convenience of having the Bī-sūt people in Bajaur-fort,[3] Yūsuf'i-'alī the taster was sent from this camp to get them on the march and take them to that fort. Also, written orders were despatched to Kābul that the army there left should join us.

(*Feb. 4th*) On Friday the 3rd of the month of Ṣafar, we dismounted at the confluence of the waters of Bajaur and Panj-kūra.

(*Feb. 6th*) On Sunday the 5th of the month, we went from that ground to Bajaur where there was a drinking-party in Khwāja Kalān's house.

[1] f. 218*b*.

[2] Bībī Mubāraka, the Afghānī Aghācha of Gul-badan. An attractive picture of her is drawn by the *Tāwārikh-i-ḥāfiẓ-i-raḥmat-khānī*. As this gives not only one of Bābur's romantic adventures but historical matter, I append it in my husband's translation [(A.Q.R. April 1901)] as Appendix K, *An Afghān Legend*.

[3] *Bī-sūt aīlī-nīng Bajaur-qūrghānī-dā manāsabatī-bār jīhatī*; a characteristic phrase.

(*g. Expedition against the Afghān clans.*)

(*Feb. 8th*) On Tuesday the 7th of the month the begs and the Dilazāk Afghān headmen were summoned, and, after consultation, matters were left at this:—"The year is at its end,[1] only a few days of the Fish are left; the plainsmen have carried in all their corn; if we went now into Sawād, the army would
Fol. 221. dwindle through getting no corn. The thing to do is to march along the Aṃbahar and Pānī-mānī road, cross the Sawād-water above Hash-nagar, and surprise the Yūsuf-zāī and Muḥammadī Afghāns who are located in the plain over against the Yūsuf-zāī *sangur* of Māhūrā. Another year, coming earlier in the harvest-time, the Afghāns of this place must be our first thought." So the matter was left.

(*Feb. 9th*) Next day, Wednesday, we bestowed horses and robes on Sl. Wais and Sl. 'Alā'u'u-dīn of Sawād, gave them leave to go, marched off ourselves and dismounted over against Bajaur.

(*Feb. 10th*) We marched next day, leaving Shāh Manṣūr's daughter in Bajaur-fort until the return of the army. We dismounted after passing Khwāja Khiẓr, and from that camp leave was given to Khwāja Kalān; and the heavy baggage, the worn-out horses and superfluous effects of the army were started off into Lamghān by the Kūnār road.

(*Feb. 11th*) Next morning Khwāja Mīr-i-mīrān was put in charge of the camel baggage-train and started off by the Qūrghā-tū and Darwāza road, through the Qarā-kūpa-pass. Riding light for the raid, we ourselves crossed the Aṃbahar-pass, and yet another great pass, and dismounted at Pānī-mālī nearer[2] the Afternoon Prayer. Aūghān-bīrdī was sent forward with a few others to learn[3] how things were.

(*Feb. 12th*) The distance between us and the Afghāns being short, we did not make an early start. Aūghān-bīrdī came back at breakfast-time.[4] He had got the better of an Afghān

[1] Perhaps the end of the early spring-harvest and the spring harvesting-year. It is not the end of the campaigning year, manifestly; and it is at the beginning of both the solar and lunar years.

[2] Perhaps, more than half-way between the Mid-day and Afternoon Prayers. So too in the annals of Feb. 12th.

[3] *tīl ālghālī* (Pers. *zabān-gīrī*), a new phrase in the B.N.

[4] *chāsht*, which, being half-way between sunrise and the meridian, is a variable hour.

and had cut his head off, but had dropped it on the road. He brought no news so sure as the heart asks (*künkül-tīladīk*). Mid-day come, we marched on, crossed the Sawād-water, and dismounted nearer[1] the Afternoon Prayer. At the Bed-time Prayer, we remounted and rode swiftly on. Fol. 221*b*.

(*Feb. 13th*) Rustam *Turkmān* had been sent scouting; when the Sun was spear-high he brought word that the Afghāns had heard about us and were shifting about, one body of them making off by the mountain-road. On this we moved the faster, sending raiders on ahead who killed a few, cut off their heads and brought a band of prisoners, some cattle and flocks. The Dilazāk Afghāns also cut off and brought in a few heads. Turning back, we dismounted near Kātlāng and from there sent a guide to meet the baggage-train under Khwāja Mīr-i-mīrān and bring it to join us in Maqām.[2]

(*Feb. 14th*) Marching on next day, we dismounted between Kātlāng and Maqām. A man of Shāh Manṣūr's arrived. Khusrau Kūkūldāsh and Aḥmadī the secretary were sent with a few more to meet the baggage-train.

(*Feb. 15th*) On Wednesday the 14th of the month, the baggage-train rejoined us while we were dismounting at Maqām.

It will have been within the previous 30 or 40 years that a heretic qalandar named Shahbāz perverted a body of Yūsuf-zāī and another of Dilazāk. His tomb was on a free and dominating height of the lower hill at the bill (*tūmshūq*) of the Maqām mountain. Thought I, "What is there to recommend the tomb of a heretic qalandar for a place in air so free?" and ordered the tomb destroyed and levelled with the ground. The place was so charming and open that we elected to sit there some time and to eat a confection (*ma'jūn*). Fol. 222.

(*h. Bābur crosses the Indus for the first time.*)

We had turned off from Bajaur with Bhīra in our thoughts.[3] Ever since we came into Kābul it had been in my mind to move on Hindūstān, but this had not been done for a variety of

[1] See n. 2, f. 221.
[2] Perhaps Maqām is the Mardān of maps.
[3] Bhīra, on the Jehlam, is now in the Shāhpūr district of the Panj-āb.

reasons. Nothing to count had fallen into the soldiers' hands during the three or four months we had been leading this army. Now that Bhīra, the borderland of Hindūstān, was so near, I thought a something might fall into our men's hands if, riding light, we went suddenly into it. To this thought I clung, but some of my well-wishers, after we had raided the Afghāns and dismounted at Maqām, set the matter in this way before me:—"If we are to go into Hindūstān, it should be on a proper basis; one part of the army stayed behind in Kābul; a body of effective braves was left behind in Bajaur; a good part of this army has gone into Lamghān because its horses were worn-out; and the horses of those who have come this far, are so poor that they have not a day's hard riding in them." Reasonable as these considerations were, yet, having made the start, we paid no Fol. 222*b*. attention to them but set off next day for the ford through the water of Sind.[1] Mīr Muḥammad the raftsman and his elder and younger brethren were sent with a few braves to examine the Sind-river (*daryā*), above and below the ford.

(*Feb. 16th*) After starting off the camp for the river, I went to hunt rhinoceros on the Sawātī side which place people call also Karg-khāna (Rhino-home).[2] A few were discovered but the jungle was dense and they did not come out of it. When one with a calf came into the open and betook itself to flight, many arrows were shot at it and it rushed into the near jungle; the jungle was fired but that same rhino was not had. Another calf was killed as it lay, scorched by the fire, writhing and palpitating. Each person took a share of the spoil. After leaving Sawātī, we wandered about a good deal; it was the Bed-time Prayer when we got to camp.

Those sent to examine the ford came back after doing it.

(*Feb. 17th*) Next day, Thursday the 16th,[3] the horses and baggage-camels crossed through the ford and the camp-bazar

[1] This will be the ford on the direct road from Mardān for the eastward (Elphinstone's *Caubul* ii, 416).

[2] The position of Sawātī is represented by the Suābī of the G. of I. map (1909 AD.). Writing in about 1813 AD. Mr. Erskine notes as worthy of record that the rhinoceros was at that date no longer found west of the Indus.

[3] Elph. MS. *ghura*, the 1st, but this is corrected to 16th by a marginal note. The Hai. MS. here, as in some other places, has the context for a number, but omits the figures. So does also the Elph. MS. in a good many places.

and foot-soldiers were put over on rafts. Some Nīl-ābīs came and saw me at the ford-head (*guzar-bāshī*), bringing a horse in mail and 300 *shāhrukhīs* as an offering. At the Mid-day Prayer of this same day, when every-one had crossed the river, we marched on; we went on until one watch of the night had passed (*circa* 9 p.m.) when we dismounted near the water of Kacha-kot.[1]

(*Feb. 18th*) Marching on next day, we crossed the Kacha-kot-water; noon returning, went through the Sangdakī-pass and dismounted. While Sayyid Qāsim Lord of the Gate was in charge of the rear (*chāghdāwal*) he overcame a few Gujūrs who had got up with the rear march, cut off and brought in 4 or 5 of their heads. Fol. 223.

(*Feb. 19th*) Marching thence at dawn and crossing the Sūhān-water, we dismounted at the Mid-day Prayer. Those behind kept coming in till midnight; the march had been mightily long, and, as many horses were weak and out-of-condition, a great number were left on the road.

(*i. The Salt-range.*)

Fourteen miles (*7 kos*) north of Bhīra lies the mountain-range written of in the *Ẓafar-nāma* and other books as the Koh-i-jūd.[2] I had not known why it was called this; I now knew. On it dwell two tribes, descendants from one parent-source, one is called Jūd, the other Janjūha. These two from of old have been the rulers and lawful commanders of the peoples and hordes (*aūlūs*) of the range and of the country between Bhīra and Nīl-āb. Their rule is friendly and brotherly however; they cannot take what their hearts might desire; the portion ancient custom has fixed is given and taken, no less and no more. The agreement is to give one *shāhrukhī*[3] for each yoke of oxen and seven for headship in a household; there is also service in the army. The Jūd and Janjūha both are divided into several

[1] This is the Harru. Mr. Erskine observes that Bābur appears to have turned sharp south after crossing it, since he ascended a pass so soon after leaving the Indus and reached the Sūhān so soon.

[2] *i.e.* the Salt-range.

[3] Mr. Erskine notes that (in his day) a *shāhrukhī* may be taken at a shilling or eleven pence sterling.

clans. The Koh-i-jūd runs for 14 miles along the Bhīra country, taking off from those Kashmīr mountains that are one with
Fol. 223*b*. Hindū-kūsh, and it draws out to the south-west as far as the foot of Dīn-kot on the Sind-river.[1] On one half of it are the Jūd, the Janjūha on the other. People call it Koh-i-jūd through connecting it with the Jūd tribe.[2] The principal headman gets the title of Rāī; others, his younger brothers and sons, are styled Malik. The Janjūha headmen are maternal uncles of Langar Khan. The ruler of the people and horde near the Sūhān-water was named Malik Hast. The name originally was Asad but as Hindūstānīs sometimes drop a vowel *e.g.* they say ***khabr*** for ***khabar*** (news), they had said Asd for Asad, and this went on to Hast.

Langar Khān was sent off to Malik Hast at once when we dismounted. He galloped off, made Malik Hast hopeful of our favour and kindness, and at the Bed-time Prayer, returned with him. Malik Hast brought an offering of a horse in mail and waited on me. He may have been 22 or 23 years old.[3]

The various flocks and herds belonging to the country-people were close round our camp. As it was always in my heart to possess Hindūstān, and as these several countries, Bhīra, Khūsh-āb, Chīn-āb and Chīnīūt[4] had once been held by the Turk, I pictured them as my own and was resolved to get them into my hands, whether peacefully or by force. For these reasons it being imperative to treat these hillmen well, this following
Fol. 224. order was given :—" Do no hurt or harm to the flocks and herds of these people, nor even to their cotton-ends and broken needles ! "

[1] It is somewhat difficult not to forget that a man who, like Bābur, records so many observations of geographical position, had no guidance from Surveys, Gazetteers and Books of Travel. Most of his records are those of personal observation.

[2] In this sentence Mr. Erskine read a reference to the Musalmān Ararat, the Koh-i-jūd on the left bank of the Tigris. What I have set down translates the Turkī words but, taking account of Bābur's eye for the double use of a word, and Erskine's careful work, done too in India, the Turkī may imply reference to the Ararat-like summit of Sakeswar.

[3] Here Dr. Leyden's version finally ends (Erskine).

[4] Bhīra, as has been noted, is on the Jehlam ; Khūsh-āb is 40 m. lower down the same river ; Chīnīūt (Chīnī-wat ?) is 50 miles south of Bhīra ; Chīn-āb (China-water ?) seems the name of a tract only and not of a residential centre ; it will be in the Bar of Kipling's border-thief. Concerning Chīnīūt *see* D. G. Barkley's letter, JRAS 1899 p. 132.

(*j. The Kalda-kahār lake.*)

(*Feb. 20th*) Marching thence next day, we dismounted at the Mid-day Prayer amongst fields of densely-growing corn in Kalda-kahār.

Kalda-kahār is some 20 miles north of Bhīra, a level land shut in [1] amongst the Jūd mountains. In the middle of it is a lake some six miles round, the in-gatherings of rain from all sides. On the north of this lake lies an excellent meadow; on the hill-skirt to the west of it there is a spring [2] having its source in the heights overlooking the lake. The place being suitable I have made a garden there, called the Bāgh-i-ṣafā,[3] as will be told later; it is a very charming place with good air.

(*Feb. 21st*) We rode from Kalda-kahār at dawn next day. When we reached the top of the Hamtātū-pass a few local people waited on me, bringing a humble gift. They were joined with 'Abdu'r-raḥīm the chief-scribe (*shaghāwal*) and sent with him to speak the Bhīra people fair and say, "The possession of this country by a Turk has come down from of old; beware not to bring ruin on its people by giving way to fear and anxiety; our eye is on this land and on this people; raid and rapine shall not be."

We dismounted near the foot of the pass at breakfast-time, Fol. 224*b*. and thence sent seven or eight men ahead, under Qurbān of Chīrkh and 'Abdu'l-malūk of Khwāst. Of those sent one Mīr Muḥammad (a servant?) of Mahdī Khwāja [4] brought in a man. A few Afghān headmen, who had come meantime with offerings and done obeisance, were joined with Langar Khān to go and speak the Bhīra people fair.

After crossing the pass and getting out of the jungle, we arrayed in right and left and centre, and moved forward for Bhīra. As

[1] *taur yīrī waqī' būlūb tūr*. As on f. 160 of the valley of Khwesh, I have taken *taur* to be Turkī, complete, shut in.

[2] *chashma* (f. 218*b* and note).

[3] The promised description is not found; there follows a mere mention only of the garden [f. 369]. This entry can be taken therefore as shewing an intention to write what is still wanting from Ṣafar 926 AH. to Ṣafar 932 AH.

[4] Mīr Muḥ. may have been a kinsman or follower of Mahdī Khwāja. The entry on the scene, unannounced by introduction as to parentage, of the Khwāja who played a part later in Bābur's family affairs is due, no doubt, to the last gap of annals. He is mentioned in the Translator's Note, *s.a.* 923 AH. (*See* Gul-badan's H.N. Biographical Appendix *s.n.*)

we got near it there came in, of the servants of Daulat Khān *Yūsuf-khail's* son 'Alī Khān, Sīktū's son Dīwa *Hindū*; with them came several of the notables of Bhīra who brought a horse and camel as an offering and did me obeisance. At the Mid-day Prayer we dismounted on the east of Bhīrá, on the bank of the Bahat (Jehlam), in a sown-field, without hurt or harm being allowed to touch the people of Bhīra.

(*k. History of Bhīra.*)

Tīmūr Beg had gone into Hindūstān; from the time he went out again these several countries *viz.* Bhīra, Khūsh-āb, Chīn-āb and Chīnīūt, had been held by his descendants and the dependants and adherents of those descendants. After the death of Sl. Mas'ūd Mīrzā and his son 'Alī *Asghar* Mīrzā, the sons of Mīr 'Alī Beg

(*Author's note on Sl. Mas'ūd Mīrzā.*) He was the son of Sūyūrghatmīsh Mīrzā, son of Shāhrukh Mīrzā, (son of Tīmūr), and was known as Sl. Mas'ūd *Kābulī* because the government and administration of Kābul and Zābul were then dependent on him (deposed 843 AH.–1440 AD.)

Fol. 225. *viz.* Bābā-i-kābulī, Daryā Khān and Apāq Khān, known later as Ghāzī Khān, all of whom Sl. Mas'ūd M. had cherished, through their dominant position, got possession of Kābul, Zābul and the afore-named countries and *parganas* of Hindūstān. In Sl. Abū-sa'īd Mīrzā's time, Kābul and Zābul went from their hands, the Hindūstān countries remaining. In 910 AH. (1504 AD.) the year

(*Author's note to 910 AH.*) That year, with the wish to enter Hindūstān, Khaibar had been crossed and Parashāwūr (*sic*) had been reached, when Bāqī *Chaghānīānī* insisted on a move against Lower Bangash *i.e.* Kohāt, a mass of Afghāns were raided and scraped clean (*qīrīb*), the Bannū plain was raided and plundered, and return was made through Dūkī (Dūgī).

I first came into Kābul, the government of Bhīra, Khūsh-āb and Chīn-āb depended on Sayyid 'Alī Khan, son of Ghāzī Khān and grandson of Mīr 'Alī Beg, who read the *khutba* for Sikandar son of Buhlūl (*Lūdī Afghān*) and was subject to him. When I led that army out (910 AH.) Sayyid 'Alī Khān left Bhīra in terror, crossed the Bahat-water, and seated himself in Sher-kot, one of the villages of Bhīra. A few years later the Afghāns became suspicious about him on my account; he, giving way to his own fears and anxieties, made these countries over to the then governor

Fol. 225*b*. in Lāhūr, Daulat Khān, son of Tātār Khān *Yūsuf-khail*, who gave them to his own eldest son 'Alī Khān, and in 'Alī Khān's possession they now were.

(*Author's note on Daulat Khān Yūsuf-khail.*) This Tātār Khān, the father of Daulat Khān, was one of six or seven *sardārs* who, sallying out and becoming dominant in Hindūstān, made Buhlūl Pādshāh. He held the country north of the Satluj (*sic*) and Sahrind,[1] the revenues of which exceeded 3 *krūrs*.[2] On Tātār Khān's death, Sl. Sikandar (*Lūdī*), as over-lord, took those countries from Tātār Khān's sons and gave Lāhūr only to Daulat Khān. That happened a year or two before I came into the country of Kābul (910 AH.).

(*l. Bābur's journey resumed.*)

(*Feb. 22nd*) Next morning foragers were sent to several convenient places; on the same day I visited Bhīra; and on the same day Sangur Khān *Janjūha* came, made offering of a horse, and did me obeisance.

(*Feb. 23rd*) On Wednesday the 22nd of the month, the headmen and *chauderis*[3] of Bhīra were summoned, a sum of 400,000 *shāhrukhīs*[4] was agreed on as the price of peace (*māl-i-amān*), and collectors were appointed. We also made an excursion, going in a boat and there eating a confection.

(*Feb. 24th*) Ḥaidar the standard-bearer had been sent to the Bilūchīs located in Bhīra and Khūsh-āb; on Thursday morning they made an offering of an almond-coloured *tīpūchāq* [horse], and did obeisance. As it was represented to me that some of the soldiery were behaving without sense and were laying-hands on Bhīra people, persons were sent who caused some of those Fol. 226. senseless people to meet their death-doom, of others slit the noses and so led them round the camp.

(*Feb. 25th*) On Friday came a dutiful letter from the Khūsh-ābīs; on this Shāh Shujā' *Arghūn's* son Shāh Ḥasan was appointed to go to Khūsh-āb.

[1] or Sihrind, mod. Sirhind or Sar-i-hind (Head of Hind). It may be noted here, for what it may be found worth, that Kh(w)āfī Khān [i, 402] calls Sar-i-hind the old name, says that the place was once held by the Ghaznī dynasty and was its Indian frontier, and that Shāh-jahān changed it to Sahrind. The W.-i-B. I.O. 217 f. 155 writes Shahrind.

[2] Three krores or crores of dāms, at 40 to the rupee, would make this 750,000 rupees, or about £75,000 sterling (Erskine); a statement from the ancient history of the rupī!

[3] This Hindustānī word in some districts signifies the head man of a trade, in others a landholder (Erskine).

[4] In Mr. Erskine's time this sum was reckoned to be nearly £20,000.

(*Feb. 26th*) On Saturday the 25th of the month,[1] Shāh Ḥasan was started for Khūsh-āb.

(*Feb. 27th*) On Sunday so much rain fell[2] that water covered all the plain. A small brackish stream[3] flowing between Bhīra and the gardens in which the army lay, had become like a great river before the Mid-day Prayer; while at the ford near Bhīra there was no footing for more than an arrow's flight; people crossing had to swim. In the afternoon I rode out to watch the water coming down (*kīrkān sū*); the rain and storm were such that on the way back there was some fear about getting in to camp. I crossed that same water (*kīrkān sū*) with my horse swimming. The army-people were much alarmed; most of them abandoned tents and heavy baggage, shouldered armour, horse-mail and arms, made their horses swim and crossed bareback. Most streams flooded the plain.

(*Feb. 28th*) Next day boats were brought from the river (Jehlam), and in these most of the army brought their tents and baggage over. Towards mid-day, Qūj Beg's men went 2 miles up the water and there found a ford by which the rest crossed.

Fol. 226*b*. (*March 1st*) After a night spent in Bhīra-fort, Jahān-nūma they call it, we marched early on the Tuesday morning out of the worry of the rain-flood to the higher ground north of Bhīra.

As there was some delay about the moneys asked for and agreed to (*taqabbul*), the country was divided into four districts and the begs were ordered to try to make an end of the matter. Khalīfa was appointed to one district, Qūj Beg to another, Nāṣir's Dost to another, Sayyid Qāsim and Muḥibb-i-'alī to another. Picturing as our own the countries once occupied by the Turk, there was to be no over-running or plundering.

(*m. Envoys sent to the court in Dihlī.*)

(*March 3rd*) People were always saying, "It could do no harm to send an envoy, for peace' sake, to countries that once depended

[1] Here originally neither the Elph. MS. nor the Ḥai. MS. had a date; it has been added to the former.

[2] This rain is too early for the s.w. monsoon; it was probably a severe fall of spring rain, which prevails at this season or rather earlier, and extends over all the west of Asia (Erskine).

[3] *aṣ ghīna shor sū*. Streams rising in the Salt-range become brackish on reaching its skirts (G. of I.).

on the Turk." Accordingly on Thursday the 1st of Rabī'u'l-awwal, Mullā Murshid was appointed to go to Sl. Ibrāhīm who through the death of his father Sl. Iskandar had attained to rule in Hindūstān some 5 or 6 months earlier(?). I sent him a goshawk (*qārchīgha*) and asked for the countries which from of old had depended on the Turk. Mullā Murshid was given charge of writings (*khāṭṭlār*) for Daulat Khān (*Yūsuf-khail*) and writings for Sl. Ibrāhīm; matters were sent also by word-of-mouth; and he was given leave to go. Far from sense and wisdom, shut off from judgment and counsel must people in Hindūstān be, the Afghāns above all; for they could not move and make stand like a foe, nor did they know ways and rules of friendliness. Fol. 227. Daulat Khān kept my man several days in Lāhūr without seeing him himself or speeding him on to Sl. Ibrāhīm; and he came back to Kābul a few months later without bringing a reply.

(*n. Birth of Hind-āl.*)

(*March 4th*) On Friday the 2nd of the month, the foot-soldiers Shaibak and Darwesh-i-'alī,—he is now a matchlockman,—bringing dutiful letters from Kābul, brought news also of Hind-āl's birth. As the news came during the expedition into Hindūstān, I took it as an omen, and gave the name Hind-āl (Taking of Hind). Dutiful letters came also from Muḥammad-i-zamān M. in Balkh, by the hand of Qambar Beg.

(*March 5th*) Next morning when the Court rose, we rode out for an excursion, entered a boat and there drank *'araq*.[1] The people of the party were Khwāja Dost-khāwand, Khusrau, Mīrīm, Mīrzā Qulī, Muḥammadī, Aḥmadī, Gadāī, Na'man, Langar Khān, Rauh-dam,[2] Qāsim-i-'alī the opium-eater (*tariyākī*), Yūsuf-i-'alī and Tīngrī-qulī. Towards the head of the boat there was a *tālār*[3] on the flat top of which I sat with a few people, a few others sitting below. There was a sitting-place also at the tail of the boat; there Muḥammadī, Gadāī and Na'man sat. *'Araq* was drunk till the Other Prayer when, disgusted by its bad flavour, by consent of those at the head of the boat, *ma'jūn* was preferred.

[1] Here this will be the fermented juice of rice or of the date-palm.
[2] *Rauḥ* is sometimes the name of a musical note.
[3] a platform, with or without a chamber above it, and supported on four posts.

Fol. 227b. Those at the other end, knowing nothing about our *ma'jūn* drank *'araq* right through. At the Bed-time Prayer we rode from the boat and got into camp late. Thinking I had been drinking *'araq* Muḥammadī and Gadāī had said to one another, "Let's do befitting service," lifted a pitcher of *'araq* up to one another in turn on their horses, and came in saying with wonderful joviality and heartiness and speaking together, "Through this dark night have we come carrying this pitcher in turns!" Later on when they knew that the party was (now) meant to be otherwise and the hilarity to differ, that is to say, that [there would be that] of the *ma'jūn* band and that of the drinkers, they were much disturbed because never does a *ma'jūn* party go well with a drinking-party. Said I, "Don't upset the party! Let those who wish to drink *'araq*, drink *'araq*; let those who wish to eat *ma'jūn*, eat *ma'jūn*. Let no-one on either side make talk or allusion to the other." Some drank *'araq*, some ate *ma'jūn*, and for a time the party went on quite politely. Bābā Jān the *qabūz*-player had not been of our party (in the boat); we invited him when we reached the tents. He asked to drink *'araq*. We invited Tardī Muḥammad *Qībchāq* also and made him a comrade of the drinkers. A *ma'jūn* party never goes well with an *'araq* or a wine-party; the drinkers began to make wild talk and chatter from all sides, mostly in allusion to *ma'jūn* and *ma'jūnīs*. Bābā Jān even, when drunk, said many wild things. The drinkers soon made Tardī Khān mad-drunk, by giving him one full bowl after another. Try as we did
Fol. 228. to keep things straight, nothing went well; there was much disgusting uproar; the party became intolerable and was broken up.

(*March 7th*) On Monday the 5th of the month, the country of Bhīra was given to Hindū Beg.

(*March 8th*) On Tuesday the Chīn-āb country was bestowed on Ḥusain *Aīkrak*(?) and leave was given to him and the Chīn-āb people to set out. At this time Sayyid 'Alī Khān's son Minūchihr Khān, having let us know (his intention), came and waited on me. He had started from Hindūstān by the upper road, had met in with Tātār Khān *Kakar*;[1] Tātār Khān had not let him pass on, but had kept him, made him a son-in-law by giving him his own daughter, and had detained him for some time.

[1] so-written in the MSS. Cf. Raverty's *Notes* and G. of I.

(*o. The Kakars.*)

In amongst the mountains of Nīl-āb and Bhīra which connect with those of Kashmīr, there are, besides the Jūd and Janjūha tribes, many Jats, Gujūrs, and others akin to them, seated in villages everywhere on every rising-ground. These are governed by headmen of the Kakar tribes, a headship like that over the Jūd and Janjūha. At this time (925 AH.), the headmen of the people of those hill-skirts were Tātār *Kakar* and Hātī *Kakar*, two descendants of one forefather; being paternal-uncles' sons.[1] Torrent-beds and ravines are their strongholds. Tātār's place, named Parhāla,[2] is a good deal below the snow-mountains; Hātī's country connects with the mountains and also he had made Bābū Khān's fief Kālanjar,[3] look towards himself. Tātār Fol. 228*b*. *Kakar* had seen Daulat Khān (*Yūsuf-khail*) and looked to him with complete obedience. Hātī had not seen Daulat Khān; his attitude towards him was bad and turbulent. At the word of the Hindūstān begs and in agreement with them, Tātār had so posted himself as to blockade Hātī from a distance. Just when we were in Bhīra, Hātī moved on pretext of hunting, fell unexpectedly on Tātār, killed him, and took his country, his wives and his having (*būlghānī*).[4]

(*p. Bābur's journey resumed.*)

Having ridden out at the Mid-day Prayer for an excursion, we got on a boat and *'araq* was drunk. The people of the party were Dost Beg, Mīrzā Qulī, Aḥmadī, Gadāī, Muḥammad 'Alī *Jang-jang*, 'Asas,[5] and Aūghān-bīrdī *Mughūl*. The musicians were Rauḥ-dam, Bābā Jān, Qāsim-i-'alī, Yūsuf-i-'alī, Tīngrī-qulī, Abū'l-qāsim, Rāmẓān *Lūlī*. We drank in the boat till the Bed-time Prayer; then getting off it, full of drink, we mounted, took torches in our hands, and went to camp from the river's bank,

[1] Anglicé, cousins on the father's side.

[2] The G. of I. describes it.

[3] Elph. MS. f. 183*b*, *manṣūb*; Ḥai. MS. and 2nd W.-i-B. *bīsūt*. The holder might be Bābā-i-kābulī of f. 225.

[4] The 1st Pers. trs. (I.O. 215 f. 188*b*) and Kehr's MS. [Ilminsky p. 293] attribute Hātī's last-recorded acts to Bābur himself. The two mistaken sources err together elsewhere. M. de Courteille corrects the defect (ii, 67).

[5] night-guard. He is the old servant to whom Bābur sent a giant *ashrafī* of the spoils of India (Gul-badan's H.N. *s.n.*).

leaning over from our horses on this side, leaning over from that, at one loose-rein gallop! Very drunk I must have been for, when they told me next day that we had galloped loose-rein into camp, carrying torches, I could not recal it in the very least. After reaching my quarters, I vomited a good deal.

(*March 11th*) On Friday we rode out on an excursion, crossed the water (Jehlam) by boat and went about amongst the orchards (*bâghât*) of blossoming trees and the lands of the sugar-cultivation. We saw the wheel with buckets, had water drawn, and asked
Fol. 229. particulars about getting it out; indeed we made them draw it again and again. During this excursion a confection was preferred. In returning we went on board a boat. A confection (*ma'jūn*) was given also to Minūchihr Khān, such a one that, to keep him standing, two people had to give him their arms. For a time the boat remained at anchor in mid-stream; we then went down-stream; after a while had it drawn up-stream again, slept in it that night and went back to camp near dawn.

(*March 12th*) On Saturday the 10th of the first Rabī', the Sun entered the Ram. Today we rode out before mid-day and got into a boat where *'araq* was drunk. The people of the party were Khwāja Dost-khāwand, Dost Beg, Mīrīm, Mīrzā Qulī, Muḥammadī, Aḥmadī, Yūnas-i-'alī, Muḥ. 'Alī *Jang-jang*, Gadāī Ṭaghāī, Mīr Khurd (and ?) 'Asas. The musicians were Rauḥ-dam, Bābā Jān, Qāsim, Yūsuf-i-'alī, Tīngrī-qulī and Ramẓān. We got into a branch-water (*shakh-i-āb*), for some time went down-stream, landed a good deal below Bhīra and on its opposite bank, and went late into camp.

This same day Shāh Ḥasan returned from Khūsh-āb whither he had been sent as envoy to demand the countries which from of old had depended on the Turk; he had settled peaceably with them and had in his hands a part of the money assessed on them.

The heats were near at hand. To reinforce Hindū Beg (in Bhīra) were appointed Shāh Muḥammad Keeper of the Seal and his younger brother Dost Beg Keeper of the Seal, together with several suitable braves; an accepted (*yārāsha*) stipend
Fol. 229b. was fixed and settled in accordance with each man's position. Khūsh-āb was bestowed, with a standard, on Langar Khān, the prime cause and mover of this expedition; we settled also that

he was to help Hindū Beg. We appointed also to help Hindū Beg, the Turk and local soldiery of Bhīra, increasing the allowances and pay of both. Amongst them was the afore-named Minūchihr Khān whose name has been mentioned; there was also Naẓar-i-'alī *Turk*, one of Minūchihr Khān's relations; there were also Sangar Khān *Janjūha* and Malik Hast *Janjūha*.

(*pp. Return for Kābul.*)

(*March 13th*) Having settled the country in every way making for hope of peace, we marched for Kābul from Bhīra on Sunday the 11th of the first Rabī'. We dismounted in Kaldah-kahār. That day too it rained amazingly; people with rain-cloaks[1] were in the same case as those who had none! The rear of the camp kept coming in till the Bed-time Prayer.

(*q. Action taken against Hātī Kakar.*)

(*March 14th*) People acquainted with the honour and glory (*āb u tāb*) of this land and government, especially the Janjūhas, old foes of these Kakars, represented, "Hātī is the bad man round-about; he it is robs on the roads; he it is brings men to ruin; he ought either to be driven out from these parts, or to be severely punished." Agreeing with this, we left Khwāja Mīr-i-mīrān and Nāṣir's Mīrīm next day with the camp, parting from them at big breakfast,[2] and moved on Hātī *Kakar*. As has been said, he had killed Tātār a few days earlier, and having taken possession of Parhāla, was in it now. Dismounting at the Other Prayer, we gave the horses corn; at the Bed-time Prayer we rode on again, our guide being a Gujūr servant of Malik Hast, named Sar-u-pā. We rode the night through and dismounted at dawn, when Beg Muhammad *Mughūl* was sent back to the Fol. 230.

[1] The *kīping* or *kīpik* is a kind of mantle covered with wool (Erskine); the root of the word is *kīp*, dry.

[2] *aūlūgh chāsht*, a term suggesting that Bābur knew the *chota ḥāẓirī*, little breakfast, of Anglo-India. It may be inferred, from several passages, that the big breakfast was taken after 9 a.m. and before 12 p.m. Just below men are said to put on their mail at *chāsht* in the same way as, *passim*, things other than prayer are said to be done at this or that Prayer; this, I think, always implies that they are done after the Prayer mentioned; a thing done shortly before a Prayer is done "close to" or "near" or when done over half-way to the following Prayer, the act is said to be done "nearer" to the second (as was noted on f. 221).

camp, and we remounted when it was growing light. At breakfast-time (9 a.m.) we put our mail on and moved forward faster. The blackness of Parhāla shewed itself from 2 miles off; the gallop was then allowed (*chāpqūn qūūldī*); the right went east of Parhāla, Qūj Beg, who was also of the right, following as its reserve; the men of the left and centre went straight for the fort, Dost Beg being their rear-reserve.

Parhāla stands amongst ravines. It has two roads; one, by which we came, leads to it from the south-east, goes along the top of ravines and on either hand has hollows worn out by the torrents. A mile from Parhāla this road, in four or five places before it reaches the Gate, becomes a one-man road with a ravine falling from its either side; there for more than an arrow's flight men must ride in single file. The other road comes from the north-west; it gets up to Parhāla by the trough of a valley and it also is a one-man road. There is no other road on any side. Parhāla though without breast-work or battlement, has no assailable place, its sides shooting perpendicu-
Fol. 230*b*. larly down for 7, 8, 10 yards.

When the van of our left, having passed the narrow place, went in a body to the Gate, Hātī, with whom were 30 to 40 men in armour, their horses in mail, and a mass of foot-soldiers, forced his assailants to retire. Dost Beg led his reserve forward, made a strong attack, dismounted a number of Hātī's men, and beat him. All the country-round, Hātī was celebrated for his daring, but try as he did, he could effect nothing; he took to flight; he could not make a stand in those narrow places; he could not make the fort fast when he got back into it. His assailants went in just behind him and ran on through the ravine and narrows of the north-west side of the fort, but he rode light and made his flight good. Here again, Dost Beg did very well and recompense was added to renown.[1]

Meantime I had gone into the fort and dismounted at Tātār *Kakar's* dwelling. Several men had joined in the attack for whom to stay with me had been arranged; amongst them were Amīn-i-muḥammad Tarkhān *Arghūn* and Qarācha.[2] For this

[1] *Juldū Dost Beg-nīng ātī-gha būldī.*

[2] The disarray of these names in the MSS. reveals confusion in their source. Similar verbal disarray occurs in the latter part of f. 229.

fault they were sent to meet the camp, without *sar-u-pā*, into the wilds and open country with Sar-u-pā [1] for their guide, the Gujūr mentioned already.

(*March 16th*) Next day we went out by the north-west ravine and dismounted in a sown field. A few serviceable braves under Wālī the treasurer were sent out to meet the camp.[2]

(*March 17th*) Marching on Thursday the 15th, we dismounted at Andarāba on the Sūhān, a fort said to have depended from of old on ancestors of Malik Hast. Hātī *Kakar* had killed Malik Hast's father and destroyed the fort; there it now lay in ruins. Fol. 231.

At the Bed-time Prayer of this same day, those left at Kalda-kahār with the camp rejoined us.

(*r. Submissions to Bābur.*)

It must have been after Hātī overcame Tātār that he started his kinsman Parbat to me with tribute and an accoutred horse. Parbat did not light upon us but, meeting in with the camp we had left behind, came on in the company of the train. With it came also Langar Khān up from Bhīra on matters of business. His affairs were put right and he, together with several local people, was allowed to leave.

(*March 18th*) Marching on and crossing the Sūhān-water, we dismounted on the rising-ground. Here Hātī's kinsman (Parbat) was robed in an honorary dress (*khil'at*), given letters of encouragement for Hātī, and despatched with a servant of Muḥammad 'Alī *Jang-jang*. Nīl-āb and the Qārlūq (Himalayan?) Hazāra had been given to Humāyūn (*aet.* 12); some of his servants under Bābā Dost and Halāhil came now for their darogha-ship.[3]

(*March 19th*) Marching early next morning, we dismounted after riding 2 miles, went to view the camp from a height and ordered that the camp-camels should be counted; it came out at 570. Fol. 231*b*.

[1] Manifestly a pun is made on the guide's name and on the *cap-à-pie* robe of honour the offenders did not receive.

[2] *aūrdū-ning aldī-gha*, a novel phrase.

[3] I understand that the servants had come to do their equivalent for "kissing hands" on an appointment *viz.* to kneel.

We had heard of the qualities of the saṃbhal plant[1]; we saw it on this ground; along this hill-skirt it grows sparsely, a plant here, a plant there; it grows abundantly and to a large size further along the skirt-hills of Hindūstān. It will be described when an account is given of the animals and plants of Hindūstān.[2]

(*March 20th*) Marching from that camp at beat of drum (*i.e.* one hour before day), we dismounted at breakfast-time (9 a.m.) below the Sangdakī-pass, at mid-day marched on, crossed the pass, crossed the torrent, and dismounted on the rising-ground.

(*March 21st*) Marching thence at midnight, we made an excursion to the ford[3] we had crossed when on our way to Bhīra. A great raft of grain had stuck in the mud of that same ford and, do what its owners would, could not be made to move. The corn was seized and shared out to those with us. Timely indeed was that corn!

Near noon we were a little below the meeting of the waters of Kābul and Sind, rather above old Nīl-āb; we dismounted there between two waters.[4] From Nīl-āb six boats were brought, and were apportioned to the right, left and centre, who busied themselves energetically in crossing the river (Indus). We got there on a Monday; they kept on crossing the water through the night preceding Tuesday (*March 22nd*), through Tuesday and up to Wednesday (*March 23rd*) and on Thursday (*24th*) also a few crossed.

Hātī's kinsman Parbat, he who from Andarāba was sent to
Fol. 232. Hātī with a servant of Muḥ. 'Alī *Jang-jang*, came to the bank of the river with Hātī's offering of an accoutred horse. Nīl-ābīs also came, brought an accoutred horse and did obeisance.

(*s. Various postings.*)

Muḥammad 'Alī *Jang-jang* had wished to stay in Bhīra but Bhīra being bestowed on Hindū Beg, he was given the countries

[1] spikenard. Speede's *Indian Handbook on Gardening* identifies *saṃbhal* with *Valeriana jatmansi* (Sir W. Jones & Roxburgh); "it is the real spikenard of the ancients, highly esteemed alike as a perfume and as a stimulant medicine; native practitioners esteeming it valuable in hysteria and epilepsy." Bābur's word *dirakht* is somewhat large for the plant.

[2] It is not given, however.

[3] *i.e.* through the Indus.

[4] Perhaps this *aīkī-sū-ārāsī* (*miyān-dū-āb*) was the angle made by the Indus itself below Atak; perhaps one made by the Indus and an affluent.

between it and the Sind-river, such as the Qāriūq Hazāra, Hātī, Ghiyāṣ-wāl and Kīb (Kitib):—

> Where one is who submits like a *ra'iyat*, so treat him;
> But him who submits not, strike, strip, crush and force to obey.

He also received a special head-wear in black velvet, a special Qīlmāq corselet, and a standard. When Hātī's kinsman was given leave to go he took for Hātī a sword and head-to-foot (*bāsh-ayāq*) with a royal letter of encouragement.

(*March 24th*) On Thursday at sunrise we marched from the river's bank. That day confection was eaten. While under its influence[1] wonderful fields of flowers were enjoyed. In some places sheets of yellow flowers bloomed in plots; in others sheets of red (*arghwānī*) flowers in plots, in some red and yellow bloomed together. We sat on a mound near the camp to enjoy the sight. There were flowers on all sides of the mound, yellow here, red there, as if arranged regularly to form a sextuple. On two sides there were fewer flowers but as far as the eye reached, flowers were in bloom. In spring near Parashāwar the fields of flowers are very beautiful indeed. Fol. 232*b*.

(*March 25th*) We marched from that ground at dawn. At one place on the road a tiger came out and roared. On hearing it, the horses, willy-nilly, flung off in terror, carrying their riders in all directions, and dashing into ravines and hollows. The tiger went again into the jungle. To bring it out, we ordered a buffalo brought and put on the edge of the jungle. The tiger again came out roaring. Arrows were shot at it from all sides[2]; I shot with the rest. Khalwī (var. Khalwā) a foot-soldier, pricked it with a spear; it bit the spear and broke off the spear-head. After tasting of those arrows, it went into the bushes (*būta*) and stayed there. Bābā the waiting-man [*yasāwal*] went with drawn sword close up to it; it sprang; he chopped at its head; 'Alī *Sīstānī*[3] chopped at its loins; it plunged into the river and was killed right in the water. It was got out and ordered to be skinned.

[1] *ma'jūnī nāklīkī*, presumably under the tranquillity induced by the drug.
[2] *massadus*, the six sides of the world, *i.e.* all sides.
[3] This is the name of one of the five champions defeated by Bābur in single combat in 914 AH. (Translator's Note *s.a.* 914 AH.).

(*March 26th*) Marching on next day, we reached Bīgrām and went to see Gūr-khattrī. This is a smallish abode, after the fashion of a hermitage (*ṣauma'at*), rather confined and dark. After entering at the door and going down a few steps, one must lie full length to get beyond. There is no getting in without a lamp. All round near the building there is let lie an enormous quantity of hair of the head and beard which men have shaved off there. There are a great many retreats (*ḥujra*) near Gūr-
Fol. 233. khattrī like those of a rest-house or a college. In the year we came into Kābul (910 AH.) and over-ran Kohāt, Bannū and the plain, we made an excursion to Bīgrām, saw its great tree and were consumed with regret at not seeing Gūr-khattrī, but it does not seem a place to regret not-seeing.[1]

On this same day an excellent hawk of mine went astray out of Shaikhīm the head-falconer's charge; it had taken many cranes and storks and had moulted (*tūlāb*) two or three times. So many things did it take that it made a fowler of a person so little keen as I!

At this place were bestowed 100 misqāls of silver, clothing (*tūnlūq*), three bullocks and one buffalo, out of the offerings of Hindūstān, on each of six persons, the chiefs of the Dilazāk Afghāns under Malik Bū Khān and Malik Mūsa; to others, in their degree, were given money, pieces of cloth, a bullock and a buffalo.

(*March 27th*) When we dismounted at 'Alī-masjid, a Dilazāk Afghān of the Yaq'ūb-khail, named Ma'rūf, brought an offering of 10 sheep, two ass-loads of rice and eight large cheeses.

(*March 28th*) Marching on from 'Alī-masjid, we dismounted at Yada-bīr; from Yada-bīr Jūī-shāhī was reached by the Mid-day Prayer and we there dismounted. Today Dost Beg was attacked by burning fever.

(*March 29th*) Marching from Jūī-shāhī at dawn, we ate our mid-day meal in the Bāgh-i-wafā. At the Mid-day Prayer we betook ourselves out of the garden, close to the Evening Prayer forded the Siyāh-āb at Gandamak, satisfied our horses' hunger in a field of green corn, and rode on in a *garī* or two (24–48 min.).

[1] f. 145*b*.

After crossing the Sūrkh-āb, we dismounted at Kark and took a sleep. Fol. 233*b*.

(*March 30th*) Riding before shoot of day from Kark, I went with 5 or 6 others by the road taking off for Qarā-tū in order to enjoy the sight of a garden there made. Khalīfa and Shāh Hasan Beg and the rest went by the other road to await me at Qūrūq-sāī.

When we reached Qarā-tū, Shāh Beg *Arghūn's* commissary (*tawāchī*) Qīzīl (Rufus) brought word that Shāh Beg had taken Kāhān, plundered it and retired.

An order had been given that no-one soever should take news of us ahead. We reached Kābul at the Mid-day Prayer, no person in it knowing about us till we got to Qūtlūq-qadam's bridge. As Humāyūn and Kāmrān heard about us only after that, there was not time to put them on horseback; they made their pages carry them, came, and did obeisance between the gates of the town and the citadel.[1] At the Other Prayer there waited on me Qāsim Beg, the town Qāẓī, the retainers left in Kābul and the notables of the place.

(*April 2nd*) At the Other Prayer of Friday the 1st of the second Rabī' there was a wine-party at which a special head-to-foot (*bāsh-ayāq*) was bestowed on Shāh Ḥasan.

(*April 3rd*) At dawn on Saturday we went on board a boat and took our morning.[2] Nūr Beg, then not obedient (*tā'ib*), played the lute at this gathering. At the Mid-day Prayer we left the boat to visit the garden made between Kul-kīna[3] and the mountain (Shāh-i-kābul). At the Evening Prayer we went to the Violet-garden where there was drinking again. From Kul-kīna I got in by the rampart and went into the citadel.

(*u. Dost Beg's death.*)

(*April 6th*) On the night of Tuesday the 5th of the month,[4] Dost Beg, who on the road had had fever, went to God's mercy. Fol. 234.

[1] Ḥumāyūn was 12, Kāmrān younger; one surmises that Bābur would have walked under the same circumstances.

[2] *ṣabuḥī*, the morning-draught. In 1623 AD. Pietro della Vallé took a *ṣabuḥī* with Mr. Thomas Rastel, the head of the merchants of Surat, which was of hot spiced wine and sipped in the mornings to comfort the stomach (Hakluyt ed. p. 20).

[3] f. 128 and note.

[4] Anglicé, in the night preceding Tuesday.

Sad and grieved enough we were! His bier and corpse were carried to Ghaznī where they laid him in front of the gate of the Sulṭān's garden (*rauza*).

Dost Beg had been a very good brave (*yīkīt*) and he was still rising in rank as a beg. Before he was made a beg, he did excellent things several times as one of the household. One time was at Rabāṭ-i-zauraq,[1] one *yīghāch* from Andijān when Sl. Aḥmad *Tambal* attacked me at night (908 AH.). I, with 10 to 15 men, by making a stand, had forced his gallopers back; when we reached his centre, he made a stand with as many as 100 men; there were then three men with me, *i.e.* there were four counting myself. Nāṣir's Dost (*i.e.* Dost Beg) was one of the three; another was Mīrzā Qulī *Kūkūldāsh*; Karīm-dād *Turkmān* was the other I was just in my *jība*[2]; Tambal and another were standing like gate-wards in front of his array; I came face to face with Tambal, shot an arrow striking his helm; shot another aiming at the attachment of his shield;[3] they shot one through my leg (*būtūm*); Tambal chopped at my head. It was wonderful! The (under)-cap of my helm was on my head; not a thread of it was cut, but on the head itself was a very bad wound. Of other help came none; no-one was left with me; of necessity I brought myself to gallop back. Dost Beg had been a little in my rear; (Tambal) on leaving me alone, chopped at him.[4]

Fol. 234*b*. Again, when we were getting out of Akhsī [908 AH.],[5] Dost Beg chopped away at Bāqī *Ḥīz*[6] who, although people called him *Ḥīz*, was a mighty master of the sword. Dost Beg was one of the eight left with me after we were out of Akhsī; he was the third they unhorsed.

Again, after he had become a beg, when Sīūnjuk Khān (*Aūzbeg*), arriving with the (Aūzbeg) sulṭāns before Tāshkīnt, besieged Aḥmad-i-qāsim [*Kohbur*] in it [918 AH.],[7] Dost Beg

[1] f. 106*b*.

[2] This would be the under-corselet to which the four plates of mail were attached when mail was worn. Bābur in this adventure wore no mail, not even his helm; on his head was the under cap of the metal helm.

[3] Index s.n. *gharīcha*.

[4] The earlier account helps to make this one clearer (f. 106*b*).

[5] f. 112 *et seq*.

[6] Catamite, mistakenly read as *khīz* on f. 112*b* (*Mémoires* ii, 82).

[7] He was acting for Bābur (Translator's Note *s.a.*; Ḥ.S. iii, 318; T.R. pp. 260, 270).

passed through them and entered the town. During the siege he risked his honoured life splendidly, but Aḥmad-i-qāsim, without a word to this honoured man,[1] flung out of the town and got away. Dost Beg for his own part got the better of the Khān and sulṭāns and made his way well out of Tāshkīnt.

Later on when Sherīm Ṭaghāī, Mazīd and their adherents were in rebellion,[2] he came swiftly up from Ghaznī with two or three hundred men, met three or four hundred effective braves sent out by those same Mughūls to meet him, unhorsed a mass of them near Sherūkān (?), cut off and brought in a number of heads.

Again, his men were first over the ramparts at the fort of Bajaur (925 AH.). At Parhāla, again, he advanced, beat Hātī, put him to flight, and won Parhāla.

After Dost Beg's death, I bestowed his district on his younger brother Nāṣir's Mīrīm.[3]

(*v. Various incidents.*)

(*April 9th*) On Friday the 8th of the second Rabī', the walled-town was left for the Chār-bāgh.

(*April 13th*) On Tuesday the 12th there arrived in Kābul the honoured Sulṭānīm Begīm, Sl. Ḥusain Mīrzā's eldest daughter, the mother of Muḥammad Sulṭān Mīrzā. During those throneless times,[4] she had settled down in Khwārizm where Yīlī-pārs Fol. 235. Sulṭān's younger brother Aīsān-qulī Sl. took her daughter. The Bāgh-i-khilwat was assigned her for her seat. When she had settled down and I went to see her in that garden, out of respect and courtesy to her, she being as my honoured elder sister, I bent the knee. She also bent the knee. We both advancing, saw one another mid-way. We always observed the same ceremony afterwards.

(*April 18th*) On Sunday the 17th, that traitor to his salt, Bābā Shaikh[5] was released from his long imprisonment, forgiven his offences and given an honorary dress.

[1] "Honoured," in this sentence, represents Bābur's honorific plural.
[2] in 921 AH. (Translator's Note *s.a.*; T.R. p. 356).
[3] *i.e.* Mīr Muḥammad son of Nāṣir.
[4] *i.e.* after the dethronement of the Bāī-qarā family by Shaibānī.
[5] He had been one of rebels of 921 AH. (Translator's Note *s.a.*; T.R. p. 356).

(*w. Visit to the Koh-dāman.*)

(*April 20th*) On Tuesday the 19th of the month, we rode out at the return of noon for Khwāja Sih-yārān. This day I was fasting. All astonished, Yūnas-i-'alī and the rest said, "A Tuesday! a journey! and a fast! This is amazing!" At Bīh-zādī we dismounted at the Qāẓī's house. In the evening when a stir was made for a social gathering, the Qāẓī set this before me, "In my house such things never are; it is for the honoured Pādshāh to command!" For his heart's content, drink was left out, though all the material for a party was ready.

(*April 21st*) On Wednesday we went to Khwāja Sih-yārān.

(*April 22nd*) On Thursday the 22nd of the month, we had a large round seat made in the garden under construction on the mountain-naze.[1]

(*April 23rd*) On Friday we got on a raft from the bridge. On our coming opposite the fowlers' houses, they brought a *dang*
Fol. 235*b*. (or *ding*)[2] they had caught. I had never seen one before; it is an odd-looking bird. It will come into the account of the birds of Hindustan.[3]

(*April 24th*) On Saturday the 23rd of the month cuttings were planted, partly of plane, partly of *tāl*,[4] above the round seat. At the Mid-day Prayer there was a wine-party at the place.

(*April 25th*) At dawn we took our morning on the new seat. At noon we mounted and started for Kābul, reached Khwāja Ḥasan quite drunk and slept awhile, rode on and by midnight got to the Chār-bāgh. At Khwāja Ḥasan, 'Abdu'l-lāh, in his drunkenness, threw himself into water just as he was in his *tūn aūfrāghī*.[5] He was frozen with cold and could not go on with us when we mounted after a little of the night had passed. He stayed on Qūtlūq Khwāja's estate that night. Next day, awakened to his past intemperance, he came on repentant. Said I, "At once! will this sort of repentance answer or not? Would to God you would repent now at once in such a way that you

[1] f. 137.

[2] This is the Adjutant-bird, Pīr-i-dang and Hargila (Bone-swallower) of Hindūstān, a migrant through Kābul. The fowlers who brought it would be the Multānīs of f. 142*b*.

[3] f. 280.

[4] *Memoirs*, p. 267, sycamore; *Mémoires* ii, 84, *saules*; f. 137.

[5] Perhaps with his long coat out-spread.

would drink nowhere except at my parties!" He agreed to this and kept the rule for a few months, but could not keep it longer.

(*x. Hindū Beg abandons Bhīra.*)

(*April 26th*) On Monday the 25th came Hindū Beg. There having been hope of peace, he had been left in those countries with somewhat scant support. No sooner was our back turned than a mass of Hindūstānīs and Afghāns gathered, disregarded us and, not listening to our words, moved against Hindū Beg in Bhīra. The local peoples also went over to the Afghāns. Hindū Beg could make no stand in Bhīra, came to Khūsh-āb, came through the Dīn-kot country, came to Nīl-āb, came on to Kābul. Fol. 236.
Sīktū's son Dīwa *Hindū* and another Hindū had been brought prisoner from Bhīra. Each now giving a considerable ransom, they were released. Horses and head-to-foot dresses having been given them, leave to go was granted.

(*April 30th*) On Friday the 29th of the month, burning fever appeared in my body. I got myself let blood. I had fever with sometimes two, sometimes three days between the attacks. In no attack did it cease till there had been sweat after sweat. After 10 or 12 days of illness, Mullā Khwāja gave me narcissus mixed with wine; I drank it once or twice; even that did no good.

(*May 15th*) On Sunday the 15th of the first Jumāda [1] Khwāja Muḥammad 'Alī came from Khwāst, bringing a saddled horse as an offering and also *taṣadduq* money.[2] Muḥ. Sharīf the astrologer and the Mīr-zādas of Khwāst came with him and waited on me.

(*May 16th*) Next day, Monday, Mullā Kabīr came from Kāshghar; he had gone round by Kāshghar on his way from Andijān to Kābul.

(*May 23rd*) On Monday the 23rd of the month, Malik Shāh Manṣūr *Yūsuf-zāī* arrived from Sawād with 6 or 7 Yūsuf-zāī chiefs, and did obeisance.

[1] The fortnight's gap of record, here ended, will be due to illness.

[2] f. 203*b* and n. to *Khams*, the Fifth. *Taṣadduq* occurs also on f. 238 denoting money sent to Bābur. Was it sent to him as Pādshāh, as the Qorān commands the *Khams* to be sent to the Imām, for the poor, the traveller and the orphan?

(*May 31st*) On Monday the 1st of the second Jumāda, the chiefs of the Yūsuf-zāī Afghāns led by Malik Shāh Manṣūr were dressed in robes of honour (*khil'at*). To Malik Shāh Manṣūr was given a long silk coat and an under-coat (?*jība*) with its buttons; to one of the other chiefs was given a coat with silk sleeves, and to six others silk coats. To all leave to go was granted. Agreement was made with them that they were not
Fol. 236*b*. to reckon as in the country of Sawād what was above Abuha (?), that they should make all the peasants belonging to it go out from amongst themselves, and also that the Afghān cultivators of Bajaur and Sawād should cast into the revenue 6000 ass-loads of rice.

(*June 2nd*) On Wednesday the 3rd, I drank *jul-āb*.[1]

(*June 5th*) On Saturday the 6th, I drank a working-draught (*dārū-i-kār*).

(*June 7th*) On Monday the 8th, arrived the wedding-gift for the marriage of Qāsim Beg's youngest son Ḥamza with Khalīfa's eldest daughter. It was of 1000 *shāhrukhī*; they offered also a saddled horse.

(*June 8th*) On Tuesday Shāh Beg's Shāh Ḥasan asked for permission to go away for a wine-party. He carried off to his house Khwāja Muḥ. 'Alī and some of the household-begs. In my presence were Yūnas-i-'alī and Gadāī Ṭaghāī. I was still abstaining from wine. Said I, "Not at all in this way is it (*hech andāq būlmāī dūr*) that I will sit sober and the party drink wine, I stay sane, full of water, and that set (*būlāk*) of people get drunk; come you and drink in my presence! I will amuse myself a little by watching what intercourse between the sober and the drunk is like."[2] The party was held in a smallish tent in which I sometimes sat, in the Plane-tree garden south-east of the Picture-hall. Later on Ghiyās the house-buffoon (*kīdī*) arrived; several times for fun he was ordered kept out, but at last he made a great disturbance and his buffooneries found him a way in. We invited Tardī Muḥammad *Qībchāq* also and

[1] Rose-water, sherbet, a purgative; English, jalap, julep.

[2] Mr. Erskine understood Bābur to say that he never had sat sober while others drank; but this does not agree with the account of Harāt entertainments [912 AH.], or with the tenses of the passage here. My impression is that he said in effect "Every-one here shall not be deprived of their wine".

Mullā *kitāb-dār* (librarian). The following quatrain, written impromptu, was sent to Shāh Ḥasan and those gathered in his house :— Fol. 237.

> In your beautiful flower-bed of banquetting friends,
> Our fashion it is not to be ;
> If there be ease (*ḥuzūr*) in that gathering of yours,
> Thank God ! there is here no un-ease [*bī ḥuzūr*].[1]

It was sent by Ibrāhīm *chuhra*. Between the two Prayers (*i.e.* afternoon) the party broke up drunk.

I used to go about in a litter while I was ill. The wine-mixture was drunk on several of the earlier days, then, as it did no good I left it off, but I drank it again at the end of my convalescence, at a party had under an apple-tree on the south-west side of the Tālār-garden.

(*June 11th*) On Friday the 12th came Aḥmad Beg and Sl. Muḥammad *Dūldāī* who had been left to help in Bajaur.

(*June 16th*) On Wednesday the 17th of the month, Tīngrī-bīrdī and other braves gave a party in Ḥaidar *Tāqī's* garden ; I also went and there drank. We rose from it at the Bed-time Prayer when a move was made to the great tent where again there was drinking.

(*June 23rd*) On Thursday the 25th of the month, Mullā Maḥmūd was appointed to read extracts from the Qorān[2] in my presence.

(*June 28th*) On Tuesday the last day of the month, Abū'l-muslim Kūkūldāsh arrived as envoy from Shāh Shujā' *Arghūn* bringing a *tīpūchāq*. After bargain made about swimming the reservoir in the Plane-tree garden, Yūsuf-i-'alī the stirrup-holder swam round it today 100 times and received a gift of a head-to-foot (dress), a saddled horse and some money.

(*July 6th*) On Wednesday the 8th of Rajab, I went to Shāh Ḥasan's house and drank there ; most of the household and of the begs were present. Fol. 237*b*.

(*July 9th*) On Saturday the 11th, there was drinking on the terrace-roof of the pigeon-house between the Afternoon and Evening Prayers. Rather late a few horsemen were observed,

[1] This verse, a difficult one to translate, may refer to the unease removed from his attendants by Bābur's permission to drink ; the pun in it might also refer to *well* and *not well*.

[2] Presumably to aid his recovery.

going from Dih-i-afghān towards the town. It was made out to be Darwīsh-i-muḥammad *Sārbān*, on his way to me as the envoy of Mīrzā Khān (Wais). We shouted to him from the roof, "Drop the envoy's forms and ceremonies! Come! come without formality!" He came and sat down in the company. He was then obedient and did not drink. Drinking went on till the end of the evening. Next day he came into the Court Session with due form and ceremony, and presented Mīrzā Khān's gifts.

(*y. Various incidents.*)

Last year[1] with 100 efforts, much promise and threats, we had got the clans to march into Kābul from the other side (of Hindū-kush). Kābul is a confined country, not easily giving summer and winter quarters to the various flocks and herds of the Turks and (Mughūl ?) clans. If the dwellers in the wilds follow their own hearts, they do not wish for Kābul! They now waited (*khidmat qīlīb*) on Qāsim Beg and made him their mediator with me for permission to re-cross to that other side. He tried very hard, so in the end, they were allowed to cross over to the Qūndūz and Bāghlān side.

Ḥāfiẓ the news-writer's elder brother had come from Samarkand; when I now gave him leave to return, I sent my *Dīwān* by him to Pūlād Sulṭān.[2] On the back of it I wrote the following

Fol. 238. verse:—

> O breeze! if thou enter that cypress' chamber (*ḥarīm*)
> Remind her of me, my heart reft by absence;
> She yearns not for Bābur; he fosters a hope
> That her heart of steel God one day may melt.[3]

(*July 15th*) On Friday the 17th of the month, Shaikh Mazīd Kūkūldāsh waited on me from Muḥammad-i-zamān Mīrzā, bringing *taṣadduq* tribute and a horse.[4] Today Shāh Beg's envoy Abū'l-muslim Kūkūldāsh was robed in an honorary dress

[1] *aūtkān yīl*, perhaps in the last and unchronicled year; perhaps in earlier ones. There are several references in the B.N. to the enforced migrations and emigrations of tribes into Kābul.

[2] Pūlād (Steel) was a son of Kūchūm, the then Khāqān of the Aūzbegs, and Mihr-bānū who may be Bābur's half-sister. [Index *s.n.*]

[3] This may be written for Mihr-bānū, Pūlād's mother and Bābur's half-sister (?) and a jest made on her heart as Pūlād's and as steel to her brother. She had not left husband and son when Bābur got the upper hand, as his half-sister Yādgār-sulṭān did and other wives of capture *e.g.* Haidar's sister *Ḥabība*. Bābur's rhymes in this verse are not of his later standard, *āī ṣubāḥ*, *kūnkūlīkā*, *kūnkūlī-kā*.

[4] *Taṣadduq* sent to Bābur would seem an acknowledgment of his suzerainty in Balkh [Index *s.n.*].

and given leave to go. Today also leave was given for their own districts of Khwāst and Andar-āb to Khwāja Muhammad 'Alī and Tīngrī-bīrdī.

(*July 21st*) On Thursday the 23rd came Muḥ. 'Alī *Jang-jang* who had been left in charge of the countries near Kacha-kot and the Qārlūq. With him came one of Hātī's people and Mīrzā-i-malū-i-qārlūq's son Shāh Ḥasan. Today Mullā 'Alī-jān waited on me, returned from fetching his wife from Samarkand.

(*z. The 'Abdu'r-raḥman Afghāns and Rustam-maidān.*)

(*July 27th*) The 'Abdu'r-raḥman Afghāns on the Gīrdīz border were satisfactory neither in their tribute nor their behaviour; they were hurtful also to the caravans which came and went. On Wednesday the 29th of Rajab we rode out to over-run them. We dismounted and ate food near Tang-i-waghchān,[1] and rode on again at the Mid-day Prayer. In the night we lost the road and got much bewildered in the ups and downs of the land to the south-east of Pātakh-i-āb-i-shakna.[2] After a time we lit on a road and by it crossed the Chashma-i-tūra[3] pass. Fol. 238*b*.

(*July 28th*) At the first prayer (*farẓ-waqt*) we got out from the valley-bottom adjacent[4] to the level land, and the raid was allowed. One detachment galloped towards the Kar-māsh[5] mountain, south-east of Gīrdīz, the left-hand of the centre led by Khusrau, Mīrzā Qulī and Sayyid 'Alī in their rear. Most of the army galloped up the dale to the east of Gīrdīz, having in their rear men under Sayyid Qāsim Lord of the Gate, Mīr Shāh *Qūchīn*, Qayyām (Aūrdū-shāh Beg?), Hindū Beg, Qūtlūq-qadam and Ḥusain [Ḥasan?]. Most of the army having gone up the dale, I followed at some distance. The dalesmen must have been a good way up; those who went after them wore their horses out and nothing to make up for this fell into their hands.

Some Afghāns on foot, some 40 or 50 of them, having appeared on the plain, the rear-reserve went towards them. A courier was sent to me and I hastened on at once. Before I got up

[1] This is the Gīrdīz-pass [Raverty's *Notes*, Route 101].
[2] Raverty (p. 677) suggests that Pātakh stands for *bātqāq*, a quagmire (f. 16 and n.).
[3] the dark, or cloudy spring.
[4] *yāqīsh-līq qūl*, an unusual phrase.
[5] var. Karmān, Kurmāh, Karmās. M. de C. read Kīr-mās, the impenetrable. The forms would give Garm-ās, hot embers.

with them, Ḥusain Ḥāsan, all alone, foolishly and thoughtlessly, put his horse at those Afghāns, got in amongst them and began to lay on with his sword. They shot his horse, thus made him fall, slashed at him as he was getting up, flung him down, knifed him from all sides and cut him to pieces, while the other braves looked on, standing still and reaching him no helping hand! On hearing news of it, I hurried still faster forward, and sent some of the household and braves galloping loose-rein ahead
Fol. 239. under Gadāī Ṭaghāī, Payānda-i-muḥammad *Qīplān*, Abū'l-ḥasan the armourer and Mūmin Ātāka. Mūmin Ātāka was the first of them to bring an Afghān down; he speared one, cut off his head and brought it in. Abū'l-ḥasan the armourer, without mail as he was, went admirably forward, stopped in front of the Afghāns, laid his horse at them, chopped at one, got him down, cut off and brought in his head. Known though both were for bravelike deeds done earlier, their action in this affair added to their fame. Every one of those 40 or 50 Afghāns, falling to the arrow, falling to the sword, was cut in pieces. After making a clean sweep of them, we dismounted in a field of growing corn and ordered a tower of their heads to be set up. As we went along the road I said, with anger and scorn, to the begs who had been with Ḥusain, "You! what men! there you stood on quite flat ground, and looked on while a few Afghāns on foot overcame such a brave in the way they did! Your rank and station must be taken from you; you must lose *pargana* and country; your beards must be shaved off and you must be exhibited in towns; for there shall be punishment assuredly for him who looks on while such a brave is beaten by such a foe
Fol. 239*b*. on dead-level land, and reaches out no hand to help!" The troop which went to Kar-māsh brought back sheep and other spoil. One of them was Bābā Qashqa[1] *Mughūl*; an Afghān had made at him with a sword; he had stood still to adjust an arrow, shot it off and brought his man down.

(*July 29th*) Next day at dawn we marched for Kābul. Pay-master Muḥammad, 'Abdu'l-'azīz Master of the Horse, and Mīr Khūrd the taster were ordered to stop at Chashma-tūra, and get pheasants from the people there.

[1] *balafré*; marked on the face; of a horse, starred.

As I had never been along the Rustam-maidān road,[1] I went with a few men to see it. Rustam-plain (*maidān*) lies amongst mountains and towards their head is not a very charming place. The dale spreads rather broad between its two ranges. To the south, on the skirt of the rising-ground is a smallish spring, having very large poplars near it. There are many trees also, but not so large, at the source on the way out of Rustam-maidān for Gīrdīz. This is a narrower dale, but still there is a plot of green meadow below the smaller trees mentioned, and the little dale is charming. From the summit of the range, looking south, the Karmāsh and Bangash mountains are seen at one's feet; and beyond the Karmāsh show pile upon pile of the rain-clouds of Hindūstān. Towards those other lands where no rain falls, not a cloud is seen. Fol. 240.

We reached Hūnī at the Mid-day Prayer and there dismounted.

(*July 30th*) Dismounting next day at Muḥammad Āghā's village,[2] we perpetrated (*irtqāb*) a *ma'jūn*. There we had a drug thrown into water for the fish; a few were taken.[3]

(*July 31st*) On Sunday the 3rd of Sha'bān, we reached Kābul.

(*August 2nd*) On Tuesday the 5th of the month, Darwīsh-i-muḥammad *Faẓlī* and Khusrau's servants were summoned and, after enquiry made into what short-comings of theirs there may have been when Ḥusain was overcome, they were deprived of place and rank. At the Mid-day Prayer there was a wine-party under a plane-tree, at which an honorary dress was given to Bābā Qashqa *Mughūl*.

(*August 5th*) On Friday the 8th Kīpa returned from the presence of Mīrzā Khān.

(*aa. Excursion to the Koh-dāman.*)

(*August 11th*) On Thursday at the Other Prayer, I mounted for an excursion to the Koh-dāman, Bārān and Khwāja Sih-yārān.[4] At the Bed-time Prayer, we dismounted at Māmā Khātūn.[5]

[1] Raverty's *Notes* (p. 457) give a full account of this valley; in it are the head-waters of the Tochī and the Zurmut stream; and in it R. locates Rustam's ancient Zābul.

[2] It is on the Kābul side of the Gīrdīz-pass and stands on the Luhugūr-water (Logar).

[3] f. 143

[4] At this point of the text there occurs in the Elph. MS. (f. 195*b*) a note, manifestly copied from one marginal in an archetype, which states that what follows is copied from Bābur's own MS. The note (and others) can be seen in JRAS 1905 p. 754 *et seq.*

[5] Masson, iii, 145.

(*August 12th*) Next day we dismounted at Istālīf; a confection was eaten on that day.

(*August 13th*) On Saturday there was a wine-party at Istālīf.

(*August 14th*) Riding at dawn from Istālīf, we crossed the space between it and the Sinjid-valley. Near Khwāja Sih-yārān a great snake was killed as thick, it may be, as the fore-arm and as long as a *qūlāch*.[1] From its inside came out a slenderer snake, that seemed to have been just swallowed, every part of it being
ol. 240b. whole; it may have been a little shorter than the larger one. From inside this slenderer snake came out a little mouse; it too was whole, broken nowhere.[2]

On reaching Khwāja Sih-yārān there was a wine-party. To-day orders were written and despatched by Kīch-kīna the night-watch (*tūnqṭār*) to the begs on that side (*i.e.* north of Hindū-kush), giving them a rendezvous and saying, "An army is being got to horse, take thought, and come to the rendezvous fixed."

(*August 15th*) We rode out at dawn and ate a confection. At the infall of the Parwān-water many fish were taken in the local way of casting a fish-drug into the water.[3] Mīr Shāh Beg set food and water (*āsh u āb*) before us; we then rode on to Gul-bahār. At a wine-party held after the Evening Prayer, Darwīsh-i-muḥammad (*Sārbān*) was present. Though a young man and a soldier, he had not yet committed the sin (*irtqāb*) of wine, but was in obedience (*tā'ib*). Qūtlūq Khwāja *Kūkūldāsh* had long before abandoned soldiering to become a darwīsh; moreover he was very old, his very beard was quite white; nevertheless he took his share of wine at these parties. Said I to Darwīsh-i-muḥammad, "Qūtlūq Khwāja's beard shames you! He, a darwīsh and an old man, always drinks wine; you, a soldier, a young man, your beard quite black, never drink! What does it mean?" My custom being not to press wine on a non-drinker, with so much said, it all passed off as a joke; he was not pressed to drink.

[1] A *qūlāch* is from finger-tip to finger-tip of the outstretched arms (Zenker p. 720 and *Mêms.* ii, 98).

[2] Neither *interne* is said to have died!

[3] f. 143.

(*August 16th*) At dawn we made our morning (*ṣubāḥī subūḥī qīldūk*).

(*August 17th*) Riding on Wednesday from Gul-i-bahār, we dismounted in Abūn-village[1] ate food, remounted, went to a summer-house in the orchards (*bāghāt-i-kham*) and there dismounted. There was a wine-party after the Mid-day Prayer. Fol. 241.

(*August 18th*) Riding on next day, we made the circuit of Khwāja Khāwand Sa'īd's tomb, went to China-fort and there got on a raft. Just where the Panjhīr-water comes in, the raft struck the naze of a hill and began to sink. Rauḥ-dam, Tīngrī-qulī and Mīr Muḥammad the raftsman were thrown into the water by the shock; Rauḥ-dam and Tīngrī-qulī were got on the raft again; a China cup and a spoon and a ṭambour went into the water. Lower down, the raft struck again opposite the Sang-i-barīda (the cut-stone), either on a branch in mid-stream or on a stake stuck in as a stop-water (*qāqghān qāzūq*). Right over on his back went Shāh Beg's Shāh Ḥasan, clutching at Mīrzā Qulī Kūkūldāsh and making him fall too. Darwīsh-i-muḥammad *Sārbān* was also thrown into the water. Mīrzā Qulī went over in his own fashion! Just when he fell, he was cutting a melon which he had in his hand; as he went over, he stuck his knife into the mat of the raft. He swam in his *tūn aūfrāghī*[2] and got out of the water without coming on the raft again. Leaving it that night, we slept at raftsmen's houses. Darwīsh-i-muḥammad *Sārbān* presented me with a seven-coloured cup exactly like the one lost in the water.

(*August 19th*) On Friday we rode away from the river's bank and dismounted below Aīndīkī on the skirt of Koh-i-bacha where, with our own hands, we gathered plenty of tooth-picks.[3] Fol. 241*b*.
Passing on, food was eaten at the houses of the Khwāja Khiẓr people. We rode on and at the Mid-day Prayer dismounted in a village of Qūtlūq Khwāja's fief in Lamghān where he made ready a hasty meal (*mā ḥaẓirī*); after partaking of this, we mounted and went to Kābul.

[1] or Atūn's-village, one granted to Bābur's mother's old governess (f. 96); Gulbadan's guest-list has also an Atūn Māmā.

[2] f. 235*b* and note.

[3] *miswāk; On les tire principalement de l'arbuste épineux appelé capparis-sodata* (de C. ii, 101 n.).

(*bb. Various incidents.*)

(*August 22nd*) On Monday the 25th, a special honorary dress and a saddled horse were bestowed on Darwīsh-i-muḥammad *Sārbān* and he was made to kneel as a retainer (*naukar*).

(*August 24th*) For 4 or 5 months I had not had my head shaved; on Wednesday the 27th, I had it done. Today there was a wine-party.

(*August 26th*) On Friday the 29th, Mīr Khūrd was made to kneel as Hind-āl's guardian.[1] He made an offering of 1000 *shāhrukhīs* (*circa* £50).

(*August 31st*) On Wednesday the 5th of Ramẓān, a dutiful letter was brought by Tūlik Kūkūldāsh's servant Barlās Jūkī(?). Aūzbeg raiders had gone into those parts (Badakhshān); Tūlik had gone out, fought and beaten them. Barlās Jūkī brought one live Aūzbeg and one head.

(*Sep. 2nd*) In the night of Saturday the 8th, we broke our fast[2] in Qāsim Beg's house; he led out a saddled horse for me

(*Sep. 3rd*) On Sunday night the fast was broken in Khalīfa's house; he offered me a saddled horse.

(*Sep. 4th*) Next day came Khwāja Muḥ. 'Alī and Jān-i-nāṣir who had been summoned from their districts for the good of the army.[3]

(*Sep. 7th*) On Wednesday the 12th, Kāmrān's maternal uncle

Fol. 242. Sl. 'Alī Mīrzā arrived.[4] As has been mentioned,[5] he had gone to Kāshghar in the year I came from Khwāst into Kābul.

(*cc. A Yūsuf-zāī campaign.*)

(*Sep. 8th*) We rode out on Thursday the 13th of the month of Ramẓān, resolved and determined to check and ward off the

[1] Gul-badan's H.N. Index s.n.

[2] This being Ramẓān, Bābur did not break his fast till sun-set. In like manner, during Ramẓān they eat in the morning before sun-rise (Erskine).

[3] A result, doubtless, of the order mentioned on f. 240*b*.

[4] Bābur's wife Gul-rukh appears to have been his sister or niece; he was a Begchīk. Cf. Gul-badan's H.N. trs. p. 233, p. 234; T.R. p. 264–5.

[5] This remark bears on the question of whether we now have all Bābur wrote of Autobiography. It refers to a date falling within the previous gap, because the man went to Kāshghar while Bābur was ruling in Samarkand (T.R. p. 265). The last time Bābur came from Khwāst to Kābul was probably in 920 AH.; if later, it was still in the gap. But an alternative explanation is that looking over and annotating the diary section, Bābur made this reference to what he fully meant to write but died before being able to do so.

Yūsuf-zāī, and we dismounted in the meadow on the Dih-i-yaq'ūb side of Kābul. When we were mounting, the equerry Bābā Jān led forward a rather good-for-nothing horse ; in my anger I struck him in the face a blow which dislocated my fist below the ring-finger.[1] The pain was not much at the time, but was rather bad when we reached our encampment-ground. For some time I suffered a good deal and could not write. It got well at last.

To this same assembly-ground were brought letters and presents (*bīlāk*) from my maternal-aunt Daulat-sulṭān Khānīm[2] in Kāshghar, by her foster-brother Daulat-i-muḥammad. On the same day Bū Khān and Mūsa, chiefs of the Dilazāk, came, bringing tribute, and did obeisance.

(*Sep. 11th*) On Sunday the 16th Qūj Beg came.

(*Sep. 14th*) Marching on Wednesday the 19th we passed through Būt-khāk and, as usual, dismounted on the Būt-khāk water.[3]

As Qūj Beg's districts, Bāmīān, Kāh-mard and Ghūrī, are close to the Aūzbeg, he was excused from going with this army and given leave to return to them from this ground. I bestowed on him a turban twisted for myself, and also a head-to-foot (*bāsh-ayāq*).

(*Sep. 16th*) On Friday the 21st, we dismounted at Badām-chashma. Fol. 242*b*.

(*Sep. 17th*) Next day we dismounted on the Bārīk-āb, I reaching the camp after a visit to Qarā-tū. On this ground honey was obtained from a tree.

(*Sep. 20th*) We went on march by march till Wednesday the 26th, and dismounted in the Bāgh-i-wafā.

(*Sep. 21st*) Thursday we just stayed in the garden.

(*Sep. 22nd*) On Friday we marched out and dismounted beyond Sulṭānpūr. Today Shāh Mīr Ḥusain came from his country. Today came also Dilazāk chiefs under Bū Khān and

[1] Anglicé, the right thumb, on which the archer's ring (*zih-gīr*) is worn.

[2] a daughter of Yūnas Khān, Ḥaidar's account of whom is worth seeing.

[3] *i.e.* the water of Luhugūr (Logar). Tradition says that Būt-khāk (Idol-dust) was so named because there Sl. Maḥmūd of Ghaznī had idols, brought by him out of Hindūstān, pounded to dust. Raverty says the place is probably the site of an ancient temple (*vahāra*).

Mūsa. My plan had been to put down the Yūsuf-zāī in Sawād, but these chiefs set forth to me that there was a large horde (*aūlūs*) in Hash-naghar and that much corn was to be had there. They were very urgent for us to go to Hash-naghar. After consultation the matter was left in this way :—As it is said there is much corn in Hash-naghar, the Afghāns there shall be overrun ; the forts of Hash-naghar and Parashāwar shall be put into order ; part of the corn shall be stored in them and they be left in charge of Shāh Mīr Ḥusain and a body of braves. To suit Shāh Mīr Ḥusain's convenience in this, he was given 15 days leave, with a rendezvous named for him to come to after going to his country and preparing his equipment.

(*Sep. 23rd*) Marching on next day, we reached Jūī-shāhī and there dismounted. On this ground Tīngrī-bīrdī and Sl. Muḥammad *Dūldāī* overtook us. Today came also Ḥamza from Qūndūz.[1]

(*Sep. 25th*) On Sunday the last day of the month (Ramẓān), we marched from Jūī-shāhī and dismounted at Qīrīq-arīq (forty-
Fol. 243. conduits), I going by raft, with a special few. The new moon of the Feast was seen at that station.[2] People had brought a few beast-loads of wine from Nūr-valley ;[3] after the Evening Prayer there was a wine-party, those present being Muḥibb-i-'alī the armourer, Khwāja Muḥ. 'Alī the librarian, Shāh Beg's Shāh Ḥasan, Sl. Muḥ. *Dūldāī* and Darwīsh-i-muḥ. *Sārbān*, then obedient (*tā'ib*). From my childhood up it had been my rule not to press wine on a non-drinker ; Darwīsh-i-muḥammad was at every party and no pressure was put on him (by me), but Khwāja Muḥ. 'Alī left him no choice ; he pressed him and pressed him till he made him drink.

(*Sep. 26th*) On Monday we marched with the dawn of the Feast-day,[4] eating a confection on the road to dispel crop-sickness. While under its composing influence (*nāklīk*), we were brought a colocynth-apple (*khunṭul*). Darwīsh-i-muḥammad had never

[1] Qāsim Beg's son, come, no doubt, in obedience to the order of f. 240*b*.

[2] The 'Īd-i-fitr is the festival at the conclusion of the feast of Ramẓān, celebrated on seeing the new moon of Shawwāl (Erskine).

[3] f. 133*b* and Appendix G, *On the names of the wines of Nūr-valley*.

[4] *i.e.* of the new moon of Shawwāl. The new moon having been seen the evening before, which to Musalmāns was Monday evening, they had celebrated the 'Īd-i-fitr on Monday eve (Erskine).

seen one; said I, "It is a melon of Hindūstān," sliced it and gave him a piece. He bit into it at once; it was night before the bitter taste went out of his mouth. At Garm-chashma we dismounted on rising-ground where cold meat was being set out for us when Langar Khān arrived to wait on me after being for a time at his own place (Koh-i-jūd). He brought an offering of a horse and a few confections. Passing on, we dismounted at Yada-bīr, at the Other Prayer got on a raft there, went for as much as two miles on it, then left it.

(*Sep. 27th*) Riding on next morning, we dismounted below the Khaibar-pass. Today arrived Sl. Bāyazīd, come up by the Fol. 243*b*. Bāra-road after hearing of us; he set forth that the Afrīdī Afghāns were seated in Bāra with their goods and families and that they had grown a mass of corn which was still standing (lit. on foot). Our plan being for the Yūsuf-zāī Afghāns of Hash-naghar, we paid him no attention. At the Mid-day Prayer there was a wine-party in Khwāja Muḥammad 'Alī's tent. During the party details about our coming in this direction were written and sent off by the hand of a sulṭān of Tīrah to Khwāja Kalān in Bajaur. I wrote this couplet on the margin of the letter (*farmān*):—

> Say sweetly o breeze, to that beautiful fawn,
> Thou hast given my head to the hills and the wild.[1]

(*Sep. 28th*) Marching on at dawn across the pass, we got through the Khaibar-narrows and dismounted at 'Alī-masjid. At the Mid-day Prayer we rode on, leaving the baggage behind, reached the Kābul-water at the second watch (midnight) and there slept awhile.

(*Sep. 29th*) A ford[2] was found at daylight; we had forded the water (*sū-dīn kīchīldī*), when news came from our scout that the Afghāns had heard of us and were in flight. We went on, passed through the Sawād-water and dismounted amongst the Afghān corn-fields. Not a half, not a fourth indeed of the promised corn was had. The plan of fitting-up Hash-naghar, made under the hope of getting corn here, came to nothing. Fol. 244.

[1] Dīwān of Ḥāfiẓ lith. ed. p. 22. The couplet seems to be another message to a woman (f. 238); here it might be to Bībī Mubāraka, still under Khwāja Kalān's charge in Bajaur (f. 221).

[2] Here and under date Sep. 30th the wording allows a ford.

The Dilazāk Afghāns, who had urged it on us, were ashamed. We next dismounted after fording the water of Sawād to its Kābul side.

(*Sep. 30th*) Marching next morning from the Sawād-water, we crossed the Kābul-water and dismounted. The Begs admitted to counsel were summoned and a consultation having been had, the matter was left at this:—that the Afrīdī Afghāns spoken of by Sl. Bāyazīd should be over-run, Pūrshāwūr-fort be fitted up on the strength of their goods and corn, and some-one left there in charge.

At this station Hindū Beg *Qūchīn* and the Mīr-zādas of Khwāst overtook us. Today *ma'jūn* was eaten, the party being Darwesh-i-muḥammad *Sārbān*, Muḥammad Kūkūldāsh, Gadāī Ṭaghāī and 'Asas; later on we invited Shāh Ḥasan also. After food had been placed before us, we went on a raft, at the Other Prayer. We called Langar Khān *Nīa-zāī* on also. At the Evening Prayer we got off the raft and went to camp.

(*Oct. 1st*) Marching at dawn, in accordance with the arrangement made on the Kābul-water, we passed Jām and dismounted at the outfall of the 'Alī-masjid water.[1]

(*dd. Badakhshān affairs.*)

Sl. 'Alī (Ṭaghāī's servant?) Abū'l-hāshim overtaking us, said, "On the night of 'Arafa,[2] I was in Jūī-shāhī with a person from Badakhshān; he told me that Sl. Sa'īd Khān had come with designs on Badakhshān, so I came on from Jūī-shāhī along the Jām-rūd, to give the news to the Pādshāh." On this the begs were summoned and advice was taken. In consequence of this
Fol. 244*b*. news, it seemed inadvisable to victual the fort (Pūrshāwūr), and we started back intending to go to Badakhshān.[3] Langar Khān was appointed to help Muḥ. 'Alī *Jang-jang*; he was given an honorary dress and allowed to go.

[1] This may be what Masson writes of (i, 149) "We reached a spot where the water supplying the rivulet (of 'Alī-masjid) gushes in a large volume from the rocks to the left. I slaked my thirst in the living spring and drank to repletion of the delightfully cool and transparent water."

[2] Mr. Erskine here notes, "This appears to be a mistake or oversight of Bābur. The eve of 'Arafa" (9th of Ẕū'l-ḥijja) "was not till the evening of Dec. 2nd 1519. He probably meant to say the 'Īd-i-fitr which had occurred only five days before, on Sep. 26th."

[3] This was an affair of frontiers (T.R. p. 354).

That night a wine-party was held in Khwāja Muḥ. 'Alī's tent. We marched on next day, crossed Khaibar and dismounted below the pass.

(ee. The Khiẓr-khail Afghāns.)

(*Oct. 3rd*) Many improper things the Khiẓr-khail had done! When the army went to and fro, they used to shoot at the laggards and at those dismounted apart, in order to get their horses. It seemed lawful therefore and right to punish them. With this plan we marched from below the pass at daybreak ate our mid-day meal in Dih-i-ghulāmān (Basaul),[1] and after feeding our horses, rode on again at the Mid-day Prayer.

Muḥ. Ḥusain the armourer was made to gallop off to Kābul with orders to keep prisoner all Khiẓr-khailīs there, and to submit to me an account of their possessions; also, to write a detailed account of whatever news there was from Badakhshān and to send a man off with it quickly from Kābul to me.

That night we moved on till the second watch (midnight), got a little beyond Sulṭānpūr, there slept awhile, then rode on again. The Khiẓr-khail were understood to have their seat from Bahār (Vihāra?) and Mīch-grām to Karā-sū (*sic*). Arriving before dawn, (*Oct. 4th*) the raid was allowed. Most of the goods of the Khiẓr-khailīs and their small children fell into the army's hands; a few tribesmen, being near the mountains, drew off to Fol. 245. them and were left.

(*Oct. 5th*) We dismounted next day at Qīlaghū where pheasants were taken on our ground. Today the baggage came up from the rear and was unloaded here. Owing to this punitive raid, the Wazīrī Afghāns who never had given in their tribute well, brought 300 sheep.

(*Oct. 9th*) I had written nothing since my hand was dislocated; here I wrote a little, on Sunday the 14th of the month.[2]

(*Oct. 10th*) Next day came Afghān chiefs leading the Khirilchī [and] Samū-khail. The Dilazāk Afghāns entreated pardon for them; we gave it and set the captured free, fixed their tribute at 4000 sheep, gave coats (*tūn*) to their chiefs, appointed and sent out collectors.

[1] Manucci gives an account of the place (Irvine iv, 439 and ii, 447).
[2] Sep. 8th to Oct. 9th.

(*Oct. 13th*) These matters settled, we marched on Thursday the 18th, and dismounted at Bahār (Vihāra?) and Mīch-grām.

(*Oct. 14th*) Next day I went to the Bāgh-i-wafā. Those were the days of the garden's beauty; its lawns were one sheet of trefoil; its pomegranate-trees yellowed to autumn splendour,[1] their fruit full red; fruit on the orange-trees green and glad (*khurram*), countless oranges but not yet as yellow as our hearts desired! The pomegranates were excellent, not equal, however, to the best ones of Wilāyat.[2] The one excellent and blessed content we have had from the Bāgh-i-wafā was had at this time. Fol. 245*b*. We were there three or four days; during the time the whole camp had pomegranates in abundance.

(*Oct. 17th*) We marched from the garden on Monday. I stayed in it till the first watch (9 a.m.) and gave away oranges; I bestowed the fruit of two trees on Shāh Ḥasan; to several begs I gave the fruit of one tree each; to some gave one tree for two persons. As we were thinking of visiting Lamghān in the winter, I ordered that they should reserve (*qūrūghlāīlār*) at least 20 of the trees growing round the reservoir. That day we dismounted at Gandamak.

(*Oct. 18th*) Next day we dismounted at Jagdālīk. Near the Evening Prayer there was a wine-party at which most of the household were present. After a time Qāsim Beg's sister's son Gadāī *bihjat*[3] used very disturbing words and, being drunk, slid down on the cushion by my side, so Gadāī Ṭaghāī picked him up and carried him out from the party.

(*Oct. 19th*) Marching next day from that ground, I made an excursion up the valley-bottom of the Bārīk-āb towards Qūrūq-sāī. A few purslain trees were in the utmost autumn beauty. On dismounting, seasonable[4] food was set out. The vintage

[1] *khūsh rang-i khizān*. Sometimes Bābur's praise of autumn allows the word *khizān* to mean the harvest-crops themselves, sometimes the autumnal colouring.

[2] This I have taken to mean the Kābul *tūmān*. The Ḥai. MS. writes *wilāyatlār* (plural) thus suggesting that *aūl* (those) may be omitted, and those countries (Trans-oxiana) be meant; but the second Pers. trs. (I.O. 217 f. 169) supports *wilāyat*, Kābul.

[3] joyous, happy.

[4] *y:lk:rān*. This word has proved a difficulty to all translators. I suggest that it stands for *aīlīkarān*, what came to hand (*aīlīk see* de C.'s Dict.); also that it contains puns referring to the sheep taken from the road (*yūlkarān*) and to the wine of the year's yield (*yīlkarān*). The way-side meal was of what came to hand, mutton and wine, probably local.

was the cause! wine was drunk! A sheep was ordered brought from the road and made into *kabābs* (*brochettes*). We amused ourselves by setting fire to branches of holm-oak.[1]

Mullā 'Abdu'l-malik *dīwāna*[2] having begged to take the news of our coming into Kābul, was sent ahead. To this place came Ḥasan Nabīra from Mīrzā Khān's presence; he must have come after letting me know [his intention of coming].[3] There was Fol. 246. drinking till the Sun's decline; we then rode off. People in our party had become very drunk, Sayyid Qāsim so much so, that two of his servants mounted him and got him into camp with difficulty. Muḥ. Bāqir's Dost was so drunk that people, headed by Amīn-i-muḥammad Tarkhān and Mastī *chuhra*, could not get him on his horse; even when they poured water on his head, nothing was effected. At that moment a body of Afghāns appeared. Amīn-i-muḥammad, who had had enough himself, had this idea, "Rather than leave him here, as he is, to be taken, let us cut his head off and carry it with us." At last after 100 efforts, they mounted him and brought him with them. We reached Kābul at midnight.

(*ff. Incidents in Kābul.*)

In Court next morning Qulī Beg waited on me. He had been to Sl. Sa'īd Khān's presence in Kāshghar as my envoy. To him as envoy to me had been added Bīshka Mīrzā *Itārchī*[4] who brought me gifts of the goods of that country.

(*Oct. 25th*) On Wednesday the 1st of Ẕū'l-qa'da, I went by myself to Qābil's tomb[5] and there took my morning. The people of the party came later by ones and twos. When the Sun waxed hot, we went to the Violet-garden and drank there, by the side of the reservoir. Mid-day coming on, we slept. At the Mid-day Prayer we drank again. At this mid-day party I gave wine to Tīngrī-qulī Beg and to Mahndī (?) to whom at any earlier party, wine had not been given. At the Bed-time Fol. 246b. Prayer, I went to the Hot-bath where I stayed the night.

[1] f. 141b.
[2] f. 217 and n.
[3] I think Bābur means that the customary announcement of an envoy or guest must have reached Kābul in his absence.
[4] He is in the T.R. list of the tribe (p. 307); to it belonged Sl. Aḥmad *Tambal* (*ib.* p. 316).
[5] *Qābil-ning kūrī-ning qāshī-ka*, lit. to the presence of the tomb of Qābil, *i.e.* Cain the eponymous hero of Kābul. The Elph. MS. has been altered to "Qābil Beg"!

(*Oct. 26th*) On Thursday honorary dresses were bestowed on the Hindūstānī traders, headed by Yaḥya *Nūḥānī*, and they were allowed to go.

(*Oct. 28th*) On Saturday the 4th, a dress and gifts were bestowed on Bīshka Mīrzā, who had come from Kāshghar, and he was given leave to go.

(*Oct. 29th*) On Sunday there was a party in the little Picture-hall over the (Chār-bāgh) gate; small retreat though it is, 16 persons were present.

(*gg. Excursion to the Koh-dāman.*)

(*Oct. 30th*) Today we went to Istālīf to see the harvest (*khizān*). Today was done the sin (? *irtikāb qīlīb aīdī*) of *ma'jūn*. Much rain fell; most of the begs and the household came into my tent, outside the Bāgh-i-kalān.

(*Oct. 31st*) Next day there was a wine-party in the same garden, lasting till night.

(*November 1st*) At dawn we took our morning (*ṣubāḥī ṣubūḥī qīldūk*) and got drunk, took a sleep, and at the Mid-day Prayer rode from Istālīf. On the road a confection was eaten. We reached Bih-zādī at the Other Prayer. The harvest-crops were very beautiful; while we were viewing them those disposed for wine began to agitate about it. The harvest-colour was extremely beautiful; wine was drunk, though *ma'jūn* had been eaten, sitting under autumnal trees. The party lasted till the Bed-time Prayer. Khalīfa's Mullā Maḥmūd arriving, we had him summoned to join the party. 'Abdu'l-lāh was very drunk

Fol. 247. indeed; a word affecting Khalīfa (*ṭarfīdīn*) being said, 'Abdu'l-lāh forgot Mullā Maḥmūd and recited this line:—

Regard whom thou wilt, he suffers from the same wound.[1]

Mullā Maḥmūd was sober; he blamed 'Abdu'l-lāh for repeating that line in jest; 'Abdu'l-lāh came to his senses, was troubled in mind, and after this talked and chatted very sweetly.

Our excursion to view the harvest was over; we dismounted, close to the Evening Prayer, in the Chār-bāgh.

(*Nov. 12th*) On Friday the 16th, after eating a confection

[1] Mr. Erskine surmised that the line was from some religious poem of mystical meaning and that its profane application gave offence.

with a few special people in the Violet-garden, we went on a boat. Humāyūn and Kāmrān were with us later; Humāyūn made a very good shot at a duck.

(*hh. A Bohemian episode.*)

(*Nov. 14th*) On Saturday the 18th, I rode out of the Chār-bāgh at midnight, sent night-watch and groom back, crossed Mullā Bābā's bridge, got out by the Dīūrīn-narrows, round by the bāzārs and *kārez* of Qūsh-nādur (var.), along the back of the Bear-house (*khirs-khāna*), and near sunrise reached Tardī Beg *Khāk-sār's*[1] *kārez.* He ran out quickly on hearing of me. His shortness (*qālāshlīghī*) was known; I had taken 100 *shāhrukhīs* (£5) with me; I gave him these and told him to get wine and other things ready as I had a fancy for a private and unrestrained party. He went for wine towards Bih-zādī[2]; I sent my horse by his slave to the valley-bottom and sat down on the slope behind the *kārez.* At the first watch (9 a.m.) Tardī Beg brought a pitcher of wine which we drank by turns. After him came Muḥammad-i-qāsim *Barlās* and Shāh-zāda who had got to know of his fetching the wine, and had followed him, their minds quite empty of any thought about me. We invited them to the party. Said Tardī Beg, "Hul-hul Anīga wishes to drink wine with you." Said I, "For my part, I never saw a woman drink wine; invite her." We also invited Shāhī a qalandar, and one of the *kārez*-men who played the rebeck. There was drinking till the Evening Prayer on the rising-ground behind the *kārez*; we then went into Tardī Beg's house and drank by lamp-light almost till the Bed-time Prayer. The party was quite free and unpretending. I lay down, the others went to another house and drank there till beat of drum (midnight). Hul-hul Anīga came in and made me much disturbance; I got rid of her at last by flinging myself down as if drunk. It was in my mind to put people off their guard, and ride off alone to Astar-ghach, but it did not come off because they got to know. In the end, I rode

Fol. 247*b*.

[1] His sobriquet *khāksār*, one who sits in the dust, suits the excavator of a *kārez*. Bābur's route can be followed in Masson's (iii, 110), apparently to the very *kārez*.

[2] In Masson's time this place was celebrated for vinegar. To reach it and return must have occupied several hours.

away at beat of drum, after letting Tardī Beg and Shāh-zāda know. We three mounted and made for Astar-ghach.

(*Nov. 15th*) We reached Khwāja Ḥasan below Istālīf by the first prayer (*farẓ waqt*); dismounted for a while, ate a confection,
Fol. 248. and went to view the harvest. When the Sun was up, we dismounted at a garden in Istālīf and ate grapes. We slept at Khwāja Shahāb, a dependency of Astar-ghach. Ātā, the Master of the Horse, must have had a house somewhere near, for before we were awake he had brought food and a pitcher of wine. The vintage was very fine. After drinking a few cups, we rode on. We next dismounted in a garden beautiful with autumn; there a party was held at which Khwāja Muḥammad Amīn joined us. Drinking went on till the Bed-time Prayer. During that day and night 'Abdu'l-lāh, 'Asas, Nūr Beg and Yūsuf-i-'alī all arrived from Kābul.

(*Nov. 16th*) After food at dawn, we rode out and visited the Bāgh-i-pādshāhī below Astar-ghach. One young apple-tree in it had turned an admirable autumn-colour; on each branch were left 5 or 6 leaves in regular array; it was such that no painter trying to depict it could have equalled. After riding from Astar-ghach we ate at Khwāja Ḥasan, and reached Bih-zādī at the Evening Prayer. There we drank in the house of Khwāja Muḥ. Amīn's servant Imām-i-muḥammad.

(*Nov. 17th*) Next day, Tuesday, we went into the Chār-bāgh of Kābul.

(*Nov. 18th*) On Thursday the 23rd, having marched (***kūchūb***), the fort was entered.

(*Nov. 19th*) On Friday Muḥammad 'Alī (son of ?) Ḥaidar the stirrup-holder brought, as an offering, a ***tūīgūn***[1] he had caught.

(*Nov. 20th*) On Saturday the 25th, there was a party in the Plane-tree garden from which I rose and mounted at the Bed-time Prayer. Sayyid Qāsim being in shame at past occurrences,[2] we dismounted at his house and drank a few cups.

Fol. 248*b*. (*Nov. 24th*) On Thursday the 1st of Ẕū'l-ḥijja, Tāju'd-dīn Maḥmūd, come from Qandahār, waited on me.

[1] Kunos, *āq tūīgūn*, white falcon; *'Amal-i-ṣāliḥ* (I.O. MS. No. 857, f. 45*b*), *taus tūīghūn*.
[2] f. 246.

(*Dec. 12th*) On Monday the 19th, Muḥ. 'Alī *Jang-jang* came from Nīl-āb.

(*Dec. 13th*) On Tuesday the . . . of the month, Sangar Khān *Janjūha*, come from Bhīra, waited on me.

(*Dec. 16th*) On Friday the 23rd, I finished (copying ?) the odes and couplets selected according to their measure from 'Alī-sher Beg's four Dīwāns.[1]

(*Dec. 20th*) On Tuesday the 27th there was a social-gathering in the citadel, at which it was ordered that if any-one went out from it drunk, that person should not be invited to a party again.

(*Dec. 23rd*) On Friday the 30th of Ẕū'l-ḥijja it was ridden out with the intention of making an excursion to Lamghān.

[1] Nawā'ī himself arranged them according to the periods of his life (Rieu's Pers Cat. p. 294).

926 AH.—DEC. 23RD 1519 TO DEC. 12TH 1520 AD.[1]

(*a. Excursion to the Koh-dāman and Kohistān.*)

(*Dec. 23rd*) On Saturday Muḥarram 1st Khwāja Sih-yārān was reached. A wine-party was had on the bank of the conduit, where this comes out on the hill.[2]

(*Dec. 24th*) Riding on next morning (2nd), we visited the moving sands (*reg-i-rawān*). A party was held in Sayyid Qāsim's *Bulbul's* house.[3]

(*Dec. 25th*) Riding on from there, we ate a confection (*ma'jūn*), went further and dismounted at Bilkir (?).

(*Dec. 26th*) At dawn (4th) we made our morning [*ṣubāḥı ṣubūḥī qīldūk*], although there might be drinking at night. We rode on at the Mid-day Prayer, dismounted at Dūr-nāma[4] and there had a wine party.

(*Dec. 27th*) We took our morning early. Ḥaq-dād, the headman of Dūr-namā made me an offering (*pesh-kash*) of his garden.

(*Dec. 28th*) Riding thence on Thursday (6th), we dismounted at the villages of the Tājiks in Nijr-aū.

(*Dec. 29th*) On Friday (7th) we hunted the hill between Forty-ploughs (*Chihil-qulba*) and the water of Bārān; many deer fell.
Fol. 249. I had not shot an arrow since my hand was hurt; now, with an easy[5] bow, I shot a deer in the shoulder, the arrow going in to half up the feather. Returning from hunting, we went on at the Other Prayer in Nijr-aū.

[1] Elph. MS. f. 202*b*; W.-i-B. I.O. 215 f. 175 (misplaced) and 217 f. 172; Mems. p. 281.

[2] *pushta aūstīda*; the Jūl-khwūsh of f. 137.

[3] The Ḥai. MS. omits a passage here; the Elph. MS. reads *Qāsim Bulbulī nīng awī*, thus making "nightingale" a sobriquet of Qāsim's own. Erskine (p. 281) has "Bulbulī-hall"; Ilminsky's words translate as, the house of Sayyid Qāsim's nightingale (p. 321).

[4] or Dūr-namā'ī, seen from afar.

[5] *narm-dīk*, the opposite of a *qātīq yāī*, a stiff bow. Some MSS. write *lāzim-dīk* which might be read to mean such a bow as his disablement allowed to be used.

(*Dec. 30th*) Next day (Saturday 8th) the tribute of the Nijr-aū people was fixed at 60 gold miṣqāls.[1]

(*Jan. 1st*) On Monday (10th) we rode on intending to visit Lamghān.[2] I had expected Humāyūn to go with us, but as he inclined to stay behind, leave was given him from Kūra-pass. We went on and dismounted in Badr-aū (Tag-aū).

(*b. Excursions in Lamghān.*)

(*Jan. . .*) Riding on, we dismounted at Aūlūgh-nūr.[3] The fishermen there took fish at one draught[4] from the water of Bārān. At the Other Prayer (afternoon) there was drinking on the raft; and there was drinking in a tent after we left the raft at the Evening Prayer.

Ḥaidar the standard-bearer had been sent from Dāwar[5] to the Kāfirs; several Kāfir headmen came now to the foot of Bād-i-pīch (pass), brought a few goat-skins of wine, and did obeisance. In descending that pass a surprising number of . . .[6] was seen.

(*Jan. . .*) Next day getting on a raft, we ate a confection, got off below Būlān and went to camp. There were two rafts.

(*Jan. 5th*) Marching on Friday (14th), we dismounted below Mandrāwar on the hill-skirt. There was a late wine-party.

(*Jan. 6th*) On Saturday (15th), we passed through the Darūta narrows by raft, got off a little above Jahān-namā'ī (Jalālābād) and went to the Bāgh-i-wafā in front of Adīnapūr. When we were leaving the raft the governor of Nīngnahār Qayyām Aūrdū Shāh came and did obeisance. Langar Khān *Nīā-zāī*,—he had Fol. 249*b*.

[1] Mr. Erskine, writing early in the 19th century, notes that this seems an easy tribute, about 400 *rupīs i.e.* £40.

[2] This is one of the three routes into Lamghān of f. 133.

[3] f. 251*b* and Appendix F, *On the name Dara-i-nūr.*

[4] This passage will be the basis of the account on f. 143*b* of the winter-supply of fish in Lamghān.

[5] This word or name is puzzling. Avoiding extreme detail as to variants, I suggest that it is Dāūr-bīn for Dūr-namā'ī if a place-name; or, if not, *dūr-bīn*, foresight (in either case the preposition requires to be supplied), and it may refer to foreseen need of and curiosity about Kāfir wines.

[6] *chīūrtika* or *chīūr-i-tika*, whether *sauterelle* as M. de Courteille understood, or *jānwār-i-ranga* and *chīkūr*, partridge as the 1st Persian trs. and as Mr. Erskine (explaining *chūr-i-tīka*) thought, must be left open. Two points arise however, (1) the time is January, the place the deadly Bād-i-pīch pass; would these suit locusts? (2) If Bābur's account of a splendid bird (f. 135) were based on this experience, this would be one of several occurrences in which what is entered in the Description of Kābul of 910 AH. is found as an experience in the diary of 925–6 AH.

been in Nīl-āb for a time,— waited upon me on the road. We dismounted in the Bāgh-i-wafā; its oranges had yellowed beautifully; its spring-bloom was well-advanced, and it was very charming. We stayed in it five or six days.

As it was my wish and inclination (*jū dagh-dagha*) to return to obedience (*tā'ib*) in my 40th year, I was drinking to excess now that less than a year was left.

(*Jan. 7th*) On Sunday the 16th, having made my morning (*ṣubūḥī*) and became sober. Mullā Yārak played an air he had composed in five-time and in the five-line measure (*makhammas*), while I chose to eat a confection (*ma'jūn*). He had composed an excellent air. I had not occupied myself with such things for some time; a wish to compose came over me now, so I composed an air in four-time, as will be mentioned in time.[1]

(*Jan. 10th*) On Wednesday (19th) it was said for fun, while we were making our morning (*ṣubūḥī*), "Let whoever speaks like a Sārt (*i.e.* in Persian) drink a cup." Through this many drank. At *sunnat-waqt*[2] again, when we were sitting under the willows in the middle of the meadow, it was said, "Let whoever speaks like a Turk, drink a cup!" Through this also numbers drank. After the sun got up, we drank under the orange-trees on the reservoir-bank.

(*Jan. 11th*) Next day (20th) we got on a raft from Darūta; got off again below Jūī-shāhī and went to Atar.

(*Jan. . .*) We rode from there to visit Nūr-valley, went as far as Sūsān (lily)-village, then turned back and dismounted in Amla.

Fol. 250. (*Jan. 14th*) As Khwāja Kalān had brought Bajaur into good order, and as he was a friend of mine, I had sent for him and had made Bajaur over to Shāh Mīr Ḥusain's charge. On Saturday the 22nd of the month (Muḥarram), Shāh Mīr Ḥusain was given leave to go. That day in Amla we drank.

(*Jan. 15th*) It rained (*yāmghūr yāghdūrūb*) next day (23rd).

[1] Ḥai. MS. *maḥali-da mazkūr bulghusīdūr*, but W.-i-B. I.O. 215 f. 176 for *maḥali-da*, in its place, has *dar majlis* [in the collection], which may point to an intended collection of Bābur's musical compositions. Either reading indicates intention to write what we now have not.

[2] Perhaps an equivalent for *farẓ-waqt*, the time of the first obligatory prayer. Much seems to happen before the sun got up high!

When we reached Kula-grām in Kūnār[1] where Malik 'Alī's house is, we dismounted at his middle son's house, overlooking an orange-orchard. We did not go into the orchard because of the rain but just drank where we were. The rain was very heavy. I taught Mullā 'Alī Khān a ṭalisman I knew; he wrote it on four pieces of paper and hung them on four sides; as he did it, the rain stopped and the air began to clear.

(*Jan. 16th*) At dawn (24th) we got on a raft; on another several braves went. People in Bajaur, Sawād, Kūnār and thereabouts make a beer (*bīr būza*)[2] the ferment of which is a thing they call *kīm*.[3] This *kīm* they make of the roots of herbs and several simples, shaped like a loaf, dried and kept by them. Some sorts of beer are surprisingly exhilarating, but bitter and distasteful. We had thought of drinking beer but, because of its bitter taste, preferred a confection. 'Asas, Ḥasan *Aīkirik*,[4] and Maṣtī, on the other raft, were ordered to drink some; they did so and became quite drunk. Ḥasan *Aīkirik* set up a disgusting disturbance; 'Asas, very drunk, did such unpleasant things that we were most uncomfortable (*bā tang*). I thought of having them put off on the far side of the water, but some of the others begged them off. Fol. 250*b*.

I had sent for Khwāja Kalān at this time and had bestowed Bajaur on Shāh Mīr Ḥusain. For why? Khwāja Kalān was a friend; his stay in Bajaur had been long; moreover the Bajaur appointment appeared an easy one.

At the ford of the Kūnār-water Shāh Mīr Ḥusain met me on his way to Bajaur. I sent for him and said a few trenchant words, gave him some special armour, and let him go.

Opposite Nūr-gal (Rock-village) an old man begged from those on the rafts; every-one gave him something, coat (*tūn*), turban, bathing-cloth and so on, so he took a good deal away.

At a bad place in mid-stream the raft struck with a great shock; there was much alarm; it did not sink but Mīr Muḥammad the raftsman was thrown into the water. We were near Atar that night.

[1] Koh-i-nūr, Rocky-mountains (?). *See* Appendix F, *On the name Dara-i-nūr*.
[2] Steingass gives *būza* as made of rice, millet, or barley.
[3] Is this connected with Arabic *kīmiyā'*, alchemy, chemistry?
[4] Turkī, a whirlpool; but perhaps the name of an office from *aīgar*, a saddle.

(*Jan. 17th*) On Tuesday (25th) we reached Mandrāwar.[1] Qūtlūq-qadam and his father had arranged a party inside the fort; though the place had no charm, a few cups were drunk there to please them. We went to camp at the Other Prayer.

(*Jan. 18th*) On Wednesday (26th) an excursion was made to Kind-kir[2] spring. Kind-kir is a dependent village of the Mandrāwar *tūmān*, the one and only village of the Lamghānāt
Fol. 251. where dates are grown. It lies rather high on the mountain-skirt, its date lands on its east side. At one edge of the date lands is the spring, in a place aside (*yān yīr*). Six or seven yards below the spring-head people have heaped up stones to make a shelter[3] for bathing and by so-doing have raised the water in the reservoir high enough for it to pour over the heads of the bathers. The water is very soft; it is felt a little cold in wintry days but is pleasant if one stays in it.

(*Jan. 19th*) On Thursday (27th) Sher Khān *Tarkalānī* got us to dismount at his house and there gave us a feast (*ẓiyāfat*). Having ridden on at the Mid-day Prayer, fish were taken out of the fish-ponds of which particulars have been given.[4]

(*Jan. 20th*) On Friday (28th) we dismounted near Khwāja Mīr-i-mīrān's village. A party was held there at the Evening Prayer.

(*Jan. 21st*) On Saturday (29th) we hunted the hill between 'Alī-shang and Alangār. One hunting-circle having been made on the 'Alī-shang side, another on the Alangār, the deer were driven down off the hill and many were killed. Returning from hunting, we dismounted in a garden belonging to the Maliks of Alangār and there had a party.

Half of one of my front-teeth had broken off, the other half remaining; this half broke off today while I was eating food.

(*Jan. 22nd*) At dawn (Ṣafar 1st) we rode out and had a fishing-net cast, at mid-day went into 'Alī-shang and drank in a garden.

[1] The river on which the rafts were used was the Kūnār, from Chītrāl.

[2] An uncertain name. I have an impression that these waters are medicinal, but I cannot trace where I found the information. The visit paid to them, and the arrangement made for bathing set them apart. The name of the place may convey this speciality.

[3] *panāhī*, the word used for the hiding-places of bird-catchers on f. 140.

[4] This will be the basis of the details about fishing given on f. 143 and f. 143*b*. The statement that particulars have been given allows the inference that the diary was annotated after the *Description of Kābul*, in which the particulars are, was written.

(*Jan. 23rd*) Next day (Ṣafar 2nd) Ḥamza Khān, Malik of 'Alī-shang was made over to the avengers-of-blood [1] for his evil deeds in shedding innocent blood, and retaliation was made.

(*Jan. 24th*) On Tuesday, after reading a chapter of the Qorān (*wird*), we turned for Kābul by the Yān-būlāgh road. At the Other Prayer, we passed the [Bārān]-water from Aūlūgh-nūr (Great-rock); reached Qarā-tū by the Evening Prayer, there gave our horses corn and had a hasty meal prepared, rode on again as soon as they had finished their barley.[2] Fol. 251*b*.

[1] *qānlīqlār*. This right of private revenge which forms part of the law of most rude nations, exists in a mitigated form under the Muhammadan law. The criminal is condemned by the judge, but is delivered up to the relations of the person murdered, to be ransomed or put to death as they think fit (Erskine).

[2] Here the text breaks off and a *lacuna* separates the diary of 11 months length which ends the Kābul section of the *Bābur-nāma* writings, from the annals of 932 AH. which begin the Hindūstān section. There seems no reason why the diary should have been discontinued.

TRANSLATOR'S NOTE ON 926 TO 932 AH.—1520 TO 1525 AD.

Bābur's diary breaks off here for five years and ten months.[1] His activities during the unrecorded period may well have left no time in which to keep one up, for in it he went thrice to Qandahār, thrice into India, once to Badakhshān, once to Balkh; twice at least he punished refractory tribesmen; he received embassies from Hindūstān, and must have had much to oversee in muster and equipment for his numerous expeditions. Over and above this, he produced the *Mubīn*, a Turkī poem of 2000 lines.

That the gap in his autobiography is not intentional several passages in his writings show;[2] he meant to fill it; there is no evidence that he ever did so; the reasonable explanation of his failure is that he died before he had reached this part of his book.

The events of these unrecorded years are less interesting than those of the preceding gap, inasmuch as their drama of human passion is simpler; it is one mainly of cross-currents of ambition, nothing in it matching the maelstrom of sectarian hate, tribal antipathy, and racial struggle which engulphed Bābur's fortunes beyond the Oxus.

None-the-less the period has its distinctive mark, the biographical one set by his personality as his long-sustained effort works out towards rule in Hindūstān. He becomes felt; his surroundings bend to his purpose; his composite following accepts his goal; he gains the southern key of Kābul and Hindūstān and presses the Arghūns out from his rear; in the Panj-āb he becomes a power; the Rājpūt Rānā of Chitor proffers him alliance against Ibrāhīm; and his intervention is sought in those warrings of the Afghāns which were the matrix of his own success.

[1] Jan. 2 th 1520 to Nov. 17th 1525 AD. (Ṣafar 926 to Ṣafar 1st 932 AH.).
[2] Index *s.nn.* Bāgh-i-ṣafā and B.N. *lacunae.*

a. Dramatis personae.

The following men played principal parts in the events of the unchronicled years :—

Bābur in Kābul, Badakhshān and Balkh,[1] his earlier following purged of Mughūl rebellion, and augmented by the various Mīrzās-in-exile in whose need of employment Shāh Beg saw Bābur's need of wider territory.[2]

Sulṭān Ibrāhīm *Lūdī* who had succeeded after his father Sikandar's death (Sunday Ẕū'l-qa'da 7th 923 AH.—Nov. 21st 1517 AD.)[3], was now embroiled in civil war, and hated for his tyranny and cruelty.

Shāh Ismā'īl *Ṣafawī*, ruling down to Rajab 19th 930 AH. (May 24th 1524 AD.) and then succeeded by his son Ṭahmāsp *aet.* 10.

Kūchūm (Kūchkūnjī) Khān, Khāqān of the Aūzbegs, Shaibānī's successor, now in possession of Transoxiana.

Sulṭān Sa'īd Khān *Chaghatāī*, with head-quarters in Kāshghar, a ruler amongst the Mughūls but not their Khāqān, the supreme Khānship being his elder brother Manṣūr's.

Shāh Shujā' Beg *Arghūn*, who, during the period, at various times held Qandahār, Shāl, Mustang, Sīwīstān, and part of Sind. He died in 930 AH. (1524 AD.) and was succeeded by his son Ḥasan who read the *khuṭba* for Bābur.

Khān Mīrzā *Mīrānshāhī*, who held Badakhshān from Bābur, with head-quarters in Qūndūz ; he died in 927 AH. (1520 AD.) and was succeeded in his appointment by Humāyūn *aet.* 13.

[1] Nominally Balkh seems to have been a Ṣafawī possession ; but it is made to seem closely dependent on Bābur by his receipt from Muḥammad-i-zamān in it of *taṣadduq* (money for alms), and by his action connected with it (*q.v.*).

[2] *Tārīkh-i-sind*, Malet's trs. p. 77 and *in loco*, p. 365.

[3] A chronogram given by Badāyūnī decides the vexed question of the date of Sikandar *Lūdī's* death—*Jannātu'l-firdūs nazlā* = 923 (Bib. Ind. ed. i, 322, Ranking trs. p. 425 n. 6). Erskine supported 924 AH. (i, 407), partly relying on an entry in Bābur's diary (f. 226*b*) *s.d.* Rabī'u'l-awwal 1st 925 AH. (March 3rd 1519 AD.) which states that on that day Mullā Murshid was sent to Ibrāhīm whose father *Sikandar had died five or six months before.*

Against this is the circumstance that the entry about Mullā Murshid is, perhaps entirely, certainly partly, of later entry than what precedes and what follows it in the diary. This can be seen on examination ; it is a passage such as the diary section shews in other places, added to the daily record and giving this the character of a draft waiting for revision and rewriting (fol. 216*b* n.).

(To save difficulty to those who may refer to the L. & E. *Memoirs* on the point, I mention that the whole passage about Mullā Murshid is displaced in that book and that the date March 3rd is omitted.)

Muḥammad-i-zamān *Bāī-qarā* who held Balkh perhaps direct from Bābur, perhaps from Ismā'īl through Bābur.

'Alā'u'd-dīn 'Ālam Khān *Lūdī*, brother of the late Sulṭān Sikandar *Lūdī* and now desiring to supersede his nephew Ibrāhīm.

Daulat Khān *Yūsuf-khail* (as Bābur uniformly describes him), or *Lūdī* (as other writers do), holding Lāhor for Ibrāhīm *Lūdī* at the beginning of the period.

SOURCES FOR THE EVENTS OF THIS GAP

A complete history of the events the *Bābur-nāma* leaves unrecorded has yet to be written. The best existing one, whether Oriental or European, is Erskine's *History of India*, but this does not exhaust the sources—notably not using the *Ḥabību's-siyar*—and could be revised here and there with advantage.

Most of the sources enumerated as useful for filling the previous gap are so here; to them must be added, for the affairs of Qandahār, Khwānd-amīr's *Ḥabību's-siyar*. This Mīr Ma'ṣūm's *Tārīkh-i-sind* supplements usefully, but its brevity and its discrepant dates make it demand adjustment; in some details it is expanded by Sayyid Jamāl's *Tarkhān-* or *Arghūn-nāma*.

For the affairs of Hindūstān the main sources are enumerated in Elliot and Dowson's *History of India* and in Nassau Lees' *Materials for the history of India*. Doubtless all will be exhausted for the coming *Cambridge History of India*.

EVENTS OF THE UNCHRONICLED YEARS

926 AH.—DEC. 23RD 1519 TO DEC. 12TH 1520 AD.

The question of which were Bābur's "Five expeditions" into Hindūstān has been often discussed; it is useful therefore to establish the dates of those known as made. I have entered one as made in this year for the following reasons;—it broke short because Shāh Beg made incursion into Bābur's territories, and that incursion was followed by a siege of Qandahār which several matters mentioned below show to have taken place in 926 AH.

a. Expedition into Hindūstān.

The march out from Kābul may have been as soon as muster and equipment allowed after the return from Lamghān chronicled in the diary. It was made through Bajaur where refractory tribesmen were brought to order. The Indus will have been forded at the usual place where, until the last one of 932 AH. (1525 AD.), all expeditions crossed on the outward march. Bhīra was traversed in which were Bābur's own Commanders, and advance was made, beyond lands yet occupied, to Siālkot, 72 miles north of Lāhor and in the Rechna *dū-āb*. It was occupied without resistance; and a further move made to what the MSS. call Sayyidpūr; this attempted defence, was taken by assault and put to the sword. No place named Sayyidpūr is given in the Gazetteer of India, but the *Āyīn-i-akbarī* mentions a Sidhpūr which from its neighbourhood to Siālkot may be what Bābur took.

Nothing indicates an intention in Bābur to join battle with Ibrāhīm at this time; Lāhor may have been his objective, after he had made a demonstration in force to strengthen his footing in Bhīra. Whatever he may have planned to do beyond Sidhpūr (?) was frustrated by the news which took him back to Kābul and thence to Qandahār, that an incursion into his territory had been made by Shāh Beg.

b. Shāh Shujā' Beg's position.

Shāh Beg was now holding Qandahār, Shāl, Mustang and Sīwīstān.[1] He knew that he held Qandahār by uncertain tenure, in face of its desirability for Bābur and his own lesser power. His ground was further weakened by its usefulness for operations on Harāt and the presence with Bābur of Bāī-qarā refugees, ready to seize a chance, if offered by Ismā'īl's waning fortunes, for recovery of their former seat. Knowing his weakness, he for several years had been pushing his way out into Sind by way of the Bolān-pass.

His relations with Bābur were ostensibly good; he had sent him envoys twice last year, the first time to announce a success

[1] Shāl (the local name of English Quetta) was taken by Ẕū'l-nūn in 884 AH. (1479 AD.); Sīwīstān Shāh Beg took, in second capture, about 917 AH. (1511 AD.), from a colony of Barlās Turks under Pīr Walī *Barlās*.

at Kāhān had in the end of 924 AH. (Nov. 1519 AD.). His son Ḥasan however, with whom he was unreconciled, had been for more than a year in Bābur's company,—a matter not unlikely to stir under-currents of unfriendliness on either side.

His relations with Shāh Ismā'īl were deferential, in appearance even vassal-like, as is shewn by Khwānd-amīr's account of his appeal for intervention against Bābur to the Shāh's officers in Harāt. Whether he read the *khuṭba* for any suzerain is doubtful; his son Ḥasan, it may be said, read it later on for Bābur.

c. The impelling cause of this siege of Qandahār.

Precisely what Shāh Beg did to bring Bābur back from the Panj-āb and down upon Qandahār is not found mentioned by any source. It seems likely to have been an affair of subordinates instigated by or for him. Its immediate agents may have been the Nīkdīrī (Nūkdīrī) and Hazāra tribes Bābur punished on his way south. Their location was the western border-land; they may have descended on the Great North Road or have raided for food in that famine year. It seems certain that Shāh Beg made no serious attempt on Kābul; he was too much occupied in Sind to allow him to do so. Some unused source may throw light on the matter incidentally; the offence may have been small in itself and yet sufficient to determine Bābur to remove risk from his rear.[1]

d. Qandahār.

The Qandahār of Bābur's sieges was difficult of capture; he had not taken it in 913 AH. (f. 208*b*) by siege or assault, but by default after one day's fight in the open. The strength of its position can be judged from the following account of its ruins as they were seen in 1879 AD., the military details of which supplement Bellew's description quoted in Appendix J.

The fortifications are of great extent with a treble line of bastioned walls and a high citadel in the centre. The place is in complete ruin and its locality now useful only as a grazing ground. . . . "The town is in three parts, each on a separate

[1] Was the attack made in reprisal for Shāh Beg's further aggression on the Barlās lands and Bābur's hereditary subjects? Had these appealed to the head of their tribe?

eminence, and capable of mutual defence. The mountain had been covered with towers united by curtains, and the one on the culminating point may be called impregnable. It commanded the citadel which stood lower down on the second eminence, and this in turn commanded the town which was on a table-land elevated above the plain. The triple walls surrounding the city were at a considerable distance from it. After exploring the citadel and ruins, we mounted by the gorge to the summit of the hill with the impregnable fort. In this gorge are the ruins of two tanks, some 80 feet square, all destroyed, with the pillars fallen; the work is *pukka* in brick and *chunām* (cement) and each tank had been domed in; they would have held about 400,000 gallons each." (Le Messurier's *Kandahar in 1879 AD.* pp. 223, 245.)

e. Bābur's sieges of Qandahār.

The term of five years is found associated with Bābur's sieges of Qandahār, sometimes suggesting a single attempt of five years' duration. This it is easy to show incorrect; its root may be Mīr Ma'ṣūm's erroneous chronology.

The day on which the keys of Qandahār were made over to Bābur is known, from the famous inscription which commemorates the event (Appendix J), as Shawwāl 13th 928 AH. Working backwards from this, it is known that in 927 AH. terms of surrender were made and that Bābur went back to Kābul; he is besieging it in 926 AH.—the year under description; his annals of 925 AH. are complete and contain no siege; the year 924 AH. appears to have had no siege, Shāh Beg was on the Indus and his son was for at least part of it with Bābur; 923 AH. was a year of intended siege, frustrated by Bābur's own illness; of any siege in 922 AH. there is as yet no record known. So that it is certain there was no unremitted beleaguerment through five years.

f. The siege of 926 AH. (1520 AD.).

When Bābur sat down to lay regular siege to Qandahār, with mining and battering of the walls,[1] famine was desolating the

[1] Le Messurier writes (*l.c.* p. 224) that at Old Qandahār "many stone balls lay about, some with a diameter of 18 inches, others of 4 or 5, chiselled out of limestone.

country round. The garrison was reduced to great distress; "pestilence," ever an ally of Qandahār, broke out within the walls, spread to Bābur's camp, and in the month of Tīr (June) led him to return to Kābul.

In the succeeding months of respite, Shāh Beg pushed on in Sind and his former slave, now commander, Mehtar Saṃbhal revictualled the town.

927 AH.—DEC. 12TH 1520 TO DEC. 1ST 1521 AD.

a. The manuscript sources.

Two accounts of the sieges of Qandahār in this and next year are available, one in Khwānd-amīr's *Ḥabību's-siyar*, the other in Ma'ṣūm *Bhakkarī's Tārīkh-i-sind.* As they have important differences, it is necessary to consider the opportunities of their authors for information.

Khwānd-amīr finished his history in 1524–29 AD. His account of these affairs of Qandahār is contemporary; he was in close touch with several of the actors in them and may have been in Harāt through their course; one of his patrons, Amīr Ghiyāṣu'd-dīn, was put to death in this year in Harāt because of suspicion that he was an ally of Bābur; his nephew, another Ghiyāṣu'd-dīn was in Qandahār, the bearer next year of its keys to Bābur; moreover he was with Bābur himself a few years later in Hindūstān.

Mīr Ma'ṣūm wrote in 1600 AD. 70 to 75 years after Khwānd-amīr. Of these sieges he tells what may have been traditional and mentions no manuscript authorities. Blochmann's biography of him (*Āyīn-i-akbarī* p. 514) shews his ample opportunity of learning orally what had happened in the Arghūn invasion of Sind, but does not mention the opportunity for hearing traditions about Qandahār which his term of office there allowed him. During that term it was that he added an inscription, commemorative of Akbar's dominion, to Bābur's own at Chihil-zīna, which records the date of the capture of Qandahār (928 AH.—1522 AD.).

These were said to have been used in sieges in the times of the Arabs and propelled from a machine called *manjanic* a sort of balista or catapult." Meantime perhaps they served Bābur!

b. The Ḥabību's-siyar account (lith. ed. iii, part 4, p. 97).

Khwānd-amīr's contemporary narrative allows Ma'ṣūm's to dovetail into it as to some matters, but contradicts it in the important ones of date, and mode of surrender by Shāh Beg to Bābur. It states that Bābur was resolved in 926 AH. (1520 AD.) to uproot Shāh Shujā' Beg from Qandahār, led an army against the place, and "opened the Gates of war". It gives no account of the siege of 926 AH. but passes on to the occurrences of 927 AH. (1521 AD.) when Shāh Beg, unable to meet Bābur in the field, shut himself up in the town and strengthened the defences. Bābur put his utmost pressure on the besieged, "often riding his piebald horse close to the moat and urging his men to fiery onset." The garrison resisted manfully, breaching the "life-fortresses" of the Kābulīs with sword, arrow, spear and death-dealing stone, but Bābur's heroes were most often victorious, and drove their assailants back through the Gates.

c. Death of Khān Mīrzā reported to Bābur.

Meantime, continues Khwānd-amīr, Khān Mīrzā had died in Badakhshān; the news was brought to Bābur and caused him great grief; he appointed Humāyūn to succeed the Mīrzā while he himself prosecuted the siege of Qandahār and the conquest of the Garm-sīr.[1]

d. Negociations with Bābur.

The Governor of Harāt at this time was Shāh Ismā'īl's son Ṭahmāsp, between six and seven years old. His guardian Amīr Khān took chief part in the diplomatic intervention with Bābur, but associated with him was Amīr Ghiyāṣu'd-dīn—the patron of Khwānd-amīr already mentioned—until put to death as an ally of Bābur. The discussion had with Bābur reveals a complexity of motives demanding attention. Nominally undertaken though intervention was on behalf of Shāh Beg, and certainly so at his request, the Persian officers seem to have been less anxious on

[1] "Just then came a letter from Badakhshān saying, 'Mīrzā Khān is dead; Mīrzā Sulaimān (his son) is young; the Aūzbegs are near; take thought for this kingdom lest (which God forbid) Badakhshān should be lost.' Mīrzā Sulaimān's mother (Sulṭān-nigār Khānīm) had brought him to Kābul" (Gul-badan's H. N. f. 8).

his account than for their own position in Khurāsān, their master's position at the time being weakened by ill-success against the Sulṭān of Rūm. To Bābur, Shāh Beg is written of as though he were an insubordinate vassal whom Bābur was reducing to order for the Shāh, but when Amīr Khān heard that Shāh Beg was hard pressed, he was much distressed because he feared a victorious Bābur might move on Khurāsān. Nothing indicates however that Bābur had Khurāsān in his thoughts; Hindūstān was his objective, and Qandahār a help on the way; but as Amīr Khān had this fear about him, a probable ground for it is provided by the presence with Bābur of Bāī-qarā exiles whose ambition it must have been to recover their former seat. Whether for Harāt, Kābul, or Hindūstān, Qandahār was strength. Another matter not fitting the avowed purpose of the diplomatic intervention is the death of Ghiyāṣu'd-dīn because an ally of Bābur; this makes Amīr Khān seem to count Bābur as Ismā'īl's enemy.

Shāh Beg's requests for intervention began in 926 AH. (1520 AD.), as also did the remonstrance of the Persian officers with Bābur; his couriers followed one another with entreaty that the Amīrs would contrive for Bābur to retire, with promise of obeisance and of yearly tribute. The Amīrs set forth to Bābur that though Shāh Shujā' Beg had offended and had been deserving of wrath and chastisement, yet, as he was penitent and had promised loyalty and tribute, it was now proper for Bābur to raise the siege (of 926 AH.) and go back to Kābul. To this Bābur answered that Shāh Beg's promise was a vain thing, on which no reliance could be placed; please God!, said he, he himself would take Qandahār and send Shāh Beg a prisoner to Harāt; and that he should be ready then to give the keys of the town and the possession of the Garm-sīr to any-one appointed to receive them.

This correspondence suits an assumption that Bābur acted for Shāh Ismā'īl, a diplomatic assumption merely, the verbal veil, on one side, for anxiety lest Bābur or those with him should attack Harāt,—on the other, for Bābur's resolve to hold Qandahār himself.

Amīr Khān was not satisfied with Bābur's answer, but had his attention distracted by another matter, presumably 'Ubaidu'l-lāh Khān's attack on Harāt in the spring of the year (March–April

1521 AD.). Negociations appear to have been resumed later, since Khwānd-amīr claims it as their result that Bābur left Qandahār this year.

e. The Tārīkh-i-sind account.

Mīr Ma'ṣūm is very brief; he says that in this year (his 922 AH.), Bābur went down to Qandahār before the year's tribute in grain had been collected, destroyed the standing crops, encompassed the town, and reduced it to extremity; that Shāh Beg, wearied under reiterated attack and pre-occupied by operations in Sind, proposed terms, and that these were made with stipulation for the town to be his during one year more and then to be given over to Bābur. These terms settled, Bābur went to Kābul, Shāh Beg to Sīwī.

The Arghūn families were removed to Shāl and Sīwī, so that the year's delay may have been an accommodation allowed for this purpose.

f. Concerning dates.

There is much discrepancy between the dates of the two historians. Khwānd-amīr's agree with the few fixed ones of the period and with the course of events; several of Ma'ṣūm's, on the contrary, are *seriatim* five (lunar) years earlier. For instance, events Khwānd-amīr places under 927 AH. Ma'ṣūm places under 922 AH. Again, while Ma'ṣum correctly gives 913 AH. (1507 AD.) as the year of Bābur's first capture of Qandahār, he sets up a discrepant series later, from the success Shāh Beg had at Kāhān; this he allots to 921 AH. (1515 AD.) whereas Bābur received news of it (f. 233*b*) in the beginning of 925 AH. (1519 AD.). Again, Ma'ṣūm makes Shāh Ḥasan go to Bābur in 921 AH. and stay two years; but Ḥasan spent the whole of 925 AH. with Bābur and is not mentioned as having left before the second month of 925 AH. Again, Ma'ṣūm makes Shāh Beg surrender the keys of Qandahār in 923 AH. (1517 AD.), but 928 AH. (1522 AD.) is shewn by Khwānd-amīr's dates and narrative, and is inscribed at Chihil-zīna.[1]

[1] *infra* and Appendix J.

928 AH.—DEC. 1ST 1521 TO NOV. 20TH 1522 AD.

a. Bābur visits Badakhshān.

Either early in this year or late in the previous one, Bābur and Māhīm went to visit Humāyūn in his government, probably to Faizābād, and stayed with him what Gul-badan calls a few days.

b. Expedition to Qandahār.

This year saw the end of the duel for possession of Qandahār. Khwānd-amīr's account of its surrender differs widely from Ma'ṣūm's. It claims that Bābur's retirement in 927 AH. was due to the remonstrances from Harāt, and that Shāh Beg, worn out by the siege, relied on the arrangement the Amīrs had made with Babūr and went to Sīwī, leaving one 'Abdu'l-bāqī in charge of the place. This man, says Khwānd-amīr, drew the line of obliteration over his duty to his master, sent to Bābur, brought him down to Qandahār, and gave him the keys of the town—by the hand of Khwānd-amīr's nephew Ghiyāṣu'd-dīn, specifies the *Tarkhān-nāma.* In this year messengers had come and gone between Bābur and Harāt; two men employed by Amīr Khān are mentioned by name; of them the last had not returned to Harāt when a courier of Bābur's, bringing a tributary gift, announced there that the town was in his master's hands. Khwānd-amīr thus fixes the year 928 AH. as that in which the town passed into Bābur's hands; this date is confirmed by the one inscribed in the monument of victory at Chihil-zīna which Bābur ordered excavated on the naze of the limestone ridge behind the town. The date there given is Shawwāl 13th 928 AH. (Sep. 6th 1522 AD.).

Ma'ṣūm's account, dated 923 AH. (1517 AD.), is of the briefest:—Shāh Beg fulfilled his promise, much to Bābur's approval, by sending him the keys of the town and royal residence.

Although Khwānd-amīr's account has good claim to be accepted, it must be admitted that several circumstances can be taken to show that Shah Beg had abandoned Qandahār, *e.g.* the removal of the families after Bābur's retirement last year, and his own absence in a remote part of Sind this year.

c. The year of Shāh Beg's death.

Of several variant years assigned for the death of Shāh Beg in the sources, two only need consideration.[1] There is consensus of opinion about the month and close agreement about the day, Sha'bān 22nd or 23rd. Ma'ṣum gives a chronogram, *Shahr-Sha'bān*, (month of Sha'bān) which yields 928, but he does not mention where he obtained it, nor does anything in his narrative shew what has fixed the day of the month.

Two objections to 928 are patent: (1) the doubt engendered by Ma'ṣūm's earlier ante-dating; (2) that if 928 be right, Shāh Beg was already dead over two months when Qandahār was surrendered. This he might have been according to Khwānd-amīr's narrative, but if he died on Sha'bān 22nd 928 (July 26th 1522), there was time for the news to have reached Qandahār, and to have gone on to Harāt before the surrender. Shāh Beg's death at that time could not have failed to be associated in Khwānd-amīr's narrative with the fate of Qandahār; it might have pleaded some excuse with him for 'Abdu'l-bāqī, who might even have had orders from Shāh Ḥasan to make the town over to Bābur whose suzerainty he had acknowledged at once on succession by reading the *khuṭba* in his name. Khwānd-amīr however does not mention what would have been a salient point in the events of the siege; his silence cannot but weigh against the 928 AH.

The year 930 AH. is given by Niẓāmu'd-dīn Aḥmad's *Ṭabaqāt-i-akbarī* (lith. ed. p. 637), and this year has been adopted by Erskine, Beale, and Ney Elias, perhaps by others. Some light on the matter may be obtained incidentally as the sources are examined for a complete history of India, perhaps coming from the affairs of Multān, which was attacked by Shāh Ḥasan after communication with Bābur.

d. Bābur's literary work in 928 AH. and earlier.

1. The *Mubīn*. This year, as is known from a chronogram within the work, Bābur wrote the Turkī poem of 2000 lines to which Abū'l-faẓl and Badāyūnī give the name *Mubīn* (The

[1] E. & D.'s *History of India*, i. 312.

Exposition), but of which the true title is said by the *Nafā'isu'l-ma'āsir* to be *Dar fiqa mubaiyan* (The Law expounded). Sprenger found it called also *Fiqa-i-bāburī* (Bābur's Law). It is a versified and highly orthodox treatise on Muḥammadan Law, written for the instruction of Kāmrān. A Commentary on it, called also *Mubīn*, was written by Shaikh Zain. Bābur quotes from it (f. 351*b*) when writing of linear measures. Berézine found and published a large portion of it as part of his *Chrestomathie Turque* (Kazan 1857); the same fragment may be what was published by Ilminsky. Teufel remarks that the MS. used by Berézine may have descended direct from one sent by Bābur to a distinguished legist of Transoxiana, because the last words of Berézine's imprint are Bābur's *Begleitschreiben* (*envoi*); he adds the expectation that the legist's name might be learned. Perhaps this recipient was the Khwāja Kalān, son of Khwāja Yaḥya, a Samarkandī whom Bābur sent a copy of his Memoirs on March 7th 15– (935 AH. f. 363).[1]

2. The *Bābur-nāma* diary of 925–6 AH. (1519–20 AD.). This is almost contemporary with the *Mubīn* and is the earliest part of the *Bābur-nāma* writings now known. It was written about a decade earlier than the narrative of 899 to 914 AH. (1494 to 1507 AD.), carries later annotations, and has now the character of a draft awaiting revision.

3. A *Dīwān* (Collection of poems). By dovetailing a few fragments of information, it becomes clear that by 925 AH. (1919 AD.) Bābur had made a Collection of poetical compositions distinct from the Rāmpūr *Dīwān*; it is what he sent to Pūlād Sulṭan in 925 AH. (f. 23–). Its date excludes the greater part of the Rāmpūr one. It may have contained those verses to which my husband drew attention in the Asiatic Quarterly Review of 1911, as quoted in the *Abūshqa*; and it may have contained, in agreement with its earlier date, the verses Bābur quotes as written in his earlier years. None of the quatrains found in the *Abūshqa* and there attributed to "Bābur Mīrzā",

[1] For accounts of the *Mubīn*, *Akbar-nāma* Bib. Ind. ed. i. 118, trs. H. Beveridge i. 278 note, Badāyūnī *ib.* i, 343, trs. Ranking p. 450, Sprenger ZDMG. 1862, Teufel *ib.* 1883. The *Akbar-nāma* account appears in Turkī in the "Fragments" associated with Kehr's transcript of the B.N. (JRAS. 1908, p. 70, A. S. B.'s art. *Bābur-nāma*. Bābur mentions the *Mubīn* (f. 252*b*, f. 351*b*).

are in the Rāmpūr *Dīwān*; nor are several of those early ones of the *Bābur-nāma*. So that the Dīwān sent to Pūlād Sulṭān may be the source from which the *Abūshqa* drew its examples.

On first examining these verses, doubt arose as to whether they were really by Bābur *Mīrānshāhī*; or whether they were by " Bābur Mīrzā " *Shāhrukhī.* Fortunately my husband lighted on one of them quoted in the *Sanglakh* and there attributed to Bābur Pādshāh. The *Abūshqa* quatrains are used as examples in de Courteille's *Dictionary*, but without an author's name; they can be traced there through my husband's articles.[1]

929 AH.—NOV. 20TH 1522 TO NOV. 10TH 1523 AD.

a. Affairs of Hindūstān.

The centre of interest in Bābur's affairs now moves from Qandahār to a Hindūstān torn by faction, of which faction one result was an appeal made at this time to Bābur by Daulat Khān *Lūdī* (*Yūsuf-khail*) and 'Alāu'd-dīn 'Ālam Khān *Lūdī* for help against Ibrāhīm.[2]

The following details are taken mostly from Aḥmad Yādgār's *Tārīkh-i-salāṭīn-i-afāghana*[3]:—Daulat Khān had been summoned to Ibrāhīm's presence; he had been afraid to go and had sent his son Dilāwar in his place; his disobedience angering Ibrāhīm, Dilāwar had a bad reception and was shewn a ghastly exhibit of disobedient commanders. Fearing a like fate for himself, he made escape and hastened to report matters to his father in Lāhor. His information strengthening Daulat Khān's previous apprehensions, decided the latter to proffer allegiance to Bābur and to ask his help against Ibrāhīm. Apparently 'Ālam Khān's interests were a part of this request. Accordingly Dilāwar (or Apāq) Khān went to Kābul, charged with his father's message, and with intent to make known to Bābur Ibrāhīm's

[1] JRAS. 1901, *Persian MSS. in Indian Libraries* (description of the Rāmpūr *Dīwān*); AQR. 1911, *Bābur's Dīwān* (*i.e.* the Rāmpūr *Dīwān*); and *Some verses of the Emperor Bābur* (the *Abūshqa* quotations).

For Dr. E. D. Ross' Reproduction and account of the Rāmpūr *Dīwān*, JASB. 1910.

[2] "After him (Ibrāhīm) was Bābur King of Dihlī, who owed his place to the Pathāns," writes the Afghān poet Khūsh-ḥāl *Khattak* (Afghān Poets of the XVII century, C. E. Biddulph, p. 5).

[3] The translation only has been available (E. & D.'s H. of I., vol. 1).

evil disposition, his cruelty and tyranny, with their fruit of discontent amongst his Commanders and soldiery.

b. Reception of Dilāwar Khān in Kābul.

Wedding festivities were in progress[1] when Dilāwar Khān reached Kābul. He presented himself, at the Chār-bāgh may be inferred, and had word taken to Bābur that an Afghan was at his Gate with a petition. When admitted, he demeaned himself as a suppliant and proceeded to set forth the distress of Hindūstān. Bābur asked why he, whose family had so long eaten the salt of the Lūdīs, had so suddenly deserted them for himself. Dilāwar answered that his family through 40 years had upheld the Lūdī throne, but that Ibrāhīm maltreated Sikandar's amīrs, had killed 25 of them without cause, some by hanging, some burned alive, and that there was no hope of safety in him. Therefore, he said, he had been sent by many amīrs to Bābur whom they were ready to obey and for whose coming they were on the anxious watch.

c. Bābur asks a sign.

At the dawn of the day following the feast, Bābur prayed in the garden for a sign of victory in Hindūstān, asking that it should be a gift to himself of mango or betel, fruits of that land. It so happened that Daulat Khān had sent him, as a present, half-ripened mangoes preserved in honey ; when these were set before him, he accepted them as the sign, and from that time forth, says the chronicler, made preparation for a move on Hindūstān.

d. 'Ālam Khān.

Although 'Ālam Khān seems to have had some amount of support for his attempt against his nephew, events show he had none valid for his purpose. That he had not Daulat Khān's, later occurrences make clear. Moreover he seems not to have been a man to win adherence or to be accepted as a trustworthy and sensible leader.[2] Dates are uncertain in the absence of

[1] The marriage is said to have been Kāmrān's (E. & D.'s trs.).

[2] Erskine calculated that 'Ālam Khān was now well over 70 years of age (H. of I. i, 421 n.).

Bābur's narrative, but it may have been in this year that 'Ālam Khān went in person to Kābul and there was promised help against Ibrāhīm.

e. Birth of Gul-badan.

Either in this year or the next was born Dil-dār's third daughter Gul-badan, the later author of an *Humāyūn-nāma* written at her nephew Akbar's command in order to provide information for the *Akbar-nāma.*

930 AH.—NOV. 10TH 1523 TO OCT. 29TH 1524 AD.

a. Bābur's fourth expedition to Hindūstān.

This expedition differs from all earlier ones by its co-operation with Afghān malcontents against Ibrāhīm *Lūdī*, and by having for its declared purpose direct attack on him through reinforcement of 'Ālam Khān.

Exactly when the start from Kābul was made is not found stated; the route taken after fording the Indus, was by the sub-montane road through the Kakar country; the Jīhlam and Chīn-āb were crossed and a move was made to within 10 miles of Lāhor.

Lāhor was Daulat Khān's head-quarters but he was not in it now; he had fled for refuge to a colony of Bilūchīs, perhaps towards Multān, on the approach against him of an army of Ibrāhīm's under Bihār Khān *Lūdī.* A battle ensued between Bābur and Bihār Khān; the latter was defeated with great slaughter; Bābur's troops followed his fugitive men into Lāhor, plundered the town and burned some of the *bāzārs.*

Four days were spent near Lāhor, then move south was made to Dībālpūr which was stormed, plundered and put to the sword. The date of this capture is known from an incidental remark of Bābur about chronograms (f. 325), to be mid-Rabī'u'l-awwal 930 AH. (*circa* Jan. 22nd 1524 AD.).[1] From Dībālpūr a start was made for Sihrind but before this could be reached news arrived which dictated return to Lāhor.

1 A. N. trs. H. Beveridge, i, 239.

b. The cause of return.

Daulat Khān's action is the obvious cause of the retirement. He and his sons had not joined Bābur until the latter was at Dībālpūr; he was not restored to his former place in charge of the important Lāhor, but was given Jalandhar and Sulṭānpūr, a town of his own foundation. Th s angered him extremely but he seems to have concealed his feelings for the time and to have given Bābur counsel as if he were content. His son Dilāwar, however, represented to Bābur that his father's advice was treacherous; it concerned a move to Multān, from which place Daulat Khān may have come up to Dībālpūr and connected with which at this time, something is recorded of co-operation by Bābur and Shāh Ḥasan *Arghūn.* But the incident is not yet found clearly described by a source. Dilāwar Khān told Bābur that his father's object was to divide and thus weaken the invading force, and as this would have been the result of taking Daulat Khān's advice, Bābur arrested him and Apāq on suspicion of treacherous intent. They were soon released, and Sulṭānpūr was given them, but they fled to the hills, there to await a chance to swoop on the Panj-āb. Daulat Khān's hostility and his non-fulfilment of his engagement with Bābur placing danger in the rear of an eastward advance, the Panj-āb was garrisoned by Bābur's own followers and he himself went back to Kābul.

It is evident from what followed that Daulat Khān commanded much strength in the Panj-āb; evident also that something counselled delay in the attack on Ibrāhīm, perhaps closer cohesion in favour of 'Ālam Khān, certainly removal of the menace of Daulat Khān in the rear; there may have been news already of the approach of the Aūzbegs on Balkh which took Bābur next year across Hindū-kush.

c. The Panj-āb garrison.

The expedition had extended Bābur's command considerably, notably by obtaining possession of Lāhor. He now posted in it Mīr 'Abdu'l-azīz his Master of the Horse; in Dībālpūr he posted, with 'Ālam Khān, Bābā Qashqa *Mughul*; in Sīālkot, Khusrau Kūkūldāsh, in Kalanūr, Muḥammad 'Alī *Tājīk.*

d. Two deaths.

This year, on Rajab 19th (May 23rd) died Ismā'īl *Ṣafawī* at the age of 38, broken by defeat from Sulṭān Salīm of Rūm.[1] He was succeeded by his son Ṭahmāsp, a child of ten.

This year may be that of the death of Shāh Shujā' *Arghūn*,[2] on Sha'bān 22nd (July 18th), the last grief of his burden being the death of his foster-brother Fāẓil concerning which, as well as Shāh Beg's own death, Mīr Ma'ṣum's account is worthy of full reproduction. Shāh Beg was succeeded in Sind by his son Ḥasan, who read the *khuṭba* for Bābur and drew closer links with Bābur's circle by marrying, either this year or the next, Khalīfa's daughter Gul-barg, with whom betrothal had been made during Ḥasan's visit to Bābur in Kābul. Moreover Khalīfa's son Muḥibb-i-'alī married Nāhīd the daughter of Qāsim Kūkūldāsh and Māh-chūchūk *Arghūn* (f. 214*b*). These alliances were made, says Ma'ṣūm, to strengthen Ḥasan's position at Bābur's Court.

e. A garden detail.

In this year and presumably on his return from the Panj-āb, Bābur, as he himself chronicles (f. 132), had plantains (bananas) brought from Hindūstān for the Bāgh-i-wafā at Adīnapūr.

931 AH.—OCT. 29TH 1524 TO OCT. 18TH 1525 AD.

a. Daulat Khān.

Daulat Khān's power in the Panj-āb is shewn by what he effected after dispossessed of Lāhor. On Bābur's return to Kābul, he came down from the hills with a small body of his immediate followers, seized his son Dilāwar, took Sulṭānpūr, gathered a large force and defeated 'Ālam Khān in Dībālpūr. He detached 5000 men against Sīālkot but Babur's begs of Lāhor attacked and overcame them. Ibrāhīm sent an army to reconquer the Panj-āb;

[1] The following old English reference to Isma'il's appearance may be quoted as found in a corner somewhat out-of-the-way from Oriental matters. In his essay on beauty Lord Bacon writes when arguing against the theory that beauty is usually not associated with highmindedness, "But this holds not always; for Augustus Cæsar, Titus Vespasianus, Philip le Bel of France, Edward the Fourth of England, Alcibiades of Athens, Isma'il the Sophy (Ṣafawī) of Persia, were all high and great spirits, and yet the most beautiful men of their times."

[2] Cf. *s.a.* 928 AH. for discussion of the year of death.

Daulat Khān, profiting by its dissensions and discontents, won over a part to himself and saw the rest break up.

b. 'Ālam Khān.

From his reverse at Dībālpūr, 'Ālam Khān fled straight to Kābul. The further help he asked was promised under the condition that while he should take Ibrāhīm's place on the throne of Dihlī, Bābur in full suzerainty should hold Lāhor and all to the west of it. This arranged, 'Ālam Khān was furnished with a body of troops, given a royal letter to the Lāhor begs ordering them to assist him, and started off, Bābur promising to follow swiftly.

'Ālam Khān's subsequent proceedings are told by Bābur in the annals of 932 AH. (1525 AD.) at the time he received details about them (f. 255*b*).

c. Bābur called to Balkh.

All we have yet found about this affair is what Bābur says in explanation of his failure to follow 'Ālam Khān as promised (f. 256), namely, that he had to go to Balkh because all the Aūzbeg Sulṭāns and Khāns had laid siege to it. Light on the affair may come from some Persian or Aūzbeg chronicle; Bābur's arrival raised the siege; and risk must have been removed, for Bābur returned to Kābul in time to set out for his fifth and last expedition to Hindūstān on the first day of the second month of next year (932 AH. 1525). A considerable body of troops was in Badakhshān with Humāyūn; their non-arrival next year delaying his father's progress, brought blame on himself.